Law, Politics and Society in Early Modern England

Law, like religion, provided one of the principal discourses through which early modern English people conceptualised the world in which they lived. Transcending traditional boundaries between social, legal and political history, this innovative and authoritative study examines the development of legal thought and practice from the later Middle Ages through to the outbreak of the English civil war, and explores the ways in which law mediated and constituted social and economic relationships within the household, the community and the state at all levels. By arguing that English common law was essentially the creation of the wider community, it challenges many current assumptions and opens new perspectives about how early modern society should be understood. Its magisterial scope and lucid exposition will make it essential reading for those interested in subjects ranging from high politics and constitutional theory to the history of the family, as well as the history of law.

CHRISTOPHER W. BROOKS is Professor of History at Durham University.

Law, Politics and Society in Early Modern England

Christopher W. Brooks

CAMBRIDGE
UNIVERSITY PRESS

CAMBRIDGE UNIVERSITY PRESS
Cambridge, New York, Melbourne, Madrid, Cape Town, Singapore,
São Paulo, Delhi, Dubai, Tokyo

Cambridge University Press
The Edinburgh Building, Cambridge CB2 8RU, UK

Published in the United States of America by Cambridge University Press,
New York

www.cambridge.org
Information on this title: www.cambridge.org/9780521323918

© Christopher W. Brooks 2008

First published 2008
Reprinted 2010

Printed in the United Kingdom at the University Press, Cambridge

A catalogue record for this publication is available from the British Library

Library of Congress Cataloguing in Publication data
Brooks, C. W
 Law, politics and society in early modern England / Christopher W. Brooks.
  p. cm.
 Includes bibliographical references and index.
 ISBN 978-0-521-32391-8 (hardback)
 1. Law–England–History–16th century. 2. Law–England–History–17th
century. I. Title.
 KD612.B76 2008
 349.42–dc22
 2008036971

ISBN 978-0-521-32391-8 hardback

Contents

Preface

The chronological scope of this book requires a word of explanation. I originally intended that it should cover an even longer period than it does by including a chapter on the 1640s and 1650s and, perhaps, an epilogue on the way that some of the principal themes played out in the later seventeenth century. In the event, an expansion of the number of areas addressed for the years prior to 1642 has effectively limited what could be included in a single volume. No less important, despite the resurgence of early modern legal history in recent years, the civil war period and the Restoration era remain particularly deep black holes in terms of existing knowledge. The more I have learned about them the more convinced I have become that it would be foolhardy, and very probably misleading, to adventure premature views without undertaking the root and branch research necessary to give the subject the treatment it deserves. While this retreat from the original strategy to a more conventional 'early modern' chronology has no doubt resulted in missed opportunities to consider legal, political and social change over a longer period and with due regard for a unique discontinuity, I hope there is some compensation in the wider range of subjects I have attempted to integrate into the present account. Indeed, the sixteenth and early seventeenth centuries were such a dynamic period in English legal history that it may eventually be concluded that from a legal perspective the 'revolution' occurred before the civil wars even though twenty years of political upheaval could hardly fail to leave their mark.

Over the years between the book's conception and its final realisation, I have accumulated many institutional and personal debts. Grants from the British Academy, Leverhulme Trust and the Huntington Library, along with periods of research leave from Durham University, helped provide the time and resources that made the research possible. A Mellon Foundation Fellowship at the National Humanities Centre in North Carolina gave me a welcomed opportunity for reflection and the development of some critical areas of the study; I am grateful to the staff there for their wonderful mixture of help and hospitality. I am also appreciative of the numerous archivists and librarians who have facilitated, or at least tolerated, my inquiries and visits. I thank Richard Fisher and Michael Watson of Cambridge University Press for their extraordinary patience in sticking with this project, and for gently, but firmly, reeling me in as it has come to completion.

So many people have in one way or another supported the work or encouraged me to keep at it that I am reluctant to make a list for fear of leaving someone out. Nevertheless, I would like to extend particular thanks to Robin Frame, Matthew Greenhall, Paul Halliday, Cynthia Herrup, Henry Horwitz, the late Mervyn James, Rebecca King, John Morrill, James Oldham, Wilfrid Prest, Tim Stretton and Keith Wrightson. Although I am of course responsible for all errors and other defects in the book, I am particularly obliged to Joanne Bailey and Adrian Green for reading large sections of it and responding with such thoughtful advice. Like other scholars working in or near the field of early modern legal history, I have benefited enormously from the counsel and works of Sir John Baker, but I would like here to pay particular tribute to his monumental bibliographic and lexicographic publications. They have provided invaluable charts through the vast seas of black ink and crabbed hand-writing that early modern lawyers have left behind as well as an essential manual for negotiating the Law French in which they chose to write.

On a personal as well as a professional level, I am grateful to Michael Lobban for valued advice, friendship and logistical support when I was working in London. As ever, my greatest debt is to my wife, Sharyn; a few lines can hardly do justice to the thanks I owe her for her patience, forbearance and enthusiasm over a very long haul. Finally, I would like to dedicate the book to the memory of John Cooper and Franco Guisberti, a teacher and a fellow graduate student of mine. Both died untimely deaths years before a single page was written, but their interest in, and encouragement of, my pursuit of this particular segment of the historical landscape when it was not a particularly fashionable thing to do has been remarkably sustaining. I wish I could offer them a better memorial, but I offer it with deepest gratitude nonetheless.

Abbreviations and conventions

Unless otherwise noted, the place of publication is London. Dates have not been modernised, but 1 January is taken as the beginning of each new year. Since so many of the manuscript sources referred to were originally written in Law French, I have not thought it worthwhile to note which are in English and which are not. In quotations, punctuation has sometimes been added, but modernisation of spelling has been kept to a minimum.

Case law in this book is cited using the standard legal abbreviations, principally to named law reporters. The vast majority of reported cases can be found in *The English Reports* (1900–32), a multi-volume collection of most of the printed law reports from the mid sixteenth to the nineteenth century. Legal citations are more fully explained in Donald Raistrick, *Index to Legal Citations and Abbreviations* (2nd edn., 1993). Because they are cited frequently, fuller bibliographical details are given below for the reports of Sir Edward Coke, Sir George Croke and Sir James Dyer.

Baildon, *Cases in Camera Stellata*	W. P. Baildon, *Les reportes del cases in Camera Stellata 1593–1609. From the Original MS. of John Hawarde of the Inner Temple, Esquire, Barrister-At-Law* (1894)
Baker, *Readers and Readings*	J. H. Baker, *Readers and Readings in the Inns of Court and Inns of Chancery* (Selden Society Supplementary Series, vol. 13, 2000)
Baker, *Serjeants*	J. H. Baker, *The Order of Serjeants at Law: a Chronicle of Creations and Related Texts with an Historical Introduction* (Selden Society Supplementary Series, vol. 5, 1984)
Bankes Papers	Papers of Attorney General Sir John Bankes deposited in the Bodleian Library, Oxford
BL	British Library, Department of Manuscripts, St Pancras, London

BLAS	Bedfordshire and Luton Archives Service, Bedford
Bodleian	Bodleian Library, Oxford
Bramston	*The Autobiography of Sir John Bramston, K.B., of Skreens, in the Hundred of Chelmsford*, ed. T. W. Bramston (Camden Society, OS, vol. 32, 1845)
Bray, *Reformatio*	G. Bray, ed., *Tudor Church Reform: the Henrician Canons of 1535 and the Reformatio Legum Ecclesiasticarum* (Church of England Record Society, vol. 8, 2000).
Brooks, *Lawyers, Litigation*	C. W. Brooks, *Lawyers, Litigation and English Society since 1450* (1998)
Brooks, *Pettyfoggers and Vipers*	C. W. Brooks, *Pettyfoggers and Vipers of the Commonwealth: the 'Lower Branch' of the Legal Profession in Early Modern England* (Cambridge, 1986)
Clarendon	*The History of the Rebellion and Civil Wars in England Begun in the Year 1641 by Edward, Earl of Clarendon*, ed. W. D. Macray (6 vols., Oxford, 1969)
CLRO	Corporation of London Record Office, The Guildhall, London
Coke on Littleton	*The First Part of the Institutes of the Laws of England; or a Commentary upon Littleton*, ed. Francis Hargrave and Charles Butler (3 vols., 1794). First published 1628
Communities and Courts	*Communities and Courts in Britain*, ed. C. W. Brooks and M. Lobban (1997)
CoRep	*Les reports de Edward Coke* (11 parts, 1600–15). A twelfth part was published posthumously in 1656.
CroCar	*The Reports of Sir George Croke Knight: Late, One of the Justices of the Court of Kings-Bench...Collected and Written in French by Himself* (1657)
CroEliz	*The First Part (though Last Published) of the Reports of Sir George Croke* (1661)
CroJac	*The Second Part of the Reports of Sir George Croke* (1659)
CSPD	*Calendar of State Papers, Domestic Series, of the Reign of Charles I*, ed. J. Bruce (1858–97)
CUL	Cambridge University Library

DHC	Dorset History Centre, Dorchester
Dyer	*Cy ensuont ascuns nouel cases, ore primierment publies* (1586)
Dyer's Reports	*Reports from the Lost Notebooks of Sir James Dyer*, ed. J. H. Baker (2 vols., Selden Society, vols. 109–10, 1994)
ECO	Exeter College Library, Oxford
Folger	Folger Shakespeare Library, Washington, DC
Guildhall	Guildhall Library, London
HALS	Hertfordshire Archives and Local Studies, Hertford
HEHL	Henry E. Huntington Library, San Marino, California
HMC	Historical Manuscripts Commission
HRO	Hampshire Record Office, Winchester
ITL	Inner Temple Library, London
Lambarde, *Eirenarcha*	William Lambarde, *Eirenarcha: or of the Office of Justices of Peace* ... (1582)
L&P	*Letters and Papers, Foreign and Domestic of the Reign of Henry VIII, 1509–47*, ed. J. S. Brewer, J. Gairdner and R. H. Brodie (21 vols., 1862–1910)
LI	Lincoln's Inn Library, London
LPL	Lambeth Palace Library, London
LRO	Lancashire Record Office, Preston
NCRO	Northamptonshire Record Office, Northampton
NLW	National Library of Wales, Aberystwyth
NORTHCRO	Northumberland Records Office, Woodhorn, Northumberland
NRO	Norfolk Record Office, Norwich
ODNB	*Oxford Dictionary of National Biography*, ed. H. C. G. Matthew and Brian Harrison (Oxford, 2004)
Petyt MS	Petyt Manuscripts, Inner Temple Library, London
POSLP	*Proceedings in the Opening Session of the Long Parliament: House of Commons*, ed. Maija Jansson (4 vols., Woodbridge, 2000–2)
PP 1628	*Proceedings in Parliament 1628*, ed. M. F. Keeler, M. J. Cole and W. B. Bidwell (6 vols., London and New Haven, 1977–84)

Prest, *Barristers*	W. R. Prest, *The Rise of the Barristers, a Social History of the English Bar 1590–1640* (Oxford, 1986)
Pulton, *De pace regis et regni*	Ferdinando Pulton, *De pace regis et regni viz A Treatise Declaring which be the Great and General Offences of the Realme and the Chiefe Impediments of the Peace of the King and Kingdome* (1609)
Readings and Moots	*Readings and Moots at the Inns of Court in the Fifteenth Century*, ed. J. H. Baker and S. E. Thorne (Selden Society, vol. 105, 1990)
Rushworth, *Collections*	John Rushworth, *Historical Collections of Private Passages of State, Weighty Matters of Law, Remarkable Proceedings in Parliament* (7 vols., 1659–1701)
SA	Shropshire Archives, Shrewsbury
SARS	Somerset Archive and Record Service, Taunton
Spelman's Reports	*The Reports of Sir John Spelman*, ed. J. H. Baker (2 vols., Selden Society, vols. 93–4, 1976–7)
SRO	Staffordshire Record Office, Stafford
ST	*Cobbett's Complete Collection of State Trials and Proceedings for High Treason and Other Crimes...*, ed. W. Cobbett, T. B. Howell *et al.* (34 vols., 1809–28)
Table-Talk	*The Table-Talk of John Selden*, ed. S. W. Singer (1860)
TNA	The National Archives, Kew, London
WCRO	Warwickshire County Record Office, Warwick
WCRS	Wakefield Court Rolls Series of the Yorkshire Archaeological Society
Whitelocke papers	Whitelocke Papers, Longleat House, Wiltshire (consulted on microfilm deposited at the Institute of Historical Research, Senate House, London)
WRO	Wiltshire and Swindon Record Office, Chippenham
Wynn Papers	Wynn of Gwydir Papers, National Library of Wales, Aberystwyth
YAS	Yorkshire Archaeological Society, Leeds

1 English history and the history of English law 1485–1642

This book seeks to reintegrate the history of law, legal institutions and the legal professions with the general political and social history of the period between the end of the Middle Ages and the outbreak of the English civil wars in 1642.

Conceived over two decades ago, it was originally inspired partly by the now-famous last chapter of Edward Thompson's work on the 'Black Acts' of the eighteenth century, *Whigs and Hunters*, in which he found, rather to his surprise, that the 'culture of the rule of law' seemed to amount to something more than the simple hegemony of the gentry over the rest of society.[1] It might be, he acknowledged, a set of values and practices that transcended the interests of any given group, one that was sometimes appropriated and used as much by the politically dispossessed as by the elite. At roughly the same time, my own studies of civil litigation and the legal profession indicated that the numbers of lawyers were rapidly increasing in the later sixteenth century, that by the beginning of the seventeenth the central courts in England were probably more heavily used than they ever had been before, and that the social range from which the litigants were drawn was surprisingly wide.[2] Both sets of findings seemed to point to the need for a fuller examination of the place of law in early modern society, and although it was already evident by the early 1980s that a considerable renaissance in legal history was taking place, the subject had been so neglected for so long that, while political as well as social historians frequently acknowledged the importance of 'the law', there was evidently a very real need for a work which attempted both a fair amount of detailed exposition as well as an interpretative overview.

During the years that have passed between the book's conception and its completion, a number of excellent works on some of the themes with which it deals have been published. There have been books on

[1] E. P. Thompson, *Whigs and Hunters: the Origins of the Black Act* (1975).
[2] Brooks, *Lawyers, Litigation*.

1

crime,[3] on the ecclesiastical courts,[4] on the legal professions,[5] on civil litigation, and on the place of common-law thinking in early modern political thought.[6] However, while all of these have contributed to the story that is told here, most have been written with a number of different agendas in mind. They have been dispersed in their chronological coverage, and none has been explicitly concerned with the role of law in politics and society broadly conceived. Those working on the lawyers have concentrated on internal professional developments and the social origins and social mobility of practitioners. Studies of crime in the seventeenth century usually draw their conclusions with little reference to the institutions and attitudes that were associated with law enforcement in the sixteenth. Those who have used quarter sessions and assize records to study crime, or ecclesiastical court depositions to examine sex and marriage, have on the whole been more concerned with the nature and incidence of crime and criminals, or the character of sexual and marital relations, than with legal thought and practice. Several recent studies have confirmed the importance of 'going to court' for ordinary people of both sexes, and have addressed questions about the relationship between law and agency, but they have for the most part been interested primarily in the value of legal records as sources for social and cultural history rather than in the social history of law itself.[7]

Indeed, many British historians would probably maintain that whilst legal records are a useful source of evidence, 'the law' itself is not a very worthwhile or rewarding subject of investigation. This lack of interest, which accounts for the relative paucity of work on the subject since the late nineteenth century, is frequently, and with some justification, blamed on the insularity and sterility of what is usually described as

---

[3] For example, J. A. Sharpe, *Crime in Early Modern England 1550–1750* (1984); C. Herrup, *The Common Peace: Legal Structure and Legal Substance in East Sussex, 1594–1640* (Cambridge, 1987); G. Walker, *Crime, Gender and the Social Order in Early Modern England* (Cambridge, 2003).

[4] R. Houlbrooke, *Church Courts and the People during the English Reformation 1520–1570* (Oxford, 1979); M. Ingram, *Church Courts, Sex and Marriage in England 1570–1640* (Cambridge, 1987); R. H. Helmholz, *Roman Canon Law in Reformation England* (Cambridge, 1990).

[5] E. W. Ives, *The Common Lawyers of Pre-Reformation England: Thomas Kebell, a Case Study* (Cambridge, 1983); Prest, *Barristers*; Brooks, *Pettyfoggers and Vipers*.

[6] For instance, J. P. Sommerville, *Politics and Ideology in England 1603–1640* (1986); G. Burgess, *The Politics of the Ancient Constitution* (Basingstoke, 1992); A. Cromartie, *The Constitutionalist Revolution: an Essay on the History of England 1450–1642* (Cambridge, 2006).

[7] L. Gowing, *Domestic Dangers: Women, Words and Sex in Early Modern London* (Oxford, 1996); T. Stretton, *Women Waging Law in Elizabethan England* (Cambridge, 1998); M. Gaskill, *Crime and Mentalities in Early Modern England* (Cambridge, 2000); A. Wood, *The Politics of Social Conflict: the Peak Country, 1520–1770* (Cambridge, 1999); S. Hindle, *The State and Social Change in Early Modern England 1550–1640* (Basingstoke, 2000).

doctrinal legal history, but its roots go more deeply into the heart of western social thought. Works of lawyer/historians such as F. W. Maitland and W. S. Holdsworth reflect a late Victorian and Edwardian tradition that regarded legal thought and institutions as keys to the understanding of any society, and a similar perspective informed the work of continental sociologists, such as Max Weber and Emile Durkheim, as well as early investigations in the relatively new discipline of anthropology.[8] Ultimately, however, other, more influential perspectives have driven scholars away from the study of law and legal history.

Although Karl Marx was educated as a lawyer, his thought, and that of his collaborator, Frederick Engels, placed little emphasis on the independent history of law as a societal institution. Instead, they regarded it as little more than an epiphenomenon of the means of production, a view that did little to promote studies of the legal organisation of society. At the same time, during the twentieth century, the overweening power of the state in western countries with democratic forms of government, no less than in the totalitarian regimes of the former Soviet empire, was accompanied by scepticism about the congruity between the law as legislated, or determined by judges, and the aspirations or values of the community at large, not to mention the realities of power.[9] According to the influential French theorist Michel Foucault, for example, in modern liberal states social and political relationships are construed with little reference to legal or constitutional structures, and there may be some justification for this view.[10] As the American legal historian Lawrence Friedman has put it, compared with other societies and other periods, western legal systems for most of the twentieth century removed the bulk of the population from any extensive voluntary contact with courts or the ideas and practices associated with them.[11] Closer to home, John Baker has observed that in the twentieth century the delegation of power to administrative bodies established by parliament meant that the rule of law was been replaced by policy.[12] No less important, twentieth-century

---

[8] E. Durkheim, *The Division of Labor in Society* (New York, 1933); *Max Weber on Law in Economy and Society*, ed. M. Rheinstein and E. Shils (Cambridge, MA, 1954); K. N. Llewellyn and E. A. Hoebel, *The Cheyenne Way: Conflict and Case Law in Primitive Jurisprudence* (Norman, OK, 1941); D. Kelley, *The Human Measure: Social Thought in the Western Legal Tradition* (Cambridge, MA, 1990).

[9] In fact an early assertion of a point similar to this can be found in Edward Jenks, *Law and Politics in the Middle Ages* (1912), ch. 1.

[10] See L. Engelstein, 'Combined underdevelopment: discipline and the law in imperial and soviet Russia', *American Historical Review*, 93(2) (1993), 338–53.

[11] L. M. Friedman, 'Opening the time capsule: a progress report on studies of courts over time', *Law and Society Review*, 24 (1990), 237–8.

[12] J. H. Baker, *An Introduction to English Legal History* (1979 edn), p. 131.

traditions amongst lawyers themselves aimed to stress the political and social neutrality of law in order to validate their discipline as a 'science' impervious to change.[13]

These contentions about the role of law in civil society also coincided in European and British history with a concern about distinctions between what have become known as 'elite' and 'popular' culture.[14] Here, a critical assumption is that in societies where levels of literacy were low, and where the equivalents of modern mass media were limited (or controlled by the few), overarching discourses such as those connected with religion or law would be dominated by the social elite in their construction and in their appropriation and use for practical purposes. In the case of religion, for instance, the argument has been put that if we want to know about the spiritual lives of 'ordinary' people, then it is better to look to magical practices and witchcraft rather than to the orthodoxies of established churches.[15] Similarly, there has been an assumption that the knowledge and use of law was effectively limited to the social elite, the aristocracy and gentry.[16] Ordinary people had little impact in shaping the law, and since they also had little opportunity to use it, they were bound to have found it so distant and unfamiliar that it was unlikely to provide the language in which they would seek to understand and articulate either political concerns or the social and economic relationships that constitute everyday life.

This construction of the past may tell us more about the sense of disenfranchisement that exists today under the House of Windsor than it does about the history of the Tudor and Stuart periods. But alternative interpretations of the relationship between law and society have been put forward. These have thus far come more frequently from American law schools than from history faculties on either side of the Atlantic, and they have had little perceptible impact on the writing of British history, but they do suggest that the subject should be approached with an open mind. Echoing Durkheim, Roberto Unger has postulated that every 'society reveals through its law the innermost secrets of the manner in which it holds men together'.[17] Writing about modern Morocco,

---

[13] M. J. Horwitz, 'The conservative tradition in the writing of American legal history', *American Journal of Legal History*, 17 (1973), 275–94; Brooks, *Lawyers, Litigation*, ch. 4.

[14] The seminal work in English is P. Burke, *Popular Culture in Early Modern Europe* (1978).

[15] Compare K. Thomas, *Religion and the Decline of Magic* (1971) with E. Duffy, *The Stripping of the Altars: Traditional Religion in England, c. 1400 – c. 1580* (New Haven, CT, 1992), p. 2.

[16] For an updated view see M. J. Braddick and J. Walter, eds., *Negotiating Power in Early Modern Society: Order, Hierarchy, and Subordination in Britain and Ireland* (Cambridge, 2001), Introduction.

[17] R. W. Unger, *Law in Modern Society* (New York, 1976), p. 47.

Lawrence Rosen found that judicial reasoning surprisingly often corresponded with everyday views within society at large.[18] Indeed, recent work on early modern English subjects such as the nature of religious conformity or attitudes towards gender relations appears to confirm the observation of R. W. Gordon that it is hard to describe any set of basic social practices without describing the legal relationships amongst the people involved.[19] While it would be a grave error to say that simply knowing the law enables us to describe any society, it is equally evident that lawsuits and legal discourse have been seriously neglected as sources for understanding the articulation of social, economic and political relationships and the ways they changed over time.

These radically differing perspectives on the place of law in society constitute an underlying problematic at the heart of this book, one that contributed greatly to the research strategies adopted in order to write it. Questions about 'the law' could only be addressed in the light of a fuller understanding of its meaning in the sixteenth and seventeenth centuries. Given the state of the historiography of the period, there was clearly a need to supplement statistical studies of crime and civil litigation with an investigation of English law as a set of discourses or ideas that involved both general assumptions about the nature of the state and society as well as the more narrow reasoning that dictated the outcome of particular cases. Yet 'the law' is a diabolically ambiguous term. Early modern jurists, like their ancient, medieval and modern counterparts, always regarded it important to provide pithy technical answers to the question, 'what is law?'. But in order for it to achieve any historical purchase, the reified abstraction must be broken down into its constituent ideas, institutions, processes and personnel. English law consisted of centuries of judicial reasoning as well as statutes passed by parliament. Lawsuits were complex transactions in which the interests and aims of the parties were contested in different fora, each of which had its own technical rules, as well as institutional peculiarities that were mediated by legal professionals. The application of the criminal law depended on the interaction of victims, lay constables, justices of the peace (JPs) and juries as well as the authority of the judges who visited the localities to supervise trials. Legal discourse and 'constitutional thought' was a creation of the profession, but it contained many different voices and may well have had different resonances amongst different social groups within the population. Furthermore, its impact on society can only be

---

[18] L. Rosen, *The Anthropology of Justice: Law as Culture in Islamic Society* (Cambridge, 1989), ch. 3.
[19] Robert W. Gordon, 'Critical legal histories', *Stanford Law Review*, 36 (1984), 57–125.

properly evaluated if it is measured against values that were associated with other sources such as religion or social custom.

The source material available for a study which aims to concentrate on the law whilst attempting to maintain a broad and multifaceted understanding of that word is abundant, but it is also in some respects frustratingly limited. Although public trials of both civil and criminal matters are an essential characteristic of English common-law procedure, there are hardly any coherent first-person accounts of one. Nor is it possible to investigate very thoroughly the critical role of juries in the process of adjudication.[20] On the other hand, court records themselves, which give some idea of the people involved and the issues they were contesting, survive in almost overwhelming quantities, and some of these have been put to good use in modern studies. Investigations of crime have thrown light on the records of quarter sessions and assize as well as the nature of crime and criminals. Historians interested in sex, marriage and gender have produced illuminating studies of ecclesiastical court records. But the civil courts and, especially, professional legal materials have received less scrutiny.

From the early sixteenth century onwards, professional legal works such as law reports, treatises and lectures delivered to law students survive in increasing numbers in both print and manuscript.[21] In addition, there are a significant number of extraparliamentary speeches that offer a tantalising opportunity to consider ideas about law that were communicated to the wider public by lawyers and JPs at meetings of courts stretching from the village leet to the twice-yearly visitation into the localities of the assize judges. Material of this kind has been essential in the process of trying to understand ideas about 'the law' in the period, and it has been supplemented by work on semi-official archives such as those of the late Elizabethan and early Stuart lord chancellor Thomas Egerton, those of Charles I's attorney general during most of the 1630s, Sir John Bankes, as well as by consulting the private collections of lawyers and gentry magistrates such as those of the Yelvertons, the Whitelockes, the Newdigates and the Wynns of Gwydir in Wales. Finally, given the objective of investigating law in society, and especially law in the community, court records at the town and manorial level as well as those of the central jurisdictions in London have also been consulted. Yet the book is not so much a study of court usage, or indeed

---

[20] J. S. Cockburn and T. Green, eds., *Twelve Good Men and True: the Criminal Trial Jury in England 1200–1800* (Princeton, 1988).

[21] See, for instance, Baker, *Readers and Readings* and J. H. Baker and J. S. Ringrose, *A Catalogue of English Legal Manuscripts in Cambridge University Library* (Woodbridge, 1996).

the development of legal doctrine, as it is an investigation of the terms on which legal arguments were made and the ways in which legal ideas mapped political and social relationships. For that reason an extremely traditional source of the legal historian, printed and manuscript law reports of cases that were brought before the courts, have proven to be a surprisingly important source.

The overall aim has been to combine an intimate familiarity with the institutional and intellectual world of early modern lawyers with as much local knowledge as possible of the streets and households of villages and market towns from Devon to Northumberland and from Wales to London and East Anglia. Yet since so many relationships, from that between the subject and the monarchy, to that between landlords and their tenants, to that between the person and the community, were contested in courts of law and discussed within the medium of legal thought, it seems inappropriate to preface the work as a whole with the kind of overview of early modern society that readers might normally expect as a background to the more detailed exposition. Since questions about how we should perceive the political, social and economic life of the past are so central to the book's agenda, these have been left to be worked out during the course of its chapters.

Nevertheless, several long-term, and generally uncontroversial, features of the period constitute an essential context for the more detailed story. In chronological order, the first amongst these was the advent of printing in the late fifteenth century and its steady growth and influence thereafter, a development that coincided with the intellectual changes associated with 'humanism' and 'the Renaissance'. Next, there are the religious changes that began in the 1530s with Henry VIII's decision to use a breach with the Roman Catholic Church in order to obtain a divorce from his wife, Catharine of Aragon, and then developed during the reign of Elizabeth (1558–1603) into the creation of a distinctly Protestant church of England that had a profound impact on the religious sensibilities of large numbers of people, rich and poor alike. Thirdly, although it was at times severely set back by epidemic disease before 1550, the sixteenth and seventeenth centuries saw a steady overall increase in the population of England from about 2.3 million at the beginning of the period to as many as 5 million by the end of it. One consequence of these demographic developments was an acceleration in the number of economic transactions as markets in both lands and goods expanded in volume and in the distances covered.[22] At the same time,

---

[22] K. Wrightson, *Earthly Necessities: Economic Lives in Early Modern Britain* (New Haven, CT, 2000).

since the economy of the country and the physical well-being of its inhabitants were heavily dependent on the land and agricultural productivity, the period saw the greater enrichment of those who were able to produce food for the market, and a greater precariousness in the economic condition of those who lived by wages alone. The extent of both the rise of the gentry and systemic poverty in the period have probably been exaggerated, but there seems little doubt that both the gentry and the lesser farmers known as the yeomen and husbandmen added to their wealth and saw improvements in their standards of living, as did many of the townsmen. By contrast, during difficult periods caused by harvest failures, stoppages of trade because of foreign wars or domestic policy, families on the margins of subsistence, the elderly and single parents (most often female), were likely to find themselves dependent on the parish relief which was increasingly made available as a result of late sixteenth-century statutory provision for the poor.[23]

Apart from these general characteristics of the period, several interlocking, but incompletely resolved historiographical issues have helped to determine the shape of the study as a whole, and the identification of these should alert readers to the fact that, for better or worse, the book has been written from the perspective of someone working in an academic history department rather than in a law faculty. Although few historians nowadays would argue that the reigns of either of the first two Tudor kings, Henry VII and his son, Henry VIII, marked an unequivocal break with the late medieval past, an ongoing tradition of interpretation has identified the period as a whole as one in which the agencies of the state became more far reaching and during which the place of ideas about law, and the rule of law, became more deeply engrained in social and political life. According to one long-standing interpretation of the later Middle Ages, if we look closely at fifteenth-century England, we see a social world in which the rule of law as we know it played a relatively small part.[24] The major common law courts were generally under-used, and in the view of some historians, largely ineffective. Amongst the aristocracy and gentry, ties of kinship and the values of an honour society were just as important for regulating behaviour as any concept of adherence to the rule of law. Private disputes were settled either by the resort to violence or by informal arbitration, and there was no very highly developed public law to which constitutional disputes could be referred. By comparison, if we turn from the fifteenth to the mid seventeenth

---

[23] P. Slack, *Poverty and Policy in Tudor and Stuart England* (1988); S. Hindle, *On the Parish? The Micro-politics of Poor Relief in Rural England c. 1550–1750* (Oxford, 2004).
[24] See below, pp. 30, 278.

century, there at first sight appears to be abundant evidence of change. The size of the legal profession had grown enormously, and between 1550 and 1640 litigation came flooding into the central courts at Westminster on an unprecedented scale. The aristocracy and gentry pursued lawsuits and service as local magistrates (JPs) rather than private feuds as a way of maintaining their hegemony over the rest of the population. Furthermore, the common law and common lawyers were deeply involved in many of the constitutional disputes of the early Stuart period.

The questions implied in these formulations, as well as the chronologically fragmented character of much of the existing work on them, accounts for the long-term narrative of the relationship between legal thought and political and constitutional issues that is found in chapters 2 to 8. In particular, while much has been written about the so-called 'common-law mind', the 'ancient constitution' and political conflict in the years prior to 1642,[25] very little of this takes much account of the content and development of Tudor legal thought, a feature of the historiography that partly explains why it has been difficult in recent years to conceptualise a coherent 'constitutional' account of the period leading up to the civil wars, one of the most turbulent periods in the political history of the nation.[26]

At the same time, thanks to the general interest over the past half-century in so many aspects of social history, including questions about the political awareness and 'agency' of people outside the landed elite, any study of law that concentrates only on high politics is bound to seem unsatisfactory and myopic. If lawyers and judges were involved in the collapse of political institutions in the mid seventeenth century, studies of the profession and of litigation have also shown that they were deeply involved in the everyday lives of ordinary people ranging down through the gentry to the so-called middling sort and even the poor. One obvious question suggested by this concerns the relationship between the legal ideas discussed in parliament, or famous state trials, and the everyday legal life of the mass of the population. No less important, though, since law was such an important factor in constituting, or inscribing, social and economic, as well as political relationships, it should have something to tell us about the posture of individuals and families not only in respect

---

[25] The original inspiration for this conceptualisation is, of course, J. G. A. Pocock, *The Ancient Constitution and the Feudal Law: a Study of English Historical Thought in the Seventeenth Century: a Reissue with a Retrospect* (Cambridge, 1987), originally published in 1957.

[26] For a good account see Thomas Cogswell, Richard Cust and Peter Lake, eds., *Politics, Religion and Popularity in Early Stuart Britain* (Cambridge, 2002), Introduction.

of the crown or the state, but in the more confined, but no less important, spheres of interpersonal relations and the community. Hence the second half of the book attempts to investigate a series of questions about the nature of local legal institutions and their impact, about economic and tenurial relationships, about privacy, gender and the family, about the powers of local authorities, and about the way in which the social elite (the aristocracy and gentry) as well as ordinary people, were characterised and affected by legal discourse. The intriguing thing about 'the law' is that it appears to offer a tantalising opportunity to transcend the divide between political and social history.

2   Courts, lawyers and legal thought under the early Tudors

Mapping jurisdictions

The later fifteenth century is sometimes depicted as a period of lawlessness and ineffective administration of justice, but from the perspective of lawyers and legal institutions the evidence for this is far from clear-cut.[1] Most of the features of the English legal system that figure significantly in its later history were already in place. Although the fortunes of lawyers were subject to some fluctuations, there were also important signs of professional vitality. Last, but hardly least, many of the intellectual foundations for thinking about the place of law in politics and society were laid before 1530.

The principal common-law courts, King's Bench, Common Pleas and the Exchequer of Pleas, all three of which dealt with civil litigation between subjects over questions concerning their movable property, money and land, were by the reign of Henry V firmly settled in the royal palace at Westminster, and their records had been carefully kept on large parchment rolls since the twelfth century. Although the volume of business involved was much smaller, the traditional responsibility of the king's council for delivering justice was also devolved in the fifteenth century into firmly established jurisdictions, the courts of Chancery and Star Chamber. For centuries previously, the Chancery had functioned primarily as that part of the royal bureaucracy which issued the original writs necessary in order to initiate suits in other royal courts. But by the reign of Richard II, chancellors had also established and developed a jurisdiction that encompassed forms of trusts, certain types of commercial litigation and cases where litigants argued that there were questions arising from particular circumstances, or matters of conscience, which meant either that they could not receive a fair hearing elsewhere, or that there 'was no remedy at common law'.[2] Although its earlier history has

---

[1] For further discussion see below, pp. 16ff.
[2] Brooks, *Lawyers, Litigation*, ch. 4; *Spelman's Reports*, II, pp. 70–5; Timothy S. Haskett, 'The medieval English court of Chancery', *Law and History Review*, 14 (1996), 245–313.

always been rather more controversial, and although it did not reach maturity until the time of the chancellorship of Cardinal Thomas Wolsey in the 1520s, the origins of Star Chamber were similar, but the remit of its business was more often associated with allegations of violent misconduct on the part of those in dispute and/or the improper exercise of their power by officers of the crown, including JPs as well as lawyers.[3]

If we move beyond the royal courts in London to the localities (including local jurisdictions in London),[4] where most legal business in fact took place, there were many hundred, manorial and borough courts of various sizes and shapes. Such tribunals were usually limited in their jurisdiction either by the geographical range of their competence or by a ceiling on the value of the goods or money at issue about which they could make decisions (usually but not invariably 40s).[5] In the fifteenth century, professional lawyers such as attorneys and pleaders, who were already well established as practitioners in the central courts, appear rarely to have acted within local jurisdictions,[6] but apart from this there were also some crucial similarities between the common-law courts in London and those in the provinces. Their procedures, and very often the form of their records, were similar. In both sets of courts, trials involved the presentation of oral testimony in a public forum and, while proceedings were supervised by a presiding officer, decisions were made by jurors composed of countrymen drawn broadly from the same locality as that in which the dispute occurred.

In this last respect common-law courts at either the central or the local level differed fundamentally from Star Chamber or Chancery, whose procedures had been adopted from Roman and canon law. Lawsuits in these courts were initiated by discursive 'bills' that were written in English rather than the terse and formulaic Latin writs used at common law. Testimony was collected by appointing commissioners in the country who would administer pre-prepared questions ('interrogatories') to witnesses under oath and record the answers in written depositions. Once the evidence had been assembled decisions were made, not by a jury, but by either the lord keeper or lord chancellor acting in Chancery, or by the members of the king's council and royal judges who constituted both judge and jury in the court of Star Chamber.

From time to time over the century and a half from the accession of Henry VII in 1485 to the outbreak of the civil wars, the claim that Chancery could over-ride the letter of the common law by dispensing

---

[3] J. A. Guy, *The Court of Star Chamber and its Records to the Reign of Elizabeth I* (1985), ch. 1.
[4] P. Tucker, *Law Courts and Lawyers in the City of London 1300–1550* (Cambridge, 2007).
[5] See below, p. 241.   [6] Brooks, *Pettyfoggers and Vipers*, ch. 3.

equitable relief, and the divergence between the procedures and practices of the conciliar courts from those of the common law, were sources
of political as well as intellectual controversy.[7] Furthermore, in terms of
their procedures, if not their jurisdictional competence, the conciliar
courts had much in common with the other major grouping of courts
within the realm, those of the church. A hierarchy of jurisdictions that
stretched from the archdioceses of Canterbury and York down through
the consistory courts of each individual episcopal see, the ecclesiastical
courts heard cases in connection with matters relating to matrimony,
sexual morality, defamation, heresy, the behaviour of the clergy and
offences that occurred in churchyards. In the early part of our period,
moreover, they played a role in the adjudication of debts, and throughout the period and beyond, the church courts were the institutions that
oversaw the administration of the last wills and testaments of village
artisans as well as peers of the realm.[8]

The centre and the localities

Since the principal royal courts, those that constituted the domain of
common-law jurisprudence and the common lawyers, sat in London,
attorneys had been employed for centuries by people in the provinces to
take their cases up to the capital and to oversee the procedural aspects of
lawsuits. In the vast majority of disputes, compromise solutions were
agreed at an early stage of proceedings, but when this proved impossible
and a case went to trial, it was normally returned to the locality from
which it arose to be heard by royal judges who travelled into the provinces on a regular basis precisely for this purpose.[9] From the late twelfth
and early thirteenth centuries, royal commissions under the great seal
were issued to panels of royal judges and senior lawyers (the serjeants-at-
law) which empowered them to hear civil pleas before juries in the
country and then report the decisions back to Westminster, and this
same mechanism was also used in connection with felonious criminal
matters such as murder or burglary. Commissions commanding named
judges to ride into the country in order to 'hear and determine' criminal

[7] See below, pp. 145ff.
[8] R. A. Houlbrooke, *Church Courts and the People during the English Reformation 1520–1570*
(Oxford, 1979); R. H. Helmholz, *The Oxford History of the Laws of England*, vol. i: *The
Canon Law and Ecclesiastical Jurisdiction from 597 to the 1640s* (Oxford, 2004).
[9] C. W. Brooks, 'Lawyers as intermediaries between people and courts: some reflections
on the English experience c. 1450–1800' in C. Dolan, ed., *Les auxiliaires de la justice:
intermédiaires entre justice et les populations de la fin du Moyen Âge à la période contemporaine*
(Presses Université Laval, 2005), pp. 279–99.

causes before local juries date back to the twelfth century. By the end of the thirteenth century, these commissioners had been divided into six 'circuits', each consisting of a number of contiguous counties, and by the fourteenth century, the civil and criminal sides of these practices had been combined into twice-yearly meetings in the localities, usually at the principal county town, of what came to be known as assizes.[10] Meanwhile, during the reign of Edward III (1327–77), parliamentary legislation defined the powers of yet another set of royal commissioners, this time consisting of leading laymen and lawyers (and, sometimes, clerics), who came to be known as the justices of the peace (JPs) for each shire, men who were required to investigate offences, and to keep their courts four times a year in order to try those cases, usually minor misdemeanours such as affrays, which were not held over to be considered by the justices of assize.

According to William Lambarde, an Elizabethan expert on the commissions of the peace, the creation of JPs marked a notable step in the decline of community peace-keeping, because it took the 'election' of conservators of the peace out of the hands of 'the common people', and 'translated' it to 'the assignment of the king'.[11] But, while there is a revealing element of truth in this view, it both idealizes the situation before the institution of the commissions of the peace, and, if taken in isolation, exaggerates the decline in the role of the community. Although justices of assize and JPs were always keen to emphasise the potency of the authority they derived from their royal appointment, the administration of the criminal law in the localities continued throughout the fifteenth and sixteenth centuries to depend on the participation of local people. The prime responsibility for the policing of the localities fell on village constables, part-time unpaid officials, who were normally elected through the institution of the manorial court to serve in office for one year.[12] No less important, the outcome of criminal matters at quarter sessions and assizes depended as much on juries drawn from local male householders as it did on justices of assize or JPs. At both types of court, grand juries were responsible for deciding whether the evidence against an accused was sufficiently strong for an indictment to be brought against them. If they thought there was, the matter went to trial before another, so-called petty jury; if they decided there was not, then the case was dropped.[13] In the criminal law, as in almost every other

---

[10] J. S. Cockburn, *A History of English Assizes 1558–1714* (Cambridge, 1972).
[11] Lambarde, *Eirenarcha*, pp. 20–1.
[12] J. Kent, *The English Village Constable, 1580–1642* (Oxford, 1986).
[13] J. S. Cockburn and T. A. Green, *Twelve Good Men and True: the Criminal Trial Jury in England, 1200–1800* (Princeton, 1988).

branch of the administration of justice, the English system depended for its operation on the initiative of individuals with a grievance who set the procedures in motion and then on the involvement of laymen from a fairly broad social spectrum who acted as local officials and jurors.

Legal education and the legal professions

Compared to the period immediately following the Black Death of the fourteenth century, or to the booming business of the Elizabethan era, usage by litigants of the royal courts in late fifteenth-century England was relatively low, and the numbers of professional lawyers, at no more than 180 or so attorneys, and 20 or 30 successful pleaders, was small even for a country with a population of around 2 million people.[14] Levels of civil litigation were quite high in the late fourteenth and first half of the fifteenth century, but there was a significant drop off and then a long trough in legal business which lasted, with some fluctuations, between the 1450s and the 1540s. Although the trough has sometimes been associated with endemic lawlessness and the ineffective administration of justice, viewed against the context of long-term trends in litigation, it seems much more likely to have been a consequence of persistent demographic and economic stagnation, with acute manifestations of epidemic disease and economic depression in particular years being associated with especially precipitate dips in the number of lawsuits.[15] Furthermore, while there is evidence that the late fifteenth and early sixteenth centuries were difficult times for the legal inns in London, the 'law schools' where the common lawyers, including attorneys, barristers and serjeants-at-law, learned their trades, this in fact followed one of the most vibrant and formative periods in their history.

Although its exact nature and institutional setting is not entirely clear, legal education associated with the royal courts in London already existed in some form at the end of the thirteenth century.[16] There is fragmentary evidence that the legal inns were beginning to take shape by the 1340s, and a document of 1388 mentions the Inner Temple, Gray's Inn and the Middle Temple, three of the four so-called 'greater' houses which have survived down to the present day. However, there is no mention of a fourth inn of court, Lincoln's Inn, until the reign of Henry V, and what is particularly noteworthy is that the records of the

---

[14] Brooks, *Lawyers, Litigation*, ch. 7.   [15] Ibid., pp. 66–7, 77–83
[16] P. Brand, *The Origins of the English Legal Profession* (Oxford, 1992).

legal inns, including those of the ten inns of chancery, only survive in quantity from the early fifteenth century.[17]

Since they were unincorporated voluntary societies, there was no official reason why the legal inns should ever have kept records,[18] and for this reason it may be hazardous to conclude that this sudden excrescence of evidence necessarily represents a profound quickening of institutional life. But, even if it is nothing more than a matter of chance survival, the early records of the inns point to a healthy uptake of legal education. Sets of statutes, such as those of Clifford's Inn, as well as the minutes of the governing bodies, such as the 'Black Books' of Lincoln's Inn or the accounts of Furnival's Inn, show a concern for the discipline of 'students' as well as evidence of a progression from junior to senior students, and the provision of teaching by senior members who were at the same time practising lawyers.[19] Apart from attending hearings in the courts, and clerking for established practitioners, which was most common amongst attorneys, the main method of instruction at the legal inns, as at the medieval universities, was through aural exercises, known as readings and moots.[20] Lecture series delivered during the vacations between legal terms, 'readings' normally took parliamentary statutes as a starting point for discussion that could range over broad areas of the law stretching from the definition of crimes such as murder or burglary to accounts of dower, the provision at common law that was made for wives in the event of the death of their husbands.[21] Moots, on the other hand, were more interactive forms of aural learning where tricky, even implausible, sets of circumstances were discussed in debates led by senior members, sometimes including the judges, in order to develop habits of professional reasoning and to allow students to get a feel for what was known as the 'common erudition' or 'common learning' that constituted the common law.

The importance of the legal inns as centres for vocational education is confirmed by the fact that their institutional records are supplemented by the survival of a large number of student manuscript notes of the learning exercises and of discussions in court.[22] But, according to a famous observation made in the 1460s by Sir John Fortescue, a former

---

[17] J. H. Baker, *The Third University of England* (Selden Society Lecture, 1990); *Readings and Moots*, p. xxix; C. W. Brooks, *The Admissions Registers of Barnard's Inn 1620–1869* (Selden Society, Supplementary Series, vol. 12, 1995), pp. 14–36.

[18] J. H. Baker, *The Legal Profession and the Common Law: Historical Essays* (1986), ch. 6.

[19] D. S. Bland, *The Early Records of Furnival's Inn* (Newcastle upon Tyne, 1975).

[20] *Readings and Moots*, pp. xxv–xxxiii.

[21] See, for example, BL, MS Lansdowne 1138 for a series of readings on *statuta antiqua*. For a list of readings see Baker, *Readers and Readings*.

[22] These have been made available in *Readings and Moots*.

chief justice of the King's Bench, the legal inns also attracted large numbers of amateur gentry residents, who joined the societies not so much to learn the law as to be near the political and cultural attractions of the royal court.[23] A comparison of Fortescue's estimate of the total membership of the inns (about 1,600 people) with the relatively small number of practitioners active in both branches of the profession at the time he wrote (at most 250) would seem to indicate that he must have been correct. Indeed, it may be that the general economic conditions of the later fifteenth century, with static but secure landed incomes, and relatively few opportunities in mercantile and retail trades, made the law a fairly attractive prospective career, or at least enabled significant numbers of the sons of the gentry to spend some time at the legal inns.[24] However, there are also indications that the reign of Henry VII, and especially the 1520s, may have seen economic difficulties amongst the memberships of the inns and, possibly, a contraction in their numbers. For instance, at the inn of chancery know as Barnard's Inn, which came into existence under that name in the 1440s, the 1490s and early 1500s appear to have been troubled times. The principal of the inn frequently found it necessary to sue members in order to force them to pay their fees, and he himself fell seriously behind on the annual rent he was obliged to pay to the dean and chapter of Lincoln for the inn's premises in Holborn.[25] Documents which record admissions to the legal inns in sufficient detail for quantitative measurements to be made from them do not survive before the early sixteenth century. It is therefore difficult to argue any more precisely about fluctuations in the size of the memberships. Nevertheless, the numbers admitted in the 1520s would appear to have been insufficient to sustain the memberships of the inns of court at the levels described by Fortescue, and it is certainly the case that the 1520s, 1530s and 1540s were decades of difficulty for all of the inns of chancery.[26]

Legal learning and legal discourse

Despite this evidence of short-term difficulty, the vigour of the early Tudor inns of court, and the virtuosity of the legal profession has been

---

[23] Sir John Fortescue, *De laudibus legum Angliae*, ed. S. B. Chrimes (Cambridge, 1942), pp. 119ff.

[24] C. Carpenter, *Locality and Polity: a Study of Warwickshire Landed Society, 1401–1499* (Cambridge, 1992), pp. 123, 130, 146; Nigel L. Ramsay, 'The English legal profession c. 1340 – c. 1450' (Cambridge University PhD thesis, 1985).

[25] Brooks, *Admissions Registers of Barnard's Inn*, pp. 15–16.

[26] W. R. Prest, *The Inns of Court under Elizabeth and the Early Stuarts, 1590–1640* (1972), pp. 5–7.

extensively demonstrated by the work of Professor Baker. Many technical innovations of the Henrician period in particular will figure frequently in the subsequent chapters of this book.[27] Furthermore, the character of the early Tudor inns as centres for the education of laymen as well as professional lawyers can be further illustrated by considering the milieu and writings of four of their members, Sir John Fortescue (c. 1394–1479) and his contemporary Sir Thomas Littleton (d. 1481), and Christopher St German (c. 1460–1541) and his contemporary, Sir Thomas More (1478–1535). The first three stand out as the most important legal authors of the late medieval and early modern periods before Sir Edward Coke, the chief justice who began publishing his famous reports, as well as a 'commentary' on Littleton, in the first decade of the seventeenth century.[28] More, the son of a judge and himself a barrister of Lincoln's Inn, a future lord chancellor and martyr for the Roman Catholic cause in the 1530s, was also a friend of the leading light of the northern European humanist movement, Desiderius Erasmus. Although the works authored by each of these lawyers were different in their aims, and readerships, each of them has something to say about the multifaceted meaning of law in the reigns of Henry VII and Henry VIII.

Since the inns of court were the places where practising lawyers resided when they were in London during the four legal terms during which the courts were in session, as well as training grounds for young students, there was an ongoing tension between their teaching function and the busy professional lives of active practitioners. Although most of those who achieved professional success participated in readings and moots, delivering a series of lectures was normally a one-off obligation. There were apparently no professional teachers of the common law, and although notes on readings often circulated in manuscript, few ever found their way into print; nor was there a strong tradition of treatise writing before 1550.

For all of these reasons, the posthumous publication of Littleton's *Tenures* in 1481 was a particularly notable event.[29] The book inaugurated legal publishing, and it was authoritative because it was written by a man whose long career was capped by his appointment as a justice of the court of Common Pleas in 1466. A didactic work addressed primarily to students, it became a classic not only because of the simplicity of the exposition, but also because it laid out the foundations of land law in a

---

[27] Sir John Baker, *The Oxford History of the Laws of England*, vol. VI: *1483–1558* (Oxford, 2003).
[28] See below, pp. 324ff.   [29] See *ODNB*.

primarily agricultural society.[30] Littleton began with the fundamental premises that all land in England was held (or seised) from a higher lord rather than owned outright, and that the occupation of land according to a dozen different types of tenure might include obligations (or services) as well as differing conditions with regard to the ability of the holder to alienate it by sale, or make intergenerational transfers to heirs or widows.[31]

Compared to what became the tradition in common-law treatise writing, Littleton's *Tenures* does not contain many references to specific cases or to the legal arguments that had surrounded them. In this it also differed significantly from the other major compilations of the common law in the later Middle Ages, the laconic notes of discussions in court that were known as the *Year Books*. Furthermore, if Littleton was authoritative, the content of the *Year Books* was more tentative and exploratory. The exchanges on points of law they contain are multilateral discussions between judges and advocates rather than adversarial confrontations between opposing lawyers arguing the cases of their clients. The effectiveness of a lawyer depended less on pursuing novel arguments than on his ability to reason sharply along the parameters of the law as it had normally been articulated in the past. At the same time there was much less emphasis on the definitive dicta, or rulings, of the judges than was to become the case from about the middle of the sixteenth century onwards.[32]

Thus, while lawyer's law in the late fifteenth century was clearly based on a sophisticated tradition of inherited learning, it does not appear to have been rigid or hide-bound; indeed Littleton accepted that he had not always taken account of recent innovations and resisted the notion that he had the final word on every subject.[33] Although the citation of older authorities was regarded as an advantage, there was no principle that previous decisions set binding precedents. Nor was there a particular reverence for old law, or a preoccupation with the idea that law should be unchanging. Senior judges on occasion acknowledged readily enough that the law on a particular issue had altered more than once in the recent past. Furthermore, given the emphasis early modern historians frequently attach to the idea that lawyers were addicted to a notion of immemorial law based on great medieval landmarks such as Magna Carta, it is worth stressing that from at least 1450 through to the reign of

[30] Not only the first law book to be published in England, it was arguably the most successful. There were more than ninety subsequent editions.
[31] For Littleton and the land law, see below pp. 325–9.
[32] Baker, *The Legal Profession and the Common Law*, ch. 23.
[33] *Coke on Littleton*, II, *Epilogus*.

Henry VIII, it was a professional commonplace that despite its name, Magna Carta was a statute ('positive law'). Rather than making a claim that they confirmed an ancient and unchanging tradition, the most typical pedagogic move in discussing Magna Carta and the other *statuta antiqua* of the Middle Ages in lectures was to explain how they were intended to remedy defects within the common law before their passage. The general, long-term history of English law was neither particularly crucial, nor, evidently, was lawyers' understanding of it particularly penetrating. But, on the other hand, they had a good idea of changes that had taken place over the past several hundred years on the technical issues with which they dealt, and an appreciation of the importance of statutory innovations introduced by parliament.[34]

Legal science was highly developed, yet it was also highly technical, and there were features of the administration of justice and professional life that limited its accessibility as a body of knowledge. When a litigant brought a dispute in the common-law courts, he did so by having his legal advisors take out a Latin writ issued by the court of Chancery, and the formal proceedings of nearly every court in the realm (on the local as well as the national level), apart from the courts of Chancery and Star Chamber, were recorded in Latin. At the same time, there were hardly any treatises or handbooks written for laymen, and although arguments in court and at the learning exercises in the legal inns were conducted in English, lawyers who took notes on them invariably did so in Law French, an archaic and specialised version of the tongue of William the Conqueror which also provided many technical terms of art. The disadvantages of these language gaps were commented upon at the beginning of a series of lectures that the future judge Anthony Fitzherbert gave at Gray's Inn in the first decade of the sixteenth century, when he acknowledged that regional government might improve and that everyone from barons to the commons would be better able to defend their 'heretages' and possessions if they were better able to understand the law.[35] But, although similar points were made fairly frequently over the ensuing 150 years, Norman French and Latin were only temporarily abolished as the languages of record in the 1650s and remained in place until the 1730s.

On the other hand, although manuscript copies remained the principal medium for legal literature throughout the sixteenth century, the new technique of printing, which had been introduced into England in the 1480s, was fairly quickly exploited for the publication of law books

---

[34] Brooks, *Lawyers, Litigation*, ch. 8.
[35] BL, MS Additional 36,079, fol. 1. Baker, *Readers and Readings*, pp. 369–71.

that followed in the wake of Littleton's *Tenures*. Anthony Fitzherbert's *Graunde Abridgement* (1514), an attempt to sum up the whole of the common law, became both a best-seller and a model for later works. While most publications appeared first in Law French, a significant proportion were subsequently released in English. The statutes of the realm, for example, had an English edition during the reign of Henry VII, and in the preface of his 1519 abridgement of the statutes, the lawyer and legal publisher John Rastell stressed the importance of making works of this kind available in the 'tong maternall'.[36]

During the course of the early 1530s, Rastell became a follower of Protestantism who died a prisoner for his beliefs,[37] and many later writers noted a parallel between the translation of the Bible into English in the wake of the Reformation and the need to make legal knowledge more widely available, but it may be a mistake to overstress the point. Fitzherbert, for instance, remained a religious conservative,[38] and there were some purely professional motivations for endorsing the public dissemination of law, or at least the ideal of the rule of law. Within the profession itself, there was a well-established rhetoric that made the point regularly on ceremonial occasions. For example, in a speech made to newly promoted serjeants-at-law, Sir Robert Brudenell (CJCP) reminded them that their services were essential to a 'publique weale' because without law no man might ride safely, all virtue and goodness would be exiled, theft, murder, rape and all other kinds of mischief would reign to the great 'disquieting of all good men'.[39]

Speeches such as these, which invariably called for the serjeants to exemplify in their own lives the virtues of law and justice, normally included language and ideas drawn from either religious or classical sources. In this respect they illustrate how the public expression of legal values was often made in a language much closer to that of learned laymen (or clerics) than the more technical jargon of legal practice. There was, moreover, a long-standing tradition of disseminating legal knowledge that began well before the age of printing, and which appears to have been reasonably well suited to a predominantly illiterate, but largely face-to-face society. In the thirteenth century, for instance, each reissue of Magna Carta was accompanied by instructions that it should be read out in county courts, and after 1265 the sheriffs of each county

---

[36] H. J. Graham, '"Our tong maternall marvellously amendyed and augmented": the first Englishing and printing of the medieval statutes at large, 1530–33', *UCLA Law Review*, 13 (1965), 58–98; Richard Ross, 'The commoning of common law: debates over printing English law 1520–1640', *University of Pennsylvania Law Review*, 146 (1998), 323–462.
[37] *ODNB.* [38] *ODNB.* [39] Baker, *Serjeants*, p. 280.

were instructed to publish the charter twice yearly.[40] While it is unclear whether this practice continued into the fifteenth and sixteenth centuries, the meetings of most kinds of local courts were regularly accompanied by lengthy speeches known as charges, which gave the presiding officer an opportunity to say something about both the law in general and those aspects of it that were relevant to the particular occasion.

At its most basic, the charge was a lengthy list of statutory and other offences with which the jurors of the court in question were supposed to concern themselves, but there was a link between these local orations and the institutions of the common law in London. Charges to manorial courts were sometimes discussed at the legal inns, and the earliest printed formulary for holding such courts, which appeared in 1512, was clearly associated with a longer manuscript tradition.[41] Similarly, *The Boke of Justices of Peace*, which appeared in 1506, contains a form of a charge that was designed for delivery at quarter sessions. Yet while charges contained a great deal of prescribed, formulaic matter, these details could be prefaced by a more individualistic preamble that provided an opportunity to dilate on the sources of authority of the court, on its general role as a social and legal institution, or indeed more general political issues. One of the earliest known examples of this kind of material is a manorial court charge delivered at Fountains Abbey (Yorkshire) in the late fifteenth century, but it is a fair guess that many more existed, and as paper became more common during the sixteenth century, so the evidence of preambles becomes more and more plentiful.[42] Furthermore, although the evidence is once again stronger from the middle of the sixteenth century than before, meetings of manorial courts and quarter sessions were hardly the only occasions when there was an opportunity for both lawyers and laymen alike to discuss law as a feature of the English polity. Lord chancellors addressed judges who were about to go on their assize circuits and gentry MPs who were returning home from London to the localities.[43] Subsidy commissioners gave speeches to freeholders who were being asked to pay parliamentary taxation, and lawyers who acted as recorders of incorporated towns regularly spoke at the annual celebrations that marked the appointment of mayors or, more rarely, on the occasions when there was a visit of the monarch. Last, but hardly least, the justices of assize 'charged' grand

---

[40] J. C. Holt, *Magna Carta* (Cambridge, 1965), p. 288.

[41] *Modus tenendi curia baronum cum visu Franci plegii* (published by Wynkyn de Worde, 1519).

[42] See below, pp. 87–92.   [43] See below, pp. 59–60.

juries at the beginning of the sessions of the courts over which they presided.[44]

It is arguable that by the seventeenth century public speeches of this kind were the most common, and perhaps the most important, medium for the expression of general political discourse, as opposed to the more systematic and rarefied ideas that contemporaries may or may not have encountered in learned treatises. By comparison, such materials are much rarer for the fifteenth century, but Sir John Fortescue's *De laudibus legum Angliae*, which was first composed in Latin in the early 1470s, is one of the most important examples in English history of a work written by a lawyer for a non-professional audience. After a long and successful legal career, Fortescue lost his office as chief justice of the King's Bench because he was a supporter of King Henry VI and the Lancastrian cause during the mid-century Wars of the Roses, and *De laudibus* was probably composed when he was in exile in France with the Lancastrian court. The literary convention employed by the work is that of a dialogue in which an elderly chancellor (Fortescue) instructs a warlike prince (the son of the deposed Henry VI) on the need for a ruler to devote as much attention to a knowledge and love of the law as he did to the military arts, and judging from the references to 'detestable civil wars', which had been raging recently in England, *De laudibus* may deserve to be read in part as a reflection of the virtues of peace and the rule of law during a time of civil convulsion. In addition, Fortescue was blatantly nationalistic in comparing English legal institutions with those of France. This may have been partly because he wanted to allay fears about the consequences of French aid for the Lancastrian cause, or the predictable hostility of an Englishman to the perpetual enemy of the Hundred Years War, but it was also part of the broader purpose of the work, which was to place English law within a more general and comparative perspective. In doing this, moreover, Fortescue argued not in the technical language associated with the English common law, but in terms that were more generally current in the political thought of medieval western Christendom.[45]

Fortescue began by quoting from Old Testament authorities to prove that law was a divine creation. He also made frequent comparisons between Roman law, the primary source for most continental juristic thought, and English common law. But the Greek philosopher Aristotle is the author to whom Fortescue refers most often, and in its general

[44] For example, see below, pp. 158–9, 226–7.
[45] See Fortescue, *De laudibus*, ed. Chrimes, pp. lxxix–c, for an analysis of some of Fortescue's sources.

account of the place of law in society, *De laudibus* is firmly within the tradition of medieval scholastic Aristotelian thought. Hence the foundations of English law are to be found in divine laws that permeate the universe, natural laws and human laws in the form of statutes and customs that had come to be associated with particular human communities.[46] Even a famous passage in chapter 9 in which he declares that English kings ruled 'politically' as well as 'regally', and therefore could not tax their subjects without their consent, is supported by the classic justification for placing limits on the power of monarchs which is found in Book III of Aristotle's *Politics*. In principle, it was better for a polity to be ruled by the best man than by the best law; but, since it was impossible to guarantee that the office of king would always be held by the best man, Fortescue agreed with St Thomas Aquinas and recommended that, in order to avoid tyranny, 'regal power' should be restrained by 'political law'.[47]

Fortescue also included some discussion of aspects of the English legal system that were relevant to his case but did not go into much technical detail. He praised legal education at the inns of court and chancery, the probity and knowledge of the judges, the relative speed with which causes were dealt with by the central courts, and the effectiveness of sheriffs as royal officials in the localities.[48] In addition, he stressed the advantages of the English system of trying cases, not simply on the evidence of witnesses collected by judges, as was the case in the Romano-canonical tradition, but by a trial before a jury consisting of twelve substantial freeholders.[49] While historians have often queried whether or not Fortescue was over-idealistic in his account of the effectiveness of the English system, it is nevertheless significant that he chose to stress aspects of it that involved the participation of the lay population, including those outside the landed elite, whilst at the same time displaying an awareness of the importance of the local dimension of the administration of justice appropriate for a lawyer who was appointed thirty-five times to serve as a JP in seventeen different counties and boroughs.[50] Whether or not Fortescue ever articulated any of his views during the course of charges delivered to meetings of the commissions of the peace, or when he served as a justice of assize, is unknown, but a mixture of general legal and political theory with an appreciation of the importance of the jury are precisely the qualities found in such speeches

---

[46] Fortescue also wrote a treatise on natural law, as well as one on the 'Governance of England' (see below, pp. 33, 281). *The Works of Sir John Fortescue*, ed. T. Fortescue (2 vols., 1869).

[47] Fortescue, *De laudibus*, ed. Chrimes, p. 27.   [48] Ibid., pp. 119ff.

[49] Ibid., pp. 43, 55, 69.   [50] Ibid., p. lxx.

of the later sixteenth and seventeenth centuries.[51] So, too, was the element of self-interest which, according to the Prince in *De laudibus*, was ultimately the most convincing reason for accepting the virtues of English law.

For who would not prefer to live under a law which makes it possible to live a secure life, rather than under a law such that it always renders him weak and defenceless against the savagery of his enemies.[52]

Unpublished until the 1540s, *De laudibus* did not figure prominently in the professional literature of the sixteenth century; it probably enjoyed a wider readership both inside and outside the profession in the seventeenth.[53] Nevertheless, the Aristotelian approach that Fortescue followed continued to provide a major element in English thinking about the relationship between law and society. The same framework was deployed by the serjeant-at-law Christopher St German in his dialogue *Doctor and Student*, which was first published, again in Latin, in 1528.[54] Essentially a discussion of the circumstances in which litigants should be allowed to seek remedies in cases of conscience from the court of Chancery, *Doctor and Student* became the fundamental early modern text about the nature of equitable relief (the relief of the strict letter of the law in favour of reason or natural justice) in the English system.[55] St German's scholastic learning was probably more profound than Fortescue's, and since he was writing primarily for a professional audience, his work was ultimately more influential, but they shared many of the same premises.[56] Thus, according to St German's 'Student of the Common Law', the laws of England were based on four grounds: the laws of God, the laws of nature (which in England are called the laws of reason), diverse general customs of the realm called maxims and, finally, diverse particular customs and statutes. The law of reason was written in the hearts of men, and 'against this lawe prescription, statute, nor custome may not prevayle, and if any be thought against it, they be no prescriptions, statutes or customs, but things void and against justice'.[57]

For St German, again like Fortescue, these 'grounds' implied that law had a moral purpose, and that it constituted the means by which the

---

[51] See below, pp. 90–2.   [52] Fortescue, *De laudibus*, ed. Chrimes, p. 67.
[53] Ibid., p. x. See below, pp. 100, 122, 139.
[54] For biographical information and the dating see, *ODNB*. Christopher St German, *Doctor and Student*, ed. T. F. T. Plucknett and J. Barton (Selden Society, vol. 91, 1974).
[55] The work also appears to have been designed to show that sources of equity existed within the secular English legal system, as well as within those of the ecclesiastical courts. J. A. Guy, ed., *Christopher St German on Chancery and Statute* (Selden Society, Supplementary Series, vol. 6, 1985), p. 21. Also, see below, pp. 145–50.
[56] Ibid., pp. 1–14.   [57] *Doctor and Student*, p. 15.

kingdom, or political society, and the community became one and the
same thing. Fortescue wrote that 'the Justice which the laws disclose . . .
is perfect because it eliminates all vice and teaches every virtue, so that it
is in itself justly called virtue.'[58] According to St German,

human law is said to be just. . .when it ordains for the common good, when it is
within the authority of the maker, and when it imposes burdens proportionally
upon the subjects for the common good. [B]ut if it imposes burdens upon the
multitude unequally, even though the object be the common good, it does not
bind in conscience.[59]

Fortescue quoted St Augustine for the view that 'A people is a body of
men united by consent of law and community of interest.' In a famous
passage he explained that

The law, indeed, by which a group of men is made a people, resembles the
nerves of the body physical, for, just as the body is held together by the nerves, so
this body mystical is bound together and united into one by the law . . . And just
as the head of the body physical is unable to change its nerves . . . so a king
who is head of the body politic is unable to change the laws of that body, or to
deprive that same people of their own substance against their wills.

Hence, although Fortescue accepted the necessity for monarchical rule
as the natural source of executive authority in a 'public weale', the law
provided the essential framework of civil society.[60] And, since law
received its authority from God and the consent of the community, for
both St German and Fortescue, it was a logical impossibility that the law
could be contrary to the interests of either the community or any individual within it.[61]

Since he himself sat as judge in the court of Chancery before his arrest
for opposing Henry VIII's proposed break from Rome, and was at the
same time engaged in polemical religious controversies with St German,
Sir Thomas More, the last of our lawyer authors, was no doubt fully
aware of the kinds of thinking that lay behind the works of both
St German and Fortescue.[62] Furthermore, while his most famous book,
Utopia (1516), depicted an ideal society that was based on similar ideals
about the common good and social wholeness, More also identified
precisely the kind of alienation of individuals from the state which
Fortescue and St German thought impossible. Although the work

---

[58] Fortescue, *De laudibus*, ed. Chrimes, p. 11.   [59] *Doctor and Student*, p. 27.
[60] Fortescue, *De laudibus*, ed. Chrimes, pp. 31–2.
[61] For some consequences of this view see below, pp. 241–42.
[62] A. Fox and J. Guy, *Reassessing the Henrician Age: Humanism, Politics, and Reform 1500–
1550* (Oxford, 1986), pp. 97ff.

contains an account of a fictional society, *Utopia* also discussed a number of abuses in the administration of justice that contemporaries must have identified easily with England. Felons were liable to be executed for stealing exceedingly small sums of money. Kings used the resurrection of out-of-use laws as a means of raising revenue, and they summonsed judges to come before them during the course of their deliberations so that they could ensure that their own interests were being maintained. Inequalities of wealth in commonwealths meant that rich men were able to take away the livings of the poor not only by frauds, but by manipulating 'public law'. In Utopia, on the other hand, there were few laws, and lawyers were absolutely banished. Laws were to be simple enough so that everyman could plead his own cause.[63]

Ultimately, the happiness of the Utopians lay in the fact that they lived in a society where all property was held in common, which probably explains why the book never seems to have been all that attractive to lawyers.[64] The first-person narrator at one point speculates that there would be 'continual bloodshed and riot' in a country where individuals could not legally keep their 'own' goods,[65] and modern scholars still debate how far More himself was committed to the most radical of the book's proposals.[66] Nevertheless, *Utopia* is an excellent illustration of the influence on at least one English lawyer of that revival of interest in Latin classics known as humanism, and this was a development that did shape the interpretations that contemporaries made of the place of law in politics and society. As Professor Skinner has suggested, the concern of *Utopia* to investigate what constitutes 'the best state of a commonwealth' raises a question that can be traced back to Book V of Aristotle's *Politics*, but which was further developed in the Middle Ages in the tradition of civic humanism associated with writers of the late Roman republic, and, in particular with the philosopher, lawyer and statesman Mark Tully Cicero. Furthermore, the debate in Book I of *Utopia* about the duty of a virtuous man to give counsel to his ruler for the improvement of the entire commonwealth is based on a set of values about participation in public life that were commonly drawn from Cicero's most popular and influential work, *De officiis* (*offices*).[67]

---

[63] *The Yale Edition of the Complete Works of St Thomas More*, vol. IV: *Utopia*, ed. Edward Surtz and J. H. Hexter (New Haven, CT, 1965), pp. 61, 68, 73, 75, 195, 241.

[64] Ibid., pp. 101, 103, 105, 165. The Utopians did maintain that contracts between private persons ought to be observed.

[65] Ibid., p. 107.

[66] See B. Bradshaw, 'More on Utopia', *Historical Journal*, 24 (1981), 1–27.

[67] Q. Skinner, 'Sir Thomas More's Utopia and the language of renaissance humanism' in A. Pagden, ed., *The Languages of Political Theory in Early Modern Europe* (Cambridge, 1987), pp. 125, 129.

Unlike *The Politics* of Aristotle, which was lost to the western tradition at the time of the fall of Rome and only rediscovered in the thirteenth century, Cicero's thought was known throughout the Middle Ages,[68] but it became an even more influential source of political, social and moral ideas as the Renaissance spread northwards from Italy during the fifteenth century.[69] In fact, many of the central political values found in the works of Cicero, including a stress on the importance of the rule of law and the consent of the people who were subject to laws in the making of them, were little different from those expressed in Aristotelian works such as Fortescue's *De laudibus*. But while Aristotle stressed that living in a political society was natural to man, Ciceronian thought emphasised that the formation of a flourishing state depended on convincing men to subordinate their baser instincts to values that would lead to a more civilised life.[70] There was scope for human agency in creating a just society, and a need for citizens to be vigilant in order to maintain one. Indeed, according to Cicero, the duty to the commonwealth was a greater duty than that to one's family. Furthermore, civil magistracy, rather than service in arms, was the most important expression of this duty, and a special stress was placed on the value of effective oratory in leading citizens to adhere to the higher public values.[71]

The magistrate's part is to consider himself as the representative of the city, and to uphold the honour and dignity of it; to observe the laws and customs; to do justice; and to remember that all these things are committed to his charge. It is the part of a private man to live with his fellow-citizens under one common bond of legal duty, neither falling so low as to make himself despicable, nor too much exalting himself; and never to entertain any thought but to the glory and peace of the commonwealth.[72]

The works of Cicero were not taught as part of the curriculum at the inns of court, but given Cicero's emphasis on the importance of the rule of law, on oratory and the fact that he was himself a lawyer, it is not

---

[68] C. J. Nederman, 'Nature, sin and the origins of society: the Ciceronian Tradition in medieval political thought', *Journal of the History of Ideas* (49) 1 (1988), 3–26.

[69] See for example, R. Tuck, 'Humanists and political thought' in A. Goodman and A. Mackay, eds., *The Impact of Humanism on Western Europe* (Harlow, 1994). E. W. Ives, *The Common Lawyers of Pre-Reformation England* (Cambridge, 1983), p. 366, shows that Thomas Keble owned a copy of *De officiis*. C. E. Moreton, 'The library of a late fifteenth-century lawyer', *The Library*, 6 (13) (1991), 338–46.

[70] Nederman, 'Nature, sin and the origins of society'. Below, pp. 56–9.

[71] *Cicero De officiis with an English Translation*, trans. Walter Miller (Cambridge, MA, 1938), pp. 59–61.

[72] Ibid., p. 127. The translation is from *Tully's Offices Turned out of Latin into English by Roger L'Estrange (1680)* (1900 edn), p. 58.

surprising that he became an iconic symbol for the legal profession.[73]
Although Ciceronian humanism had little impact on the technical
content of English law, it did have a profound one on the way in which
the concept of the law was discussed in public speeches and debate.
Moreover, while there was much in Cicero's works that appealed to
lawyers, he was by no means their own private property. Latin works,
including those of Cicero, were already becoming part of the curriculum
at Oxford and Cambridge colleges during the first two decades of the
sixteenth century. By the end of the century, Cicero's works, and
especially *De officiis*, had become a fundamental part of the curriculum
of schools because of its use in the teaching of Latin grammar. Hence
one of the most interesting features of the relationship between law and
society in the Tudor and Stuart periods is that works mined for aphoristic truths by lawyers and statesmen were also well known to school
boys. If the technicalities of the common law frequently appeared 'darke
and farr off', there was a more general political and legal discourse that
was part and parcel of the common intellectual currency of the day. It
was, furthermore, one which could be used either to investigate, or at
least question, the ways in which the native polity could be made better,
or to advocate the maintenance of established legal and political
authority in order to keep a chaotic state of nature at bay.

[73] See below, pp. 62–3.

3 The initiatives of the crown and the break from Rome

Historiography

The early Tudor period is one of the few in English history where questions about the administration of justice and the effectiveness of the rule of law have been linked with considerations of the causes and impact of political instability and the capacity of one monarchical regime to govern more effectively than another. According to Polydore Vergil in the early sixteenth century, and Sir Francis Bacon in the early seventeenth, Henry VII was the monarch who restored law and order after the Wars of the Roses, a period in which political uncertainty and civil war were accompanied by magnate challenges to royal authority.[1] Later on, early twentieth-century historians persistently depicted Henry VII as a 'new monarch', who released the nation from the thrall of 'bastard feudalism'. In the 1950s and 1960s, Sir Geoffrey Elton shifted the emphasis from the first Tudor to his son, Henry VIII, and postulated a 'revolution in government', a view of the Tudor period that is reflected still in studies which see the sixteenth century as a critical stage in the making of the English state.[2]

Although Elton's original insights arose primarily in connection with the organisation of the king's council and focused on the administrative genius and reforming character of the king's principal secretary during the 1530s, Thomas Cromwell, he subsequently attempted to show that Cromwell's general approach to governance included expansion of the use of legislation to accomplish policy objectives (including of course the jurisdictional breach with Rome), and a considerable interest in law reform. Significantly, moreover, this picture was compatible with a series of technical, but important, changes in the common law. First noted in print by the mid-seventeenth-century jurist Sir Mathew Hale and illustrated in detail by the studies of J. H. Baker, these included an expansion

---

[1] Denys Hay, *Polydore Vergil: Renaissance Historian and Man of Letters* (Oxford, 1952).
[2] For a recent example, see K. J. Kesselring, *Mercy and Authority in the Tudor State* (Cambridge, 2003).

in the volume of central court litigation and a decline in local jurisdictions; an increase in the number of legal practitioners (especially attorneys); a multiplication in the number of statutes; and the decline of some of the traditional common-law actions and their replacement by a new form of action, actions on the case, which provided both a new way for people to litigate about their debts and which also opened up entirely new areas of jurisdiction, especially in connection with actions of slander.[3]

Many of the themes raised by these interpretations, including the attitudes of the nobility and gentry towards the rule of law, the fate of local jurisdictions and the connections between litigation and social and economic change, constitute the subjects of subsequent chapters in this book,[4] but concentrating on the significance of the 'new' Tudor monarchs, it is important to stress from the outset that many of the planks in the older interpretations are now subject to considerable doubt. First, as we saw in the last chapter, the life-signs of both the legal profession and the common law were strong rather than weak in the fifteenth century. Second, while Elton tended to downplay the achievement of Henry VII, his own 'Tudor revolution in government' was challenged by interpretations that stressed continuities in connection with important matters such as anti-papal legislation and the changes in the way the king delegated authority and took advice from his councillors.[5] Elton's interpretation, and the school of scholarship he founded, devoted little attention to the relationship between the centre of government in London and the reaction of the localities.[6] No less important, apart from the passage of statutes, some of which will be considered in due course below, there are apparently surprisingly few links between the initiatives of Henrician government and technical innovation in the courts.

Indeed, when comparing the earlier fifteenth century with the rule of the Tudors, it is worth keeping in mind a few basic observations with regard to public order. While the years from the outbreak of the Wars of the Roses in 1450 to the victory of Henry Tudor over Richard III at Bosworth (in Leicestershire) in 1485 involved the crown and nobility in the bloody business of civil war on an uncomfortably regular basis, the

---

[3] G. R. Elton, *The Tudor Revolution in Government: Administrative Changes in the Reign of Henry VIII* (Cambridge, 1953) and *Reform and Renewal: Thomas Cromwell and the Common Weal* (Cambridge, 1973); Christopher Coleman and David Starkey, eds., *Revolution Reassessed: Revisions in the History of Tudor Government and Administration* (Oxford, 1986).

[4] Below, chs. 9–11.

[5] The revision of Elton began with P. Williams and G. L. Harriss, 'A revolution in Tudor history?', *Past and Present*, 25 (1963), 87–96.

[6] Stephen Ellis, *Tudor Frontiers and Noble Power: the Making of the British State* (Oxford, 1995) is a significant exception.

following century was hardly free from major civil unrest. Himself a usurper, Henry VII lived in fear of threats to his throne, a paranoia at least partially justified by the schemes of pretenders. Although his son succeeded peacefully in 1509, economic difficulties coupled with demands for taxation in connection with war created popular unrest in the 1520s.[7] The commons and nobility of much of northern England joined in the Pilgrimage of Grace of 1536, an open rebellion against the direction of Henrician policy under Thomas Cromwell and a perceived threat to traditional Catholicism.[8] There were risings in Devon, Cornwall and East Anglia in 1549, and armed men were raised both for and against the succession of Mary Tudor to the throne in 1553. After the aristocratically inspired and religiously motivated rising of the northern earls in 1569, the reign of Elizabeth finally saw the return of greater domestic tranquillity.[9] But by then the opening up of confessional differences amongst the subjects at a time when the country was threatened by invasions from Spain, and questions about who would succeed the virgin queen, continued to contribute to political uncertainty. Ultimately, it is easier to understand the sometimes desperate appeals to law as a source of social stability in the light of these disturbances than it is to see them as the product of successful state-building projects by either the reigning monarchs or their advisers.

Henry VII and 'fiscal feudalism'

Comparing the reign of Henry VII with that of the later Tudors is difficult because of discrepancies in the evidence. From the 1510s onwards, the survival of vast quantities of state papers, which were accumulated by monarchs and their ministers, provides insights into the problems they faced as well as their aims and ambitions, but material of this kind is virtually non-existent for the reign of Henry VII. Thus comparisons of 'government policy' are not founded on the same documentary base, and the first Tudor has to be judged almost wholly on the basis of his deeds.[10] As it happens, however, some of these were recorded soon after Henry's death by the London lawyer Edward Hall, who produced a

---

[7] G. W. Bernard, *War, Taxation, and Rebellion in Early Tudor England: Henry VIII, Wolsey, and the Amicable Grant of 1525* (Brighton, 1986).

[8] The most recent major treatment is R. W. Hoyle, *The Pilgrimage of Grace and the Politics of the 1530s* (Oxford, 2001).

[9] A. Fletcher, *Tudor Rebellions* (1983 edn).

[10] See for example, C. G. Bayne and W. H. Dunham, eds., *Select Cases in the Council of Henry VII* (Selden Society, vol. 75, 1958), p. xlvi, for the dangers of comparing the later with early Tudor councils.

chronicle-like account of the reign, and his view was that while Henry sometimes made a show of governing according to law, this did not always correspond with the reality in the eyes of his subjects.[11]

Henry appointed a council learned in the law that was supposed to see to the maintenance of 'justice' and 'equity'. In addition, he called parliaments charged with passing laws for the benefit of the commonwealth, and the overall legislative achievement of the reign was not negligible.[12] A total of 192 statutes were passed in an era when parliament sat for relatively short periods of time, including a ground-breaking measure that enabled JPs to regulate alehouses by giving them the power to grant licences.[13] Yet only one statute actually aimed to improve administration of justice in the localities, and the programme as a whole did not depart radically from fairly impressive legislative achievements of the Lancastrian and Yorkist kings.[14]

For contemporaries, especially amongst the landowning classes, the more striking legacy of Henry VII was associated with his efforts to use the law to raise money. One of the problems that contributed to the civil wars from the 1450s onwards was the fact that the crown was so impoverished that it was unable to pay its debts. Facing endless demands for taxation to support the lost English cause in France, parliament had in 1450 gone so far as to pass Acts of Resumption, which abrogated royal grants of crown lands to private individuals in the hope that this would enable the king more effectively to live on his own. In *The Governance of England*, another unpublished treatise that he wrote to advise the king, Sir John Fortescue argued that members of the nobility had rebelled during the Wars of the Roses in part because they had the wealth that enabled them to do so. Therefore he stressed that the crown should be richer than any other peer in the realm, advising that the king should create a kind of trust for the royal patrimony so that it could never be alienated without the assent of parliament.[15] Although they did not go this far, the Yorkist kings, especially Edward IV, took some steps to improve royal finances, primarily by remodelling the administration of crown income, so that it could more effectively collect what was due to it, especially the rents from crown lands. The resulting reforms, which involved the bypassing of the Exchequer and the accumulation of revenues in the Chamber, an office of the royal household, has been

---

[11] *Hall's Chronicle: Containing the History of England During the Reign of Henry the Fourth, and the Succeeding Monarchs to the End of the Reign of Henry the Eighth*, ed. H. Ellis (1809), pp. 498.
[12] Ibid., pp. 424, 498. [13] Below, p. 411. [14] S. B. Chrimes, *Henry VII* (1972), p. 166.
[15] Sir John Fortescue, *The Governance of England: Otherwise Called the Difference between an Absolute and a Limited Monarchy*, ed. C. H. Plummer (Oxford, 1885), p. 152.

described as a change whereby the monarch began to administer his financial assets in much the same way as ordinary landed magnates did theirs, and Henry VII pursued this policy even further.[16]

Henry was able to augment the size of the royal estate as a result of confiscations and attainders that followed the defeat of his enemies at Bosworth. He also created machinery, in the form of escheators and commissioners, that would enable him to exploit more effectively income due from the tenurial obligations of those who held land from the crown. The principal targets were so-called tenants-in-chief, those whose lands had a direct tenurial link with the crown, and who usually happened to be amongst the wealthiest landholders in the realm. The object was not so much to raise revenue in the form of rents as to exploit traditional seigneurial rights in those circumstances where the existing tenant died when his heir was still under age. The first of these, *primer seisin*, entitled the crown to enjoy the profits of any such lands until the heir was old enough to have them granted to him once again; the second, wardship, made the heir a ward of the crown, while he or she was still under age, and thereby in essence gave the king the power to oversee the education of the ward, and to dispose of him or her in marriage.

The claim of the crown to these seigneurial incidents was laid out in a legal text known as the *Prerogativa regis*, that was composed during the thirteenth century, and which had been the subject of occasional readings at the inns of court during the middle years of the fifteenth century. Declarative rather than historical in nature, the fact that *Prerogativa regis* was the subject of readings implies that it was considered a statute, but the question was openly debated by the lawyers. There was no doubt about the nature of the rights of the crown that it outlined, but it is equally important that English kings since the thirteenth century had gradually allowed these to atrophy. In addition, methods of devising the descent of land from one generation to another, most notably the enfeoffment to use, had either bypassed or ignored such obligations for generations.[17]

Given these circumstances, it seems more than a coincidence that two newly appointed serjeants-at-law, Robert Constable and Thomas Frowyk, gave readings on *Prerogativa regis* at the inns of court in 1495.[18] But, although King Henry attended the readers' feast that was held to

---

[16] B. P. Wolffe, *The Crown Lands, 1461–1536: an Aspect of Yorkist and Early Tudor Government* (New York, 1970).

[17] For a recent treatment, see Margaret McGlynn, *The Royal Prerogative and the Learning of the Inns of Court* (Cambridge, 2003).

[18] Ibid. and *Prerogativa Regis. Tertia lectura Roberti Constable de Lycolnis Inne anno 11 H. 7*, ed. S. E. Thorne (New Haven, CT, and London, 1949).

celebrate their promotion, it is unclear how far the choice of topic was politically motivated. Furthermore, though the approaches of the two were in many ways similar, there were also some interesting differences. Constable held that *Prerogativa regis* was a statute while Frowyk said it was merely a lawyer's treatise. Constable tended to emphasise the king's rights, while Frowyk took a more balanced view of the rights of the crown versus those of the tenants.[19] But Frowyk, who was appointed chief justice of the Common Pleas in 1502, was a much more obvious beneficiary of the king's favour.[20]

While these readings, and those that followed on the same subject during the first couple of decades of the sixteenth century, reflect cautious differences of opinion amongst lawyers about the issues at stake, the lawyer Edmund Dudley, who became president of the king's council in 1506, and Sir Richard Empson, chairman of the King's Council Learned in the Law, became directly associated with revenue-raising policies that were strictly speaking legal, but which involved the resurrection of long-out-of-use legal obligations that also emphasised the ultimate tenurial superiority of the crown in connection with the holding of land.[21] This was the first, but hardly the last, time in the Tudor and Stuart periods when such issues came to the fore.[22] Furthermore, just as was the case in the 1530s and again in the 1630s, royal attempts to exploit 'fiscal feudalism' were unpopular amongst those they affected, and since the king's tenants-in-chief tended to be the richer subjects of the realm, members of the aristocracy and gentry, this had political implications. Edward Hall put the best gloss on the case for the king when he commented that this 'good and modest prince' had pursued the policy in order to quell the rebellious inclinations of his subjects, but Hall also alleged that the inquests the Council Learned carried out in order to prove the king's tenurial claims were fixed in his favour. He observed that 'some' people argued that the policy owed more to the king's personal desire for 'gain and profit' than for any prudent policy or politic provision.[23] He disliked Empson and Dudley, a view so widely shared that Henry VIII responded by sending the pair to the Tower on the day after he acceded to the throne in 1509. According to another contemporary barrister, Sir John Spelman, this was because they, along with other 'promoters', had sought to carry out the covetous purposes of Henry VII rather than advance the good of the commonwealth. Edmund

---

[19] CUL, MS Hh.2.1, fols. 1ff.   [20] McGlynn, *The Royal Prerogative*, p. 247.
[21] J. B. Hurstfield, 'The revival of feudalism in early Tudor England', *History*, 37 (1952), 131–45.
[22] See below, pp. 42–5, 194, 325.   [23] *Hall's Chronicle*, p. 502.

Dudley subsequently admitted as much himself, and both were executed soon thereafter.[24]

Wolsey and justice

Thus Henry VIII began his reign with a demonstration that he intended to rule according to justice, equity and the law.[25] His council quickly called for a compilation of reports on recent proceedings in connection with commissions of *oyer and terminer* so that these could be shown to the king. William Wareham, archbishop of Canterbury and lord chancellor, made a speech before parliament in which he stressed that the proper administration of the law was high up on the new government's agenda.[26] While doubtless sincere, these moves were hardly novel, probably reflecting little more than an attempt by the new monarch to win moral legitimation by promising to fulfil the age-old monarchical obligation to provide impartial justice. Nor is it likely that this aspect of royal policy would have resulted in anything very remarkable if Henry had not decided in 1515 to make the cleric Thomas Wolsey his lord chancellor and chief minister.

Wolsey, the son of an Ipswich butcher who eventually became archbishop of York and a cardinal of Rome, achieved a virtual monopoly over the reins of government between 1515 and 1529, a period in which Henry VIII's aggressive European foreign policy and war were principal preoccupations of the regime. Yet, although Wolsey was an extremely busy man, he attached importance to the role the lord chancellorship gave him in the judicial system, and he made a dynamic, if controversial, impact. In effect the crown's chief law officer, he was the presiding judge in the court of Chancery and a powerful figure in the court of Star Chamber, a nascent manifestation of conciliar justice that had received some statutory recognition in the previous reign. On several occasions in the 1510s, Wolsey spoke before the king and council of the need for the effective administration of justice, and he also undertook the exemplary prosecution of some notable men, including the earl of Northumberland. In November 1519 he reiterated his objectives at the ceremonial swearing-in of new JPs, and the articles of instruction that he referred to in his speech were subsequently put into print.[27]

---

[24] *Spelman's Reports, II*, p. 49. Dudley enjoyed a good reputation in the profession earlier in his career.

[25] This course was also recommended by Edmund Dudley's allegorical *The Tree of Commonwealth*, ed. D. M. Brodie (Cambridge, 1948), which was composed in prison.

[26] HEHL, MS Ellesmere 2652.

[27] J. A. Guy, *The Cardinal's Court: the Impact of Thomas Wolsey in Star Chamber* (Hassocks, 1976), pp. 30–2.

Wolsey's speeches are known about only because notes on them were extracted, along with other memoranda about the proceedings of the court of Star Chamber, from now lost records of the council during the later sixteenth century.[28] This may be why they seem stronger on generalised conventional rhetoric than on detailing particular problems and specific solutions for dealing with them. On the other hand, while the nature of the evidence makes it dangerous to speculate about whether the charges to JPs were an innovation, they appear to mark the first recorded instances of a practice which subsequently became a regular feature of Tudor and Stuart government thereafter. Furthermore, by relaxing procedural requirements, Wolsey made it easier for litigants to seek conciliar justice, especially in Star Chamber.[29] Even Edward Hall who, like many other contemporaries, had very little to say in favour of Wolsey, commented that his willingness to punish lords and knights, as well as ordinary men, encouraged many poorer people to approach his courts, and there is evidence that he used Star Chamber to punish the excesses of sheriffs and JPs, especially in the north.[30] Business in the court of Chancery in fact increased hardly at all, but the number of bills brought in Star Chamber, which frequently alleged that the offences being complained about caused the hindrance of the due administration of justice, grew from not much more than a dozen a year in the reign of Henry VII to an average of about 100 a year during Wolsey's ascendancy. The number of cases from people who claimed that they were too impoverished to sue through the normal courts also became so numerous that Wolsey eventually found himself overwhelmed by the business and set up the court of Whitehall, the forerunner of the later court of Requests, to relieve the pressure upon himself.[31]

Historians have endlessly debated exactly what motivated Wolsey's approach and his impact. There is little reason to doubt an element of sincerity; he may even have been influenced by 'humanist' ideology.[32] But his judicial powers provided him with weapons that could be used against his political enemies while the populist element may well have been associated with a persistent quest for personal aggrandisement that was such a dominant feature of his character. No less important, Wolsey as a judge was also Wolsey the royal minister who needed to raise money for the king in order to pursue an ambitious foreign policy during a

---

[28] HEHL, MS Ellesmere 2652–5. [29] Guy, *Cardinal's Court*, p. 81.
[30] *Hall's Chronicle*, p. 587; John Guy, 'Wolsey and the Tudor polity' in S.J. Gunn and P.G. Lindley, eds., *Cardinal Wolsey: Church, State and Art* (Cambridge, 1991), p. 69.
[31] For comparative figures for litigation, see Brooks, *Pettyfoggers and Vipers*, pp. 54–5.
[32] See, for example, J.J. Scarisbrick, 'Wolsey and the common weal' in E.W. Ives, R.J. Knecht and J.J. Scarisbrick, eds., *Wealth and Power in Tudor England* (1978).

decade and a half when the economy was frequently in difficulties.[33] Edward Hall praised some of Wolsey's achievements, particularly those that were carried out with the 'consent of the body of the whole realm' in parliament, but he was distinctly critical about 'forced loans' of the early 1520s, which Wolsey and the king attempted to raise in lieu of parliamentary taxation. On Hall's account, the common complaint in London and the provinces was a kind of echo of Fortescue's dictum in *De laudibus*: 'if men should give their goodes by a Commission, then were it no worse then the taxes of Fraunce, and so England should be bond and not free'. A common counsellor of London reportedly told Wolsey that there were statute laws against levies of the kind he was trying to raise.[34] In Suffolk, a clothier called John Green impressed a leading lawyer, Sir John Wingfield, with his learned arguments against the levy.[35]

When Wolsey fell from power in 1529 because he failed to facilitate a divorce from Catherine of Aragon that Henry needed in order to marry Anne Boleyn, large numbers of 'common people' turned out to watch the cardinal as he made his way by boat from Westminster to Putney. According to Wolsey's contemporary biographer, George Cavendish, they 'rejoysed' at his fall partly because the 'common people' always disdain those in authority, and Cavendish also claimed that Wolsey had suffered the fate of 'all good Iusticers' who 'mynestreth equytie to all men Indifferently'.[36] Yet, there was certainly more to the story. In a collection of notes he made on Hall's *Chronicle* during the first half of the reign of Elizabeth, the future lord chancellor Thomas Egerton was impressed by the claim that, although the cardinal's courts were initially popular, the people eventually discovered that few of their lawsuits were ever concluded, and that the decisions delivered were liable to be challenged in the common-law courts. Consequently, they quickly turned away from Wolsey's tribunals towards common-law jurisdictions such as King's Bench and Common Pleas.[37]

It is unclear exactly how far this was the case, but Egerton seems to have known the Henrician archives quite well. If Star Chamber bills from Wolsey's period in office frequently contain allegations about the damage done to the administration of justice, the answers of defendants just as often began by making the counter-claim that the court had no lawful jurisdiction because the matter could more properly have been

---

[33] Bernard, *The Amicable Grant*.   [34] *Hall's Chronicle*, pp. 698–9.

[35] D. MacCulloch, *Suffolk and The Tudors: Politics and Religion in an English County 1500–1600* (Oxford, 1986), p. 294.

[36] *The Life and Death of Cardinal Wolsey by George Cavendish*, ed. R. S. Sylvester (Early English Text Society, 1959), pp. 100–1.

[37] HEHL, MS Ellesmere 2810.

heard at common law. Although many common lawyers practised before the courts where he presided, Wolsey apparently earned the general antipathy of the legal profession. Some of this may have been due to shifts of business away from King's Bench and Common Pleas in a period when rates of litigation were generally low, but there were other matters of style and substance at stake. Edward Hall criticised Wolsey's mendacity and the excessive ambition that made him one of the most hated royal councillors since the duke of Suffolk in the 1450s.[38] In the works he wrote about the exercise of the equitable jurisdiction in England, Christopher St German raised questions about the dangers of courts, like the Chancery, that were presided over by single judges, who might or might not act according to the common law of the realm.[39] In 1527, the members of Gray's Inn put on a Christmas play that had been written some twenty years earlier by one of their members, John Roo, which depicted the dangers of allowing good government to become overwhelmed by dissipation. Evidently taking the matter personally, Wolsey subjected the author to the profound disgrace of being expelled from the order of the serjeants-at-law,[40] and the cardinal's animosity towards the common lawyers may well have been even more wide-ranging than this. In 1528, the lawyer Richard Rich, one of the more sinister political operators of the period,[41] wrote Wolsey a fawning letter in which he said he knew Wolsey had long been interested in reforming the common law. Rich went on to suggest that if he and the cardinal could meet in private, he would provide a list of abuses that might be suitable for action.[42]

Unfortunately, Rich's request for secrecy has made it impossible to establish what he had in mind, and it is uncertain exactly how systematic or far-ranging any of Wolsey's plans may have been. What is clear is that he injected dynamism into Star Chamber, a jurisdiction that went on to establish itself as one of the major courts in the realm until its abolition in 1641, but one whose Romano-canonical forms of procedure were sometimes questioned, and where the fact that the king's council acted as both judge and jury made it a potential instrument of abuse.[43] At the time of Wolsey's fall in 1529, one of the formal charges laid against him was that he had committed the statutory offence of *praemunire*, that is removing to other jurisdictions cases which should have been heard at

---

[38] *Hall's Chronicle*, p. 774

[39] Christopher St German, *Doctor and Student*, ed. T. F. T. Plucknett and J. Barton (Selden Society, vol. 91, 1974), p. 129; J. A. Guy, ed., *Christopher St German on Chancery and Statute* (Selden Society, vol. 6, 1985), pp. 65–85, 102–5.

[40] Ibid. *Spelman's Reports*, II, pp. 77–9.   [41] *ODNB*.

[42] *L & P*, vol. 4 (pt 2), no. 4937. Dated 16 Nov.   [43] See below, p. 232.

common law, and by the early seventeenth century, if not earlier, he was clearly regarded by lawyers as symptomatic of everything bad that could happen when jurisdictional power was put in the hands of a clergyman.[44] His fall and replacement by Sir Thomas More nearly ended the tradition of appointing clerical chancellors that stretched back to the Middle Ages. Although several churchmen were given the great seal during the brief reign of Queen Mary, the common lawyers dominated the post for the remainder of the sixteenth century.[45]

Law reform and 'uses'

During his brief tenure as chancellor in the early 1530s, Thomas More managed to smooth relations between the common law judges and the courts over which he presided, whilst at the same time overseeing a significant increase in the amount of business entertained by them.[46] But, if for no other reason than that he soon became preoccupied with combating the heresies he associated with Henry's strategy of using a break from the Roman church as a way of securing a divorce, More made none of the radical proposals for law reform that might have been expected from the author of *Utopia*.[47] Nevertheless, during the course of the 1530s, several schemes relating to the law, some of them evidently inspired by humanist and commonwealth ideals of social improvement, were in circulation amongst those who advised the government or who wanted to exert influence on it.[48] In fact, one of the most interesting of these came from More's polemical opponent in the debate over the divorce and the break from Rome, Christopher St German, who was responsible for a parliamentary draft, dated 1531, which combined a number ideas for reforming the clergy and the church courts with a programme designed to help the deserving poor and punish, or put on work, the undeserving.[49]

St German, whose advocacy of a united campaign by the crown and parliament to reform clerical abuses was useful to Henry VIII's broader political objectives, does not appear to have been all that close to the centre of government in connection with other business, and his

---

[44] See below, p. 148.
[45] J. A. Guy, *The Public Career of Sir Thomas More* (Brighton, 1980), pp. 31–2. The churchmen were Thomas Goodrich, bishop of Ely, Stephen Gardiner, bishop of Winchester and Nicholas Heath, archbishop of York. The last clerical lord keeper, John Williams, bishop of Lincoln, was appointed in 1621. See below, pp. 150–1.
[46] Brooks, *Pettyfoggers and Vipers*, pp. 54–5.   [47] See above, pp. 26–7.
[48] For the context see P. Slack, *From Reformation to Improvement: Public Welfare in Early Modern England* (Oxford, 1998), chs. 1–2.
[49] Guy, *Christopher St German*, pp. 127ff.

proposals were in any case probably too radical to get very far. On the other hand, the voluminous papers of Thomas Cromwell, Henry's chief minister in the 1530s, make it abundantly clear that he took considerable interest in judicial administration and that those associated with him were at times actively suggesting schemes of reform of greater or lesser degrees of radicalism. There are, for instance, reports from the localities of particular problems associated with recalcitrant juries, the performance of clerks of the peace, and the loyalty of JPs, but the archive also contains a number of more adventurous materials.[50] In 1534, for example, Cromwell was at least considering a proposal for creating a statutory court charged with the more effective enforcement of social and economic legislation passed by parliament since the beginning of the reign of Henry VII. The tribunal was to consist of six 'discrete' men, of whom at least three were supposed to be utter barristers, and they were to be called 'conservators of the commonweal'. Sitting at Whitehall, and employing a seal which depicted industry and handicraft, they would be empowered to appoint agents in the counties and to bring before them anyone they thought guilty of violating the laws in question.[51] Even more ambitiously, the government went so far in the later 1530s as to establish a commission consisting of three lawyers, Thomas Denton, Nicholas Bacon (the future lord keeper) and Robert Carey, who were supposed to report on the nature and organisation of the inns of court, evidently with a view towards either converting some of them into royal academies for training young gentlemen and noblemen in Latin, French and a smattering of law, or creating parallel institutions with a similar purpose.[52]

Along with calls from humanists such as Richard Morison and Thomas Starkey that the lawyers be brought into order, and that their barbaric Latin and Law French be replaced by classically correct Latin and English, none of these more ambitious plans ever seems to have come close to implementation.[53] Henrician government was certainly willing to use statute law as a way of undertaking social and political engineering,[54] but while the 1530s and 1540s were also decades in which significant measures of law reform were mooted, it is not in the end clear how highly they figured on the otherwise busy political agenda

---

[50] *L & P*, vol. 8, no. 157; vol. 11, no. 158; vol. 13 (pt 1), pp. 41, 128, 541; (pt 2), p. 485.

[51] Ibid., vol. 7, p. 603. Discussed by Elton in *Reform and Renewal*, ch. 6.

[52] R. M. Fisher, 'Thomas Cromwell, humanism and educational reform 1530–1540', *Bulletin of the Institute of Historical Research*, 50 (1977), 153–63. For the details see Edward Waterhous, *Fortescutus illustratus: or a Commentary on that nervous treatise De laudibus legum Angliae* (1663).

[53] *Spelman's Reports*, ii, p. 36.

[54] Sir John Baker, *The Oxford History of the Laws of England*. vol. vi: *1483–1558* (Oxford, 2003), p. 35.

of Thomas Cromwell.[55] From the perspective of the common law and its practitioners, apart from some relatively minor technical changes introduced in parliament in 1540, the really important measures were the statutes passed in 1543 which integrated Wales into the English legal system,[56] and the passage of the Statute of Uses in 1536 and the Statute of Wills in 1541.

The history of the Statutes of Uses and Wills is directly linked to the attempts, discussed earlier, of Henry VII and Henry VIII to increase revenues from the seigneurial obligations tenants-in-chief owed to the crown, but they cannot properly be understood without explaining a legal device, known as the 'use', which was widely employed by landholders in the late medieval and early Tudor periods for a number of purposes, most notably the intergenerational settlement of land. In order to create a 'use', the holder of land transferred the legal ownership of it to trustees ('feoffees') who then held it 'to the use of' himself and/or anyone else he nominated (the beneficiary was in either case known as the *cestuy que use*). The popularity of the device lay principally in the fact that it overcame the common-law rule that prohibited land from being passed to nominated heirs by means of a will. It worked because a testator *cestuy que use* passed on the 'use' (occupation and profits) of the property, but not the ownership itself, which remained in the hands of the trustees. With the aid of the use, a landowner could overcome the law of primogeniture and pass his property to whomever he wished.[57]

However, the use also generated several problems, all of which lay in the background to the passage of the statute. First, since the beneficiary of the use, *cestuy que use*, divested himself of ownership of the property but continued to enjoy the profits from it, the nature of his estate in the eyes of the common law was problematic. Second, the creation of uses frequently involved legal instruments, such as the 'bargain and sale', which did not require public notoriety, traditionally a necessary part of land conveyancing. Hence uses were negotiated through 'secret', informal, agreements which were sometimes associated with attempts to defraud creditors or future purchasers. Finally, and most importantly in connection with the passage of the statute, the beneficiary of a use could evade seigneurial incidents such as wardship and *primer seisin* (whereby the lord enjoyed one year's profits of the land), which were due when a lesser tenant died and his heir came into ownership. Since *cestuy que use* had transferred the legal estate of his property to a self-perpetuating group of trustees, the owner of his land never died.

[55] Elton, *Reform and Renewal*, ch. 6.   [56] See below, pp. 124–8.
[57] *Spelman's Reports*, II, pp. 192–204.

Because the crown was a major landlord, it had long suffered significant losses of income as a result of uses, and statutory attempts to remedy this state of affairs were made during the reign of Henry VII, but the sustained attack on uses as a means of evading 'feudal' obligations appears to have begun in 1526 when the council ordered the rigorous prosecution of royal rights. In the same year, Thomas Audley, evidently attempting to find favour with the crown whilst at the same time attacking Wolsey, delivered a lecture at the Inner Temple in which he developed the legal case against the practice.[58] Then, in 1529, Lord Chancellor More signed an agreement with thirty members of the peerage in which the king agreed to forego two-thirds of his income from feudal incidents in return for a package deal in which the crown and all other feudal lords would be guaranteed the other third regardless of whether land was devised by will or held through uses.

Bills based on this agreement were put to parliament on several occasions in the early 1530s, but rejected by the Commons who apparently saw less for themselves in the compromise than the peers had. In 1532 Henry was so exasperated by their refusal that he threatened to withdraw the deal and 'search out the extremitie of the law'. An opportunity to do just this was found in 1535 when the crown brought a lawsuit against the testamentary settlement that a recently deceased peer, Lord Dacre of the South, had made of his estate. Under considerable pressure from the king, the judges sitting in Exchequer Chamber ruled that uses and a will could not be employed to establish the inheritance of land.

The decision in *Dacre's Case* did not, as is sometimes said, make uses illegal. It did, however, threaten the tenure of anyone who held his land as a result of a will, and this was enough to force parliament to accept a tough bill on uses, which became law in the spring of 1536. The preamble to the statute rehearsed alleged abuses that had long been associated with uses, but the body of the bill was ingeniously simple. It declared that where several persons held land to the use of another person, the *cestuy que use*, not the trustees, would be deemed to have the ownership.[59] The advantage of this change to the crown and other feudal lords was that since the beneficiary of the use, and not the self-perpetuating trustees, was henceforth considered the owner of the land, feudal incidents could be collected when he died because ownership would clearly pass to his heir. Wills of land were also in effect abolished. Furthermore, while the statute protected the rights of married women who had an income, or 'jointure', settled on them for their maintenance

---

[58] Ibid., pp. 198–9. BL, MS Hargrave 87, fols. 427–57. [59] 27 Henry VIII, c. 10.

in the event of the death of their husbands, it also stipulated that in those cases where a jointure had been established, the woman was to be deemed to have forfeited her common-law right of 'dower', which entitled her to claim one-third of the estate of her deceased spouse. Finally, there was one concession to the landowning classes, which must have been suffering considerable anxiety. The last clause specifies that wills made before 1 May 1536 were to be considered valid despite anything in the Act, or any previous judicial decision to the contrary, and thereby protected existing titles to land against the potentially disastrous consequences of the judgment in *Dacre's Case*.[60]

Since the Statute of Uses enabled the crown to exploit feudal incidents to the full, and limited the possibility of making grants of land in wills, it was intensely unpopular. By the later fifteenth century, service as trustees in connection with uses was a regular source of income for lawyers. Since most landholders from the gentry down through the yeomanry frequently employed uses and disposed of land by will, it is not surprising that opposition to the statute figured as one of the grievances raised by the participants in the Pilgrimage of Grace of 1536; by 1538 Thomas Cromwell seems to have been aware that the lawyers were busily at work devising legal instruments designed to overcome the restrictions created by the statute.[61]

By 1540, these considerations, along with the willingness of the king to make concessions to more conservative counsel as the influence of Cromwell waned, led to a compromise solution to the problem of uses that was enacted in the Statute of Wills. Based on the principle that obligations such as wardship and *primer seisin* would be levied on only one-third of the land technically liable to them, the statute in effect meant that two-thirds of all lands held directly from the crown (tenure-in-chief) could be devised by will at the 'pleasure' of the owner. Similarly, in those cases where land was held by military tenure (knight's service) of a lord other than a king, that lord could collect feudal incidents on a third. Landowners who held land neither from the king nor by military tenures were completely free to dispose of all of their land by will.[62] Thus, in return for a clear obligation to pay a part of their feudal dues, landholders were released from the pressure that the Statute of

---

[60] *Spelman's Reports*, II, pp. 192–202. See also E. W. Ives, 'The genesis of the Statute of Uses', *English Historical Review*, 82 (1967), 673–97.

[61] N. L. Ramsay, 'The English legal profession c. 1340 – c.1450' (Cambridge University PhD thesis, 1985), pp. 70–3; S. J. Gunn, 'Peers, commons and gentry in the Lincolnshire revolt of 1536', *Past and Present*, 123 (1989), 52–79.

[62] 32 Henry VIII, c. 1. See also J. M. W. Bean, *The Decline of English Feudalism 1215–1540* (1968).

Uses had put them under to pay all. In addition, although legal devices involving uses had made it possible before 1535 to dispose of land by will, the Statute of Wills marked the first full recognition of the legality of doing so. This was important because it enabled landowners to break the custom of primogeniture and provide for their children as they pleased.[63]

The break from Rome

Accompanied by the creation of the court of Wards, the history of the statutes concerning uses and wills amply illustrates Henry VIII's willingness to use the law in order to bully his subjects, and the statutes were significant because of the impact they had in shaping the subsequent history of the land law.[64] Even so, in the general political history of the period they understandably take second place to the legislation Henry passed through parliament in order to divorce his wife, Catherine of Aragon, and marry Anne Boleyn in the hopes of producing a male heir to the throne: the Act in Restraint of Appeals (1532) which declared England an 'empire' subject to no other earthly authority, and the Act of Supremacy (1534), which proclaimed that the king was the head of the church in England.[65]

Despite its powerful wording, the Act in Restraint of Appeals was primarily a technical measure designed to prevent Catherine of Aragon, and hence any other subject, from appealing decisions made in English church courts to Rome. In this respect it probably reflected, or appealed to, a brand of hostility to the ecclesiastical court jurisdiction that seems already to have been popular amongst common lawyers. Recent research has shown that from the later fifteenth century onwards, common-law writs of prohibition, and actions based on the Statute of Praemunire, had been used by litigants and their lawyers to attack the competence of the ecclesiastical courts in England to hear certain types of case, most notably actions of debt and those involving defamation not involving allegations of sexual immorality. As Professor Helmholz has written, as far as the church's loss of jurisdiction is concerned, by the time of the official Reformation, a jurisdictional reformation had already commenced.[66]

---

[63] For subsequent developments see N. G. Jones, 'The influence of revenue considerations upon the remedial practice of Chancery in trust cases 1536–1660' in *Communities and Courts*, pp. 99–114.

[64] See below, pp. 326–7.   [65] 24 Henry VIII, c. 12; 26 Henry VIII, c. 1.

[66] R. H. Helmholz, *Roman Canon Law in Reformation England* (Cambridge, 1990), pp. 26–33.

The chronicler Edward Hall, himself a sympathiser with the Reform cause, recorded the famous case of Richard Hunne, who was found dead in prison in 1514 after having been arrested for failure to pay a mortuary fee, and which evidently stirred up feelings of Londoners in the 1520s against the church courts there.[67] Parliamentary legislation in 1529 empowered parishioners all over the country to use the common law courts to sue clerics who sold their parish livings or became non-resident and thereby left their flocks without a priest.[68] As noted already, although apparently a traditionalist in religion, in the 1530s Christopher St German engaged in open pamphlet warfare with Sir Thomas More, advocating the use of the authority of parliament in order to reform the church in the name of efficiency and good government.[69] His *Treatise Concerning the Power of the Clergy and the Law of the Realm* (1534/5), which argued for the subordination of canon law to English common law, provided a foretaste of conflict between the common lawyers and the churchmen that remained a dynamic element in shaping the relationship between law and politics throughout the later sixteenth and early seventeenth centuries.[70]

Nevertheless, although circumstances as well as professional inclination may have made them a minority, lawyers who remained attached to the old religion and the connection with Rome could find legalistic arguments supporting their position. The most important of these was, of course, More, but another was Robert Aske, a barrister of Gray's Inn, who was a principal player in the major revolt that took place in the north of England in 1536, the Pilgrimage of Grace. As a result of his opposition to the relaxation of the laws against Protestant 'heretics', and his refusal to accept the consequences of the break from Rome, More fell into disfavour with the king and resigned the great seal in 1532. Subsequently, his involvement with the Catholic prophetess, the Nun of Kent, and general hostility to the king's policies, led to his indictment for treason and execution in the summer of 1535.[71] At his trial, More rejected the 'Reformation' legislation on two grounds. First, the Acts of parliament concerned were null and void because they attempted to alter the laws of God and the church, 'the supreme government of which, or any part thereof, may no temporal prince presume by any law to take upon him'. Second, the new legislation was, he held, contrary to Magna Carta,

[67] *Hall's Chronicle*, p. 573.
[68] R. C. Palmer, *The Selling of the Church: the English Parish in Law, Commerce, and Religion 1350–1550* (Chapel Hill, NC, 2002).
[69] Guy, *Christopher St German*, pp. 38–9.   [70] See below, pp. 52, 97ff.
[71] Alaistair Fox and John Guy, *Reassessing the Henrician Age: Humanism, Politics, and Reform 1500–1550* (Oxford, 1986), pp. 97–119.

the first chapter of which guaranteed the liberties of the English church (*Ecclesia Anglicani*).[72] Similarly, Robert Aske maintained that Magna Carta was a legitimate warrant for the rebellion of the Pilgrims because, he claimed, Lord Darcy had told him that it had been a common practice in the House of Lords for members to declare at the opening of parliaments that they affirmed the liberties of the church granted in the charter.[73]

These denunciations of the novelty of the 'Reformation' statutes were in effect the bases of Elton's claim for their constitutional significance as the point at which the 'omni-competence of parliamentary statute' was firmly established.[74] Yet arguments such as those of More and Aske were hardly self-evidently true in terms of contemporary jurisprudence. Although there was a theoretical adherence to the view that English laws had to conform to the laws of God, the extensive competence of positive laws made in parliament was also recognised. If Magna Carta, 'though called a charter' was in fact a statute made by parliament, then parliament could change it.[75] There were legislative precedents for limitations on the jurisdiction of Rome in the form of the Statute of Provisors and Statute of Praemunire of the reign of Richard II that were frequently referred to in ordinary litigation. Finally, many practices of the English ecclesiastical courts were in any case based on local practices rather than ordinances of the church in Rome, and as St German wrote in the 1520s, there were many examples of laws of the church that were merely the reflection of policy rather than divine institution.[76]

It seems unlikely that the Reformation statutes fundamentally altered common law practice or jurisprudence,[77] but there is little doubt about the long-term political and constitutional consequences of the confessional diversity unleashed by the fact that Henry VIII's desperate desire to marry a younger woman coincided with the gradual spread of the ideas of continental religious reformers. If there was ever a moment when English men and women had to face up to the prospect that there was a policy of the state which might not necessarily be one with which they could feel content in the way idealised by medieval theories which held that there was no distinction between the community and the institutions which governed it, the 1530s must be a prime candidate. In

[72] Quoted in Faith Thompson, *Magna Carta: Its Role in the Making of the English Constitution 1300–1629* (Minneapolis, 1948), p. 140.
[73] Ibid., p. 141.
[74] G. R. Elton, *The Parliament of England 1559–1581* (Cambridge, 1986), p. 34.
[75] Above, pp. 19–20.
[76] St German, *Doctor and Student*, pp. 21–3; Helmholz, *Roman Canon Law*, p. 29.
[77] *Spelman's Reports*, II, pp. 44–5.

1534, Richard Morison, an advisor of Cromwell's who is sometimes described as an English Machiavellian, warned the minister that the 'ship of state was in danger'. Cromwell had to act as the pilot and Morison advised him to banish those who harmed the commonwealth.[78] As one historian has put it, the Pilgrimage of Grace, an armed protest against just about everything that had gone on in the 1530s, forced people to make calculations which balanced their duties of civic loyalty to the state against the dictates of their consciences, a dilemma that was henceforth to be created again and again during the course of the sixteenth and seventeenth centuries.[79]

In 1534, the controversy surrounding Henry's policies led to a statutory expansion of the law of treason so that it was henceforth an offence to speak against the king as well as to take direct action against him or his government.[80] Since Henry broke with Rome but chose to maintain a church that was essentially Catholic in doctrine, it also became possible by the end of the decade to be executed as a traitor for maintaining the supremacy of the bishop of Rome, or as a heretic for advancing the doctrines of the Protestant faith.[81] In 1539, a total of fifty-three names, the largest number in English history, were included in a single parliamentary Act of attainder. In 1540, Thomas Cromwell himself and seventeen other people were condemned.[82]

In declaring England an empire, the Statute of Appeals gave to the king the spiritual headship over the church that had been previously exercised by the pope, and in the 1530s the legal system was utilised to promote royal policy in both church and state. In January or February 1538, for instance, Cromwell wrote a note to himself to remind Lord Chancellor Audley to have all the JPs in London come before him in Star Chamber so that they could be charged to suppress the 'bruiting of n[ews] as well as vagabonds and unlawful games'.[83] In the same year, he had a circular letter sent to justices thanking them for what they had done in carrying out previous orders and directing them to see that the king's supremacy was set forth. Maintainers of the bishop of Rome were to suffer condign punishment. Beckett of Canterbury, that defender of the independence of the Roman church in England, should be denounced as a traitor. The justices had been doing their duties so well that the king's subjects were quiet, but the clergy were stirring them up.[84] In early 1540

[78] *L&P*, vol. 7, p. 504.
[79] E. H. Shagan, *Popular Politics and the English Reformation* (Cambrdige, 2003), p. 127.
[80] 26 Henry VIII, c. 13.   [81] *Spelman's Reports*, II, pp. 44–5.
[82] S. E. Lehmberg, *The Later Parliaments of Henry VIII, 1536–1547* (Cambridge, 1977), pp. 119, 126, 268.
[83] *L&P*, vol. 13 (pt 2), p. 451.   [84] Ibid., p. 485.

Audley made a speech in Star Chamber that addressed 'readers' from the inns of court and Chancery. He 'admonished and warned' them to truly and justly interpret and expound the king's laws and statutes in readings and moots, and to advise the subjects without 'subtile practise and imagination or deceipt'. In concluding, he reported on the fate of three senior figures, including the serjeants-at-law Sir Humphrey Brown and Nicholas Hare, who, despite being in receipt of the king's fee, had advised Sir John Shelton about how he might avoid wardships. In addition to having the king's fee withdrawn from them, Brown and Hare, having pleaded guilty, were committed to the Tower to await the king's pleasure regarding further punishment.[85]

Doubtless as a result of pressure such as this, at least some of the exercises at the inns of court increasingly reflected the royal position on the church and the authority of the crown. At the start of a reading on chapter I of Magna Carta, which was given at one of the legal inns between 1532 and 1536, the lecturer noted that another recent reading had shown that the king, and not the pope, had always been considered the supreme head of the spirituality. The reading then went on to limit the discussion of the liberties of the church to a consideration of the privileges of ecclesiastical personnel, the nature of sanctuary and the jurisdiction of the church courts. In addition, this reader offered elaborate prefatory remarks which raised a number of historical issues that were relatively rarely considered in the first half of the sixteenth century. He noted that the laws of England had existed long before the making of the Charter. Some of them had been made by King Lucius, some by Edward the Confessor and some by William the Conqueror. By the time of King John these had fallen out of use, and large amounts of blood had been shed in the Barons' Wars in order to have them restored. The point was that rule of law was essential to the maintenance of peace and prosperity, and for the rule of law to be effective, the king's authority had to be recognised. 'If Law be taken from the Prince, what tormoyle is like to grow amongst the subjects.'[86]

At about the same time, Richard Morison put forward a plan for making a direct impression on people right the way through the social order. Noting that the 'common people' had traditionally used recently abolished summer holy days in order to celebrate 'Robin Hood' and 'disobedience . . . to [the king's] officers', he recommended that they should be made instead into occasions that attacked the bishop of Rome

---

[85] BL, MS Stowe 424, fol. 116v.
[86] BL, MS Harleian 4990, fols. 154–6, 163. For the dating of this see Brooks, *Lawyers, Litigation*, ch. 8, note 64.

and showed the people 'the obedience that yo[u]r subjectes by Goddes and mans Lawes owe unto yo[u]r ma[jes]tie'.[87] Like Morison's other law reform proposals, this one was evidently unsuccessful, but the general thrust of his thinking is reflected in a manuscript 'book of things inquirable at inferiour courts', which appears to date from the 1530s, possibly 1538, and was evidently composed for the use of lawyers acting as stewards in town courts, sheriff's tourns and manorial courts. Acknowledging that in the past only matters technically within the jurisdiction of such local courts had been given in charges to jurors, it goes on to explain that the king now wanted the unlearned and 'ignorant' people to be better educated in their 'dewtie first to God, then to his highness as Godes vicar'. Along with a long list of matters dealing with the administration of justice and the defence of Henrician church policy, the manual also contains a message to be passed on to jurymen: the king had been appointed by God to rule over the commonwealth and any disobedience to the monarch was a violation of holy ordinances.[88] If More was unable to use the law of God to defend the church, these works of the 1530s used it to justify a call for obedience to the monarch.

---

[87] BL, MS Cotton Faustina C.II, 'A Discours touching the Reformation of the Lawes of England', fol. 18.
[88] BL, MS Additional 48047, fols. 59–61. Found in the papers of Robert Beale, the charge may have been collected, or composed, by John Hales.

4 Political realities and legal discourse in the later sixteenth century

Mid-Tudor turmoil

The immediate impact of the Henrician regime on political ideas and political discourse engaged in by lawyers was less than clear-cut. Lawyers were sometimes bullied by Henry VIII, but the more important point is that legal institutions, including the inns of court, survived largely unscathed, and on some important secular issues, such as uses and wills, the profession contributed to political compromise. Henry VIII may personally have believed that the king ruled under God rather than under the law, and, as we have seen, some legal rhetoric communicated to the public appears to have endorsed such a view.[1] Nevertheless, there is considerable truth in the contention that Henrician political thought contained unresolved tensions between ascending and descending theories of where ultimate political authority lay,[2] and there was much that blurred the distinctions. The break from Rome, the dissolution of the monasteries, and the subsequent changes in the church were all carried out through parliament. Indeed, in the 1540s Henry even went so far as to encourage parliament to pass a statute that enabled him to determine the succession to the throne by will so that he could ensure that his son Edward would succeed in preference to his eldest surviving child, Mary, daughter of Catherine of Aragon.[3]

Despite all of his efforts, however, Henry was ultimately unable to completely resolve the problem that had launched his 'empire' in the first place, the succession to the throne. When he died in 1547, the crown passed to the adolescent Edward VI, who had been raised by reformers, and under whom government was administered by a regency

---

[1] See above, pp. 47–50.

[2] J. A. Guy, *Politics, Law and Counsel in Tudor and Early Stuart England* (2000), pp. vi–x, chs. 11–12.

[3] 35 Henry VIII, c. 1 (1543): An Act concerning the establishment of the King's Majesty's succession to the Imperial Crown. The immediate cause was the king's imminent departure for France. The statute allowed the king to give the crown to whomever he pleased if there was a failure of legitimate issue.

51

council, controlled first by Edward Seymour, the 'Protector' Somerset, and then by John Dudley, the duke of Northumberland. After a brief contest with a usurper, the Boy King was succeeded in 1553 by Catholic Queen Mary. In 1558, Mary died and was replaced by the daughter of Anne Boleyn, the anti-papal, but unmarried, Elizabeth I.

Since these quick turnovers in regime were accompanied by potential alterations in spiritual as well as temporal affairs, not to mention the unprecedented accession of female monarchs, the rule of law was sometimes compromised by political expediency. Yet the mid-Tudor period was also one in which law was inevitably turned to as a source of stability in troubled times. John Hales, an ardent Protestant reformer, who was also an official in the court of Chancery, went so far as to suggest that the need for the ecclesiastical court jurisdictions to adapt to the Reformed religion might provide the opportunity to write down all of English law into a vernacular written code that might be better understood by everyone who was subject to it.[4] Although this idea failed to materialise, during the late 1540s and early 1550s reforming zeal and faith in the salutary power of statutory measures produced a spate of parliamentary law-making that resulted in the introduction of an English form of church service, the appointment of a parliamentary commission to investigate and reform English canon law,[5] a number of measures addressing social problems such as unemployment,[6] and the abrogation of Henry VIII's Treason Act of 1534.[7] Even highly technical measures designed to address abuses in the court of King's Bench were prefaced with remarks that acknowledged the need for laws to change in order to take account of the times.[8] Furthermore, although a reformer like John Hales accepted that royal authority was divinely ordained, he quoted Aristotle for the view that those who desire written laws to rule over them desire the rule of god, 'But they that will haue it unwritten, to depende in mens heades, make their rulers an unreasonable treasure.'[9]

Nevertheless, the notorious confessional switchbacks of the decade 1548–58 made life as dangerous for judges and lawyers as it was for other members of the population. The problem was anticipated in a speech Sir Edward Montague, chief justice of the King's Bench, made

---

[4] BL, MS Harleian 4990: 'An oration in commendation of the laws', fols. 14–18. The work is addressed to Sir Anthony Browne, knight of the garter and master of the king's horse, who is to asked to show it to Henry VIII. It is not known whether or not the king saw the work.
[5] Bray, *Reformatio*; see below, pp. 97–100.
[6] M. Bush, *Government Policy of Protector Somerset* (1975).
[7] 1 Edward VI, c. 12 (1548). Some of the social legislation is discussed below, pp. 378, 411.
[8] TNA, SP 46/162, pp. 122–51.   [9] BL, MS Harleian 4990, fol. 16.

on the appointment of new serjeants-at-law in 1540. Noting that it had in the past been customary to exhort new serjeants about the importance of their vocation by expounding on a text of scripture, he explained why he was not going to stick to tradition. Although he had nothing against the scriptures, and was aware that the king had lately spent large sums of money in order to make the Bible available in every parish church, the scriptures were 'difficult' to understand, much less expound.[10] Thirteen years later, Montague was dismissed from office and imprisoned by the new Queen Mary because he had reluctantly agreed to the demand of the duke of Northumberland that he draw up the instrument that disinherited Mary from the throne in favour of Lady Jane Grey, a Protestant claimant apparently favoured by King Edward, who also happened to be the wife of Northumberland's son.[11]

Montague later petitioned the queen claiming that he and his fellow judges had in fact advised against the 'devise', and many others, including the future judge James Dyer appear to have signed the document, which he took to be the young king's 'last will', without having any confidence that it was 'legal'.[12] Perhaps because so many judges and prominent lawyers were implicated in the failed plot, most managed to survive relatively unscathed, and it was of course the man with the most inflexible conscience who suffered the most. Sir James Hales, a devoted Protestant who had acted earlier in his career as legal council to Archbishop Cranmer,[13] actually opposed the attempt to exclude the Catholic Mary from the throne because it was done without consulting parliament. But Hales soon earned the displeasure of the new queen by making speeches on the Home assize circuit that encouraged the enforcement of anti-papal legislation from the two previous reigns that had not yet been reversed. On his return to London, he was arrested in Westminster Hall and imprisoned. Evidently driven to distraction by his predicament, he attempted to commit suicide by slitting his wrists with a pen-knife. When this failed, the man who once told Bishop Stephen Gardiner that he was ready to 'adventure as well my life as my substance' for religion drowned himself.[14]

---

[10] Baker, *Serjeants*, p. 294; *ODNB*.

[11] L. Abbott, 'Public office and private profit: the legal establishment in the reign of Mary Tudor' in J. Loach and R. Tittler, eds., *The Mid Tudor Polity c. 1540–1560* (1980), pp. 137–8.

[12] *Dyer's Reports*, I, p. xlvii. The device is printed in J. G. Nichols, ed., *The Chronicle of Queen Jane* (Camden Society, vol. 48, 1850), pp. 91–100.

[13] *ODNB*. D. MacCulloch, *Thomas Cranmer: a Life* (1996), p. 202.

[14] John Foxe, *The Acts and Monuments of the Christian Martyrs* (8 vols., London, 1863), VI, pp. 712–13; BL, MS Lansdowne 389, fols. 333–8.

Well known at the time, Hales's story was included by John Foxe in his *Book of Martyrs*, but it is not evidence that the legal profession as a whole was hostile to the old religion, or to frame the question more narrowly, unwilling to accept the legitimacy of Mary's regime once it had been established.[15] Although few of them subsequently displayed the loyalty to Catholicism of Edmund Plowden, whose public career was effectively ended when Elizabeth came to the throne in 1558,[16] Mary was able to find plenty of lawyers to serve her. Hardly any prominent legal figures went into exile; many, including William Cecil, Nicholas Bacon and William Fleetwood, either lay low or ended up accepting the new regime even if they disagreed with its policies, which of course included the queen's marriage to Philip II of Spain as well as the reversal of the Protestant Reformation.[17]

The return to Rome, and the penal legislation accompanying it, was steered through parliament by the notable lawyers William Stanford and James Dyer. A statute was also passed against the spreading of seditious rumours, and the treason laws were reformed once again so that words as well as deeds could be taken as sufficient evidence of the offence having been committed.[18] Lack of sources makes it difficult to say how much debate there was about the legislation, but there does appear to have been some controversy about the extent to which a woman could claim to enjoy the same monarchical power as a man since most of the sources outlining those powers, including acts of parliament, only mentioned male kings. According to a treatise written in 1575 by William Fleetwood,[19] some of Mary's English legal advisors, including, perhaps, Anthony Browne, joined with the Spanish ambassador Renard in proposing that the best solution would be for the queen to claim that she ruled by conquest rather than succession, thereby enabling her 'at her pleasure' to retake the dissolved monastic lands and otherwise 'do what she list'.[20] But to be fair, Fleetwood, who was no friend of the regime, also noted within a few lines of the same manuscript that neither

---

[15] R. M. Fisher, 'The inns of court and the Reformation 1530–1580' (Cambridge University PhD thesis, 1974) demonstrates the complexity of the situation. By 1558, the benchers of at least three out of four of the inns seem to have been 'conservative', and Elizabeth's government was apparently concerned about papists at the inns of court in the 1570s and 1580s.

[16] Geoffrey de C. Parmiter, *Edmund Plowden: an Elizabethan Recusant Lawyer* (Catholic Record Society, 1987).

[17] C. H. Garrett, *The Marian Exiles* (Cambridge, 1938); *ODNB*.

[18] 1 & 2 Philip and Mary, c. 9.

[19] See J. D. Alsop, 'The Act for the Queen's regal power, 1554', *Parliamentary History*, 13(3) (1994), 261–76.

[20] BL, MS Harleian 6234, fols. 21v–2. Fleetwood does not directly name Browne, but his description fits him. *ODNB*.

Mary nor her chancellor, Bishop Stephen Gardiner, were interested in following this course of action. Gardiner's solution to the problem was a statute simply making it clear that Mary enjoyed the 'imperial crown' on the same terms as her predecessors had done.[21]

Equally, the articles of marriage between Mary and Philip II, which put severe limits on the new king's authority, were also confirmed by parliament, but the Spanish match was the principal cause of the rebellion of Kentishmen led by Sir Thomas Wyatt in 1554. Furthermore, the confessional reversals and the enforcement of a policy of religious conformity that resulted in the burning to death of some 300 people for heresy, and the exile of several times that many, was bound on occasion to leave both the judges and the law in a compromised position. Another martyr's life recounted by Foxe tells of a remarkable confrontation that occurred when Anthony Browne was interrogating Thomas Watts, a linen-draper of Billericay (Essex), at Chelmsford assizes in connection with a charge of heresy that would soon lead to his execution. When Browne asked him how he had come to hold Protestant opinions, Watts replied that he had learned them from the mouth of Browne himself, who had spoken against Catholicism in 'open sessions' as vehemently as any preacher during the reign of Edward, while at the same time declaring that it was treason to 'bring in any foreign power to rule here'.[22]

At their trials in 1554 following Wyatt's rebellion, two brothers, Sir John and Sir Nicholas Throckmorton, found that the same evidence resulted in radically different verdicts being given against them. While Sir John Throckmorton was convicted of treason, Sir Nicholas was famously acquitted on a similar charge by a London jury. Although neither actively participated in the rising, Sir Nicholas readily admitted that he was opposed to the Spanish match, and that he had spoken on numerous occasions to people who were planning the revolt.[23] Indeed, he claimed that the expressions of discontent about the marriage he heard in private conversations were little different from discussions of it in the House of Commons, and Sir Nicholas's well-informed defence was that the Henrician statute that brought 'words' uttered against the crown within the scope of treason had been reversed by the more recent Edwardian Act.[24] His point was that this abrogation of the recent statute meant that the treason Act of Edward III had come back into force and

[21] 1 Mary, Session 3, c. 1. This is followed in the statute books by the confirmation of the articles of marriage of the queen with Philip II.

[22] Foxe, *Acts and Monuments*, VI, pp. 118–19.

[23] *ST*, I, cols. 895ff. For Throckmorton's later, highly successful career, see *ODNB*.

[24] 1 Edward VI, c. 12. The trial took place before the passage of the Marian statute.

that there was consequently an important distinction between words and deeds. When the crown's lawyers, including Stanford and Dyer, countered that he was nevertheless guilty of the [common law] crime of procuring treason, Throckmorton accused them of betraying their own principles. Stanford, he claimed, had previously described the Henrician Act as draconian in speeches in parliament.[25] Addressing the jury that eventually acquitted him against the instructions of the judges, Sir Nicholas wondered whether the subject might not be better off with explicitly cruel laws like the Henrician statute, which at least enabled people to know exactly where they stood. The new laws appeared at first sight to deliver us 'from our old bondage . . . .But when it pleaseth the higher powers to call any man's life and sayings in question, then there be constructions, interpretations, and extensions reserved to the justices and judges equity, that the party tryable, as I am now, shall find himself in much worse case, than before those cruel laws stood in force.' He went on to admonish the 'judges [who] be rather agreeable to the time, than to the truth; for their judgments be repugnant to their own principle, repugnant to their godly and best learned predecessors opinions, repugnant, I say, to the Proviso in the Statute of Repeal made in the last parliament'.[26]

As Throckmorton's testimony suggests, controversy and debate in the Marian period extended to bold speeches in parliament of a kind that were later suppressed under Queen Elizabeth.[27] In a less direct way, the political climate is also reflected in a major literary project that was being undertaken at about the same time within the social milieu of the inns of court. The collection of cautionary tales published as *The Mirror for Magistrates* drew on examples from British history in order to demonstrate the dire consequences of bad government. Allegedly suppressed by Lord Chancellor Stephen Gardiner, and so not published until 1559, the *Mirror* consisted of contributions from people such as William Baldwin, Thomas Phayer and George Ferrers, active publicists with legal training, and the editorial team also included Thomas Norton and Thomas Sackville (the future Lord Buckhurst), two figures who became active players on the Elizabethan political scene. Conceived as an elaboration on John Lydgate's early fifteenth-century translation of Boccaccio's *Fall of Princes*, the exemplary 'histories' reflected what have

---

[25] *ST*, I, col. 896.   [26] Ibid., col. 897.

[27] According to an account later written by William Fleetwood, some MPs thought they had 'litle to loose, and much lesse to care for what we spoke . . . for our speeches tended to a troath, and by any meanes might be a furtherance to God's glorie, the honour and safetie of the Prince, and the publique wealth of the realme'. BL, MS Harleian 6234, fol. 21v.

come to be known as the classic Florentine values of service for the good of the commonweal, and the importance of maintaining the rule of reason and law as guarantees of social and political stability. For example, the moral that Ferrers drew from the crimes of the fourteenth-century judge Thomas Tresilian was that the abuse of the law ultimately led to tyranny, and eventually the overthrow of the king, Richard III.[28]

> So wrukyng lawe lyke waxe, the subiecte was not sure
> of lyfe, lande, nor goods, but at the princes wyll
> which caused his kingdome the shorter tyme to dure
> For clayming power absolute both to save and spyll
> The prince therby presumed his people for pyll:
> And set his lustes for law, and will had reasons place . . .[29]

In fact, the *Mirror* was often ardently pro-monarchical in tone, but the stories collectively suggested a distinction between the person of the king or queen and the institutions and life of the body politic. Consideration was sometimes given to alternative forms of government, but what comes through most consistently is the idea that sound administration and the maintenance of law and equity were the essential benefits of government that any self-respecting commonwealth should expect, and this same need for institutional stability in uncertain times was also the principal point of a play called the *Tragedy of Gorboduc*, which was performed at the Inner Temple in 1561. Written by Norton and Sackville, and generally recognised as the first blank-verse tragedy in English as well as the prototype for Shakespeare's King Lear, *Gorboduc* addressed the thorny questions of the succession to the throne, and how the new queen should dispose of herself in marriage.[30] At least one person who attended thought the authors favoured a marriage between Elizabeth and her favourite, the earl of Leicester, but he also noted that the more general conclusion of the work was that 'civil discention bredeth morning. And many things were said for the succession to put things in certainty.'[31]

Gorboduc falls into the erratic pattern of inns of court entertainments that occasionally came to notice because they touched closely on current

---

[28] L. B. Campbell, *The Mirror for Magistrates Edited from Original Texts in the Huntington Library* (Cambridge, 1933). See also *ODNB*.

[29] Ibid., p. 77.

[30] *The Tragedie of Gorboduc: Whereof Three Actes Were Wrytten by Thomas Nortone, and the Two Laste by Thomas Sackvyle* (1565).

[31] BL, MS Additional MS 48023, fol. 359v. See also Susan Doran, 'Juno versus Diana: the treatment of Elizabeth I's marriage in plays and entertainments, 1561–1581', *Historical Journal*, 38(2) (1995), 257–74.

political issues.[32] But the play was also performed at court before the queen, and in this respect *Gorboduc*, like *The Mirror for Magistrates*, also illustrates the humanist project of influencing political affairs through learned public debate. Furthermore, they also coincided with the publication of Thomas Wilson's influential treatise *The Arte of Rhetoric* (1553), which drew a much more general connection between law, public speaking and the maintenance of a civilised society.

While the works of the lawyer Cicero were key texts for the study of Latin grammar, dialectic and disputation at grammar schools as well as in the universities, there is little evidence that there was anything particularly distinctive about the training of English lawyers in courtroom oratory or advocacy. Indeed, Wilson's book suggests instead that there was a convergence between professional and lay approaches to rhetoric. Essentially a recycling into English of Latin material that had for some time been available in schools and colleges,[33] most of its set-piece examples are based either on legal affairs or on 'matters of state', and Wilson's definition of rhetoric seems to have been written with lawyers in mind. It was the art to

set forth by utteraunce of words, matter at large, or (as Cicero doth say) it is a learned, or rather an artificiall declaration of the mynd, in the handling of any cause . . . An Orator must be able to speake fully of al those questions, which by lawe [and] mans ordinance are enacted, and appointed for the vse and profite of man . . .[34]

No less important, Wilson stressed that public rhetoric was an essential constituent in the maintenance of a civilised society. Although the loss of reason was a consequence of the Fall, and caused the world to descend into barbarity, God had subsequently stirred his 'faithful and elect to persuade with reason all men to society'.

Neither can I see that men could haue beene brought by any other meanes, to liue together in fellowship of life, to maintaine Cities, to deale truely, and willingly obeye one an other, if men at the first had not by art and eloquence perswaded that which they oft found out by reason.[35]

Indeed, the medium was in part the message; Aristotle had taught that speech and reason set man apart from the beasts. They gave him

---

[32] See above, p. 39. Marie Axton, *The Queen's Two Bodies: Drama and the Elizabethan Succession Question* (1977), pp. 61–2, 71, suggests that the establishment of a public theatre by William Burbage in 1576 shifted theatrical initiative from the inns to the public stage.

[33] Peter Mack, *Elizabethan Rhetoric: Theory and Practice* (Cambridge, 2002), esp. pp. 79–83.

[34] Thomas Wilson, *The Arte of Rhetorique 1560*, ed. G. H. Mair (Oxford, 1909), p. 1.

[35] Ibid.

the capacity to use political organisation in order to promote civilised society.

Civilising rhetoric, the increase in litigation and the legal profession

As the reign of Elizabeth began, therefore, law and rhetoric were extolled in print as essential constituents of the civilising process. Quite apart from the uncertain political circumstances, the intellectual culture of the time made it almost second nature for technical legal argument to be merged with more general observations on the nature of the rule of law into modes of general public political discourse that were sometimes repeated with almost platitudinous regularity.[36] Even so, the extent to which this happened also owed something to the influence of individuals. Since the common law remained a highly technical and largely self-contained intellectual discipline, it would be misleading to depict an instantaneous overwhelming impact of humanist rhetoric on its practitioners or its technical doctrines.[37] On the other hand, it is significant that two of the most senior appointments in the Elizabethan regime went to men with legal training, William Cecil (1520–98) and Nicholas Bacon (1510–79), who had prefaced their legal studies with time spent at Cambridge University, and who maintained notable associations with the Protestant humanist movement. Cecil, who later became Lord Burghley and the queen's principal political advisor, was the son of a Northamptonshire squire. Having studied Greek at St John's College, he was said always to have carried a copy of Cicero's *Offices* in his pocket. His brother-in-law, Bacon, who descended from Suffolk yeoman stock, became lord keeper of the great seal, and hence the queen's leading law officer in 1558.[38]

Cecil and Bacon were practical men of business whose careers demonstrated a typically Elizabethan capacity for combining public service with personal material advancement. Nevertheless, both also brought a certain amount of humanist-inspired idealism to their work, a point illustrated by a series of orations Bacon delivered in London to the assize judges as they were going off on their circuits, when he was seeing off MPs as they returned home to the shires at the end of parliaments, and on other public occasions. As he himself noted in 1559, speeches of this kind were in many respects traditional, and his aims in making them were no doubt little different from those of Wareham or Wolsey earlier in the century, but Bacon's speeches survive in several different

[36] See pp. 62–3.   [37] For example, *Dyer's Reports*, I, pp. xxiii–xxiv, 445.   [38] *ODNB*.

manuscript copies, and they appear to have been particularly well regarded at the time.[39]

At the end of Elizabeth's first parliament in 1559 Bacon declared that nothing decided in parliament, where matters had been freely and frankly discussed, should be infringed by any private man. The queen's 'goode, humble, and obedient subiect*es*' should 'willingly *and* humbly *yeeld and submit themselves to the Lawe as to the thinge whereby each man enioyeth his lyvinge libertye and lief*'.[40] The 'heads' for a country magistrate to keep in mind were the maintenance of the queen's peace, the doing of justice between the subjects and the safe-guarding of one order in religion. When it came to the reasons for undertaking the task, Bacon reverted to familiar, almost proverbial, language. A man with a torch would be foolish to stumble about in the dark; a gardener with good tools should use them to cultivate. But Bacon also lamented that there were too many magistrates who were too 'slothful' to be bothered to attend quarter sessions. While such men might tell themselves that they were merely 'good and quiet', in reality they were selfish and more interested in themselves than the 'common good'. In a speech made to assembled nobles and justices in the Trinity Term of the same year, Bacon warned that the council wanted examples made of ineffective 'ministers of justice' because of the government's concerns about tumults, conspiracies and conventiclers, as well as crimes such as burglary, regrating, forestalling and vagrancy.[41] But he also had a more general vision. Given the importance of the administration of justice, it was essential that the task be done well. Ministers of justice had to set an example for others. Everything rested on the shoulders of these 'servants', who were the 'executors of all good government amongst the people'.[42]

Judging from some of the practical plans that they came up with at the beginning of Elizabeth's reign, it would appear that these rhetorical exhortations arose in part from the fact that councillors such as Cecil and Bacon were not particularly impressed with the state of the magistracy as they found it. For example, an unattributed plan from 1559 to improve the militia and make the commissions of the peace more effective proposed to cut the number of JPs down to ten 'besides the lords', and suggested that henceforth only lawyers should be appointed to the office of *custos rotulorum*, the effective head of each county commission, and a place hitherto nearly always filled by a notable country

---

[39] George Puttenham, *The Arte of English Poesie, Contriued into three Bookes*. . . . (1589), pp. 116–17, described Bacon as 'a most eloquent man, and of rare learning and wisedome, as ever I knew England to breed'.

[40] Folger, MS V.a.143, fol. 12. Italics here represent contemporary underlining.

[41] Ibid. Star Chamber speech, Trinity Term 1559.   [42] Ibid., fol. 21.

gentleman.[43] In 1566, Cecil was evidently so concerned about a drift towards lawlessness that he considered reforming the lawyers and remodelling the commissions of the peace.[44] In 1568 Bacon announced in a Star Chamber speech that the queen was aware of a failure to enforce the laws that 'concerne god*es* hono[u]r and his true religion established in parliament by the whole consent of the three estates of the Realme'.[45] In the 1570s the two ministers collaborated in trying to find ways to make certain that the penal laws were more effectively enforced, and the state papers are filled with letters directed to particular localities to chivvy activity. In 1569, for example, twenty-four Shropshire gentle-men were issued with a special commission to put down unlawful games and return the names of those who neglected the statutory requirement to practise their archery.[46]

It is not easy to measure the practical impact of either the rhetoric or the administrative prodding on the quality of the commissions of the peace.[47] Yet, despite rather than because of government initiatives, a gradual increase in court usage in the form of litigation between private parties, which began in the later part of the reign of Henry VIII, turned into what can only be described as a flood during the Elizabethan period. Caused largely by demographic and economic change, this led in turn to an unprecedented increase in the size of both the upper and lower branches of the legal profession. Whereas common lawyers were thin on the ground in most counties in 1560, by 1600 they had become such common fixtures that complaints began to be expressed about excessive numbers.[48] If the 'commonwealths man' John Hales, writing in the 1540s, could claim that one of the disadvantages of the Catholic faith was that it encouraged young men to waste their lives in monasteries and thereby diverted good wits from the study of the law,[49] by the end of the reign of Elizabeth the well-known Puritan theologian William Perkins lamented the fact that in his day all of the best young minds became lawyers rather than clergymen because of the better career prospects that were available in law.[50] While political historians have recognised the

---

[43] HEHL, MS Ellesmere 2580.
[44] C. Read, *Mr Secretary Cecil and Queen Elizabeth* (1955), pp. 437–9, suggests that the document was composed when Cecil was worried about disorder and a general lack of respect for government policy.
[45] Folger, MS V.a.143, fol. 71: 'A Speach in Star Chamber to the Justices, 1568'.
[46] SA, Shavington Collection, p. 113.   [47] For more on this, see pp. 294–5.
[48] Brooks, *Lawyers, Litigation*, chs. 2, 4, 5; Brooks, *Pettyfoggers and Vipers*, chs. 3–6.
[49] BL, MS Harleian 4990, fol. 20.
[50] William Perkins, *Of the Calling of the Ministerie, Two Treatises*. . . . (1607), p. 6–7. The work was published posthumously by William Crawshaw, who had been appointed preacher at the Inner and Middle Temples in February 1605. His epistle is addressed to

significance of lawyer 'men of business' such as Thomas Norton and William Fleetwood as features of the Elizabethan political scene,[51] they were merely one manifestation of a more general development which saw common lawyers making themselves more evident as clerks of the peace, town clerks, manorial stewards, recorders of incorporated towns and members of parliament.[52]

Increasing amounts of litigation and growing numbers of lawyers were accompanied by a distinctive cast of legal mindedness that became a feature of Elizabethan culture. Moreover, the profession itself appears to have fashioned its own self-image largely in terms that would have corresponded nicely to the public rhetoric of Lord Keeper Bacon. With both amateur gentry and professional admissions to them increasing steadily in the years after 1560, the inns of court expanded physically and appear to have been places of self-confidence and intellectual vitality,[53] a measure of which can be gauged by the personal remarks with which readers prefaced the lectures they delivered to the young. Before his reading at Gray's Inn in 1588, for example, Edmund Pelham explained the honour which had been bestowed upon him. By being asked to read, he was joining a list of gifted men, 'whose memory remaineth fresh and hath left a deeper impression then continuance of time can [e]race out', men who were qualified to judge of matters and govern in societies.[54]

The even more celebratory oration Christopher Yelverton delivered to the membership of Gray's Inn on the eve of his appointment as a serjeant-at-law in 1589 referred to Cicero's *Orations* in order to illustrate the importance of legal learning and encourage his listeners to persist in their studies. There is no commonwealth, he told them, in which the professors of the law are not 'advanced to honour . . . The Laweyers houses saith Lucius Crasus be as it were thoracles of the whole citie. They decide what is consonant to ryght, determine what is agreable to reason, forsee that men liue not uppon wrong *and* violence *and* doe defend the hope, life, fame and prosperitie of their clientes.'[55]

Later on, when he went into the court of Chancery to be formally inducted into the order of the coif, a second speech tied in the values of

---

Sir Edward Coke, then attorney general, and Sir Thomas Hesketh, attorney of the court of Wards.

[51] P. Collinson 'Puritans, men of business and Elizabethan parliaments', *Parliamentary History*, 7 (1988), 189–211, and M. A. R. Graves, 'The common lawyers and the privy council's parliamentary men-of-business, 1584–1601', *Parliamentary History*, 8(2) (1989), 189–215.

[52] Prest, *Barristers*; Brooks, *Pettyfoggers and Vipers*, chs. 9–10.

[53] W. R. Prest, *The Inns of Court under Elizabeth and the Early Stuarts* (1972).

[54] BL, MS Hargrave 398, fols. 143ff.   [55] BL, MS Additional 48109, fol. 13.

law with the good fortune England was then enjoying in comparison with countries (such as France) that had been ravaged by civil war. 'The lawe is the perfeccon of pure [and] tried reason, the frame of politicke [and] prudent gouerment, the rule of staied [and] contented subieccon, the scepter of sweete [and] happy peace [and] the life of the common wealth.' While other Christian kingdoms were tearing themselves apart, Elizabeth had honoured the law, and law and peace were like Hippocrates twins. His speech then turns to a couple of folios of boundless praise for the queen, but the motto on the serjeants' rings that he and his fellow serjeants had made to commemorate the call were inscribed with the Latin tag 'Lex Reipublicae vitae'.[56]

Like other Elizabethan lawyers, Yelverton was well aware that English law was not written down or delivered with the approval of the prince in the same way as the famous law code of the Roman emperor Justinian, The Corpus Juris Imperii, had been.[57] One reason for the importance of lawyers was their collective possession of the law, largely through discussion at the inns or in what were still mainly unpublished learning aids. In fact, legal knowledge existed primarily in the commonplace books compiled by individuals, in the decisions they reported by observing arguments in court, and in the notes that were taken by students who attended the readings of the legal inns.[58] Some of this material had long circulated in the form of scribal copies, but, as the population of the legal inns increased, there were also further developments in legal publishing.

Composed in the 1540s, but not published until 1567, Sir William Stanford's Exposition on the King's Prerogative was arranged as a series of explanatory essays on relevant subjects taken from Fitzherbert's Graund Abridgment. It has been described as the first example of an English legal treatise, and the preface expressed the hope that similar works on other subjects might help shed some light on the 'dark and farr off' nature of the common law.[59] In 1577, the indefatigable recorder of London, William Fleetwood, wrote Lord Burghley that he was attempting to compose a 'general table for the hole body of the Common Law that I maie turne to anything at the first that is sett down in our bookes'.[60] A few years earlier, Edmund Plowden published his famous Commentaries,

---

[56] Ibid., fols. 8v–10v.   [57] Ibid., fol. 14.

[58] While the educational efficacy of the learning exercises at the inns of court is debatable, an enormous amount of manuscript material survives from the readings and the notes students made on them during the late sixteenth and seventeenth centuries. Baker, Readers and Readings.

[59] W. Stanford, An Exposicion of the Kinges Prerogative Collected Out of the Great Abridgement of Justice Fitzherbert. . . . (1567).

[60] BL, MS Lansdowne 82, fol. 198.

law reports that provided a much fuller account of arguments in court than could be found in most manuscripts of the time and which were completely unprecedented in print. Begun when he was a student in 1550, Plowden explained that his approach was to 'be present at, and . . . give diligent attention to, the debates and questions of law', and particularly to the arguments of those who were men of the greatest note and reputation for learning. Believing that there 'were few arguments so pure as not to have some refuse in them', he did not quote verbatim, but he did preface each report with a transcription of the pleadings from the court record, and he tried to verify the accuracy of the arguments he presented by consulting the judges and other lawyers who had made them, sometimes by showing them his version.[61] In 1586, the executors of Sir James Dyer, who was appointed chief justice of the Common Pleas in 1559, published roughly 1,000 cases from his personal legal note-books.[62] The first reports to be published under a judge's name, they remained authoritative into the early seventeenth century, and all of these works reflect what Professor Baker has identified as a development that saw the older common-law learning of the legal inns giving way both to a greater emphasis on contrasting arguments and to the authoritative dicta of the judges.[63] Litigants evidently wanted decisions and they wanted to know the reasons for those decisions.

There is no doubt that print made an important contribution to this process by rendering decisions more easily and reliably retrievable, but given these advantages, it is notable that no further reports of similar stature were published until those of Sir Edward Coke began to emerge in the first decade of the seventeenth century.[64] Indeed, in comparison with major professional works, books for students of varying degrees of originality, and books addressed primarily to magistrates constituted the greatest volume of print.[65] Some of these may have been encouraged by government, or at least have arisen out of projects initiated by leading figures in it. In the 1570s, for instance, Sir Nicholas Bacon devised a plan for utilising professional talent at the legal inns in order to weed out redundant statutes with a view to publishing a more coherent and authoritative volume containing those that remained in force.[66]

---

[61] *Les commentaries ou reports . . . de divers cases . . . .* (1571), Preface.
[62] *Dyer's Reports*, I, pp. xxxv–xxxvi.
[63] J. H. Baker, *The Legal Profession and the Common Law* (London, 1986), ch. 23.
[64] See below, pp. 152–3.
[65] Richard Ross, 'The commoning of the common law: the Renaissance debate over printing English law, 1520–1640', *University of Pennsylvania Law Review*, 146 (1998), 323–461.
[66] BL, MS Harleian 249, fols. 117v–18.

Although this scheme was not fully implemented, Ferdinando Pulton subsequently produced an edition of the penal statutes, which he dedicated to crown law officers, and his introductory remarks constituted a particularly fulsome argument in favour of publishing laws which was based largely on historical precedents. After the Romans had banished their kings, the Senate had the laws published in brass throughout their city. Although the English were already aware of many of their laws through the process of 'sinderisis', the effect natural law had on the conscience of men, he noted that there were medieval ordinances that positive laws such as Magna Carta should be read regularly in parish churches. Princes had always taken care that the laws should be published in places of justice, places of commerce and places of prayer. The need of the subject for knowledge of temporal laws was little different from his need to know the Ten Commandments, which were supposed to be discussed within every household.[67]

One reason for abstracting the penal statutes was of course that they needed to be known to the non-professional magistrates in the localities, and another popular Elizabethan genre consisted of works aimed specifically at the instruction of JPs. Within the space of a few years in the late 1570s and early 1580s, three notable barristers, William Fleetwood, Richard Crompton and William Lambarde, all produced a guidebook. In terms of their form and content, all of them were based on an unpublished, but well-known, fifteenth-century reading by Thomas Marrow, as well as a print tradition begun by Fitzherbert in the early sixteenth century.[68] In fact, the works of Fleetwood and Crompton did not extend very far beyond mere reproduction of the earlier text, and Crompton, who published in Law French, appears to have been aiming primarily at the student and professional market.[69] William Lambarde's *Eirenarcha* (1582) was by contrast both a better guide and a more interesting book. Punctilious about keeping the work up to date, his dedication to Sir Thomas Bromley, the man who succeeded Nicholas Bacon as lord keeper, says that he had originally gathered together the

---

[67] Ferdinando Pulton, *An abstract of al the penall statutes which be generall, in force....* (1577), 'Epistle'. The book regularly appeared in subsequent editions.

[68] B. Putnam, *Early Treatises on the Practice of Justices of the Peace in the Fifteenth and Sixteenth Centuries* (Oxford, 1924); B. Putnam, 'The earliest form of Lambarde's "Eirenarcha"', *English Historical Review*, 41 (1926), 260–73; Baker, *Readers and Readings*, p. 72; A. Fitzherbert, *The Boke of Justices of Peas* (?1506).

[69] Though not published until the mid-seventeenth century as *The office of a justice of peace...by W. Fleetwood, Esq; sometime recorder of London* (1658), numerous earlier commercial manuscript copies survive; e.g. CUL, MS Additional 3295, BL Harleian 72 and Hargrave 15. *L'office et aucthoritie de justice de peace, in part collect per le tres reverend, Monsieur Fitzherbert...per R. Crompton* (1584).

material for his own use. The claim was probably true enough, since there are many surviving manuscript compilations which follow roughly the same form. But what set Lambarde's work apart, and no doubt led his 'friends' to encourage publication, was the fact that he brought to it an historical knowledge that had been displayed earlier in the publication of his Latin compilation of Saxon laws as well as a more general jurisprudential outlook, which he evidently developed in part by reading continental text books.[70]

The Elizabethan common-law mind

Partly because of this increasing use of print, but mainly because of the extensive survival of manuscript reports, commonplace books and notes on lectures, it is possible to assemble a fairly detailed picture of some of the ideas about politics and society current within the Elizabethan legal world and the ways in which these were articulated in speeches intended for wider public dissemination.

For lawyers and laymen alike, the technique known as 'commonplacing' was the principal pedagogic tool for organising reading, and hence stocks of knowledge about topics ranging from law to divinity and political theory. Commonplacing involved taking notes from a range of sources on subjects that were organised under a series of alphabetical headings so that the information could then be drawn upon as a resource for formulating a legal brief or making a speech. Essentially a means of collecting together a series of views on any given subject, it was a perfect medium for studying law, which was at least partly a matter of collecting the dicta from the *Year Books* or law reports under various technical headings such as the forms of actions or the terms of art associated with the land law. One consequence of commonplacing was that it was perfectly possible to assemble contradictory views on any given subject, something that became increasingly frequent as the range of source material widened. Another, which followed from this, was that when contemporaries wrote down their own opinions, they frequently began with a collection of contradictory points of view, which explains the tendency in most forms of early modern writing either to refute some authorities in favour of others, or to reconcile competing views with greater or lesser degrees of conviction and clarity.

---

[70] Lambarde, *Eirenarcha*. A substantially revised and enlarged edition in 1588 was followed by others through the 1590s. See also, W. Dunkel, *William Lambarde, Elizabethan Jurist 1536–1601* (New Brunswick, NJ, 1965).

In the case of technical common-law learning, while there was an established canon of texts, and a body of common learning, there was not necessarily a settled authority on any given topic.[71] This was even more true of the general stock of knowledge about the nature of society, government and the place of law within it. Lawyers inevitably had a tendency to begin with the resources of the common law such as the *Year Books* or reports,[72] and in the later sixteenth century, as earlier, Greek and Roman authors, in particular Aristotle and Cicero, also featured prominently. Yet, in the Elizabethan period there was also a distinct interest in what continental authors had to say as well as a significantly greater concern with religious ideas and the long-term history of England as a polity. There are identifiable patterns of reading, and a number of standard positions that can be confidently associated with Elizabethan legal thought, but it is probably best described as a mode of discourse containing a number of intellectual ingredients that could be assembled in different ways rather than a single, prescribed ideology.

As far as the influence of the Greeks and Romans is concerned, for instance, although many could be given, there is no better illustration than the ceiling of Sir Nicholas Bacon's library at his house at Gorhambury in Hertfordshire. Drawing largely on the works of Cicero and Seneca, he assembled there epigrams which attempted to distil human experience into pithy expressions of wisdom. 'Sententia' of this kind no doubt appealed to a common lawyer bred up on maxims of the law, and Bacon's collection centred on the humanistic, and lawyerly, view that the foundation of political behaviour should be rational and humane conduct coupled with the rule of law.[73] It has even been argued that by making these choices he was expressly rejecting the political arts of the 'lion and the little fox', which Machiavelli thought the prince must know how to use.

Although the exact nature of Bacon's religious beliefs have been debated,[74] he, like many other Elizabethans, no doubt had occasion to find out something about the works of John Calvin, whose *Institutes of the Christian Religion* were translated into English by the barrister of the

---

[71] See, for example, the prefatory remarks in Lambarde's *Eirenarcha*.

[72] In addition, during the Elizabethan period, much older 'classics' such as *Bracton* and 'Glanvill', became more widely available. See, for instance, D. E. C. Yale, ' "Of no mean authority": some later uses of Bracton' in M. S. Arnold, T. A. Green, S. A. Scully and S. D. White, eds., *On the Laws and Customs of England: Essays in Honor of Samuel E. Thorne* (Chapel Hill, NC, 1981), who suggests that Thomas Norton may have written the preface of the first edition.

[73] Elizabeth McCutcheon, *Sir Nicholas Bacon's Great House Sententiae* (English Literary Renaissance Supplements, 3, Amherst, MA, 1977), p. 31; P. Collinson, 'Sir Nicholas Bacon and the Elizabethan *via media*', *Historical Journal*, 23 (1980), 255–78.

[74] Ibid., pp. 266–73.

Inner Temple (and son-in-law of Archbishop Cranmer), Thomas Norton in 1561.[75] The interesting thing about Calvin is less any direct influence he may have had than the surprising extent to which his thoughts on 'civil government' would have been both familiar and broadly acceptable to sixteenth-century English legal minds. Having trained as a civil lawyer in France, Calvin's earliest published work was an essay on Seneca's 'Treatise on Clemency'.[76] His account of the relationship between the law of God and natural law, like his treatment of equity, is, at least in Norton's translation, not unlike that given these subjects by Christopher St German in the 1520s and 1530s.[77] Drawing as heavily on the familiar classical sources as on the scriptures for most of his general observations about the nature and purpose of civil government, Calvin held that the pride, obstinacy and wickedness of men made government necessary, but he also repudiated a draconian approach to law enforcement by stressing that strictness needed to be moderated by mercy and Christian charity.[78]

Calvin said little about the origins of political society but his analysis of the different forms of government was essentially Aristotelian. So long as their laws 'tende all together to one mark of equity' (the law of nature), different cities, different nations, would have their distinct laws and constitutions. He also rehearsed the three principal types of government – monarchy, aristocracy and democracy – and the pitfalls each was prone to.[79] While he cautiously advised that it was dangerous to weigh up the strengths of each of these without taking careful account of the circumstances, he concluded, along with Aristotle, that the best form of government would be one where monarchy was mixed, 'or tempered' by 'common government', because

it most seldome chaunceth that kinges so temper themselves that their will never swarveth from that which is just and right . . . [T]he fault, or default, of men maketh that it is safer and more tollerable that many should haue the gouernment, that they may mutually one help an other, one teach and admonish an other, and if any aduance himselfe hier than is meet, there may be ouerseers and maisters to restraine his wilfulnes.[80]

---

[75] M. A. R. Graves, *Thomas Norton: the Parliament Man* (Oxford, 1994).

[76] BL, MS Additional 48104, fol. 6 for a note by William Stanford illustrating a point by reference to Seneca's *De Consolatione*.

[77] *The Institution of Christian Religion, Written in Latine by M. Iohn Calvine, and Translated into English According to the Authors Last Edition, by Thomas Norton* (1582), p. 502. *John Calvin, Institutes of the Christian Religion*, trans. Henry Beveridge (3 vols., Edinburgh, 1846), III, p. 538. I have at a number of points compared the second, corrected, edition of Norton with a more recent translation. For St German, see above, pp. 25–6.

[78] *Calvin, Institutes of the Christian Religion*, III, p. 533. For a contemporary English view on this issue, see below, p. 301.

[79] Norton, *Institution of Christian Religion*, p. 527.   [80] Ibid.

On the other hand, while Calvin stressed that the purposes of government included the maintenance of public quiet, the protection of property and innocent commerce, as well as public religion and 'humanity' amongst men, he also embraced authority. He warned against those who argued that Christian liberty, the equality of men and women before God, should be applied to temporal affairs since the 'spiritual kingdom of Christ and civil government are things far separated'. Furthermore, since divine providence had arranged that different polities should be ruled differently, it was foolish to attack what God had established. It was 'unlawful' for private men to 'consult of the framing of any common weale'. Kings and magistrates had their commissions from God, 'whose steede they do after a certaine maner supplie'.[81] Even laws were in a sense secondary in importance to the magistrate, but, like most lawyers, Calvin ultimately concluded that what was important was a symbiotic relationship in which the magistrate ruled by enforcing the law.

Next to the magistrate in civile states are lawes, the most strong sinewes of common wealthes, or (as Cicero calleth them according to Plato) the soules, without which the Magistrate can not stande, as they againe without the Magistrate haue no liuely force. Therefore nothing coulde be more truely sayde, than that the lawe is a dumbe Magistrate, and that the Magistrat is a liuing lawe.[82]

Although Calvin was not regularly referred to by name as a source by English lawyers, it is striking how frequently similar questions and similar treatments of them were raised in contemporary legal discourse. Despite his emphasis on law enforcement, for example, some of Lord Keeper Bacon's speeches also stressed the importance of striving to reform malefactors as well as punishing them; judges often needed to take account of time, place and circumstances in dealing with those before them.[83] Like the Elizabethan 'Homily of Obedience', which was supposed to be read in every parish church at least once a year, charges addressed to quarter sessions and assizes harped on the rule of law as the only guarantee of the interests of the private man and his family whilst at the same time maintaining it as a corollary that the rule of law could only be sustained by obedience to the person of Queen Elizabeth, the magistrate God had appointed to rule. As Richard Crompton once put it, the laws of God, no less than the laws of man, demanded absolute obedience to the monarch.[84]

---

[81] Ibid., p. 497v.   [82] Ibid., p. 501v.   [83] See above, p. 60.
[84] Richard Crompton, *A Short Declaration of the Ende of Traytors and False Conspirators Against the State, and the Duetie of Subjectes to Theyr Soueraigne Gouernour* (1587).

Reverence for the monarch as the source of justice and political stability was already by 1550 a commonplace theme, but it was inevitably
reinforced in the Elizabethan period when persistent doubts about the
succession to the throne, confessional conflict, and then foreign wars
which lasted for two decades, always inclined lawyers to the view that
some government, any government, was better than no government and
civil war. Sometimes identified as the doctrine known as political neo-
Stoicism, this view also lay at the core of works by continental jurists
such as Jean Bodin, whose works were becoming increasingly well
known long before Richard Knolles's English translation of *The Six
Books of a Commonwealth* in 1606.[85] While Bodin was an advocate of the
absolute power of sovereign kings, he was also preoccupied with how
social life, civility and the rule of law could be maintained during a
period of intense civil unrest in France. This aspect of his thought was
naturally appealing to lawyers, and in England it helps to explain why a
group of mature males often found it expedient to express a high view of
the majesty and power of a female monarch.[86] Offences against the law
were breaches of the queen's peace. In a speech he drafted in anticipation of a visit by the queen to Northampton, for example, Christopher
Yelverton pulled out all the stops, just as the occasion demanded. The
visit of the most 'gratious, best and most dear sovereign' was a source of
'harty and unrepenting joy'.[87] One of the most memorable episodes in
Yelverton's life occurred when the queen gave him her ungloved hand to
kiss after he had been confirmed as speaker of the 1597 parliament and
then put her hands about his neck 'and staid a good space'. Yelverton
coyly recorded that gossip had it that the queen, who at this stage in her
life suffered from stinking breath and wore a wig, had told her ladies that
she was 'sorry she knew me no sooner'.[88] Afterwards he wrote a grov-
elling letter thanking his most sacred sovereign for the favour she had
bestowed upon him.[89]

Yet even such lavish manifestations of loyalty were often accompanied
by a more worldly-wise sense of reality.[90] Once again referring to the
comparatively bad state of affairs overseas, Yelverton was able to praise
the queen in his speech at Northampton because of the 'abounding
felicitie' with which Elizabeth had 'run the course of your most happy
and well-ruled government'. Only the Roman emperor Vespasian had a

---

[85] Bodin's work was first published in 1576.
[86] BL, MS Harleian 249, fol. 115; Graves, *Norton*, pp. 101, 396–7.
[87] BL, MS Additional 48109, fol. 35.   [88] Ibid., fol. 30.   [89] Ibid.
[90] Elizabeth once accused William Lambarde of identifying her with the deposed fourteenth-
century king, Richard II. John Nichols, *Bibliotheca Topographica Britannica* (10 vols.,
1780–90), I, pp. 525–6.

similar record of ending his long reign with the same temperance and clemency with which he had begun.[91] Using one of the most familiar tropes in late sixteenth-century legal rhetoric, he described Elizabeth as a good monarch because she had allowed herself to be ruled by the law, just as her royal progenitors had always done.[92]

Unresolved tensions about the place of the monarchy in the constitution were, moreover, brought into high relief by the question of what would happen if the unmarried female monarch died heirless and without a plan of succession that dealt effectively with the claims of the Catholic and pro-French Mary of Scotland.[93] The problem became acute early in the reign when Elizabeth suffered a near-fatal bout of smallpox in late 1562. Although the queen was consistently hostile to speculation by anyone other than herself, the issue was lobbied consistently in parliament with the connivance of her councillors, and as early as 1566 Cecil hit on the idea that if the queen would not marry then the best course of action was a statute that would in case of an interregnum put the government of the realm into the hands of a specified group of councillors until the two houses of parliament could name a new monarch.[94] Although this did not materialise in any concrete way, in 1584 Cecil, who had subsequently become Lord Treasurer Burghley, supervised Attorney General Sir John Popham's production of a document known as the 'Bond of Association'. Essentially an agreement in a form that was a commonplace in all kinds of business affairs at the time, the bond was to be entered into by members of the aristocracy and gentry, as well as other important elements of the political nation, including members of the inns of court. In signing it, they pledged revenge in the event of the queen's death, with an implication that the future disposition of the crown would be in the hands of parliament.[95]

During the first three decades of the reign, moreover, the machinations of the politicians were matched by several significant treatises that either supported the claims of Mary, or offered alternatives to it. Although written to persuade wider audiences rather than for presentation in a court of law, succession treatises involved their authors in close discussion of the nature of the crown and its relationship to the

---

[91] BL, Additional 48109, fol. 35v.   [92] Ibid.
[93] See, also, A. N. McLaren, *Political Culture in the Reign of Elizabeth I. Queen and Commonwealth 1558–1585* (Cambridge, 1999).
[94] Stephen Alford, *The Early Elizabethan Polity: William Cecil and the British Succession Crisis, 1558–1569* (Cambridge, 1998), pp. 36, 70, 105–16.
[95] P. Collinson, 'The monarchical republic of Queen Elizabeth I', *Bulletin of the John Rylands Library*, 69(2), (1986–7), 394–424; D. Cressy, 'Binding the nation: the Bonds of Association, 1584 and 1596' in D. J. Guth and John W. McKenna, eds., *Tudor Rule and Revolution: Essays for G.R. Elton from his American Friends* (Cambridge, 1982).

wider political nation, as well as questions about nationality and political allegiance. Writing them could also be dangerous, not least because they involved unprecedented consideration of the nature of the 'constitution'.

In 1563, for instance, John Hales, who had spent the Marian years in exile in Germany, and who was sitting in parliament as MP for Lancaster, composed an argument supporting Lady Katherine Grey, the sister of 'Queen' Lady Jane Grey, and the presumptive claimant under the will of Henry VIII and the Act of Succession of 1544. Written as though it was intended as a speech in parliament,[96] but unlikely to have been delivered, Hales's brief acknowledged that there was a problem with the authenticity of Henry's will (no signed copy could be found), but his tract played heavily on the idea that parliamentary authority had been granted to Henry so that 'the state' would not 'after his life . . . be destitute of a lawfull governor'.[97]

Shall we then with cavilling wordes subvert the state when by the true meaning of the Statute [and] w[i]thout iniury to any p[er]son wee may preserve our Countrey in safety . . .[98]

Unfortunately for Hales, Lady Katherine had recently been sent to the Tower by the queen for entering into a clandestine marriage with the earl of Hertford, the son of Protector Somerset, by whom she subsequently became pregnant. Although Hales was ostensibly punished by the queen for meddling in this affair, there is little doubt that the treatise also explains why he himself was imprisoned and subjected to a period of house arrest that lasted almost until his death in 1572,[99] and the suspicion that Nicholas Bacon had been complicit in the work also cost him a short period in the political wilderness.[100] Nevertheless political speculation of this kind was so widespread that the queen pressured the judges into ruling in 1566 that members of parliament could be imprisoned for making unseemly speeches touching her marriage and the succession to the throne.[101] Given this, it is perhaps surprising that at about the same time, two distinguished lawyers, Sir Anthony Browne, now a justice of the Common Pleas, and the recusant Edmund Plowden,

---

[96] BL, MS Sloane MS 1608; J. E. Neale, *Elizabeth I and Her Parliaments 1559–1581* (1953) notes a vehement speech calling for the settlement of the succession that was *probably* given either in 1563 or 1566 by Sir Ralph Sadler (p. 104), who was a longtime associate and, possibly, a patron of Hales. P. W. Hasler, *The House of Commons 1558–1603* (1981), pp. 238–9.

[97] BL, MS Sloane 1608, fols. 3–4.   [98] Ibid., fol. 4.

[99] *Dyer's Reports*, I, pp. xlviii–xlix.

[100] Ibid., p. xlix. Dyer's notes confirm the suspicion of Bacon's involvement, which he denied. Cecil also felt himself under suspicion in the matter.

[101] Ibid., p. xlix.

took up their pens in favour of Mary of Scotland, and managed to survive, perhaps because they enjoyed the protection of the duke of Norfolk.[102]

For Browne, and for Plowden who wrote explicitly to improve on Browne's case, the central issues were whether or not the crown of England descended by the ordinary rules of common law, which would exclude a foreigner, or by laws that were unique to the crown, and which would therefore not preclude Mary who was the legitimate heir by birth, even though she was a Scot. Both works accepted that there was a distinction between the person of the monarch and the crown. Indeed, developing the standard Aristotelian line about the origins of political society, Browne accepted that the first princes had reigned as a result of 'choice and election'.[103] But, the world had subsequently been 'constrained' to repudiate election, and although this raised the problem that the throne might be occupied by one who was not well qualified for the task, there was a compensatory benefit in the peace and quiet that resulted from successions by blood.[104] Although Mary was disqualified at common law, this was in fact no impediment because the common law, like Roman civil law, dealt 'only w[i]th private mens Causes', not questions about the succession to the throne. Furthermore, the monarch came to the crown, not only by descent (as in a case of the inheritance of a piece of land), but by succession, as was the case in connection with a corporation, and hence the occupation of the throne did not follow the same rules of inheritance that applied to goods or land.[105]

Plowden's longer treatise, which was written in December 1566, took into account Hales as well as Browne, and accepted that there was no legal objection to statutory provision for the disposal of the crown of the kind that had been made for Henry VIII to name his successor by will but, unlike Hales, Plowden was unconvinced that a valid will survived.[106] This opened the way for the succession of Mary; in order to make a case for her, Plowden relied on a point he himself had reported in the *Case of the Duchy of Lancaster*, which was that there was a distinction between the physical person of the king and the office, or body politic, of the monarch, and he went on to describe the political body of the king as a corporation. This in turn led to a consideration of the ways corporate bodies, such as towns or religious foundations, were created, and the rules of succession that applied to them, namely election, presentation or donation. However, the crown was clearly different from other corporations insofar as it had been created for the 'necessity of the people'

---

[102] Parmiter, *Edmund Plowden*, pp. 85–5.   [103] BL, MS Harleian 555, fol. 11v.
[104] Ibid., fols. 11–12v.   [105] Ibid., fols. 15r–v, 26.   [106] BL, MS Harleian 849, fol. 31.

rather than by letters patent, and in England the crown descended by blood.[107]

This still left the question of whether or not a foreigner like Mary might be allowed to succeed, and here Plowden developed a two-fold answer. On the one hand, the kings of Scotland, despite years of enmity, had in fact long owed homage to the kings of England, and hence Mary was not out of allegiance to England.[108] On the other hand, he also put together a more subtle legal and constitutional argument, which once again depended on the body politic of the king being similar to a corporation. It was clearly intolerable for someone who owed allegiance to one kingdom to become the king of another. Hence the crown as a corporate body in effect extinguished all other allegiances. It was unreasonable that 'the pryvate p[er]son of a man shoulde by reason of his office bryng a su[b]jecon to all those ov[er] whom he hath rule by reason of his office, and which were before free'.[109] 'Where a whole realme hathe interest in the body of one, shall not that interest take away the pryvate interest of the king?'[110]

Plowden shored up his legal points by making the political ones that the succession of Mary would in effect bring to fruition the union of the two crowns that had been foreseen when Henry VII had married his daughter Margaret to the king of Scotland, and he was confident that if such an event came to pass, the king of Scotland would always have a tendency to come to England, as the 'lesser' always would come to the head of the island.[111] Nevertheless, Plowden's central constitutional argument was that the corporate character of the English throne effectively placed restraints on whoever occupied it, and many of the ingredients in his case could with some further manipulation be made to yield an argument that in the event of a 'vacancy', the succession to the throne of England could be determined by parliament, a point, it will be recalled, that Plowden himself did not deny.

Although it has hitherto received less attention than the works of Browne and Plowden, this was precisely the aim of a manuscript treatise with a title that was cumbersome even by Elizabethan standards: 'Certaine errors upon the statute made the xxvth year of King Edward the Third of Children Borne beyond sea, conceived by Serjeant Browne and Confuted by Sergeant Fairfax in the manner of a dialogue'.[112] Despite

---

[107] Ibid., fols. 1, 2, 7, 15.   [108] Ibid., fols. 9v, 18vff.   [109] Ibid., fol. 15.
[110] Ibid., fol. 29v.   [111] Ibid., fol. 29.
[112] CUL, MS Additional 9212 appears to be a corrected autograph copy. Bodleian, MS Rawlinson C.85 is also referred to below. For the location of other copies, see, J. H. Baker and J. S. Ringrose, *A Catalogue of English Legal Manuscripts in Cambridge University Library* (Woodbridge, 1996). Sir Edward Coke owned a copy.

the suggestion in the title that it was concerned primarily with the capacity of foreigners to succeed to the throne, 'Certaine errors' disposes quickly with the prospect of a Scottish succession, and then moves to a consideration of what might happen if Mary was effectively ruled out and there was no obvious heir in the event of Queen Elizabeth's death.

Though the Serjeant Browne of the dialogue holds views similar to those of Sir Anthony (and Plowden), and although the text of 'Certaine errors' exploits the connection in the name, the disputants in the dialogue are evidently fictional. The nature of the work, and its conclusions, indicate that the manuscript was composed (or put into final form) in the early to mid 1580s, probably in connection with the Bonds of Association project of 1584.[113] There is no known attribution of authorship, and no conclusive internal evidence, but 'Certaine errors' was certainly written by a common lawyer, and the strongest candidate is William Fleetwood, a political ally of Cecil's, who was recorder of London for twenty years between 1571 and 1591. The handwriting of the autograph corrected copy has a similarity to Fleetwood's, and although the hand is not so distinctive as to make it a certainty that it is his, circumstantial evidence also points in his direction. Fleetwood authored many manuscript treatises, and his political track-record puts him firmly into the camp of those hostile to Mary and sympathetic to a parliamentary solution to the succession. He had seen John Hales's brief in favour of Lady Katherine Grey, and he spoke frequently against the succession of Mary of Scotland in parliamentary debates during the 1570s and 1580s.[114] Fleetwood also had a connection with Plowden, having provided an analytical index to the second edition of *The Commentaries*, and he would certainly have known of Browne's treatise as well.[115]

Contending first of all with the arguments in favour of a Scottish succession, 'Certaine errors' begins by disposing of the idea that England was in any respect a feudal state. Referring to the points Browne, and especially Plowden, had made about Scots being within the allegiance of England because Scottish kings had done homage to English kings, 'Certaine errors' described homage as a French invention dating from the time of Hugh Capet which was associated with the gift of '*feodes* (I meane tenements to be holden by service either of knight hode)' or of free socage, by lords to tenants.[116] Yet the oath of homage made it clear that any obligation owed by a tenant to a lord was superseded by

---

[113] See above, p. 71. [114] *ODNB*.

[115] *Les commentaries, ou reportes de Edmunde Plowden . . . Ouesque vn table perfect des choses notables contenus en ycell, nouelment compose per William Fletewoode recorder de Loundres . . .* (1578).

[116] CUL, MS Additional 9212, fol. 6.

allegiance owed to the king. Far from being based on tenure, allegiance could not exist without a nation of people. Furthermore, allegiance transcended the individual existence of any given king because, even in those circumstances were the throne was vacant, 'the crowne in question, which is as well taken for the universal state of the realm, as for jurisdiction over the same, abideth still, whereunto every leige man, oweth by the law of nature and nations . . . legience'.[117]

It followed from these premises that it was impossible for a Scot, or the subject of any other country, to owe allegiance to more than one crown, but if Mary's claim to the throne of England could on this basis be proven invalid, that still left the question of how it should be filled in the event of a 'vacancy', that is if Elizabeth died without creating an heir or naming a successor. Here, 'Certaine errors' exploited the analogies Browne and Plowden had made between the succession to the throne and the succession of the heads of ecclesiastical corporations by making the polemical point that such an argument should consider temporal rather than ecclesiastical examples. According to 'Certaine errors', the crown of England was similar to the electorships of the German states, where the electorship was a dignity that had offices and possessions annexed to it, the right to which descended by inheritance.[118] But the author also referred to the early Tudor judge Sir John Fyneux for the view that the crown was a corporation created by the common law, and he concluded that the most useful analogy might be between the crown and an urban corporation. If we stand 'with the king as the commonaltie incorporate with the mayor [of a town] then may we be sawcie to controwle his grantes without our consent'.[119]

The next move involved showing that the common law and parliament had the power to interpret or make laws that affected the crown, its occupants and its prerogatives. Whereas Sir Anthony Browne had stressed that the succession to the throne was a matter beyond the determination of the common law, 'Certaine errors' sought to show that this amounted to an assertion that English monarchs were 'loose' from, or not bound by any law, and that consequently the prerogatives of the crown came from nowhere (figuratively, that they were 'bastards').[120] In refuting this point, 'Certaine errors' referred to statutes, fifteenth-century *Year Book* cases, and the deal worked out in parliament between Henry VI and the duke of York in the 1450s as part of a demonstration

---

[117] Ibid.   [118] Bodleian, MS Rawlinson C.85, fol. 23v.   [119] Ibid., fol. 20v.

[120] Ibid., fol. 26. Browne's position was that there are two kinds of prerogative, one given to the king by the laws, and another, which could not be severed from the crown, including the power to grant pardons, make corporations, dispense with laws and statutes etc., and that no act of parliament could bind the king's prerogatives.

that prerogatives had been gradually annexed to the crown over the course of time. Although the crown existed before the prerogatives, both the highest and the lowest of them were created by the law and were subject to regulation by it.[121]

Aware that the greatest of the royal prerogatives was the idea that the king was above the law, 'Certaine errors' goes on to argue that this concept was not a part of the universal law of nations, the *ius gentium*, because it was clear from historical examples that the exercise of the prerogative had differed in different times and places. For example, Aristotle said that the Lacedemonian kings ruled 'not by power but by law onely'; Tacitus showed that many Roman kings were subject themselves to the laws they made. The prerogative of being 'loose from laws' in Rome was not immemorial, but granted for the first time to Augustus.[122] Since the crown of England was imperial and had no superior except God, the prerogatives attached to it can only have come from the law or usurpation. It was to the greater glory of the crown that they were based on law, 'thereby taking away all manner of exceptions that man may object to impune or disobey any of them'.[123] At common law, the prerogative was a particular custom, but even the authors of the Roman laws always described such powers as laws, and so too did the French: 'so what mean you to say that the prerogatives of the crown [of England] are base born when they have a mother the same as those of the French or the Romans'. The law, which is reasonable policy, gave the prince the powers necessary to govern, but this did not imply that the law and parliament could not 'sequester' them from the natural body of an individual ruler (as in the case of lunacy) or alter them.[124]

Yet even if it was accepted that parliament and/or the common law might intercede to determine the succession of the crown, there was another problem. After the death of the monarch the courts would be shut up, and there would be no way to call a parliament since the necessary royal writ could not be issued. In these circumstances, according to Browne, the country would have to fall back upon the laws of God and nature to determine the descent of the crown, but while 'Certaine errors' acknowledges that this might be a problem, Serjeant Fairfax also points out that the implied return to the state of nature would have the unacceptable consequence that 'all common inherit-ances' would suffer the same fate during the interregnum.[125] In any case, the law of nations revealed that different countries had different methods of selecting their king, and, furthermore, there were two further

[121] Ibid., fols. 26v–7.   [122] Ibid., fol. 27.   [123] Ibid.   [124] Ibid., fols. 28–31v.
[125] Ibid., fol. 39v.

laws of nature that needed to be taken into consideration. The first was the natural inclination to self-preservation (termed by lawyers, the instinct of nature).[126] The second was reason,[127] which enabled man to look into the necessity of human things and provide for them so that civil society might be maintained. Furthermore, 'The most common and best means for the preservation and conservation as well of private as publick tranquilitie and society used in all ages and by all means is by way of a lawful assembly [which] we call a parliament.'[128]

Political bodies differ from natural bodies in that if the head is taken away, the 'politicall bodie remayneth quicke'. As nature forms the head out of its natural body, 'soe consent of voices at the first produced the political head out of the political body', and the law of God and nature permits a people to assemble themselves together to form a new head when the old one is removed. It is true that the king should be present to call a parliament, but, if he is not, then it is necessary to fall back on the law of nature and nations. Despite the death of the monarch, judges, constables, JPs and other officials with lawful authority continued to exist. Although the king of England had more power than the doge of Venice, England, like Venice, was an 'equal' [i.e. mixed] common-wealth, consisting of monarchy, aristocracy and democracy. Even if the monarchical part died, 'aristocratia and democratia, that is the nobility and commons' remain still alive and in force.[129]

The constitutional ideas expressed in 'Certaine errors' should no doubt be seen as a response to a set of particular circumstances that in the eyes of many contemporaries constituted nothing less than a national emergency. Nevertheless, they reflect a legalistic version of what Professor Collinson once described as the republican 'virus' within Elizabethan thought that was also evident in other kinds of writing, including, for example, Sir Thomas Smith's *De republica Anglorum*, which was composed in 1565 although not published until twenty years later.[130] Furthermore, the interest in and influence of the succession issue should not be underestimated. In 1566 William Thornton, a reader at Lincoln's Inn, was imprisoned for allowing students to undertake some kind of disputation about it,[131] but Sir Anthony Browne mentioned

---

[126] Ibid.
[127] The exact words are 'a minde whereby we are moved and drawn to do justly'.
[128] Ibid., fols. 39v–40.   [129] CUL, MS Additional 9219, fols. 40, 52.
[130] A. McLaren, 'Reading Sir Thomas Smith's *De republica Anglorum* as Protestant apologetic', *Historical Journal*, 42(4) (1999), 911–39, esp. 927, argues that Smith was concerned with mixed monarchy in which common consent constrained the queen in defence of Protestantism.
[131] M. Levine, *The Early Elizabethan Succession Question, 1558–1568* (Stanford, 1966), p. 170.

in his treatise that briefs on the subject were appearing all the time, and it is evident that the kinds of thinking about the constitution that were involved in the succession treatises were also sometimes being expounded in lectures at the legal inns even when they were not devoted explicitly to that question. In 1578, for instance, James Morice, reader at the Middle Temple gave a series of lectures on the royal prerogative, but instead of following the traditional method of basing the text on *Prerogativa regis* and discussing the king's tenurial rights,[132] he read on chapter 50 of the Statute of Westminster I, and produced what is probably the most complete analysis of the constitution by a common lawyer to have survived from the reign of Elizabeth.

Morice argued that the powers of the monarch must constitute a worthy subject for study: 'For what cann A Right or Prerogative Roiall most aptly signifie or expresse unto us, then that a Lawfull Prynce by Justice and not by pleasure doth rule and governe the People commytted to his Charge.'[133] Everyone agreed that nothing was better than good government, or worse than anarchy, and it had been long disputed what 'state' or form of government might 'take place and be preferred for the best'. Following Aristotle's account of the different forms in considerable detail, Morice began by taking a wrecking ball to democracy, and finished by advocating mixed monarchy bounded by law. The trouble with rule by the 'Inconstant rude *and* Ignorant multitude (how gloriously soever it be adorned with the goodly name of Isonomia, equality of justice)', was that 'where all beare rule, there none doe well obey . . . The nature of the common sorte is eyther humbly to serve or with Arrogancie to commaunde. Libertie which is the meane neither can they use nor moderately refuse.'

On the other hand, although Roman history demonstrated that all states tended ultimately towards monarchy, the sovereign rule and absolute authority of single persons had frequently broken the 'sacred bounds of Justice' and degenerated into 'Tirany, and Insolent oppression'. Since

good kynges and Prynces are neyther by Nature Immortals, nor of them selves being Men, Imutable, an other State of kingdome and better kind of monarchy hath been by common Assent ordayned and establyshed, wherein the Prince (not by Lycentious will and Immoderate affections, but by the Lawe, that is by

---

[132] For Morice, see *ODNB* and below, pp. 100ff. At least two versions of the reading survive. BL, MS Egerton 3376 is a fair copy of the first three 'divisions', and contains a preface addressed to Burghley. The only date on it pertains to its ownership in 1682, and the hand could be seventeenth century. BL, MS Additional 36081 also appears to be a scribal copy, but it contains headings for fourteen divisions of the reading, although the content survives only for the first two.

[133] BL, MS Additional 36081, fol. 230.

the prudent Rules and Precepts of Reason agreaed upon and made [in] the Covenant of the Comon Wealth) may Justly governe and com*m*ande, and the People in one obedience saflie lyve and quyetly enioye their own.[134]

Yet Morice did not aim to undermine the extensive prerogatives of the English king, those 'Lawfull Authoryties, Prehyemences, dignyties and Royall Prevyledges, whereby he Ruleth, excelleth, is preferred and magnyfied over and above all other persons within this kingdom [by the common laws and customs of the same]'.[135] Like others at this time, he accepted the legal tradition, dating from the reign of Edward IV, that a usurper could take on all the privileges of a rightful king, the reason being that justice and the benefits of government simply could not be maintained without a ruler.[136] According to Morice, the king learned the grievances of the subject through parliament, which was established and called by the king alone.[137] The role of the lords and commons in parliament was to consult and consent in deliberations over the making of laws, but statutes had the force of law only through the royal assent.[138] Nevertheless, in what appears to be an appropriation of a point made by Bodin, although parliament was not sovereign, the system worked because 'what cawse agaiyne haue the Comens to murmor or rebell agaynst the Lawes and Statutes by which they are governed since they themselves are of Counsell and Consent to the makinge of the same'.[139] Furthermore, while it was a 'common saying' that the king by his prerogative was above the law, to 'say that the kyng is so A Emperor over his Lawes and Act*es* of Parliament (because he hath power to make them) as that he is not bounde to governme by the same but at his will and pleasure, is an opinion altogeather repugnant to the wise and politicke State of government established within the realm'.[140] As *Bracton* had pointed out, the king was bound by his coronation oath. In any case, it was contrary to reason that any prince should overthrow decisions made by 'so grave a Counsel, uppon so great deliberatcon, and by the Com*m*on assent of all'.[141]

Morice's own interest in the royal prerogative probably focused primarily on the section of the reading that dealt with the monarch's powers in connection with the government of the church and ecclesiastical

---

[134] Ibid., fols. 230–1v.
[135] Ibid., fol. 235v. The phrase in square brackets was added to the fair copy manuscript in a contemporary hand.
[136] Ibid., fol. 242v.
[137] Ibid., fol. 239v. A marginal note in another hand says that similar points had been made by Fortescue.
[138] Ibid., fols. 237–8.   [139] Ibid., fol. 239v.   [140] Ibid., fols. 243v–44.
[141] Ibid., fol. 244.

causes, an issue that earned him the displeasure of the queen in 1593.[142] Yet there is no indication that the views he expressed in 1578 were particularly controversial. One version of this reading contains an epistle to Burghley, which indicates that he had asked Morice for a copy of the text after it had been delivered rather than that he had any fore-knowledge of, or influence on, what had been said. Morice himself seems to have anticipated that the work, though 'unworthy to be read of the wise and learned', might be suitable for the instruction of young law students.[143] In fact, there is no evidence that any steps were taken to make the text more widely available, but Morice and Burghley remained on good terms for another twenty years, and the latter helped to obtain for Morice an appointment as one of the four attorneys in the court of Wards.[144]

Nevertheless, readings that went as far into the nature of the consti-tution as Morice's were rare in Elizabethan England. Furthermore, while Morice's lecture would have had an audience at the inns of court, and indirectly reached the ears of Burghley, it was one of hundreds of lectures given, and its circulation in manuscript seems to have been moderate at best.[145] 'Certaine errors', on the other hand, was probably designed to be read and contemplated by a learned lay audience as well as professional lawyers. Thus, although two manuscript treatises alone cannot necessarily be taken to represent professional opinion in the 1570s or 1580s, there is equally little reason to doubt that the essentially mixed-monarchical interpretations of the English constitution that they put forward would have been both instantly recognised and considered fairly conventional. It is true that Lord Keeper Bacon declined to comment on a lengthy account of the various forms of government, 'Monarchia; Aristocratia; Democratia', which had been included in a speech delivered by the speaker of the House of Commons in 1575,[146] but, while they always, and not surprisingly, came down in favour of monarchy, discourses of this kind evidently continued to be common at least up until 1597, when Christopher Yelverton included similar matter in his own opening address as speaker of the House.[147]

At the same time, works such as 'Certaine errors' and James Morice's reading also demonstrate how Elizabethan legal writing on consti-tutional subjects integrated technical common law learning with the broader tradition of European juristic humanism, a finding that is not surprising when it is considered how similar some of the problems faced

---

[142] See below, pp. 108–9.   [143] BL, MS Egerton 3376, fol. 2.   [144] *ODNB.*
[145] Baker, *Readers and Readings*, p. 165.   [146] Folger, MS V.a.197, fol. 59v.
[147] HEHL, MS Ellesmere 2585.

by countries such as England and France were at this time. John Hales is said to have sent Robert Beale, who would later become a secretary of state to Queen Elizabeth, on a grand tour of European centres of learning in order to find support for his arguments.[148] Sir John Dodderidge, William Lambarde and Sir Christopher Yelverton were all familiar with the work of Joachim Hopperus, a Flemish civil lawyer who enjoyed a successful career under Philip II of Spain.[149] A list of relevant authors Dodderidge compiled in connection with a work on the royal prerogative he undertook at the instigation of Thomas Sackville, Lord Buckhurst, included the Bible and the works of Thomas Aquinas as well as Plato, Aristotle and the ancient and modern interpreters of Aristotle. Then there were Machiavelli, Justus Lipsius and a number of French lawyers, including Bodin and François Hotman.[150] A bibliography assembled from the printed and manuscript works of William Fleetwood would include Aristotle, Bodin, Erasmus, Cicero, Plutarch and the French civilian Joachimus Perionius; if we accept that Fleetwood was the author of 'Certaine errors', then the list would have to be expanded to include works on the civil law, including the *Corpus juris imperii*.[151] Similarly, although the titles are not specified, James Morice's will mentions a bequest to his eldest son of his 'books of the laws of England' as well as 'Latin, French & Greek books'.[152]

Although much of the historiography on the relationship between legal and political thought over the past century or so has stressed the relative insularity of English common-law thinking, this misses the point that the Elizabethans in particular embraced classical and continental learning with some enthusiasm and used it to develop a more thoughtful appreciation of the nature and history of their own institutions.[153] One of the most immediately apparent characteristics of Aristotle's *Politics* is

---

[148] For the connection between Hales and Beale, see *ODNB*.

[149] Lambarde's copy of *Tractatus de iuris arte, duorum clarissimorum Iurisconsul Ioannis Corassii et Ioachim Hopperi* (Cologne, 1582) was purchased in 1583; it is copiously annotated. BL, Department of Printed Books, shelf mark 516.a.55.

[150] BL, MS Harleian 5220, fols. 3–21.

[151] BL, MS Stowe 423, fols. 106ff. *Bibliotheca Monastica-Fletewodiana. A Catalogue of Rare Books and Tracts in Various Languages and Faculties: including the Antient Conventual Library of Missenden Abbey in Buckinhamshire: Together with some choice remains of that of the late Eminent Serjeant at Law, William Fletewode, Esq.* (1744) lists a number of titles that may well have been in Fleetwood's library. While it is impossible to prove that he bought all of them, the history of the collection suggests that this was most likely the case. Relevant items include several early sixteenth-century French works on the laws of Burgundy and Normandy, Montaigne's *Essays* (1572 edition), Norton's translation of Calvin, and Seneca's *Tragedies*.

[152] *ODNB*.

[153] Cf. J. G. A. Pocock, *The Ancient Constitution and the Feudal Law* (Cambridge, 1987 edn).

the way it employs accounts of the individual Greek city states to
illustrate different types of polity, along with their different systems of
laws, and the ways these changed over time. A reading by Francis Rhodes
in 1575 includes a list of lawgivers that began with Solon (Athens) and
Lycurgus (Lacedemonians), and then proceeded through the early British
kings before concluding with William the Conqueror and Henry II.[154]
Equally, it was apparently commonplace for Elizabethans to describe
their system as more like that of the Lacedemonians (Spartans), who had
unwritten laws, than like that of the Athenians, who used a code.

The fact that English law could be categorised in this way provided
a means of recognising its distinctiveness, while at the same time maintaining that it could be understood within a broader intellectual framework that included other national systems, past or present. Moreover,
although the authority of customary practices was increasingly significant in several technical branches of the common law from the mid
sixteenth century onwards,[155] there is little evidence to suggest that 'long
usage' alone was very often taken as decisive in general political and
constitutional works at this time. Apart from anything else, in an age
when the 'truth' of the scripturally based Protestant religion was regularly contrasted with the tendency of Catholics to follow theirs purely in
the name of custom, arguments based merely on tradition were bound to
seem problematic.[156] For instance, in a pamphlet he wrote in order
to win the loyalty of northerners tempted to participate in the rebellion
of the earls in 1569, Thomas Norton warned that they should not be
misled by claims that the rebels were going to restore ancient customs
and liberties to the church and the realm: 'Are all customes, without
respect of good or bad, to be restored; are not rather the bad to be
reformed: and so it is true liberty to be delivered from them, and not
remayne in thrall and bounde unto them.'[157] Equally, John Hales confidently claimed that the laws of the realm 'do teach us' that if a custom
is contrary to reason or a higher law, it should be abolished as a great evil
no matter how long it had been in use.[158]

On the other hand, histories, and in particular national histories were
becoming increasingly significant. It was perfectly possible to practise
law proficiently without knowing much history, but this only makes it

---

[154] Guildhall MS 86, fol. 164.   [155] See below, pp. 328, 386.

[156] See HEHL, MS Ellesmere 6202, fol. 44a, a dialogue between verity and custom where
this idea is applied to a consideration of the doctrine of the Eucharist. 'A dialogue
between custom and truth' was printed in Foxe, *Acts and Monuments*, VI, pp. 336–49.

[157] Thomas Norton, *To the Quenes Maiesties Poore Deceyued Subiectes of the Northe Countrey
Drawen into Rebellion by the Earles of Northumberland and Westmerland* (1569), sig. Gi.

[158] BL, MS Sloane 1608, fol. 12v.

more striking that the major archival collections of lawyers' papers in this period nearly all reflect an interest in history in general, and of the common law in particular. William Fleetwood, for instance, attributed his appreciation of the subject to the Greek 'historiographer' Nicephorus and to Cicero, whose *De oratore* commended history as the life of memory and a candle of truth,[159] and many of his works reveal what he himself described as an enthusiasm for the antiquities of England that stretched from accounts of the ancient kings to the etymologies of some of the local place names of London.[160] Even more significantly, lawyers very quickly became interested in historical accounts of the reformed religion in England, which argued that, far from being revolutionary, the religious changes brought about by Henry VIII and Elizabeth were merely a restoration of the primitive, and true, Christianity that had long existed in the country before the usurpations of the bishops of Rome.

Thomas Norton, for example, wrote an account of the political and religious history of England that showed how the Tudors came out of Wales, where the Anglo-Saxons had centuries before been forced to seek refuge, and brought the reformed religion with them.[161] Fleetwood was particularly interested in the mid Tudor critics of the Italian historiographer Polydore Vergil.[162] Like William Lambarde, and the young Edward Coke, Fleetwood also had connections with, and borrowed books from, Archbishop Matthew Parker, the central figure in the circle of historical apologists for Protestant England.[163] While Fleetwood's own major historical investigations concentrated on the rather narrow subject of the history of the forest laws,[164] it is striking that the most complete version of his work placed them within the context of a thoroughly anti-papal account of the general history of English law, while another prefaces the subject with an investigation of the waves of immigration that had shaped the population of Britain since the time of the Flood.[165]

Especially in terms of his published works, a much more important figure in marrying English history to legal learning was the Kentish barrister William Lambarde. His first book, a translation of Anglo-Saxon laws and customs into Latin was undertaken in collaboration with the antiquarian and map-maker Laurence Nowell.[166] His *Perambulation of*

---

[159] CUL, MS Dd.9.17, fol. 3.
[160] BL, MS Harleian 6234, fol. 11. See, also, *ODNB*.   [161] Graves, *Norton*, p. 227.
[162] Stowe 423, fol. 133r–v. Mentions the work of Sir John Price, Sir Brian Tuke, Humphrey Lloyd, John Leyland and John Bale.
[163] CUL, MS Dd.9.17, fol. 4.   [164] See below, pp. 195 and 335–6.
[165] Guildhall, MS 86, fols. 40, 60 (for the religious emphasis); CUL, MS Dd.9.17, fol. 3r–v.
[166] *Archaionomia, siue de priscis anglorum legibus libri sermone Anglico. . . .Gulielmo Lambardo interprete* (1568). For Nowell, see *ODNB*.

Kent (1576) was the prototype both for Camden's *Britannia* as well as the large number of county histories produced during the seventeenth century.[167] While the translation of Anglo-Saxon laws provided a source book that was mined by subsequent generations of scholars and lawyers who wanted to argue about the longevity and pedigree of the laws of England, and while Lambarde himself was certainly nationalistic, he very often appears to have taken the history of the British Isles more or less as he found it. For example, he concluded a discussion of the laws of the pre-Norman British kingdoms in *Perambulation* with the observation that while most of Mercia had its own laws, some parts were subject to that of the Danes. After the Conquest, William of Normandy collected together all of the existing laws of his new kingdom and, with the advice of his council, allowed some, altered others, and quite abrogated a great many, in place of which he established the laws of his own country.[168]

In fact, it is Lambarde's last work, *Archion; or A Discourse upon the High Courts of Justice in England*, which was probably completed in 1591, but not published until the 1630s, that best demonstrates how the classical and historical strains of thought could be brought together to create a nationalistic, and essentially populist view of English legal institutions, including the High Court of Parliament.[169] The 'archeion' in the title referred to the governing body of ancient Athens, and although Lambarde did not elaborate the point, he and his contemporaries would have been aware that the history of the *archeion* had been described by Aristotle and others as involving the gradual evolution of the dynastic rule of kings into aristocracy and then democracy.[170] The preface declares that 'Next the Knowledge of God and our selves, that of our Country takes place, as most usefull and necessary.' The first few pages of the text are devoted to an account of the foundation of civil societies that drew largely on Cicero's *De officiis*. In the beginning the only political society was the family governed by the patriarch; but as population grew, the weak and helpless began to be oppressed by the

---

[167] The first edition of *Perambulation* contains commendatory verses by Fleetwood.

[168] W. Lambarde, *The Perambulation of Kent. Contaeining the description, Hystorie and Customes of that Shyre* (1576), pp. 5, 11.

[169] William Lambarde, *Archion; or A Discourse upon the High Courts of Justice in England* (first published London, 1635, but the preface is dated 1591). The autograph copy is in LI, MS Miscellaneous 599. There are differences between the printed version and the manuscript. A modern edition was published by C. H. McIlwain and P. L. Ward, *Archeion or, A Discourse upon the High Courts of Justice in England by William Lambarde* (Cambridge, MA, 1957). A similar, but more technical work had been published earlier by Richard Crompton, *L'authoritie et jurisdiction des courts de la maiestie de la roygne* (2nd edn, 1594).

[170] Hugo Grotius also had an interest in Athenian history. Richard Tuck, *Philosophy and Government, 1572–1651* (Cambridge, 1993), p. 162.

strong. Consequently, the people went to the man who was most distinguished for his virtue and established him as their king. He protected the weak and set up an equitable system of government that united the highest and lowest in equal rights. Inevitably, however, rulers were subject to human frailty and corruption, and it was for this reason that 'Lawes and rules of Justice were devised, within the which as within certaine Limits, the power of governors should from henceforth be bounded'.[171] Although Lambarde acknowledged that William the Conqueror ruled 'by the sword',[172] and made a number of changes in the operation of the courts, he downplayed the significance of the alterations, claiming that in most instances there were changes in the names of things rather than in their substance.[173] Finally, citing Tacitus, Lambarde traced the origins of representative government back to the Germans (Saxons) who brought the English manner of 'consultation' with them. Before the Conquest, the institutions themselves were supposedly known as 'synods . . . now appropriated to the Ecclesiasticall meetings only'. Thus while the word 'parliament' was itself a Norman innovation, the practice was much more ancient, having had Germanic origins similar, in fact, to those which the Frenchman François Hotman had described for the Franks.[174]

The subsequent chapters in *Archion*, which offered accounts of the various courts within the legal system, were technically useful and largely uncontroversial,[175] just the sort of thing that lawyers such as William Fleetwood had been striving to create some time earlier; given Lambarde's distinction as a legal author, it is surprising that it remained unpublished for so long. Perhaps the polemical content was less palatable in the 1590s than it would have been a decade or so earlier, a point suggested by the fact that Robert Cecil, to whom it was dedicated, evidently declined to sponsor it.[176] On the other hand, the 1590s were not particularly easy times in legal publishing, and Lambarde himself may have been preoccupied with other business as a result of his appointment as a master in Chancery. Nevertheless, the work circulated widely in manuscript. Henry Yelverton collected over 100 folios of abstracts from

---

[171] Lambarde, *Archion*, pp. 1–5. Lambarde also refers frequently to the historical works of Lorenzo Valla.

[172] Ibid., p. 20–1. William and his son, Rufus, governed by 'a meere and absolute power, as in a Realme obtayned by Conquest'.

[173] Ibid., p. 9.   [174] Ibid., pp. 239–41. Brooks, *Lawyers, Litigation*, ch. 8.

[175] Although some points Lambarde made about equity were later referred to by Sir Robert Filmer (below, pp. 304–05).

[176] Dunkel, *Lambarde*, pp. 130, 133, 139, suggests he may have intended the work as a contribution to the debate between the common law and the prerogative courts. See below, pp. 97ff.

it when he was studying for the bar in the 1590s, concentrating in particular on Lambarde's assertion that both written and unwritten law in the form of prescription demonstrated the long-standing history of parliament.[177] In 1593, Edward Coke, as speaker of the House of Commons, treated MPs to a long discourse on the history of the institution that followed much the same path Lambarde had taken.[178]

Public discourse

The increasing richness of Elizabethan thought about the nature of law and the polity can be traced in manuscripts and in printed works intended primarily for professional or magisterial audiences. But thanks to the better survival of evidence in the form of charges given to grand juries and other local courts,[179] from about 1550 onwards it is also possible to piece together a fuller picture of the transmission of juristic ideas into the localities, and the ways in which they were articulated for those outside the social and political elite.

In *Eirenarcha*, Lambarde traced the practice of charging back to the time of Canute, and commended the custom in *Bracton*'s day, which was that the justices in eyre would deliver a preamble, or prefatory remarks, and then leave it to one of the jurors to read out the relevant statutes that constituted the charge itself.[180] However, since the numbers of statutes had increased so greatly in the intervening period, he concluded that the tedious exposition of them should be shortened in order to make way for more lengthy and speculative preambles ('whereof there is greater use and necessity').[181] At the same time, he also supported what seems to have become a common practice by Elizabethan times, if it had not been so before, which was that the opening of courts of quarter sessions, as well as assizes, should include a sermon as well as a charge: 'seeing that the laws of men must be obeyed for God, it doeth of necessitie ensue that he which will seek to have man obeyed rightly, must first cause god to be preached truely'.[182]

For Lambarde the purpose of the charge was instructive ('to enforme the people'), and the oratorical possibilities of the preamble were doubtless well understood by the rhetoric-conscious Elizabethans. One general guideline, which was that the issues covered should be divided into matters ecclesiastical and matters temporal, may only have become

---

[177] BL, MS Hargrave 398, fols. 135ff.
[178] J. E. Neale, *Elizabeth and Her Parliaments 1584–1601* (1957), pp. 319–20.
[179] See above, pp. 21–3.   [180] Lambarde, *Eirenarcha*, pp. 310–11.   [181] Ibid., p. 312.
[182] Ibid., p. 310. For a discussion of sermons, see below, pp. 211–14.

common after the break from Rome in the 1530s, but it was a regular feature of charges from the mid sixteenth century onwards. In addition, Lambarde advised that preambles should focus on an 'exhortation' to obey the laws and 'dehortation' from the things which they forbade. Beyond this, however, the direction of a charge was left largely to the person who gave the speech. There were some printed templates,[183] but since courts such as quarter sessions met four times a year, the chairman of the bench would often find himself obliged to address a similar audience on more than one occasion, and monotonous repetition was to be avoided. Hence, Lambarde's advice included several different openings. One was to divide the subject according to the concerns of God, the prince and the subject. Another began with the proposition that all laws prohibited something contrary to the four cardinal virtues: prudence, justice, fortitude, or temperance. A third would be to organise the discussion around the Ten Commandments.

Apart from twenty-nine charges written by Lambarde himself, no more than two dozen or so Elizabethan charges survive out of the hundreds that were given,[184] but even this relatively small sample shows that there was considerable scope for the orator to draw on his own fund of reading in order to elaborate on a range of legal and political issues in speeches that probably lasted at least as long as forty minutes.[185] Stressing that jurors who failed to make honest presentments would suffer in the eyes of God as well as in those of men, many charges probably consisted of little more than 'exhortations' to juries to make the criminal legal system work effectively by acting as the eyes of the magistrates. Brief notes from a charge that was probably delivered in Cheshire in the 1560s, for example, stuck largely to basics. Presentments at quarter sessions were for the advancement of justice, the punishment of 'misdoers', and the conservation of the peace. In performing the service well, jurors were seeking God's glory, the preservation of the prince and their own safety. They should report any deviations from the Book of Common Prayer as well as anyone who had dealings with foreign princes.[186]

---

[183] Most notably the example given in Crompton, *L'office et aucthoritie de justices de peace*, sig. cci.

[184] Conyers Read, ed., *William Lambarde and Local Government: His 'Ephemeris' and Twenty-nine Charges to Juries and Commissions* (Ithaca, NY, 1962), p. 57, knew of only one other charge and thought that the practice may not have been common. In addition to the charges given by lawyers, which are discussed here, they were also given by non-professional country gentlemen; see below, pp. 298ff.

[185] Read, *Lambarde and Local Government*, p. 56, notes that Lambarde mentioned that the reading out of the statutes may have taken up to two hours.

[186] HEHL, MS Ellesmere 481a, fols. 231ff: a charge that belonged originally to the Harpur family in Cheshire.

Others, however, were a good deal bolder.[187] A fragmentary charge for a manorial court, which must date from the reign of Queen Mary, and which appears to refer to the earlier dissolution of monastic lands, drew on Plutarch's account of Aratus and Cleomenes to make the point that it was wise policy for those who returned to power after exile to respect tenures as they existed, even if there had been in the interval many unlawful disseisins.[188] Although they shared many common elements, the suite of seven charges that Christopher Yelverton gave at meetings of the Northamptonshire commissions of the peace in the years around 1569 each developed an aspect of his personal interpretation of the Elizabethan polity. The first stressed that while parliament passed many laws for remedying the ills of the commonwealth, effective administration of them depended on the service of the jury, who were selected as 'instrumentes to serve not your own private affections, but the necessities of the publick state, not by mallice to wreke your own gall, but by indifferencie to proceed in your duties'.[189] The second, by contrast, used a distinctly Protestant view of human nature to persuade listeners of the value of the rule of law. Given man's boundless inclination for sin and evil, 'public order' could only be maintained by the vigilance of juries in presenting offenders against the 'civill societie of this state'.[190]

The third of Yelverton's speeches criticised the 'common state' of the realm for failing to act in order to stem the tide of 'outrageous offences', but this particular theme was developed with surprising complexity. While it was obvious that the 'baser sort' could hardly be restrained without the 'rod' of 'civil discipline', even the 'better and discreetor sort', those who seemed 'more evenlie to weigh both their private duties towards God, and their publique service towards their countrie', might slip into 'misorder' if it were not for the dread of law. Indeed, every member of the body politic was subject to potential failings. The 'haughtie raigne of an unskilful prince' could slip into tyranny; the 'insolent rule of noble and mightie personages' might fall into contempt of their sovereign; the 'rising authority of a great Magistrate' might decline into oppression. It was wrong to think that what was wrong for one person was right for another. Murder by a great prince was just as much a crime as murder by a private soldier.[191] Mischief caused by the greatest person was the greatest mischief, 'for when mallice is armed

---

[187] Also, see above, p. 50.   [188] TNA, SP 46/26.
[189] BL, MS Additional 48109, fol. 36.   [190] Ibid., fol. 36v.
[191] Ibid. Retails the story of Alexander the Great being told by a pirate that what the pirate did on a small scale to keep himself alive, Alexander did on a large scale.

w[i]th soueraigntie and power . . . neither is it so soone decerned by the simple, nor so soone resisted by the wise . . . ' His advice, therefore, was that jurors should 'w[i]th a more percing eie look into the state'.[192]

In most speeches, including those of Yelverton, there was an attempt to persuade people that their personal, private, interests coincided with those of the broader civil society in enforcing the rule of law, that 'constant and perpetuall good thing w[i]thout wh[i]ch noe house, no Citie, no countrie, no state of men, no naturall creature' can exist.[193] But national political crises brought forth much more direct arguments for obedience. In a charge apparently composed at the time of the 1569 rebellion of the northern earls, Yelverton began by noting that:

So fowle and deformed is become the beautifull face of humble subiection and so far from frame the right course of dutifull obedience, that where to begin the front of good perswasion, or where to set end to just reprehension, where in these tempestuous times, the greatest travaile of the Orator.

He then went on to praise the rule of Elizabeth and to refute the arguments the rebels had used in order to persuade the 'vulgar' to join them (redress of religion, removing evil counsellors, preservation of the nobility, the restitution of ancient and frank liberties).[194]

A similar approach was illustrated by two charges published in the 1580s by the Middle Templar, Richard Crompton. The first, which was printed as a specimen in his handbook for JPs in 1583, made the usual points about the necessity of law enforcement for peaceful enjoyment of wives, children, lands and goods, but it was generally authoritarian in tone. Crompton drew heavily on the biblical story of the creation of the world in order to make the point that law, rule and government were instituted by God, and he stressed to jurors that there would be divine retribution for them if they failed to abide by their oaths and make presentments.[195] The second charge, which was printed in 1587, had originally been given by Crompton at a meeting of the sessions of the peace in Staffordshire. Making a number of references to the recently executed Mary Queen of Scots, and clearly aware of the deterioration in relations between England and Spain, Crompton was no less insistent in this one than in the first that obedience to established authority was enjoined by the laws of God and nature. Yet he also drew heavily on the works of Cicero (especially *De legibus*), Aristotle and Marsilius of Padua to show 'what law and iustice is and in particularity, some of the great benefits *and* profittes which growe by the same to the commonwealth

---

[192] Ibid., fols. 37–8.   [193] Ibid., fol. 38v.   [194] Ibid., fol. 39v.
[195] Crompton, *L'office et aucthoritie de justices de peace*, sig. cci.

and state of every kingdome'.[196] Towards the end of the tract, he pointed out how fortunate the English were to live under laws like that of 9 Henry III, c. 28 (Magna Carta), which laid it down that no man should be taken or imprisoned, disseised of his freehold, put out of his liberties or free customs, or outlawed except by judgment of his peers. The prince, by her coronation oath, was bound to maintain the laws of the realm. '[H]er Maiestie is also well pleased, (albeit shee be aboue her lawes in some respect) yet to be ordered in the same, as other her noble progenitors have doone . . .'[197]

Many of William Lambarde's charges similarly combined eloquent 'commendations' of the laws with rebukes of Kentish grand juries for failing to take adequate advantage of them by making presentments, but on occasion he also distilled some of his historical learning for a wider audience.[198] In 1585 he told a jury at Maidstone that they were lucky to be living in an epoch of peace and good rule. There were obvious distempers abroad, and even in comparison with other periods in English history, there was much to be thankful for:

the times hath been when the nobility and commons of this realm have (with all humility and heart's desire) begged at the hands of their princes the continuation of their country laws and customs; and not prevailing so, they have armed themselves and have sought by force and with the adventure of their honors, goods, and lives to extort it from them. But we (God's name be blessed for it) do live in such a time and under such a prince as we need not to make suit, much less to move war, for our country laws and liberties. We have no cause to strive so much and so long about Magna Charta, the Great Charter of England, as it was called. For our prince hath therein already prevented us, so that not only the parts of that Great Charter but also many other laws and statutes no less fit and profitable for us than they are freely yielded unto us, and that not to be fetched afar off by us but sent home by her even to our own doors; not to be administered by foreign judges and spies but by our own friends, familiars, and countrymen.[199]

These same themes were developed even more fully in a charge Lambarde delivered on 28 September 1591. Pointing out that he was going to depart from the typical exhortation based on justice and religion, he proceeded instead to describe the unique features of the English polity ('thinking thereby to inflame the minds of the hearer with such a love of the same'), while at the same time warning that some of these might be lost if jurors failed to perform their duties. Not borrowed from the imperial or Roman law ('as be the laws of the most part of other

---

[196] Crompton, *Short Declaration of the Ende of Traytors*, sig. Eii.   [197] Ibid., sig. Eiv–F.
[198] Read, *Lambarde and Local Government*, pp. 74, 77, 87, 90, 109, 119.
[199] Ibid., pp. 78–9.

Christian nations'), the critical difference between the law of England and that of other nations was that both civil and criminal disputes were settled through trial by jury:

> we are not to be peremptorily sentenced by the mouth of the judge, as other peoples are, but by the oath and verdict of jurors that be our equals, and the same not strangers born but our own countrymen, nor far dwelling but of the nearest neighborhood that we have.[200]

The problem, according to Lambarde, was that grand juries were not as active as they should be. Most of the business coming before quarter sessions came there by way of indictments rather than by the ancient course of jury presentments. A consequence of this was that parliament and the council had taken measures to remove many matters from their jurisdiction, and more of the same was likely to follow. The court of Star Chamber had been created to deal with riots, retainers, maintenance and embraceries. Informers were relied on to enforce penal statutes, and a number of offences could be tried by the discretion of the JPs, without the benefit of a jury. Most recently, the queen and council had 'invented' the office of provost marshal to deal with 'rogues' because constables would not do so. The point Lambarde wanted to bring home was that as a result of the

> default of jurors and inquests the native liberty and ancient preeminence of the English policy is already little by little exceeding shred off and diminished, very like also in short time to be utterly lost and taken from us if you lay not better hands and hold upon it. Which thing if it should happen in our days . . . we shall be condemned by all posterity to have been the most ungracious and base-minded age of men that have lived here since the general conquest of our nation and country.[201]

---

[200] Ibid., p. 102.
[201] Ibid, p. 107. Lambarde had a general concern that social policy might be enforced by the 'absolute' power of the crown rather than through traditional institutions. See P. Slack, *From Reformation to Improvement: Public Welfare in Early Modern England* (Oxford, 1998), pp. 53ff.

5   The politics of jurisdiction I: the liberty of the subject and the ecclesiastical polity 1560–c. 1610

The rule of law and personal liberty

In the long history of the relationship between law and society in England, the later sixteenth century must be reckoned one of the most dynamic. Increases in the amount of legal business entering courts at all levels occurred on a scale that had not been seen for at least two hundred years previously. There had never before been a higher ratio of lawyers to population than had emerged by the end of the sixteenth century.[1] It is not surprising that the first fifty years of the life of Sir Edward Coke, a Jacobean judge whose professional writings exerted an influence for at least two centuries after his death, coincided almost exactly with the period from the accession of Edward VI to the death of Elizabeth, or that his law reports reflect so much of the social and economic life of middle England.[2]

Thanks, moreover, to the intellectual structures of the time, as well as confessional conflict and uncertainties about the succession to the throne, political rhetoric and constitutional thought were cast in a mode of discourse that merged technical legal learning with a more general emphasis on the role and benefits of law as a defining characteristic of the state and civil society. Potentially nationalistic, and capable of being given an historical dimension, this was also broadcast surprisingly deeply into the localities, often with the avowed oratorical purpose of persuading people to maintain their loyalty to government but at the same time encouraging them to participate in it. Divine ordinance certainly figured in calls for allegiance, but it was frequently accompanied by the argument that in return for his loyalty, the subject could expect justice, the predictability of the rule of law, and the protection of his person, his family and his property.

---

[1] Brooks, *Lawyers, Litigation*, chs. 4, 7.
[2] See below, pp. 152, 323ff. See also, A. D. Boyer, *Sir Edward Coke and the Elizabethan Age* (Stanford, 2003).

Although the flood of civil litigation between private parties led to conflicts between office-holders, accusations of bureaucratic peculation and the pettifogging practices of swarms of lawyers,[3] people evidently went to law because they thought they had something to gain from doing so, and on the whole, the Elizabethan legal system was reasonably successful in maintaining property rights.[4] By contrast, the regime was much less convincing in living up to its own rhetoric when it came to matters having to do with the liberty and protection of the subject.

Though treason trials were less frequent than they had been in the time of Henry VIII, they were more common under Elizabeth than the early Stuarts. Mary of Scotland was judicially executed.[5] In 1571, the duke of Norfolk, who had consorted with Mary and planned to marry her, begged the judges to allow legal counsel to help him answer his indictment but was categorically refused before being convicted of treason, at least partially on the testimony of another of the defendants.[6] Even some contemporaries were taken aback by the hectoring invective that Attorney General Coke used in making the case for the crown against the earl of Essex in 1598 and Sir Walter Raleigh in 1603.[7] There is some evidence of the use of torture in ordinary criminal cases as well as those of Catholic priests, but this appears to have been exceptional rather than routine.[8] Nevertheless, Elizabeth executed Catholic priests for treason, and from 1570 Catholics who refused to attend Anglican church services were subjected to increasingly severe recusancy fines imposed by parliamentary legislation. Nor were Catholics the only ones to suffer. In 1579, a barrister of Lincoln's Inn, John Stubbs, was imprisoned and had his right hand lopped off for writing a pamphlet opposing the proposed marriage of the queen to the French duke of Alençon.[9] In the 1580s, gentry members of the commission of the peace in Suffolk took the unusual step of protesting to the privy council about the harsh treatment

---

[3] Brooks, *Pettyfoggers and Vipers*, chs. 6–7.   [4] See below, ch. 11.

[5] *Dyer's Reports*, I, p. lxiii. Professor Baker observes that treason and sedition make little showing in professional law books, evidently because the technicalities of treason were thought unfit for discussion. Nevertheless, while the judges showed considerable independence in their preliminary rulings on questions of law in even the most highly charged case, they did co-operate with the law officers in drafting indictments.

[6] *ST*, I, cols. 965–7.   [7] *ST*, II, cols. 5–7.

[8] BL, MS Harleian 4943, fol. 129: a letter from the privy council to Somerset JPs investigating the murder of Thomas Stower appears to anticipate that torture might be used. M. A. R. Graves, *Thomas Norton: the Parliament Man* (Oxford, 1994), esp. pp. 244, 262, discusses Norton's reputation amongst Catholics as a torturer.

[9] N. Mears, 'Counsel, public debate, and queenship: John Stubbs's *Discoverie of A Gaping Gulf*, 1579', *Historical Journal*, 44(3), (2001), 629–50.

of Godly ministers by the assize judges.[10] Chief justice of the Common Pleas, Edmund Anderson, was particularly well known for his hostility to Protestant as well as Catholic non-conformity. He presided over the trial of John Udall in 1590, who was convicted and executed for his alleged role in the publication of the Martin Marprelate tracts, scurrilous pamphlets that attacked episcopacy and the church courts, and in 1596 there were complaints about his severity towards Protestant preachers in Lincolnshire.[11] Last but hardly least, Elizabeth and her council arrested, and held without trial, individuals who had for one reason or another found themselves on the wrong side of the royal will, a fate to which lawyer 'men of business' such as William Fleetwood, Thomas Norton and James Morice seem to have been particularly susceptible.[12]

The harsh treason trials are doubtless explained by the contemporary sense of the dangerousness of the times. As Lord Treasurer Burghley explained in *The Execution of Justice in England*, a pamphlet published under his name in 1584, political adherence to the pope, or attempts to overthrow the government were punishable as treason rather than heresy. But, as long as Catholics maintained outward conformity by attending services in their parish church, or paid the fines for refusing to do so,[13] they were free to hold whatever spiritual views they thought fit, and ordinary Catholics were apparently treated with a good deal more leniency in the localities than the rhetoric of MPs in parliament might suggest.[14] Although periods of imprisonment at the order of the queen or council were hardly pleasant, they were rarely indefinite, and often ended with neither a tidy conclusion nor any sharp exemplary punishment. In this light, the judicial mutilation of John Stubbs was particularly harsh, but it was apparently widely rumoured in the profession that the sentence was illegal because the Marian statute against seditious libel on which it was based had lapsed and not been renewed; in fact, Robert Monson, a justice of the Common Pleas, was imprisoned for several months and eventually lost his position for questioning it. Typically, Stubbs himself continued to enjoy the patronage of Burghley, and he ended his days as steward of Great Yarmouth.[15]

---

[10] D. MacCulloch, *Suffolk and the Tudors: Politics and Religion in an English County 1500–1600* (Oxford, 1986), p. 343. BL, MS Harleian 367, fol. 24.

[11] BL, MS Lansdowne 83, article 53. W. Pierce, *Historical Introduction to the Marprelate Tracts* (1908).

[12] See below, p. 109.

[13] *The Execution of Justice in England by William Cecil; and A True, Sincere, and Modest Defense of English Catholics, by William Allen*, ed. R. M. Kingdon (Ithaca, NY, 1965).

[14] M. Questier, *Conversion, Politics and Religion in England 1580–1625* (Cambridge, 1996).

[15] *ODNB*.

Perhaps because so many of them had witnessed the Marian persecution, and been aware of the confessional and career choices involved, the judiciary was not notably bloodthirsty on matters of religion. Although denied public office, the ardently Catholic Edmund Plowden continued to practise law, and he was an influential member of the Inner Temple, where he supervised the building of a new hall.[16] This would have been impossible without the acquiescence of the judges.[17] Furthermore, in a case that was frequently referred to later on, in 1565, the judges granted a writ of *habeas corpus* to an attorney of the Common Pleas, Thomas Lee (or Leigh), who had been imprisoned by the ecclesiastical court of High Commission because of his adherence to the Catholic mass.[18]

As we shall see in chapter 13, Elizabethan judges were increasingly willing to grant writs of *habeas corpus*, which were based on the due process clauses of Magna Carta, to individuals who claimed that they had been unlawfully imprisoned by local officials,[19] and they also gave some thought to the use, or abuse, of arbitrary state power. In 1592, Chief Justice Anderson and his colleagues went so far as to inform the privy council that they were concerned about the unlawful arrest and imprisonment of individuals on the order of the lords of the council or other 'great men'. Sometimes, they alleged, people involved in private suits were brought up to London and subjected to unlawful imprisonment until they withdrew their claims. In other cases, officials had been interfered with or arrested as they went about their business delivering writs. In addition, they cautiously questioned the use of imprisonment by the privy council, or on the express order of the queen, without any charge being specified. James Morice had maintained in his law lecture of 1578 that while the monarch could imprison for any cause, he was nevertheless obliged to bring charges and allow the subject to be tried by his peers, but there was clearly doubt about the point of law, especially in the light of contemporary practice.[20] Stressing that detentions without charges should be limited to the most serious matters involving the security of the state, the judges' not altogether straightforward conclusion in 1592 was that persons committed by the monarch or council should *normally* have charges laid against them. They also maintained

[16] *ODNB*.
[17] However, there was a case in 1577 which involved the punishment of lawyers who gave counsel to Catholic women. *Dyer's Reports*, II, p. 361.
[18] *Dyer's Reports*, I, pp. lxxix, 143.   [19] See below, pp. 402ff.
[20] See above, p. 79. BL, MS Egerton 3376, fol. 27: '. . . for this is the libertie of the Subiect confermed by the great Charter of England that no freeman shalbe taken imprisoned outlawed or exiled, but by lawful judgement . . .'.

the legitimacy of issuing writs of *habeas corpus* in such circumstances, and of demanding a certification of the cause of the commitment.[21]

The crown, the common law and the ecclesiastical polity

Evidence of this judicial initiative resurfaced during parliamentary debates about arbitrary arrest in the later 1620s, but imprisonment by order of the council continued until the end of the reign of Elizabeth.[22] Nevertheless, questions about the liberty of the subject remained significant in the 1580s and 1590s primarily because of unresolved jurisdictional questions about the relationship between the secular and ecclesiastical courts that went back to the 1530s. The most important issue was the questionable legality of so-called *ex officio* procedures, which enabled ecclesiastical court officials to cite individuals to appear before them and to swear that they would truthfully answer any questions that were put to them on pain of imprisonment, even if no specific charges had been made. Debates on this issue exposed some of the difficulties created by the emergence of confessional differences amongst Protestants, and also raised questions about the authority of the crown. Ultimately, they impacted on attitudes towards secular as well as religious liberty, and they can only properly be understood in the light of the 'ecclesiastical polity' that evolved during the course of the later sixteenth century.

The break from Rome in the 1530s was made by statutes passed in parliament that vested responsibility for the spirituality in the crown. But, even at the time, there were differences of opinion about the significance of this. Henry VIII, not surprisingly, thought that the unification of the temporal and spiritual power conferred on the crown divine as well as human authority. At least some of the clergy, most notably Bishop Stephen Gardiner, maintained what might be described as a 'high church' interpretation, which was that in matters spiritual, the ecclesiastical establishment, including its courts, were answerable to God and the king rather than the common law.[23] The lawyers, on the other hand, were by virtue of their profession, naturally inclined to favour the view that the break, and the subsequent acts of the Reformation, had

---

[21] There are a number of contemporary manuscript copies. W. S. Holdsworth, *A History of English Law* (16 vols., 1966 edn), v, pp. 495–97, prints two versions.

[22] See below, pp. 171, 174.

[23] G. R. Elton, '*Lex terrae victrix*: the triumph of parliamentary law in the sixteenth century', in D. M. Dean and N. L. Jones, eds., *The Parliaments of Elizabethan England* (1990), pp. 20–1.

been made by statute, and that the spiritual, no less than the temporal, jurisdictions therefore fell within the authority of the common law courts as well as that of the king and parliament.[24] Indeed, the fundamental issues arose during a brief exchange in the 1530s when Lord Chancellor Audley reportedly made it clear to Gardiner that there was a potential for absolutism in the royal supremacy of the church, and that it would therefore be carefully monitored, if necessary by invoking the late fourteenth-century Statute of Praemunire against churchmen who attempted to ignore the secular common law.[25]

Having already been used in the charges against Cardinal Wolsey, *praemunire* sanctioned legal action in the secular courts against anyone who took to Rome a legal dispute that could be settled according to the common law of England.[26] In Reformation historiography therefore, the statute was often referenced as a particularly good example of earlier English attempts to thwart papal pretensions, but in the post-Reformation period, far from becoming irrelevant, it continued to be seen by the common lawyers as a way of limiting the jurisdiction of the ecclesiastical courts in England, even though they were no longer subject to Rome.[27] At the same time, jurisdictional rivalries between the secular and ecclesiastical courts over significant areas of litigation, including debt and slander, were well underway in the late fifteenth century, and in connection with these the judges had increasingly been willing to countenance the use of a prerogative writ, the writ of prohibition, in order to stay actions in the ecclesiastical courts where one of the parties claimed that the matter in question involved a temporal as well as a spiritual issue.[28]

In the wake of the break, therefore, the authority of the ecclesiastical courts was unresolved, and common-law procedures existed for challenging their jurisdiction. From as early as the 1540s, moreover, radical Protestants such as John Hales argued that 'spiritual' matters, including marriage, sexual incontinency and blasphemy, should be incorporated into a unified law of the realm that was based on parliamentary statute, and while the king's headship of the church as well as the laity was seen as a crucial source of authority for such a project, Hales was explicitly hostile to any suggestion that this new English code should be based on

---

[24] J. A. Guy, *Christopher St German on Chancery and Statute* (Selden Society, Supplementary Series, vol. 6, 1985), pp. 21–5, 38–9.

[25] Elton, 'Lex terrae victrix', p. 25. See also G. R. Elton, *Reform and Renewal: Thomas Cromwell and the Commonweal* (Cambridge, 1973), pp. 137–8, 152.

[26] 16 Richard II, c. 5.   [27] See below, pp. 100–1.

[28] R. H. Helmholz, *Roman Canon Law in Reformation England* (Cambridge, 1990), p. 26.

the English canon or Roman civil law.[29] It is far from clear how widespread views such as these were at the time, but lingering doubts about the Roman origins of English ecclesiastical law did result in the appointment of a parliamentary commission to consider its reform and codification in the light of the Reformation.[30] Led by Archbishop Thomas Cranmer, and including a team of churchmen and common lawyers, the commissioners succeeded in producing a new codification known as the *Reformatio legum ecclesiasticarum*, which was presented to parliament in 1553. Although it proposed the novel possibility of a form of divorce that permitted remarriage, the *Reformatio* was not a radical document. Nevertheless, it was evidently suppressed by the duke of Northumberland and then became redundant with the accession of Queen Mary.[31] Consequently, with the accession of Elizabeth, the powers of the ecclesiastical courts rested on statutes of 1559 that merely recreated the jurisdictional break from Rome and reasserted the restoration (following papal usurpation) of the crown's ancient jurisdiction 'over the estate ecclesiastical and spiritual'.[32]

Under these circumstances the resurrection of the *Reformatio* might have seemed a worthwhile way of clarifying ambiguities, but, although it was printed by John Foxe and may have been raised by Cranmer's son-in-law, Thomas Norton, in the 1571 parliament, there seems to have been surprisingly little enthusiasm for the project, which thereafter died a nearly complete death, probably because none of those with an interest in the ecclesiastical jurisdiction really wanted to see it implemented.[33] Since it did not propose the creation of a unified jurisdiction, from the point of view of common lawyers, legislating a new code into existence would have had the effect of setting into stone jurisdictional distinctions that might otherwise be contested through litigation in the common-law courts. Church-court lawyers, on the other hand, no doubt found it hard to see how they could enjoy legislative recognition without accepting their ultimate subjection to the common-law judges, since, even in the pre-Reformation period, claiming that a legal question involved a breach of a statute had long been grounds for claiming that it should be heard by the common-law judges rather than those of the church courts.[34]

---

[29] BL, MS Harleian 4990, fol. 21. It is worth noting that Hales was also a translator of Plutarch's works on medicine.
[30] See above, pp. 52–4.   [31] Bray, *Reformatio*, pp. xliv, xlvi, lxxiii.
[32] 1 Elizabeth, c. i: An Act restoring to the Crown the ancient jurisdiction over the state Ecclesiasticall and Spirituall, and abolishing all foreign power repugnant to the same.
[33] Bray, *Reformatio*, pp. lxxviii–c.
[34] Robert Beale, for example, who was a protégé of Hales, continued to lament in the 1590s that the ecclesiastical law had not been reformed. BL, MS Additional 48039, fols. 63–7v.

Last, but hardly least, there were bound to be questions about who had the authority to implement a measure such as the *Reformatio*. Should it be parliament, which Elizabeth tried to exclude from discussing matters of religion, or should it be Convocation, which, according to most lawyers, had authority over the clergy, but which could not be taken to speak for the lay membership of the Church of England as a whole?

The queen's vehement claim that she, like her father, was the sole governor of the Church of England was accompanied by her largely successful attempt to prevent discussion of ecclesiastical policy in parliament, a stand that sometimes led to spells in the Tower for MPs who opposed her.[35] Yet from the juridical point of view the royal supremacy of the church was a double-edged sword that could be exploited by Godly reformers as well as used against them.[36] For example, although James Morice's 1578 lecture at the Middle Temple articulated a mixed-monarchical view of English government,[37] his discussion of the crown's power over the church stressed the role of the monarchy in the historic struggles against the bishop of Rome, and described the king as the undisputed head of the English church as well as the authority responsible for its ongoing reform in the name of 'true Religion'.[38]

Rejecting the view of the 'popish' Polydore Vergil in favour of that of Sir John Fortescue, Morice argued that there was a continuity in the history of the common law stretching from the time of the early Britons, and running through the Norman Conquest. For him this showed that kings had traditionally controlled patronage over the church (including the appointment of bishops) up until the time of Henry II, or indeed that of King John, periods when 'that son of a Saracyne' Thomas Beckett and the 'false apostle' Innocent I, had forced them to give it up in the name of the liberties of the [Roman] English church.[39] Nevertheless, these powers had been won back with the passage of the Statutes of Provisors in the time of Edward III and the Statute of Praemunire in the reign of Richard II, precursors of the Act in Restraint of Appeals (24 Henry VIII, c. 12). The consequence of all this history was that Convocation could not act without being called by the king,[40] and the church courts and 'Constitutions Ecclesiastical' were part of the law by which the realm

---

[35] These episodes are recounted in Sir John Neale's *Elizabeth I and Her Parliaments* (2 vols., 1953, 1957).

[36] Thomas Norton, for example, thought royal authority should be used to ensure that only good Protestants should be allowed to practise law. BL, MS Lansdowne 155, fols. 105–6.

[37] See above, p. 79.   [38] BL, MS Egerton 3376, fol. 45.

[39] Ibid., fol. 46.   [40] Ibid., fol. 56v.

was governed, having such 'place, power and authroitie as the auncient Customes and vsage of the Realme hath assigned vnto them'.[41]

Morice's reading demonstrates how the royal supremacy, the view that the monarch was the 'only sole and imediate Governor [of the church] under God',[42] might be employed by common lawyers as a stick with which to beat the ecclesiastical jurisdiction. If the church courts were the king's courts then they, like all other royal jurisdictions, were ultimately answerable to the common law and its judges. Although they cited chapter 29 of Magna Carta, writs of prohibition were issued in the king's name, and praemunire was an offence against the king as well as the common law. Crucially, moreover, these legal fine points became acutely relevant in the 1580s when John Whitgift, a newly appointed archbishop of Canterbury, launched a vigorous campaign to enforce conformity to the established church, and turned to the ecclesiastical courts to help him carry it out.

Responding in large part to the recent success of the English Presbyterian movement, Whitgift required clergymen to subscribe to three articles declaring that the Book of Common Prayer, and the organisation of the spirituality into bishops, priests and deacons, contained nothing contrary to the word of God.[43] In addition, he undertook to breathe new life into the court of High Commission, a jurisdiction created by royal letters patent based on the authority of the 1559 Act of Supremacy. Having branches in each of the English dioceses, the court was charged with the investigation and punishment of crimes against the spiritual laws of the realm. Common lawyers, including judges, and figures like the Recorder of London, William Fleetwood, were appointed to sit on the commission alongside bishops and civil lawyers, and in 1577, the common-law judges agreed that it should have the power to fine and imprison.[44] In addition, Whitgift's campaign also exploited the power of ecclesiastical court judges to summon people to appear before them, and then to administer an oath that required the suspect to answer truthfully whatever questions were put to them before they had been informed of the charges, a process known as *ex officio mero*.

By 1584 Whitgift's project had led to the suspension of 300 to 400 ministers, and there was sufficient opposition to the methods used for bills to have been presented in parliament for the abolition of the oath

---

[41] Ibid., fol. 58v.   [42] Ibid., fol. 59v.

[43] F. Heal, *Reformation in Britain and Ireland* (Oxford, 2003), pp. 417–19.

[44] R. H. Helmholz, *The Oxford History of the Laws of England*, vol. I: *The Canon Law and Ecclesiastical Jurisdiction from 597 to the 1640s* (Oxford, 2004), p. 287, notes that legislative authority of High Commission in fact created doubt about whether it was a spiritual or a temporal jurisdiction.

and High Commission.[45] Although these were unsuccessful, and although Whitgift had the support of the queen, critical members of the privy council, and, it seems, some of the judges were much more doubtful about his methods. Burghley once declared that the 'Inquisitors of Spain use not so many questions to comprehend and to trap their preys . . . According to my simple judgment, this kind of proceeding is too much savouring of the Romish Inquisition . . . .'[46] More surprisingly, a charge given to jurors at the trial of one of the Martin Marprelate pamphleteers, probably by Edmund Anderson, was clear that radical Protestants, no less than papists, were guilty of attempting to withdraw themselves from the yoke of the civil magistrate and make laws and ordinances for themselves, but in endorsing the royal supremacy, the speaker also made it clear that the ecclesiastical authorities were also subject to the same secular power.[47] Peter, the first pope, had not been given primacy by Christ. Nor had Christ given bishops 'power or auctoritye to holde courtes or consistories, to call princes subiectes before them, nor to exact oathes of them . . . .'[48] Evidently aware that these remarks might be potentially inflammatory, the speaker was careful to add that he did not mean to disparage the authority of the bishops or their courts, but the speech helps to explain why the queen herself was said to be suspicious that the judges were sympathetic to the Marprelate position.

By the mid 1580s Whitgift had moderated his campaign in most parts of the country, but in the diocese of London, Bishop John Aylmer continued the crack-down on non-conformity.[49] Furthermore, Aylmer was also instrumental in bringing one of the clergymen within his diocese, Robert Caudry of North Luffenham (Rutland), before High Commission in 1586, and then depriving him of his living, because he had reportedly disparaged the Book of Common Prayer in a sermon. Almost certainly at the instigation of Burghley, and thinking it unseemly for a lawyer to refuse help to someone who had been wronged, James Morice rather reluctantly agreed to act as counsel for Caudry in what became an important leading case.[50]

Doubtful about the chances of success considering the 'present time and p[er]sons',[51] Morice initially tried to convince Aylmer that he had acted outside the law and that he should allow the case to be reconsidered by High Commission on this basis. But while Caudry was given several opportunities over the space of three years to repudiate his earlier

---

[45] Heal, *Reformation in Britain*, pp. 419–20.
[46] As quoted in S. B. Babbage, *Puritanism and Richard Bancroft* (1962), pp. 18–19.
[47] BL, MS Harleian 361, fols. 68–9.   [48] Ibid., fol. 72.
[49] Heal, *Reformation in Britain*, p. 418.   [50] BL, MS Lansdowne 68, fols. 104–9.
[51] Ibid., fol. 125.

opinions, the bishop refused to back down on the question of whether or not he had acted illegally. In 1591, therefore, Morice advised Caudry to bring an action of trespass against the clergyman who had been inserted into his living at North Luffenham,[52] and following a trial at assizes, the case was returned to Westminster for argument before the judges on the points of law. Although Morice mentioned *ex officio* procedure and the oath in his accounts of the case, these were not in themselves the principal points in contention, and they were not mentioned in the judges' decision. Instead, Morice's key question was whether or not the actions of High Commission were legal in the light of the Elizabethan Act of Uniformity, which specified that deprivations should only take place after three convictions before juries at assizes for 'depraving' the Book of Common Prayer.[53] Although Caudry's deprivation had not followed this course, the judges nevertheless ruled against him, their point being that while the Act of Uniformity made convictions at assize a possibility, the statute also preserved the traditional ecclesiastical jurisdiction, and according to this, High Commission had the power to degrade clergymen from the ministry and deprive them of their livings.[54]

Meanwhile, while Caudry was fighting for his living, Thomas Cartwright and other leaders of the Presbyterian movement were prosecuted in High Commission and imprisoned in 1590 for declining to take the oath *ex officio* and refusing to answer questions put to them.[55] As Professor Collinson has so aptly put it, the proceedings against the ministers had a Kafkaesque quality that was typically Elizabethan.[56] They were harassed with imprisonment, but they were never subjected to the more severe penalties that might have been the result of the Star Chamber proceedings that were threatened, but never initiated, against them. Even so, their case was a *cause célèbre*, and as it was progressing the churchmen, including Whitgift, Aylmer and the future archbishop of Canterbury, Richard Bancroft,[57] took steps to justify their authority in print. In 1591, a former pupil of Whitgift's at Cambridge, the civilian

---

[52] Ibid., fol. 108v.   [53] Ibid., fol. 106r–v.

[54] There is a concise report of the case in 79 *ER* 1175 (reports of Sir John Popham). For Coke's more extensive treatment, see below, pp. 119–21.

[55] Cartwright's view was that if the *ex officio* proceedings were allowed in ecclesiastical causes, then there was a real danger that they would be introduced into the secular administration of justice, where the authority of the crown was even more 'absolute', a development that would be to the prejudice of the liberty of the subject and contrary to the ancient laws. HMC, *Report on the Manuscripts of R. R. Hastings, of the Manor House, Ashby de la Zouche* (4 vols., 1928–47), I, p. 442.

[56] P. Collinson, *Elizabethan Puritan Movement* (1967), p. 430.

[57] Babbage, *Puritanism and Richard Bancroft*, pp. 18–19.

Richard Cosin, published *An Apologie for Sundrie Proceedings by Jurisdiction Ecclesiastical*.[58]

The *Apologie* made a sturdy defence of the use of *ex officio* proceedings in connection with the perceived problem of non-conformity, but the general aim of the book was to defend all aspects of the ecclesiastical courts' jurisdiction, from matrimonial causes to those involving tithes and defamation, from the attacks on it by those who advanced a 'new discipline' for the church, and others, influenced by the common lawyers, who aimed to take exception to the jurisdiction of the courts in general, and here James Morice was certainly someone that Cosin had in mind, although he was not the only one.[59] From at least the mid 1580s, Morice had been collecting examples from Essex, which was within the diocese of London, of cases where ordinary people had been put to considerable trouble and expense as a result of being obliged to answer on oath in cases that were made against them on the basis of rumours, or mere suspicion.[60] In 1590, furthermore, the commissary of the archdeaconry of Norfolk, Thomas Hunt,[61] was indicted at a meeting of Norfolk quarter sessions for proceeding according to the oath on secret complaints, allegedly under colour of a reformation of manners, but according to Morice, primarily for the sake of lining his own purse.[62]

The catalyst for the indictment of Hunt was a charge given to the grand jury in Norfolk by justice of the Common Pleas, Francis Wyndham, and his fellow countryman the then Mr Edward Coke, in which they had declared that the ordinary could not cite men to appear *pro salute anime* to answer upon oath. According to an account written by Wyndham himself, moreover, the incident subsequently had repercussions in London. In February 1591 Whitgift claimed at a meeting of the privy council (from which Burghley was absent because of illness) that the ecclesiastical courts were 'lyke cleane to be overthrowen by reason' of the charge, the rumour of which had 'bred a scruple to all the byshops in Englande that they dowbt how to procede in theyr courtes for that they have every synce the Conquest used no other course'.[63]

---

[58] A second, enlarged, edition of *An Apologie* was published in 1593 under the title *An Apologie for Sundrie Proceedings by Iurisdiction Ecclesiasticall, of late times by some challenged, and also diuersly by them impugned . . .*

[59] Ibid., Preface, A2v.   [60] For more on this see below, p. 405.

[61] BL, MS Additional 48039, fol. 89.

[62] LPL, MS 234, 'A Iust and Necessarie Defence of a Briefe Treatise made ageinst generall oathes exacted by Ordinaries and Iudges Ecclesiasticall to answer to all such articles as pleaseth them to propounde, and against their forced oathes, Ex Officio Mero . . .', fol. 99.

[63] A. Hassell Smith and G. M. Baker, eds., *The Papers of Nathaniel Bacon of Stiffkey* (Norfolk Record Society, vol. 53, 1987–8), p. 118: letter from Francis Wyndham to Nathaniel Bacon, dated 18 February 1590/91.

The queen herself was sufficiently displeased to demand that all the judges be assembled before going on circuit and warned not to repeat anything similar in their charges.[64] In addition, a group of civil lawyers, that probably included Cosin, was assembled to give their opinion on the matter. They argued that if there was a suspicion of a crime, even without any formal presentment or charge, the ecclesiastical court judges could swear witnesses, and if this process indicated that there was a case to answer, then the suspect could be proceeded against by oath.[65]

Licensed in July 1591, it is hard to say exactly how directly connected Cosin's *Apologie* was to these incidents as opposed to more high-profile prosecutions, such as those of Caudry and Cartwright.[66] Reaching to almost 200 pages, it would have taken some time to assemble, and, as we have seen, many of the issues were already controversial before the charge of Coke and Wyndham. In any case, during the summer vacation between the law terms in 1591,[67] James Morice composed a treatise attacking the use of oaths in ecclesiastical courts, which was eventually published at Middleburg in 1591 or early 1592.[68] Although he does not mention it in the treatise, Morice was probably at this stage acting as legal counsel for Cartwright and the other puritan ministers, and he and the clerk of the crown Robert Beale,[69] who had collaborated with John Hales in the 1560s, worked together to compile a large dossier of historical and legal material supporting their case. Beale addressed a lengthy manuscript attack on the legality and political efficacy of the oath directly to Whitgift, and it is significant that the two men continued to enjoy at least the tacit support of Burghley, although he was evidently unable to gain sufficient backing in the council for a curb on the oath *ex officio*.[70] At the same time, the exchange of learned treatises escalated. Cosin issued a revised edition of his *Apologie* in 1593, which attacked the works of both Morice and Beale, even though it did not directly name them.[71] In response, Morice wrote an even longer work that aimed to pick apart Cosin point by point; but, much to his chagrin, this remained in manuscript.[72]

---

[64] Ibid.   [65] LPL, MS 234, fol. 100.
[66] The epistle to the reader in the 1593 edition of *An Apologie* mentions the previous opinion of diverse civilians.
[67] TNA, SP 12/238, fol. 107.
[68] James Morice, *A Briefe Treatise of Oathes Exacted by Ordinaries and Ecclesiasticall Iudges, to Answere Generallie to all such articles or interrogatories, as pleaseth them to propound . . .*
[69] *ODNB*.
[70] BL, MS Additional 48039, fols. 78ff. Heal, *Reformation in Britain*, p. 418.
[71] Cosin, *Apologie* (1593 edn), Epistle.
[72] LPL, MS 234, 'A Just and Necessarie Defence . . . .'

The arguments surrounding the oath *ex officio* were historical as well as jurisprudential. It had in fact been opposed as recently as the reign of Henry VIII, and a principal statutory authority justifying its use, *De heretico carburendo* (2 Henry IV, c. 15), which had been aimed at the Lollards, was abrogated in 1534.[73] In defending the oath, Richard Cosin claimed that it had always been employed in English spiritual courts, a point he illustrated by examining cases associated with writs of prohibition, in which litigants had tried to transfer their cases to the common-law courts but been refused permission to do so.[74] Sensitive to the rivalry between the church courts and the common law, he defended the clergy as well as the civil and canon law against the negative imputations that the works of Morice and Beale had allegedly made against them, which included reproaches and wounds delivered through 'the sides of papists'.[75] The overall thrust was that the spiritual courts and their procedures were an integral part of the jurisdiction that was reinvested in the crown by the statute establishing the Elizabethan supremacy, and were therefore perfectly legal.

The argument of Morice and Beale on the other hand was essentially two-pronged. *A Brief Treatise of Oaths* sought to demonstrate that the oath *ex officio* was not justified by scripture, the civil law, or, indeed, the canon law of the church. But at the same time Morice and Beale argued that the oath was contrary to common-law practices, as well as those of other secular courts, such as Star Chamber and Chancery, where oaths were indeed used, but only after the defendant had been obliged to appear on a specified charge taken out by a named individual.[76] In effect, they followed, with only a little elaboration, the position outlined in Morice's reading on the royal prerogative in 1578. Thus, for instance, the use in former times of oaths in cases other than those involving matrimony or testamentary matters (where it was agreed they could be used) was merely a reflection of the extent to which the usurped power of Rome had been at its most intense, in the time of Beckett, King John and, of course, Thomas Wolsey.[77] But thanks to the ecclesiastical legislation of Henry VIII and Elizabeth, England had been declared an

---

[73] Ibid., fol 2. See also Brooks, *Lawyers, Litigation*, p. 218.
[74] Cosin, *An Apologie* (1593 edn), pp. 33, 46–50.   [75] Ibid., sig. B4, C–Cv.
[76] Morice, *Brief Treatise of Oathes*, pp. 33–4, 38–9, 47; LPL, MS 234, fols. 122v–4.
[77] BL, MS Cotton Cleopatra F I, fols. 5–12: 'A collection shewing what jurisdiction the clergy hath heretofore lawfully used and may lawfully use in the realm of England'. For a discussion of the exact authorship of this contribution see James E. Hampson, 'Richard Cosin and the rehabilitation of the clerical estate in late Elizabethan England' (St Andrews University PhD, 1997), p. 74. The manuscript also contains a version of Morice's treatise on oaths.

empire governed by a single head responsible for the spirituality as well as the temporality. The English were consequently free from subjection to any laws other than those which had been devised and made by them, or such others as had been taken at their free liberty by their own consent and used amongst them.[78] History showed that the common-law judges through the use of writs of prohibition, and the king and parliament in passing legislation such as the Statute of Provisors and the Statute of Praemunire, had long resisted clerical pretensions that were contrary to the laws of the realm.

According to Beale and Morice, the weight of these arguments was so strong that no man 'learned in the common lawe should allow' the legality of the *ex officio* proceedings,[79] but they elaborated their general historical points in order to illustrate the ways in which kings and people throughout English history had tried to keep clerical usurpation at bay. Between the foundation of Christianity and the Norman Conquest, control over the church had clearly been exercised by the king and councils of the realm. When King Lucius asked Pope Elutherius what he should do about the introduction of ecclesiastical laws into the realm, he was advised to consult with his lawyers about which to accept and which to reject.[80] This wise policy had been forced into abeyance during the tyrannical rule of the Normans, who were after all conquerors. But thanks to the sacrifice of 'more English subjects then be at this day living in the land', the ancient liberties of the English were restored through the repeated passage of that 'Lawe of Lawes', Magna Carta, which clearly declared that 'in an accusation upon the bare information of any man, judge, or accuser, without lawful witnesses, none ought to be put to his oath or proceeded against without better proofs'.[81]

While Morice and Beale made a point of maintaining that all English monarchs had an obligation to reform the church as it proved necessary,[82] they were also more explicit than Morice had been in his lecture that the Elizabethan statutes had made the spirituality subject to the king in parliament and not the king alone. Such 'absolut authoritie without consent of p[ar]liament, never was lawfully in pope, prelate or other spiritual or Ecclesiastical power in England what so ev[er] . . .'.[83] Although the Elizabethan statutes gave the crown power and authority to rule over all sorts of persons, it did not follow that any 'absolute authority' was transferred in causes either ecclesiastical or temporal, or that the prince

---

[78] BL, MS Cleopatra F I, fol. 6.   [79] BL, MS Additional 48039, fol. 83.
[80] Ibid., fol. 100.   [81] BL, MS Cotton Cleopatra F I, fols. 22v–3.
[82] BL, MS Additional 48039, fol. 101.   [83] Ibid., fol. 80.

may absolutly w[i]thout parliament doe what he list, or that the p[ar]liament men may not deale in suche causes. It was nev[er] ment, nor ever so much assumed by anie: and briefly neither the pope nor anie prince ev[er] had that absolut authoritie in this realme either in Ecclesiastical causes or Temporall, and if in one then in both, and if not in one, then neither in thother.[84]

True to these principles, and evidently not satisfied merely to debate the matter in print, in February 1593 Morice, sitting as MP for the Puritan borough of Colchester (Essex), delivered two bills concerning the oath *ex officio* to the speaker of the House, Sir Edward Coke. The first essentially reiterated chapter 29 of Magna Carta, which laid it down that no subject would have to make an answer in any criminal cause without the existence of a formal indictment specifying the charges. The second proposed that anyone attempting in the future to use the oath *ex officio* should be subject to punishment under the Statutes of Provisors and Praemunire.[85] In the lengthy, but cogent, speech that he delivered in proposing the bills, Morice touched on many of the previously rehearsed issues but there was also an unmistakable rhetorical thrust which demonstrated his passionate concern for the liberty of the subject and the moral integrity of the monarchy.

God and *our* Prince by certaine abuses (as I take it) lately crept in amongst us, *and* that under colour *and* pretence of lawfull Aucthority, are highlie dishonoured, Law *and* Common Justice by Lordely *and* licentious pleasure are violated *and* perverted; *and* we in all our free *and* lawfull liberties suffer great wronge *and* injury . . .[86]

According to Morice's account of the debate in the House that followed, there was considerable, though not universal support for his position, even though the House had been warned by a privy councillor that they were forbidden to consider matters of 'estate, *and* these thinges touched ecclesiasticall Government'.[87] In the end, Burghley's son, Sir Robert Cecil, asked for a delay in considering the bills, and Coke, leafing through them, supported him on the grounds that it would take some time to consider the details in full. Coke also promised that he would keep the contents of the proposed legislation secret until the bills were brought before the House again, but that same evening he was summonsed to court and told to bring them with him. This was the last heard of them, and the next day Morice was called before the privy

---

[84] Ibid., fol. 80.
[85] Neale, *Elizabeth I and Her Parliaments*, II, 267–79: what appears to be a first-person account by Morice is in CUL, MS Mm.1.51, fols. 112–17.
[86] Ibid., fols. 106, 107.   [87] Ibid., fol. 117.

council, told of the queen's displeasure, and summarily sentenced to a period of not too uncomfortable house arrest in the London home of Sir John Fortescue.

Judging from Morice's extraordinary first-person account of these events, there was amongst the councillors some degree of support for him. Lord Buckhurst appreciated that Morice had acted out of conscience rather than malice.[88] Burghley thought it an error to argue that the Henrician abrogation of the 'heresy statute' implied that the oath *ex officio*, as applied to lesser offences, was illegal; nevertheless, he acknowledged that Morice had made a number of fair points, and in the end, he appears to have been more concerned with the form than the content of Morice's intervention. Some two months after his imprisonment, Morice was summonsed to appear in the bed-chamber of Burghley, who was suffering from gout. Announcing his release, Cecil told Morice that the queen wanted him admonished on two points. The first was that, whenever he found anything amiss in the church or commonwealth, he should not 'straight-waie make it known to the Comon Sort, but declare it to hir Majestie'. The next was that if anyone came to seek his advice in such a matter, he should make it known immediately to Her Majesty or the privy council. For his part, although Morice apologised for giving offence to the queen, and had to ask powerful friends to intercede in his favour, he appears to have maintained his indignation that matters such as the oath *ex officio* could not be handled by parliament. He told the councillors at his first interview that he hoped the queen would not 'deny her Subjects to complain to hirselfe in Parliament of wronge *and* oppression offered them', just as had been done in all 'other Princes times'.[89] In a letter that thanked Burghley for his support, Morice complained that 'Bills of Assize of Breade, shippinge of Fyshe *and* such like maie be offered *and* receyved into the House, *and* no offence to hir Maj[es]ties Royall Commaundment. . . But the great things of the Lawe *and* publique Justice maie not be touched without offence.'[90]

Prohibitions

In the short term, James Morice's campaign against *ex officio* procedures and in favour of deprived ministers resulted in little more than his own discomfiture. Caudry lost his living; neither High Commission nor the

---

[88] LPL, MS 3470, fol. 174: in a letter to Buckhurst, Whitgift complained that he had been vehemently criticised in the council, probably by Burghley, for telling the queen about Morice's speech in parliament.
[89] CUL, MS Mm.1.51, fol. 120.   [90] Ibid., fols. 121–3.

ex officio oath were extirpated. Morice was denied further official advancement,[91] and he even lost his manuscript attack on Cosin. Having lent it to Whitgift, it was never returned to him, and, as Morice explained to Burghley, he never succeeded in making the archbishop understand that there was a difference between the *ex officio* oath and the procedures used in courts such as Star Chamber or Chancery.[92] On the other hand, Morice perfectly illustrates Sir John Neale's contention that there was a connection between late sixteenth-century radical Protestantism and the determination of members of the House of Commons to discuss matters the queen contended they had no right to meddle in. Even more importantly, the controversies over the oath, the powers of High Commission, and the relationship between the temporal and spiritual jurisdictions were regularly resurrected in litigation and in parliament throughout the 1590s and well into the seventeenth century.

The association of the oath with the campaign to maintain clerical uniformity through High Commission was the most notorious bone of contention, but, as we have seen, the campaigns of Morice and Beale also owed much to long-standing animosity between the laity and the ecclesiastical court officials in Essex and other parts of East Anglia.[93] Morice in particular attached great importance to what he saw as the misuse of *ex officio* proceedings as part of the 'office' jurisdiction of the church courts. The greater part of Cosin's lengthy *Apologie* was devoted to matters other than the use of the oath by High Commission to ferret out heterodox beliefs, and in his manuscript reply to Cosin, Morice retailed a long list of cases from Essex that illustrated how the oath was used, sometimes unscrupulously, by ecclesiastical court officials to force unsuspecting laymen to come into their courts and pay fees.[94]

It is difficult to know how far these concerns about potential abuses of their powers were influential in shaping general public attitudes towards the ecclesiastical courts in the years between 1585 and the middle of the reign of James VI and I. The best recent studies of the jurisdiction have tended to stress that contemporaries found the ecclesiastical courts useful and resorted to them in large numbers. But it is worth recalling that there was a wide area of church court jurisdiction involving marriage and last wills and testaments that was largely uncontroversial, while there were others, especially that having to do with tithes, which were highly contentious.[95] At the same time, there were those, like Morice

---

[91] He died in 1597.   [92] BL, MS Lansdowne 82, fol. 150r–v.   [93] See above, pp. 104–5.
[94] LPL, MS 234, fol. 14v. For some of the details, see below, p. 405.
[95] Helmholz, *Canon Law*; M. Ingram, *Church Courts, Sex and Marriage in England, 1570–1640* (Cambridge, 1987); but see some qualifications in C. Haigh, *The Plain Man's Pathways to Heaven* (Oxford, 2007), pp. 153–7.

and Beale, who felt that the church courts were more effective at har-
assing people for trivial offences and collecting fees than in policing
serious breaches of morality, which they thought should in any case be
dealt with by the secular authorities. Furthermore, it also appears that
the legal questions over High Commission (in the dioceses of Canterbury and London) were exacerbated by an increase in the amounts of
ordinary litigation that it began to attract, and by the fact that in dealing
with these matters, as well as those involving serious threats to the
spiritual well-being of the country, it used the distinctly temporal powers
of imprisonment both to enforce summonses and to punish offenders
once they had been excommunicated.

For all of these reasons, during the course of the 1590s, the ecclesiastical authorities found that writs of prohibition, which had been so
crucial in the debate over the oath, were being taken out with increasing
frequency by litigants attempting to gain an advantage over their
adversaries by asking the common law courts to stay, and then consider,
cases that had originally been brought in church courts. Obtaining a
prohibition was evidently easy and not all that expensive. In order to
take one out of the court of Common Pleas, for example, the party or
his attorney had merely to go to one of the prothonotaries' clerks in the
court, pay the requisite fees, and have the writ drawn. After that, he
needed to have it signed by one of the judges in his chambers, and then
sealed.[96] Nearly always beginning with a recitation of how the action in
the ecclesiastical court amounted to a breach of chapter 29 of Magna
Carta, the broad principle upon which prohibitions were based was that
the question at issue contained sufficient matter to bring it within the
cognisance of the secular courts, which should in such circumstances
have precedence over the ecclesiastical jurisdiction.[97]

From the point of view of the common lawyers, the measure was
guaranteed a high level of success because it was left up to the common-
law judges (who also had a share in the fees) to determine what issues
came into this category. Indeed, by the early seventeenth century, a new
procedural innovation enabled the legal advisors of litigants to obtain a
writ of prohibition on what was known as 'surmise', a stipulation that
although the action was on the face of it an ecclesiastical matter it might,
if looked at in a largely fictitious way, be taken to be one of concern to
the common-law courts. An extreme example of this was allegedly the
case of a man accused in an ecclesiastical court of laying hands on a

---

[96] The details, including material on costs, are laid out in BL, MS Cotton Cleopatra F II,
fol. 440.
[97] BL, Stowe 424, fol. 158: reports of cases in High Commission, dated 1611.

clergyman in a churchyard, who then applied for a prohibition on the surmise that his action would have been legal if he had been a constable, even though this had not been mentioned in the original ecclesiastical court case.[98] In 1598, papers that were probably drawn up by Whitgift, Bancroft and Cosin, and then passed to the privy council, complained about the number of prohibitions being taken out, and even went so far as to suggest that since the Act of Supremacy had united the temporal and spiritual jurisdictions of the crown, the writ itself was unnecessary and redundant. More realistically, they asked that no writ of prohibition be granted on the mere assertion of a lawyer that the ecclesiastical court was hearing what might be construed as a temporal matter.[99]

As R. G. Usher pointed out in his pioneering studies, the churchmen's efforts were evidently unsuccessful in suppressing challenges to the ecclesiastical jurisdiction, or convincing the common-law judges that they should stem the tide of prohibitions. The number of writs issued continued to rise after 1598, and it would appear that a significant number of them involved questions about the payment of tithes, cases in which groups of parishioners joined together in going to law, and were therefore able to carry on their actions with the benefit of a common purse. In addition, whereas High Commission and clerical conformity were mentioned as only part of the problem in 1598, they once again achieved a much greater significance after the accession of James I in 1603. The new king and Richard Bancroft, who succeeded Whitgift as archbishop of Canterbury in early 1604, aimed to put the ecclesiastical government on a more secure footing. The first comprehensive revisions of the canons of the post-Reformation church were passed later that year, and there were fresh episcopal attempts to purge non-conforming ministers.[100] A surviving manuscript critique of the canons of 1604 in the papers of the future judge William Jones argued that they would result in the unjust molestation of the people by drawing them into the ecclesiastical courts on trivial matters and lead to unjust gains for the officials that would amount annually to the value of a subsidy in the reign of Henry VIII.[101] The critique also claimed that it was an abuse to use excommunication as a weapon against clergymen who failed to conform, and it appears from other sources that Bancroft's policy was

---

[98] BL, MS Stowe 420 (notes on prohibitions ascribed to Attorney General Hobart), fols. 18ff.

[99] R. G. Usher, *The Reconstruction of the English Church* (2 vols., 1910), II, pp. 77–8.

[100] Ibid., II, pp. 362–5; R. G. Usher, *The Rise and Fall of High Commission* (Oxford, 1968 edn, first published 1910), p. 167.

[101] ECO, MS 137, fols. 19–21.

countered by the dissemination of legal advice about how the writ of
prohibition could be used to block deprivations.

Bills hostile to the jurisdiction of the church courts were put forward
in the House of Commons throughout James's first English parliament,
which sat in several sessions between 1603 and 1610, and members of
the gentry from Northamptonshire and Essex mounted a petitioning
campaign on behalf of non-conforming clergy.[102] In 1604, for example,
a draft bill, described rather elegantly as a measure for the 'Due
Observation of the Great Charter of England', received a second reading; amongst other things, it declared that canons passed by Convocation had no legal validity unless they were approved in parliament.[103]
Another measure aimed to lay down specific procedures that would
make it possible for a sentence of excommunication to be passed only
after there had been three attempts to summons individuals to answer
citations against them.[104] Still another went so far as to advocate the
suppression of what were known as the three-weeks' courts, a level of
jurisdiction below that of the bishop's consistory court. One clerical
opponent of this last measure compared it with the dissolution of the
smaller monasteries, the thin end of the wedge that would eventually
undermine the entire system because the increased costs to litigants of
having to take their cases to the bishop's courts instead of the three-
weeks' courts would eventually drive them away from the ecclesiastical
jurisdiction altogether. A third bill, which proposed to grant the costs of
prohibitions to litigants who successfully brought them, was evidently
passed by the House of Commons before being rejected by the Lords.[105]
As a contemporary critic put it, the thrust of this bill was to overthrow
the ecclesiastical jurisdiction in its entirety, not just that which was
exercised by High Commission. The granting of costs for prohibitions,
especially when none was awarded to those who successfully sought
consultations, would drive away litigants and lead to 'great injury' of the
ecclesiastical court officials.[106]

In the wake of the petitioning campaign, the king came to the support
of Bancroft, and called a meeting in Star Chamber of the judges and
members of the gentry prior to Lent assizes in 1605, where directions
were given for the enforcement of the new canons. In response to
questions from the lord chancellor, the common-law judges delivered an
extra-curial opinion in which they held 'it clear that the King without
Parliament might make orders and Constitutions for the government of

---

[102] Usher, *Reconstruction*, II, 361ff.   [103] Babbage, *Puritanism and Bancroft*, p. 101.
[104] Petyt MS 538 (38), fol. 208.   [105] BL, MS Cotton Cleopatra, F II, fol. 436v.
[106] Ibid.

the clergie and might deprive them if they obeyed not, and so the Commissioners might deprive them'.[107] They also agreed that common-law process should not be used to block the ordinary process of High Commission. But, despite this resolution, prohibitions continued to be sought, and granted, in cases involving High Commission as well as ordinary ecclesiastical causes. Furthermore, while it would be wrong to overstress the intensity or success of this campaign against the ecclesiastical jurisdiction, the sensitivities of Archbishop Bancroft and church court officials were clearly aroused. The Cambridge civilian Dr John Cowell published his *Institutiones juris anglicani*, which sought to demonstrate that there was an essential unity between the practice of the common law and ecclesiastical courts;[108] similar points were also made by William Fulbecke, an author who claimed some training in both the common and civil law.[109]

In late 1605, moreover, the bishops drew up a lengthy document consisting of over twenty articles of complaint against the widespread use of prohibitions, which the king then required the common-law judges to answer in some detail. Apart from noticing that writs of *habeas corpus* had recently been utilised as yet another way of interfering with the use of the oath *ex officio* in High Commission,[110] these *Articuli Clerci*, as Coke later mockingly described them,[111] also included quantitative evidence collected by ecclesiastical court officials to demonstrate how 'the humour of the time is growne to be too eager against all ecclesiastical jurisdiction'. Whereas, during the entire reign of Elizabeth, there had been only 488 prohibitions, since 1603, 82 had been issued to the court of Arches alone, and they suspected that much the same was true of all the other ecclesiastical courts in the realm.[112]

In their response, the judges reported that their own searches indicated these figures were an exaggeration. They found that since the beginning of the reign of James I, only 251 prohibitions had been granted by the King's Bench, of which 149 concerned tithes; and no more than 62 (of which 31 involved tithes) had been issued by the justices of Common Pleas. Since it is unclear precisely how the statistics were arrived at, it is probably unwise to read too much into them.[113] Nevertheless, the detailed responses of the judges indicate that they were

[107] Usher, *High Commission*, p. 167.
[108] *Institutiones iuris Anglicani ad methodum et seriem institutionum imperialium compositae & digestae . . . . Authore Iohanne Cowello* (1605).
[109] Usher, *Reconstruction*, II, p. 211.   [110] *ST*, II, col. 153.   [111] Ibid., cols. 131–4.
[112] Ibid., cols. 136–7.
[113] It is most likely that the judges had counts made from the *scria facias* rolls of the King's Bench. TNA, KB 165/1.

not inclined to make concessions. They insisted on the right of the king's common-law courts to intervene in any question where there was the least suspicion that a temporal matter might be at issue.[114] They rejected the claim that they were wrong in asserting that any matter about which there had been legislation automatically became a matter for their interpretation.[115] They argued that if more cases concerning tithes were coming to their attention, this was simply because the clergy had in recent years become more greedy and were no longer willing to accept traditional assessments of how much their parishioners should pay them. Finally, they insisted that any alterations in the way the relationship between the two jurisdictions was managed would have to be approved in parliament. Although they did not directly oppose the proposal that prohibitions should henceforth be issued by the lord chancellor out of Chancery, they found it a

strange presumption in the ecclesiasticall judges to require that the kings courts should not doe that which by law they ought to doe, and always have done, and which by oath they are bound to doe and if this shall be holden inconvenient, and they can in discharge of us obtaine some act of parliament to take it from all other courts then the chancery, they shall doe unto us a great ease: but the law of the realme cannot be changed, but by parliament: and what reliefe or ease such an act may worke to the subject, wise men will soone finde out and discerne: but by these articles thus dispersed abroad, there is a general unbeseeming aspersion of that upon the judges, which ought to have been forborn.[116]

Given the previous interest of the House of Commons in these matters, the judicial invitation for questions about the relationship between the spiritual courts and the ecclesiastical courts to be handled in parliament can only be seen as deliberately provocative. Nevertheless, King James, whose assistance was frequently sought by Bancroft, called for further conferences between the judges and the clergy, and by late spring 1606, he appears to have been satisfied that a compromise had been reached. In the event, however, this proved illusory, or at least very short lived. For most of 1607, the Puritan barrister Nicholas Fuller,[117] who had acted in the 1590s for Cartwright, fashioned a series of legal proceedings that once again called the legality of High Commission into question. Claiming at one point to have been encouraged by the common-law judges to defend individuals who had been brought before the church courts, he sought prohibitions at common law with the aim of freeing two different groups of Puritans, one from East Anglia, and another from Yorkshire, who had been imprisoned by High Commission.

---

[114] *ST*, II, col. 135.   [115] Ibid., col. 151.   [116] Ibid., col. 145.   [117] *ODNB*.

In speaking to the first of the writs, he went so far as to attempt to revive, and slightly refashion, the argument against the oath *ex officio*, alleging that the procedure could not have been 'saved' by the Elizabethan Act of Supremacy, because prior to 1559 the clergy had never had the power to fine and imprison. Since he accompanied his remarks in open court with the assertion that High Commission was 'popish' and the ecclesiastical courts 'not of Christ but of Antichrist', he was summonsed before High Commission, fined £200 and imprisoned, but not before he himself had brought a prohibition and a *habeas corpus*, and argued the matter further in court. Apparently divided amongst themselves, the common-law judges refused to claim jurisdiction in the case, which is what Fuller wanted, but their acknowledgment of the authority of High Commission was limited. It could proceed according to ecclesiastical authority against schism, heresy, or impious error, but, since the principal charges against Fuller included slander and contempt of court, it was left unclear whether these were legitimate areas over which it could have cognisance, and it was only because heresy and schism had been included amongst the additional charges that High Commission was entitled to proceed against him.[118]

After making something of a submission, Fuller was released from prison in early 1608, but a pamphlet published in his name concerning the first of the cases, that of Ladd and Maunsell from Norfolk, rehearsed many of the arguments that had been made in the 1580s and 1590s by Morice and Beale. The laws of England were the inheritance of the realm, which directed the king as well as the people. The judges were the principal preservers of that law, and the king could not either alter or dispense with it at will.[119] In the same year, moreover, Archbishop Bancroft, apparently responding to complaints from ecclesiastical court officials about further losses of business, implored King James once again to take steps to establish boundaries between the two jurisdictions and stem the tide of prohibitions.[120] Once again James presided over a series of conferences between the judges and the churchmen. In November 1608, Sir Edward Coke, who had been promoted to chief justice of the Common Pleas two years earlier, explained the judges' view that the ecclesiastical courts should have cognisance over cases only so long as there was no temporal matter at stake. Acknowledging that

---

[118] Usher, *Reconstruction*, II, pp. 143–4. The key document is BL, MS Lansdowne MS 1172, fol. 97.

[119] *The argument of Master Nicholas Fuller, in the case of Thomas Lad, and Richard Maunsell, his clients Wherein it is plainely proved, that the Ecclesiasticall Commissioners have no power, by vertue of their commission, to imprison, to put to the Oath ex officio . . .* (1607).

[120] Usher, *Reconstruction*, II, pp. 214ff.

the civilians had a different opinion, he asserted that this had no authority in England because it was for the common-law judges alone to determine the law of the realm.[121] At this point, famously, King James intervened, remarking that the judges argued just like the papists, maintaining that they based their authority on texts (in this case statute law) and then proceeded to claim that theirs was the only acceptable interpretation of them. But, according to the king, the truth was far otherwise. Although he vowed to protect the common law, the king was the supreme fountain of justice and the courts, and there was nothing to prevent him from sitting on the judicial bench himself if he chose to do so. Apparently reading much into these remarks, Coke interrupted to counter that 'the common law protecteth the King'. James shouted in anger that this was 'a traiterous speech'; the king protected the law and not the law the king. Rising from his chair, he is said to have shaken his fist in Coke's face, at which point the chief justice 'fell flat on all fower' and begged the king's pardon if his zeal had carried him beyond his duty and allegiance.[122]

Having apologised and sought the intercession of Robert Cecil, the earl of Salisbury, Coke held on to his office, but this was the first of the major confrontations between the judge and the king that would ultimately result in his dismissal in 1616.[123] Furthermore, a circular letter written by Bancroft in early 1609 provides a unique, if biased, insight into the public relations dimension of the controversy. The archbishop was aggrieved that some people were spreading ('seditiouslie in my opinion') the view that his reliance on the king in order to defend the ecclesiastical court jurisdiction meant that he intended to make the 'Kinge belieue that he is one absolut Monarch and maie *iure Regio* doe what he list and that I am an Enimie to all the professors of the Comon Lawe.'[124] Yet he also said that he thought it would be proper for some of the judges to be bridled, and he complained that 'they affect to much to be populer w[hi]ch was never approued in anye Comon wealth by men of solid and grounded iudgement, nor is p[er]haps tollerable in this'.[125] He went on to suggest that gentry MPs and the lawyers preferred common law to ecclesiastical law mainly because jury trials in the country were easier for them to influence in their favour. If the poor commons really knew how badly they were being done by in, for example, enclosure disputes, they would willingly look to the king, the '*pater patrium*', rather than the judges as the upholders of their birthright.[126]

[121] Ibid.   [122] Ibid., p. 215.   [123] See below, p. 150.
[124] BL, MS Cotton Cleopatra F II, fol. 121.   [125] Ibid., fol. 121v.
[126] Ibid., fols. 121v–2.

There is no evidence as candid as this about exactly where the common-law judges stood on these issues, but despite the confrontation with James, Coke continued issuing prohibitions brought to limit High Commission's intervention in ordinary litigation that did not involve serious offences threatening the unity of the church.[127] Furthermore, as the debate continued to rumble on through numerous conferences chaired by the king, the focus shifted more directly towards the issue of tithes. Here the judges maintained their right to issue prohibitions because the customary basis of the payment of tithes, which varied from parish to parish, was, they claimed, a matter for the common law to decide. This was, moreover, a jurisdictional gap that laymen were inevitably keen to exploit because it meant that cases involving tithes would be heard by common-law juries rather than by the ecclesiastical court judges, and lay juries could be expected to be sympathetic to other laymen who were reluctant to pay any more than absolutely necessary to support the church.[128]

The history of the English church and the 'ancient constitution'

Perhaps distracted by other matters, James did not pursue the jurisdictional controversy to a definitive conclusion, but, as we shall see, many of the issues dividing the churchmen and the common lawyers returned again in much the same form in the 1620s, and especially the 1630s.[129] At the same time, there may well have been some truth in Bancroft's allegation that Coke and the other judges were courting 'popularity'. In East Anglia, at least, the questions had been aired at meetings of quarter sessions and assize, and the debates since the 1590s had also been fuelled by the persistence of litigants and their lawyers in bringing writs of prohibition. For the common-law judges, and for Coke, in particular, the most obvious reason for maintaining their power to issue prohibitions can be put down to a desire for jurisdictional omnicompetence, the view that they had the right to be the final arbiters of the law of the land whether it was ecclesiastical or temporal, and of course, there were fees at stake as well. As his opponents occasionally pointed out, Coke seemed keen enough on High Commission when, as

---

[127] Usher, *Reconstruction*, II, p. 216; BL, MS Stowe 424, fol. 158.
[128] Usher, *Reconstruction*, II, p. 226.
[129] LI, MS Miscellaneous 586, fol. 41 suggests that from about 1614 it became necessary to sue for prohibitions in open court, which did effectively cut down the number being sought.

attorney general, he had been responsible for drawing several of the patents outlining its powers.

Yet Coke in particular may also have been driven by a more complex set of motives that can be traced back to the first fifty years of his life during the reign of Elizabeth. Although there is nothing to suggest that he was anything other than a conforming Protestant adherent to the Church of England that had been established by statute in 1559, he had been a member of Whitgift's college in Cambridge at the very time when Thomas Cartwright was advancing the Presbyterian views that would subsequently cause him to lose his professorship there. Coke also had ties with 'Godly' lawyers and magistrates in his native Norfolk, and he was related by marriage to 'Left-handed' John Stubbs, the mutilated author of pamphlet advice to Queen Elizabeth about her marriage.[130] As we have seen, in 1591 he and Wyndham had criticised the use of *ex officio* proceedings in Norfolk. He owned a copy of James Morice's 1578 reading on the royal prerogative, and he was the last person known to have had custody of the bills Morice presented to parliament in 1593. Although he was writing some years after he had been directly involved in the controversies, Coke later claimed that he and another prominent judge, Sir John Popham, had always believed that the powers of High Commission to fine and imprison were illegal.[131] Moreover, though it does not go so far, the account Coke published of *Caudry's Case* in his *Fifth Reports*, seems to have followed Morice's lead in the way it configured the relationship between the church, royal authority and the common law.

Coke's report reiterated the original judicial decision upholding the power of High Commission to deprive ministers for non-conformity. It also acknowledged that there were within the realm two sets of laws, the temporal, which were there to correct the outward wrongdoings of men, and the spiritual, which were supposed to reform the inward man, '*pro salute animae*'. Yet whereas the only other contemporary published report of the case, that by Popham, manages to make these points briefly, Coke needed many pages. Not only did he outline in full the arguments Morice made for Caudry; he also launched into a much more expansive consideration of the relationship between the temporal and spiritual laws that included some of his most classic expressions about the essentially unchanging nature of the English polity, as well as explanation of Elizabethan policy regarding Catholics.[132] Hence the

---

[130] Boyer, *Sir Edward Coke*, pp. 179–88.   [131] 12 *CoRep*, 19, 26.
[132] 5 *CoRep*, 42–5. The Jesuits and priests were not condemned and executed for their priesthood and profession, but for their treasonable and damnable persuasions and practices against the crown and dignities of monarchs.

Elizabethan acts did not annex to the crown any jurisdiction except that which ought to have been due to it according to the ancient laws. The king could act through High Commission because this 'ancient prerogative' was sanctioned by the law of England. Although Coke paraphrased the familiar words of the Henrician Act in Restraint of Appeals – that England was an absolute empire with one head – he also pointed out that the realm consisted of a body politic, and the remainder of his report is a history lesson ranging from Saxon times to his own which demonstrated, usually by an example from each reign, the authority that kings, or kings in parliament, exercised over the churchmen and spiritual courts. Just as laws which the Romans had borrowed from the Greeks nevertheless became known as Roman laws, so too any ecclesiastical laws that had been adopted by the kings of England had become English laws because they had been 'approved, and allowed here, by and with a general consent'.[133] The upshot of the argument was that the ecclesiastical courts had a role to play, but they were the king's courts (even if they were held in the name of bishops), and since they were the king's courts it was natural that their proceedings should be directed by the king's laws (as interpreted by the common-law judges).[134]

Bound by the decision in *Caudry's Case*, Coke was unable to argue as a result of all this that High Commission did not have the power to deprive ministers, or that *ex officio* proceedings were illegal because they were contrary to the principles of English law laid down in Magna Carta. Nor was he as explicit as some Elizabethan writers had been about the mixed monarchical implications of the argument that the king in parliament, as well as the king alone, had authority over the church. Nevertheless, he employed familiar sixteenth-century arguments about the history of the English polity in relation to the usurpations of the bishops of Rome, and the place of Roman canon law within the realm, to maintain implicitly the case for the right of the judges, common law and parliament to determine the disputed jurisdictional boundaries between the temporal and the spiritual spheres. Furthermore, although Coke did not invent this particular version of what has frequently been described by later historians as the 'ancient constitution', he was the first to publish it in an authoritative law report, and he also gave it a self-consciously patriotic and anti-papal gloss. Indeed, in finishing he explained that he was writing in English as well as Latin in order to better instruct his 'dear

[133] Ibid., 11.
[134] Ibid., 45. Just because the ecclesiastical courts are held in the bishop's name, does not mean that they are not the king's courts.

countrymen' and make them acquainted with 'the laws of this realm, their own birth-right and inheritance . . . .'.[135]

In the long run the historical gloss Coke put on *Caudry's Case* was as significant as the decision itself. This was amplified, moreover, by the fact that in 1605, the year of the Gunpowder Plot, the leading English Jesuit of the day, Robert Parsons, published *An Answere to the Fifth Part of the Reports*. Responding to Coke's assertion at the trial of the seminary priest Henry Garnett that the Protestant Church of England had existed since the advent of Christianity in the country, Parsons also attacked Coke's claim in his report of *Caudry's Case* that the Elizabethan Acts of Supremacy and Uniformity had merely declared the ancient laws of England, primarily by questioning the antiquity of those laws. Criticising the reliability of evidence for periods before the Conquest, and the absence of any authoritative statutes before the reign of Henry III, Parsons made a root and branch assault on Coke's notion that English common law had an unbroken history. Indeed, Parsons went even further than this, claiming that the common law had been brought in by the Normans at the time of the Conquest as a means of oppressing the English. If the common law was 'our birth-right' only the few who had grown rich on the backs of the many were the beneficiaries.[136]

The intervention of Parsons can only have lent patriotic colour to Coke's stress on the timelessness of English legal institutions, a point on which he clearly played in the prefaces to his next published reports in which he wrote that he was developing the historical dimension of his writing on law in order to address the ignorance of those who had challenged his views.[137] Meanwhile at the inns of court, arguments very similar to those Coke made in *Caudry's Case* were being adopted to reiterate the jurisdictional superiority of the common law over the spirituality, especially in connection with the vital matter of tithes. In a widely circulated reading given at the Inner Temple in 1606, Richard Gwyn, the recorder of Great Yarmouth (where Stubbs was steward), mixed godly zeal, history and anti-popery in order to prove that the payment of tithes was determinable at common law. Gwyn claimed that over the course of English history the common law had been adapted by king and people to reach a perfection that was 'most agreeable to the law of God'.[138] The 'common law of England extendeth itself as well to the

---

[135] Ibid., 46.

[136] *An Answere to the Fifth Part of Reports, Lately Set Forth by Syr Edward Cooke, Knight, the Kings Attorney Generall, Concerning the Ancient and Moderne Muncipall Lawes of England Which Do Apperteyne to Spiritual Power et Iurisdiction. By a Catholic Divine* ([St Omer], 1606), Preface, pp. 12–16.

[137] Brooks, *Lawyers, Litigation*, pp. 225–7. [138] BL, MS Additional 11405, fol. 5v.

states and causes ecclesiastical as temporal', and parliament, rather than convocation was the true representative of all the estates of the church.[139] Although he admitted that Roman civil law was studied in England, and that it was widely used in other countries, Gwyn was clear that the common law had never allowed in either the usurping jurisdiction of the pope or its fellow-traveller, the canon law.[140]

Yet, although Gwyn was even more forthright than Coke had been about supremacy of the common law in the ecclesiastical polity, he was notably less dogmatic than Coke about the unbroken history of the laws of England. While Gwyn maintained that the perfection of English law had evolved over time, he was much more willing to acknowledge that its continuity might have been broken from time to time either by papal intrusions or numerous foreign invasions. In this respect, Gwyn was in fact much closer than Coke to both the Elizabethan exponents of this view, such as Morice and Beale, and to the positions taken by other, younger lawyer historians. For instance, in a paper he delivered to the Elizabethan Society of Antiquaries, William Hakewill argued that English laws compared well with those of any other nation because they agreed with 'the written law of God, the law of primary reason, and the old laws of Greece (of all lawes humane the most ancient) in very many points . . .'.[141] However, he rejected the importance of antiquity alone, and explicitly questioned Sir John Fortescue's claims for the unbroken continuity of English legal institutions.[142] He pointed out that the ongoing influence of civil law in Scotland demonstrated how significant the Roman invasion of Britain had been. But although the Romans had extinguished the law of the ancient Britons, in England subsequent invasions by the Saxons, Danes, and then the Normans had brought further transformations. Indeed, since trial by jury was such a fundamental part of the law of both nations, he ascribed particular importance to the influence of the Danes, even though their ascendancy had been short-lived.[143] Similarly, in the preface to the edition of Fortescue's *De laudibus* that was published in 1616, the young John Selden questioned the accuracy of Fortescue's history and offered instead a vision of the English constitution as one that had evolved over time through a series of renegotiations between king and people until it had achieved its distinctive national character.[144]

---

[139] Ibid.   [140] Ibid., fol. 6.
[141] Thomas Hearne, *A Collection of Curious Discourses, Written by Eminent Antiquaries Upon Several Heads in our English Antiquities* (2 vols., Oxford, 1720, 1771), I, pp. 1–2.
[142] Ibid., pp. 2–3.   [143] Ibid., pp. 9–12.
[144] J. Selden, *De laudibus legum Angliae writen by Sir Iohn Fortescue L. Ch. Iustice, and after L. Chancellor to K. Henry VI . . .* (1616).

Thus while the history of English law had come to be inscribed in parallel with the history of the English church, the details of that history might by the early seventeenth century be interpreted in different ways. Yet its polemical purpose remained essentially the same, namely the delineation of the relationship between the temporal and spiritual jurisdictions. In 1616, Selden published *A History of Tithes*, which used European-wide comparisons of laws, and natural law theory, to demonstrate, much to the dissatisfaction of the churchmen, that the payment of tithes had always been a matter for local secular courts rather than being determinable by the laws of God in ecclesiastical courts.[145] Towards the end of his life, in the 1640s, he produced a multi-volume Latin treatise which demonstrated that there had been a unity of the temporal and spiritual jurisdiction in the time of the ancient Hebrews.[146] As he is reported to have summed it up in his *Table-Talk*, 'There's no such Thing as Spiritual Jurisdiction; all is Civil; the Church's is the same with the Lord Mayor's.'[147] Coke, if he thought the same, was never able to say as much even though John Hales had almost certainly arrived at a similar conclusion in the 1540s.

---

[145] J. Selden, *The Historie of Tithes that is, the Practice of Payment of Them* (1618). See also Paul Christianson, *Discourse on History, Law and Governance in the Public Career of John Selden, 1610–1635* (Toronto, 1996), p. 79 and Reid Barbour, *John Selden: Measures of the Holy Commonwealth in Seventeenth Century England* (Toronto, 2003).

[146] *Ioannis Seldeni De synedriis & praefecturis iuridicis veterum Ebraeorum* (3 vols., 1650).

[147] *Table-Talk*, p. 171.

6 The politics of jurisdiction II: multiple kingdoms and questions about royal authority

Wales and Ireland

The clash between the common law and the ecclesiastical courts involved questions that had generated debate since before the Break from Rome in the 1530s. That they came to a head in the last decade or so of the reign of Elizabeth was due largely to the attempt by the ecclesiastical authorities to maintain the unity of the Church of England in the face of Protestantism's tendency to generate alternative visions of church government. The problem was that their methods involved invoking sources of authority, and using procedures, that were liable to attract the hostility of common lawyers. This quarrel about the relationship between the two 'systems' of law that coexisted within the realm would have been significant enough if it had taken place in isolation, but circumstances conspired in such a way that it did not. By the first decade of the seventeenth century, contemporaries also found themselves comparing English legal institutions with those in other parts of the British Isles, namely Wales, Ireland and Scotland.[1] In the cases of Wales and Ireland, the underlying issues arose out of the medieval conquest and colonisation by the English of territories that had formerly been independent and enjoyed their own distinctive customary laws. Scotland, on the other hand, was an independent and historically hostile nation, whose king acceded peacefully to the throne of England in 1603 in the person of James VI and I.

Writing in the 1590s, the Pembrokeshire antiquarian George Owen explained that following the invasion of England by the Saxons, the ancient Britons had retreated to Wales where they managed to maintain their independence, and traditional laws, up to, and indeed after the Norman Conquest. However, following the subsequent English subjection of Wales, the country came under the government of marcher

[1] By 1603, there was also a well-established international dimension. See, for example, K. MacMillan, *Sovereignty and Possession in the English New World: the Legal Foundations of Empire, 1576–1640* (Cambridge, 2006).

lordships, and there was an incomplete introduction of English law. While the English prohibited the Welsh from inheriting land in boroughs so that they could secure control of the towns, the Welsh were permitted to maintain their customs, including partible inheritance, so long as they were not repugnant to the laws of England, which meant that many localities had Welsh as well as English courts at the level of the manor and village. Government by 'marcher law' continued until the time of Henry VIII, when, according to Owen, the king concluded that the Welsh had become sufficiently peaceful to enjoy the benefits of English law.[2] In fact, the Henrician legislation creating a legal union of England and Wales was driven by a perceived administrative need in London for more effective means of enforcing the Reformation as well as petitions from parts of the principality requesting an extension of English law to the Welsh.[3] Statutes passed between 1536 and 1542 divided Wales into twelve shires and created quarter sessions and JPs as well as the courts of Great Session, a jurisdiction which in effect administered English civil and criminal law in Wales through a bench of judges appointed by the king from amongst the English bar. In addition, this typically Tudor combination of integration and devolution was overseen by a Council in the Marches, which was authorised by commissions granted by royal letters patent that gave it administrative powers along with the capacity to determine civil and criminal causes, including, unusually, accusations of sexual incontinency such as fornication and adultery.[4]

Judging from the available contemporary comment, and the conclusions of later historians, the extension of English law to Wales was largely successful. In a fictional dialogue between a German doctor of civil law and a Pembrokeshire gentleman he composed in 1594, George Owen claimed that great improvements in the peace and prosperity of Wales had occurred over the past 100 years; along with the introduction of grammar schools, 'wholesome laws' had enabled the people to thrive by husbandry.[5] Many other sources suggest that the Welsh were highly litigious, and apart from anything else, the extension of English law to Wales meant that Welshmen began attending the inns of court in greater

[2] BL, MS Harleian 141, fols. 1–4v. For Owen, who was a significant landholder in Wales, and educated at least in part as a lawyer, see *ODNB* and B. G. Charles, *George Owen of Henllys: a Welsh Elizabethan* (1973). Owen's treatises on Wales are published in Henry Owen, *The Description of Pembrokeshire by George Owen of Henllys, Lord of Kemes* (Cymmrodorion Record Series, 1, 1892–1902).

[3] Peter Roberts, 'The English crown, the principality of Wales and the Council in the Marches 1534–1641' in B. Bradshaw and J. S. Morrill, eds., *The British Problem c.1534–1707* (Basingstoke, 1996), p. 123.

[4] Penry Williams, *The Council in the Marches of Wales under Elizabeth I* (Cardiff, 1958).

[5] BL, MS Harleian 141, fols. 28, 38, 55v, 75.

numbers so that by the early seventeenth century, barristers and judges from Wales were making an impact on the profession in England as well as in Wales.

The Council in the Marches, on the other hand, was more controversial. Since the Council's judicial authority was based exclusively on letters patent from the crown, it was arguably accountable only to the monarch rather than the privy council, and it was outside the supervision of any other royal court. Furthermore, its equitable and criminal jurisdiction meant that it attracted cases that might otherwise have been handled by the ordinary course of law in both England and Wales, and like all other courts it was vulnerable to accusations of administrative abuse. In the balanced account he gave of the Council, Owen acknowledged the uncertain authority of the jurisdiction, and some of the alleged abuses, but although he accepted that some people argued that the current peace and prosperity of Wales had in a sense rendered the Council unnecessary, he was on balance in favour of reform through the offices of the lord president rather than outright abolition.[6]

This may well have reflected opinion in Wales, but another peculiarity of the Council was that marches of Wales were traditionally taken to encompass the four English border counties (Hereford, Worcester, Shropshire and Cheshire) as well as the new Welsh shires. Consequently there were complaints from Englishmen that the Council was being used by opposing litigants to tie them up in actions before the Council that should have been heard either by English local courts or the king's courts in London.[7] Chester and Bristol had, for example, sought measures to protect their courts in the 1560s, and more general calls for limitations on the Council were made in parliament by gentry MPs.[8] A bill designed to restrict the jurisdiction of the Council was passed by the House of Commons in 1598, but rejected by the Lords.[9] At the same time, litigants also began to seek writs of *habeas corpus* and prohibition from the royal courts in order to interrupt actions before the Council. In 1603 its refusal to acknowledge a *habeas corpus* from the King's Bench in *Fareley's Case* led to a long series of legal arguments about the extent of its jurisdiction,[10] which were accompanied by unsuccessful lobbying in

[6] Ibid., fols. 41–3v.
[7] Penry Williams, 'The attack on the Council in the Marches, 1603–1642', *Transactions of the Honourable Society of Cymmrodorion* (1961), 1–2.
[8] David Dean, *Law-Making and Society in Late Elizabethan England: the Parliament of England, 1584–1601* (Cambridge, 1996), pp. 194–5.
[9] Ibid., p. 253.
[10] The best account of the arguments is in J. Spedding, R. L. Ellis and D. D. Heath, *The Letters and Life of Francis Bacon* (7 vols., 1857–74), VII (pt 2), pp. 569ff. In 1592, *Cornwall's Case* raised the issue of whether parts of the 'four counties' might once have

parliament by MPs from 'the four shires' for legislation making it clear
that the English counties were not part of either Wales or the Welsh
marches.

It has been argued that the English gentry who opposed the Council
did so largely because they resented the supervisory powers it wielded over
the four shires, and that the lawyers who supported them at Westminster
did so primarily because they were anxious to augment their fees by
attracting business away from the Council and towards the Westminster
courts.[11] Since Sir Edward Coke, then attorney general, was one of the
leading lawyers making the case against the Council, it is plausible that
his particular brand of East Anglian legal imperialism was at play, but
evidence of a scramble for fees is in fact extremely thin, especially given
the boom in English litigation that was currently underway. Some of
the legal arguments, which focused on the grammatical conundrum of
whether or not the marches of Wales actually meant the four English
counties as well as those in Wales, seem tendentiously pedantic, but there
was a real comparative question to consider since it was clear that the
marches towards Scotland did not include counties in northern England.

For contemporaries there were also broader constitutional issues at
stake, and these were similar to those raised in connection with the oath
ex officio and the ecclesiastical courts. The Council's opponents claimed
that its English jurisdiction deprived Englishmen of their 'birthright',
which was to have their causes heard before one of the established
common law courts either in the localities or in London. The Council's
supporters, on the other hand, argued that populist lawyers and country
squires challenged it primarily because it prevented them from oppressing
their poorer neighbours by exercising undue influence over juries.[12] The
solicitor general's defence of the royal prerogative powers that under-
wrote the jurisdiction maintained that it was beneficial to the subjects of
the four counties to have access to a court that could provide 'summary'
justice permitting the quick and equitable resolution of disputes.[13]

After hearing the legal arguments, King James at first took steps to
limit the jurisdiction of the Council somewhat but then changed his
mind and by 1610 restored it to what it had been before he came to the

been in Wales since it involved the question of whether ancient Welsh laws were the
legitimate customs of a manor in Herefordshire (BL, MS Harleian 141, fols. 25–6).

[11] This is the argument of Williams, 'The attack on the Council in the Marches, 1603–1642',
11, 14.

[12] ECO, MS 154 contains a series of MS separates on the subject collected by either Sir
William Jones or his son Charles, Welsh lawyers who later became involved in Ireland.
See *ODNB* and below, p. 163. The collection also contains material on Ireland and on
prohibitions.

[13] *Letters and Life of Francis Bacon*, VII (pt 2), pp. 589, 602.

throne. Despite their lack of success, the opposers, including Coke, continued to raise the question of the four counties in nearly all of the parliaments of the 1620s,[14] and the jurisdiction of the Council suffered a massive onslaught, which led eventually to its abolition, once the Long Parliament met in 1640.[15] Yet while the Council in Wales was controversial, the exportation of English law to Wales, and the principles that underlay it, were much less so. Defending the Council during one of the early Elizabethan challenges, the earl of Pembroke, then lord president, maintained that a communion of laws was the best way to reconcile the differences in languages, customs and dispositions that existed on either side of the border, and that the introduction of English law had been the means of turning barbarism into civility.[16]

Ideas very similar to these were also used to construct a justification for Jacobean policies in Ireland. Like Wales, Ireland was an independent kingdom appended to the crown of England, but to a much greater extent than Wales, Ireland had been a constant problem for the privy council and the lord deputies sent to govern it during the Tudor period. Though colonised in the thirteenth century by Norman English families, who inhabited the Pale around Dublin and enjoyed the benefits of English law, the native Irish inhabitants of the country, still in the majority, maintained their native language, culture and legal traditions, and were denied access to the English courts. During the 1590s, Hugh O'Neill, the earl of Tyrone, led a major uprising of the Gaelic Irish, and its eventual suppression in 1603 gave James I's government a fresh opportunity to establish a firmer grip on the rebellious lordship. By the end of the decade, royal policy supported the introduction of English legal institutions and tenures to those parts of the island that were still under Brehon law alongside a concerted programme of colonisation through the establishment of 'plantations' of English and Scottish settlers on land confiscated from Tyrone and other Irish lords.[17]

The legal aspects of the policy were articulated mainly by Sir John Davies, a barrister from Wiltshire, who became solicitor general in Ireland in 1603, and who went on to become attorney general there between 1609 and 1619. Davies was genuinely appalled by the conditions he found in the lordship,[18] and wrote at length about how the 'barbarity' of the 'mere' Irish and their perpetual propensity to rebellion were caused

---

[14] 21 James I, c. 10, 'An Act for Wales', repealed parts of the Henrician legislation that enabled the monarch to alter Welsh legal practices without consulting parliament.
[15] Below, p. 232.   [16] ECO, MS 113, fols. 84–5v.
[17] Nicholas Canny, *Making Ireland British, 1580–1650* (Oxford, 2001).
[18] Hans S. Pawlisch, *Sir John Davies and the Conquest of Ireland: a Study in Legal Imperialism* (Cambridge, 1985), p. 59.

by the failure of previous English rulers to conquer the country effect-ively, establish their 'sovereignty' and introduce that most vital of institutions for the maintenance of civilised life, English common law.[19] Strikingly unselfconscious apologies for cultural imperialism, Davies's works reveal the way in which an English lawyer might conceive of legal institutions as instruments of social engineering. If the Irish had been granted English laws much earlier, there would have been a 'perfect union between the two nations'. As long as the Irish were unprotected by English law, they could be oppressed by the English to the extent that it was not a capital offence to kill an Irishman.[20] If they had been forced to hold their land by English tenures, if they had been granted markets, fairs and other franchises, and been allowed to erect corporate towns, they would have been 'long since' reduced to peace, plenty and civility. They would have built houses and ships, enjoyed their orchards, and made provision for their posterity. Ireland would have become an island of prosperous freeholders not unlike England.[21]

Instead the Irish had continued to use native Brehon customs, in particular the form of land tenure known as tanistry, which according to Davies was at the heart of everything wrong with 'mere' Irish society. An inheritance custom with many variants, tanistry, was sometimes seen by common lawyers as a custom, such as gavelkind in Kent or some of those in Wales, that was at least to a degree compatible with common law. But tanistry was also associated with the election of chiefs, or heads of Irish clans, and was evidently capable of changing from one blood line to the next in each generation. It was therefore unclear, at least to the English, what, if any, security tenants might enjoy in property they held from greater lords, and, according to Davies, this uncertainty about the possession of lands and goods explained why conflict and 'incivility' continued in those parts of Ireland where tanistry was still in use.[22]

Davies praised King James for introducing English institutions such as shires and commissions of the peace and assize. Furthermore, he parti-cipated in and subsequently reported on a test case in the Irish King's Bench in 1608, which declared that tanistry was not a legal tenure, a decision that forced the 'mere' Irish to surrender their lands to the crown in the hope of regrants in the form of English tenures. The judgment declared tanistry illegal because it prejudiced the king in the collection of incidents such as wardship, because it was oppressive to smallholders,

---

[19] Sir John Davies, *A Discoverie of the True Causes why Ireland was neuer entirely Subdued, nor brought under Obedience of the Crowne of England, vntill the Beginning of his Maiesties happie Raigne* (1612), p. 14.
[20] Ibid., pp. 116–17.
[21] Ibid., pp. 5, 74, 99, 118, 120, 268, 271, 272, 276–8, 289.   [22] Ibid., pp. 167ff.

and because it was unreasonable insofar as it made titles to land uncertain, and a 'commonwealth cannot exist without certainty of ownership'.[23]

The legal arguments associated with Jacobean policy in Ireland raised questions about the role of conquest in shaping the powers of kings, and ultimately about the history of English as well as Irish tenures.[24] For Davies they also led to a reflection on English law in general that he appended in the form of a preface to a collection of Irish Reports he published in 1615 and dedicated to Lord Chancellor Ellesmere.[25] Writing, he said, for the Irish rather than the English profession, Davies began with a brief account of the fractured introduction of English law into Ireland in the reign of Henry II. But he devoted most space to a laudatory account of English law that stressed the way English lawyers, in making reports of cases, had, over the generations, recorded the growth of a system of judge-made law that was free from any external influences and arguably even better adapted to the needs of English society than parliamentary statutes.[26] Aiming to validate, or commend, English law to Irish practitioners as the best way of 'making Ireland English', Davies was at the same time anxious to defend it against criticisms levelled by civilians or other detractors who picked on the fact that it was written in French and disparaged its uncertainty costs and delays. As an English lawyer, it is not surprising that he was inclined to select the common law as his imperial law of preference, but Davies appears to have been aware that some of his contemporaries might well have maintained that other systems, including Roman civil law, or indeed the laws of Scotland, were equally worthy of consideration.[27]

Scotland and England

Developments in Wales and Ireland contributed to association of the common law with an acute sense of English nationalism that had already found fertile soil in the sixteenth century.[28] In retrospect, it seems almost inevitable that the accession of James VI to the English throne

---

[23] Sir John Davies, *Le primer report des cases & matters en ley resolves & adiudges en les Courts del Roy en Ireland* (Dublin, 1615), pp. 28–42.

[24] See below, p. 341.

[25] Though frequently cited by modern historians as indicative of the 'common-law mind', it is unclear how Davies's preface was received by his contemporaries, though *The Reports* were fairly frequently cited in the 1620s.

[26] Although he did not develop the point all that fully in the preface, he wrote in *A Discoverie*, p. 127, that though William I had put law into French, the Normans had ruled both Normandy and England 'by the common law of England'.

[27] Davies, *Le primer report*, 'A preface dedicatory' [no pagination].

[28] See above, pp. 83–5.

following the death of Elizabeth in 1603 should have had the potential for disagreements, or at the very least misunderstandings, about the place of the national law of England in the composite monarchy that resulted when the crowns of two countries that had been enemies for centuries were both perched on the head of a single person, who also happened to be a Scot. Apart from anything else, Queen Elizabeth had been an unmarried female monarch advised largely by a group of males, many of whom had been trained as common lawyers, and who seem frequently to have seen themselves governing the realm in her name as trustees.[29] James was a mature and well-educated male, who had a distinctive view of the nature of monarchy, which he advertised to his subjects in printed books and pamphlets. No less important, his greatest political ambition in the decade following 1603 was a complete union of the two separate realms over which he ruled, one that should, if possible, include an amalgamation of two distinct legal systems into one.[30]

In fact, given the debates that had surrounded the status of his mother, Mary of Scotland, the succession of James VI and I was at first sight accompanied by much less turbulence than might have been expected, evidently because his accession to the English throne at last provided a solution to a half-century of acute anxiety about the central institution of the English state. Yet, James was one of a generation of European princes who had been educated for government, and who had an intellectual as well as a practical political view of his role in it. Having been tutored in Scotland by George Buchanan, one of the leading monarchomach writers of the later sixteenth century, he was a capable political theorist. His avowedly propagandistic pamphlet, *The Trew Law of Free Monarchy* (1598), which was designed as a political primer, contains instructive discussion of most of the ways of looking at political obligation and political society that were currently in play. Reissued when James came to the English throne in 1603, many of the points it makes about the duty of subjects to obey, and the responsibility of monarchs to rule well, were commonplaces that could have been accepted easily enough by Englishmen. There may even have been something reassuring about the essentially scholastic quality of his thought and his subsequent willingness to discuss religious and political issues in disputations between the judges and the bishops, such as that which occurred in connection with prohibitions. On the other hand, James concluded in *The Trew Law* that he ruled Scotland by conquest, and he saw the role and power of

---

[29] See above, pp. 70ff.
[30] Many of the legal aspects of the union project are discussed in R. B. Galloway, *The Union of England and Scotland, 1603–1608* (Edinburgh, 1986).

monarchs as ultimately patriarchal; that is, all powerful but responsible to the good of the people. Acknowledging that kings were subject to the laws of nature, and answerable to God, James in the strictest sense may not have been an absolutist, but he made it clear that he thought kings were not necessarily bound by the human laws of the countries over which they ruled.[31]

Whether or not we should explain it by reference to this particular aspect of James's thought, or to the simple fact that he was a foreign king, there are in the prefaces to Coke's reports, which were coming from the press at just about the same time, unmistakable reminders to his countrymen that they should value English legal institutions as birthrights that protected their liberties and property.[32] But James's proposal for a perfect union between the kingdoms involved detailed consideration of whether or not the laws of the two could be reconciled into one, a point that was particularly problematic since the English regarded Scots law as being heavily influenced by Roman civil law. Although some crown lawyers, most notably Francis Bacon, wrote briefs in support of the proposal, the plan encountered a great deal of nationalistic opposition on both sides of the border.[33] Under these circumstances, a defence of the integrity of English law was not necessarily critical to the defeat of the union, but it was certainly a useful position to take up by those who wanted to prevent it. After looking abroad at other European examples in the age of composite monarchies, even the relatively balanced paper on the subject written by solicitor general John Dodderidge concluded by repeating one of the commonplaces of late sixteenth-century juristic thought: it was dangerous to introduce changes in the native laws of any kingdom unless some ambitious programme of social reconstruction was intended. Thus in his view the union of Welsh and English law during the reign of Henry VIII had been beneficial to the Welsh because of its civilising influence, but it was difficult to make similar arguments about the union with Scotland without either alienating the Scots and/or implying that the law of England might itself be ripe for change.[34]

Parliamentary opposition in England, as well as in Scotland, ultimately forced James to give up on plans for a complete, or 'perfect union',

---

[31] 'The trew law of free monarchies: or the reciprock and mutuall duetie betwixt a free king and his natural subjects' in *The Political Works of James I*, ed. C. H. McIlwain (Cambridge, MA, 1918), pp. 61–4.

[32] Brooks, *Lawyers, Litigation*, pp. 224–6.

[33] *ST*, II, cols. 578–95; LI, MS Maynard 83 is an extensive legal collection regarding the union negotiations in the period up to 1607.

[34] BL, MS Sloane 3479, fols. 60–1.

but he was successful in having himself declared King of Great Britain, and, although it was generally agreed that the private law of the two realms, as opposed to public law, should remain separate, the practical need to establish whether Scots born after James's English accession could inherit land in England led to a test case on the question that forced the English judges to pronounce on the nature of the allegiance that was created when one crowned head ruled both England and Scotland. *Calvin's Case*, or the case of the *post-nati* as it was known, was a collusive action brought by the trustees of a three-year-old Scot, Robert Colville, in 1607, just at the time when negotiations were under way between English and Scottish lawyers about the nature of the union that might be proposed for acceptance in parliament, and some of the issues raised were debated in the House of Commons as well as in the Exchequer chamber where the question was eventually sent for resolution. The defendants in the action argued that since Colville was born in Scotland of Scottish parents, and hence owed allegiance to the kingdom of Scotland, he could not at the same time owe allegiance to the kingdom of England: consequently, the writs aimed at enforcing his inheritance in England were invalid.[35]

It was clearly seen at the time that *Calvin's Case* touched directly on one of the issues that led so many Englishmen to oppose a union, namely the real or imagined threat that numberless Scots would join James VI in a colonisation of England that would be economic as well as political. Yet, despite this political disadvantage, and vigorous arguments against Colville's inheritance, the English judges decided by a large majority that it was valid, and in doing so they departed significantly from modes of thought that had been used both for and against the right of Mary of Scotland to inherit the throne in the early years of Queen Elizabeth. Those who opposed the right of Colville to inherit argued their case along the same lines as those outlined in 'Certaine errors upon the statute 24 Ed III (*De natis ultra mare*)',[36] which used the theory of the king's two bodies to show that political allegiance was owed not to the person of the king, but to the 'crown', that collection of laws and institutions that constituted a particular body politic. The case in favour of the *post-nati*, which was argued by Francis Bacon and Henry Hobart, on the other hand explicitly rejected the argument for two bodies, and aimed to demonstrate that allegiance was owed to the person of the monarch.[37]

---

[35] Galloway, *The Union*, p. 148; *ST*, II, cols. 559ff.

[36] See above, p. 76. Though the earlier treatise is not referred to directly, *De natis ultra mare* was. *ST*, II, cols. 566, 572, 581–2.

[37] Galloway, *The Union*, pp. 152–4.

Since the king of England was also king of Scotland, someone who was born in Scotland in effect had a single allegiance which was the necessary qualification for inheritance.

Many of the judges, including Lord Chancellor Ellesmere, seem to have thought that the question was so novel and difficult that it should have been handled in parliament rather than by the bench, but since this was politically impractical, James is said to have used his influence to gain a favourable decision.[38] Chief Justice Fleming declared that the distinction between the two bodies of the king was unprecedented in constitutional argument. Justice Christopher Yelverton thought that the idea of allegiance to a body politic was a 'light imaginaire conceit', and he also made the interesting, and valid, point that if it were accepted then the Irish and the townsfolk of the northern border town Berwick-upon-Tweed would have to be considered 'aliens'.[39] In his widely quoted argument in favour of the *post-nati*, Ellesmere elaborated these points further and went out of his way to discredit any of the 'republican' implications that figured so intriguingly in the Elizabethan succession treatises.[40]

While Ellesmere emphasised that the case was being argued according to the common law of England, he also noted that there were no obvious precedents for the question at hand; under these circumstances common lawyers as well as continental civilians agreed that it was necessary to resort to reason and the maxims of the law. These taught that it was dangerous to draw a distinction between the king and his crown. Allegiance could only be due to a natural body. Only papists, puritans, sectaries and famous monarchomachs like the king's tutor, George Buchanan, held otherwise. Furthermore, Ellesmere also refused to enter into speculation about whether kings came before laws, or to engage with the views of the likes of Aristotle and Plato, who were enemies, or 'at least mislikers', of monarchies. He concluded with the provocative remark that he would not cast upon the common-law judges the aspersion that they held that the 'common law doe not attribute as great power and authoritie to their Soveraignes . . . as the Romane lawes did to their Emperours'.[41]

---

[38] Ibid., p. 149. However, a note in the commonplace book of one of the judges, Peter Walmesley, who had dissented from the majority decision, says King James had not withdrawn his favour as a consequence. LRO, MS DD, Pt/46/1.

[39] Galloway, *The Union*, p. 154.

[40] Printed in L. A. Knafla, *Law and Politics in Jacobean England: the Tracts of Lord Chancellor Ellesmere* (Cambridge, 1977).

[41] Ibid., pp. 215–48.

Since this last point was one that the author of 'Certaine errors' was at pains to explicitly repudiate, it is hard not to read Ellesmere's opinion, and that of the majority in the case of the *post-nati*, as marking a potentially significant turning point, and this also seems to have been the opinion of Sir Edward Coke, the long-lived Elizabethan, who published his account of the case in his *Seventh Reports*. Although Coke was obliged to accept the majority decision, and although he went out of his way to praise the arguments of Ellesmere and Bacon, he also engaged in a characteristic elaboration of the judgment that attempted to regain as much lost ground as possible. Whereas Ellesmere had rejected the classical pagan authors, Coke explicitly embraced Aristotle and Cicero, explaining that government was a natural feature of human society, and then going on to express the importance of laws within it in traditional Elizabethan language. He accepted that allegiance to the natural body of the king arose from the law of nature, at the very beginning of political society, and before the existence of municipal laws. But this did not prevent Coke from finding ways to limit the temporal authority of subsequent kings, which he managed in part by resurrecting the king's two bodies. The natural allegiance to the king was given in return for the king's protection. Although the sort of natural allegiance that tied both Englishmen and Scots to James I transcended municipal laws, most other areas of human experience were subject to those laws, and therefore were not alterable by the will of the monarch. If a Christian king conquered an infidel kingdom, he would be right to abolish the laws of that kingdom and rule according to natural equity; but kings like James I, who inherited Christian kingdoms by descent, could not change the native laws without the consent of parliament.[42]

Reason of state and the public good

By salvaging aspects of Elizabethan corporation theory, Coke was able to achieve the objective of maintaining the jurisdictional barriers between James's two realms. They were distinct kingdoms, governed by distinct laws and having a distinct nobility. But as in his report of *Caudry's Case*, and in his dealings with the ecclesiastical courts, he was fighting a rearguard action that was only partially successful. Although James failed to get a union of kingdoms to match his union of the crowns, the rhetorical and political resonances of the issues concerned were summed up memorably by the future judge James Whitelocke in a speech in the House of Commons in 1610. Looking back, he said that consideration

[42] 7 *CoRep*, 17b–18.

of the union had hitherto been the most important matter discussed by the long parliament that began in 1603. Although the House had shown itself unwilling to 'leave the name [England] by which our ancestors made our nation famous', they had 'lost it', saving only in those cases where our ancient and faithful protector, the common law doth retain it' (because 'the name of Britain' was not admitted in legal proceedings).[43]

Within the context of early seventeenth-century politics, moreover, questions about the union were compounded by the fact that in addition to being a Scot, James VI and I was famously short of money largely because suspicions about his extravagancy gave parliament men an easy excuse for not granting him sufficient sources of ordinary revenue. James's failure to gain parliamentary grants led him to resort to extra-parliamentary expedients for augmenting the royal revenue, the most contentious of which was a decision to raise the customs duties on the import from overseas of certain named goods, including currants.[44]

Challenged by the Levantine merchant John Bate, whose goods had been impounded for failure to pay the additional levy, arguments over the legality of impositions, as they became known, were heard before the barons of the Exchequer in 1606,[45] and following the introduction of the matter as a grievance in parliament, there was subsequently a major set-piece debate in the House of Commons in 1610. Curiously, although the crown was evidently keen that full reports of the Exchequer decision in favour of the legality of the impost should be made widely available, these do not survive in large numbers and their quality was impaired by the fact a couple of the barons of the Exchequer failed to speak loudly enough for their opinions to be heard in detail. Turning in part on technical questions about possible flaws in the crown's proceedings against Bate, the judicial decision was based ultimately on interpretations of the royal prerogative, the extent to which it was subject to the common law, and how far the private interests of the subject should be subordinated to the public good as defined by the crown.

Since a parliamentary statute granting customs duties to the king at a fixed rate had been passed by parliament in 1603, the central argument of Bate's counsel, Thomas Hitchcock and Humphrey Davenport, was that further increases levied by royal letters patent were not legal, a point

---

[43] *ST*, ii, col. 481.
[44] The background to the case is elucidated in P. Croft, 'Fresh light on Bate's case', *Historical Journal*, 30(3) (1987), 523–39. James's efforts to investigate his new English 'estate' for revenue are detailed in John Cramsie, *Kingship and Crown Finance under James VI and I* (2002).
[45] G. D. H. Hall, 'Impositions and the courts 1554–1606', *Law Quarterly Review*, 69 (1953), 203–4.

Hitchcock emphasised by challenging the crown's failure to mention any legal grounds that justified the seizure of Bate's goods. In addition, they also cited chapters of Magna Carta which guaranteed the liberties of Londoners, the freedom of merchants to enter and leave the realm without restraint, and the liberty of the subject not to pay taxes without his consent in parliament.[46] They accepted that there were some *arcani regni*, such as making war and peace, that were solely determinable according to the royal prerogative, and not subject to ordinary law, but Hitchcock argued that taxes and customs duties fell instead within the prerogative that was under the law. While the king could raise impositions that were temporary and clearly for the common good, or levied out of necessity in time of war, James I's imposition on currants did not meet these tests. It contributed instead to the decay of trade, was levied *mera authoritate*, and did more harm than good. Although the king's lawyers, Sir Francis Bacon and Sir John Dodderidge, had suggested that he needed the power to raise impositions in order to sustain an equal footing with other monarchs, Hitchcock dismissed these arguments, pointing out that the case was being decided by the law of England, not that of France or Spain, 'And in our kingdom our princes have all times ruled by the golden letter of the law.'[47]

Bate's counsel drew on precedents stretching back to the *Year Book* period as well as statutes and a handful of relatively obscure Elizabethan citations. In giving judgment in favour of the king, however, Barons Clarke and Snigg (one of the inaudible ones) relied primarily on an early Elizabethan Exchequer case, the so-called *Case of Mines* (1567), in which the queen successfully claimed against the earl of Northumberland that all the gold or silver mines within the realm, regardless of whether they were on her lands or anyone else's, belonged to the crown.[48] Here, counsel for the queen argued that the precious metal was due to the crown because the crown had a duty according to the prerogative to defend the realm and maintain the coinage for the 'universal benefit', and that the prerogative was furthermore a customary one established by prescription. By analogy, according to Clarke, the king's duty to defend the realm gave him 'customary' prerogative powers, including the power to make impositions on merchants, who enjoyed his protection in times of peace as well as in wartime.[49]

Although it also maintained that impositions should be seen as a *quid pro quo* for royal protection, and also cited the *Case of Mines*, the most

---

[46] BL, MS Hargrave 34, fol. 57v.   [47] Ibid., fol. 62.
[48] *Les commentaries, ou reports de Edmund Plowden . . . .* (1571), p. 310.
[49] BL, MS Hargrave 34, fol. 66v.

well-known judgment in *Bate's Case*, that of Chief Baron Sir Thomas Fleming, was much more clear-cut in its logic. Drawing on the language of the Roman civil law that he quoted from *Bracton*, Fleming declared that the royal prerogative had a two-fold nature: ordinary and absolute. The ordinary prerogative, which included, most importantly, the administration of justice in cases of private law, was for the profit of 'particular' (individual) people, and could be argued over in the courts. The absolute prerogative, on the other hand, which in his opinion included the powers to create impositions, applied to the general benefit of the people and was not controlled by the common law or bound by 'respect for private right'. It was *salus populi*, and therefore was most properly 'named Pollicy and Government'; as matters of state varied, 'so varieth this absolute law, according to the wisdom of the king, for the common good'.[50]

Probably reflecting the views of the king and his council, Fleming also maintained that an imposition on currants, which were hardly a necessary commodity for the welfare of the subjects, could not be considered harmful, and he pointed out that it was much better to have an imposition on such luxuries than additional subsidies on land. Nevertheless, the judicial decision was manifestly controversial. When it was debated in parliament, the narrow legal points were frequently opened up into a more general discussion about the nature of the English constitution.

Significantly, in giving their decision in favour of the king, the barons did not refer to what may have seemed the most obvious precedent, which was a badly reported decision of 1559 that apparently upheld an imposition laid on cloths during the reign of Queen Mary, but which was itself evidently controversial at the time.[51] Sir James Dyer, who reported the case, indicated in his unpublished reports that the judges had been unwilling to countenance impositions assessed by the 'absolute power' of the crown rather than in parliament, especially if they had a tendency to infringe on the property rights of one of the subjects.[52] Furthermore, an argument by Edmund Plowden against the imposition on cloths, which followed much the same line as that of the counsel for Bates, was known in the early seventeenth century.[53] It is no doubt because of this uncertain ground that the barons, and Fleming in particular, moved the argument onto a consideration of 'policy' and the public good, but in doing so Fleming also developed a clear distinction between the 'ordinary'

---

[50] *ST*, ɪɪ, cols. 389–90.   [51] *Dyer* 165(b).
[52] *Dyer's Reports*, ɪ, p. xlvi. Dyer also seems to have disagreed with the decision in the *Case of Mines* (p. liv).
[53] BL, MS Hargrave 27, fols. 84–5v.

and 'absolute' prerogative of the crown, an issue that was subject to some ambiguity in the Elizabethan period. For example, although Thomas Norton once explained the dual nature of the prerogative in terms almost identical to those of Fleming, the author of 'Certaine errors' maintained that English monarchs were not so 'absolute' as to have any prerogatives that were 'loose from laws'.[54]

The most intellectually coherent parliamentary speech against impositions, that by James Whitelocke, was the one that had most in common with the familiar Elizabethan arguments observed in chapter 4. A relative rarity amongst the common lawyers, Whitelocke had a doctorate in civil law from Oxford, and he was plainly familiar with the classic Aristotelian typology of governments as well as the writings of Jean Bodin. Although he nodded towards the words and wisdom of Sir John Fortescue, and the traditional methods of government used in the realm,[55] his position was essentially that England was a mixed monarchy, where 'sovereignty' lay with the king in parliament rather than the king alone, and that therefore the king could not impose without the consent of parliament.[56] He claimed that Wolsey had been the last to attempt such measures, and he introduced an analogy (that may well have come from Bodin) which remained familiar in early Stuart parliamentary debates. If the king had the right 'to alter the property of that which is ours without our consent, we are but tenants at his will of that which we have'. If, instead, such alterations could only be made by the king in parliament, then 'we are tenants at our own will, for that which is done in parliament is done by all our wills and consents'.[57] '[I]f you give this power to the kings patent, you subject the law, and take away all rules and bounds of settled government, and leave in the subject no property of his own.'[58] Allowing the king to make financial exactions such as impositions would eventually lead to the withering away of the political significance of parliament, just as had happened in France.[59]

A feature of the impositions debates is that those who supported the king, no less than those who opposed him, appear to have been deeply conscious of a distinction, which had hitherto not been so highly developed, between the interests of the crown as distinct from those of its subjects, and between the public interests of the nation as a whole versus those of private individuals. Sir John Davies, for example, argued that while 'subjects may live as privately as they please ... a king, by

[54] See above, pp. 76–7.   [55] *ST*, ii, col. 481.   [56] Ibid., cols. 482–3.
[57] Ibid., col. 479.   [58] Ibid., col. 486.
[59] A similar line was taken in a speech made by the future judge William Jones, then recorder of Beaumaris (HEHL, MS Ellesmere 2511).

reason of the majesty of his estate, cannot well abridge his charge, and would be in a poor situation, if he had no power of himself, without their leave, to improve his revenue'.[60] Perhaps surprisingly for the author of one of the most famous accounts of the immemorial common law, Davies claimed that the law of nations and the civil law both proved that monarchs could enjoy such power as part of the royal prerogative.[61] By contrast with this, William Hakewill was acutely sensitive to the potentially disproportionate power of the crown versus that of the subject.[62] If the king was allowed to make the levy, it would threaten the 'bounds of limitation and certainty' between the king and his poor subject, and open the way to 'oppression and bondage'.[63]

Thus while there was sufficient ambiguity about the nature and extent of the royal prerogative to make plausible Fleming's contention that it had a two-fold nature, it is also evident that a number of his contemporaries associated the notion that there was an extraordinary prerogative beyond the reach of the courts, and immeasurable by law, with a style of government that they came close to identifying with tyranny. Furthermore, although such power might well have been bounded by divine and natural law, and hence in that sense limited, Elizabethan writers had already labelled government 'loose from' positive laws as absolutist.[64] What needs explaining, therefore, is how the king's position came to achieve as much support as it did. In the case of the barons of the Exchequer, a natural inclination of the king's judges to support the royal quest for solvency is a sufficient explanation. Similarly for ambitious lawyers in an age when there was intense competition for advancement, self-interest doubtless helped to shape some of the arguments put forward, but there also appear to have been philosophical shifts in the early seventeenth century that began to incline some towards the acceptance of the need for a more exalted interpretation of executive power, especially if it was used to promote the public good.[65]

A rare, but enlightening example of such thought is provided by a manuscript treatise, 'God before all and all after the king', which was written by the government insider and future recorder of London Anthony Benn, probably between 1610 and his death in 1618.[66] With

---

[60] *ST*, II, col. 402.   [61] Ibid., col. 404.

[62] Ibid., cols. 412, 414.   [63] Ibid., cols. 414–15.

[64] Above, pp. 76, 107–8.

[65] The public policy context of this is explained in P. Slack, *From Reformation to Improvement: Public Welfare in Early Modern England* (Oxford, 1998).

[66] BLAS, L28/49, no pagination. The title may be a kind of paraphrase from *Bracton*, 'Omnes sub eo, et ipse sub nullo, nisi tantum sub Deo'. See also *Sir Robert Filmer, Patriarcha and other Writings*, ed. J. P. Sommerville (Cambridge, 1991), p. 38.

the financial worries of the crown and the judgment in *Bate's Case* clearly in mind,[67] Benn maintained that the absolute prerogative of the crown 'carries with it Caesar's superscription and must be left to Caesar himself'. *Ragion di stato*, reason of state, was essential to governing, and there was no doubt, according to Benn, that 'the lawe is not soe regular and positive as that it byndes or geves bowndes to Soveraigne Power but submittes itselfe to the kinge'. It was 'most certaine that when a prince prest by necessity seems to doe somethinge against the lawe yet is it not against Justice because through him and by his support the law receaves life and Continewance'. The king was a 'mixt' person between God and man.

Like previous common-law authors writing generally about the nature of government, Benn's range of reference went well beyond the technical shifts of the common law, but his treatise is notable for the almost complete lack of reliance on either familiar milestones in English legal history, or those favourites of Elizabethan lawyers, Cicero and Aristotle.[68] Heavily influenced by the philosophical scepticism of the French essayist Michel de Montaigne, Benn's political outlook was informed primarily by a reading of Roman authors such as Tacitus and Livy, as well as moderns, most notably Bodin. Although he began with what was in many ways a familiar refrain, that it was the role of government to secure defence in time of war and plenty in time of peace so that each man 'could goe on in his own way of his calling and thereby . . . gather wealth', he drew the conclusion from this that the (rather disengaged) subject should leave government to the king. This is not to say that he approved of bad government or tyranny, but it was to his mind an exaggeration to think that his countrymen had to contend with such circumstances. 'People in these daies (god be blessed) doe not see king*es* sway as they reade of the Tirant*es* of old time who weare the verey slaughtermen of mankynd and that only for their pleasure or ambition . . .'.[69]

Aware that present controversies about the 'liberty of all' versus the 'power of one' were a threat to the commonwealth, Benn was content to keep his private thoughts to himself and accept the Stoic principle that it was imprudent to challenge the prince.[70] He suspected that all men were over-inclined to privilege their own opinions, to make their judgments on the shifting sands of 'discourse'. Those who opposed the king and his ministers were misguided.[71] For him, patriotism meant accepting the rule of the king in the same way that children accepted the governance of

[67] BLAS, L28/49, [4].
[68] He does cite some case law in order to prove that the king was like a father to his subjects.
[69] BLAS, L28/49, [4].   [70] BLAS, L28/46, 'Of discretion'.   [71] BLAS, L28/49.

their father, because 'our lawe presupposeth him a publique and comon father of his people so that, noe more then a naturall father should willingly destroy his owne childe, noe more is it to be presupposed that the king would willingly hurt any of his subjects'. Time and the indulgence of good kings had rendered 'monarchical and absolute' government not only supple and sufferable but even 'behovefull' and necessary. Anxious about the claims ordinary people were making for a greater say in public life, Benn thought that challenges to the prerogative would lead to '*dysnomia*', chaos, and ultimately the utter destroying of all government, 'like as wee see the humour of Puritanism that for the most part ever inclyneth toward*es* Anabaptism which after many wynding*es*, changinge and alterations is seene at last to end in flatt confusion'.

Ideological uncertainty and the meaning of equity

In their efforts to revise older interpretations that depicted the Jacobean period as one in which ideological conflict about the relative powers of king and people was growing, some recent historians have described the years between 1603 and the king's death in 1625 as a time of consensus.[72] Yet, although this may well have seemed true to royalist writers of the 1640s, or even the 1660s, the controversies surrounding prohibitions, the union of the kingdoms of England and Scotland, and impositions reveal a growing differentiation in the stock of political ideas that informed the role of law in the English polity, and disagreement about how they should be applied. Broadly reflecting the Elizabethan outlook in which he was brought up, the prefaces to Sir Edward Coke's famous law reports countered both the implied threat of the union with Scotland and the pretensions of the churchmen with an adapted version of the history of Protestant England that he used to maintain the centrality of the common law and the common-law judges in the political process. Above all a legalist, he never himself seems to have made the point clearly, but his approach was at least compatible with those of lawyers like Whitelocke, who maintained the essentially Aristotelian notion of mixed monarchy that had underlain the 'monarchical republic' of Queen Elizabeth. But for much of the period Coke was on the defensive. His views were only partially shared on the bench, and other influential figures, not least Lord Chancellor Ellesmere, were evidently willing to promote a higher view of monarchical authority. Within the second rank

---

[72] See, for example, Glenn Burgess, *Absolute Monarchy and the Stuart Constitution* (1996) and David Smith *Constitutional Royalism and the Search for Settlement 1640–60* (Cambridge, 1993).

of the profession, moreover, there were still others, like Sir Anthony Benn, who were drinking in, and finding applicable, the wisdom of continental sceptics and Roman authors such as Tacitus, which uncovered a darker political reality that contrasted with the Aristotelian idealism of the previous reign.[73] Yet this view, too, could be questioned on its own terms. In the speech he gave during the impositions debates, the Lincolnshire lawyer and MP Thomas Hedley cited Tacitus, but concluded that Rome was strongest when there was a mixture in its government between the sovereignty of the king and the freedom of the subjects. Apparently influenced by the republican thinking in Machiavelli's *Discourses*, he warned that if liberty were taken away from the commons, and they found that their goods were not really their own, then the military might of the nation would be reduced to a 'drooping dismayedness'.[74]

Hedley's speech also contains one of the most elegant and complete cases ever made for the power of an immemorial common law in defending the rights of the subjects, but his argument contained important qualifications that are often overlooked. Although he maintained that custom was a part of the common law, he followed Coke's dicta in the famous case of tithes (*Modus Decimandi*) that the common law was not the same as custom.[75] Laws were to be tested by their convenience or inconvenience to the commonwealth, and in this respect, reason was the essence of the common law, which differed from custom as much as 'artificial reason' did from bare principles. For Hedley, the value of long usage was largely an epistemological one. Time was the best way to test reason; it was wiser than judges, wiser than parliament, wiser than the wit of man. It provided a way to argue for the certainty of a set of legal and political values in an age in the grip of philosophical doubt.[76]

It is difficult to be certain what proportions of lawyers and educated laymen followed any one of these routes towards understanding the nature of political society, or indeed occupied one of the many crossroads that ran between them. It is not even clear how differences in political opinion might have manifested themselves within the legal community. Despite the apparent incompatibility in their political outlooks, for example, James Whitelocke and Anthony Benn were 'ancient friends'; in making a note of Benn's early death Whitelocke seems to have regarded

---

[73] The significance of this kind of thinking is developed in Richard Tuck, *Philosophy and Government 1572–1651* (Cambridge, 1993).

[74] *Proceedings in Parliament 1610*, ed. E. R. Foster (2 vols., New Haven, CT, 1966), II, pp. 189–96.

[75] 13 *CoRep*, The case of *Modus Decimandi* (1609).

[76] *Proceedings in Parliament 1610*, II, pp. 170–97. ECO, MS 128, fols. 154ff. appears to be a fuller account of the speech.

him well.[77] Far from behaving like a tyrant, King James was notable for allowing extensive discussion of all of the controversial issues that came to the fore. Many of those lawyers who spoke against his policies sooner or later benefited from royal advancement. Nevertheless, James on at least one occasion expressed exasperation that lawyers were constantly trying to define the limits of his powers for him.[78] The controversies about prohibitions, about the union, and about impositions all touched on a similar range of questions about the exact scope of the law within the English polity, and increasingly they all came to be articulated in the same terms. Indeed, there were times at which all three of the issues came together in the same person or place. In the House of Commons, Nicholas Fuller expressed hostility to the union and royal plans for taxation whilst falling foul of the ecclesiastical court of High Commission in his attempts to defend Puritan ministers from deprivation.[79] At the end of the 1610 parliament, the House of Commons petitioned the king against impositions and asked that something be done to redress the wrongs committed by High Commission, which under colour of the Elizabethan religious statutes, fined and imprisoned, and exercised 'other authority not belonging to the ecclesiastical jurisdiction'. The people, they asserted, had 'always been careful of their own liberties and rights'.[80]

While Anthony Benn claimed to be aware that conflicts between the king's prerogatives and the liberties of the subject were a great danger to the stability of states, and therefore to be avoided, he clearly observed such conflicts in his own lifetime. Even after Archbishop Bancroft's death and replacement in 1610 by George Abbot, who was a good deal more sympathetic to Puritans, the jurisdictional troubles over prohibitions continued. A set of papers collected together to make the clerical case in 1612 pointed out that prohibitions were still being issued, and accused Coke of granting them to, amongst others, a cross-dressing adulteress, and a husband and wife who disturbed sermons, reviled ministers and published schismatic books.[81]

Evidently following up an idea that had been suggested previously by the churchmen, this brief also contains precedents from the reign of Henry VIII describing how lawyers who had acted for clients against the king's interests had been severely punished,[82] and there were two well-known incidents in the years immediately following the impositions

[77] *The Liber Famelicus of Sir James Whitelocke, a Judge of the Court of King's Bench in the Reigns of James I and Charles I*, ed. John Bruce (Camden Society, os, vol. 70, 1858), p. 63.
[78] BL, MS Hargrave 132, fol. 68v.   [79] See above, pp. 115–16.
[80] *ST*, II, cols. 519ff., 522.   [81] BL, MS Stowe 424, fols. 158ff.
[82] Ibid., fol. 166v.

debates where lawyers were censured for the advice they gave. In 1613, James Whitelocke was proceeded against in Star Chamber for advising the Vice-Admiral, Sir Robert Maunsel, that the king could not legally appoint a commission for examining and reforming abuses in the navy.[83] Two years later, Oliver St John was prosecuted in the same court for slandering the king when he counselled the mayor of Marlborough that the town was not obliged to pay a recently introduced 'benevolence' because financial levies by the crown without the consent of parliament were contrary to Magna Carta. According to Ellesmere's notes on the case, St John was spreading ideas that would have the effect of turning monarchical government into democracy.[84]

Since both incidents touched directly on the extent to which the subject was entitled to legal counsel,[85] it is hard to believe that they were not well known in the close-knit world of the legal inns in Holborn. There was, moreover, yet another controversy, that between Sir Edward Coke and Lord Chancellor Ellesmere over the scope of the jurisdiction of the equitable court of Chancery which kept alive, during the years 1615 and 1616, many of the fundamental jurisdictional issues that had already generated so much heated discussion.

As we have seen, the jurisprudential questions surrounding the place of a separate equitable jurisdiction within the English legal system went back at least as far as Wolsey and St German's *Doctor and Student*.[86] These were explored again in the 1590s in a manuscript treatise by Edward Hake, which, following St German, pointed out the dangers inherent in a jurisdiction that depended entirely on the judgment of one man, the chancellor, while suggesting that the common-law judges themselves should not be so hide-bound by the constraints of the highly technical forms of action that they completely neglected equitable considerations.[87] At the same time, Chancery procedures, which included a summons enforceable by imprisonment, the taking of evidence in sworn depositions, and decision-making by the chancellor rather than a jury trial, broadly followed the Roman-canonical tradition and therefore had similarities with those used in the ecclesiastical courts, a point Richard Cosin had exploited in the 1590s.[88]

[83] *ST*, II, col. 766.
[84] Ibid., col. 899. HEHL, MSS Ellesmere 454, 2502, 2506.
[85] *ST*, II, col. 766. In making the case against Whitelocke, Sir Francis Bacon said that 'the asking and taking, and giving of counsel in law is an essential part of justice'. But the liberty was not infinite or without limits.
[86] See above, p. 39.
[87] *Epiekeia: a Dialogue on Equity in Three Parts*, ed. D. E. C. Yale (Yale Law Library Publications, 13, New Haven, CT, 1953).
[88] See above, p. 106.

Even their supporters appreciated that courts such as Chancery and Star Chamber reflected departures from normal common-law procedures.[89] Yet the chancellor had powers litigants might be keen to exploit, most notably the power to issue injunctions to stay actions at common law until his court determined whether or not there were equitable considerations to be taken into account.[90] That these issues became a source of controversy in the years around 1615 seems to have owed something to the overall increase in litigation that had been taking place since the mid sixteenth century, something to political circumstances, and, probably, a great deal to the respective personalities and political outlooks of Thomas Egerton, Lord Chancellor Ellesmere and Sir Edward Coke, now chief justice of the King's Bench.[91]

In general, Ellesmere's watch as chancellor, though not without sordid episodes of bureaucratic infighting, appears to have been one in which Chancery practice became considerably more settled than it had been previously. But litigation in Chancery had probably doubled between the accession of Elizabeth and the early seventeenth century,[92] and a manuscript separate written between 1610 and 1616 provided some provocative explanations of why Ellesmere's court was apparently becoming increasingly popular. The critical point was that litigants had come to appreciate that Chancery offered them significant advantages.[93] Since people 'spend more money now a dayes in Suites then in former times', they wanted a better understanding of what they were doing, and this was easier in courts like Chancery, which used English, than at common law where formal proceedings were in Latin ('an unknowne tongue') and written down in 'an unlegible hand'. While it was true that the common-law judges were attempting to adapt their law to modern ways of doing business, this often resulted in conflicting judgments, many of which, as King James had pointed out in a speech in 1610, were subsequently overturned.

---

[89] [William Hudson], 'A treatise of the Court of Star Chamber' in *Collectanea Juridica. Consisting of Tracts Relative to the Law and Constitution of England* (2 vols., n.d.), ed. Francis Hargrave, pp. 3–5.

[90] See below, pp. 313–14.

[91] J. H. Baker, *The Legal Profession and the Common Law. Historical Essays* (1986), ch. 13.

[92] W. J. Jones, *The Elizabethan Court of Chancery* (Oxford, 1967); Brooks, *Pettyfoggers and Vipers*, ch. 5.

[93] BLAS, MS L28/47: 'A Problem Whence it comes to passe that the Courte of Chancery of late especially now in the time of the present Chancellor is so frequented above other the Common law Courtes at Westminster'. There are other copies (e.g. ECO, MS 113, fols. 1ff.) , but the fact that one of them survives amongst the papers of Sir Anthony Benn may suggest that he was the author. Also, see below, pp. 148–9.

In addition, according to this tract, litigants valued the finality of decisions arrived at by a single judge and not having to worry about potential injustices wrought by ignorant or partial juries. Although some criticised Chancery procedure because it did not permit the questioning of witnesses in open court, written depositions enabled Chancery to look more deeply into the circumstances of a case than was possible given the constraints of time that operated at trials at *nisi prius* in the country, especially in cases involving fraud and deceit. Finally, Ellesmere had proven himself a formidable judge. Though unquiet spirits had challenged some of his decisions in parliament and elsewhere, his decrees stood the test of time. Ellesmere was efficient in dealing with business and came down hard on professional malpractice; those who questioned him found themselves 'unprosperous'. In the end, according to this author, the increasing recourse to Chancery might best be seen as part of a necessary process of change. Since religion and 'empires' were subject to alteration, why should judicature not be the same, especially since it was 'not greatly materiall how or by what meane or in what Courte' so long as 'right be done'.

Although the tract's suggestion that Chancery was 'frequented above the other Common law Courtes at Westminster' is not borne out by modern statistical studies,[94] its plausible account of the court's progress towards juridical domination was intrinsically inflammatory for the large legal establishments, including barristers, attorneys, court officials, judges and serjeants-at-law that made their livings from work in the common-law courts. Exactly how these considerations weighed in the mind of Chief Justice Coke is not entirely clear, but it is extremely unlikely he was unaware of them. Furthermore, Ellesmere had fairly consistently, though quietly, supported the churchmen and the king in the other jurisdictional disputes; ageing and not always well, he seems to have become increasingly interventionist, even going so far as to issue injunctions from Chancery in those cases where a final verdict had been given at common law, a practice that had in fact been ruled against in the late 1590s. In 1613, Fleming raised objections to his interference, and from 1614 Coke began a campaign to reign in the chancellor which relied on judicial writs and forms of argument that closely paralleled the conflict between the common-law courts and the ecclesiastical jurisdiction. In the cases of Glanville and Apsley, he allowed a writ of *habeas corpus* to a litigant in Chancery who had been imprisoned for contempt, and in 1616, he permitted an action on the Statute of Praemunire to issue against Sergeant Francis More, supposedly a favourite of Ellesmere's, and several

---

[94] Brooks, *Pettyfoggers and Vipers*, pp. 85–8, 90, 96.

Chancery officials who had applied to obtain equitable relief after a judgment had been given at common law.[95]

Coke's suggestion that the chancellor was committing *praemunire* was so weak technically that it suggests a degree of desperation, and while the dispute must in many respects be seen in terms of the relationship between the two principal protagonists, it also reflected the intellectual and political profiles they had come to represent in the minds of contemporaries. Ellesmere frequently warned against the dangers of 'popularity' in general[96] and did everything but name Coke in particular of being guilty of what he considered a grave offence in a judge. On the other hand, by 1614 Coke was making speeches at professional occasions that warned of dangers confronting the common law. Addressing new serjeants-at-law at the Middle Temple in 1614, he proclaimed that the common law had always had adversaries, wrestlers and perverters. One enemy had been the 'Romanists' (did he mean papists, civilians, or both?); more recently there was Wolsey, a chancellor who proposed abrogating the common law and replacing it with Roman civil law, but who had been cast down by a charge of *praemunire*.[97]

Despite the rhetorical flourishes, however, the trouble with the argument that Ellesmere had committed *praemunire* was that it was relatively easy to counter. Taking a line little different from that of Coke himself in *Caudry's Case*, William Hakewill produced a brief supporting Ellesmere which demonstrated that the relevant statutes had been designed to exclude papal jurisdiction from England. They were milestones in the history of the English church, but they had nothing to do with the chancellor, whose jurisdiction was a traditional and recognised feature of the laws of England.[98] Although the boundaries of equity had been questioned by St German, his ultimate defence of its necessity had always been an accepted feature of sixteenth-century legal thought. In this respect, it is hard to see how Hakewill's moderate argument would not have been convincing, even amongst those who thought that Ellesmere had been over-extending the legitimate reach of the chancellor's acknowledged power.[99]

Yet some of Ellesmere's supporters went a good deal further than this. Anthony Benn, a leading Chancery barrister, and the possible author of

---

[95] Baker, *Legal Profession and Common Law*, pp. 210–16.
[96] See, for example, HEHL, MS Ellesmere 466, notes on the Millenary Petition, which accuses clergymen of stirring up a desire for reformation in the people.
[97] BL, MS Stowe 422, fols. 108ff. Cf. the rather bland version in Baker, *Serjeants*, p. 324.
[98] BL, MS Lansdowne 174, fols. 226–35v.
[99] A similar argument is contained in a brief on the matter written by Sir John Davies. HEHL, MS Ellesmere 2748.

the previously discussed tract explaining the popularity of Chancery,[100] wrote a brief covering many of the same historical points as Hakewill's, but which elaborated on their significance. Benn accepted that some people disliked Chancery because its procedures differed from those at common law, but in his view the laws of nature and reason transcended any national laws. The common people took it as a commonplace that conscience and equity existed before Magna Carta. No national law could be forever just or profitable to the state, therefore changes had to be undertaken by the fountain of justice, the king. Indeed, for Benn the jurisdiction of Chancery was directly associated with powers inherent in the monarchy. Equity originated in the king's power to hear and determine disputes the subjects petitioned him to resolve for them. The law lived by the countenance and protection it received from the king: 'God before all and all after the King.'[101]

Soon after writing in support of Ellesmere, Hakewill was made solicitor to Queen Anne and Benn became recorder of London.[102] While Benn's statement of the case may have been more forceful than Ellesmere himself would have made it, such reactions to the controversy as have survived suggest that it captures fairly accurately what other observers thought the chancellor stood for. James Whitelocke noted Ellesmere's death in 1617 with unrestrained joy, writing that it would have been better for the commonwealth if he had died twenty years earlier. He was the greatest enemy of the common law that ever held office, an achievement legal wags evidently commemorated by turning one of his titles, Viscount Brackley, into the uncomplimentary 'Viscount Breaklaw'.[103] These sentiments were shared by Timothy Turner, a young law student from Shropshire, who elaborated on them in sixteen 'Poyntes Daungerous et absurd affirme dev[an]t le Roy par Egerton Chancellor'. Roughly half of these were assertions by Ellesmere that the king could judge any matter concerning the jurisdiction of the courts at his will, with particular emphasis on Ellesmere's support for the churchmen on all of the outstanding questions about the relationship between the church courts and the common law. The remainder concentrated on Chancery, including Ellesmere's alleged attempts to discredit judgments at common law, his reproaches to Fleming and Coke, and his claim that the chancellor was the keeper of the king's conscience so that whatever he decided in any case could be decreed accordingly.[104] Turner also

---

[100] Above, note 93.   [101] BL, MS Stowe 177, fols. 190–8v.
[102] *ODNB*.   [103] *Liber Famelicus of Sir James Whitelocke*, p. 53.
[104] University College London, MS Ogden 29, fols. 568v–9. It is worth noting that much of the rest of the manuscript notebook contains extracts from Coke's published reports, and a fair commercial copy of Richard Gwyn's reading on tithes (above, p. 121).

noted a speech by King James in Star Chamber in which he tried to cool the controversy by stating that he had no intention of changing English law or introducing the civil law, but Turner concluded nonetheless that the king had raised the prerogative above the law of the realm so that the law could no longer intervene in disputes between the subject and the crown.[105]

Unusually long-lived (and the oldest man ever to have been made a serjeant-at-law), Turner was probably a royalist during the civil wars, but judging from marginal memoranda that he added to these notes in 1658, he thought that by convincing the king that the prerogative was 'transcendent' to the common law, Ellesmere had set a course that eventually brought the 'whole nation under a fewe into that slavery under which it now Labours'.[106] Maybe this is an example of apocalyptic hindsight, but the events of 1616 marked a significant turning point. For James I, the conflict over Chancery was merely the last straw in the long list of jurisdictional disputes in which Coke had been involved. Taking a step that was largely unprecedented, he dismissed Coke from his office as chief justice of the King's Bench, and Ellesmere had the satisfaction of bitterly attacking Coke in a speech he gave on the appointment of his successor. Yet Coke would reappear within a few years as a leading member of the parliaments of the 1620s, an unusual role for an elderly former lord chief justice of England,[107] while Ellesmere soon afterwards retired and then died. In his place, James appointed the polymath genius Sir Francis Bacon, who had been an active supporter of royal policy in general and of Ellesmere in the dispute with Coke.[108] A trained common lawyer of note, jurisdictional conflict between Chancery and the common-law courts appears to have subsided during Bacon's tenure, but when preparations were in hand for the parliament called in 1621, the court of Chancery was still a significant item on the political agenda.

Alongside the jurisdictional controversies, Chancery, like all of the major royal courts, was vulnerable to practical criticisms that resulted directly from the bureaucratic expansion (and peculation) that was an inevitable consequence of the increase in legal business.[109] According to his critics, Bacon made this situation worse by finding new ways of

---

[105] BL, MS Additional 35957, fols. 55–6v.   [106] Ibid., fol. 56v. *ODNB*.
[107] See below, pp. 173, 176.
[108] See, for example, ECO, MS 113, fol. 33: Bacon's speech on the appointment of Baron Denman in 1617, where the new judge was advised to maintain the king's prerogative and to be clear that the prerogative and the law were not two different things, but that the prerogative was the law. J. Martin, *Francis Bacon, The State, and the Reform of Natural Philosophy* (Cambridge, 1992), ch. 4.
[109] Brooks, *Pettyfoggers and Vipers*, ch. 7.

improving his own income, including the taking of bribes from litigants involved in cases being heard before him. As has frequently been pointed out, the extent of Bacon's departure from past practice in this regard is probably debatable, but the allegations were exploited by his political enemies both within and outside the royal court.[110] Indeed, according to advice offered to the king by John Williams, a rising churchman who had served as a chaplain in Ellesmere's household,[111] the best course of action for James was to acknowledge some of the problems in Chancery, including Bacon's avarice, and promise reforms in order to prohibit MPs from sinking their teeth into the matter.[112]

Some of Williams's reasons for deflecting parliamentary reform were astute. He warned that the House might not be able to distinguish between the abuses and legitimate uses of the court. More tendentiously, he reminded the king that 'All the Lower Howse consist of Lawyers and Justices of ye peace both w[hi]ch ... are often iustly Controled & Countermanded by the Ch[ancer]y w[hi]ch they would hardly forgett in this reformacon.'[113] Yet, since Williams secured the great seal for himself after Bacon had been driven from office in 1621, it is worth noting where he stood on the jurisdiction in general. Whereas ordinary courts of justice were governed by past practice (precedent), in the court of equity, 'the king governes (like God himselfe) by his owne individuall goodnes and Justice' even though the actual exercise of the office was put in the hands of another. The jurisdiction had never given offence to the 'Commonalty', because 'the sweet temper of equity, which is the will of god and good men,' had for the past six hundred years kept the 'customs of Normandy (which we call our Common Law)' from oppressing the subjects.[114]

Reminiscent of Father Parson's attack on Coke's account of English history,[115] this was one of the period's most penetrating examples of the use of the theory of the Norman yoke to attack the common law. Unfortunately, we are left to wonder exactly what King James himself thought of it, and, not surprisingly, Williams disingenuously moderated his tone when he addressed the largely legal audience that gathered in Westminster Hall to witness his receipt of the great seal in October 1621. Having just been created bishop of Lincoln as well as lord keeper, he wished he had the kind of professional legal training that would better equip him for the post. The king's choice of a cleric rather than a lawyer

---

[110] *ODNB*.
[111] John Hackett, *Scrinia Reserata: a Memorial Offer'd to the Great Deservings of John Williams, D. D. . . ..* (1692 edn), pp. 17, 27–8.
[112] CUL, MS Gg.2.31, fol. 334r–v.   [113] Ibid., fol. 334v.
[114] Ibid., fol. 334.   [115] See above, p. 121.

for the position had been a 'decision of state' that had little to do with him personally. While Williams could not resist an opportunity to suggest that someone who was above the taking of fees for legal business might be in a better position than a professional advocate to make impartial judgments, he also stressed that it would be absurd to set the king's conscience in equity above the laws and statutes of the realm.[116]

Mixed messages?

Although Williams himself had to step down three years later in the wake of professional and political malice surrounding the parliament of 1624,[117] his appointment in 1621 is in many ways an appropriate point from which to assess the history of the previous three decades. The first clerical holder of the great seal for over seventy years, he was also the last churchman ever to do so, but in conjunction with the dismissal of Coke and the failure of Bacon, his tenure in the office marked the king's determination to keep English lawyers in their place and to demonstrate that he was the fountain from which all justice flowed in the kingdom. Though Williams was a friend of lawyers as distinguished as John Selden and James Whitelocke, the symbolic significance of the appointment of a churchman as the king's principal law officer after the earlier controversies over High Commission and the oath *ex officio* could not have been more obvious. Nor would the fact that Williams had served as Ellesmere's chaplain, and acted as a kind of solicitor for clerics with litigious causes, have made it any easier to take.[118]

On the other hand, of course, as a result of his position as a judge and the publication of his authoritative law reports, Sir Edward Coke had emerged as a significant political figure. Expressing legal values formed in the Elizabethan period, Coke encouraged his readers in the time of the Scottish King James to think of English law as an ancient, national birthright – a defence against rival notions that were at best foreign and at worst popish. But Coke was also gradually being driven outside royal circles of power and influence. The king's Star Chamber speeches of 1610 and 1617 were frequently quoted by later writers to document his respect for England's legal institutions, but the conferences and disputations he held on controversial questions often ended with Coke either figuratively or literally down on his knees. The chief justice's removal from office was the first instance of what became an increasingly standard practice under Stuart kings.

---

[116] BL, MS Egerton 2651, fols. 38–40v.   [117] Below, p. 164.
[118] Hackett, *Scrinia reserata*, pp. 14, 59.

James was arguably the most intellectually qualified monarch to sit on the English throne since the Conquest, and the circumstances of his reign, not least his foreign birth and the attempt by Catholic terrorists to blow up parliament in 1605, raised important questions about the nature of political power and its application in terms of practical policy. The result was a striking diversity in the range of political discourse with which contemporaries had to contend. The dearth of published law reports in the 1590s made Coke's production of a multi-volume series a major professional development; at least according to Francis Bacon, yet another reason for his dismissal was the king's fear that he was about to bring out a new book in 1617. Yet the works of Coke were matched by those of English civilians who followed in the wake of Richard Cosin, not to mention the major apology for the episcopal Church of England as it had emerged at the end of Elizabeth's reign, Richard Hooker's *Laws of Ecclesiastical Polity*, or John Cowell's law dictionary, *The Interpreter*, which seemed to imply a view of government in which there were few bounds on the authority of the monarch.[119] In addition, there were works by the king himself, works debating the union with Scotland, works on the history of the common law published by John Selden,[120] and translations of important foreign works such as Bodin's *Six Books of the Commonweale*.[121] At the same time, accounts of the debates over impositions, and in other leading law cases, such as that of the *post-nati*, or that concerning the jurisdiction of the Council in Wales, circulated in commercial copies as manuscript separates, apparently on a significantly greater scale than before 1603.

One measure of the nature and variety of political discourse is the large number of surviving manuscript treatises, many of them anonymous, in which authors attempted to put together the existing stock of ideas into a coherent legal or political outlook. Amongst the more radical of these was an attempt to reconcile English law with Mosaic law and the law of the Old Testament,[122] but several reflect more closely the kinds of issues reviewed in this and the previous chapter. For instance, an anonymous writer on Littleton's *Tenures* was concerned to attack the

---

[119] R. Hooker, *Of the Lawes of Ecclesiastical Polity* (1593). For a general survey of civilian writing see B. Levack, *The Civil Lawyers in England* (Oxford, 1972). See also C. W. A. Prior, 'Ecclesiology and political thought in England 1580–1630', *Historical Journal*, 48(4) (2005), 855–84.

[120] Selden's works include *Jani Anglorum facies altera* (1610); *Titles of Honour* (1614), and *De laudibus legum Angliae writen by Sir Iohn Fortescue L. Ch. Iustice, and after L. Chancellor to K. Henry VI . . .* (1616), which includes Selden's notes on Fortescue.

[121] Jean Bodin, *The Six Bookes of a Commonweale: out of the French and Latine Copies, Done into English by Richard Knolles* (1606).

[122] BL, MS Sloane 2716, fols. 47ff.

'vulgar imputation of uncertainty cast upon the common law'.[123] Attempting to write English legal history by taking copious notes from the works of Coke and Selden, he accepted that William I had ruled by conquest, but concluded that it was

> a maxime in policy and a tryal by experience that the alteration of any fundamental point of the ancient comon laws and customs of this realm is most dangerous for that which hath been refined and perfected by all the wisest men in former successions of ages . . . to be good and profitable to the commonwealth . . . cannot without great danger be altered . . .[124]

Another anonymous work, 'A Treatise approueinge the Monarchy gov[ern]m[en]t of this Kingdom from the Saxons' is even more heroic in its endeavour to bring a wide range of reading into a consideration of the Jacobean political and legal scene.[125] Referring to works stretching from Plato and late sixteenth-century continental jurisprudence to the pronouncements of Ellesmere in *Calvin's Case*, this author began by lavishing praise on King James. Not only was he a religious, learned and philosophical king, but, 'knowinge right well what absolute power and authoritie accompanyeth Monarchy [he] pleaseth nevertheless to remitte the ampliture *and* fullnes thereof and to admit law and Justice . . . to interpose betweene his sovereignty and his subjects'.[126] Natural law obliged (inclined) good kings to rule by law and according to their coronation oath, but this author was also clear that a coronation was merely a public relations ceremony.[127] The substance of royal right was invested in the new ruler at the time of the death of the previous one, 'so that the sovereignty ever liveth, for the body politique no more then the natural body may endure the least moment of time to be without a head'.[128] Nevertheless, examples from the time of the Caesars showed that good emperors, including Augustus, professed themselves to be subject to law, and the actions of tyrants were clearly distinguished from those of good kings. In what must be a swipe at Jacobean impecunity and court corruption, Antonius Pius (from Suetonius) is held up as an exemplary king because he resisted the counsel of 'certain clawbackes and bloodsuckers of his court to leavy a thousand sorts of imposition on the people', declaring instead his intention to abate his 'ordinary expenses' and strive for the increase of the 'common wealth'.[129] Philip II, by

---

[123] BL, MS Harleian 1621, fol. 1.   [124] Ibid., fols. 12, 25v.
[125] The fullest version is in BL, MS Lansdowne 798. There is a copy in the Yelverton papers (BL, MS Additional 48104), and the author mentions that he had attended Gray's Inn in his youth, which may point to Henry Yelverton.
[126] BL, MS Lansdowne 798, fol. 105.   [127] Ibid., fol. 108.
[128] Ibid, fol. 106v.   [129] Ibid., fol. 110.

contrast, lost the Netherlands because he would not yield to the requests of his subjects. Tyrants considered the lives and livelihood of their people to be their own and managed things by 'absolute authority'; good and virtuous kings gloried in peace and tranquillity.[130] Moving on from these points to a full-scale discussion of government below the king that included a consideration of local courts, this author concluded that English government was a mixture of monarchy, the primary ingredient, and the other two, aristocracy and democracy.[131] Observing that a large portion of government in England was left to 'the people', he found that the democratic element in the constitution existed both in local office-holding and in the role of knights and burgesses in parliament, who, like Roman tribunes, were trustees for the people's welfare.[132]

Plausible, but unpublished, treatises such as these reflect many of the issues that apparently preoccupied legal thoughts about the nature of the polity in the early seventeenth century, but it is difficult to be certain about how commonplace the conclusions were. Sir Anthony Benn used similar ingredients to arrive at distinctly more pro-royalist conclusions, and while his closeness to Ellesmere may be one explanation for this,[133] many lawyers of his generation had to think about the ways in which what they said or wrote could affect their careers. The Jacobean legal profession suffered from overcrowding as the numbers of lawyers began to outpace the growth in legal work. By the late 1610s, contemporaries talked openly about the exchange of money in return for royal promotions, including selection for the prestigious position of serjeant-at-law.[134] There was intense competition for clients. Professional advancement that might make a difference between a mediocre and a highly successful career usually depended on the goodwill of the crown or of leading figures such as Ellesmere and Williams.

Most of the everyday work of lawyers did not in any case involve controversial political or constitutional issues. Some topical readings, such as that of Richard Gwyn on tithes, or James Whitelocke on benefices, appear to have circulated widely in manuscript, but these were the exceptions rather than the rule.[135] Although seventeenth-century law students were assiduous note-takers, the surviving evidence suggests that scores of lectures were given without the speaker ever raising the history of the common law or its relationship with the church or the crown. For example, a student who attended Sir Anthony Benn's uncontroversial reading on forcible entries at the Middle Temple in 1611 appears to have paid more attention to what he described as a successful social

---

[130] Ibid., fols. 110v–11.   [131] Ibid., fol. 116v–17.   [132] Ibid., fol. 118v.
[133] Above, p. 149.   [134] Prest, *Barristers*, ch. 5.   [135] Baker, *Readers and Readings*.

event than to the substance of the reading (which was on a potentially interesting topic!).[136]

It is also difficult to judge the exact connotation of words that may well have been carefully chosen in order to leave contemporaries guessing exactly where, if anywhere, the speaker stood. In 1623, for example, Sir James Lea's speech to newly appointed serjeants-at-law included praise for the 'laws of this kingdome', because they 'are soe inveterate to this people and soe incorporate and soe proportioned and peculiar unto them as I may say they are become even an other law of nature'. '[N]ot borrowed of any other kingdome', they had made the people happy and prosperous for many ages.[137] Given the event, such remarks were no doubt uncontroversial enough, but, then again, the adoption of Cokeian language in a ceremony that had in the sixteenth century frequently consisted primarily of moral and religious platitudes should not be dismissed as altogether meaningless.

Some of the ambiguities in Jacobean legal discourse are well summed up by the surviving manuscript notes on a reading on chapter 29 of Magna Carta that Francis Ashley delivered in Michaelmas Term 1616. One version of Ashley's prefatory remarks reveal that he was aware that the subject might be a potentially dangerous one.[138] Hoping that he would reach an 'offenceless' conclusion, he began by maintaining that Duke William had 'purchased an English Monarchy' with a Norman sword and that the passage of Magna Carta had been achieved when the barons and commons had demanded the restitution of laws that had been suspended by the Conquest.[139] Referring to the age-old question about whether Magna Carta was a new statute or merely a declaration of the ancient common law, he stated that he personally believed that it contained 'the sum and substance' of the laws that were in use during the time of Edward the Confessor.[140]

The reading itself refers frequently to Coke's *Reports* for illustrative cases, and it can be seen as an attempt to sum up, in a fairly traditional way, many of the principles of English due process law in the light of Coke's monumental compilation.[141] Yet despite the rhetorical flourishes, it is not entirely clear how polemical Ashley intended it to be. A Puritan from the 'Godly' stronghold of Dorchester (Dorset),[142] he was clear that without Magna Carta and prohibitions there would be no way to restrain the 'swelling and exhorbitant' power of the ecclesiastics.[143]

---

[136] CUL, MS Dd.5.14, fol. 8.   [137] Baker, *Serjeants*, p. 354.
[138] BL, MS Harleian 4841, fol. 1r–v.   [139] Ibid., fols. 2–3.
[140] Ibid., fol. 3.   [141] See below, pp. 420–2 for the substance of the lecture.
[142] *ODNB*.   [143] BL, MS Harleian 4841, fols. 4, 51.

On the other hand, while there was little else in the reading that was liable to cause political offence, in 'an accompt' of it that Ashley evidently prepared himself, he left out his thoughts on the Norman Conquest and history of the statute, resorting instead to the familiar metaphor of the body politic, which stressed the reciprocal duties of the head and other parts in maintaining its harmony. Two years later, when he was promoted to the order of the coif, Ashley was lavish in his praise of the new lord keeper, Sir Francis Bacon, and came close to blasphemy in declaring that he would take 'Jacob's vow', and consider King James his god.[144] Ashley appears to have defined discretion in much the same way as Sir Anthony Benn, who occupied the chamber next to his in the Temple: it taught what to speak and what to leave unspoken. He knew how to frame his public utterances to fit the occasion.

When we come, finally, to consider how Jacobean legal thought was expressed to the public beyond the profession, the speeches of lawyers in parliament, such as those in connection with impositions or the union, can be supplemented by orations given on other occasions, most notably charges to grand juries at quarter sessions and assize. Although more of this kind of public rhetoric exists for the Jacobean than the Elizabethan period,[145] it is still only a fraction of what was written and delivered, and the sample is distorted in favour of speeches given by those who were professionally and politically successful, as well as by the mere chance of survival. Just as was the case in earlier periods, moreover, there is virtually no evidence indicating exactly what any individual listener may have made of what he heard on one of these occasions. Yet speakers continued to elicit the participation of grand juries by finding ways to convince them of the benefits to themselves of the rule of law, and the ideological consequences of this could be rich. It was a way of thinking summed up nicely in an observation jotted down by Sir James White-locke: 'there is no greater motive to make one a good Citisen of the commonwealth then to interest him in the gouernment of it . . . The reason is bycause all men do naturally incline to uphold [and] maintein their owne interests as that which comes nearst them in poynt of righte.'[146]

Some speakers went into great detail about the nature of law in general as well as the matters in the remit of the particular service. For example, a pair of anonymous manorial charges explained the relationship between the laws of God, nature and the positive laws of man by combining a mind-numbing barrage of Latin quotations from Aristotle, Fortescue and St German with the evocation of the image of justice as a figure with

---

[144] Ibid., fol. 5. [145] Above, p. 88. [146] Whitelocke papers, vol. xxi, fol. 125.

a pair of scales in one hand and a sword in the other.[147] Perhaps because it aimed for a similar impact through a less scholastic approach, a widely copied charge given by Sir John Davies at York assizes in 1620 seems to have been particularly admired.[148] Noting that the grand jury was in a sense representative of the whole county, Davies reminded them that they had been assembled to 'maintain and Continue the publique peace by the execucion of the publique Justice, a worke soe noble and soe worthie, as I doubt whether any Temporall business that can be done in the life of man be Comparable unto it'. Implicitly praising the rule of King James, he observed that the peace and prosperity of the times meant that 'In these Halcyon dayes ... all Arts and Sciences, both Liberall and Mechanicall, have bin brought to perfection; and haue produced, and dailie doe produce, innumerable things, as well for pleasure and ornament as for the necesarie use for the lief of Man.' Justice was the mother of peace:

she keepeth watch and ward over every mans goodes and maketh everymans Cottage a Castle of defence, nay she herselfe is a Castle [and] a fortresse for the weake to retyre vnto. She is a Sanctuary for the oppressed to flye vnto; and haveinge the vertue of Orpheus harpe she charmeth the fiercenes of the Lyon and the Tiger, soe as the Lambe may walke in Safetie by them.[149]

While many speeches were expressed largely in secular terms, Jacobean orators, no less than their predecessors, also employed religious rhetoric from time to time. Both Sir John Croke and Henry Sherfield referred to justice as a 'sacred thing'.[150] Sir John Dodderidge's approach had much in common with the preface to the charge that Richard Crompton had published in the 1580s.[151] Starting off with a rehearsal of the biblical account of Creation, he progressed to the expulsion of Adam and Eve from the Garden of Eden. After the Fall, people began to multiply and in the first age they were guided by the law of nature until after the great Flood, when God

knowinge by his wisdome how necessary good Lawes should be, gaue the Law of the ten Com*m*andm[ent]tes. . .wherein is contayned first our duty to God next unto our Neighbours and after he gaue diuers Lawes and Statutes and ordayned

---

[147] Ibid., fols. 65ff.
[148] There is a printed version in J. S. Cockburn, *A History of English Assizes* (Cambridge, 1972), pp. 308–11. Manuscript copies are in BL, MS Hargrave 282, fols. 1ff. and CUL MS Dd.3.85, fols. 2ff.
[149] Ibid., fol. 2r–v.
[150] BL, MS Harleian 583, fol. 25. HRO, MSS 44M69/L36/1; L36/12/2.
[151] See above, p. 90.

rulers and governers and gave them power *and* authoritie to punishe such as should transgresse against the same. And w[i]thall gaue authority to kings *and* princes to make good Lawes for the goverment of their Country and subiect*es*.[152]

Even at the present day, the law of nature was the fundamental ground of all the national laws in the whole world.[153]

Despite the animosity that infected the dispute between the clergy and the common lawyers over prohibitions, many charges were emphatic in their condemnation of popery and defence of the established church. In a charge delivered at the Norfolk assizes held at Bury St Edmunds in 1609, Sir Edward Coke praised Elizabeth's handling of religious divisions and emphasised that it was the treasonable activity of the Catholic priests that had been responsible for bringing lawful persecution down upon them.[154] Dodderidge, reflecting the controversy over the Oath of Allegiance that followed in the wake of the Gunpowder Plot, on one occasion warned against seminary priests and Jesuits, the pope's instruments, 'sent abroad onely to seduce and steale away the hearts of the people and to withdraw the Subjecte from their legall and regall obedience to *the* State'.[155] Yet neither he nor Coke gave any quarter to Protestant non-conformity. Stressing that the government of the church and the government of the commonwealth were two great pillars supporting the state, Dodderidge ridiculed those 'Puritani nay rather Pruritani which have an ich in their braine which well [sic] never suffer them to bee quiett'. They opposed the existing ecclesiastical government and questioned the sacraments of the Church of England, meeting 'together in private conventicles where every one, Doctor like, taketh upon him[self] to teach, as being filled with the sperit, but it is the spirit of giddinesse and vanity . . .'.[156] According to Coke, 'Take away reverence fro*m the* minstrye, *and* the peple will pull away obedience quicklye. . .'[157]

The main objective of such orations was to stress that the benefits of justice could not be achieved unless the subjects gave their obedience to the king who was responsible for administering the law, but the emphasis in Jacobean speeches on this point was often less intense than

---

[152] CUL, MS Gg.3.26, fols. 149–51. Similar views are expressed in another version of one of his charges, BL, MS Harleian 583, fols. 13ff.

[153] Ibid., fol. 13v.

[154] Folger, MS V.b.303, fols. 348ff. Typically, Coke had a professional observation to make: Edmund Plowden had gone to church until Elizabeth was excommunicated. The content here is much the same in most respects to *The Lord Coke His Speeche and Charge* which was published without Coke's permission in 1607, and where he is alleged to have given an account of the English Reformation similar to that he gave in the report of *Caudry's Case.*

[155] BL, MS Harleian 583, fol. 15.   [156] Ibid., fols. 55–6.

[157] Folger, MS V.b.303, fol. 348v.

it had been in the more dangerous Elizabethan years. A notable, if pre-dictable, exception to this was Sir Anthony Benn, who, as recorder of London, was responsible for giving speeches on the occasion of the appointment of new lord mayors. Evidently maintaining the same political philosophy we have already seen him express elsewhere, he reminded Londoners in 1617 that the face of the king was 'imprest' by God himself to make a presence that commanded both love and awe. The glory of the appointment of the new mayor was merely the reflected glory of the king. The king, next to God, was the 'settler' of peace and plenty. Anyone who imagines anything other than 'simple and pure obedience imagines a vaine thinge'.[158]

Yet this tone was not universally adopted. Apart from anything else, different occasions called for different approaches. The very rare survival of the addresses Sir John Croke made as recorder of London in con-nection with the collection of the parliamentary subsidy show that he stressed instead the mutual obligation of the prince and people to co-operate together. In the late 1590s, he noted that public services such as the making of grants of taxation always involved public discussion.[159] Although the words themselves reflected the particular concerns of the Jacobean period, the tone of the subsidy speech Lord Keeper Williams delivered at the Guildhall in 1621 was no less emollient. Noting that in a body politic every individual should have a care for the public good in just the same way as they were concerned for their private welfare, he added that whereas in former times subsidies had been collected at the will of the king, Magna Carta had established that in England they could only be granted with agreement of the three estates of the realm in parliament.[160]

Despite this further example of Williams's ability to manipulate the political languages of the day, less elevated views of royal authority were probably more commonly expressed in the earlier rather than the later part of the period. While he was quick to point out the great power of the monarch, who after all was the source of commissions that authorised the holding of assizes and meetings of quarter sessions, and while he praised the learning of the king, Coke made a point at Bury St Edmunds of praising the independence and wisdom of the common law. Adding, furthermore, that 'Englishmen of all other are most jealous of their custome', he could not resist recording that the king had promised that

---

[158] BL, MS Lansdowne 157, fols. 110ff.   [159] All Souls College, Oxford, MS 180.
[160] BL, MS Additional 4149, fols. 323ff. Saxon kings did not receive, but imposed. So, too, did William the Conqueror.

no man would do more than himself in advancing the common law of the realm.[161] Even more interestingly, James Whitelocke's charges at quarter sessions sometimes invoked the participation of the jurors by briefly outlining an Aristotelian theory of citizenship. While men naturally had a care to the ('oeconomick') prosperity of their own private families, a commonwealth was made up of an aggregation of 'well-ordered' families, which implied a public duty on every householder in the government of the whole. As he had done in the impositions debates, moreover, Whitelocke sometimes spelt out his view that English government was a mixture of monarchy, aristocracy and democracy.[162] By contrast, a charge copied out by an attorney, Nathaniel Rogers, in the early 1620s also went through the Aristotelian forms, but concluded that democracy was by far the worst and suggested, in a somewhat garbled passage, that the best government was based on divine or ecclesiastical law.[163]

Just as was the case in the Elizabethan period, early seventeenth-century charges and public speeches show how the political languages of London, the court and parliament were regularly transmitted to the broader public in the localities. Nor was the mixture of ingredients rigidly prescribed. It was within this nexus that Coke courted his 'popularity', and apart from the need for circumspection, it is hard to believe that other speakers at other times did not refer, at least obliquely, to questions such as the plight of the 'four counties' on the Marches of Wales, the consequences of a union with Scotland, or the legality of impositions. Croke's subsidy speech clearly assumed that the subjects would be actively engaged in the issues that necessitated royal calls for money. Whitelocke evidently envisioned a political nation composed of well-informed citizens, and, as far as we can tell, one of the most characteristic themes may well have been that developed by Davies, who stressed the function of grand juries as a kind of representative institution within the constitution. Even so, diversity was also a hallmark of the legal and political discourse of the period, and, as we shall see in chapter 10, no assessment of the transmission of political ideas into the localities can be complete without considering the way in which legal and political thought was digested and then recapitulated by non-professional members of the landed gentry, who were also sometimes obliged to give public speeches before local courts.[164]

---

[161] Folger, MS V.b.303, fol. 348v.
[162] Whitelocke papers, vol. XXI, fol. 109. This was also the gist of his charge at Chester in 1621 in BL, MS Harleian 583, fol. 48r–v.
[163] BL, MS Harleian 1603, fol. 24v. [164] See below, pp. 294ff.

7   The *absoluta potestas* of a sovereign and
     the liberty of the subject: law and
     political controversy in the 1620s

Ireland and the fall of Lord Keeper Williams

England's involvement in conflict against France and Spain, and the ever-increasing influence of the duke of Buckingham in the councils of the early Stuart kings, ultimately made the political circumstances of the 1620s considerably different from those prior to the appointment of Bishop Williams as lord keeper of the great seal in 1621. Yet heated debates in the parliaments of the second half of the decade, as well as a number of well-publicised state trials, put legal questions and, indeed, the common-law judges at the centre of political controversy in a way that matched even the most highly charged episodes of the reign of James VI and I, including the dismissal of Coke.[1] But while the changes in the political climate are absolutely critical to the way in which events unfolded, there were also significant continuities in many of the ideas and issues involved. Indeed, critical questions having to do with the liberty of the subject to criticise policies of the crown, and the power of the crown to respond through the use of imprisonment, had already been ventilated to some degree in the reign of Elizabeth.

Similarly, the parliament of 1621 is known for the dismissal of Bacon from the lord keepership, and misunderstandings between the king and MPs about the best course of policy to follow in order to recover the Palatinate for James's son-in-law, the Elector Frederick V. But from the juridical point of view a no less interesting feature of the early 1620s was the attempt by the government to investigate and reform conditions in Ireland. There, policies centred on the creation of plantations and the extension of English justice were being compromised by infighting between the diverse groups of inhabitants, and by the inevitable peculation that went with the confiscation and resale of large quantities of land.[2] The Irish lords and gentry presented a petition of grievances to

---

[1] See above, pp. 117, 150.   [2] See above, p. 128.

the lord deputy in the spring of 1621. Concerns about policy in Ireland were expressed in parliament, and during the course of 1622 and 1623, Lord Treasurer Middlesex appointed two commissions to investigate some of the complaints, at least in part as a way of attacking the credibility at court of the duke of Buckingham, whose brother was deeply involved in Irish land transactions.[3] The first of the commissions was charged with a general investigation of the civil and ecclesiastical state of the lordship while the second focused more narrowly on the settlement of estates in the wake of the tenurial changes of the previous decade.

Both commissions were chaired by Sir William Jones, a native of North Wales, who had served as chief justice in Ireland from 1616 until 1620, before being made a justice of the Common Pleas in England in 1621.[4] They also involved several parliament men, including the lawyers William Noy and Thomas Crew; indeed, Sir Edward Coke would evidently have been named as well if his appointment had not been blocked by Buckingham.[5] Jones and his colleagues made visits into the provinces, took evidence from the Irish judges in Dublin and received petitions from Irish peers and gentry. The report they submitted to the king later in 1622 contains lists of those taking pensions and annuities out of the Irish revenue; further sections cover monopolies, grants of leases of church lands and trade and commerce. There is also a certificate concerning church government as well as a lengthy consideration of the state of the courts, which addressed questions about whether justice was being administered without interruption or delay and whether litigants were using the ordinary courts as they should, rather than bringing their actions for resolution before the Irish privy council in Dublin.[6]

Although those aspects of the commissioners' work that impinged directly on the plantation policy were ultimately side-tracked by political machinations associated with the parliament of 1624,[7] Jones and his colleagues produced a lengthy set of proposals that were quite quickly translated into royal 'directions' for the Irish courts that were published in 1622. The commissioners wanted to reduce meddling by the lord deputy's council in legal disputes concerning titles to land and aimed to curb the granting of protections or pardons in criminal and civil cases

---

[3] Victor Treadwell, *Buckingham and Ireland 1616–1628: a Study in Anglo-Irish Politics* (Dublin, 1998), ch. 5.

[4] *ODNB.* Jones's son, Charles, a barrister, served as clerk for the commissioners. The order book of the commission is in the Jones MSS at ECO (MS 95). Jones also owned several other manuscript works on Ireland, including notes on Davies's *Discovery* (MS 154).

[5] Treadwell, *Buckingham in Ireland*, p. 192.

[6] BL, MS Additional 4756, contains a fair-copy of the report of the commissioners.

[7] Treadwell, *Buckingham in Ireland*, p. 241.

alike. Following up matters raised by the Irish judges (who were Englishmen), they also considered the problems of finding impartial juries in counties and towns where kinship ties were still a powerful force; they therefore advised allowing limited breeches of the rules of venue, so that, with the agreement of the parties, cases could be removed from the counties in which they arose. In addition, the commissioners were concerned to maintain proper jurisdictional boundaries between the courts. Several of the orders published in the *Directions* dealt with the relationship between the common law and the ecclesiastical courts, including the laying down of guidelines for the granting of prohibitions, while others were devoted to the problem of maintaining the proper distinction between common law and equity as it was administered through the Irish Chancery.[8]

Although some of these problems, most notably partisan juries and the interference of the privy council, may have been seen by contemporaries as peculiar to Ireland, others, such as prohibitions and the relationship between common law and equity, were familiar in England as well. Indeed, by the time a new parliament met in 1624, Bishop Williams was in the process of becoming another victim to the controversies surrounding the English court of Chancery. To some extent, Williams's difficulties were purely political. Having been appointed a royal chaplain in addition to his other duties, he had become a close advisor of the king, but this involved him in machinations and quarrelling at court.[9] In 1622, he fell out with Middlesex over a pension he favoured granting to Bacon[10] and doubtless further alienated the lord treasurer by advising Buckingham to quash the findings of the Irish commissioners because they were liable to be detrimental to the duke's interest.[11] But Williams's position as a clerical head of the court of Chancery also made him vulnerable to enemies within the legal profession.[12] Although it is not clear what the common-law judges thought of him, he apparently avoided confrontations. Indeed, while sitting in Star Chamber he once went so far as to say that the English clergy had traditionally enjoyed only such privileges as they were allowed by the

---

[8] *His Maiesties Directions for the Ordering and Setling of the Courts, and Course of Justice, Within His Kingdome of Ireland* (Dublin, 1622).

[9] John Hacket, *Scrinia reserata: a Memorial Offer'd to the Great Deservings of John Williams, D. D. Who some time held the Places of Ld Keeper of the Great Seal of England, Ld Bishop of Lincoln, and Ld Archbishop of York* . . . . (1692), pp. 106, 108, 130ff; G. W. Thomas, 'Archbishop John Williams: politics and prerogative law 1621–1642' (Oxford University DPhil thesis, 1974), pp. 151, 187, 200, 205.

[10] Wynn Papers 1046: Owen Wynn to Sir John Wynn, November 1622. Hacket, *Scrinia reserata*, p. 105.

[11] Treadwell, *Buckingham in Ireland*, pp. 207, 216.   [12] *Clarendon*, i, §96.

secular courts,[13] and, according to his contemporary biographer, he thought that its dependence on the vague wording of the Act of Supremacy made High Commission a potential instrument of tyranny.[14] Judging from the letters of some of the Welshmen in his entourage, Williams worked long hours in Chancery and was successful in getting through even more business than Ellesmere had managed.[15] Nevertheless when parliament met in 1624, petitions concerning courts of justice included accusations that he took bribes,[16] and, while these came to nothing, bills were also forwarded that suggested he was using equity to encroach on the common law.[17] Following the death of James, to whom Williams ministered in his last hours, he lost favour with the duke of Buckingham and went quietly from office in 1625 under the face-saving pretext that he had only taken on the great seal for a probationary period of three years.[18]

The Forced Loan, the Five Knights and the Petition of Right

The fall of Williams removed at a stroke a potential source of disquiet between the common lawyers and the crown. His successor, Thomas Coventry, was the son of a judge, and as a young barrister he had been so closely connected with Coke that Francis Bacon wrote to the king in a futile attempt to prevent him becoming recorder of London in 1616. A year later he was knighted and became solicitor general before being promoted to attorney general in 1621.[19] By all accounts Coventry was an extremely able common lawyer with acute political instincts. Early in his tenure as lord keeper he presided over a case in Star Chamber in which disgruntled Chancery litigants, and their lawyers, were fined and imprisoned for slandering the court by entering a bill in which they claimed that Chancery was a mere spiritual court, which had no jurisdiction over property, but the case was almost certainly a residual legacy of Williams's term in office.[20] There appears to have been no significant conflict between Coventry and the common-law judges over the jurisdiction of Chancery, a point underlined by his referral of cases pending

---

[13] BL, MS Lansdowne 620, fol. 5.
[14] Hacket, *Scrinia reserata*, p. 97. Williams also shared an interest in early church history with his friend John Selden.
[15] Wynn Papers 1006, letter dated February 1622.
[16] SARS, DD/PH 216/66. Petitions concerning courts of justice, 1624.
[17] Wynn Papers 1198, 1206. According to the Wynns, Williams had done nothing that had not been done in Ellesmere's time.
[18] Wynn Papers 1379. Thomas, 'Archbishop John Williams', pp. 193, 205.   [19] *ODNB*.
[20] BL, MS Lansdowne 620, fol. 13.

before him to individual justices for their opinions or adjudication. On the other hand, his position, like that of Williams, was never completely insulated from political circumstances. It was, for example, rumoured in May 1627 that Coventry was going to be sacked and replaced by William Laud, then bishop of St David's, because of the hostility of Buckingham.[21] Hence, although Coventry was later said to have combined a clear 'conception' of the whole policy of government in church and state with an awareness of how this impacted on public opinion, he evidently chose not to speak up in meetings of the council where they were discussed.[22] This approach enabled him to hold on to the great seal until his death in 1640; at the same time, it may be a back-handed measure of his judicial impartiality that he was never granted the more elevated title of lord chancellor by the king. Nevertheless, despite Coventry's moderation, he almost immediately found himself in the middle of a series of controversies about the power of the king and the liberty of the subject that were played out in the courts as well as in parliament, a situation that was largely unprecedented over the course of the long period since the accession of Henry VII.

The power and patronage of the duke of Buckingham had been such a key feature in the political life of the nation since the late 1610s that there were few people who had not at one time or another been obliged to vie for his favour, and this included leading lawyers such as Coke and Coventry as well as courtiers, office-holders and country squires. Yet when the wars against Spain, and then France, that king Charles I and Buckingham embarked on in 1625 went badly, Buckingham's political enemies both in the council and in parliament began to target him. In 1626, Sir John Eliot and Sir Dudley Digges presented articles of impeachment in the House of Commons against the duke and were immediately imprisoned by the king for their pains.[23] In response, members of the House spoke out against the action, claiming that the arrest was a breach of the parliamentary privilege of freedom of speech. Notes made by Edward Littleton, a Shropshire lawyer and future lord keeper, indicate that he, and the parliamentary committee he sat on, supported claims for freedom of speech that went considerably further than that allowed by Queen Elizabeth, and which had so frustrated James Morice in 1593.[24] A draft petition that Littleton discussed with

---

[21] NCRO, Montague Letters, I, fol. 74. Robert Tanfield to Lord Montague.
[22] *Clarendon*, I, §96–8. Some of Coventry's official work can be followed in *A Calendar of the Docquets of Lord Keeper Coventry 1625–1640*, ed. J. Broadway, R. Cust and S. Roberts (List and Index Society, Special Series 34, 2004).
[23] C. Russell, *Parliaments and English Politics 1621–1629* (Oxford, 1979), ch. 5.
[24] Above, p. 109.

his friend John Selden insisted that it had been 'consistently held' in the past that the commons had enjoyed, and ought to continue to enjoy, freedom of speech concerning all business involving the commonwealth, including that touching the defence of the realm and the Church of England as well as the making of laws for redress of mischiefs and grievances. John Bankes, another future crown law officer, noted in the debates that the privileges of parliament were not granted by the king but were as ancient as the commonweal, and due by prescription.[25]

King Charles's response to the situation was to dismiss parliament early in the summer of 1626 in order to protect Buckingham.[26] He was, however, still in need of money in order to finance the war. In a political atmosphere that included a good deal of speculation about the future of parliament, a divided privy council agreed a plan for raising money through a series of (assessed) non-parliamentary loans to be made by the subjects to the crown. No one expected the money to be repaid, and the incentive for making the loan, or the force behind the 'Forced Loan', was the prospect that refusers would be called before the privy council in order to explain their reasons for failing to comply.[27] Although measures such as this were not entirely unprecedented (the last major example came from the time of Wolsey), and although the loan was largely successful in meeting its targets, the council accurately gauged that its collection would be met with resistance and several notable treatises were written by objectors to it who claimed that non-parliamentary levies of money were illegal.[28]

In anticipation of these arguments, and in order to encourage compliance, the judges were called before the privy council on 13 October 1626. The king opened the meeting by asking Chief Justice Sir Randolf Crewe to report any observations the judges may have made whilst riding the assize circuits about how 'the people' reacted to previous attempts to raise money. Charles then outlined the plan for the loan, and ordered them to pass on the news of it to the serjeants-at-law and the benchers of the inns of court, evidently in the expectation that the lawyers would provide a lead to the rest of the country.[29] According to

---

[25] CUL MS Mm. 6.62, fols. 90, 97. *Proceedings in Parliament 1626*, ed. W. B. Bidwell and M. Jansson (4 vols., New Haven, CT, 1991–6), II, p. 331.

[26] M. Kishlansky, 'Tyranny denied: Charles I, Attorney General Heath, and the Five Knights' case', *Historical Journal*, 42(1) (1999), 55–83, p. 59.

[27] Richard Cust, *The Forced Loan and English Politics, 1626–1628* (Oxford, 1987).

[28] Ibid., pp. 39–55, ch. 2. For more on gentry opposition, see below, pp. 301–3.

[29] NCRO, Letters to the Montague family, vol. 1, fol. 54. Robert Tanfield to Lord Montague, from the Temple, 18 October 1626, noted that the judges called the benchers of each inn before them at Lincoln's Inn and explained the council's 'pleasure' concerning the loan.

the first-hand account of Sir Richard Hutton, the judges were glad to agree to pay the loan themselves, but when they were asked two weeks later (26 October) for a written declaration of its legality, they refused, feeling that this might be taken as an authoritative ex-camera decision of a kind that had rarely been requested in such politically sensitive circumstances.[30] After negotiation with the council through Coventry, the judges eventually hit on a form of words that were intended to make it clear that while they themselves were willing to pay, this should not be taken as an 'example to others' about the legality of the measure. In response, Charles called in Crewe for an interview and dismissed him on the spot,[31] creating a 'cloude et storme', that, according to some reports, led the remaining judges to fear that the same thing would happen to them.[32] Invited to appear one-by-one before the lord keeper, they were encouraged to leave out the last part of the subscription because it hindered the king's service. According to Hutton, they were told that the king was not any longer demanding a judgment about the legality of the measure. Charles, said Coventry, did not want to involve them in anything that might compromise their oaths to uphold the laws of the realm, but the immediate needs of the state made the money necessary for the safety of the realm and its religion.[33]

In the event the remaining judges did not lose their places, but the loan, and the questions surrounding it, were widely discussed in legal circles and beyond.[34] Writing in his commonplace book, Sir James Whitelocke thanked God for the death of Sir John Davies, a supporter of impositions in 1610, who had been picked by the king as first choice to replace Crewe as the new chief justice.[35] A Star Chamber reporter recorded speeches by lords of the privy council in favour of the loan.[36] But, while it was whispered that Coventry had defected from the interest

---

[30] *The Diary of Sir Richard Hutton 1614–1639 with Related Texts*, ed. W. R. Prest (Selden Society, Supplementary Series, vol. 9, 1991), pp. 64ff.

[31] Ibid.; Prest, *Barristers*, p. 267. The episode is well told in S. R. Gardiner, *The History of England from the Accession of James I to the Outbreak of the Civil War, 1603–1642* (10 vols., 1886), VI, pp. 149–50.

[32] NCRO, Letters to the Montague family, vol. I, fol. 58. Robert Palmer to Montague, from the Middle Temple, 14 November 1626.

[33] *Diary of Sir Richard Hutton*, p. 64.

[34] Cust, *Forced Loan*, p. 87, notes that subsidy men in Hertfordshire eventually refused to subscribe because they were aware that the judges had declined to declare it legal.

[35] *Liber Famelicus of Sir James Whitelocke, a Judge of the Court of King's Bench in the Reigns of James I and Charles I*, ed. John Bruce (Camden Society, OS, vol. 70, 1858), p. 105.

[36] Folger MS V.b.70. Similar material, recorded in connection with the trial of the earl of Lincoln for writing a pamphlet against the loan, appears to have been scratched out in BL, MS Lansdowne 620, fol. 38, another version of the same reports.

of the 'commonwealth' to that of the court,[37] the profession as a whole, unlike some country squires, appears to have avoided open confrontation. George Radcliffe, a barrister of Gray's Inn and associate of Thomas Wentworth, was imprisoned in the Marshalsea for his refusal to contribute to the loan,[38] but speaking in Star Chamber, Coventry played this down. He said that all the judges of England had given voluntarily to the loan, and that there was only one 'mean and obscure' lawyer who had declared that the loan was against the law.[39]

Coventry attempted to keep questions about the legality of the loan out of the courts by advising that no formal action be taken against refusers, but eventually the need to silence opposition made this impossible.[40] In the autumn of 1627 five squires were imprisoned in the Marshalsea on the mandate of the king, but without charges being specified, following their refusal either to pay the loan, or to leave London as the king had ordered, and they subsequently brought writs of *habeas corpus* in the King's Bench requesting their release.[41] The counsel for the Five Knights, as they soon became known, included some of the most able lawyers of the day, John Selden, William Noy and Henry Calthorpe, but one of the knights, Sir Thomas Darnell, claimed in court that although he had asked many, he had not been able to find a lawyer willing to speak for him. The truth of this is hard to verify, but the new chief justice, Sir Nicholas Hyde, made a declaration that no lawyer would be penalised for acting, and John Bramston, himself a future chief justice who was already acting for Sir Arthur Havingham, was appointed for Darnell as he walked into Westminster Hall.

The hearing itself attracted a large crowd into court,[42] but although the political circumstances were exceptional, many of the legal issues were in some respects quite familiar to the lawyers of the time.[43] As we have seen, arrest by the council or queen, without charges being specified, was common enough in the time of Elizabeth, but at the same time since then the writ of *habeas corpus* had been increasingly employed in a wide range of cases by prisoners who questioned the circumstances of their arrest and imprisonment in all kinds of jurisdictions, including,

---

[37] Folger MS V.b.70, fol. 74.
[38] A Yorkshireman, Radcliffe flourished as a principal servant of Wentworth's during the 1630s. *ODNB*.
[39] BL, MS Lansdowne 620, fol. 38; Folger MS V.b.70, fol. 73v.
[40] Cust, *Forced Loan*, pp. 59–60.
[41] Kishlansky, 'Tyranny denied', p. 58, plausibly suggests that the object was to hold the knights without being drawn into a legal wrangle until the loan was collected. However, this may underestimate the extent to which the arrest was also supposed to provide a lesson to would-be refusers (*PP 1628*, II, 152).
[42] Kishlansky, 'Tyranny denied', p. 61.   [43] See above, p. 96.

of course, Chancery and the ecclesiastical courts.[44] Francis Ashley explored many of the relevant legal issues in a reading at the Middle Temple in 1616, and it appears to have been generally understood that the role of the writ in normal circumstances was to bring a prisoner before the judges so that they could consider the charge that had been brought against him, and then decide whether he should be bailed, re-committed to face trial, or released.[45]

The strategy of counsel therefore was to attack the legitimacy of the mandate of the king and counsel ('*per speciale mandatum domini regis*'), claiming that it was too general and uncertain to amount to a charge the judges could consider. The argument most lavish in its use of prece-dents, that of Henry Calthorpe, concluded that the king or council could not commit someone to prison without clearly stating the offence.[46] All of the lawyers for the knights made the rhetorical point that the writ of *habeas corpus* was the means by which the subject maintained his liberty, but Selden put the case at its most general while at the same time making a connection between the knights' case and more ordinary ones. He argued that the settled laws of the country, and especially Magna Carta (which he described as a statute), guaranteed that the subject could not be imprisoned without the cause being stated. While he accepted that there was some ambiguity in the words '*Nullus liber homo capiatur vel imprisonatur nisi per legem terrae*', he concluded that 'by the laws of the land' could only mean by due process as understood by the common law: that is by either presentment or indictment.[47]

Speaking for the crown, Attorney General Sir Robert Heath dismissed the precedents cited by Calthorpe and the others on the grounds that they applied only to ordinary judicature. Following the line of argument used by Fleming in *Bate's Case*, he drew a distinction between ordinary legal acts and that *absoluta potestas* exercised by a sovereign king. Although he acknowledged that this did not mean that the king could rule just as he pleased, he argued that while the subject had an interest in his liberty, the king also had an interest as sovereign in the commonwealth.

And sure I am, that the first stone of sovereignty was no sooner laid, but this power was given to the sovereign: if you ask me whether it be unlimited . . . I say it is not the question now in hand: but the common law, which hath long flourished under the government of our king and his progenitors . . . hath ever had that reverend respect for their sovereign as that it hath concluded the king can do no wrong.[48]

---

[44] The point was alluded to in some of the statements at the hearing. *ST*, iii, cols. 6, 38.
[45] See above, p. 156 and below, p. 420.
[46] *ST*, iii, cols. 19–29. The printed account of Calthorpe's remarks is substantially the same as that in his own 'select cases', BL, MS Hargrave 35, fols. 74ff.
[47] *ST*, iii, cols. 17ff.   [48] Ibid., col. 44.

He advised the knights that they could try petitioning the king for their release, and he also maintained that if the judges remanded them on this occasion, they would still be free to take out another writ later on.[49]

Evidently pressed for time, the judges' decision, which was delivered by Chief Justice Hyde, was brief, and maintained that they were following accepted practices by not making a judgment on the case, but delaying it.[50] According to Hyde, all of Calthorpe's precedents were irrelevant because in those instances where a charge was laid, the practice was indeed either to bail the prisoner, release him, or redeliver him to await trial. But in those cases where imprisonment had been ordered by the king or council without the charge being declared, all the precedents in their view showed that it was the practice to send the prisoner back to gaol to await further developments. If no cause of commitment was expressed, it was presumed to be for a matter of state, 'which we cannot take notice of'.[51] From the judges' point of view, their act was legally neutral insofar as no decision was made on whether to bail or not to bail, but the remand in effect maintained the distinction between an imprisonment by the crown and those that occurred during the ordinary course of justice.

As we have seen, while imprisonments of this kind had been made during the reign of Elizabeth, there was even then some doubt about their legality. In his reading on the royal prerogative in 1578, James Morice argued with characteristic certainty that the king could imprison for any cause, but that he was obliged to publish the charges, and let the subject be tried by his peers, according to law ('this is the Great Charter').[52] In 1592, the judges had expressed concern about political imprisonments, but had been more circumspect in allowing the crown the benefit of the doubt even though they were clear that imprisonment should not take place indefinitely without cause being shown.[53] Thus although it would be wrong to state that the power of the crown to imprison without cause had hitherto been completely uncontroversial,[54] the unanimous answer the judges gave to Charles I when he questioned them on the matter was certainly a reasonable account of the most

---

[49] Kishlansky, 'Tyranny denied', p. 62.
[50] For an account from the perspective of one of them see D. Powell, *Sir James White-locke's Liber Famelicus 1570–1632: Law and Politics in Early Stuart England* (Bern, 2000), pp. 131–4.
[51] *ST*, III, cols. 57.   [52] See above, p. 79.   [53] See above, p. 96.
[54] This is the opinion of Kishlansky, 'Tyranny denied', p. 62.

relevant past practice: 'the king may commit a subject without showing cause, for a convenient time'.[55]

The judges had in effect limited the scope and consequences of their decision as far as they possibly could; they did not deliver a judgment, they made a judicial order. But this strategy did not enable them to avoid controversy. The political reality was that the knights were being held in prison because they had failed to pay the loan. It was rumoured in London, and no doubt elsewhere, that the judges had ruled that the king could commit for not lending the money,[56] and this view was shared by leading parliament men such as Sir Robert Phelips, who began complaining about both the loan and imprisonment 'without remedy by law' as soon as the House of Commons met in March 1628.[57]

Even more so than was the case with impositions in 1610, the parliamentary debates about the disposition of the Five Knights for the most part repeated arguments that had already been heard in court. But the political climate was more intense in the late 1620s, not least because the legality of the Forced Loan itself, as well as questions about the introduction of martial law and billeting soldiers on the country, was also at issue at the same time.[58] Furthermore, the situation was inflamed when John Selden alleged in the House of Commons that Attorney General Heath had attempted to have the judicial order entered as a judgment in the records of the King's Bench so that it could serve thereafter as a precedent that the king could order the indefinite imprisonment of the subject without cause being shown.[59] This allegation undermined the claims of the crown's lawyers that the order was neither novel, final, or conclusive.[60] A few weeks after the opening of parliament, for example, Phelips said that while he was aware of the argument that the judges' action did not amount to a decision, the prospect of an entry once again threw the matter into doubt in his mind.[61] Following considerable debate in the lower House and two conferences with the Lords,

---

[55] Quoted by Kishlansky, ibid., p. 70, from *PP 1628*, VI, p. 47. There is an account of this in *Bramston*, pp. 40ff, which suggests that Charles was in fact not all that satisfied with the judges' decision.

[56] *PP 1628*, II, p. 152.   [57] Ibid., p. 212.

[58] L. Boynton, 'Martial law and the Petition of Right', *English Historical Review*, 79 (1964), 255–84. Coventry's speech at the opening of the parliament stressed that if subsidies were granted then there would be less pressure on the king to use other means: 'just and good kings, finding the Love of their people, and the reddinesse of their suppplyes, may the bettter forbear the use of their prerogatives, and moderate the rigor of their laws towards their subjects' (BL Harleian 37, fol. 209).

[59] This issue has been the subject of a detailed debate between Kishlansky, 'Tyranny denied', and John Guy, who originally raised it. See J. Guy, 'The origins of the Petition of Right reconsidered', *Historical Journal*, 25(2) (1982), 289–312.

[60] *PP 1628*, II, p. 203–4.   [61] Ibid., p. 212.

the king's councillors, including the duke of Buckingham, agreed to an unprecedented motion that the judges should be called before the Lords to explain what they had done.[62]

Aware that he and his colleagues were again being subjected to unusual levels of political scrutiny, Chief Justice Hyde at first expressed doubts about whether they should appear without the permission of the king, to whom they were 'sworn truly [to] account . . . in body, lands, and goods'.[63] But after some debate, several of them gave an account of their proceedings to the Lords as a matter of courtesy. They confirmed their view that the prisoners had merely been remanded until they were formally charged, or until they applied again for release, but a couple of them did elaborate a little more fully. Dodderidge expressed the view that the imperial crown of England was held of none but God, and that judicature flowed from this relationship, but he also made much of the point that the proceedings had involved the hearing of counsel at the bar, and that the decision had been reached in public.[64] In a statement that may have appeared baffling, Justice Jones noted that he had been 'pro liberties' in his time in Ireland, and that he was no less obliged to follow his conscience in English affairs. His oath of office required that he serve both king and commonwealth. He was not willing to advance the king's prerogative against his conscience, or to court popularity by wronging the king.[65]

Given the previous intimidation of the judges over the question of the legality of the Forced Loan, it is difficult to be certain exactly where they stood on the imprisonment of the knights, but it is unlikely that they wanted anything other than the most narrow construction to be put on their decision.[66] When he was called before the House of Lords to explain the entry made on the King's Bench record, the official concerned, John Keeling,[67] the clerk of the crown, confirmed that though Attorney General Heath visited him often, he had obeyed the strict instructions given him by Justice Jones, which were that nothing should be entered except the legal phrase *remitter*, which recorded that the knights had been remanded into custody, but which stated nothing more by way of decision.[68] The King's Bench judges were not censured by parliament, and in the end the validity of their legal position was to some degree acknowledged. In the Commons, Sir Edward Coke movingly described his own discomfiture when he had been imprisoned by the

---

[62] *PP 1628*, v, pp. 204–5.
[63] Ibid., p. 218. There is no mention of this episode in Hyde's commonplace book, BL MS Hargrave 247.
[64] *PP 1628*, v, p. 230.   [65] Ibid.   [66] Powell, *Sir James Whitelocke*, pp. 130–1.
[67] *PP 1628*, v, pp. 229–30.   [68] Ibid.

king's mandate at the end of the parliament of 1621, but he was nevertheless obliged to explain away decisions he had made during his tenure as a judge that could be construed as supporting the king's position, even admitting that he had previously misunderstood the treatment of the subject that had been given by William Stanford in his work on pleas of the crown.[69] As it happened, furthermore, a son of the late Chief Justice Sir Edmund Anderson was a loan refuser, and he had a fair copy of the late Elizabethan paper on imprisonment that was widely circulated.[70] But this was, of course, an ambiguous precedent. It was mentioned by Heath in his submission for the king during the trial,[71] and a very plausible gloss was put on it by Sir Francis Ashley when he spoke to the royal brief in the House of Lords.

Arguably one of the greatest living experts on the subject of unlawful imprisonment,[72] Ashley drew attention to a practical procedural issue that troubled many, including some of those who spoke against the detention of the knights. Everyone realised that JPs and constables found themselves from time to time in circumstances where it was necessary to imprison a suspected malefactor before charges could be brought. On the broader question, moreover, he fell back on some well-worn arguments about the nature of *lex terrae* that had been expressed by no less an authority than Coke in *Caudry's Case*.[73] The common law and statutes like Magna Carta were not the sole components of the law of the land. Referring to his lecture of 1616, he said that he had shown then that there was also a law of state, when necessity of state required it.[74] It was clear to him that in cases of state government, the king or his counsel had lawful power to punish without showing particular cause, where to do otherwise might tend to the disclosure of secrets of state.[75]

As against this, the position Selden and Edward Littleton put forward in both the King's Bench and parliament, which was that it was impossible for *lex terrae* to include anything other than common law and statutes such as Magna Carta, was the more novel of the two,[76] but there was of course a powerful polemical attraction in an argument that made the predicament of the knights a 'fundamental point of personal

---

[69] *PP 1628*, III, p. 150.
[70] It is, for example, included in a collection of parliamentary materials connected with the case in BL, MS Harleian 37, fols. 112ff.
[71] *ST*, III, col. 44.
[72] He referred directly to the fact that many people knew of his earlier labours concerning the liberty of the subject. *PP 1628*, v, p. 284.
[73] See above, p. 119.   [74] See below, p. 420.   [75] *PP 1628*, v, pp. 218–84.
[76] See also, [William Hudson], 'A treatise of the Court of Star Chamber' in *Collectanea Juridica. Consisting of Tracts Relative to the Law and Constitution of England* (2 vols., n.d.), ed. Francis Hargrave, II, p. 4.

liberty'.[77] No less important, the Forced Loan and the Five Knights were not the only grievances members of parliament brought with them from the provinces to London in 1628. During the interludes between military campaigns abroad, large numbers of soldiers had been billeted on the countryside, and a declaration of martial law had been extended to cover civilian populations as well as the troops. Although this subject did not make much impact on legal sources outside parliament, largely because it seems not to have been tested in the courts, lawyer MPs were amongst the most vocal critics of martial law in parliament. For example, speaking before a committee of the whole House on 16 April 1628, the future attorney general John Bankes maintained that questions about the legality of martial law were questions about the life and physical well-being of the subject. He acknowledged that kings had prerogatives just as subjects had their liberties, but claimed that these did not include the power to make commissions of martial law that were unanswerable to the common-law courts: 'The ocean itself bounds itself within its bounds.' Clearly referring to the familiar subject of the relationship between the common-law judges and the church courts, as well as their dealings with the councils in the north and Wales, he pointed out that prohibitions were used regularly by the King's Bench to regulate other jurisdictions. The king by a commission under the great seal could not alter the common law.[78]

There is no better summary of the general political situation in 1628 than the remarks of Ashley as he was concluding his speech before the House of Lords on the *Five Knights' Case* and *habeas corpus*. In his view the debate resolved itself onto the horns of an unsatisfactory dilemma.

> If the subject prevail, [he gains] liberty but loses the benefit of that state government without which a monarchy may too soon become an anarchy; or, if the state prevail, it gains absolute sovereignty but loses the subjects, not their subjection (for obedience we must yeild, though nothing be left us but prayers and tears); but it loses the best part of them, which is their affections, whereby sovereignty is established and the crown firmly fixed on his royal head.[79]

Given the gravity of the question, Ashley recommended moderation and compromise, but this was not easily achieved. Parliament resolved

---

[77] Rough notes made by the earl of Bridgewater on the parliamentary discussion of the issues on 20 March 1628 associate the name of Littleton with 'personal liberty' and 'magna carta'. Lord Saye and Sele is mentioned in conjunction with the phrase 'fundamental point of personal liberty'. HEHL, MSS Ellesmere 7785–6.

[78] *PP 1628*, II, p. 481.

[79] *PP 1628*, V, p. 284. Ashley was censured by the House of Lords for introducing this opinion on the grounds that it went beyond what had been asked of him.

that if the liberties of the subject did not already exist as part of the law of the land then they would make them so by passing a statute that clarified the question. Proposals were made for a statute confirming Magna Carta, an idea that had many precedents in English history both in the distant past and more recently. As Coke and others were fond of pointing out, the Great Charter had had up to thirty previous confirmations, and, as we have seen, similar legislation was put forward by James Morice in 1593 and had been revived again in the first decade of the seventeenth century in connection with the powers exercised by High Commission.[80] In 1628, however, it quickly became evident that King Charles was unwilling to agree this course of action, and in response Coke proposed that the House of Commons should draft a Petition of Right that could be presented to the king for his assent.[81] This called for Charles to acknowledge that the Great Charter was still in force; that no tax or tallage could be levied without parliament; that martial law was illegal; and that no man could be imprisoned, outlawed, or disseised of his freehold, liberties, or free customs except after judgment by his peers or according to the law of the land.

The king, however, remained reluctant to give ground or acknowledge the petition, and the critical issue was still the question of his power to imprison without showing cause. According to Attorney General Heath, Charles had been the driving force behind the effort to have a 'judgment' to show for the remand of the Five Knights, and the king continued in his efforts to get a more definitive opinion on the matter out of the judges. Chief Justice Hyde and Sir Thomas Richardson, the chief justice of the Common Pleas, were invited to a private audience with the king just two days before the Lords agreed to send him the petition of the '*liberties del people*'. At this meeting he ordered them to assemble the other judges and secretly produce written answers to three questions: whether the king could commit a subject without cause in 'any case whatsoever'; whether the judges should release a prisoner who brought a *habeas corpus* after being imprisoned without cause showing before they 'understood' the cause from the king; and whether, if the king granted the Petition of Right, he would 'conclude' himself from committing or restraining a subject for any time or cause whatsoever without showing cause. Their answer to the first two questions was essentially the same, and hardly broke new ground. As a general rule of law, the cause of commitment ought to be shown, but in some cases 'secrecie' might

---

[80] See above, p. 108. In fact, Heath mentioned Morice's bill in his submission to the House of Lords, ibid., pp. 273–4.
[81] Russell, *Parliaments and English Politics*, pp. 369, 389.

require the king to commit for a 'convenient time' without showing cause. Their answer to the third question, though somewhat ambiguous, appears to acknowledge that in granting the petition, as it was currently worded, the king and parliament would in effect be making a new law indistinguishable from statute. If that was the situation, then a specific case would need to be brought before the question could be determined in court.[82]

Although the judges' third answer offered the encouraging, if enigmatic, view that the granting of the petition should not lead to 'feare of conclusion as is intimated in the question', it would seem fair to say that their emphasis on the importance of secrecy, and a 'convenient time', might well have put limits on royal actions that would probably have made it difficult to detain prisoners like the knights for any length of time without showing cause. In any case, despite their advice not to fear the granting of the petition, Charles was very reluctant to do so. On 2 June he issued a written statement maintaining that he willed right to be done according to the laws and customs of the realm and agreeing that his prerogative required him to protect the just rights and liberties of the subjects. When the Houses 'conceited this answer' not to be full and satisfactory, they asked that the king come in person to the House to make his response. On 7 June Charles maintained that he thought his previous answer had been satisfactory, but asked the clerk to read the petition and replied in Norman French 'soit droit fuit come est desirer', the medieval formula used for the royal assent to a statute.[83]

Seditious speech

The royal acknowledgment of the Petition of Right, which was widely celebrated around the country by the lighting of bonfires, was a momentous point in constitutional history, and in some respects it marked a successful assertion of limitations on the authority of the crown. In the short term at least, martial law and the levy of money by unparliamentary means were discontinued. However, as the earlier arrest of Digges and Eliot in 1626 and the subsequent imprisonment of the Five Knights indicated, the events of the last four years of the 1620s that touched most dramatically on the liberty of the person, as opposed to that of his property, were concerned mainly with the extent to which government

---

[82] What appears to be Hyde's account of these events is given in BL, MS Hargrave 27, fols. 105–6v. *Bramston*, p. 48, gives a similar account. See also J. Reeve, 'The legal status of the Petition of Right', *Historical Journal*, 29 (1986), 260–61.

[83] BL, MS Hargrave 27, fol. 106v.

ministers, or government policy itself, might be discussed and criticised, and where and in what circumstances this might or might not be possible. The king's consultation with the judges in connection with the Forced Loan was aimed primarily at obtaining a declaration of the measure's legality, one that was necessitated in part by the fact that it was known that criticisms of the loan, some of them in writing, were circulating in London and the localities. In this respect, although the Five Knights were targeted because of their opposition to the loan, and the prospect that this would become widely known if they remained in London, the notable feature of their case was precisely that the crown evidently could not identify evidence of any offence for which they could be charged. This was unusual because royal paranoia about public opinion did result in charges being brought in several other cases at about the same time, and this tendency was exacerbated by the implied demand in the Petition of Right that henceforth they should be.

Although many of the most notable cases concerning the limits of political speech were connected with events in parliament, by no means all of them were. Furthermore, it is worth keeping in mind that throughout early modern society the limits of acceptable speech were set a good deal more narrowly than they are today, even though the boundaries were constantly being tested and defined.[84] Given this background, it is difficult to be certain whether or not there was an increase in defamatory political speech during the later 1620s, but contemporaries thought there had been.[85] A taste of the climate in the second half of the decade is provided by the Star Chamber prosecution in Michaelmas 1627 of a group of alehouse musicians (fiddlers) from Hertfordshire who confessed to having sung a series of satirical songs that were critical of the 'state', the king and the privy council in general, but of the duke of Buckingham in particular. In presenting the case to the court, Attorney General Heath described libels as the 'epidemic disease' of the day.

The musicians were initially fined the large sum of £500, even though they did not write the verses themselves. But since they were poor men it was decided that it would be more appropriate for them to be whipped and pilloried in Cheapside and at Ware (Hertfordshire). In the course of his judgment, Chief Justice Richardson noted that such libels created bad feeling between king and people. He recalled a case from the time of Henry VII in which a libeller had been hung for treason, and he hoped

---

[84] See below, pp. 391ff, for a fuller discussion.
[85] A. Fox, 'Ballads, libels and popular ridicule in Jacobean England', *Past and Present*, 145 (1994), 47–83; see also N. Mears, *Queenship and Political Discourse in the Elizabethan Realms* (Cambridge, 2005), ch. 6.

the punishment of the musicians at Ware, a key stopping point on the Great North Road, would cause the news of it to spread into the north and north-west. Interestingly, however, Lord Keeper Coventry's remarks pursued a much lower key. He suggested that the traditional method of dealing with such cases had been for them to be punished in manorial leet courts.[86] Acknowledging that these had much decayed in recent years, he went on to indicate that the most suitable course of action in the future would be for the assize judges to alert JPs to the need to keep an eye out for similar incidents. By suggesting that this would be a 'readier' way of approaching the problem than bringing bills in Star Chamber, he was on the one hand relegating such libels into the realm of a minor communal jurisdiction, and on the other suggesting that they should be handled locally where juries would presumably have been left to decide whether a breach of the peace had occurred or not.[87]

Coventry may have been trying to avoid making a political meal out of what he suspected might become a flood of similar incidents in the localities, but his moderation was not universally shared. When a servant of the earl of Lincoln was charged in Star Chamber with distributing letters thought to have been written by the earl himself (who was imprisoned), which encouraged non-payment of the Forced Loan, Bishops William Laud and Richard Neile reportedly argued that political dissidence expressed in words or writing amounted to treason.[88] Soon afterwards, Heath asked the judges for an extrajudicial decision about whether a charge of treason could be brought against a Somerset squire, Hugh Pine, who was reported to have made disparaging remarks about the king during a conversation within his own house, one of which was that the king was less fit for his job than Pine's elderly shepherd. After reviewing a long list of precedents relating to indictments for treason from the reign of Henry IV to the end of Henry VIII's, the judges declared that however 'wicked' the words were, they did not amount to treason. The king's death had not been imagined according to the treason statute then in force, that of Edward III. Justice Yelverton pointed out that it had already been decided in *Peacham's Case* that to charge the king with a personal vice, 'that he was the greatest whore-monger and drunkard in the kingdom', was not treason, a decision which clearly drew a distinction between a slander and the more serious offence.[89]

Yet if 'wicked words' about the king or government were not trea-sonous, they could still be punished in Star Chamber as libels. In 1630,

---

[86] See below, pp. 256ff.   [87] BL, MS Lansdowne 620, fols. 50–1.
[88] Ibid., fol. 38.   [89] *ST*, III, cols. 359, 368.

Dr Alexander Leighton, a Scottish clergyman, was sentenced to a fine of £10,000 and life imprisonment at the pleasure of the king for publishing and distributing a book addressed to the 1628–9 parliament that attacked episcopacy as 'antichristian and satanical', appeared to commend the recent assassination of Buckingham, and slandered the king and his government in connection with its powers to make laws for the church. Although Leighton claimed that he was merely bringing grievances in church and state to the attention of parliament, the fact that five or six hundred copies of the book were published and the vehemence of his language led the two chief justices to comment that he was lucky he was being tried in Star Chamber because they would have been inclined to find him guilty of treason if he had been tried at common law.[90] At the same time, less obviously incendiary words were also punished severely. In mid 1629, Chief Justice Hyde reported that one John Maude was fined £5,000 for bruiting it about that the king went to mass with the queen, and at about the same time the merchant Richard Chambers was fined and imprisoned by Star Chamber for saying during an audience before the privy council that English merchants were more screwed for customs duties payable to the king than those of Turkey.[91] Comparing an English government with Oriental despotism was indeed a profound insult in contemporary terms, but although he was certainly combative, Chambers subsequently claimed that he was talking about the customs officials rather than the king's government as a whole. Nevertheless, even though he had not spoken the words in public, the court decided that he should be fined and imprisoned as an example to others.[92]

By this time, furthermore, questions about dissident words and actions had once again become an issue in the relationship between the king and parliament. On 2 March 1629, Sir John Eliot, John Selden, William Strode, Walter Long and several others disrupted the adjournment of parliament that had been ordered by the king by holding the speaker, Sir John Finch, down in his chair while a vote was taken on a protestation of the House against popery, the rise of Arminianism, and the collection of tonnage and poundage not granted by parliament.[93] The offending MPs were ordered the next day to appear before the council, and the judges were once again called on to deliver an opinion about what actions might be taken against them. Hyde, Richardson, Chief Baron Walter and several others were supplied with a written account of what had

---

[90] Ibid., cols. 353–6.   [91] BL, MS Hargrave 27, fol. 121v.

[92] HEHL, MS Ellesmere 7901 contains material on the case that does not appear in the account of it given in *ST*. The Star Chamber bill against Chambers mentioned that his insolence and disobedience might become a dangerous example.

[93] *ST*, III, col. 236.

happened in parliament and told to meet with Attorney General Heath and other crown lawyers to answer questions about the case.[94]

In their response the judges confirmed that the king had the power to call, dissolve and adjourn parliament, but they were more circumspect when it came to offering an opinion about exactly how this should be done, a technical matter that had added to the confusion on the day of the disrupted proceedings. They also 'humbly conceived' that 'earnest though disorderly and confused' proceedings in the House might be called 'tumultuous', and yet be warranted by the privileges of parliament. On the other hand, they were clear that MPs could be punished out of parliament (by some other court) if they offended the king 'criminally or contemptuously in the parliament house'. But they were unwilling to define the offences of conspiring to defame the king's government, and delivering the subjects from obeying or assisting the king, without considering the circumstances. Not satisfied with this answer, the king wrote back to them in his own hand saying in essence that he wanted them to state, or name, the offence the MPs had committed, but the judges reiterated that they could not give further answers until more of the particulars of the case were known.[95]

After they returned to London following the Lent assizes (25 April), the judges were once again asked a similar set of questions, but on this occasion the focus was primarily on the case the crown was building against Sir John Eliot, who had made a speech prior to the disrupted adjournment in which he stated that the king was led by ill counsel, that the lord treasurer was the leader of the country's papists, and that the privy council and the judges had conspired to trample on the liberties of parliament and the people. Given the aspersions it cast on themselves, the judges not surprisingly responded that they disliked the speech and thought it went beyond what was acceptable in a parliamentary proceeding, but they declined to go any further than this because they anticipated, quite rightly, that the matter would probably come before them in a judicial proceeding. In addition, although they were clear that actions and words done or spoken in parliament could be tried outside parliament, they advised against proceeding *ore tenus* in Star Chamber because the rules of the court did not allow counsel to be heard in such proceedings, and they thought it important that there should be expert argument on the points of law at issue.[96]

---

[94] BL, MS Hargrave 27, fol. 117v.   [95] Ibid., fols. 117v–18.
[96] Ibid., fol. 119v–21. They are also asked about *Strode's Case* (from the time of Henry VIII), which involved an Act of parliament exonerating Strode and others for anything they said in parliament.

Not long after this, the imprisoned MPs brought writs of *habeas corpus* to obtain their release from prison, and the Petition of Right figured strongly in the arguments made on their behalf by counsel.[97] Although the warrants ordering the arrest of the members specified that they were committed at the pleasure of the king for 'notable contempts' against 'our self and our government, and for stirring up sedition against us', Richard Aske and Robert Mason, the counsel for Strode and Long, maintained that these returns were too general to amount to charges within the terms demanded in the Petition of Right, and even if they did, the offences were not felonious crimes of the sort that could justify the withholding of bail. Introducing a point developed by those who spoke after him, Aske remarked that he could find no evidence in 'our books' of sedition, except when it was used 'adjectively as in seditious books or seditious news'. Mason drove the point home by stating that sedition was not a 'determined offence within our law . . . there is no crime in our law called Sedition'.[98] Arguing for John Selden, and no doubt having consulted with him, Edward Littleton employed a barrage of etymological arguments in support of the same point, but he concentrated on showing that whatever else it was, sedition was not treason. Nor was it any other variety of capital offence that could justify denial of bail.[99]

Speaking for the king and against the granting of bail, the future judge Robert Berkeley stressed, on the other hand, that the cause of the imprisonment was specific enough to satisfy the Petition of Right, and though he did not press hard for the point that sedition amounted to treason, he claimed that it was a 'special offence'. It was perfectly justifiable to hold in prison those who had made themselves into 'incendiaries of the state'. It was after all justifiable to pull down the house next door to a house that was already on fire to prevent the harm from spreading further.[100] According to Attorney General Heath, who elaborated on the medical metaphor he had used in the case of the fiddlers of Ware, 'A seditious man is as a madman, in the public state of the Commonwealth, and therefore ought to be restrained' in the same way as lepers were restrained in order to prevent the spread of the disease. 'The infection of Sedition is as dangerous as any of these diseases, therefore it is not safe to let seditious men to bail or at liberty . . . in dangerous cases, the wisest way is to make all safe.'[101]

---

[97] *ST*, III, cols. 235ff.   [98] Ibid., col. 242.
[99] Ibid., cols. 252, 254, 260. Littleton's argument, written in his own hand, is contained in his notebook of parliamentary precedents. CUL, MS Mm.6.63, fol. 96.
[100] *ST*, III, cols. 247–50.   [101] Ibid., col. 284.

The king delayed the proceedings over the summer of 1629 by refusing to allow the prisoners to appear before the court on the first day appointed for the delivery of a judgment. But, despite further efforts to lobby them,[102] the judges made it clear at the beginning of the following Michaelmas Term that they accepted the argument that the MPs were not guilty of any capital offence, and that they should therefore be bailed, 'giving security for their good behaviour'. The king was so annoyed with resistance to his policies that had been expressed by the chief baron of the exchequer, Sir John Walter, that he ordered him to stop acting as a judge.[103] Nevertheless, Charles eventually expressed himself willing both to desist from further proceedings in Star Chamber and to see the prisoners bailed, even though they had not apologised.

At this point, however, the prisoners declared themselves dissatisfied with the compromise. Though content to be bailed, they all agreed that they could not accept being bound for their 'good behaviour'. At the hearing, Selden argued that such a course implied that they were guilty of the offences charged against them, and that this amounted to an offence against parliament. Walter Long, who initially found sureties, renounced them, noting that the sum involved, £2,000, was a large one, and that the 'good behaviour was a ticklish point'.[104] Since the giving of sureties of the kind requested was well established as standard legal procedure prior to hearings in all kinds of cases, the MPs were deliberately standing on a technicality in order to make a point.[105] Clearly considering themselves political prisoners, Selden and the others stayed in gaol until they were released in the 1630s.

Much the same happened to three of the MPs, Eliot, Valentine and Holles, against whom formal charges were brought in King's Bench for 'publically and maliciously' raising sedition between the king, nobles and people, with attention focusing specifically on the speech of Eliot's that accused the council and the judges of conspiring to trample

---

[102] Ibid., 287–8. According to James Whitelocke's son, Bulstrode Whitelocke, *Memorials of English Affairs* (1682 edn), p. 13, they were 'somewhat perplexed' about the case of the parliament men and wrote the king before the adjournment saying that they intended to bail them, but their letter was blocked by Coventry, who nevertheless invited them to another audience before the king. Bulstrode also claimed that his father often complained against the way in which the judges were constantly being asked their opinion before cases were heard (p. 11).

[103] The differences between Walter and the king in fact went back to the *Five Knights' Case*. See *ODNB*.

[104] *ST*, III, cols. 289–90.

[105] HALS, MS Gorhambury XII. B. 25. A defence of Justice George Croke's actions during this period that was prepared for delivery in the Long Parliament noted that if the king had not been judged entitled to bind those charged to good behaviour, then he would have been in a weaker position than the meanest of his subjects.

underfoot the liberties of the subject.[106] Presenting the case for the crown, Heath, described the offences themselves as 'mutinous' and, while he acknowledged that MPs could present grievances in a parliamentary manner, he maintained that they could not move things that tended to the distraction of the king and his government.[107] As against this, the accused and their counsel claimed that only parliament could judge them, and therefore pleaded against the jurisdiction of King's Bench rather than defending against the offence itself. Mason, who acted as assigned[108] counsel for Eliot, maintained that the deliberations of parliament were like those of the court leet or a grand jury; they were to be kept secret and not passed on to third parties such as the king and council before they saw fit to reveal them. Since parliament was a high court, MPs could make accusations there in the same way as accusations were made in the normal course of law. For example, if a man exhibited articles before JPs, the person he accused could not have an action on the case for slander even if the articles contained abuses and misdemeanours. If parliamentary privilege was limited, then MPs would find it impossible to put forward grievances without fear of imprisonment. Consequently, the role of parliament as a great council would be undermined.[109]

On the critical point of jurisdiction, however, the judges were clear that the defendants had no case. Although everyone accepted that parliament was the higher court, they were able to draw on analogies with other jurisdictions, such as the relationship between assizes and quarter sessions, which made it fairly easy to argue that an offence committed in a higher court could be tried in a lower one if the superior tribunal was no longer in session. Furthermore, although the judges accepted that MPs had privileges, they saw these in exactly the same way as they saw those accorded themselves as judges. If an action went beyond what was acceptable conduct for the office, then there was a liability to legal action. Finally, there were precedents from the mid-Tudor and Elizabethan period, which they took to provide unqualified support for their position.[110]

Ruling that by challenging the jurisdiction, the defendants had in effect confessed the offences, the judges declared that most of Mason's points about the limits of speech in parliament were irrelevant. Once they had determined that they had jurisdiction, they found Eliot and the others guilty by default. Even Justice George Croke, who was later

---

[106] The king decided not to proceed in Star Chamber.   [107] *ST*, III, cols. 204–5.
[108] BL, MS Hargrave 24, fol. 12v.   [109] Ibid.; *ST*, III, cols. 295–9.
[110] Ibid., cols. 306, 309.

revered for ruling against the legality of Ship Money, held that the offence in question had not been done in a 'parliamentary course, but it was done manuforti, ilicite et seditiose'.[111] He appears to have been thinking particularly of the action of holding the speaker in his chair to prevent the dissolution, and he expressed the same concern as the others, which was that if the offence went unpunished because parliament had been dissolved, then there was a danger of a failure of justice.

Given the extreme nature of Eliot's speech, which included accusing the lord treasurer of heading an army of papists, and the use of force in holding the speaker in his chair, even parliamentary partisans may well have thought the king had a plausible case. As Mason admitted, Eliot's words would certainly have warranted an action for slander at common law or libel in Star Chamber if they had been spoken outside parliament. His strongest point was probably the one that the deliberations of courts should be secret, but of course by the end of the 1620s what was said in parliament already had a broader circulation through news books or manuscript separates. In any case, it was also true that most early modern jurisdictions from the court leet to the meetings of town councils, or trade guilds, took it upon themselves to lay down rules and regulations for what they considered legitimate and proper speech.[112]

Dissidence and paranoia

The 1620s have in recent years become a problematic decade for students of political and constitutional history. While older Whiggish interpretations tended to depict the debates in parliament and the famous law cases that went with them as landmarks on the high road to civil war, 'revisionist historians' of the late twentieth century were inclined instead to downplay their long-term significance by suggesting that despite serious disagreements, there was relatively little linkage in the underlying issues that lay behind events, and that nothing pointed inevitably to the political crisis that was just over a decade away. At the same time, while many modern historians subscribe to the view that the common law was increasingly seen as providing the ideological foundation for 'constitutionalist' opposition to the crown in an age of increasing political awareness, others point out that in the late 1620s the manipulation and vacillation of the judges were perhaps more likely to have proven to contemporaries that reliance on the courts might not be an adequate means of resolving anxiety about the liberties and property of the subject – a point that marked the beginning of the marginalisation

---

[111] BL, MS Hargrave 24, fol. 27v.   [112] See below, pp. 391–9.

of the common law in the most serious political debates for the remainder of the century.

Viewed largely from the inside of the legal world, there would appear to be both an element of truth and an element of error in nearly all of these propositions. Justice Jones's commissions in Ireland reflected a general vision of the rule of the common law in the British Isles that went back at least as far as the reign of Elizabeth, and which was in some form or another echoed in the localities in hundreds of public speeches to freeholders and subsidy men. At the same time, since the accession of James I in 1603, a series of questions had been raised about the king's relationship to English law, but the Stuarts were able in most instances to maintain their supremacy. The loss of the great seal by Bishop Williams, and his replacement by Coventry, resolved one the areas of potential disagreement, but while King Charles felt the need to legitimate his policies and actions with judicial approval, he put unprecedented pressure on the bench in order to gain it. The dismissal of Sir Randolf Crewe, and the sequestration of Chief Baron Walter, undoubtedly left a lasting mark on the judges themselves, if no one else. In 1630 Sir George Croke made a memorandum of Walter's death, which praised his courage and integrity in not surrendering his patent when told by the king that he should stop exercising his office. But while Croke noted that Walter had stood on the terms of his appointment, *quamdiu se bene gesserit*, he also observed that it now appeared to be the case that all of the judges in fact held their positions *durante bene placito regis*, 'so they are determinable at the king's pleasure'.[113]

Nevertheless, to say that either the judges or the common law itself were completely subservient to the crown would also be misleading. They held their own over the Forced Loan. The position they took on the *habeas corpus* of the Five Knights was justified by precedent. As the earlier controversies over High Commission and the ecclesiastical courts had demonstrated, the common lawyers had not, *pace* what Littleton and others said in the late 1620s, established that *lex terrae*, the law of the land, included only common-law procedures and determinations by the common-law courts. Yet though there was a large political price to pay in terms of trust between the king and the people, the Petition of Right appeared to secure the point through a resounding appeal to a plausible account of native legal traditions.

The judges also managed on the whole to distinguish between sedition and treason, but what is most striking about dissident words in the 1620s is less their novelty than the vehemence of the dissidents and the

---

[113] *CroCar*, 778.

paranoia of the crown. While Elizabethan parliament men such as James Morice were evidently willing to accept periods of arrest by order of the council, despite his own opinion that it was illegal in those circumstances where no charges were laid, his Caroline successors were not.[114] In part, this is attributable to the changed political circumstances, the unpopularity of the war, the Forced Loan and martial law, but it was also a product of more mundane changes in legal practices. If the evolution of the law of libel and slander lent a degree of plausibility to the crown's position in the cases of seditious libel, so the development of the use of the writ of *habeas corpus* in connection with High Commission as well as secular jurisdictions made it an obvious tool for resisting arbitrary arrest by the crown. As Justice Dodderidge pointed out, it was important that the cases heard came before open courts where the points of law were debated by counsel. It is clear that large audiences were often present and that the lawyers' briefs enjoyed a fairly wide manuscript circulation, which made the arguments available to those who were not there in person. Furthermore, the 'political prisoners' of the 1620s had long memories. Many of their cases were resurrected and reviewed in the early stages of the Long Parliament.[115]

Of course, crown prosecutions against those who wrote or spoke against great officers of state were nothing new. In 1603, for example, Ellesmere made a point of warning assize judges and JPs that they should be particularly vigilant in seeking out maintainers and movers of sedition, in particular deprived clergymen who spoke or wrote against the ecclesiastical authorities.[116] But it would appear from the repeated remarks of Attorney General Heath that royal anxiety about dissident words misleading or stirring the people reached new levels in the late 1620s, and it is also evident that the prosecution of libels began to raise questions about precisely how far legitimate grievances against the government or its officers should be made known. In notes he made while sitting as a judge in Star Chamber in 1630 at the trial of the bookseller Bonham Norton, who alleged that he had bribed Lord Keeper Coventry in connection with a Chancery case, Ellesmere's son, the earl of Bridgewater, expressed concern about the breeding of dislikes between the king and his people, yet he also felt bound to say that his view of Norton's punishment would have been far different if the allegations had been true, because greatness of place could not excuse miscarriages or misdemeanours by officials.[117] In the same year, a JP and Exchequer official called Long was unsuccessful in bringing an

---

[114] See above, p. 109.   [115] See below, p. 229.
[116] Baildon, *Cases in Camera Stellata*, p. 186.   [117] HEHL, MS Ellesmere 7950.

action of slander against someone who had delivered a petition against him to the House of Commons, and while the decision against him held that it was legitimate to make accusations in parliament that could not be made elsewhere, it is easy enough given the times to see why Long thought that he might have been successful.[118]

In the end, there is probably no better illustration of the political and legal climate at the end of the decade than the case brought in Star Chamber in 1630 against the earl of Bedford, the earl of Clare, the earl of Somerset, Sir Robert Cotton, John Selden, Oliver St John and several others for the possession and alleged distribution of a short manuscript treatise entitled 'A proposition for his Majesty's Service to Bridle the Impertinence of Parliaments', which had apparently been written (probably in Italy) by Sir Robert Dudley sometime in the reign of James I. The tract itself may or may not have been composed as a satire rather than a serious piece of political advice, but it is an unusually good example of how contemporaries imagined tyranny. Disclaiming any suggestion that parliament should be suppressed outright, it described ways of bridling the subjects through the garrisoning of soldiers in towns and restrictions on the movement of people. It also recommended that there should be a universal oath acknowledging that the king of England was as 'absolute a king and monarch' within his dominions as any Christian ruler, and it proposed that royal proclamations could be used to make laws without the consent of parliament. The second half suggested that royal revenue might be increased by taking fines for the licences of inns and alehouses, taxing lawyers' fees and the sale of land, and making office-holders pay a proportion of their income to the crown.[119]

In bringing the case for the king, Attorney General Heath stressed that the elevated quality of the defendants aggravated their offence, because the multitude of people were likely to be led by those of whom they thought well. During the course of the hearing Lord Keeper Coventry repeated the by now familiar point that if the meanest subject could have an action of slander, the king was entitled to no less, and Chief Justice Richardson recommended that a commission should be established to search the study of Sir Robert Cotton for additional material.[120] The defendants claimed, on the other hand, that they possessed copies of the tract purely for its curiosity-value, and maintained that they had no intention of publishing it more widely. Bedford in particular expressed loyalty to the crown and stated his conviction that the king did not intend any innovations of the sort Dudley had suggested. In the event,

---

[118] BL, MS Hargrave 30, fol. 251v. *Longe and Dowells Case* (1630).
[119] *ST*, III, cols. 387–98.   [120] Folger, MS X.d.337, fol. 2.

Charles I personally ordered the charges dropped in celebration of the birth of his first son, but the remarkable point about the episode is the fact that the king and his law officers clearly thought it likely that large numbers of subjects would readily believe that proposals such as those contained in the libel were being seriously considered for implementation.[121]

---

[121] Cf. R. Cust, 'Charles I and popularity' in T. Cogswell, R. Cust and P. Lake, eds., *Politics, Religion and Popularity in Early Stuart Britain* (Cambridge, 2002).

8   The degeneration of civil society into a state of war 1629–1642

Subjects or slaves?

Writing within the privacy of his study in the 1610s, Sir Anthony Benn concluded that there was no need to worry that strong monarchical government would lead to tyranny. All the 'hartburning and the quarrell' in his day was about nothing more than 'money tribute, taxes and impositions'. It was not about 'our lives, nor our liberties, nor that our sonnes are to be made slaves'.[1] One wonders, therefore, how he would have described the later 1620s, when according to many a speech in parliament, and a fair number of courtroom briefs, the liberty of the subject was in great peril.[2] Indeed, one of the most recurring rhetorical devices in the parliamentary debates of 1628 and 1629 probed the heart of the relationship between subjects and monarchical states: a people whose property could be taken from them at the will of the monarch were slaves, not subjects. Or, to put it in tenurial terms familiar in English land law, they were serfs or villeins rather than free tenants whose rights to property were protected by law.[3]

First enunciated in a parliamentary setting during the Impositions debates, by the late 1620s this formula was as likely to fall from the lips of laymen such as Sir Dudley Digges as it was from lawyer MPs such as Sir Edward Coke.[4] Although it can be found in works within the English legal tradition such as *Bracton*, it was probably more familiar outside the courtroom than within it. Implicit in the works of authors such as Cicero, Tacitus and Livy, which had become such important sources for general political discourse in England, it is also found in continental works informed by Roman civil law, which explained the relationship

---

[1] BLAS, L28/49.
[2] 'Though our liberties have bene in fact invaded, yet they may revive in time.' HRO, MS 44M69, L 23/1, fol. 1v.
[3] See below, p. 348.   [4] *PP 1628*, II, pp. 64, 66, 358; III, pp. 358, 494.

between jurisdiction and authority.[5] Slaves, like unfree tenants, were subject to arbitrary jurisdiction over which they had no control. Their lives and property were determined by the will of a lord rather than by law.

According to Professor Skinner, the idea that freedom was preferable to slavery or subjection was often associated in the seventeenth century with republican forms of government,[6] yet while this appears often to have been implicit in Elizabethan legal writing, it is not a connection that arises consistently or unambiguously in the surviving legal discourse of the late 1620s or 1630s, which produced little in the way of systematically thought-out analyses of the forms of government such as James Whitelocke had enunciated in 1610.[7] Instead, it would seem that the most common way of looking at the relationship between freedom and slavery was in terms that evidently owed a great deal to the French jurist Bodin, the writer on 'absolutism', who nevertheless distinguished between a legal monarchy, where property rights were secured by law, and a lordly, or regal monarchy, essentially a tyranny, where they were not.[8]

The distinction is central to understanding the legal life of the Personal Rule because it made it possible to maintain familiar arguments about the rule of law as a civic value, while not requiring clear-cut answers to more difficult questions about where sovereignty, or ultimate authority, in the state lay. Furthermore, a logical consequence of the distinction between a legal and a lordly monarchy was that a government that could show itself to be acting legally could not justifiably be accused of tyranny. Hence, many of the policies of the Personal Rule had a legal dimension, and judicial decisions became the focus of political controversy in a way that was unprecedented, even taking into account the reign of Henry VIII, or the turbulent times of Queen Mary.

From the perspective of the crown and leading ministers such as Thomas Wentworth and William Laud, the 1630s were about reforming church and state. But, unwilling to call a parliament, the king was also desperately short of money while the Thirty Years' War was raging in Europe, and there was growing controversy between the English and the Dutch about the narrow seas that separated them. The tension between

---

[5] See, for instance, T. Boccalini, *The New-found Politicke Disclosing the Secret Natures and Dispositions as Well of Private Persons as of Statesmen and Courtiers . . . .* (1626), which praises Tacitus because he gave the people the power to see the true intention of princes.

[6] Quentin Skinner, *Liberty before Liberalism* (Cambridge, 1998), pp. 38–41.

[7] See above, p. 139.

[8] *The Six Bookes of a Commonweale: a Facsimile Reprint of the English Translation of 1606 Corrected and Supplemented in the Light of a New Comparison with the French and Latin Texts*, ed. Kenneth D. McRae (Cambridge, MA, 1962), esp. pp. 199–201, 210–12.

the crown's ambitions and its limited ability to finance them sharpened distinctions between the public good and private interests, and that between ordinary acts of government and those necessitated by the king's responsibility for the welfare of the realm. No less than Sir Anthony Benn, Caroline crown lawyers accepted that one of the roles of the state was to safeguard the private interests of individuals, but they also maintained that 'necessities of state' justified actions, or financial levies, which put the public interest first. One of their more effective points was that private selfishness was a systemic cause of a lack of sufficient concern amongst the subjects for the public good, and much of the government rhetoric in the 1630s had a reforming gloss that may well have had a positive purchase outside Whitehall. For example, an historical work on the reign of King Alfred published by a Somerset attorney, Robert Powell, described the Saxon king as a state-builder who united the warring kingdoms of Britain under a new set of institutions (hundreds, shires, leet courts and so on) and laws. Acknowledging that Charles I had not yet achieved so much, Powell nevertheless declared great expectations of him as a reforming king: 'where there are such glorious sovereigns, would it not well become their people to be gracious subjects'.[9]

Maintaining a reforming regime that was interested at the same time in raising revenue did not necessarily imply that there should be any fundamental alteration in the way the 'constitution' and political institutions were conceptualised. But Archbishop Laud's religious policy was accompanied by such an unambiguously high view of the royal supremacy over the church that the 1630s proved to be a critical phase in the ongoing process of integrating the ecclesiastical polity into the English state.[10] At the same time, in the absence of parliament, the realisation of secular reform depended on the prerogative power of the crown,[11] and it was accompanied within court circles by constitutional position papers that went so far as to propose the subordination of the liberty and property of the subject to the prerogative in a way that was only a little less extreme than that floated in Sir Robert Dudley's 'advice'.[12] For instance, the Irish lawyer and projector John Cusacke argued that the common law had been made by the king in the same way that Roman

---

[9] Robert Powell, *The Life of Alfred or Alured: the first Institutior of Subordinate Government in this Kingdome, and Refounder of the Vniversity of Oxford. Together with a Parallell of our Soveraigne Lord, K Charles* . . . (1634), pp. A5, 70, 67ff, 130, 153.

[10] See above, pp. 97ff.

[11] See also, P. Slack, *From Reformation to Improvement: Public Welfare in Early Modern England* (Oxford, 1998).

[12] Above, p. 188.

law had been the pronouncement of Roman emperors.[13] His conclusion was that the prerogative powers of the crown could be used both to shape social policy and to augment royal revenue, and in this respect, his work, like the Dudley Libel itself, does reflect some of the policies of the Personal Rule, namely attempts to raise money by taking fines from landholders worth £40 p.a. who had not taken up knighthoods, the resurrection of the forest laws, and dozens of more modest 'projects' that were invariably clothed in the language of the public interest while at the same time promising profit for the crown as well as those suggesting them.

Projects

Yet while there was an unmistakable effort to present an acceptable face of English absolutism in the 1630s, views as extreme as Cusacke's were rarely used to justify the fiscal expedients of the Personal Rule, most of which were based directly on the resurrection of measures that had been used in the past, and many of which were founded on interpretations of the prerogative powers of the crown that were very difficult to challenge at law. The immediate background to the Caroline fiscal expedients appears to have lain in a position paper produced early in 1629 by the keeper of the records in the Tower, Sir John Borough, at the request of Sir Julius Caesar, which concentrated on the way King Edward I had exploited the royal forests and financed wars through the distraint of knighthood.[14] The implementation of the measures fell to the prominent common lawyers, William Noy, John Bankes and Edward Littleton. All three had played a notable part in parliamentary opposition in the 1620s, but, perhaps for slightly different reasons, all were willing to take up employment for the crown in the 1630s.

Noy, who was appointed attorney general in 1631, was apparently close to Laud, and quickly became unpopular amongst Puritans for prosecuting William Prynne's attack on the theatres, *Histriomatix*, and for supporting the publication of the Caroline *Book of Sports*, which permitted parishioners to play games on a Sunday rather than spending all day on religious exercises.[15] Littleton, who was a close friend of John

---

[13] Bankes Papers, 48/13: discourse by John Cusacke showing that the king of England by his prerogative without an Act of parliament may compel his subjects to give way to his royal design for the improvement of their lands. See also L. L. Peck, 'Beyond the Pale: John Cusacke and the language of absolutism in early Stuart Britain', *Historical Journal*, 41(1), (1998), 121–49.

[14] BL, MS Additional 34324, fols. 269ff.

[15] W. J. Jones, ' "The Great Gamaliel of the law". Mr Attorney Noye', *Huntington Library Quarterly*, 40(2) (1977), 197–226; Nehemiah Wallington, *Historical Notices of Events*

Selden, was widely considered the most deeply learned practitioner of his day. The descendant of a long line of lawyers, including Sir Thomas, the author of the fifteenth-century *Tenures*, he may have seen royal advancement as the best way of achieving his aim of becoming chief justice of the Common Pleas, but he also appears to have been sympathetic to the pursuit of a more assertive foreign policy.[16] Bankes's early professional life is more obscure than that of the other two, but he profited the most conspicuously from royal office. The post of attorney general was worth £10,000 a year when he took it over on Noy's death in 1634, and the proceeds enabled Bankes to buy Corfe Castle on the Isle of Purbeck from the estranged widow of Sir Edward Coke.[17]

Noy and Bankes were doubtless able to see the royal revenue problem within the context of more general landlord/tenant relations over the past century or so in which landowners of all kinds employed any legal advantage they could find in order to increase their income.[18] Henry VII had, of course, attempted to raise money in this way, and while there seems to have been a relaxation under Elizabeth, James I's cash-starved government undertook the more effective exploitation of crown lands, including the duchies of Cornwall and the crown estates in Wales.[19] In this respect it is relevant that Noy, and to a lesser extent Littleton, had acted as advocates both for and against the king in the Exchequer,[20] the principal revenue court of the crown, and Bankes was a long-time legal advisor to the northern magnate Lord Howard of Naworth.

A feature of early modern land law was that it often involved historical questions about custom and long usage.[21] Yet although the financial expedients of the Personal Rule are often described as 'fiscal feudalism', and although the word 'feudal' was sometimes employed in the 1630s, the phrase itself is an anachronism, and technically misleading, since there was no systematic attempt to assert that England was a feudal monarchy, or, indeed, that it ever had been. For example, in *Stevens's Case*, which was brought in 1631 as a legal challenge to the levy of fines on those with lands valued at more than £40 p.a., but who failed to become knights, Littleton, who was employed by the plaintiff and not yet in the king's service, admitted that historical sources and records in the Tower

---

Occurring Chiefly in the Reign of Charles I (2 vols., 1869), I, pp. 64–8; P. Kopperman, *Sir Robert Heath 1575–1649: Window on an Age* (1989), p. 242.
[16] *ODNB*.   [17] *ODNB*.   [18] See below, pp. 345ff.
[19] R. W. Hoyle, ed., *The Estates of the English Crown, 1558–1640* (Cambridge, 1992). Although written many years earlier at the request of Lord Buckhurst, James I's lord treasurer, Sir John Doddridge's *History of the Ancient and Modern Estate of the Pricipality of Wales, Dutchy of Cornewall, and Earldome of Chester* was published in 1630.
[20] BL MS Hargrave 30.   [21] See below, pp. 344ff.

showed that the right to levy such fines 'had been used by kings in all ages'. Clearly aware of the unpopularity of the measure, the presiding baron of the Exchequer, Sir Thomas Trevor, expanded the point further. Like his obligation to exercise wardship in order to look after the heirs of tenants-in-chief, the king had a common-law 'duty to compell them that are of ability to come and defend the realm'. Even the 'strictest men of Parliament will confesse . . . that the king ought to be mainteyned'. However, while Trevor concluded that 'noe gentleman should think themselves Champions for the country by taking away any Right from the king', he also went out of his way to deny that knighthood fines were a 'feudal' imposition.[22]

Compared to knighthood fines, which involved the resurrection of obligations that had hardly been mentioned for several hundred years, the crown's rights in connection with royal forests were such a venerable feature of legal learning that it is surprising they had not been more effectively exploited before the reign of Charles I. There was a widely circulated early sixteenth-century law lecture on Edward I's charter of the forest, and the subject was an ongoing spare-time hobby of the Elizabethan recorder of London, William Fleetwood.[23] Following these footsteps, the barrister John Manwood published a treatise on the laws of the forest in 1598, which was reprinted and enlarged in 1615. Tracing them back to the time of King Canute, Manwood, like his predecessors, maintained that royal rights in the forest were princely prerogatives associated with the special needs of kings for recreation that would offer relief from the heavy burdens of office.[24]

A critical implication of these accounts was that the forest laws were unquestionably outside, or completely apart from, the competence of the common law, set and enforced solely by the will of the king. They also describe how the forest laws had subsequently either gone completely out of use, or how the courts (or 'justice seats') that claimed jurisdiction under them were used merely for the self-government of local communities. In either case, the interests of the crown had been neglected while incursions had been made on the bounds of royal forests, either by those who cut timber in them or by those who built cottages or otherwise appropriated royal land. Furthermore, while Fleetwood seems merely to have commented on this fact, Manwood, who was a justice of the New Forest, dedicated his work to Charles Howard, the earl of Nottingham, the courtier who held the position of chief justice of the

---

[22] Bodleian, MS Tanner 288, fols. 90–6, 112v, 120v–5.   [23] See below, pp. 344–5.
[24] J. Manwood, *A Treatise of the Lawes of the Forest: Wherein is declared not onely those Lawes, as they are now in force, but also the originall and beginning of Forests . . .* (1615), pp. iiii–vi.

Forest Eyre south of the Trent, and pointed out that 'spoils and trespasses' were taking place daily to the detriment of the king's interest.[25]

In 1629 the then attorney general Sir Robert Heath brought an
Exchequer case against a man called Harris for cutting timber in the
Forest of Dean and converting it to charcoal for use in local iron works,
contrary to a statute passed against such transactions in 1560.[26] In this
case, Noy argued unsuccessfully for the defendant, but, having taken
over the attorney generalship himself, he soon moved on from using a
penal statute to relying on the prerogative powers of the crown to exploit
its rights when he ordered an inquest to be held for Windsor Forest.
Working alongside him, Sir John Finch, who had spoken for the king in
Harris's Case, then elaborated this approach further in connection with
an investigation of the Forest of Dean in 1633 and 1634. The procedures employed in this and subsequent cases involved calling a meeting of
the forest court in the name of the king, pressuring juries to make presentments of encroachments, and then levying fines. Defendants could
justify their encroachment by claiming and proving earlier licences, or by
showing that their holdings had been accepted in earlier deforestations,
but these could be countered by evidence produced for the crown.
Although it is clear that some of them consulted lawyers,[27] it was quickly
ruled that defendants could not have recourse to the common-law courts
because the royal forests were outside the remit of the common law. In
the case of the Forest of Dean some 800 presentments led to fines
totalling £130,000, though considerably less than this was collected.[28]

Although the enforcement of the forest laws was undoubtedly inspired
by revenue considerations, crown lawyers attempted to justify it, and
defuse hostility, by claiming that the process served a greater public
purpose. A memorandum that may have been drawn up by Bankes in
connection with a commission appointed to investigate royal forests
in Yorkshire, Nottinghamshire and Derbyshire included advice to the
presiding officers about how to deflect objections. The best reply to
anyone who said that the proceedings trenched on the liberties of the
forests was that the commissions were in fact acting to repair and

---

[25] Ibid., Dedication, p. iv.   [26] BL, MS Hargrave 30, fol. 266v. Trinity 1629.
[27] A letter from Noy to the assize judges, dated 10 March 1631 (o/s), refers to a suit at
Worcester assizes concerning an action of barratry that had been brought by the
inhabitants of Bewdley against Thomas Howard because he presented bills against them
in the Exchequer for wastes done to the king's wood. Whitelocke Papers, vol. v, p. 209.
[28] George Hammersley, 'The revival of the Forest Laws under Charles I', *History*,
45 (1960), 85–102. Proceedings in connection with the Forest of Dean are recorded in
BL, MS Harleian 4850. The cases are reported in *Les reports de Sir William Jones
chevalier . . .* (1672), pp. 266ff, 347ff.

preserve them. 'Legal and just' the commissions would be approved of by parliament (if one were sitting). They promised speedy profits to the king, but they would also be a source of 'content to the people'.[29]

This same mixture of policy and venality also characterised other legal measures that became defining features of the Personal Rule, namely the use of the prerogative power of the crown to make grants through letters patent for the regulation of certain trades, and the utilisation of royal commissions under the great seal to undertake reforms or enforce penal laws. Policies of this kind had long been features of early modern government, and in some respects the 1630s represent a logical, if not necessarily popular, conclusion to long-term developments. Queen Elizabeth made grants of patents of monopoly to individual courtiers that in effect enabled them to profit by establishing measures, mostly in the form of fines, to 'regulate' trades such as the boiling of starch, the manufacture of playing cards, or the importation of German wines.[30] Evidently seen primarily as a way of providing patronage to supporters of the regime, the Elizabethan patents were sometimes garnished with claims that they had been created for the public good, but they were unpopular amongst the tradesmen caught in their web. They were also generally criticised by the lawyers, and a steady record of parliamentary opposition was concluded in 1624 with the passage of a Statute of Monopolies, the most notable feature of which was an attempt to limit grants primarily to those who invented or instituted new trades or industrial processes.[31]

However, the statute contained many loopholes, including some that recognised the long-standing delegation of jurisdictional powers by charters of incorporation to groups of tradesmen in order to regulate trades through guilds or companies, a practice that was both acknowledged at common law and an essential part of the social and economic fabric of many large or medium-sized towns.[32] Taking advantage of these openings, Attorney General Noy, who had been a leading opponent of monopolies in the 1620s, oversaw the grant of a notorious patent to a group of Catholic courtiers (the soapers of Westminster), who were incorporated in 1632 to manufacture a new kind of soap, and who were given at the same time powers to inspect the wares of other London producers, which in effect controlled their trade.[33] Faced with protests, Noy brought a Star Chamber prosecution against sixteen London manufacturers that resulted in fines of as much as £1,000 each

---

[29] Bankes Papers, 16/7.   [30] P. Williams, *The Tudor Regime* (Oxford, 1979), ch. 5.
[31] See below, p. 387. 21 James I, c. 3.   [32] See below, pp. 386–90.
[33] K. Sharpe, *The Personal Rule of Charles I* (1992), pp. 121–2.

being levied against them.[34] Furthermore, the Westminster soapers' patent was replaced in 1637 by another one which in effect incorporated all of the soapmakers in England, including the opposers.[35] Allegedly designed to maintain the good government of the trade and to ensure the price and quality of the soap made available to the public, a key feature of the grant was that London production was to be tightly controlled and the king would receive a levy of £8 for every ton of soap manufactured.[36]

As the extensive archive that has survived from Bankes's tenure as attorney general testifies, deals of this kind became fairly common in the later 1630s, and many of them directly reflected the traditional language found in grants of corporate status to guilds, or livery companies, as they were known in London.[37] In fact, many of them were a response to the economic diversification that had accompanied London's dramatic growth over the past century, which had resulted by the 1630s in the flourishing of new occupations that were not subject to traditional company regulation. Evidently instigated by groups of such tradesmen, there are a dozen proposals in the Bankes papers for new London companies, including those for Combmakers, Glass-sellers, Distillers, Musicians, Gunmakers, Pinmakers, Brick- and Tilemakers and Vintners.[38] In addition, since a sizable proportion of this demographic and economic change took place in the suburbs to the south of the Thames and west of Temple Bar, areas that fell largely outside the jurisdictional reach of the City within the walls and its livery companies, there was also a proposal in 1636 for a charter of incorporation for all the trades practised in the suburbs within three miles of the City.[39] Accompanied by the creation of governing bodies with powers to discipline members, and to make searches, the grants normally claimed that the company had been proposed in order to secure better government of the trade and to prohibit the sale of faulty wares to consumers, but most of them also included a novel ingredient, which was that in return for making the grant, the king could expect to receive an annual payment of between £500 and £1,000.

Alongside grants of corporate powers of this kind for the ongoing regulation of trades, the other principal tools available to Tudor and Stuart governments for the implementation of reform were the use of letters patent either to appoint commissions to investigate abuses or to

---

[34] *Articles of Accusation Exhibited by the Commons House of Parliament now assembled Against Sir John Bramston . . . Sir Robert Berkley . . . Sir Francis Crawley . . . Sir Humphrey Davenport . . . Sir Richard Weston . . . Sir Thomas Trevor . . . .* (1641), pp. 2–3.
[35] Several of them were forgiven their Star Chamber fines. Bankes Papers, 12/9.
[36] Ibid. There was also a £40,000 compensation package for the Westminster soapers.
[37] See below, pp. 386–91.   [38] Bankes Papers, 12/14, 19, 20, 24, 25, 33; 50/9.
[39] Ibid., 9/6, 12/46.

erect new offices created with the promise of improving administration. Cardinal Wolsey had appointed commissions in the 1520s to investigate the conversion of arable land to pasture, the erection of enclosures, and the resulting rural depopulation thought to have resulted from them. Commissions were also a regular feature of Elizabethan government, and in fact very good illustrations of the processes involved can be drawn from the legal system.[40] As bureaucratic problems arose in the wake of the increase in litigation, 'projectors' brought forward proposals that would remedy the abuses in return for being granted a new office, the fees of which they would be permitted to enjoy. At the same time, from the late 1590s onwards commissions were appointed on a regular basis to investigate increases in court fees, which were the cause of ongoing public complaint. Including major figures such as William Noy and John Selden, the Caroline commissions collected enormous amounts of information. They may well have helped to prevent excessive increases in the cost of litigation, but they also exemplify another feature of this method of reform that had become common by the 1630s, which was that once abuses were identified, the perpetrators were threatened with prosecution (usually in Star Chamber), but then allowed to make a 'composition' with the crown, involving the payment of a cash sum, in return for which they could continue to levy the increased fees.[41]

Amongst the commissions and offices dealt with by Bankes from 1634 onwards, some may have been judged useful but others must have seemed little more than vexatious. It is, for example, hard to imagine much public enthusiasm for the commission to investigate the decline of archery and the increase in unlawful games, especially since archery had long since gone out of use as a pastime.[42] On the other hand, a proposal for regulating dovecotes quite correctly pointed out that there was no provision at common law for controlling them in places where they caused nuisances that could not be brought before manorial courts.[43] Both Bankes and Solicitor General Littleton supported a commission for the more effective execution of writs of excommunication, the most severe sanction of the ecclesiastical courts,[44] and Bankes concluded that a proposal for enumerating the number of foreigners in London, and granting them licences to take up lodgings, was agreeable to the 'old Roman law called *Lex peregrinaria*', and to the 'modern rules' of policy and sound government pursued in other countries.[45]

---

[40] Williams, *Tudor Regime*, ch. 12.   [41] Brooks, *Pettyfoggers and Vipers*, chs. 6–7.
[42] Bankes Papers, 17/37.   [43] Ibid., 17/36, and see below, p. 267.
[44] Ibid., 17/25. This proposal had originally been put forward in 1627, but not then pursued by the projector.
[45] Ibid., 6/12.

It is an interesting comment on early modern legal sensibilities that Sir Edward Coke thought that a Jacobean scheme similar to this last one would 'infer a terror',[46] which would at the same time lead to retaliatory measures being taken against Englishmen by other states, but in comparison with some of the 'modern' measures, other Caroline commissions aimed to apply traditional solutions to traditional social problems, most notably the decay of tillage due to enclosure and depopulation, and the hoarding of foodstuffs by forstallers and engrossers. Although these commissions, no less than those aimed at seeking out defective titles, must ultimately have been of little consequence because the policy of compounding permitted offenders to continue with their existing practices so long as they paid the king for a licence to do so, they could attract the support of contemporaries, and evidently caught the attention of the gentry.[47] Having himself participated in an enclosure commission in Wiltshire, for example, Robert Powell published a tract in 1636 which argued eloquently that depopulation and the decay of tillage undermined the quality of the nation's population. It made people thriftless and idle, causing 'them [to become] aliens and strangers to their national government', while at the same time weakening the tax base and straining the resources available for poor relief.[48]

Since interests of the commonwealth had precedence over the estates of individuals, Powell concluded that the king had 'full and absolute power to award commissions for the welfare of the kingdom'. Nevertheless, the overall contemporary verdict on the use of prerogative powers in this way during the 1630s, and the projects in particular, was perhaps best summed up by the future royalist Nicholas Culpeper during the early stages of the Long Parliament. 'These, like the frogs of Egypt, have got possession of our dwellings, and we have scarce a room free from them: they sup in our cup, they dip in our dish, they sit by our fire; we find them in the dye-vat, wash-bowl, and powdering-tub; . . . they have marked and sealed us from head to foot.'[49] According to Edward Hyde's retrospective evaluation, projects of all kinds had taken as much as £200,000 p.a. from the king's subjects, but scarcely £1,500 of that came into the hands of the king.[50]

---

[46] 12 *CoRep*, 116: *Walter Chute's Case.*   [47] Sharpe, *Personal Rule*, pp. 471–3.

[48] *Depopulation Arraigned, Convicted and Condemned by the Lawes of God and Man: a Treatise Necessary in these Times by R. P. of Wells, one of the Societie of New Inne* (1636), pp. 4, 42–3, 45, 61. There is a dedication to Bankes.

[49] Quoted in J. R. Tanner, *English Constitutional Conflicts of the Seventeenth Century* (1962 edn), p. 76.

[50] *Clarendon*, I, §148.

Ship Money

Although major Caroline schemes such as those associated with the forests, and a large-scale 'project' to drain the fens in Lincolnshire led to considerable local discontent, many of them were merely irritating rather than *causes célèbres*.[51] The fate of John Waller, a haberdasher who had to chase around London in order to recover a number of hats that had been wrongly confiscated from his warehouse by people claiming to have been acting for the Corporation of Beavermakers, is a fair measure of their impact.[52] By comparison, the most well-known revenue-raising measure of the Personal Rule, the extension of the levy known as Ship Money to inland as well as maritime counties, on a regular basis reached much more systematically into the pockets of people all over the country. It led to one of the longest hearings in early modern legal history, and at the same time obliged the judiciary to say exactly where they stood with regard to the king's claims on the property of his subjects.

Like the other financial measures, Ship Money began with an acknowledged right of the crown. It was uncontroversial that the king could make levies on coastal towns to provide ships for maintaining the royal dominion over the seas. Ship Money had been collected with little protest during the wartime years of Elizabeth's reign. The council contemplated a revival of the levy, including an extension of it to inland as well coastal areas, in the late 1620s. The significant innovation of the 1630s was, therefore, the decision to carry through the policy, including the provisions for making collections across the entire country. The justification was that the king's duty to defend the realm entitled him to make such a levy in those circumstances where, in his opinion, the safety and welfare of the country was in danger. The writs issued in 1635 mentioned pirates as the immediate threat, but the king and his councillors almost certainly had wider strategic issues in mind.[53] The Thirty Years' War was raging, the king's brother-in-law, Louis XIII of France, was building up his navy, and the English were becoming increasingly aware of commercial rivalry with the Dutch, a matter with significant jurisprudential ramifications. In response to the claims of the Dutch jurist Hugo Grotius that the seas were a free territory outside the jurisdiction of any land-based power, in 1635 John Selden published his *Mare clausum*, an argument that states could exercise dominion over the

---

[51] L. Lindley, *Fenland Riots and the English Revolution* (1982); B. Sharp, *In Contempt of all Authority: Rural Artisans and Riot in the West of England 1586–1660* (1980), ch. 8.

[52] Bankes Papers, 63/2.

[53] R. J. W. Swales, 'The Ship Money levy of 1628', *Bulletin of the Institute of Historical Research*, 50 (1977), 164–76, Sharpe, *Personal Rule*, pp. 545ff; *CSPD 1634–5*, p. 100.

seas which bordered their shores.[54] Edward Littleton, who spoke for the king at the Ship Money trial, conferred with Selden while it was being heard,[55] and at least one common lawyer, the future judge David Jenkins, later said that he thought Selden's work had been in itself a justification for making the levy.[56]

According to a letter written in 1637 by Archbishop Laud, the law officers were less involved with the formulation of the policy than with its detailed implementation.[57] In July 1634, just weeks before his death, Noy, Lord Keeper Coventry and Bankes had a meeting to discuss the 'King's great business for guarding the seas'. Although Noy was concerned at this stage that efforts should be made to encourage 'persons of quality' to voluntarily participate in order to add 'lustre to the business', their discussions were primarily about finding the best ways of framing the writs and how the assessments were to be made.[58] Bankes undertook to search records in Chancery, but it is unlikely that extensive collections of precedents were made, or that detailed legal arguments were composed, prior to the test case of the matter that was eventually heard in 1637.

Assessed repeatedly over a period of years during which the king declined to call a parliament, Ship Money reached further down the social scale than most contemporary taxation because local officials were expected to collect the amounts demanded by assessing individual householders. Historians debate the overall success of the levy, but there was certainly hostility to it in London as early as 1635 and 1636, as well as recalcitrance in the localities.[59] At the same time, a fair number of resisters resorted to legal process, usually in the form of writs taken out against collectors who attempted to distrain property in order to enforce payment.[60] Against this background, and wishing to prevent litigation arising from

---

[54] The work had been written in the reign of James I. There were rumours at the time that Selden, who had recently been released from prison, was about to make a reconciliation with the king. HMC, *Report on the Manuscripts of R. R. Hastings of the Manor House, Ashby de la Zouche* (4 vols., 1928–47), II p. 77.

[55] LI, MS Hale 12, contains autograph notes by Selden. Littleton also consulted with Selden about the implementation of the forest laws and about knighthood fines.

[56] Oleg M. Roslak, 'John Selden and the laws of England: jurisprudence and constitutional theory, 1584–1654', (Cambridge University PhD thesis, 1999), p. 83.

[57] *The Works of William Laud* (57 vols., Library of Anglo-Catholic Theology, 1847), VII, p. 333.

[58] *CSPD 1634–5*, pp. 161, 234.

[59] William Knowler, *The Earl of Strafforde's Letters and Dispatches, with an Essay towards his Life by Sir George Radcliffe* (1739), p. 359. Thomas Gerrard to Wentworth, 11 January 1635, notes that the City lawyers were called before the lords and were admonished to take heed how they advised the city in a case so clear for the king. Henrik Langelüddecke, ' "I finde all men & my officers all soe unwilling": the collection of Ship Money, 1635–1640', *Journal of British Studies*, 46 (2007), 509–42.

[60] Joan R. Kent, *The English Village Constable 1580–1642* (Oxford, 1986), pp. 162, 246.

the erroneous opinions of his subjects, Charles decided in February 1637 to ask 'his' judges to provide a written opinion about its legality.[61]

In response to specific questions, the judges' collective response was that where the good and safety of the kingdom was concerned, the king could command his subjects to provide ships for such time as he 'shall think fit', and they added that the king was the 'sole Judge both of the danger and when and how the same is to be prevented and avoyded'.[62] Addressing them as they were about to depart for the assize circuits on 14 February, Coventry explained that the king had decided their opinion should be published in all parts of the kingdom, and that they had cause to declare it with 'joy' that in so high a point of sovereignty the king had consulted with them.[63] Despite this publicity, however, the judicial opinion failed to quiet discontent, and although the judges had previously refused to hear cases in connection with the measure, in August 1637 the king permitted a writ to be issued against a Buckinghamshire gentleman, John Hampden, for his failure to pay his assessment of 20 shillings.[64]

The wide-ranging arguments presented by the lawyers in Hampden's case included abstract considerations of the limits of the rule of law but, since the questions raised were for the most part novel to the Tudor and Stuart periods, there were also heroic references to records stretching back to pre-Conquest times, moves that were in fact unusual in common or garden litigation. Hampden's counsel, Robert Holborne and Oliver St John, began traditionally enough by maintaining that the levy was unlawful because it breached both Magna Carta and the Petition of Right, which were taken to uphold the principal that the king could not take the property of the subject without the consent of parliament. On the other hand, Bankes and Littleton, speaking for the crown, acknowledged that the statute 1 Edward III, c. 5 appeared to prohibit novel charges being laid on the subject for defence, but maintained that there could be exceptions when there were was a sudden 'necessity'. They then produced precedents from pre-Conquest times which demonstrated obligations to defend the realm, 'as well with ships as otherwise when need shall require . . . in case of common necessity'.[65] In other words,

---

[61] *CSPD 1636–8*, pp. 412–17 (2 February 1636/7).

[62] Ibid., p. 418. For the discussions of the judges amongst themselves, see below, p. 206.

[63] Ibid. Writing from Whitehall, a North correspondent noted the public-relations aspect of this. 'The Judges with one consent haue declared their opinion that his Ma[jes]ties demand of Ship-money is according to law & he the sole & lawfull Judge wher it is fit to be don. This was published the last day of the Term in the Star Chamber & ordered to be entred in all Courts of Justice & made knowne openly at the next Assizes in euery County.' Bodleian, MS North C4, fol. 22.

[64] Sharpe, *Personal Rule*, pp. 720–1.

[65] DHC, DBKL, 'Reasons for the shipping business and answers to objections.'

one part of their argument was that the levy was based on ancient laws and powers of the crown, not on new ones.

Despite this historical dimension, however, the essential questions boiled down to a consideration of what constituted an immediate danger to the realm, who should judge whether or not a necessity arising out of such a situation existed, and whether the emergency had been such as to preclude the calling of a parliament to deal with the problem. All the lawyers agreed that property was a human invention, defined and maintained by known positive laws, but the crown claimed that in times of danger to the state, necessity overthrew purely private interests, and obliged everyone to contribute. Sir Edward Littleton, now solicitor general, argued that it was self-evident that the 'law of necessity of arms to defend' was superior to all other laws. It was, he said, inconceivable that the king should be authorised to issue writs to settle disputes over Whiteacre and Blackacre, mere clods of earth, but not be entitled to issue writs, such as those for collecting Ship Money, when the kingdom was in imminent danger. Private interest had to give way to common good, and in any case public and private were 'so nearly connext' that they could not easily be separated because 'public loss falls immediately, and by consequence upon particular persons'.[66] Everyone knew, for instance, that it was lawful for a man to pull down the house of another when it was next to one that was on fire in order to stop the damage from spreading.[67]

In response, Holborne and St John noted that Littleton's argument might easily lead to the conclusion that an emergency returned society to a state of nature where any man, not just the king, could lay claim to the property of another in the name of necessity. But they focused primarily on two points. First, the king was already provided with sufficient legal means to finance the defence of the realm. Secondly, the tests of danger and necessity were not satisfied by the Ship Money writs, which mentioned the need to suppress pirates on the open seas, not a threat to the realm equivalent to an invasion or occupation. St John produced a *tour de force* history of military tenures in order to show that obligations such as those connected with knights' fees provided sufficient revenue for the king to meet his undoubted responsibility for defending the realm; beyond this, the subject had no general obligation to make a contribution without the consent of parliament.[68] In any case, the circumstances of the 1630s did not amount to a state of war, which St John demonstrated by several examples, including the obvious fact that the courts had not been forced to shut.[69]

[66] *ST*, iii, cols. 926–7.   [67] Ibid., cols. 927, 929.   [68] Ibid., cols. 865, 869.
[69] Ibid., cols. 902, 903, 905.

Taking this argument further, Holborne maintained that the king's assessment of the danger was insufficient to be binding in a court of law. Aware that he was skating on thin ice, he developed the point with a veiled reference to the Aristotelian commonplace that one of the problems with monarchical government was that the individuals holding the office were human beings as liable to err as anyone else.[70] It was difficult to be certain that an heir of Charles I would inherit his virtue along with his crown. Since the king might err in his natural body, it followed that he should be prevented from doing so in his political capacity. The risk of allowing the king a right to his subjects' property was greater than the risk of limiting his powers, even in times of potential danger.[71] Consequently, the 'fundamental policy of England' was that the king could not charge the subject, except through parliament. Throwing down the gauntlet to Littleton, who used a 'beadroll of precedents' to demonstrate the making of similar levies from the time of the Saxons and Danes onwards, Holborne declared that he was only going to refer to times of good government, 'when the liberties of the subject had not been trampled upon'.[72] Far from depending on an unchanging 'ancient constitution', the accounts he and St John provided of English history had much in common with the familiar struggle between popery and the English church. In the relationship between kings and their subjects, there had been periods when bad practices had crept in, but these had always been corrected by parliament.[73] The Petition of Right, in reaffirming Magna Carta, had been a notable and relevant example of this process at work.

Holborne's vision of England as a mixed polity ruled by law was in sharp contrast with that of Attorney General Bankes, who argued that there was an absolute power in the king to make levies such as Ship Money, one which was inherent in the crown and not granted by 'the people' at any point in history. Such prerogatives were part of the *'antiques leges et consuetudines Angliae'*, which had survived from Saxon times, unchanged even by the Conquest in 1066.[74] Although they go further into detail than what he said in court, notes Bankes made on this part of his argument appeal to the laws of God and nature, as well as references to Grotius and Bodin, to make the case that kings were endowed with 'Absolute power' by God. The law of nature, and the law

---

[70] Ibid., cols. 971, 977. Holborne was cautioned several times during his argument by Chief Justice Finch.
[71] Ibid., cols. 979–80, 1000.   [72] Ibid., col. 969.
[73] Ibid., col. 989.   [74] Ibid., cols. 1019–21.

of nations, bound subjects to love their country and to 'defend the state they live in' with their goods as well as their bodies.[75]

Despite the length and complexity of the arguments in Hampden's case, they apparently had relatively little influence on the decisions of the judges, who ruled by a majority of seven to five in favour of the king's right to make the levy. Although it is admittedly a retrospective account dating from November 1641, a letter from Sir George Croke to Sir John Bramston states clearly that the judges had already been divided on the wording of the extrajudicial decision they had given at the king's request in February 1637 before the trial began. According to Croke, he and Sir Richard Hutton were deeply reluctant to sign the declaration no matter what the form of words, and Bramston, with the support of two other judges, Berkeley and Davenport, had instigated a lengthy debate about whether they should qualify their approval of the measure by amending the words 'as the king sees fit' to an 'apparent or im*m*anent or publique danger which is in tyme only of necessity when all other usual wayes doe fail'. Furthermore, according to Croke, almost half of the judges were close to adding 'and only during the continuance of such danger' as well. At this point, however, Sir John Finch, recently promoted to chief justice of the Common Pleas, reportedly told the meeting that the 'king would utterly dislike to have any such addition', adding with the agreement of Sir William Jones, that he thought the original phrasing ('as he shall think fit'), implied 'that it should be only for the tyme of danger and if he thought it should be otherwise intended to make it often or annuall he would never Consente or subscribe unto yt'.[76]

Hence although all of the judges subscribed to the majority view in the extrajudicial opinion, all of them, with the exception of Berkeley, subsequently adhered broadly to the general positions they had taken in the discussions of it. While they clearly felt some pressure, and no doubt recalled the incidents of the late 1620s, it is not clear exactly how heavily this weighed in the outcome.[77] Ruling for the king, Sir Robert Berkeley stressed his adherence to the principle that Englishmen were freemen

---

[75] DHC, DBKL, 'Touching the king's power in commanding aydes for defence of the Realme.'

[76] LPL, MS 3391, fol. 62. Letter from Sir George Croke to Sir John Bramston, from Waterstock, 8 November 1641. Finch told the Long Parliament (*POSLP*, II, pp. 9–10) that 'my opinion of that cause has lain heavy upon me', but he denied attempting to influence the other judges. Hutton and Croke eventually subscribed because they were told by the rest of the judges that it was convention for them all to do so where there was a majority view. *Bramston*, p. 68 also seems to be based on Croke's letter.

[77] In December 1640, MPs were dispatched to ask the surviving judges whether they had been threatened (*POSLP*, I, p. 488), but no evidence, other than Croke's letter, appears to have survived. See, also, Sharpe, *Personal Rule*, pp. 723–5.

and not slaves. Ship Money was a contribution made *pro bono publico*, not a tribute amounting to regular taxation. But he also said that he could not accept that the king could have nothing from his subjects except through parliament, specifically referring to the possibility that a parliament might prove so fractious or disruptive that it would not act with sufficient speed to meet the emergency.[78] Putting it more boldly, baron of the Exchequer Sir Thomas Trevor said that the kingdom of England had always been monarchical rather than democratic, and this was also the thrust of the ruling by Sir John Finch, which was later described as particularly controversial. Referring to his experience as speaker of the House of Commons, and being held down in his chair by Eliot and the other MPs in 1629, Finch wished that parliament had not encouraged 'private humours' to create discontent in the commonwealth. As for historical proofs, he was clear that kings had existed before parliaments, and 'it cannot be denied but originally the King had a sovereignty of the whole kingdom'. The same law that gave him a responsibility for defending and governing the kingdom also gave 'the King power to charge his subjects for the necessary defence and good thereof'.[79]

Two of the judges who ruled against the crown, Chief Baron Davenport and Lord Chief Justice Bramston, accepted that the king had a right to take levies such as Ship Money in times of danger, but argued that technical faults in the writs (a failure to say to whom the money was to be paid) rendered them invalid.[80] Croke and Hutton, were, however, much more forthright in their conclusions. Observing that the case was the greatest that 'ever came in question before any judges', Sir George Croke said that he thought it was a matter more fit for debate in 'the public assembly of the whole state' rather than before the judges alone. Echoing Sir Francis Ashley's speech in the *habeas corpus* debates of 1628, he noted that the case involved a weighing up of the royal prerogative against the liberty of the subject in his property and goods. The levy was:

Against the common law of the land, which gives a man a freedom and property in his goods and estate, that it cannot be taken from him, but by his assent in specie, in parliament, or by his particular assent: for the law puts a difference between a freeman and a bondman. A bondman's goods may be taken without his consent; but not so a freeman . . . [N]o necessity nor danger can allow a charge which is a breach of the laws.[81]

---

[78] *ST*, III, cols. 1090, 1095, 1097, 1098, 1101.   [79] Ibid., 1114.

[80] Ibid., 1245, 1247, 1251. Bramston said that he in fact agreed with much of what Finch had to say and referred to Selden's *Mare clausum* for confirmation that it was an ancient practice to charge inland as well as maritime counties in case of necessity.

[81] Ibid., 1129, 1134.

Sir Richard Hutton was even more dismissive than Croke of the entire project. Looking at the historical arguments, he agreed with Holborne and St John that whatever the bases of ancient levies such as *danegelt* had been, subsequent legislation from medieval times down to the Petition of Right had outlawed them. Indeed, he drew a distinction between ancient methods of kingship and more 'modern' ones where kings ruled through parliaments, and lamented that government by parliament was 'so much out of use nowadays.' He attacked what must have seemed to contemporaries the most obvious weakness in the crown's case: the lack of clear and convincing evidence that there was a danger to the realm that could justify allowing the law of necessity to override the law of property. Hutton pointed out that the first Ship Money writ failed to specify any danger at all. True, the second writ, issued two years later certified '*quod salus regni periclitubatur*', and named pirates as the danger, but this was added because the crown's legal advisors were aware that the first one had been unsatisfactory. The second writ could not overcome the invalidity of the first; furthermore, the passage of two years seemed to undermine the need to act immediately.[82]

Lawyers and the clergy

Ship Money was collected reasonably successfully until the later 1630s when another royal levy, that for 'coat and conduct money' to support Charles's campaign against the rebellious Scots, led to a collapse of both. But there is no doubt that the arguments in *Hampden's Case* were widely discussed outside Westminster, and on ale benches as well as in the parlours of the gentry. Yet while this public debate was unquestionably important, from the juristic point of view the terms of the argument were not much different from those in the debate over impositions several decades earlier: exactly how far could the prerogative of the crown alone be used to further the interests of the state without the consent of the people in parliament? More importantly, the emphasis on taxation and secular policy should not obscure the fact that the other long-standing 'constitutional' problem of the early modern state, namely questions about the nature of the ecclesiastical polity, were no less contentious in the 1630s than they had been earlier.

If the mid-Tudor legal profession had been as divided as the rest of English society on confessional issues,[83] subsequent generations of English lawyers were demonstrably influenced by 'Godly' evangelicalism.[84] From at least the 1590s onwards, young barristers such as Henry

[82] Ibid., 1199.   [83] See above, pp. 52–4.   [84] Prest, *Barristers*, ch. 7.

Yelverton or Oliver St John, assiduously took notes on the sermons they heard when they were out in the country riding the assize circuits. Lawyers wrote religious 'meditations', and many had close connections with individual members of the clergy, mentioning them in their wills, or even undertaking the task of editing some of their sermons.[85] As we have seen, Bishop Williams was apparently friendly with Whitelocke and Selden. Archbishop Laud was influential in gaining the release from prison of Selden,[86] and he was, it seems, one of the few people who expressed much of a sense of loss at the death of Attorney General Noy in 1634.

There were, moreover, many points of intersection between legal and religious discourse, so many indeed that the potential for complex, even unexpected, combinations of ideas was only limited by the number of individuals who gave them some thought. Sir Robert Heath saw a parallel between popery and witchcraft and the political and religious aspirations of the 'unruly people'; all three expressed a fatal inclination to privilege human agency over the quiet acceptance of divine authority.[87] By contrast, one of the most important influences on St John was *The Theatre of God's Judgments*, a work translated from the French by Oliver Cromwell's schoolmaster, Thomas Beard, which used historical and biblical sources to show how the wrath of God brought down rulers and statesmen who transgressed His commandments. More conventionally, perhaps, Michael Dalton's 'Breviary of the State of the Roman (or Western) Church and Empire . . . from the time of Christ till Luther' brought the familiar struggle between true religion and popery down to his own day, and praised the 'Godly' progress that had been made under both James I and Charles I.[88]

But, if Dalton was evidently satisfied with the evolution of the ecclesiastical polity, others were the intellectual heirs of Robert Beale and James Morice, the Elizabethans who led the campaign against High Commission and the oath *ex officio*.[89] Beale's daughter married Henry Yelverton, who inherited many of her father's manuscripts. The Yelvertons joined with several other Northamptonshire gentry families to press

[85] BL, MS Additional 48016, contains Sir Henry Yelverton's observations on the Bible, as well as notes taken on assize sermons. St John's 'theological' commonplace (BL, MS Additional 25285) contains notes on secular as well as religious authors. MS Additional 25278 contains a meditation on Grace based on St Paul's Epistle to the Ephesians. Sir John Bankes also wrote a meditation on the passion and resurrection of Christ, which contains a number of references to sermons he had read or heard (DHC, DBKL). Prest, *Barristers*, pp. 219–21.

[86] HMC, *Hastings*, IV, p. 76.

[87] BL, MS Egerton 2982, fols. 87ff. Heath's meditation on 1 Samuel 15, 23.

[88] BL, MS Sloane 4359.   [89] See above, pp. 100ff.

for religious reform just after James's accession, and they were subsequently involved in long-term controversies with the local ecclesiastical court official Sir John Lambe.[90] In Essex, Sir Harbottle Grimston was imprisoned in 1626 for refusing to pay the Forced Loan and was involved in the 1630s in controversies concerning the clergy in Colchester, the town for which Morice had acted as recorder. He and his son, Harbottle II, who was a barrister and son-in-law of the judge Sir George Croke kept a close eye on national political and religious developments, and Harbottle II was a significant figure in the opening stages of the Long Parliament.[91]

Furthermore, controversy continued, especially in the early 1630s, over prohibitions and about the relationship between the ecclesiastical and secular legal systems. In May 1631, Laud and other council members were commissioned by the king to investigate problems associated with the granting of prohibitions by the common-law judges.[92] In 1633, the archbishop was concerned about the decline in the number of civil lawyers. As he explained to the privy council, this was partly because business in the ecclesiastical courts was insufficient to attract new practitioners, but he was aware that common lawyers were intruding into ecclesiastical administration. In response to the attempt by the bishop of Chester, John Bridgeman, to appoint his son, Orlando, a common lawyer, as his diocesan chancellor, the doctors of the court of Arches had petitioned the king to prohibit the practice.[93] In February 1633, moreover, propositions formulated for the consideration of the judges included a restatement of the Jacobean view that, according to the fundamental constitutions of the kingdom, there were two several and distinct jurisdictions governed and managed by two several and distinct learnings and professions. But the paper also complained that the ecclesiastical court judges were so interrupted in their business by prohibitions that it was as though there were no ecclesiastical jurisdiction at all, especially in matters relating to tithes, testamentary cases, repairs of churches, pews, burial places and the selection of churchwardens.[94]

[90] *The British Library Catalogue of Additions to the Manuscripts. The Yelverton Manuscripts. Part I. Descriptions. Additional Manuscripts 48000–48196* (1994), p. x; Diana Newton, *The Making of the Jacobean Regime: James VI and I and the Government of England, 1603–1605* (Woodbridge, 2005), chs. 3–4. A. J. Fielding, 'Conformists, puritans and the church courts: the diocese of Peterborough, 1603–1642' (University of Birmingham PhD thesis, 1989), pp. 22, 34–6, 61, 76.

[91] *ODNB*. See below, p. 229.   [92] HEHL, MS Ellesmere 7928.

[93] SRO, P/399/110: Laud to Bridgeman, 12 August 1633. Laud actively discouraged the promotion of Orlando, who was 'altogether unskilled in ecclesiastical laws and government'.

[94] Petyt MS 518, fol. 97v. Propositions presented to the consideration of the reverend judges by direction of his Majesty in Council.

Nevertheless, in the 1630s, no less than in earlier periods, it was still a commonplace that religion and law were the two columns that supported the commonwealth, an architectural metaphor that was turned into a virtual reality at every meeting of quarter sessions and assize. As we have seen, the prefaces to charges in both jurisdictions were always divided into two sections, one dealing with secular and the other with ecclesiastical affairs. What has not hitherto been stressed is that by Elizabethan times, if not earlier, it had become common practice on the first morning of the meetings of the courts to have a sermon, which offered the clergymen an opportunity to cast a theological eye on the institutions and personnel of secular justice, and, sometimes, to speculate more generally on political or religious questions.[95]

Infinitely more sermons were given than have survived in the historical record, but sermons were much more likely than charges to be printed, and the number published was much higher in the seventeenth century than in the sixteenth.[96] The fact that sermons went into print more often than charges is one reason why it is much easier to capture the nuances of religious, as opposed to legal, political thought. Publishing was part of the career pattern for clergy, many of whom taught at some point within the universities, but successful lawyers were mostly too busy to write for print.[97] At the same time, while clergymen were appointed on a one-off basis to give a single sermon,[98] lawyer and gentry magistrates were often faced with giving similar speeches over and over again, which presumably made publishing counterproductive. Some surviving sermons are found in the collected works of notable preachers, such as Robert Bolton or Edward Reynolds, but many of those produced as separates make a point of saying that they were published at the request of those who heard them, often naming either the sheriff who selected the preacher, or, indeed, the judges before whom the sermon was preached.[99]

[95] Above, p. 87. William Kethe, *A Sermon Made at Blandford Forum in the Countie of Dorset on Wednesday the 17 of January last past at the session holden there, before the honorable and worshyppeful of that Shyre* (1571) is a rare example of early publication.

[96] Godfrey Davies, 'English political sermons 1603–1640', *Huntington Library Quarterly*, 1 (1939) 1–22; J. S. Cockburn, *A History of English Assizes* (Cambridge, 1972), contains a fairly complete bibliography of assize sermons.

[97] See above, p. 18.

[98] William Leigh, *The Dampe of Death: Beaten Back with the Glorious Light of Iesus Christ . . . In a Sermon Preached at Lancaster Assizes* (1613), p. 1, mentions that this was his second appearance. Robert Bolton, *Two Sermons Preached at Northampton at Two Several Assizes There One in 1621, the Other in 1629* (1634).

[99] For example, Leigh, *Dampe of Death*; William Sclater, *A Sermon Preached At the last generall Assise holden for the County of Sommerset at Taunton* (1616); Robert Harris, *Two Sermons: The One Preached before the Judges of Assize at Oxford, The Other to the University* (1628); Theophilus Taylor, *The Mappe of Moses or, A Guide for Governors. Two Sermons*

The fact that lawyers attending meetings of assizes and quarter sessions took notes on both sermons and charges demonstrates that attention was paid to them, but it is no easier to interpret the impact of sermons than it is charges. Prior to 1632, when Richard Neile circulated a letter from the council warning the bishops in the province of York that they should make certain that sheriffs selected only grave and discrete ministers, who would say nothing prejudicial to the laws or 'present government', there is little direct evidence of attempts to control sermons.[100] But given the setting, sermons must not all that often have veered away from the bounds of political acceptability, and it hardly needs saying that those that found their way into print were even less likely to have done so. Nevertheless, the sophistication of the political ideas expressed in sermons is sometimes striking.

In the early seventeenth century, in the wake of the Gunpowder Plot of 1605 and the subsequent controversy of the introduction by James I of an oath of allegiance, a recurrent theme centred around the question of whether government and laws were the creation of human or divine agency. Invariably coming to the conclusion that the king and laws were given by God for the sake of preserving a divinely ordained order,[101] the typical rhetorical strategy involved associating popular or demotic theories of government with Jesuits such as Robert Parsons, or the Spanish writers Bellarmine and Molina, who were accused of endorsing the proposition that 'the people' could overthrow existing authority on the grounds of religious conscience.[102]

By the later 1620s or 1630s this line of thought was frequently accompanied by warnings that the idea of Christian liberty did not extend so far as to make ordinary people the same as kings, or to justify the 'poysonfull papal doctrine of the Churche of Rome, which tolerateth, yea animateth subiects to take arm*es* against their sovereign Princes'.[103] According to a sermon preached before the earl of Bridgewater at Ludlow in 1639, kings in the modern age did not crave bondage from

---

lately Preached before the Iudges of Assize, and Magistrates of the Towne of Reading, at two seuerall assemblies there held for the Countie of Berks (London, 1629), dedicated the work to a country squire and magistrate who had been his student.

[100] HMC, *Fourteenth Report (appendix, part 4). The Manuscripts of Lord Kenyon* (London, 1849), p. 49.

[101] Sclater, *A Sermon Preached.*

[102] Bartholomew Parsons, *The Magistrates Charter Examined or His Duty and Dignity Opened in A Sermon Preached at an Assizes held at Sarum in the County of Wilt[shire]* (1616), pp. 8–9. Bellarmine makes magistrates, even kings, 'the supreme Homagers both to people and pope'. William Dickinson, *The Kings Right Briefely set downe in a Sermon preached before the Reuerend Iudges at the Assizes held in Reading for the County of Berks, Iune 28, 1619* (1619), sig. c2.

[103] Taylor, *Mappe of Moses*, p. 18.

their subjects, but ingenious subjection; not servitude but obedience. Christ taught us the proper posture to assume before those in authority. He obeyed his parents with humility, the emperor with piety and the law with integrity. Only papists and schismatics took it upon themselves to judge kings and to kill them if they decided that they merited the title of 'tyrant'.[104]

Based on a text from scripture, and drawing on current theological works, sermons were distinctly different in content from secular charges, where, as we have seen, political histories, the 'pagan' thinkers Aristotle and Cicero and an articulation of self-interest as a reason for political allegiance were more likely to be emphasised.[105] On the other hand, although Elizabethan charges more often stressed human agency alongside divine will in the formation of civil society, seventeenth-century lawyers such as Sir Anthony Benn, or indeed Attorney General Bankes, often connected royal power to divine ordination, and in this respect the theological perspective clearly had an impact. Furthermore, no less a legal figure than Coke had expressed the importance of religious obedience to established authority as an essential prerequisite of political stability,[106] and when it came to the everyday exercise of magistracy and the administration of justice, the clerics often spoke the same language as the jurists.[107] Many assize sermons retailed commonplaces about the value of justice and the rule of law, and lawyers could hardly have objected to the general proposition that the administration of justice should be undertaken in accordance with the principles of 'Godly' religion.[108] In 1619, William Pemberton noted that since both kings and magistrates were created by divine authority, both had an obligation to judge righteously without respect of persons, and to pilot the 'ship of the commonwealth' to peace and prosperity. Grand jurymen should be patient in their decisions and not jump to conclusions about innocence or guilt until all the evidence had been thoroughly sifted and examined.[109]

There were, therefore, many points on which clerical and legal thought were highly compatible or complementary. In 1613, for instance, William Leigh even managed to draw a fairly plausible parallel between preaching

---

[104] HEHL, MS Ellesmere 6873.   [105] See above, pp. 87ff.   [106] See above, p. 159.

[107] BL, MS Additional 48016. Henry Yelverton frequently seems to have been interested in the legal implications of the theological remarks.

[108] Samuel Garey, *Ientaculum Iudicum: or, A Breakefast for the Bench: Prepared, Presented and Preached in two Sacred Seruices, or Sermons, The Morning Sacrifice before the two Assizes: at Thetford, at Norwich: 1619. Containing monitory Meditation, to execute Iustice and Law-Businesse with a good Conscience* (1623), p.16.

[109] William Pemberton, *The Charge of God and the King, To Judges and Magistrates for Execution of Justice [at Hereford assizes]* (1619), pp. Bi, 2, 21, 24, 82, 101; Taylor, *Mappe of Moses*, pp. 24–39.

and pleading. The body of the law lay in books in the same way as God's truth was found in the Bible, but just as the saving of souls required preaching, so too, the soul of the law was found in the moots and pleadings, the oral exercises, of the lawyers.[110] Yet if there were elements of professional mutual respect, and a good deal of common interest with regard to magistracy, there were also points of potential discord. The most formulaic element in sermons was a warning that lawyers should not delay lawsuits in order to increase fees, or engage in chicanery or lies in order to gain undue advantage for their clients. These were nearly timeless tropes that stretched back at least as far as the fifteenth century, and so too did professional rivalry between the two occupations,[111] but there are signs that these old saws were cutting more sharply in the reign of Charles I.

In weighing up the comparative standing of the learned professions, contemporaries often began by considering the significance of the field of knowledge with which each was concerned. The divines came first because they dealt with the soul; the medics second because they worked on the body; and the lawyers last because they dealt merely with the temporal goods and affairs of men, and were sometimes obliged to implement laws that were either unjust or enabled the rich to dominate the poor.[112] While such comparisons were probably most often the stuff of after-dinner debate, there was nevertheless potential within these distinctions for the creation of a hierarchy of authority. For example, John Gauden, a future post-Restoration bishop, prefaced his sermon at Chelmsford assizes in 1642 with the remark that 'The Customary solemnity of *publike Assise*, and administration of Justice . . .' was for the judges to receive 'advice from the *Pulpit*, before you goe to the *Bench*, and hear *God's charge* to you before you give *your charge* to others', thereby ascending with 'Moses first to the Mount, and talke with God, before you judge and teach the people'.[113]

At the level of national politics, moreover, the professional rivalry between the churchmen and the lawyers that we have seen in connection with Lord Keeper Williams in 1621 was hardly relieved by the political prominence of William Laud, who had notable run-ins with lawyers in the 1630s.[114] In 1632, for example, he instigated the censure before the privy council of Chief Justice Sir Thomas Richardson for suppressing church ales in Somerset, and some of his correspondence with Bankes

---

[110] Leigh, *Dampe of Death*, Preface.   [111] Above, p. 61.
[112] Petyt MS 538, fols. 80ff. Comparison between 'physique and law wherein is proved that the profession of phisique is far more excellent'.
[113] John Gauden, *Three Sermons Preached upon Severall Publike Occasions* (1642), pp. 39.
[114] Above, pp. 151, 164.

reflects both his vigilance for clerical interests and a clear sense that his views were supported by the authority of the king.[115] In the course of giving a sentence in Star Chamber against Henry Sherfield, a lawyer from Salisbury who was prosecuted for knocking down a stained-glass window, Laud noted that just as it was a 'great offence in a divine to infringe the law of the kingdom ... so it was a great offence if those of the law profession vilify the poor laws of the Church'. Addressing the common lawyers in general, he warned that 'there was a time when Churchmen were as great in this kingdom as you are now; and let me be bold to prophesy, there will be a time when you will be as low as the Church is now, if you go on thus to condemn the church'.[116]

Calls like this one for clergymen and lawyers to keep themselves within the bounds of their disciplines were uttered largely because some of those in each field were trespassing, and there was a sense of a growing incommensurability between the two in connection with political authority. In response to instructions from Laud, sermons in favour of the Forced Loan in 1626 by Matthew Wren, Robert Sibthorpe, Isaac Bargrave and Roger Mainwaring argued, or were taken to argue, that the divine rights of kings included the right to make levies on the wealth of their subjects.[117] Some years after the fact, John Selden recalled that Dr Mosely, a clergyman who visited him during his imprisonment, had said that 'he found no such words as parliament, habeas corpus, return, tower, etc in either the schoolmen or the fathers'. Though Selden described Mosely as a 'good, discrete man', he thought this had been a kind of 'Satire upon all those Clergymen that meddle with Matters they do not understand'; the clergyman 'goes not a dram further than this, you ought to obey your prince in general'.[118]

This background helps to explain the mutual recrimination between lawyers and clergymen that formed part of the fall-out from the Ship Money trial. Writing to Wentworth in December 1637, Laud noted that Holborne, 'was very bold, to say no more', in making his points about the need for safeguards against bad kings.[119] Yet in the course of giving his opinion, Justice Jones remarked that he and his colleagues were supposed to judge according to the fundamental customs and laws of the realm, rather pointedly adding that he would leave it to the divines to talk about the king's power, 'who under favour take more liberty than is fitting in the pulpit'.[120] It is impossible to judge exactly how far this may have been true, but Thomas Hurste, one of the king's chaplains, referred

---

[115] Cockburn, *History of English Assizes*, p. 233.   [116] Laud, *Works*, VI(I), p. 20.
[117] Richard Cust, *The Forced Loan and English Politics, 1626–1628* (Oxford, 1987), p. 164.
[118] *Table-Talk*, p. 133.   [119] Laud, *Works*, VII, p. 397.   [120] *ST*, III, cols. 1186.

to the issue in a sermon preached at Lincoln assizes in March 1637, which was tellingly entitled *The Descent of Authoritie: or The Magistrates Patent from Heaven*. Observing that most men would agree that preachers should have something to say about death, God's mercy, man's proneness to sin and so on, he quipped that by contrast the subject of his sermon, 'the just power of one man over another . . . may seeme to be Apocryphall, or an Exchecker-chamber case'.[121]

Professional sensitivities were even more strikingly exposed in May 1638 when Thomas Harrison, the vicar of Crick in Northamptonshire, walked into Westminster Hall and publicly accused Justice Richard Hutton of high treason because of his ruling against the king in *Hampden's Case*.[122] Everyone, including Charles I, was clear that Harrison should be punished, and while the lawyers found him slightly unhinged, they were exasperated by his opinions.[123] Content to admit that he understood little about the common law, Harrison also acknowledged that he had no first-hand knowledge of Hutton's judgment, which he had heard of only through 'reports'. Maintaining that the function of judges was similar to that of the moderators of theological disputations in the examination schools at the universities, he based his allegation on the Jacobean Oath of Allegiance, which he interpreted as meaning that the king's prerogative should always be upheld no matter what the case. Adding for good measure that every 'orthodox' divine in the land agreed that Ship Money was legal, Harrison saw it as his duty to expose Hutton, whose views were the main reason why so many in Northamptonshire were refusing to pay.[124]

Lord Chief Justice Bramston was incredulous at the suggestion that the Oath of Allegiance was relevant.[125] According to Hutton's own notes, Harrison refused to back down and behaved like a man who did not understand that the government of the realm rested upon its laws.[126] Attorney General Bankes, who prosecuted the case at the king's request, pointed out that Harrison evidently understood neither the common law or the role of the judges and called for a severe censure.[127] After being found guilty in Star Chamber, Harrison was fined, imprisoned and carted

---

[121] Thomas Hurste, *The Descent of Authority or The Magistrates Patent from Heaven Manifested in a Sermon preached at Lincolnes Assizes, March 13, 1636* (1637), pp. 1–2; Clive Holmes, *Seventeenth-Century Lincolnshire* (Lincoln, 1980), pp. 112, 195.
[122] There is an eye-witness account in the Bankes Papers, 44/10.
[123] Bankes led the prosecution with the full support of the king.
[124] Ibid., 18/16; *ST*, III, cols. 1373–4.
[125] Bankes Papers, 44/11; *ST*, III, cols. 1378–80.
[126] W. R. Prest, *The Diary of Sir Richard Hutton, 1614–1639* (Selden Society Supplementary Series, vol. 9, 1991), p. 131.
[127] Bankes Papers, 44/11.

around all the courts at Westminster with a paper on his head declaring his offence.[128] Hutton later sued him for slander and was awarded £10,000 damages by a Middlesex jury.[129]

If Harrison was a clergyman who ran foul of the professional territory of the lawyers, only a year before William Prynne, a barrister of Lincoln's Inn, was tried in Star Chamber along with John Bastwick (a physician) and Henry Burton (a clergyman) for attacking in print the actions and authority of the bishops and stirring up the people by alleging that there were plans to alter the religion of the realm. Having already been judicially mutilated as a result of a Star Chamber sentence given against him for publishing *Historiomastix*, an attack on stage plays, Prynne was described at the trial by Attorney General Bankes as

not unlearned in the profession of the law, as far as learning is acquired by the mere reading of books; but being a person of great industry [he] had spent more time in reading divinity; and which marred that divinity, in the conversation of factious and hot-headed divines; and so, by a mixture of all three, with the rudeness and arrogance of his own nature, had contracted a proud and venomous dislike to the discipline of the Church of England; and so by degrees, as the progress is very natural, an equal irreverence to the government of the state too.[130]

Driven by his dislike for the policies being promoted by Laud and his colleagues, Prynne explicitly attacked what Laud himself referred to as the *jure divinio* view of episcopal authority, the idea that the office of bishop had been created by God, not by the human agency of kings, or kings in parliament.[131] In doing this, Prynne probably went further than any previous common lawyer had done in print, and he inflamed clerical animosity by outlining in one of his books some fifty parallels between the devil and the prelates.[132] Yet as we have seen, common-law writing on similar subjects had in the past focused on the struggles against the pope by king and people to retain control of the Church of England, including the appointment of bishops.[133] Despite the violence of his language, therefore, when Prynne claimed that it behoved 'the king and state to look' into the proceedings of the bishops, he could certainly claim to be fighting a longstanding cause in defence of the crown as well as the people.[134]

---

[128] BL, MS Hargrave 46, fols. 225v–6.   [129] Ibid., fols. 229v–30.

[130] *ST*, III, col. 713.   [131] Laud, *Works*, VI(I), p. 43.

[132] Bankes, who prosecuted the case, collected several pages of slanderous anti-episcopal phrases from *The Pontificall Lordly Prelates of England*. DHC, DBKL, Bankes Papers.

[133] See above, pp. 84, 100.

[134] DHC, DBKL, Bankes Papers: notes taken from a letter from Prynne to Lady Waldegrave (no date).

In delivering sentence against Prynne, Bastwick and Burton, Laud recognised that the three learned professions were represented in the persons of the accused. Claiming that he honoured the law 'with his heart', he went on to observe that 'Mr Prynn may seek all the Inns of Court (and with a candle too if he will), and scarce find such a malevolent as himself against State and Church'.[135] Yet while Laud may well have been correct with regard to the vehemence of Prynne's views, in February and March 1640 he was directly involved in suppressing a series of readings delivered at the Middle Temple by a Northamptonshire barrister, Edward Bagshawe, which recapitulated many of the issues that had traditionally divided lawyers from churchmen.[136]

A committed Protestant, close friend of the distinguished clergyman Robert Bolton, and connected with the future parliamentary leader Lord Saye and Sele,[137] Bagshawe began his reading by explaining that he had picked a statute relating to benefices and ecclesiastical patronage (25 Edward III, c. 7) in order to avoid controversial questions about the jurisdiction of the ecclesiastical courts.[138] But, despite the disclaimer, he managed to work his way from prohibitions and High Commission to the Petition of Right and Thomas Harrison's slander of Justice Hutton. His intention, or so he explained it to the students of the Temple, was to find a subject that would enable him to advance the common law above the civil and canon laws, and to prove that the common law was more 'agreeable' to the law of God than either of the other two. He aimed to show that it was more effective in advancing 'true religion and worship', that it was a greater defender of the 'people's liberties', and that, though it was a 'paradox to some', it was a 'solid truth' that it was also more advantageous to the king's prerogative.[139] In fact, Bagshawe expressed outrage that despite these qualities,

this Law so ancient & so honourable together with the professors of it have been of late years traduced in pamphlets, jeered and derided in plays and play books, and openly reviled and slandered at our bars of law, and by churchmen themselves whom my statute favours, and of whome I dare not only speak it here, but in any ecclesiastical consistory in the land, that they are more beholden to the common law of England, then the civil and canon laws, put them together.

---

[135] Laud, *Works*, VI(I), p. 39.
[136] There is a printed account in Rushworth, *Collections*, II, p. 990. For manuscript versions see Baker, *Readers and Readings*.
[137] *ODNB*. Fielding, 'Conformists, Puritans and the church courts', pp. 15–16. Bagshawe left parliament and joined the king in 1645. He explained his political evolution in *A Just Vindication of the Questioned Part of the Reading of Edward Bagshaw* (London, 1660).
[138] BL, MS Hargrave 206, fol. 2v; MS Harleian 1222, fols. 108–9; pp. 1–7; MS Stowe 424, fol. 3.
[139] Ibid.

We are not such ignoramuses but that we know this to be true, nor such dull men but we can be sensible when we are kickt.[140]

Maintaining that English common law, unlike the laws of the Greeks and Romans, was derived from the laws of God rather than human authority, Bagshawe demonstrated his point by recapitulating the centuries-long struggles of the English people and their rulers against clerical pretensions.[141] In the first 500 years after the death of Christ, there had been virtually no distinction between temporal and ecclesiastical causes. In the next 500 years the clergy were allowed jurisdiction over marriage and testaments on the grounds that, since they were sacraments, they were thought fit to be handled as spiritual matters. For most of the final 500 years, roughly from the time of the Norman Conquest onwards, the clergy had accumulated greater and greater powers, a process that might well have continued if they had not tried during the time of Wolsey to suppress the common law in favour of the civil and canon laws.[142] Furthermore, according to Bagshawe, in primitive times the laity had a voice in the election of bishops, and ordinations had been conducted by bishops by 'the laying on of hands', and without any further ceremony.[143]

Although these views could certainly be described as sympathetic to Presbyterianism,[144] Bagshawe's principal aim was less to attack episcopacy than to illustrate that it, like every other jurisdictional feature of the English church, had been sanctioned either by the king or by the king in parliament, and was therefore subject to limitations or alterations by temporal powers, including the common-law judges.[145] Although it is uncertain whether or not he actually covered all of them in the lectures as delivered, notes on the reading also contain familiar lawyerly points about prohibitions, including a remark that heresy should be tried as a temporal rather than a spiritual offence, and swipes at the authority of the court of High Commission.[146] Noting, inaccurately, that the latter was a court where both the judges and the pleaders were civil lawyers who adhered to the doctrine that whatever pleased the king was the rule of law (*Quicquid placuit Principi legis vigorem habet*), he alleged that it was a misunderstanding of this dictum that had led Thomas Harrison to declare Justice Hutton a traitor.[147]

---

[140] Ibid.   [141] Ibid., fol. 4.   [142] Ibid., fols. 1, 4v–15.   [143] Ibid., fol. 9.

[144] Writing after the fact, Whitelocke, *Memorials*, p. 31, described Bagshawe as 'much inclined to the Nonconformist way'.

[145] Stowe 424, fol. 3v.

[146] Ibid. fols. 9v, 18v, 24, 28. He was critical of Cosin's work of the 1590s, and mentioned *Caudry's Case*, as well as that of Fuller.

[147] Ibid., fol. 25.

There is some doubt about how much of this Bagshawe was actually able to deliver because the lecture series was cut short by the intervention of Laud, who persuaded the king to suppress it.[148] At a meeting with Laud and Finch, who had recently become lord keeper, Bagshawe claimed that he avoided questions about High Commission and prohibitions. But, Laud was more concerned with what Bagshawe had said about the role of the clergy in temporal affairs. Raising the question of whether a valid act of parliament could be made when the bishops were not sitting in the House of Lords, Bagshawe argued that bishops held their seats as a result of the temporal baronies that had been attached to their sees rather than in respect of their ecclesiastical offices. Hence statutes such as the Elizabethan Act of Supremacy were good laws even though the bishops had not been present when they were passed. In addition, although he later claimed not to have meddled with the appointment in the present day of clergymen as JPs, he did point out that in the reign of Edward III bishops and clergymen had not been allowed to exercise any temporal jurisdiction.[149]

When Finch informed Bagshawe of the king's decision to stop the reading, he criticised the timing in the light of the outbreak of the Bishops' War in Scotland rather than the content, and advised Bagshawe to see Laud once again.[150] But Laud was unimpressed by Bagshawe's claim that he had chosen his subject two years earlier and saw no connection between his remarks and developments in Scotland. In response to the archbishop's suggestion that he should perhaps have changed topics, Bagshawe said he 'hoped hee neede not feare any mans power in regard his cause was Lawfull and warrentable' and humbly desired leave to finish what he had begun. Laud informed him that the king had decided otherwise and threatened him with a citation before High Commission.[151]

Professional life and public discourse

The popularity of Prynne's works and the star-status he, along with Bastwick and Burton, achieved in the wake of their prosecutions is well

---

[148] There is some confusion over the dates on which Bagshawe read. He apparently began on 24 February, and *The Vindication*, pp. 1–12, indicates that he read on three days, but gives the dates as 25, 27 and 29 March.

[149] There is an account, apparently by Bagshawe himself, of his dealings with Laud in BL, MS Harleian 1222, fols. 103ff. There is a copy in the papers of Sir Edward Littleton, CUL, MS Mm.6.62, esp. fol. 30.

[150] BL, MS Harleian 1222, fol. 107v.

[151] Ibid., fols. 108–9. Bagshawe also told Laud that up until twelve months earlier, he had never heard any opposition to bishops. For Laud's version see his *Works*, IV, p. 133.

known.[152] Bagshawe's reading is less famous, but manuscript copies circulated widely, and the incidents associated with it made an impact at the time. On Friday, 6 March 1640, he rode out of London towards Northamptonshire accompanied by fifty or sixty members of the inns of court. Along with another barrister, John White, who had accompanied him on the visit to Laud, he was offered a seat in the Short and Long Parliaments by the borough of Southwark largely on the basis of the reputation his reading had established.[153]

As Laud suggested when sentencing Prynne, however, it is difficult to be certain exactly how these confrontations over the ecclesiastical polity, or the arguments in the Ship Money case, played out within the broader legal culture associated with the inns in London or in the speeches that judges and lawyers gave in the localities. In purely professional terms, circumstances may well have inclined people to keep their heads down and pursue the private business of getting and spending as best they could. The 1630s were a period of mixed fortunes for lawyers within both the upper and lower branches of the profession, and in these conditions obtaining an office or gaining an audience before a judge was liable to be an important consideration.[154] The sad fate of Henry Sherfield, who died a broken man soon after being sentenced in Star Chamber for breaking the stained-glass window in Salisbury, was a warning about the consequences of indiscrete political or religious actions, and, later on in the decade, crown law officers sometimes made the point more explicitly.

Taken as a whole, speeches given on the appointment of new serjeants-at-law or judges were as anodyne in the 1630s as they had been earlier, but there were a few sharp, and possibly revealing, phrases. In 1631 when Sir Thomas Richardson (CJKB) agreed with Fortescue that no Christian country could be governed or subsist without laws and that English laws, essentially unchanged over the centuries, were the best

---

[152] A. Bellany, 'Libels in action: ritual, subversion and the English literary underground' in T. Harris, ed., *The Politics of the Excluded, c. 1580–1850* (Basingstoke, 2001), pp. 110–16. SRO, P399/158: Neile to Bridgman from Bishopsthorp, 26 November 1637, gives an account of proceedings in the High Commission at York that were taken out against a number of the inhabitants of Chester, who were distributing pictures of Prynne.

[153] BL, MS Harleian 1222, fol. 109. White (*ODNB*), also a member of the Middle Temple, was one of the members of the feoffees of impropriations, which was declared illegal in an Exchequer case brought by Noy in 1633. A severe critic of clerical impropriety as well as bishops, he was the author of *The First Century of Scandalous, Malignant Priests* (1643). Bagshawe, *A Just Vindication*, pp. 1–7.

[154] Prest, *Barristers*, pp. 80–2; Brooks, *Pettyfoggers and Vipers*, ch. 11; New College Library, Oxford, MS 9502, Robert Woodford's diary, provides many insights into the personal concerns of a local practitioner during this period.

laws of all nations, he was undoubtedly mouthing a commonplace. But it could be taken to have some polemical import, especially since he concluded by wondering how, given all this, anyone could speak ill of the common lawyers.[155] In 1634, he could not resist pointing out that the great preferments of state had been going in recent years to the divines, leaving it to his auditors to make a connection, if they wanted, to either the time of Cardinal Wolsey, or, indeed, Coke's reference to the cardinal on a similar occasion in 1614.[156]

As the decade progressed, political developments, or at least the language of reform, clearly had some impact on professional life. In 1633, the chief justice of the Common Pleas pointed out to a jury of attorneys appointed to investigate abuses amongst practitioners that the time was ripe for such measures, and that there 'was no company, or society, no order of men, but time and neglect doth bring in disorders and misdemeanours' that required correction.[157] When Lord Keeper Coventry addressed the judges and serjeants-at-law about to leave London for the assizes in 1635, he stressed that their charges should acquaint the people with the king's thinking about Ship Money, which was that he intended to maintain the defence of the country on land and at sea by the creation of a powerful fleet.[158] After 1635, on the other hand, the language of the crown law officers often seems defensive, and sometimes threatening. In 1637, Coventry reminded a call of new serjeants that they must respect the king as next unto God, and not court popularity; on the same occasion Chief Justice Bramston complained that he had recently noticed a 'boldness' in lawyers who would even go so far as to contest the opinion of a judge.[159] Similarly, a regular feature of speeches Sir John Bankes made at Gray's Inn was a reminder that kings had always done great honour to the law, and the professors of the law have 'allways in former times (and I hoppe in these times) retorned their duties to the Crowne to acknowledge him to be an absolute king'.[160] By 1640, Finch put it more bluntly. Newly appointed serjeants should study to preserve the prerogative of the king, not countenancing the factious spirits of the times. While majesty cherished the obedient, it would grind the opposed into powder.[161]

Orders for the better regulation of the inns of court published by the judges in 1634 at the instigation of the privy council were mainly about

---

[155] Baker, *Serjeants*, p. 363.   [156] Ibid., p. 370. See above, p. 148.
[157] BL, MS Hargrave 46, fol. 190.   [158] Rushworth, *Collections*, II, p. 357.
[159] Ibid., p. 377.
[160] DHC, DBKL, Bankes's speech to new serjeants when they were leaving Gray's Inn, January 1637.
[161] Rushworth, *Collections*, II, pp. 395–6.

decorum and personal behaviour, but a general atmosphere of political circumspection was reflected in Thomas Shirley's masque, *The Triumph of Peace*, which was performed jointly by members of the inns before the king in 1634. Shirley's stress on the interrelationship between peace, justice and the rule of law repeated familiar commonplaces that could hardly have given offence to the king.[162] But some contemporaries were more struck by that part of the masque which attacked monopolists and projectors,[163] and at least one of its more memorable lines – that the laws made a temple of the forest – must have resonated with multiple meanings for contemporaries. On the one hand, this was a metaphor for the role of the law in facilitating the triumph of civility over barbarity, but on the other, it was exactly the line of thought that the government tried to promote in putting the best case for the policy of exploiting its rights in the royal forests. Furthermore, the king responded to the *Triumph* by inviting 120 lawyers to a performance at court of Thomas Carew's *Coelm Britannicum*, which described the mythical return to civility of a great city (Rome standing for London) in terms of some of the measures of reform that King Charles had introduced through proclamations.[164]

Compared with the up-beat Ciceronianism that was so evident in the thought of Christopher Yelverton in the 1580s,[165] the tone of professional discourse in the 1630s was more subdued, and, acting through the positions they held as officers of the inns, the crown lawyers exerted influence on them.[166] Confronted by an outbreak of domestic disharmony at Gray's Inn in 1639, which was evidently not connected with national politics, Bankes, who was treasurer of the House, reminded members that not everyone could be a governor; the younger generation should accept authority so that they could look forward to exercising it themselves when they eventually came to govern the inn or hold office in the commonwealth.[167] Figures like Bankes were also in the habit of attending readings at the inns, but there is no clear evidence about the impact of this,[168] and the controversy surrounding Bagshawe's lectures seems exceptional.[169]

---

[162] M. Butler, 'Politics and the masque: *The Triumph of Peace*', *The Seventeenth Century*, 2(2) (1987), 117–41.

[163] Whitelocke, *Memorials*, p. 23.

[164] Butler, 'Politics and the masque'; see also K. M. Sharpe, *Criticism and Compliment: the Politics of Literature in the England of Charles I* (Cambridge, 1987).

[165] See above, pp. 62–3.

[166] For a general account of the 1630s, see W. R. Prest, *The Inns of Court Under Elizabeth and the Early Stuarts* (1972).

[167] DHC, DBKL, speech given 'at the cupboard' touching the contribution to St Paul's, Michaelmas 1638.

[168] DHC, DBKL, speeches to readers in February and March 1637/8.

[169] BL, MS Additional 10114, fols. 1ff. In his reading in 1637, the future speaker of the Long Parliament, William Lenthall, maintained that William I had not claimed his

On the other hand, the Caroline readings that survive most plentifully in manuscript are those given by people like Bankes, Edward Littleton and Henry Calthorpe, who was made attorney of the court of Wards in 1634, and these tended to support the current government line, particularly in connection with royal revenue.[170] For instance, Littleton's lectures in 1632 on the Edwardian statute on Merchant Strangers (27 Edward III, c. 17) aimed to justify the king's power to issue letters of marque, warrants that empowered subjects to take reprisals against foreigners in those circumstances where they could not obtain justice in connection with losses overseas. Referring to the use of letters of marque during Elizabeth's undeclared naval war against Spain, Littleton may have been floating an idea for asserting naval power without putting a strain on royal finances, but the lectures gave him the opportunity to introduce a discussion of some of the ideas of Grotius, and he also touched on a number of the recent cases relevant to the policy of using the prerogative to raise revenue.[171]

Yet, if professional life was in all these subtle ways more heavily influenced by the royal interest than at any time since the reign of Henry VIII, the other unmistakable feature of the 1630s is that the celebrated court cases of the period were followed closely. The attorney Robert Woodford went to hear the judges give their decisions in the case of Ship Money, and Coventry noted the large number of gentry and lawyers who assembled in the Star Chamber to hear the outcome of the case against Henry Sherfield.[172] Apart from the appearance of the first volume of Coke's *Institutes*, and the fact that Lambarde's *Archion* was finally published in 1635,[173] the Personal Rule was not a notable period in legal publishing, but commercial manuscript separates relating to important cases circulated widely. It was said that the opinion of Justice Croke in the case of Ship Money was so well known that it was a country witticism that the levy could be collected by hook, but not by crook.[174]

There are relatively few surviving accounts of lawyerly public speeches in the form of addresses to meetings of quarter sessions and assizes, especially if we discount those that were made by judges. An unattributed fragment, which refers to the 'guardian angel' of the law as a counter to tyrannical oppression, appears to be of a piece with country opinion in

---

throne by conquest, but used all means to get the love of the people. MS Additional 27380, fols. 5ff., an elaborate reading by Thomas Tempest, in August 1639, which included some history of the Exchequer, seems on the other hand to have avoided making any significant political comment.

[170] See Baker, *Readers and Readings*.   [171] BL, MS Hargrave 372, fols. 55, 59.
[172] New College Library, Oxford, MS 9502. HALS, MS Gorhambury XII.A.3, fol. 22.
[173] See above, p. 85.   [174] *ODNB*.

the late 1620s, but for this reason it is perhaps not surprising that its survival is unusual.[175] No doubt because of his subsequent promotions into the judiciary, the later speeches of Sir James Whitelocke up to his death in 1632 do not repeat the striking advocacy of the idea of mixed monarchy that had characterised his efforts in the wake of the early parliaments of James I,[176] but they did contain many of the traditional tropes of legal discourse. He often began by remarking that the doing of justice was a civil (or civic) as well as a moral duty, and on one occasion explained that jury service was for the peace of the commonwealth as well as its good and health.[177] He could account for delegated authority either in terms of English history from the Saxons onwards or by way of analogies with the creation of local jurisdictions mentioned in the Old Testament, and on at least one occasion he touched on the relationship between the secular and ecclesiastical jurisdictions. Speaking in 1628 in Durham Cathedral before an audience that doubtless contained many clergymen, he argued that it was a mistake for anyone to think that the Reformation had greatly reduced the reach of the ecclesiastical courts. On the contrary, the fact that the jurisdiction now flowed from the king rather than the pope made it stronger than ever. Even so, he also pointed out that in the modern age tithe disputes were likely to be more common than they had been in the past, and in this connection, as well as others, he was not willing to go along with those who claimed that prohibitions by the common-law courts should not be issued at all.[178]

In comparison with Whitelocke's, a set of speeches delivered by Francis Parlett, the recorder of King's Lynn, in the first half of the 1630s are perhaps more revealing of the conformist climate of the times, and they are particularly valuable because they include addresses made on occasions such as the appointment of mayors as well as charges to courts.[179] A firm Protestant, even a Puritan in his religious outlook, Parlett had no time for either non-conformists or Papists, believing that both deviancies were the product of pride, a sin that made the pope want to overthrow kings and led schismatics to believe that they alone had discovered the truths of salvation.[180] Having confiscated a copy of Prynne's *Historiomastix* that he discovered in the town library, he was concerned that it might be dangerous to be caught in possession of such a libellous book.[181] Although he distinguished between matters of

---

[175] CUL, MS Dd.xiv.3, fol. 213.   [176] See above, p. 161.
[177] Whitelocke papers, iii, fols. 107, 114.   [178] Ibid., fols. 115–16.
[179] NRO, MF/RO 396/13. Parlett was a member of Lincoln's Inn.
[180] Ibid., fols. 2–3, 13v.
[181] Ibid., fols. 54v, 83v. In response to Parlett's queries about this, Attorney General Noy told him to hand the book over to the Stationers' Company.

conscience, which were largely a question of the relationship between God and man, and overt acts, which were the legitimate concern of secular laws, his thought exemplifies the links between what Patrick Collinson has called 'magistracy and ministry'.[182] Addressing the Grand Inquest at Lynn in August 1632, he noted that the greatest enemy of man was man himself: 'Sin is a transgression of the lawe of God, *and* whosoever is a transgressor ag[ain]st the lawe of God is also a transgressor ag[ain]st the law of man.'[183]

There was also, however, a more secular side to Parlett's thought, which had much in common with a strain of patriarchal political thought that was evidently popular at the Caroline court. In one of his addresses on the installation of a new mayor, he began with an explanation of the Aristotelian connection between 'oeconomical' and political duty. Government began with the first marriage between Adam and Eve, and thereafter grew within families, cities and commonwealths. Yet, while 'natural necessity' was the reason for the origins of states, the government of Lynn itself was a 'civille subordinate delegacon from him that is ye supreme natural parent of all the families of this realm, the king, our natural liege lord'.[184] Parlett often referred to the relationship between rulers and ruled, between the mayor of the town and its citizens, in the language of matrimony. The mayor's oath of office was like the wedding vow; he was the civil husband of a civil wife. The civic leader, like the head of household, had an obligation to instruct his family in goodness because the failure to do so would 'shutt the gates to civilie discipline *and* . . . open them to disorder, w[hi]ch ending brings in Confuscon, ruin *and* desolacon'.[185] While the aim of government at all levels was the 'amitie and Correspondencie betwene man *and* man in a co*m*mon societye or publique state', this could only be achieved through obedience to 'the king our Sov[er]aigne, To whom the apostle bids us all submitt *and* obey for Conscience sake'.[186]

After 1635, the evidence of public speeches relates mostly to the judges, who were evidently unable to escape the controversy surrounding the Ship Money case. One of the accusations Thomas Harrision made against Sir Richard Hutton was that the judge had used his speeches at assizes to advance his view that that levy was not lawful. On the other hand, Sir Robert Berkeley was alleged to have said in a charge at York in Lent 1636 that it was a lawful and inseparable flower of the crown for the king to command Ship Money from inland as well as maritime

---

[182] Ibid., fols. 5–5v. P. Collinson, *The Religion of Protestants* (Oxford, 1982), ch. 4.
[183] NRO, MF/RO 396/13, fols. 2–3.   [184] Ibid., fol. 7v.
[185] Ibid., fols. 11v, 12.   [186] Ibid., fols. 18v, 72v.

counties.[187] According to an account of it that Francis Cheynell included in a letter to his uncle, Sir William Jones used his charge at the Oxford assizes in Lent 1638 to cover many of the arguments in support of Ship Money that had been made by Coventry in his own speech to the judges just before they went on circuit, and which in most respects merely rehearsed arguments from the trial. However, Cheynell was particularly struck by one of the points Jones made in order to quiet fears about the long-term constitutional consequences of the levy: 'a King is in truth and propriety no Kinge (but only in respect of God's permission) but a tyrant, if hee abuse his power to the oppression of his people'.[188]

At the very least, therefore, it is clear that judicial differences of opinion in the London trials were accompanied by parallel discussions out in the country.[189] Furthermore, meetings of quarter sessions and assize frequently provided the setting for the ventilation of political issues. Presentments by grand juries in the localities that in effect criticised aspects of royal policy by bringing them to the attention of justices as offences that needed redress were a notable feature of the 1630s.[190] One matter that came up again and again was the distaste in the shires for the modest financial exactions connected with the equipping and training of the militia, a matter that at this time languished in legal ambiguity. According to a defence of his actions as a judge that was drawn up by his son-in-law at the time of the Long Parliament, Sir George Croke had been willing to accept such presentments, which frequently claimed that the fees to employ professional muster-masters were against the Petition of Right, even though he had suffered a dressing-down by the privy council for his pains.[191] In a well-known but hardly untypical case from Shropshire, when discussion took place at quarter sessions about whether or not to accept a presentment over this issue in 1635, one of the JPs, Sir John Corbet, had the clerk of the peace read out the Petition to the assembled court, and wondered why one of his colleagues, the lawyer Timothy Turner, was so touchy about allowing a grand jury to do exactly what it was supposed to do.[192] Evidently responding to a charge

---

[187] *Articles of Accusation Exhibited . . . Against Sir John Bramston . . . [et al.],* pp. 5–6. Sir Humphrey Davenport imprisoned a defendant at Gloucester assizes for speaking against Ship Money (*ODNB*).

[188] HMC, *Various,* vol. 7, 417–18.

[189] Sharpe, *Personal Rule* and E. S. Cope, *Politics without Parliaments, 1629–1640* (1987), pp. 116–29, give many examples of discussion of the case in the localities.

[190] Ibid., pp. 101–6, 150–1, 185–6, 194.   [191] HALS, MS Gorhambury, xii.B.25.

[192] HEHL, MS Ellesmere 7631–32. The episode is discussed in M. Braddick, 'Administrative performance: the representation of political authority in early modern England' in M. J. Braddick and J. Walter, eds., *Negotiating Power in Early Modern England* (Cambridge, 2001), pp. 166–87.

by Sergeant Atkins that encouraged them to present innovations in religion, a grand jury at the Hertfordshire assizes in 1639 presented the removal of a communion table in All Saints Hertford from its traditional position so that it could be situated 'altarwise' in the manner prescribed by Caroline religious initiatives.[193]

While it is true that presentments of this kind were perhaps inevitable in a period when there was no parliament, they were also entirely consistent with, if not the outcome of, a kind of participatory rhetoric that had been retailed by lawyers since the sixteenth century, if not earlier.[194] As soon as the Short Parliament met in the spring of 1640, moreover, a flood of county petitions complained about nearly all of the religious and political initiatives of the Personal Rule.[195]

'Hannibal at the Gates'

When Charles I travelled north in March 1639 to meet a Scottish army that had been raised in rebellion against his rule there, it fell to the recorder of York, Thomas Widdrington, to give the customary address welcoming the king and his entourage to the city. Developing a familiar theme, Widdrington proclaimed that the king had established his throne on two columns made out of diamonds, piety and justice. At York and a little later on at Berwick, where he repeated the task, Widdrington went on to say that the king's English subjects were satisfied with his performance in connection with both. Any conspiracies against his rule were mere 'bubbles'.[196]

Widdrington's speeches evoked lavish, but decorous, neo-classical pillars gracefully supporting the throne, a masque-like image that was sometimes reproduced in frontispieces and prints. Yet a more realistic evocation might have been of twisted and stressed baroque columns, each composed of words, paper and human actions, that sometimes merged into one with a throne perched rather precariously on the top. It is true that the road that ended in the outbreak of civil war in England began with the rebellion of the Scots, largely in response to the introduction of a prayer book that had been composed under the supervision of an English archbishop, William Laud, but there is no doubting the pent-up discontent of the subjects south of the border as well. By the end of the 1630s, crown-law officers were having to deal with

---

[193] *Articles of Accusation Exhibited . . . Against Sir John Bramston . . . [et al.]*, p. 6.
[194] See above, pp. 89–90.
[195] *Proceedings of the Short Parliament of 1640*, ed. E. S. Cope and W. H. Coates (Royal Historical Society, Camden Fourth Series, vol. 19, 1977), pp. 275ff.
[196] Petyt MS 538 (51), fols. 206v–7.

seditious words and rumoured conspiracies, mostly involving indiscrete Londoners of small substance and influence.[197] Much more seriously, measures had to be taken against a large number of sheriffs who were backward in accounting to the Exchequer for the Ship Money they were supposed to be collecting, and significant numbers of people were being imprisoned for refusing to pay 'coat and conduct money', a levy to support the king's strategy of using county-trained bands to stop the advance of the Scots into England.[198] In the spring and summer of 1640, large demonstrations, composed mainly of apprentices, frequently took to the streets of London, and on several occasions Laud's episcopal palace at Lambeth was surrounded.[199] When the king was finally obliged to call first the Short and then the Long Parliaments in May and November in order to meet the demands the Scots were making in return for halting their invasion at Newcastle, royal financial measures of the previous decade and the judges who had countenanced them, no less than the high churchmen, immediately came under attack.

Lord Keeper Finch opened the Short Parliament with a speech that tried to align recent royal policy with the ancient constitution under which England had flourished as a nation that had never 'suffered any Conqueror to give any new law, nor the old law was never changed'.[200] But as the son of Lord Chief Justice Bramston perceptively noted some years after the event, the membership of parliament included many people who had in one way or another fallen foul of the policies of the Personal Rule, and their demands for retribution produced inflammatory speeches.[201] Consequently, one of the first orders of business in the House of Commons when what became the Long Parliament met in November 1640 was the presentation by John Hampden, the defendant in the Ship Money case, of a petition from Alexander Ginnis (or Jennings), who had also refused to pay the levy, and who had been imprisoned by the Council for making scandalous speeches against the king's government.[202] On the same day, Harbottle Grimston, the son-in-law of Justice Croke, launched a powerfully worded polemical attack. 'Judges have overthrowne the Lawe and Bishops Religion and some of both

[197] Bankes Papers, MSS 18/1–2,21; 37/54, 57; 44/46; 58/1; 62/28, 63; 65/28.
[198] Ibid., 5/51. HEHL, MS Ellesmere 7845, letter to the earl of Bridgewater.
[199] HEHL, MS Ellesmere 7834. Letter from John Castle to the earl of Bridgewater, 15 May 1640.
[200] *Proceedings of the Short Parliament of 1640*, pp. 115–16.
[201] *Bramston*, p. 73; *The Diary of Bulstrode Whitelocke 1605–1675*, ed. R. Spalding (Oxford, 1990), pp. 123–4.
[202] *POSLP*, I, p. 31.

have been the authors of all these miseries and wee hope wee shall have . . . punishment against them.'[203]

Inside parliament, Oliver St John, one of Hampden's counsel, and an ally of the earl of Bedford, stressed that Ship Money violated the express words of the Petition of Right and was made chairman of the committee investigating it.[204] Outside parliament, Henry Parker, a barrister of Lincoln's Inn, who was closely associated with Lord Saye and Sele, another leading aristocratic opponent of the regime, published a fierce denunciation of the judicial decision itself. Going only a little further than Robert Holborne had during the trial, he pointed out that of all the possible forms of government, the monarchical was worst because of the unpredictable quality of the holder of the office,[205] and he was particularly scathing of Justice Jones's acceptance of the trustworthiness of the king. Describing the levy as 'a pickelocke tricke' desiged to overthrow all liberty and property of goods, he repeated the line of thought enunciated so frequently at the end of the 1620s: a people who were not governed by known and certain laws with regard to their property were no better than slaves.[206] The royal prerogative could only extend so far as it protected the liberty and property of the subject.

Although argued with much greater reference to history and legal precedent, a similar point was made in a tract on the Oath of Allegiance that the attorney of Wells (Somerset), Robert Powell, appended to an otherwise unremarkable treatise on the jurisdiction of the court leet. Tracing English liberties back beyond the Conquest, he also drew on the calculation of self-interest that had frequently informed charges in Elizabethan times. While it was the duty of the subject to obey the monarch, this obedience was given in return for the expectation that he would receive protection and the liberty to enjoy his spiritual and temporal estate, free from 'rapine, expilation and all unjust encroachments, restraints, confinements, imprisonments and oppressions whatsover'.[207]

---

[203] *The Journal of Sir Simonds D'Ewes From the Beginning of the Long Parliament to the Opening of the Trial of the Earl of Strafford*, ed. Wallace Notestein (New Haven, CT, 1923), p. 6, *POSLP*, I, p. 33. He mentioned the case of Sir Thomas Tresilian, who was appealed of treason and hanged in 1388 for giving an opinion that measures taken to limit Richard II's powers were illegal. See above, p. 57.

[204] Ibid., pp. 337, 341.

[205] Henry Parker, *The Case of Ship Money briefly discoursed, According to the Grounds of Law, Policy and Conscience* (1640), pp. 22–3. See also, M. Mendle, *Henry Parker and the English Civil War: the Political Thought of the Public's 'Privado'* (Cambridge, 1995).

[206] Parker, *Ship Money*, p. 22.

[207] Robert Powell, *A Treatise of the Antiquity, Authority, Vses and Iurisdiction of the Ancient Courts of Leet, or view of Franck-Pledge, . . . With a large Explication of the old Oath of Allegiance and the Kings Royall office of Protection annexed* (1642), pp. 205–6.

Both Powell and Parker looked to parliament to redress wrongs and re-establish the subjects' rights, and at Westminster the emergence of individual cases spurred on the condemnation of allegedly illegal measures stretching back to the later 1620s, when, according to some, the 'legal government' of the realm had first been undermined.[208] In early December 1640 the Long Parliament demanded to know the whereabouts of the papers of Sir Edward Coke, which had been confiscated after his death in 1634, and ordered the publication of parts of his *Institutes* that had not yet gone to the press.[209] At precisely the same moment, the future royalists Viscount Falkland and Edward Hyde made speeches calling for the impeachment of the surviving members of the judicial bench on the ground that a number of their decisions, but especially that in the Ship Money case, had undermined the laws and liberties of the realm.[210] According to the memoirs he wrote many years later, Hyde thought the judges had let down the nation by failing to stand up to the king in the same way as their predecessors had done, but he also noted that it was the public speeches they had made in support of royal policies, as much as the decisions themselves, that had 'incensed the people'.[211] Since the majority decision in Hampden's case was at odds with the apparently unanimous extrajudicial opinion given to the king in February 1637, the focus of attention locked onto Sir John Finch who was accused by Falkland of having lobbied and threatened the others.

Called before the House of Lords to explain himself, Finch was rather disingenuous about some of his activities during the Personal Rule, especially in connection with the royal forests,[212] but, while it seems certain that he encouraged the other judges to support the king, there is no concrete evidence that he used direct threats.[213] Similarly, Sir Robert Berkeley was singled out for close scrutiny because he had allegedly tried to change Sir George Croke's mind about Ship Money, but, according to Croke himself, Berkeley had in fact been in favour of adding the words 'in times of immediate danger' to the extrajudicial opinion. Accused at just about the same time as the two houses were organising a case of treason against the earl of Strafford, the pressure on Finch was so great that he fled to Holland and stayed there until 1660.[214] In 1641, *Articles of Accusation* were published against all of the surviving judges who had ruled in favour of Ship Money. Prefaced with a passage from Chronicles 'Take heed what ye do: for ye judge not for man, but for the Lord', these included general charges of having 'traitorously and wickedly

---

[208] HALS, MS Gorhambury XII.B.25.   [209] *POSLP*, I, pp. 469, 473–4.
[210] Ibid., pp. 479.   [211] *Clarendon*, I, §151–3.   [212] *POSLP*, II, pp. 5–11.
[213] *POSLP*, I, pp. 561. Above, p. 206.   [214] *ODNB*.

endeavoured to subvert the fundamental laws and established government of the Realm of England, and instead thereof to introduce an
Arbitrarie, and Tyrannicall government against law'.[215]

Alongside the condemnation of the common-law judges, there were
also concerted, and largely successful, attacks on nearly all of the courts in
the realm that based their jurisdiction on the royal prerogative alone.
Since their personnel and actions were indelibly linked with the prosecution of cases such as those of Burton, Bastwick and Prynne, Star
Chamber and High Commission were condemned as illegal jurisdictions
largely on the basis of the sentences they had passed. Although the
oath *ex officio* was referred to in connection with High Commission, and
although the traditional lawyerly suspicion of the courts helped make
them vulnerable, the Commons debates suggest that it was their 'political'
use during the Personal Rule, rather than the procedural anomalies James
Morice had been so concerned about, that accounted for their downfall.[216] In the Short Parliament, Star Chamber was said to have become
merely a means of raising money through the exaction of heavy fines in
connection with the 'projects'.[217] According to Harbottle Grimston's notes
on the *Case of Bishop Williams*, who had been hounded in the courts after
writing a book against the making of communion tables into altars, the
use of Star Chamber and High Commission in such cases 'reflect[ed] a
daunger vpon all other Subiectes of England'. Star Chamber had become
'in the moderne practise very arbitrarie, referring too much to the private
opinion of the judges, that begin the sentence who have no direction in
Law to guide their judgments'. Some of them 'mainetayne doctrines of
dangerous consequence, that the Acts of this Court (soe variable and
mingled . . .) are not questionable elswhere, noe not in Parliament . . .'.[218]

An attack against the Council in the Marches of Wales was led by the
Shropshire squire Sir John Corbet, who was intent on revenge against
the lord president of the Council, the earl of Bridgewater, whose reports
to London resulted in the fines and imprisonment imposed on Corbet
after he had called for the Petition of Right to be read at quarter sessions
in 1635.[219] Although there were plausible allegations about the taking of

---

[215] *Articles of Accusation Exhibited . . . Against Sir John Bramston . . . [et al.]*, p.1.
[216] *POSLP*, II, p. 269. In March 1641, Dr Arthur Duck, chancellor of the diocese of
London and a member of High Commission gave the only testimony in support of its
jurisdiction (ibid., p. 616).
[217] HALS, MS Gorhambury XII.A.2a.   [218] HALS, MS Gorhambury XII.A.19.
[219] HEHL, MSS Ellesmere 7701–11. Serjeant Wilde said in committee that Corbet,
'a man of worth and quality', and a father of many children, had been imprisoned, not
for offending against the law, but for doing what the law required him to do. In June
1641, the Commons ordered the Star Chamber judgment against him be taken off the
file, and it was agreed that Bridgewater ought to make reparations (*POSLP*, IV, p. 714).

irregular fees, and the use of the court to make money out of cases involving sexual misconduct, the abolition of the jurisdiction by statute must also be seen in the context of the ongoing campaign against it that had been waged since the 1590s.[220] Similarly, allegations against the Council of the North included the charge that Strafford, during his tenure as lord president, had made it into a 'new kind of Chancery'.[221] In April 1641, Edward Hyde alluded to the general question of whether the king could issue commissions that in effect 'cantoned' out the country. He stressed that the jurisdiction was outside the superintendence of the courts at Westminster and consequently denied northerners their rights as Englishmen at common law.[222]

Alongside these secular issues, of course, religion figured prominently in the reaction of parliament to the Personal Rule, and the intensity of confessional feelings inflamed political discourse. Petitions were regularly received from the localities concerning either the maltreatment of Puritan clergymen by the ecclesiastical authorities, or, alternatively, protesting against the actions of those who had supported the religious policies of Archbishop Laud and the king. Spurred by the receipt in December 1640 of the 'Root and Branch' petition from London, MPs debated whether to reform the church by suppressing Laudian innovations or by completely transforming it. Bishops were, therefore, subjected to an intimidating range of threats that began with charges of treason and progressed to exclusion from the House of Lords and complete abolition. Furthermore, while the attack was driven by accusations that Laud and his colleagues had betrayed English Protestantism to 'popery', the long-standing juridical issues that divided the churchmen and the common lawyers were also prominent.

Henry Parker's pamphlets referred to Thomas Harrison's slander of Justice Hutton and denounced the intellectual and political pretensions of the clerical estate. They claimed to supersede the opinions of statesmen and lawyers and poisoned the king against parliament. They aimed to extend their jurisdiction further and further into secular life; they preached 'an unlimitable prerogative and condemne all liberty as

---

[220] Above, pp. 126–8. The background is ably described in C. A. J. Skeel, *The Council in the Marches of Wales: a Study in Local Government during the Sixteenth and Seventeenth Centuries* (1904). Many details survive in the Bridgewater papers in the Huntington Library. There had also been controversy in 1637 concerning prohibitions issued in connection with the Council's jurisdiction over legacies and sexual incontinency, which had led to clashes with the prerogative court at Canterbury (Ellesemere 7482). There is additional correspondence in SA, Ludlow Papers Box 212.

[221] *POSLP*, III, p. 86. [222] Ibid., IV, p. 102.

injurious to Kings and monarchy'.[223] Robert Powell complained that the clergy argued about government in such general terms that they took no account of local laws, customs and constitutions.[224] Inside parliament, a number of lawyers, including Edward Bagshawe, castigated the ecclesiastical canons of 1640 on the grounds that they promoted the view that divine right kings could make claims on the property of the subject.[225] Having been appointed to a committee investigating Laud's involvement in the formulation of the canons, Harbottle Grimston plumbed the rhetorical depths in denouncing the archbishop as 'the stye of all Pestilent filth, that hath infected the State, and Government of the Church and Common-wealth . . .'.[226]

Along with John Pym, the lawyer-MPs John Glynn, Bulstrode Whitelocke and Edward Bagshawe were involved in drafting a bill in the House of Commons for the exclusion of bishops from the House of Lords. Drawing heavily on arguments from Bagshawe's suppressed reading at the Temple, the point was that if the bishops held their seats only through their temporal baronies, and not as representatives of a separate clerical estate, the confiscation of these would eliminate their right to sit.[227] Although the House of Lords rejected a bill along these lines that narrowly passed the Commons in the spring of 1641,[228] Bishop Williams, now out of disfavour and leading the defence of episcopacy, instigated an alternative set of measures that promised instead the reform and regulation of ecclesiastical government. As if taking its agenda from that of Morice in the 1590s, this proposed a thorough reformation of the church court system, including a redefinition of rules of procedure and the elimination of offensive features such as the oath *ex officio*. Furthermore, it stipulated that from henceforth no clergyman should sit on any secular court, including Star Chamber and commissions of the peace.[229]

The bishops were eventually excluded from parliament in early 1642, following claims by Williams and others that any votes taken in the House of Lords in their absence were invalid. He and eleven others were accused of treason and imprisoned, but no bill to reform the government

---

[223] Parker, *Case of Ship Money*, p. 33; *A Discourse Concerning Puritans. A vindication of those, who uniustly suffer by the mistake, abuse, and misapplication of that Name* (1641).
[224] Powell, *A Treatise of the Antiquity [of] Courts of Leet*, p. 194.
[225] *POSLP*, I, pp. 164, 307, 530–41, 803.
[226] Ibid., pp. 658–9; *Mr Grymstons Speech in Parliament upon the Accusation and Impeachment of William Laud, Arch-Bishop of Canterbury, upon high Treason* (1641), p. 2.
[227] G.W. Thomas, 'Archbishop John Williams: politics and prerogative law 1621–1642' (Oxford DPhil thesis, 1974), pp. 299–319. *POSLP*, II, pp. 390, 696–703, 709; IV, p. 39.
[228] Ibid., III, pp. 605, 707, 715–16.   [229] Thomas, 'Archbishop John Williams', p. 316.

and jurisdiction of the church was agreed upon, a matter of some significance since both remained in a state of flux for most of the next two decades. While the traditional jurisdictional conflicts between the common-law and the spiritual courts meant that lawyers were well placed to express the grievances of the laity against the clerical establishment, they were not necessarily in a better position than anyone else in the 1640s and 1650s to resolve the profound questions that lay at the heart of church/state relations. If Erastianism, the view that the spirituality was ultimately subject to secular authority, was the likely default position of most, that still left many outstanding issues over which there could be critical differences of opinion. Writing in the tradition of *praemunire*, Parker on the one hand maintained that the pretensions of the clergy subverted the power and authority of the king, while at the same time arguing that the clerics had depended on royal authority in order to increase their own influence.[230] In the mid 1640s John Selden and other parliamentarian lawyers were amongst the most vocal critics of attempts to replace episcopacy with *jure divino* Presbyterianism,[231] but in the Long Parliament Selden had argued against Bagshawe's tenurial interpretation of episcopal seats in the House of Lords, maintaining that the clerical estate needed to have a means of expressing its interests in parliament.[232]

As was the case for many lay MPs, for many lawyers, agreement that the church needed reform in 1641 did not necessarily translate into the view that institutions that had been a part of English life for hundreds of years should simply be abolished. Consequently the issue of episcopacy emerged as one of those that eventually divided supporters of the king from those of parliament. At the same time, by the autumn of 1641 the king had assented to legislation that addressed many of the secular legal grievances. In an unprecedented act, the House of Lords ordered that the lord keeper, the master of the rolls and the two lord chief justices should bring the record of the judgment in the Ship Money case into the house so that a note could be entered on the court rolls that the judgment had been vacated and declared illegal by parliament.[233] Writing in July 1641, the Welsh MP John Bodvell mentioned the 'great blessings' of the taking away of Star Chamber and High Commission by bill and royal assent, and he looked forward to the downfall of the Council in Wales.[234]

---

[230] Parker, *Discourse Concerning Puritans*, pp. 13, 17, 29.
[231] Whitelocke, *Memorials*, pp. 68, 105.   [232] *POSLP*, II, p. 696.
[233] DHC, DBKL, Ship Money paper dated 26 February 1641. An account of the reversal was also to be announced by the judges at assize.
[234] Wynn Papers, MS 1689.

It is a sign of how far things had gone by the end of October that the parliamentary diarist Simonds D'Ewes puzzled over a speech given by a little-known lawyer called Smith. Since it was concerned primarily with the defence of property, D'Ewes could only conclude that it had been penned before the Ship Money was taken away. Even more significantly, in the midst of the same debate, which concerned the degree of control the two houses were entitled to exercise over the appointment of royal councillors, Hyde spoke in favour of moderation, claiming that the taking away of Star Chamber, High Commission and the Ship Money was enough to satisfy the concerns of the subjects.[235] Soon afterwards, D'Ewes suggested that the impeachment cases against the judges, which had languished in the face of more pressing business, should be pursued with greater vigour so that they could be put to 'fine and ransom, whose scarlet robes may blush for their crimes because they themselves will not'. Yet, at this stage he advocated the measure largely as a way of showing 'the people' that the financial burdens facing the country should not be laid entirely upon them, and nothing came of the proposal.[236] Despite the intense political hostility that had come down on them, from a strictly legal point of view the parliamentary charges against the judiciary were unprecedented and had a good deal in common with Thomas Harrison's slander of Justice Hutton, a point that may have been recognised by many of the lawyers in the House. A number of them had spoken earlier against the idea that Sir Robert Berkeley's actions could be said to have amounted to treason.[237] Although the case against the judges was taken up occasionally in the spring of 1642, it lapsed thereafter, and Berkeley and several others continued to act.[238]

In November 1641, news of rebellion in Ireland reached London, a development that radically shifted the political emphasis away from demands for retribution for the acts of the Personal Rule towards the question of whether parliament should have a say in naming the king's councillors and in the control of the army needed to suppress it. This controversy, which led eventually to the raising of the forces that fought the opening battles of the civil war, was exacerbated when King Charles left London for York in January 1642, having failed in his attempt to arrest five MPs on suspicion of treason. In March, after much debate, the two houses passed a Militia Ordinance in order to put county forces in a state of readiness. Although not unprecedented, ordinances passed

---

[235] *The Journal of Sir Simonds D'Ewes From the First Recess of the Long Parliament To the Withdrawal of King Charles From London*, ed. W. H. Coates (New Haven, CT, 1942), pp. 44–5.
[236] Ibid., p. 121.   [237] *POSLP*, II pp. 431–3.   [238] *ODNB*.

by one, but not all of the constituent parts of the English parliament (king, lords and commons) were extraordinary, and, although precedents were discussed, the legality of the Militia Ordinance was inevitably a matter of doubt, a point the king exploited by denouncing it as illegal and issuing alternative commands to the localities in the form of royal commissions of array.

Appropriately enough for the last major legal dispute before the outbreak of civil war, the questions surrounding the Militia Ordinance were intractable and ultimately boiled down to arguments that were surprisingly similar to those in the Ship Money case. Although it earned them the displeasure of a king they both would eventually support, Sir John Bankes, now chief justice of the Common Pleas, and Sir Edward Littleton, now lord keeper, were widely known to have endorsed the legality of the Militia Ordinance, presumably on the grounds that the danger to the realm from the Irish rebellion necessitated action, and since the king was not in London to oversee it, something had to be done by the two houses.[239] On the other hand, other leading legal figures questioned the legality of the measure,[240] and the formidable legal scholar John Selden, who remained in London throughout the civil wars, at one stage in the summer of 1642 gave a speech in the Commons that made his doubts about the Militia Ordinance absolutely clear: 'the people may justly dislike it, for here is a power given by an ordinance [not a statute with the legal assent of the king] to dispose of their goods and persons because they are to muster and train as often as they shall be required'.[241] While the actions of the two houses might be necessary because of the emergency, the powers they claimed could potentially be used to make levies on the subject as arbitrary as those of the 1630s.

By the time Selden spoke, moreover, the issue of parliamentary, as opposed to royal, tyranny had been identified and exploited by the most effective royal propaganda of the period, *The Answer to the Nineteen Propositions*, which was published in the name of Charles, but ghostwritten by Nicholas Culpeper and Viscount Falkland. According to the *Answer*,

---

[239] Whitelocke, *Memorials*, p. 56. The importance of the position of the crown law officers is revealed in two remarkable letters from Lord Francis Willoughby to the king in June 1642, which explained that he had personally acted on the Militia Ordinance largely because their widely reported opinions had led him to think that it was legal (DHC, DPKL). George Bankes, *The Story of Corfe Castle, and of Many who Have Lived there . . .* (1853), p. 133.

[240] Whitelocke, *Memorials*, p. 59. See also, R. Tuck, ' "The ancient law of freedom": John Selden and the English civil war' in J. S. Morrill, ed., *Reactions to the English Civil War 1642–46* (Basingstoke, 1982), pp. 137–62.

[241] *The Private Journals of the Long Parliament 3 January to 5 March 1642*, ed. W. H. Coates, A. S. Young and Vernon Snow (New Haven, CT, 1982), p. 161.

the two houses of parliament were sustaining their position by undermining the constitution, and replacing the law of the land by their will.
'They have thought fit to remove a troublesome Rub in their way, The
Law . . . Orders and ordinances are pressed upon the people as Laws,
and their obedience required of them.'[242] The king, by contrast, promised to uphold the fundamental laws of the land, and, in addition, the
Answer, though perhaps not the king himself, put forward the proposition that the constitution of England was essentially a mixed monarchy, where rule was shared equally by king, lords and commons.[243]

In response, Henry Parker published an argument for the two houses
that focused on two points. Maintaining that the authority for government derived from 'the people', he asserted that the king's power and
office were held in trust for them and not based on either hereditary
right or divine ordination.[244] Acknowledging that the two houses were
claiming extraordinary powers, he explained that this was because of the
extraordinary circumstances created by the king's breach of trust, which
meant that there was no option but to call on the 'law of necessity'.
Referring to the Latin dictum that the welfare of the people was above
the rule of law, he asked his readers in the end to consider which part of
the fracturing English polity, the king or the two houses, was most likely
to use power in the interests of the people as a whole.

There was much in Parker's argument, including the claim that the
people were the root of all authority, that was compatible with thinking
that we have seen expressed at one point or another in writings and
speeches by lawyers stretching back at least as far as the reign of
Elizabeth.[245] Furthermore, at least one other lawyer, John Marsh of
Lincoln's Inn published a defence of the Militia Ordinance that argued
along similar lines, and many others may well have been convinced by
the same considerations.[246] Nevertheless, lawyer allegiance in the civil
wars appears to have divided along roughly the same lines as that of
other groups in the population, and while there are of course many
different reasons why this may have been so, one of them was that from

---

[242] *His Maiesties Answer to the XIX Propositions of Both Houses of Parliament (Reprinted by
His Maiesties Command)* (Oxford, 1642), p. 2. D. Smith, *Constitutional Royalism and
the Search for Settlement, c. 1640–1649* (Cambridge, 1994), pp. 9, 90.
[243] *His Maiesties Answer*, pp. 22–7.
[244] [Henry Parker], *Observations upon some of his Majesties late Answers and Expressions*
(1642), pp. 1–6.
[245] See above, pp. 76–81, 86, 91.
[246] [John Marsh], *An Argument or, Debate in Law* (1642). See also, BL, MS Additional
46500, fol. 27: letter dated 21 May 1642 from Roger Hill to his wife, which explains
that if the king makes war on parliament that would be a 'breach of the Trust reposed
in him by his People'.

the point of view of a common lawyer, there were problems with the kinds of arguments that Parker and Marsh were making.

The notion that the crown was held in trust was an effective polemical tool precisely because it immediately brought to mind mundane everyday circumstances and a well-known legal device. It was a long-standing practice for landholders of all kinds to have their lawyers draw up enfeoffments to use, instruments that put their property into trust, most often to secure intergenerational transferrals and secure the interests of their wives and children.[247] Conveyances were drawn appointing trustees who were supposed to manage the estate in the interests of the beneficiary. Guidelines might be stipulated about how the trustees were supposed to exercise their office, and alleged breaches of the trust, or challenges to the authority of the trustees were one of the principal sources of business of the court of Chancery.

As we have seen, however, although the equitable jurisdiction of Chancery was part and parcel of the legal system, common lawyers since the time of St German had raised concerns about a jurisdiction based on conscience rather than the strict letter of the law, and pamphlets like those of Parker or Marsh read more like bills submitted in Chancery than as arguments at common law.[248] Furthermore, both consistently maintained that, given the circumstances, the overthrow of the strict letter of the law was necessary in order to achieve justice or a greater good. As Marsh put it, 'without question, the rigour of all Lawes, ought to receive such qualification, and equitable construction, that the Common-wealth doe not suffer to be indamaged. The Law was made to support the common good, and therefore that Law is against Law, that is against the common good.'[249]

Yet while such arguments might well have been recognised in the past as a justification for passing parliamentary legislation, they were less compelling when made in favour of ordinances that did not carry the authority of the king in parliament. One problem was that it was difficult to prove that the king held the crown as a trustee rather than by a hereditary right at common law. While the Elizabethan author of 'Certaine errors' had come close, the divine origins of royal authority had just as often in the recent past been stressed.[250] More importantly, since the idea that obligations should be strictly kept was a bedrock of common-law thinking about economic and political life, equitable claims that they could be loosened or qualified, even by necessity, threatened a chaos of

---

[247] See above, p. 42. [248] Below, pp. 313–16. [249] Marsh, *An Argument*, p. 9.
[250] Above, pp. 74–8, 140–2, 152–61.

uncertainty that might ultimately undermine the rule of law, and it was hard to know where this might end.[251]

The other major problem with arguments such as those of Parker and Marsh concerned the consequences of living in a state where the law of necessity applied. As in *Hampden's Case*, there was a question about who had the authority to declare that the law of necessity was in force, and if it was then 'Hannibal was at the gates'; the courts of justice were closed, there was no law and civil society was effectively dissolved so that no one could call their property their own. In June 1642, as war seemed increasingly likely, there was discussion in the House of Commons about how preparations for war might actually lead to war, and several speakers pointed out that war would destroy the law and consequently all differences between man and man.[252] For lawyers who paid attention to their own rhetoric, the state of war was also the antithesis of the peace that the rule of law was supposed to provide. The traditional common-law view of the state of nature was in fact not all that much different from Hobbes's war of all against all. Consequently a descent into civil war was the equivalent of professional failure, and a palpable source of emotional distress. Lord Keeper Littleton, who eventually joined the king at York in May 1642, was evidently a depressed and temporarily broken man.[253] The correspondence of Attorney General Bankes with leading parliamentarians in London reveals a profound anxiety about the outbreak of war, even though he was unable to think of any means of preventing it.[254] The Ship Money judge Sir John Bramston claimed that he could not join the king at York in May 1642 because of ill health and the danger of being captured by parliamentary militia on his journey north. According to his son, however, another reason for his reluctance was that Sir Edward Coke had once explained to him that in case of civil war, it was one of the duties of the chief justice of England to go into the field after a battle to identify the dead so that the property and goods of rebels could be confiscated for the king.[255] That was not something he wanted to do.

---

[251] Above, pp. 39, 145–7.   [252] *Private Journals of the Long Parliament*, pp. 43–5.
[253] *ODNB*.   [254] Bankes, *Story of Corfe Castle*, pp. 121–48.
[255] *Bramston*, pp. 83–4. Dismissed from his office by the king for failing to attend, Bramston was subsequently courted by parliament for the remainder of the 1640s.

9   Law and 'community'

Persons and polities

Focusing often on debates in parliament, or well-known trials before the royal courts in London, the first half of this book concentrated on the legal dimensions of political, religious and 'constitutional' debate. It also showed that the legal discourses constituting these debates were refracted back into the localities in literally thousands of speeches before country squires, farmers and citizens. Nevertheless, when we turn away from high politics at Westminster, it is difficult to determine how juristic values resonated in provincial England. Direct evidence about the reception of legal language is limited. In any case discussions of the royal prerogative do not necessarily tell us all that much about the legal matrix within which people of vastly different levels of affluence earned their livings, raised their children, or interacted on the streets. Yet, just as early Stuart political and religious controversies were very often played out before judges, so too the great wave of litigation characteristic of the period brought a wide range of issues, stretching nearly from the cradle to the grave, into the courts and consequently into the law reports or readings that were given at the inns of court and chancery. The gap between metropolitan high politics and the provincial 'politics of the parish' is perhaps more readily bridged through legal materials than almost any other kind of source.

As we shall see in this and the following chapters, moreover, two of the most common ideas about the role of law in the polity were as relevant to the ways juristic thought handled social and economic issues as they were to general political questions. On the one hand, ideas derived from Ciceronian humanism postulated that the origins of civil society involved a process in which heads of families in the state of nature had agreed to seek peace and protection for themselves and their families by placing themselves first under kings, and subsequently under laws. The implication was that submission to government involved a calculation of self-interest, and the rhetorical expression of this, which was found in sources as diverse as the Elizabethan *Homily on Obedience* and countless public speeches, was that the purpose of law was to protect the property, wives, children and livelihoods of individual householders, a notion that was increasingly associated as the period wore on with the 'private interests' of individuals as against those of the 'public' or the state.[1]

On the other hand, however, this view coexisted with a no less venerable emphasis on the Aristotelian teleology of the state. Since polities were by definition created for the good of the people who composed them, it was logically impossible that the commonwealth should act against the interests of its individual members.[2] Most thinkers were more interested in discussing the origins of states, and the reasons why people should subject themselves to them, than they were with questions of the extension of state power over individuals. There was no generally acknowledged human right that could be mobilised to protect the person of the subject from any obligation or constraint that the community or the commonwealth thought it appropriate to impose upon him in the name of the common good. Furthermore, at least up until the civil war period, it was generally accepted that an individual's interest in his lands or goods existed, not through any natural right, but as a result of humanly constructed laws. When the Leveller Richard Overton claimed in the 1640s that every individual had a 'propriety in his own person', he was advancing a proposition that had previously had little direct purchase in English legal thought.[3]

No less important, it is worth recalling that when Sir John Davies argued for the implementation of English law in Ireland, he emphasised that the quality of Irish life would improve through the enjoyment of some of the less celebrated features of English government: markets, fairs, corporate towns and other franchises.[4] His imperial vision is a reminder that it is impossible to describe the place of the person within early modern civil society without referring to the large number of intermediate institutions that stood between him or her and the apex of the polity. Including manorial courts and craft guilds, the palatinates of Durham and Chester, as well as incorporated and unincorporated towns, these institutions have normally been discussed since the nineteenth century in terms of 'local' jurisdictions or 'local government', but these were not early modern usages. The subordination of the local to

---

[1] See above, pp. 190–2.   [2] See above, pp. 23–6.
[3] Richard Overton, *An Arrow Against All Tyrants and Tyrany, shot from the Prison of Newgate into the Prerogative Bowels of the Arbitrary House of Lords and all other Usurpers and Tyrants Whatsoever* (1646), p. 3.
[4] See above, pp. 128–9.

the state was more ambiguously conceived in the sixteenth and seventeenth centuries than it is today.

On one level, for instance, analogies were drawn between English towns and the Greek city-states that had been the focus of Aristotle's *Politics*. Thus manuscript treatises celebrating the towns of Winchester and Great Yarmouth, composed by their respective town clerks, John Trussell and Henry Manship, referred to the teachings of John Case, the leading expositor of Aristotelian thought in late Elizabethan Oxford.[5] Both described their towns as historic voluntary associations founded for the economic and social benefit of their inhabitants. By the 1620s, this view appears to have been more conflicted than it had been earlier, but that it was not altogether extinguished is illustrated by a speech the recorder of London, Sir Heneage Finch, gave at Greenwich in June 1622 when he introduced the newly selected lord mayor to the king. Noting that Londoners did not 'pretende to be Aboriginies', who would claim that they had their beginning as a polity from any other source than the crown, he nevertheless maintained that the City could trace its own history back more than 1,000 years.[6]

The point is that whether they were validated by a charter of incorporation granted by the crown, or by a prescriptive claim based on long continuance, lesser polities saw themselves, and were seen in law, as 'corporate and pollitique'[7] bodies that could perfectly legitimately make bylaws, hold courts and establish various other kinds of regulations concerning the economic and social life of their communities. Consequently, an exploration of law in the community which concentrates on the most local of all secular jurisdictions, the manorial court, can shed light on a number of issues that have recently been of interest to historians but which are often approached from diverse points of reference. These include the articulation of the state, the significance of neighbourliness, the relationship between the community and individuals, and the character of political consciousness and 'law-mindedness' amongst social groups outside the landed elite.[8]

---

[5] HRO, MS 107M88/W23; C. J. Palmer, ed., *The History of Great Yarmouth by Henry Manship, Town Clerk* (Yarmouth, 1854), pp. 24–6, 62, 191–2; C. B. Schmitt, *John Case and Aristotelianism in Renaissance England* (Kingston and Montreal, 1983).

[6] BL, MS Additional 18016, fol. 169v. For the development of some of these themes see P. Withington, *The Politics of Commonwealth: Citizens and Freemen in Early Modern England* (Cambridge, 2005).

[7] Bankes Papers, 12/11: the humble petition of the inhabitants of the town of Colbrooke in 'Buckinghamshire and Middlesex', c. 1637.

[8] Relevant work includes K. Wrightson, 'Two concepts of order: justices, constables and jurymen in seventeenth-century England' in John Brewer and John Styles, eds., *An Ungovernable People? The English and Their Law in the Seventeenth and Eighteenth Centuries*

244 Law and 'community'

Communal courts

Courts associated with the manor and the borough were unquestionably the jurisdictions most familiar to early modern men and women. Yet, over the past century or so, early modern historians, as opposed to medievalists,[9] have paid relatively little attention to them.[10] Historiographical fashions have had something to do with this, but another reason for the neglect is that the subject is difficult to treat in a systematic way. There were probably as many as 10,000 manors in England, and local variations, often accompanied by differences in terminology, make it difficult to sum up the theoretical nature of 'franchise' jurisdictions or to generalise confidently from the study of individual examples.[11]

There were, for example, significant differences between the institutions of corporate towns, which normally had a royal charter of incorporation, and manors, where jurisdiction was usually based on custom and closely tied to land tenure. Nevertheless, many significant unincorporated towns, such as Leeds, Manchester and Trowbridge (Wiltshire), were governed largely through manorial institutions that were in principle little different from those operating at village level.[12] At the same time, while some villages were subject to more than one manorial jurisdiction, in other places manorial structures were relatively insignificant even at the beginning of our period.[13] In still others, such as the thirty square miles covered by the largest manor in England,

---

(1980), pp. 21–47; Brooks, *Lawyers, Litigation*, ch. 7; A. Wood, 'The place of custom in plebeian political culture: England 1550–1800', *Social History*, 22 (1997), 46–60; S. Hindle, *The State and Social Change in Early Modern England, 1550–1640* (Basingstoke, 2000); A. Shepard and P. Withington, eds., *Communities in Early Modern England: Networks, Place, Rhetoric* (Manchester, 2000); K. Wrightson, 'Mutualities and obligations: changing social relationships in early modern England', *Proceedings of the British Academy*, 139 (2006), 157–94.

[9] See, for example, Zvi Razi and Richard Smith, eds., *Medieval Society and the Manor Court* (Oxford, 1996).

[10] For important exceptions see S. and B. Webb, *English Local Government from the Revolution to the Municipal Corporation Act: the Manor and the Borough* (2nd impression, 1924); J. F. C. Hearnshaw, *Leet Jurisdiction in England* (Southampton Record Society, 1908); J. P. Dawson, *A History of Lay Judges* (Cambridge, MA, 1960); F. G. Emmison, *Elizabethan Life: Home, Land and Work* (Chelmsford, 1976); M. K. McIntosh, *A Community Transformed. The Manor and Liberty of Havering 1500–1620* (Cambridge, 1991); A. Winchester, *The Harvest of the Hills: Rural Life in Northern England and the Scottish Borders 1400–1700* (Edinburgh, 2000).

[11] A. Wood, *Politics of Social Conflict: The Peak Country 1520–1770* (Cambridge, 1999) is a study of a mining district where a local customary court was central to the trade.

[12] Arthur Redford, *History of Local Government in Manchester* (3 vols., 1939–40); R. G. H. Whitty, *The Court of Taunton in the Sixteenth and Seventeenth Centuries* (Taunton, 1934).

[13] Significantly this was the case at Terling (Essex). K. Wrightson and D. Levine, *Poverty and Piety in an English Village: Terling 1525–1700* (2nd edn, Oxford, 1995).

Wakefield in Yorkshire, there were manors within manors, which meant that submanors associated with individual vils owed suit to a principal manorial court that had supervisory authority over them.[14]

Last but hardly least, the blanket term manorial court covered what were in effect two separate types of jurisdiction. According to the lawyers, the 'court baron' was concerned primarily with the conditions on which land was held by tenants from the lord of the manor, with its intergenerational transfer, and with civil pleas between parties in connection with economic transactions. Courts leet, on the other hand, dealt with what we would describe as the regulation of social and economic life within the community. They were responsible for 'common nuisances', minor breaches of the peace (affrays), and the enforcement of local bylaws as well as relevant parliamentary statutes. Yet while these distinctions made sense to professional lawyers, manorial records very often mixed the two sorts of activities together into the meeting of a single court, which ordinarily took place at least twice a year, but which in some places could occur weekly, or once every three weeks.[15]

Moot halls in larger towns and some villages reflect the extent to which local courts were vital local institutions, and while some of these, like that of Hexham in Northumberland, dated from before the fifteenth century, there were also a fair number erected during the middle and later parts of the Tudor period.[16] Even so, the majority of courts probably met in inns or alehouses, and conviviality was evidently a traditional part of the process.[17] Before 1600, the lawday at Southampton was accompanied by feasting and drinking participated in by a significant cross-section of the community. In other places, lords of manors are known to have laid on quite considerable amounts of drink, a practice which was evidently a traditional seigneurial responsibility.[18]

To date, however, no one has uncovered a narrative, or descriptive, account of a meeting of a manorial court; any picture of what went on has to be pieced together from the surviving official records. Proceedings

---

[14] D. J. H. Michelmore and M. K. E. Edwards, 'The records of the Manor of Wakefield', *Journal of the Society of Archivists*, 5 (1975), 245–50.

[15] Hearnshaw, *Leet Jurisdiction*, pp. 11–12.

[16] R. Titler, *Architecture and Power: The Town Hall and the English Urban Community c.1500–1640* (Oxford, 1991).

[17] C. Harrison, 'Manor courts and the governance of Tudor England' in *Communities and Courts*, pp. 51–3.

[18] Ibid.; Hearnshaw, *Leet Jurisdiction*, p. 167; HEHL, MSS Ellesmere 6722, 6726. Accounts for dinners at Ellesmere's courts at Pitchelsthorne and Ivinghoe. The fare included bread and beer, as well as boiled and roast meat. In addition there were charges for two pigs, two geese, three capons and a dozen pigeons, as well as a cask of claret, fruit and cheese.

were carried out in public, but stewards, the presiding officers, were expected to write out a formal Latin record on parchment or (later on) in a paper court book. Consequently, the surviving evidence is usually either super-abundant, but not very revealing, or totally non-existent. Since court rolls were potentially important to both the lords of manors and their tenants, there was a presumption, and a legal obligation, that they should be carefully kept.[19] Some manors, such as those at Battle Abbey in Sussex or Wakefield, have records that cover hundreds of years.[20] But, due the ravages of time, fire, flood and rodents, continuous series of records in fact survive for only a tiny proportion of the total number of manors, and it is usually the smaller and less significant places that are most poorly documented. Although the court rolls of the manor of Wakefield, and in particular those which recorded the transfer of copyhold land, run from the thirteenth to the eighteenth century, those of the submanors that made up its constituent parts are much less well preserved, a circumstance that seriously limits the overall picture of court activity. But even when records do survive, the formal entry of transfers of land, or presentments for affrays or other infractions, are brief and laconic. In those cases where it is possible to make one, a comparison of the parchment rolls with the 'rough papers', or working notes, made by stewards before or during court sessions, invariably reveals a greater volume and range of activity than the formal parchment rolls.

The distinctive characteristics of manorial courts were that jurisdiction was normally vested in the lord of the manor, and that those tenants who held land from the manor owed suit of court and were therefore subject to its jurisdiction.[21] Hence manors were defined by land tenure rather than geography, but beyond this their exact nature and legal status was not straightforward. Contemporaries often found it difficult to decide whether the courts should be designated seigneurial, communal, or royal institutions, and it would seem that the confusion actually increased in the century before the outbreak of civil war. In a lecture delivered at the Inner Temple in 1630, for instance, John Wilde seemed to endorse the very highest form of seigneurialism when he described the lord of the manor as ruling over his tenants more or less as

[19] See below, pp. 274, 331.
[20] J.H. Baker, 'Personal actions in the High Court of Battle Abbey 1450–1602', *Cambridge Law Journal*, 51(3) (1992), 508–29. John Charlesworth, ed. *Wakefield Manor Book, 1709* (Yorkshire Archaeological Society, Record Series, vol. 101, 1939). The main series of Wakefield manorial court rolls have been published starting with C. M. Fraser and Kenneth Emsley, eds., *The Court Rolls of the Manor of Wakefield from October 1639 to September 1640* (WCRS, vol. 1, 1977).
[21] For more on the tenurial implications, see below, pp. 328ff.

an absolute monarch. The manor was a petty kingdom, where the lord was the king, the tenants the subjects, and the courts equivalent to the equitable and common-law jurisdictions at Westminster Hall.[22] Such an interpretation would, moreover, appear to coincide with the surviving bylaws for the manors of Whitchurch and Bodington (Shropshire), which were issued rather imperiously by the earl of Bridgewater in 1637 so that his tenants would not be ignorant of such orders as they were 'by custom' required to obey.[23]

Yet, by this date, Bridgewater's bylaws would have had a distinctly neo-feudal air about them, and even Wilde's analogy was ambiguous enough to warrant multiple interpretations. While he appears to have been implying some form of absolute lordship verging on that of a satrap, his listeners would have been aware that, on some interpretations at least, the rule of King Charles himself was cumbered with limitations in favour of his subjects. If the king, like lords of manors, was obliged to provide justice, neither he nor they sat regularly on the justice seat themselves since the king had his judges and the lord appointed a steward to preside over the court in his name. No less important, while the notion that the manor was some-how independent of, or an alternative to, royal justice, was more likely to have been articulated in the 1620s or 1630s than it would have been earlier, it was never a serious contention in any part of our period.[24]

Indeed, the multifaceted nature of manorial courts was already widely acknowledged, if not subjected to detailed analysis, in the later fifteenth century. The charge used at the manorial courts associated with the estates of Fountains Abbey, for example, stressed that the purpose of the courts was to protect the interests and enforce the responsibilities of the king, the lord and the tenants. Jurors were required to present alienations of lands by tenants that adversely affected the interests of the abbey. But the steward also reminded them to look out for matters of a broader individual or community concern: the unlawful taking of land from 'neighbours'; the protection of water courses; the repair of houses. Although the legal status of the Fountains Abbey courts meant that royal officials were forbidden to enter the jurisdiction in order to serve legal process, the tenants were reminded that they were the king's liege subjects and hence obliged to protect his person and keep his peace. They were to inquire about the presence of Lollards, seek out coun-terfeiters, present thieves, maintain weights and measures, and prevent anything, including unlawful games, forbidden by either common or statute law.[25]

---

[22] BL, MS Hargrave 372, fol. 3v.   [23] SA, Bridgewater Collection, Whitchurch Manor.
[24] See below, p. 249.   [25] BL, MS Additional 40010, fol. 186r–v.

Throughout the sixteenth and seventeenth centuries, the obligation to keep manorial courts, which included feeing the steward and maintaining instruments of punishment such as pillories and tumbrels, was an essential condition of lordship.[26] In fact, the cost to lords of 'seigneurial' justice must frequently have outweighed the benefits. In one of his early Elizabethan Star Chamber speeches, Lord Keeper Bacon reminded manorial lords that they should diligently and severely investigate, correct and punish all offences examinable within inferior courts such as leets, wapentakes and tourns. Such courts, he said, had been 'divised and ordeyned principally for the good order of tenants and residents', but 'nowadays' they were kept merely for the sake of profit, or allowed to atrophy.[27]

Since manorial law courts were financed entirely by the taking of fees and fines, the role of profit and conflicts over it were important issues,[28] but the legal and constitutional status of the institution was subject to a complex set of glosses. In the Elizabethan period, printed and manuscript charges stressed the prescriptive, or customary, nature of the jurisdiction, while at the same time taking up the lawyerly perspective that it was merely another manifestation of the king's responsibility to provide justice. In *Le court leet et le court baron* (1580), the most important professional text on the subject, John Kitchen wrote that manorial courts were in effect royal jurisdictions just like any other. Quoting from sources as diverse as Seneca, the testaments, *Bracton* and Fortescue, he explained that the king had been appointed to rule by law over his subjects. In return for obedience, the subjects could expect to enjoy rights at law. Kitchen's account of the historical background was a bland assertion that as the number of people in the realm began to multiply (at some imprecise date) the courts had been created. The leet was for the punishment of enormities prohibited by statute as well as 'public nuisances' committed within the jurisdiction. The court baron was designed to determine injuries, trespasses, debts and other actions where the value was less than 40s. It was also supposed to maintain the rights and interests of both tenants and lords.[29]

---

[26] *CroEliz*, 698, *Steverton* v. *Scroggs; Dyer's Reports*, 1, p. 178. For stewards, see Brooks, *Pettyfoggers and Vipers*, pp. 197–203.

[27] Folger, MS V.a.143, fol. 22.

[28] Dawson, *Lay Judges*, p. 223. The statute, 2 James I, c. 5, noted the increasing profits that were being taken from manorial courts, and in an effort to prevent stewards overcharging for work in connection with them, forbade them from pocketing the fees themselves.

[29] *Le court leet et court baron, collect per Iohn Kytchin de Greys Inne vn apprentice en le ley. . .* (1580), fols. 1–4v. Kitchen stressed in this work that lords should appoint professional (legally trained) stewards so that the courts would be kept properly, which was the best way to prevent the possibility of forfeitures arising from *quo warranto* proceedings in the Exchequer.

By the early seventeenth century, and thanks in part to the writings of William Lambarde, it was possible to argue that local jurisdictions stretched back to the days before the Conquest, and that they constituted one of the principal democratic elements within the constitution.[30] Such views may have given weight to the claims of radical reformers in the 1640s and 1650s that true English justice was to be found in traditional local courts where laymen sat as both judges and juries. But, on the other hand, royalist propaganda made effective play with the fact that the oath of allegiance, which all males over the age of twelve were obliged to take in the court leet, bound them to be loyal to the king. The author of one tract on the subject noted that the oath was instituted by King Arthur and included in the *Legis Edwardi regis ante conquestum*. Its import was that nearly every male in the realm has sworn to 'be trew and faithfull to our sovereign Lord Kinge Charles and his heirs . . . and you shall neither know nor heare of anie ill or damage intended to him that you shall not defend, soe healpe you God'.[31] Given this, it is not surprising that some Levellers preferred to stress analogies between manorial lordship and monarchy, concluding that both were absurdly outdated in modern social and economic conditions.[32]

Despite these political ambiguities, however, the lawyers had maintained since well before 1500 that manorial courts and their proceedings were potentially subject to the rulings of the king's judges at Westminster. There was no point in the period covered by this book when common and statute law were not so intimately involved in village life that social relations might be discussed entirely without reference to them. Practice within manorial courts was the subject of study at the fifteenth-century legal inns, and there was a long manuscript tradition of guides about how the courts should be 'kept' and their records written.[33] The form and content of manorial court rolls often resembles those of the common-law courts at Westminster. At Hatfield Chase in Yorkshire in 1510, for example, an entry concerning a problematic succession to land records that one of the parties was '*non compos mentis cum a comon legum in Nat[ura] Brev[ium]*'.[34] Even more importantly, cases from

---

[30] William Lambarde, *Archion, or A Commentary Upon the High Courts of Iustice in England* (1635), pp. 9–11. For historical treatments, see below, pp. 334–41.

[31] BL, MS Sloane 1818, fol. 195.

[32] D. Veall, *The Popular Movement for Law Reform, 1640–1660* (Oxford, 1970); N. L. Matthews, *William Sheppard, Cromwell's law reformer* (Cambridge, 1984).

[33] Z. Razi and R. Smith, 'The origins of the English manorial court rolls as a written record: a puzzle' in Razi and Smith, eds., *Medieval Society and the Manor Court*, p. 36. The first printed guide for holding a manorial court was *Modus tenendi curia baronum cum visu Franci plegii* (1510).

[34] Leeds City Archives, DB 205/Box 6.

manorial courts had been coming to Westminster Hall in sufficient numbers throughout the Middle Ages for the royal judges to have had a significant role in shaping the character of the jurisdiction. When John Kitchen set about writing *Le court leet and le court baron*, he was able to draw on a wealth of material from the *Year Book* period that stretched back as far as the reign of Edward II.

Yet while manorial courts were hardly perfect examples of prelapsarian communal justice, they were evidently valued in the localities. Villages and townships sometimes wrote to the king's law officers demanding the reinstatement of courts that had fallen into disuse. The inhabitants of Knutsford (Cheshire) complained to Lord Chancellor Ellesmere that the failure of their manorial lord to keep his court had led to an escalation of disorders such as brawling and scolding. In a not dissimilar case considered by Lord Keeper Bacon a few years later a group of tenants, including a medical doctor, claimed that the failure of the lord of their manor to keep a court baron prejudiced their tenurial rights.[35] According to the 'chief inhabitants' of Swallowfield (Wiltshire), the collapse of their manorial court, and the lack of nearby JPs, had led them to draw up a set of bylaws in 1596 so that villagers might 'more quyetly live together in good love and amytie to the praise of God, and for the better serving of her Majestie'. They were particularly concerned about problems relating to the bearing of illegitimate children, provision of the poor, and the suppression of 'pilfereres, backbyters, hedge-breakers, mischievous persons, and all such as be prowde, dissentious and arrogant'. They agreed to maintain a written record of their proceedings and pledged not to sue each other at law without first attempting to resolve the matter amongst themselves.[36]

With the exception of looking after the poor, most of these matters were within the traditional jurisdiction of manorial courts. Furthermore, while the residents of Swallowfield did not exclude the possibility that disputes might be taken to JPs or to the central common-law courts, their bylaws stressed participation and the elimination of contention. One of the ordinances specified that none should do 'any thing one gainst another or against any man by word or deed upon affection, or

---

[35] HEHL, MS Ellesmere 678; John Ritchie, *Reports of Cases Decided by Francis Bacon Baron Verulam, Viscount St Albans, Lord Chancellor of England, in the High Court of Chancery 1617–1621* (1932), p. 71.

[36] HEHL, MS Ellesmere 6195. The document has been published, along with a useful introduction, by S. Hindle, 'Hierarchy and community in the Elizabethan parish: the Swallowfield articles of 1596', *Historical Journal*, 42(3) (1999), 835–51. The authors apparently saw themselves creating an institution that was somewhere between a parish and a leet, although they are most likely to have been drawing on the experience of a local manorial institution.

malice, in our meeting nor to be discontented . . . since none of us is ruler of himself, but the whole company or the most part is ruler of us all'. Another reiterated that 'none of us shall disdayne one another, nor seek to hinder one another nether by words nor deeds, but rather to be helpers, assisters, and councellors of one another, and all our doings to be good, honest, lovying and juste one to another'.[37]

Words such as these appear to confirm the element of communal self-regulation that impressed J. P. Dawson in his study of the manor of Redgrave in Suffolk.[38] More recently, Patrick Collinson has referred to the 'Bylaws of Swallowfield' as an illustration of the participatory tradition which, arguably, lay at the heart of English social and political life.[39] Although he did not allude to the more general political implication, the Elizabethan Sir Thomas Smith's well-known *De republica Anglorum* noted that the court baron was the place for men 'that can be content to be ordered by their neighbours, and which love their quiet and profit in their husbandrie, more than to be busie in the law'.[40] That the spirit of Smith's remarks was sometimes translated into practice is suggested by a letter written in April 1584 by Thomas Goddard to his uncle, the steward of Selkley Hundred in Wiltshire. Goddard asked that he and other tenants of the submanor of Clatford might be excused from the next meeting of the hundred court on the grounds that they had 'some special business in hand this day concerning the commonwealth of our little lordship'.[41]

Procedure and jurisdiction

The steward, the jurors (or homage) and the tenants constituted a manorial court. A warrant from the lord to the steward instructed him to summons those who owed suit to court, but before the middle of the sixteenth century, it was rare for a steward to be named on the court roll, and many who acted in this anonymous capacity were probably amateur court-holders rather than professional lawyers. After 1550, by contrast, the recording of the names of stewards appears to have been associated with the growing involvement of professional practitioners, mainly country attorneys who also worked in London.[42]

In some places this change led to a greater degree of formality in the records, but the impact on the proceedings themselves may not have

---

[37] Ibid., p. 849.   [38] Dawson, *Lay Judges*, passim.
[39] P. Collinson, 'The monarchical republic of Queen Elizabeth I', *Bulletin of the John Rylands Library*, 69(2) (1987), 394–424.
[40] Sir Thomas Smith, *De republica Anglorum*, ed. M. Dewar (Cambridge, 1982), p. 102.
[41] WRO, Acc. 192/12B (inserted sheet).   [42] Brooks, *Pettyfoggers and Vipers*, ch. 3.

been very profound. By the Elizabethan period, it was conventional wisdom that lords should employ professionals in order to protect their interests, and for the lawyers, who frequently held a number of courts belonging to different lords, local knowledge and a rapport with the tenants doubtless competed with the collection of fees as a primary consideration.[43] Given the steward's intermediary position, there was scope for differences of opinion between them and suitors, but it is hard to weigh the general significance of individual examples. In the Elizabethan period cases came before the central courts involving disputes between stewards and manorial juries who refused to make presentments. Particularly in those jurisdictions where the lord was distant, or an institution rather than an individual, stewards could raise local ire. In 1592, for example, the tenants of Gimingham (Norfolk) claimed in a bill they put into the court of the Duchy Chamber that they were resorting to law because 'friendly' and 'gentle' approaches had failed to dissuade the steward from indulging in bribery and extortion in connection with access to documents.[44] On the other hand, in many jurisdictions it is likely that the custom of the manor continued to exert a considerable influence on local practices even when there was a steady turnover of stewards or a change in the lord. At Nettleton in Wiltshire, for example, a single court-book records sittings over nearly forty years and under at least four different stewards, while maintaining throughout the unusual local custom of recording presentments in English rather than Latin.[45]

By comparison with those of stewards, the names of jurors and tenants who owed suit were normally recorded at length. In theory every tenant of a court baron had to enter an *essoin*, sometimes including a small fine, for failure to attend.[46] At the court leet, every male inhabitant over the age of twelve was required by a statute of Edward III to swear homage to the lord and the king. It is impossible to be certain whether court meetings were consequently full of teenage boys as well as men, but the possibility should not be ruled out. Peter Graunt, a middle-aged tenant of the manor of Wakefield claimed in 1598 that he could remember discussions he had heard in the court there when he had attended as a boy with his father.[47] Local orders specifically requiring that lists be

---

[43] Ibid., pp. 197–203.   [44] TNA, DL 1/165, fol. 4.

[45] BL, MS Additional 23151, fols. 45ff.

[46] WRO, Acc. 192/12J: notes of deaths of tenants as well as *essoins* entered for failure to attend.

[47] TNA, DL 4/40/12. For additional examples of how knowledge of local customs was accumulated see A. Wood, 'Custom and the social organisation of writing in early modern England', *Transactions of the Royal Historical Society*, 6th series, 9 (1999), 257–69.

drawn up of those who owed suit, and that young men be duly sworn, were common in the seventeenth century.[48]

Even in the later sixteenth century, when there was a rapid turnover in agricultural land, individuals appear rarely to have claimed that they did not owe suit to a court. On the other hand, disputes about what would appear at first sight to have been a more clear-cut matter, whether an entire submanor was obliged either to attend or send representatives to a higher jurisdiction, sometimes did take place. For instance in 1613 tenants at Walton (Yorkshire) enlisted the support of the lord of their manor in a campaign to limit the obligations they owed to the court at Wakefield.[49] In doing so, they expressed a sense of collective identity that is one of the most striking features of cases that came from manors into the central courts of law. Often paid for by a 'common purse', actions brought by such groups of tenants against lords, stewards, un-cooperative neighbours, or the tenants of adjoining manors were such a regular feature of litigation from the reign of Elizabeth onwards that higher jurisdictions sometimes ordered groups of manorial tenants to proceed in this way.[50]

According to a speculative treatise written in the Jacobean period, presentment juries at manorial courts, like grand juries at quarter sessions and assize, constituted the democratic element in the English constitution, but it is unclear to what extent this form of democracy involved elections.[51] Although lesser officials, including constables, bailiffs and ale-tasters, that manorial courts were responsible for appointing were usually elected, the juries (or homages) evidently were not. *Year Book* cases from the reigns of Henry VI and Henry VII determined that stewards could distrain a manorial tenant for refusal to serve on the inquest or leet.[52] In some places, such as Worstead in Norfolk, service was described as being based on tenure, but it seems likely that in most cases the steward selected jurors from lists of tenants who owed suit.[53] While this must sometimes have made the selection of jurors a bone of contention, there is in fact surprisingly little evidence of complaints about any collusion or corruption that may have resulted, although the actions of jurors themselves were certainly liable to criticism.

[48] For example, BL, MS Additional 23151, fol. 68: thirteen named people, who had dwelt in the lordship (Nettleton) for a year and a day, and who were over twelve years of age were ordered to appear in court to be sworn 'to the king's majesty'.

[49] YAS, MD 225/329A.

[50] Roger B. Manning, *Village Revolts: Social Protest and Popular Disturbances in England, 1509–1640* (Oxford, 1988), pp. 45, 79, 84.

[51] BL, MS Additional 48104, fol. 38.

[52] Kitchen, *Court leet et court baron*, pp. 43–4.   [53] NRO, DCN 60/38/4.

Jurors were almost certainly drawn from older tenants who would normally have had a significant stake in the manor concerned, people who constituted the local elite.[54] Nevertheless, there was often a high turnover in the membership of such juries, and it was not unusual for men who served as jurors to be amongst those who also came before the court in connection with pleas for small debts or misdemeanours, such as unlawful gaming or engaging in affrays.[55] At Worstead in 1585, for example, the court on one occasion adjourned to the house of John Taylor, a sometime juror, who had in the past been presented as a common 'tipler'.[56]

In theory, jurors were expected to undertake their tasks with an appropriate sense of purpose and according to standards of behaviour that transcended personal or factional interest. At Southampton, for example, where the leet jury was composed of men rising up the ladder of civic office, the confidentiality of deliberations was sternly enforced. When one of the jurors who was appointed to act as secretary hired a clerk to write up proceedings for him, he suffered the humiliating punishment of having to sit for one day, alone and unspoken to, in the moot chamber.[57] At the same time, despite their evident proximity to the political and administrative establishment of the town, the South-ampton jurors often repeated from one year to the next criticisms of the town governors for failing to reform abuses that had been presented at the leet.[58] This suggests a sense of responsibility in carrying out the service which is borne out by other evidence. William Lambarde's charges to grand jurors at quarter sessions occasionally reveal frustration that they sometimes took it upon themselves to act as judges as well as juries in matters that came before them, a mode of behaviour which may well reflect the greater powers enjoyed by manorial juries as opposed to those at quarter sessions.[59] On the other hand, in seventeenth-century Lancashire a steward on one occasion told a manorial jury lumbered with a difficult arbitration that if they failed to agree an award, he would be forced to take the matter before the JPs, which 'will be a great dis-credit to you'.[60] If the doing of justice was a responsibility and source of honour for the king, aristocracy and gentry, so too was it for the villagers who sat on manorial juries.

---

[54] Dawson, *Lay Judges*, p. 221; Winchester, *Harvest of the Hills*, p. 41.
[55] See, for example, H. Richardson, ed., *The Court Rolls of the Manor of Acomb* (Yorkshire Archaeological Society Record Series, vols. 131, 137, 1969).
[56] NRO, DCN 60/38/19.
[57] J. F. C. and D. M. Hearnshaw, *[Southampton] Court Leet Records*, vol. I (3 parts, Southampton Record Society, 1905–7), pt 1, p. 18.
[58] Ibid., pp. 22, 42, 83, 103, 174, 201.   [59] Above, p. 91.   [60] LRO, DD Ar 21–2.

Although it is not recorded in court rolls, meetings of seigneurial courts in theory opened with an 'oyer, oyer', as well as a more specific call for graves or constables to come forward. At this point the steward was also supposed to address a charge to the jurors in order to remind them of the matters within the competence of the court. While it is difficult to prove that charges were regularly given,[61] printed and manuscript versions of what was known as the 'Uniform Order of the Charge' were widely available. The *Modus tenendi curia baronum*, first published in 1512, was undoubtedly the product of a long manuscript tradition, but hand-copied versions of charges also survive in numbers from the later sixteenth century.[62]

Manorial charges, like those delivered at quarter sessions or assizes, contained two elements. The preamble gave the holder of the court an opportunity to dilate on its historical and legal functions or to address more general issues.[63] The second part, known as the order of the charge, listed the criminal and civil matters within the jurisdictional competence of the court, and about which the jury were expected to make presentments. The theoretical responsibilities of the court leet were extremely wide, stretching from high treason, murder and heresy to the maintenance of weights and measures, the regulation of personal behaviour, and the protection of the environment. The court baron, on the other hand, was supposed to deal with land transferrals, the enforcement of debts, the control of agriculture and commerce. According to the early Tudor guidebooks, the protection of the interests of lord and king could extend to taking note of the activities of unfree tenants (serfs), including the marriage of their daughters and the placing of sons in apprenticeships, as well as the more mundane recording of the deaths of tenants and the disposition of their holdings. In fact, however, by the later fifteenth century there were already limits on the jurisdiction. Court rolls from the Tudor and Stuart periods never record cases reflecting the control of lords over the family lives of base tenants, presumably because the power of enforcing such obligations had been lost during the relative glut of land that followed the fourteenth-century Black Death and the withering away of serfdom.[64] Similarly, although the manorial court at Wakefield had the right to use its guillotine to

---

[61] TNA, DL 4/14/32. Deposition by a tenant at Gimingham in Norfolk that mentions something he heard a steward give in charge to the court.

[62] DHC, DBKL/CF1/1/73 (Kingston Lacey); Acc. 5712 (Broadwindsor): 'Instruction for holding a Leet and Court Baron'.

[63] Above, pp. 87, 89, 157, for some discussion of the content of manorial preambles.

[64] See, D. MacCulloch, 'Bondmen under the Tudors' in C. Cross *et al.*, eds. *Law and Government under the Tudors* (Cambridge, 1988), pp. 91–108.

summarily execute thieves caught in the possession of stolen goods, there is otherwise little evidence of the presentment by manorial juries of murder, treason, heresy, or, indeed, other felonious crimes, including the thefts of significant amounts of money. When the King's Bench made an authoritative decision in 1534 that murder was not inquirable at a court leet,[65] such serious crimes had already become matters primarily for coroners and the justices of assize, but the traditional scope of the manorial jurisdiction continued to figure for some time in the handbooks.[66] It was not until the 1590s that they regularly point out that juries were simply to take note of offences such as murder rather than to formally inquire into them, a point of view also found in seventeenth-century manuscript versions.[67] In practice, the parts of the charge that mattered most, and which were reflected most often in the formal records, were a series of more minor issues. These included the recording of copyhold titles, the trying of petty debts, the punishment of affrays, and maintaining the quality of victuals and the water supply. In addition there was the invigilation of personal behaviour: drunkenness, gambling, eavesdropping and scolding.

At the leet, issues were brought before the court via 'presentments' made in the name of the homage, which in effect acted as prosecutor as well as jury. A consequence of this, and of the relatively intermittent court sittings, was that much of a jury's work was done between meetings. Notes of infractions appear to have been accumulated and then written out in anticipation of the formal sitting. At Upholland in Lancashire, for example, the steward and jurors met four times a year to review presentments informally, and evidently consumed 144 quarts of ale in the process.[68] The rough paper notes from which stewards composed the formal rolls indicate that juries frequently came to court armed with their presentments written out on separate pieces of paper.

The public meeting of the court was, nevertheless, important. At Selkley in Wiltshire, for instance, the hundred court made an order in 1591 that Richard Signet should be brought to the next court by the tithingman to answer a charge against him.[69] The refusal of an inhabitant who owed suit to come,[70] or 'stand up in court', could result in the

[65] *Spelman's Reports*, I, p. 159.
[66] For example, DHC, DBKL/CF1/1/73 (Kingston Lacey).
[67] DHC, Acc. 5712 (Broadwindsor).
[68] W. J. King, 'Leet jurors and the search for law and order in seventeenth-century England: "galling persecution" or reasonable justice', *Histoire Sociale/Social History*, 26 (1980), 305–23, p. 313.
[69] WRO, Acc. 192/12F (10 Sept., 33 Elizabeth).
[70] T. Lawson-Tanckred, *Records of a Yorkshire Manor* (1937), p. 68.

distraint of livestock.[71] The Latin formula used at Blickling in Norfolk to indicate that an individual had done business in person 'in open court before all the homage' is unusual in its precise language, but it probably conveys something of the importance of open discussion.[72] Where the transferral of copyhold land was involved, it was not uncommon for one, or both, of the parties concerned to act through 'an attorney', who was as likely to be a neighbour as a professional lawyer, and by the later Elizabethan period the public transferral may in many instances have already become little more than a formality. Yet juries were sometimes asked to adjudicate on customs or descents of land. At Wakefield it was common practice to interview widows to determine their rights after the death of their husbands, and in civil cases verbal statements, even if they amounted to little more than 'confessions of the debt' would have been necessary.[73]

Apart from the stewards, professional lawyers appear rarely to have been involved in manorial business. Although they had long-practised before the courts of the City of London, professionals did not act regularly in lesser urban jurisdictions until the 1580s. While country attorneys were working in the unusually active hundred courts of Devonshire and Somerset by the early seventeenth century, they had not penetrated very far into smaller manorial jurisdictions before 1650. There is, moreover, surprisingly little case law from Westminster, or in manorial court records themselves, about the regulation or recognition of lawyers.[74] Given their growing ubiquity from the reign of Elizabeth onwards, this is in some respects surprising, but lawyers may hardly have seemed worth retaining in most cases. The value of disputes was usually small, and by the reign of Henry VII, it was already common for serious conflicts regarding land tenure to be taken to the higher courts.[75] Furthermore, presentments at courts leet allowed little scope for sophisticated legal argument. According to a judgment in the court of Common Pleas in 1505, presentments at leets were like the gospels. They had to be made by twelve men, and in those cases where the penalties touched only the goods or money of an inhabitant, they were not traversable; that is, they could not be challenged on the basis of law.[76]

This characteristic of the jurisdiction was reflected in the court rolls, which invariably record little more than the offence allegedly committed together with a note of the fine or punishment inflicted as consequence.

---

[71] NRO, MS 3370.   [72] NRO, NRS 11,261 (26A4), 9 March 1614/15.
[73] YAS, MD225/1/392A. Jurors were regularly appointed to determine inheritances of copyhold land, and then report to the court. See also *Court Rolls of Acomb*, I, p. 6.
[74] Brooks, *Pettyfoggers and Vipers*, ch. 3.   [75] See below, p. 274.
[76] *Spelman's Reports*, I, p. 160. *Dyer*, 13b.

It also lies at the heart of questions about how the leet mediated between the community and the individual. In theory, the manorial homage had surprisingly broad scope for intervening in the personal affairs of their neighbours.[77] Although most of the evidence suggests that jurors rotated in some pattern or other, it is easy to see how they might sometimes have been seen as biased or oppressive. For instance, the steward at Selkley Hundred in Wiltshire on one occasion in the 'rough papers' described the jurors as much 'misliking' the actions of one Alice Palmer, who had failed adequately to maintain her lane.[78] On the other hand, despite the rules about traversing, the accused must frequently have had a say.[79] To take another instance from Selkley, in 1585, a villager who had committed an environmental misdemeanour by placing a large stone in a stream was said to have come to court to explain his actions.[80] Many court rolls also mention instances where individuals found it impossible to restrain themselves to the satisfaction of the court. At Upholland in Lancashire, for example, tenants were fined for railing at the homage; at Paston in Norfolk in 1638, a man accused the jury of lying.[81]

There were undoubtedly customary guidelines about how to speak and behave before a manorial court. At Blickling (Norfolk), for instance, an inhabitant was fined for laughing and talking during a perambulation of the manorial boundaries.[82] Other incidents in which people were fined for 'ill' (*inhonesta*) or 'litigious' words reflect a tradition of public behaviour familiar from other contemporary institutions, or forms of association, such as meetings of the governing bodies of towns or guilds, where there was an emphasis on 'honesty', and self-control. Although norms for speech and decorum were not normally written out, the bylaws of Swallowfield devoted considerable space to the matter. According to the first of the substantive articles, each speaker should be allowed to state his grievance, or make his 'defence' without interruption or 'skorn'. Every individual was supposed to 'submit himself to the censure of the whole company or to the most in number, so that no man in our meeting shall think himself wiseth or greatest'.[83]

This rhetoric is not incompatible with the quest for resolution and reconciliation associated with the 'loveday', the ancient communal practice whereby opponents settled their differences and reaffirmed their

---

[77] See below, pp. 268–9.   [78] WRO, Acc. 192/12C, inserted sheet, April 1581.
[79] Fraser and Emsley, eds., *Wakefield 1639–40*, p. xx.   [80] Ibid., 27 Elizabeth.
[81] King, 'Leet jurors and the search for law and order', pp. 319–21. NRO, MS 3370.
[82] NRO, NRS 11,275 (26A6), 2 August, 2 Philip and Mary; DCN 60/38/20, fine for *verba litigosa*, 1575. R. L. Hine, *The History of Hitchin* (1927), p. 56 (railing at a steward, and calling him a 'mountebank attorney').
[83] Hindle, 'Swallowfield articles', pp. 848–9.

love and care for one another outside a formal adjudication, but lovedays apparently went out of use before the sixteenth century. While they appear in the mid fourteenth-century records of Wakefield, for instance, they are not found thereafter.[84] But this is not to say that the mixture of authority and reconciliation expressed in the bylaws of Swallowfield were unique. Manorial courts punished barrators and scolds, males and females respectively, who were accused of causing unnecessary or excessive conflict within a locality.[85] In 1618, for example, a Paston woman was presented for stirring up discord within her 'quarter' or 'neighbourhood' (*'discordia seminator inter vicucos suas'*).[86] At the same time, the use of arbitrators, rather than fighting to the finish in court, was a popular method of resolving conflicts over debts or damage to livestock.[87]

While manorial records normally reflect a less keen sense of corporate identity and civic pride than those associated with towns, it has been plausibly argued that the courts were the venues where the concept of 'community', or the interests of communities, had their earliest expression.[88] Similarly the words 'neighbour' and 'neighbourhood' appeared frequently. If literate contemporaries were inclined to describe the world of the manor as a little 'commonwealth', from the perspective of the common lawyers, there was substance to the claim. According to the judges at Westminster, the leet jurisdiction was by definition concerned with 'common' (commune), or to use the modern expression, public, as opposed to private wrongs.[89] The pursuit of 'neighbourliness' or 'visonage' between individuals or, indeed, entire villages was a positive value,[90] and the importance of collective decision-making was both implicit and explicit. In Yorkshire, bylaws were described in the Latin as *plebecets*, or decrees of the commonalty.[91] According to the common-law judges, those wishing to enforce bylaws had to show successfully that they had been made by the assent of all the tenants or the majority of

---

[84] S. S. Walker, *Court Rolls of the Manor of Wakefield 1331–1333* (WCRS, vol. III, 1982), pp. xii–xiii.

[85] M. J. Ingram, ' "Scolding women cucked or washed": a crisis in gender relations in early modern England?' in Jenny Kermode and Garthine Walker, eds., *Women, Crime and the Courts in Early Modern England* (1994), pp. 48–91.

[86] NRO, NRS 3372. For other examples see NRO, NRS 11265 (26A.5), 38 Henry VI (common barrator); BL, MS 23151, fol. 48v (a common 'scold', whose punishment was abated after she promised to reform, 1612).

[87] NRO, 11,275 (26A.6), 1 Mary–14 Elizabeth.

[88] J. H. Baker, 'The changing concept of a court' in *The Legal Profession and the Common Law: Historical Essays* (1986), p. 165.

[89] Sir Edward Coke, *The Fourth Part of the Institutes of the Laws of England: Concerning the Jurisdiction of Courts* (1644), p. 263.

[90] TNA, DL 4/21/13; DL 4/24/6. [91] YAS, MD225/1/252 (October 1530).

them.[92] Although manorial officials were appointed by a number of means, including tenure, it is worth noticing that those of Elizabethan Gimingham (Norfolk) made a point of saying in a case they put to the Duchy Chamber that they had been duly chosen and elected, according to the 'time out of mind' custom of the manor.[93]

Even so, and as was the case in many early modern institutions, the emphasis on love, neighbourliness and the common good was constantly juxtaposed against a reality of lively conflict. The coercive powers of leets were based largely on the levying of small fines, followed by the distraint of goods or animals for failing to pay. Straying cattle or pigs that invaded common land, or the land of another inhabitant, were frequently taken to pound by officials until their owners made satisfaction for the damage done. Consequently, conflicts over the right of officials to distrain, and the breaking of pounds by owners intent on recovering their beasts, appear to have been the occasion of many small dramas, some of which led to bloodshed. In 1596, for instance, Anthony Harris assaulted Thomas Lyddiard while Lyddiard was taking to the pound a sheep that had trespassed on his corn.[94] At Broughton Gifford (Wiltshire) in 1624, a man was literally dragged to the pound himself when he refused to explain satisfactorily why his sheep were on the common.[95]

Harsh words might be directed at stewards or presentment juries, and disputes over the enforcement of local decisions also resulted in a regular flow of litigation from the localities to London. In 1570, John Oake took out a writ of trespass from King's Bench against the manorial officers of Gimingham, who were allegedly conspiring against him and who had entered his house unlawfully.[96] At Wakefield in 1613, a group of yeomen went to the county court at York to obtain a writ of *replevin* in order to recover impounded draught animals essential for the 'practice of their husbandry'. Their adversary, the steward John Benson, responded that a countermeasure as effective as a writ from York could be found under any hedge, but he must have known that the common-law action of *replevin*, which answered to precisely these circumstances, had long been available from the Westminster courts.[97] From this perspective, the frequent claims by manorial and urban jurisdictions that they restricted

---

[92] *Moore's Reports*, 452; A. Weikel, *Court Rolls of the Manor of Wakefield 1583–85* (WCRS, vol. IV, 1983), p. 154, for a presentment with the 'hole assent of the township'.

[93] TNA, DL 1/80, fol. 27.

[94] WRO, Acc. 192/12F, October 1632; DHC, Acc. 4831B (Litton Cheney, 1635), fol. 12.

[95] WRO, Acc. 34/21.

[96] TNA, DL 1/80, fols. 27–8; DL 5/15, fols. 86–7. The case involved the transfer of copyhold land.

[97] TNA, DL 4/59/24.

recourse by inhabitants to higher jurisdictions in order to maintain 'neighbourliness' and harmony ring true; nevertheless they conceal the fact that in some instances local people might well have felt they could pursue their interests more effectively through another forum. This is evidently exactly what happened in Elizabethan Gimingham. The tenants there told the Duchy Court that they had tried for years to use 'friendly admonitions' in order to reform their abusive steward. These having failed, they were now asking for a punishment that would provide both a good example, and a 'terror' to others.[98]

Questions about survival

A long tradition in nineteenth- and twentieth-century historiography identified the sixteenth and seventeenth centuries as a period of decline for communal jurisdictions. But, while this view is not without foundation based on particular case studies, there have always been caveats and counter-instances. For example, although the Webbs concluded their pioneering studies with the oft-quoted observation that by 1660 there was no place in England where manorial courts were still in their prime, they also commented on the exceptions to their generalisation.[99] Furthermore, since the Webbs wrote in the 1890s, county record offices have accumulated many thousands more court rolls than were available to them. There are more than enough long series to bear witness to the lasting vitality of local institutions well into the eighteenth century, especially, but not exclusively in unincorporated towns.

Nevertheless, in some localities the picture was more variable. Professor Knafla detected very little manorial activity in his exhaustive study of Kent at law in the year 1602.[100] While the prevalence of gavelkind tenure probably made Kent unusual in this respect, contemporary comment suggests that many courts were caught up in a series of jurisdictional shifts, or changes in local preoccupations that may have begun by about 1600 to undermine their traditional role and function. Late Elizabethan parliamentary statutes aiming to restrict the flow of petty lawsuits into the Westminster courts reflect concern about the tide of litigation moving away from the localities and going to London instead. From about the same period, local jurisdictions as geographically distant as Acomb (contiguous with the city of York), Chippenham in Wiltshire

---

[98] TNA, DL 1/165.
[99] Webbs, *The Manor and the Borough*, p. 31; Winchester, *Harvest of the Hills*, pp. 47–8.
[100] Louis A. Knafla, *Kent at Law 1602: the County Jurisdiction: Assizes and Sessions of the Peace* (1994).

and the London livery companies issued ordinances penalising individuals who took out actions at Westminster in connection with cases
that could have been tried locally.[101] While courts all over the country
continued to hear petty civil actions, the smaller manorial jurisdictions
did not see increases on anything like the scale observed in some towns.
Similarly, the number of regulatory presentments in leet records fail to
demonstrate anything like the increases that might be expected in the
course of a century-and-a-half of population expansion that was often
accompanied by economic hardship and social dislocation. Jacobean
treatise writers sometimes dismissed local bylaws as infinite in number
but of relatively little practical significance. During the reign of Charles
I, Lord Keeper Coventry found a correlation between the decline of the
leet and increases in the number of libel cases in Star Chamber.[102] Royal
officials in the 1620s and 1630s apparently had a nostalgic and probably
unrealistic view about the potential of the leet jurisdiction as a means of
maintaining local harmony.[103] But in the posthumously published
Fourth Institutes, Coke suggested that quality control of victuals was the
only important function remaining to the leet.[104]

Insofar as all of this indicates the waning of some manorial jurisdictions, the role of the judiciary and the legal profession as a whole was
probably less decisive than has sometimes been suggested.[105] The legal
parameters remained largely as they had been before 1485. Although
judicial decisions of the sixteenth and seventeenth centuries certainly
impacted on the manorial court, there is little to suggest that they aimed
to undermine it.[106] Indeed, a decree in the Duchy Chamber from 1586
indicates that royal judges were on occasion exasperated that a jurisdiction with as many courts as the manor of Wakefield was evidently
incapable of settling internal disputes.[107] Both Coke and his Jacobean
colleague, Sir Henry Hobart, owned Norfolk jurisdictions (the hundred
court at Gimingham and the manor of Blickling respectively) which
operated largely along traditional lines well into the seventeenth century.
Writs of error and actions of *replevin* were available to those who wanted
to challenge local jurisdictions in the central courts, but, they do not

---

[101] Brooks, *Pettyfoggers and Vipers*, pp. 97–101, SA, Bridgewater Collection, Whitchurch
manorial bylaws, 1636, p. 3, F. H. Goldney, *Records of Chippenham* (Chippenham,
1889), p. 34.
[102] A. Fox, 'Ballads, libels and popular ridicule in Jacobean England', *Past and Present*,
145 (1994), 47–83, p. 55.
[103] See above, p. 179.   [104] Coke, *Fourth Institutes*, p. 261.
[105] Webbs, *The Manor and the Borough*, pp. 121–4. Hearnshaw, *Leet Jurisdiction*, pp. 21.
[106] See below, pp. 332–4.
[107] TNA, DL 4/29/43: dispute over an enclosure referred back to the manorial court.

necessarily appear to have been responsible for terminally undermining local courts.[108]

Even so, in an age of rapidly rising inflation, the traditional proscription against actions involving more than 40s being heard in manorial courts must have made it necessary for increasing numbers of people to seek satisfaction in the larger hundred or borough jurisdictions, if not the courts at Westminster or those of the regional councils. Even long-lived courts, such as those in and around Wakefield, saw an Elizabethan increase in the number of cases that for one reason or another were being taken to higher courts. Litigation involving the conflicting property rights of landlords and copyhold tenants became an important category of common-law work.[109] At the same time, Sir Francis Bacon's early Jacobean opinion on the procedure for appointing constables confirms the observation that, although practices continued to vary, there was a growing tendency for these local officials to be named by JPs rather than for them to be elected by manorial courts, a trend that may well have arisen from the difficulty of getting individuals to act, but which nevertheless represented a significant shift in the chain of command in the maintenance of local law and order.[110]

These circumstances, plus a large increase in the turnover of agricultural land, which meant that many small farmers held title from, and therefore owed allegiance to, more than one manor, inevitably undermined communal courts based largely on tenure. But local variables were also significant in determining whether, and for how long, a court played a role in any given locality. In the small Norfolk town of Cawston (population c. 600 in 1600), for example, where the manor was held by the crown through the Boleyn inheritance, poverty due to the decay of husbandry was already in 1558 such a significant problem that local notables asked JPs to intervene.[111] They requested meetings of quarter sessions to deal with begging, the stealing of fruit and wood by children, and disorders in alehouses.[112] More often, absentee landlords, including

---

[108] Edmund Plowden's law lecture at the Middle Temple in 1552 was concerned in part with removing actions from 'base' courts (BL, MS Hargrave 89, fol. 42v).

[109] See below, pp. 329–30.

[110] 'The answers to questions propounded by Sir Alexander Hay, Knt, touching the office of constable (1608)' in *The Works of Francis Bacon*, ed. J. Spedding *et al.* (14 vols., 1857–74), VI, pp. 749–54. See also, J. Kent, *The English Village Constable, 1580–1642: a Social and Administrative Study* (Oxford, 1986).

[111] F. Blomefield and Charles Parkin, *An Essay Towards a Topographical History of the County of Norfolk* (11 vols., 1805–10), VI, pp. 258–9; W. Rye, *An Account of the Church and Parish of Cawston in the County of Norfolk* (Norwich, 1898), pp. 60–3. See also S. Amussen, *An Ordered Society; Gender and Class in Early Modern England* (Oxford, 1988), pp. 28–9.

[112] NRO, MC 148/37.

the crown itself, or discontinuity of ownership, threatened the credibility of particular courts. Before the dissolution of the monasteries, Worstead (Norfolk) was a manorial village attached to a priory. After subsequently coming into the hands of the dean and chapter of Lincoln, it was sublet by them during the reign of Elizabeth to various laymen who were also responsible for keeping the court, developments accompanied by irregularity in the records and, probably, interruptions to the sittings of the court.[113] The records for the years from 1569 to about 1585 are chaotic and survive in two different books. Between 1585 and 1587, there was apparently ongoing conflict about who should act as steward, and following an argument in 1587, a sitting was adjourned to the house of William Taylor, an ale seller. From this day forward, although the court continued to record transfers of land, it seems to have done little else.[114]

The collapse of the manorial jurisdiction at Swallowfield (Wiltshire) coincided with changes in ownership, and at Aldborough in Yorkshire, the sale of the manor by the crown to a local gentleman apparently led to a radical reduction in the activity of the tourn and the three-weekly court.[115] This may have been due to alterations in local practices that reduced the attractiveness of the courts, but a failure of the lord to maintain them is also a possibility. There must have been a good many cases where the expense of providing a steward to run a court would not have been compensated for by the profits which it would bring in. Even at the small and reasonably active gentry-owned manor of Nettleton (Wiltshire), the tenants had trouble getting the lords to pay for the maintenance of the pillory, stocks and 'cucking stool'.[116]

By contrast, the survival of manorial courts can often be associated with active and continuous ownership. At Blickling in Norfolk, where the crown-law officer and judge, Sir Henry Hobart built a handsome Jacobean manor house, the manorial court was well kept and busy at least up until the time of the civil wars.[117] At Paston, which was owned by the famous gentry family of the same name, although there were increasing numbers of fines for failure to attend during the early seventeenth century, civil pleas and regulatory business were quite lively through the 1620s, and much the same appears to have been the case with the manors of the Lucy and Ferrar families of Warwickshire.[118]

---

[113] Blomefield, *Norfolk*, XI, pp. 87–9. The local vicar reported 296 communicants in 1603.
[114] NRO, DCN 60/38/19–20.
[115] Lawson-Tanckred, *Records of a Yorkshire Manor*, pp. 10, 63.
[116] BL, MS Additional 23151, fols. 52v–68.
[117] Blomefield, *Norfolk*, VI, pp. 382–408; NRO, NRS 11,261 (26A.4).
[118] NRO, NRS MS 3372; WCRO, CR 136/L6/29.

No less important, tenants and inhabitants frequently had reasons of their own for maintaining manorial identity. Elizabethan villagers at Coniston in Wharfedale agreed amongst themselves to establish town meetings to replace the manorial court despite the fact that their lord had sold away his jurisdictional rights.[119] At Cawston in Norfolk, tenants joined together in the first decade of the seventeenth century in order to defend their interests.[120] The Jacobean reformulation of custumals concerning the holding and alienation of land is a reminder that whatever changes they underwent, many manorial courts certainly continued throughout the seventeenth century to play a central role in the culture associated with the farming of land by husbandmen, yeomen and the lesser squirearchy.[121]

In some localities there was, moreover, a need for small debt and regulatory courts that served larger populations than those normally associated with single manors. It is evident in this regard that the demise of the rural hundred court has undoubtedly been overwritten. For example, despite several conflicts in the later sixteenth century with 'farmers' who held the ancient demesne jurisdiction from the crown, the hundred court at Gimingham on the Norfolk coast remained quite vigorous until the civil war. Remote from both Norwich and London, and comprising nine separate townships (and submanors), it was available to a population of as many as three to four thousand people.[122] Similarly, Professor Baker has shown how the former monastic manor court at Battle Abbey saw an increasing number of civil pleas as the sixteenth century progressed.[123] At Selkley Hundred in Wiltshire, a court which also consisted of a number of submanors, civil pleas were still being heard in considerable numbers in the later seventeenth century, a pattern that may have been particularly typical of West Country hundred jurisdictions. For instance, although there is evidence for the decline of one of its submanors, Kingston Lacey, during the early Stuart period, the records of the three-weekly court of Badbury Hundred in Dorset are quite full up until the 1690s, and information collected by the Caroline commissions on court fees indicates that many Devonshire hundred courts were busy in the 1620s and 1630s, a situation which again persisted in some places until the mid eighteenth century.[124]

Finally, it was undoubtedly in unincorporated urban areas that franchise courts demonstrated their greatest flexibility and survived longest.

[119] R. W. Hoyle, 'Land and landed relations in Craven, Yorkshire c. 1520–1600' (Oxford University DPhil thesis, 1986), p. 47.
[120] Blomefield, *Norfolk*, VI, pp. 258–9.   [121] See below, pp. 273–4.
[122] NRO, NRS 16,738, 16,739; MS 6000.   [123] Baker, 'Battle Abbey', pp. 524–6.
[124] DHC, DBKL CG 1/40 (Kingston Lacey); CF 2/1/3(Badbury Hundred); TNA, E 215/1507.

At Havering in Essex, the ancient demesne manor formed the administrative foundation for a claim to a special charter of incorporation during the reign of Henry VII.[125] Far from contracting in the face of the great increase in legal business which came into Westminster Hall between 1560 and 1640, many borough and hundred courts also saw a growth in litigation.[126] Jurisdictions as geographically distant as those of Hexham in Northumberland and Trowbridge in Wiltshire formed the basis of town government,[127] and the same was true of places which later far outgrew most towns of their type, Southampton, Leeds and Manchester. Many such jurisdictions remained in place up until the Municipal Corporation Act of 1835.

Business

The business of franchise courts fell within two broad, and not always well-defined, categories. One included the invigilation of personal behaviour and community welfare. The other was more directly concerned with economic and agricultural aspects of local life. In juridical terms, the first category was associated with the leet jurisdiction, and from the perspective of Westminster Hall, the authority exercised by the courts stemmed from their responsibilities according to common and statute law, but they also had powers of their own. These flowed in part from their capacity to pass and enforce bylaws, but, most critically, from their competence over legal wrongs known as common nuisances, offences that affected more than another single person. Writing in the 1640s, for example, the legal publicist William Shepard summed up the jurisdiction of the leet largely in terms of this capacity to regulate nuisances to the whole community rather than those that affected single individuals.[128] In the court records themselves, presentments of such matters, whether in Latin or in English, frequently contained formal wording which described offences as harming (*ad nocumentum*) either the 'inhabitants', the 'community' (*commune*), or 'neighbours'. In a case dating from the reign of Henry VI, it was held that the leet was supposed to enquire of common nuisances 'fait al common people',[129] but later

---

[125] McIntosh, *A Community Transformed*, pp. 66ff.
[126] C. Muldrew, 'Rural credit, market areas and legal institutions in the English countryside' in *Communities and Courts*, pp. 166–7. For an overview see also Brooks, *Lawyers, Litigation*, ch. 4.
[127] NORTHCRO, Allendale MS P 2–3; BB 19/1–4. WRO, Acc. 192/19 P.
[128] W. Sheppard, *The Court Keepers Guide* (1650 edn), pp. 12–13 .
[129] *Year Book*: 9 Henry VI, 45.

discussions reflect some of the ambiguities noted earlier in this chapter, most notably whether the leet was in essence a royal or a communal court. In the Jacobean case *Prat* v. *Stern*, for instance, there was some doubt in King's Bench about whether a manorial presentment against a freeholder for erecting a dovecote should have described the offence as *ad commune nocumentum* or *ad nocumentum legiorum domini regis*.[130]

Yet the critical distinction for the lawyers remained whether or not the nuisance affected more than one person. In the time of Henry VII, Justice Fairfax ruled that in the case of affrays and bloodshed only those incidents that 'disturbed the king's people could be presented'. Hence breaking the close of an individual, or drawing the blood of a single person in an affray, were private, not 'common' wrongs, and private wrongs were not within the competence of the leet.[131] According to Coke, the reason why the freeholder who erected a dovecote should be presented at the leet was that otherwise the nature of the offence (which posed the threat of pigeons feeding on the crops of neighbours) would lead to an infinite number of individual personal actions for damages.[132] Apparently following similar logic, royal judges were usually willing to leave genuine common nuisances to leets, but to define them rather narrowly when called upon to do so. For example, in 1594 an inhabitant within the leet of Spalding (Lincolnshire) brought an action of trespass at common law against manorial officials for distraining animals of his that were alleged to have caused *nocumentum inhabitantum*. Although he admitted that the animals escaped because he left his gate open, the judges ruled in his favour because he was able to demonstrate that the damage was 'a private injury [to another individual] and not a nuisance inquirable at the leet'.[133]

Nevertheless, a number of environmental issues remained within the remit of presentment juries, and local courts were the principal means by which early modern towns and villages regulated the material conditions in which they lived. Quite apart from passing bylaws establishing quotas on the number of animals allowed to be pastured on common land, most courts were involved at one time or another in protecting the quality and flow of water-courses, scouring drains and ditches, maintaining footpaths, roads and highways, controlling the erection of fences or stiles, ringing swine and cleaning streets. Bylaws and presentments relating to such matters were of course more extensive in towns than in villages, but the nature of the regulation was much the same. For instance, the Elizabethan leet jury at Southampton, a town of about 3,500

[130] *CroJac*, 382.   [131] As quoted by Kitchen, *Le court leet et court baron*, p. 39.
[132] 5 *CoRep*, 104. *Boulston's Case*.   [133] *CroEliz*, 415.

inhabitants, concerned itself with the enforcement of measures about the keeping of hogs in town, the hanging out of laundry belonging to the 'sick and pocksy', the killing of animals in butchers' shops, the price of victuals and the making safe of stairways which led from street level to basements because they had proven to be 'very dangerous to men and children'.[134] But even in early seventeenth-century Nettleton, a village with no more than seventy-five households, there were presentments about the overstocking of commons, the water supply, a pit which had been dug in the road and the unsatisfactory disposal of garbage by one of the inhabitants.[135]

Thanks to its responsibility for offences committed against the community, the leet could also regulate individuals.[136] At Castle Combe in Dorset in the late fifteenth century, for instance, individual inhabitants were described as 'common nuisances', and 'common malefactors' feature regularly in the records of many courts, usually in conjunction with petty theft from common lands.[137] Barrators, like scolds, were described as sowers of discord amongst neighbours, and it is within the manorial jurisdictions that we find formulaic expressions describing individuals whose reputation alone was sufficient for them to be presented as offences. According to a note in the rough papers at Selkley Hundred (Wiltshire), the jury presented that 'Richard Signet of Ogborne Meysey is a person w[hi]ch liveth a suspicoas lyfe *and* evell behaviour'. In the formal court record he was 'homo male fame et conversacois et vixit vitam suspiciasam'.[138]

In towns, the scope of this kind of jurisdiction over behaviour could be extended quite liberally. Martin Ingram has shown how urban jurisdictions in the fifteenth and sixteenth centuries frequently imposed public punishments for moral infractions and breaches by wives of proper behaviour towards their husbands.[139] At Devizes in Wiltshire, for instance, the mid-sixteenth-century records include punishments meted out to a daughter who stole from her father, to an apprentice who threw away yarn belonging to his master, and to a couple who were playing 'the

---

[134] Hearnshaws, *[Southampton] Court Leet Records*, pt I, pp. 6, 10, 12, 22, 23; pt II, p. 167.

[135] BL, MS Additional 23151, fols. 54v, 55, 58, 82v. Similar measures figure frequently in the presentments of jurors at Chard in Somerset. SARS, D/B/ch, 11/1/1.

[136] For a long-term treatment see, Marjorie K. McIntosh, *Controlling Misbehavior in England 1370–1600* (Cambridge 1998).

[137] G. Poulett Scrope, *History of the Manor and Ancient Barony of Castle Combe in the County of Wilts* (1852), pp. 323–4.

[138] WRO, 192/12F (10 Sept. 1591).

[139] M. Ingram, 'Juridical folklore in England illustrated by rough music' in *Communities and Courts*, pp. 61–82.

whore and the knave' together in a public place.[140] At Southampton householders were at one point warned to acquire clubs they could use to suppress disorder in the streets, and Elizabethan jurors called regularly for the erection of a ducking-stool for the punishment of 'harlots and scolds'.[141]

In rural areas, on the other hand, presentments such as these were comparatively rare. In order of their frequency a number of other matters were normally more significant: the spilling of blood (affrays); presentments surrounding the drink trade; those having to do with unlawful games. Leet presentments of petty violence could in theory have been limited by the need to show that they disturbed more than one of the king's liege subjects, but in fact this was of course conceptually little different from the phrase 'against the king's peace', which was the formal basis on which similar offences were brought before JPs. Consequently, such cases were numerous, and, if they are added to those which have been assembled by historians in connection with quarter sessions, they add an important dimension to our understanding of the levels of violence in early modern society.[142]

Viewed from the perspective of the manorial court, village communities were potentially contentious places. Housewives were sometimes accused of attacking one another, brothers might quarrel over an inheritance and accusations of slander were not unknown. Indeed, some villages contained individuals, and not necessarily the poorest inhabitants, who made careers out of petty disruptiveness. One presentment at Selkley in the early years of James I apparently refers to a duel.[143] At Worstead in the 1570s, Robert Shilling, who frequently served as a juror, also appeared regularly as a 'common tipler' and a perpetrator of assaults directed fairly indiscriminately against his neighbours. In 1575, he was involved in a fight with several local pin-makers, but he was also named for affray as a result of pushing Henry Tymperly, esq., who in return hit him with a walking stick. In 1580, Shilling allegedly entered the house of Christopher Ryall (another sometime juror) and assaulted Ryall, his wife and his brother, Richard.[144]

Like the punishment of affrays and the letting of blood, many of the regulatory activities of local courts were based either on statutory

[140] B. Howard Cunnington, *Some Annals of the Borough of Devizes: Being a Series of Extracts from the Corporation Records, 1551–1791* (Devizes, 1925), pp. 15, 30, 36.
[141] Hearnshaws, *[Southampton] Leet Records*, pt II, pp. 174, 285.
[142] Harrison, 'Manor courts and governance', pp. 43–4.
[143] WRO, 192/12G (April 1605). The two protagonists are described as assaulting each other with swords and daggers.
[144] NRO, DCN 60/38/4 (1580–81); DCN 60/38/19 (1575).

authority or on the power to punish behaviour disruptive to the community. Drunkenness (Wakefield, 1580s), the drawing of apprentices or servants into alehouses after hours, and the playing of cards and other unlawful games (Acomb, 1550s) could all be presented and fined as acts which annoyed 'neighbours'. In addition, there was scope within the assizes of bread and ale for the control of these consumables, one that was no doubt both used and abused. For example, the large number of presentments, particularly of women, for unlawful brewing at Wakefield in the 1480s and 1490s gives the strong impression that they were made primarily for the value of the fines that might be collected rather than for the suppression of disorderly behaviour. On the other hand, at Selkley in the late 1570s, an ale-seller was accused of keeping ill rule, and the tithingmen were requested to present him to the JPs if he persisted.[145]

There was variation from community to community in the extent to which such powers were implemented, but the fact that a good deal of the social regulation carried out within the leet was supported by parliamentary legislation is significant because it confounds two common working assumptions of historians about early modern government. The first of these is the view that there was little regulation of local communities based on statute law before the reign of Elizabeth. The second is the presumption that legislation from London had little impact on the localities because what went on in St Stephen's Chapel and what went on in the average village were worlds apart. In fact, legislation covering many of the matters inquirable at leets, most notably statutes relating to nightwalkers, rogues and vagabonds (7 Richard II, c. 5), and that relating to the unlawful playing of games went back as far as the late fourteenth century.[146] The first statute controlling alehouses, which was enforceable in the leet, dates from 1496.[147] While much of this legislation was regularly updated, though not altered much in scope, during the fifteenth and sixteenth centuries, it is difficult to measure the precise impact of any given act. Manorial charges normally mention the types of offences to be inquired into without specifying which statutes were being enforced. Nonetheless, juries made presentments that reflected matters covered by statutes, no doubt because many of the statutory measures coincided with local concerns. Furthermore, this process was already well advanced before the advent of the 'Puritan' movement for moral reform of the later Elizabethan and early Stuart years.[148] At Castle Combe in Dorset, for instance, there were late fifteenth-century

---

[145] WRO, 192/12F.
[146] Many details are provided by Hearnshaw, *Leet Jurisdiction*, pp. 89, 123.
[147] See below, pp. 410–11.   [148] McIntosh, *Controlling Misbehavior*.

presentments of householders for harbouring inmates (i.e. strangers).[149] At Wakefield and Acomb, presentments of those indulging in unlawful games, and against vagabonds, strangers and nightwalkers commonly occurred as early as the 1530s and 1550s.[150]

Statutes were sometimes viewed with scepticism. For instance, the lord of the manor and inhabitants at seventeenth-century Nettleton enforced penal statutes by introducing a set fine of 5s. on each householder, but not bothering to name the offences in detail.[151] But, given the importance of local participation in the making of presentments, and since much of the legislation coincided with traditional perceptions, it would seem that legislation and communal control of behaviour shared many common assumptions. It was not unknown for juries to describe some offences as both 'annoyances to neighbours' and contrary to statute. There are, furthermore, several examples from the later sixteenth and seventeenth centuries where matters within the customary scope of the leet were subsequently refined by statute law. For instance, the petty theft of wood or turfs from common land or from orchards figured in leet business throughout the period, but such acts only became punishable by statute in 1601.[152] Equally, suspicion of strangers and concerns about the cost of maintaining impoverished newcomers are reflected in manorial orders issued throughout the period against the taking in of strangers by householders, but these appear to have become more common from the later sixteenth century.[153] In addition, leet juries frequently used their powers of presentment against those who erected cottages on common land to prevent the establishment of new households by poor people thought not to have the economic wherewithal to support themselves. In the Elizabethan period, however, the judges became concerned that the erecting of cottages in this way could only be described legally as a private offence against the lord of the manor rather than a common nuisance presentable at the leet.[154] Consequently the deficiency was remedied by a statute of 1589 that empowered leets to penalise those who took in inmates and fine those who erected cottages on less than four acres of land.[155]

---

[149] Poulett Scrope, *History of the Manor and Ancient Barony of Castle Combe*, p. 323.
[150] Richardson, ed., *The Court Rolls of the Manor of Acomb*, I; YAS, MD225/1/263A.
[151] BL, MS Additional 23151, fol. 50v.
[152] 43 Elizabeth, c. 6: An Act to avoid and prevent divers misdemeanours in lewd and idle persons.
[153] 2 *Bulstrode* 264; *Godbolt* 383; *Hobart* 250.   [154] 1 *Wm Saunders*, 135.
[155] 31 Elizabeth, c. 7. At Selkley (Wiltshire), there were several presentments on the statute in the following year (WRO, 192/12F).

It is true that when either social behaviour or environmental issues became the subject of statute, authority for dealing with them was extended beyond the leet to the JPs and, ultimately, the royal courts. Yet this potential alteration in jurisdictional geography was not necessarily resented by local communities. In this respect it was entirely typical that the leading inhabitants of Swallowfield planned to delve so far into people's lives that they would instruct vicars not to marry couples judged to be economically incompetent while at the same time allowing that any particularly difficult matters might be taken to the JPs. It was evidently in a similar spirit that the early seventeenth-century residents of Tamworth (Staffordshire) presented to the JP a young man who was successfully attracting the local girls, and otherwise behaving in ways which annoyed his neighbours.[156]

The history of manorial business associated with the court baron was, if anything, even more complex during the sixteenth and early seventeenth centuries than that of the leet. As historians have long pointed out the traditional 40s. limit on the value of matters in dispute that could be heard in such courts was a distinct disadvantage in an inflationary age. Even in rural areas this was by the end of the sixteenth century a relatively small sum, and it is evident from the plea rolls of the central courts that by this date yeoman and husbandman farmers from all over England regularly took their disputes to London. Consequently, although pleas for small debts, including some valued at 39s. 11d. so that they could be slipped in under the jurisdictional bar, can be found in sixteenth-century manorial records, in rural areas there were rarely more than a handful for each court sitting, and in general the numbers declined as the period progressed. On the other hand, many larger franchise and borough courts successfully claimed exemptions from the 40s. rule. At places such as Hexham (Northumberland) or Trowbidge (Wiltshire), for example, local franchise courts entertained cases for goods sold, the performance of marriage contracts, slander and the payment of rent on market stalls.[157] A recent survey shows that most areas of rural England would have been within the catchment area of a local court of this kind, and, as has been noted already, the evident response to this need for venues for local adjudication accounts for what appear to have been the most long-lived jurisdictions.[158]

[156] Shakespeare's Birthplace Trust, Stratford, Archer Collection Box 83.
[157] NORTHCRO, Allendale MS P2; BB19/1–14. WRO, 192/19P.
[158] Muldrew, 'Rural credit, market areas and legal institutions in the countryside', pp. 155–78.

However, where local courts survived with increasing amounts of business into the early seventeenth century, this was often accompanied by a process of professionalisation in the bureaucracy, the advent of professional lawyers and the regularisation of procedures.[159] This did not rule out local participation, either through appointment of court keepers and attorneys or service on juries, but local jurisdictions in this sense were becoming one of several routes, including recourse to central courts, that were available to potential litigants. At Hexham in 1624, for instance, a plaintiff sued in the local court for costs he had incurred in a case that had previously been taken before the Council of the North at York, and many of those who appear most often as principal players before hundred or borough courts must also have sued occasionally in the central courts.[160] A franchise or borough court involved lower costs in terms of travel and professional fees, but the substantive differences from common-law adjudication were becoming increasingly small. Indeed, it may be a mistake to think that they were ever that great. From the beginning of the period, set procedures such as the use of distraint and the common-law forms of action were in use in franchise courts. Amongst most of the jurisdictions in the realm, from those at Westminster Hall to those sitting in a moot hall somewhere in the provinces, the use of the general issue, not guilty, and trial by jury meant that the settlement of cases of debt and trespass depended primarily on local practices and knowledge which were left largely to the jury to determine.[161]

Of course for the majority of inhabitants of rural England, who relied largely on agriculture for their livings, the enduring importance of the court baron was associated primarily with its role in connection with land tenures and the regulation of farming practices. Most interests in land, whether they were those of a smallholder or those of the greatest magnate, were very likely to be associated with a manor and a court baron in some way or another.[162] Issues regarding the exploitation of land, its alienability and its intergenerational transferral were determined by customary practices that had arisen between lords of manors and

---

[159] W. A. Champion, 'Recourse to law and the meaning of the great litigation decline 1650–1750: some clues from the Shrewsbury local courts' in *Communities and Courts*, pp. 179–98.

[160] NORTHCRO, Allendale MS P2 (June 1624). Tenants at Wakefield had been taking cases to the central courts in the fourteenth century. Walker, *Court Rolls of the Manor of Wakefield 1331–1333*, p. xi.

[161] W. A. Champion, 'Litigation in the boroughs: the Shrewsbury *Curia Parva* 1480–1730', *Legal History*, 15(3) (1994), 201–22.

[162] For further discussion see below, pp. 327–8.

their tenants.[163] The vast bulk of early modern manorial court records consist primarily of surrenders in court of parcels of land to the lord so that they could be regranted either to heirs, widows, or those to whom the interest in them had been sold. Manorial courts in this respect functioned as vehicles for recording the holding and transfer of land according to a range of local customs. By the early seventeenth century, the formal record at Wakefield, for instance, consisted almost entirely of such transactions. The steward levied a standard charge for making searches and kept an alphabetical docket, or index, to help to facilitate the process.[164]

Furthermore, while manorial juries were charged with looking out for the interests of the lord of the manor, the homage of the court baron was also said by the lawyers to function as both the judge and jury, which meant in practice that the tenants, as opposed to the lord, had a potentially powerful voice in determining the matters that came before them. Much of this business was conducted with little contention, but manorial records in fact rarely record disputes between individuals over landholding, probably because by 1485 it was already common for such matters to be referred either to courts of equity or (later on) the common-law courts in London.[165] The number of such cases certainly increased with the demographic and economic changes of the sixteenth century, but their incidence should be kept in perspective. Over the course of the reign of Elizabeth, large manors such as Wakefield or Gimingham, which were within the jurisdiction of the duchy of Lancaster, gave rise to no more than a handful of disputes in London. Others, like Blickling, sent hardly any at all.

Nevertheless, as chapter 11 shows, disputes between landlords and manorial tenants that were determined in the central courts ultimately had a significant impact on both the theory and practice of landholding, and already by the mid sixteenth century there is ample evidence that the inhabitants of manors were able, if necessary, to contend quite vigorously amongst themselves or with their landlords. A record inserted in the court rolls of Portesham (Dorset) in 1565 referred to a Chancery case that had settled the fate of a ninety-acre tenement.[166] Cases brought into equity courts, which frequently alleged the enclosure of common land, reveal that villagers could have conflicting views about what

---

[163] J. Beckerman, 'Towards a theory of medieval manorial adjudication', *Law and History Review*, 13(1) (1995), 1–22, p. 11, notes that there had since the thirteenth century been a growing trend towards reducing manorial customs to writing.

[164] Michelmore and Edwards, 'Records of the manor of Wakefield', p. 248; Fraser and Emsley, eds., *Wakefield Court Rolls 1639–40*, p. xxviii.

[165] See below, pp. 328ff.   [166] DHC, Fry 11/6 (Portesham).

constituted customary practice, and that far from stretching beyond the memory of man, the practical time limit was in fact closer to sixty years.[167] At the same time, the practices of individuals and their families also caused complications that eventually ended up in court. Many women who sued in the court of Requests were seeking the enforcement of their rights as widows according to local custom.[168] One case from Wakefield involved a dispute arising from an attempt to demise land according to a will, and another that went to London involved a manorial holding that had become subject to a common-law use.[169]

In many of the cases that flowed from manors to Westminster, groups of tenants joined together in collective actions. Since customs that affected one tenant were in theory exactly the same as those applied to all the others, there were common interests, and for this reason franchise jurisdictions provided an institutional framework for organising and paying for lawsuits.[170] At Wakefield there was a long-running and hotly contested battle between the local manorial official who ran the common bake house and residents over the extent to which householders were obliged to do their baking in the common oven (as opposed to in their own kitchens).[171] At Gimingham in the 1550s, and again in the 1570s, tenants sued the king's farmer about those classic bones of contention in East Anglia, labour services, free-fold and warren.[172] In addition, there were controversies over enclosures, but central court litigation brought by groups of tenants as often involved disputes between communities as it did conflict between landlords (or their representatives) and their tenants. In 1595, for example, and probably due to population pressures, tenants of the neighbouring Nottinghamshire villages of Stockwith and Misterton clashed over their respective rights to the common they shared in a dispute that centred on the collection of reeds and thatch used for roofing materials.[173] The inhabitants of Pontefract regularly went to court to seek reductions in the tolls inflicted upon them by the manorial officials at Wakefield. In cases such as these, yeomen and husbandmen farmers gave evidence to local commissioners recruited from the local gentry and the legal profession, and there is every indication that smallholders were quite familiar with the workings of 'professional' law. In 1572, a deponent from Gimingham alleged that a kinship connection had been responsible for a prejudiced decision by the

---

[167] TNA, DL 4/49/3 (Sloley Heath, Worstead).
[168] T. Stretton, *Women Waging Law in Elizabethan England* (Cambridge, 1998), pp. 158–72.
[169] TNA, DL 4/21/13, *Holdsworth* v. *Waterhouse*.   [170] See above, pp. 253.
[171] TNA, DL 4/40/12; DL 5/22, fols. 51, 54.
[172] TNA, DL 4/24/6; DL 5/17, fols. 493, 539, 594.
[173] TNA, DL 4/37/21; DL 5/19, fol. 195.

duchy court in a previous hearing.[174] According to the residents of Stockwith, those of Misterton secretly obtained an order from Sir Christopher Wray (LCJ) which allowed them to build a bridge over the river Bickerdick so that they could more ruthlessly exploit the common they were supposed to share between them.[175]

Although formally drafted by counsel rather than by the tenants themselves, the bills put into the equity courts to initiate proceedings in the Elizabethan period argued their cases in several different ways: on the basis of customary rights, reasonableness, or general social values. Thus in 1586, when the inhabitants of Wakefield sued several men for engrossing and enclosing open-field land around the town (which had traditionally been used after harvest as common pasture), their claim was that the new development had taken away their rights to commonage 'to their dissheritaunce and impov[er]ishment' because rents for such land, as well as the price of hay, had increased. The engrossers, on the other hand, argued that the right of enclosure was a 'time out of mind' custom, and that their actions had brought positive economic benefits to the town by enhancing the quantity of 'merchandize' available to satisfy 'the greate traffick *and* resorte of straungers into Wakefield'.[176]

Apparently unable to reach a clear-cut decision, the duchy court ruled in this case that the enclosures should stand, but on the condition that the enclosers pay 6d. per acre in perpetuity to the poor and that no new enclosures should be erected without the approval of a manorial jury in one of the Wakefield courts and the authorisation of the duchy of Lancaster.[177] Although it may not have made for perfect consistency, it is likely that similar efforts to weigh common sense, reasonableness and local custom lay behind most decisions reached by the equity courts during the late sixteenth century, and a significant number of cases were at about the same time coming before the common-law courts in response to copyholders who brought litigation against their landlords for raising excessively high entry fines and rents. In fact, while the manorial milieu cannot be said to have determined the fate of lesser landholders in the period, neither landholding or agricultural life can be properly understood without taking it into account.[178]

As chapter 11 demonstrates in more detail, by the early seventeenth century the language employed in describing the tenurial relationship between lords of manors and their tenants had become incorporated into the political discourse at Westminster that was used in negotiating the relationship between the king and his subjects. In much the same

---

[174] TNA, DL 4/24/6.   [175] TNA, DL 5/19, fol. 195.   [176] TNA, DL 4/29/43.
[177] TNA, DL 5/19, fol. 7v.   [178] See below, pp. 327–34.

way, although it is tempting to differentiate between the kinds of communal justice represented by manorial courts and the 'professional' law
dispensed by the tribunals in London, or to postulate the decline of the
communal in the face of the centralising tendencies of the common law,
the evidence of this chapter suggests that such distinctions oversimplify
and at the same time miss out an important dimension of the legal
culture of the period.[179] Legal institutions were so imbricated in the
fabric of local life that they provided a vehicle for those with some
proprietary interest in their communities to have a role in governing
them, and this could be as true of a free miner in Derbyshire as it was for
a smallholder in Norfolk.[180] At the same time, the long-standing recognition of the manorial jurisdiction by the professional lawyers contributed to the ease with which ordinary people in this period were able
to cast their interests in legal language; indeed, they had little choice but
to do so. Yet the local also had an impact on the 'national'. The recognition of manorial custom, and the rights of lesser polities and their
inhabitants, was at least as important a feature of the early modern
'common-law mind' as the more familiar references to the 'ancient
constitution' and debate over the royal prerogative. Concepts such as
neighbourhood and community had a legal as well as a social or moral
valence.

[179] Cf. Wrightson, 'Two concepts of order', pp. 21–33.
[180] M. Goldie, 'The unacknowledged Republic: office-holding in Early Modern England'
in T. Harris, ed., *The Politics of the Excluded* (Basingstoke, 2001), pp. 153–94; Wood,
Politics of Social Conflict.

10 The aristocracy, the gentry and the rule of law

The problem of the 'over-mighty'

A simple observation that emerges from the previous survey of early modern franchise jurisdictions is that the landed elite, the aristocracy and gentry, enjoyed surprisingly little power and influence directly as a result of being lords of the manor. Although advanced without reference to questions about land tenure and economic relationships that will be discussed in the next chapter, the point can be illustrated by some striking examples from the fifteenth century. On 30 December 1460, Richard of York, the principal antagonist of King Henry VI in the Wars of the Roses, was slain within the precincts of his manor of Wakefield, evidently unable to depend on support from his tenants, copyholders who had long enjoyed considerable control over their holdings.[1] Similarly, given the nature of the charge that was used at Fountains Abbey at about the same time, it is not surprising that the jury at another Yorkshire manor, Aldborough, presented some of their fellow tenants for riding in support of Richard, the earl of Salisbury and Sir John Neville contrary to proclamations and mandates of King Henry.[2]

It would probably not be technically accurate to describe any period covered by this book as one in which England was simply a collection of noble fiefdoms,[3] and as we shall see, the common law took only limited notice of the status terms associated with either peers of the realm (earl, baron, duke, etc.), or country squires (knight, esquire, gentleman). Yet an excessively legalistic approach to landed power can easily be dismissed as myopic. Apart from anything else, the affairs of the landed classes provided plenty of employment for lawyers, and their wealth must inevitably have given them advantages as litigants. While manorial courts may not have been seats of power, places on the commissions of

---

[1] P. A. Johnson, *Duke Richard of York 1411–1460* (Oxford, 1988), pp. 222–3.
[2] Thomas Lawson-Tanckred, *Records of a Yorkshire Manor* (1937), p. 67.
[3] G. W. Bernard, *The Power of the Early Tudor Nobility: a Study of the Fourth and Fifth Earls of Shrewsbury* (Brighton, 1985), p. 180.

the peace, which imparted magisterial authority to individuals drawn largely from the landed elite, bestowed more than enough compensatory local influence.

Questions about elite attitudes towards the rule of law have long been central to discussions of the nature of the English polity in the late medieval and early modern periods. One influential line of thought going back to the time of the Tudors connected shortcomings in the administration of justice with a disregard for the law amongst the aristocracy and gentry, a point illustrated, but not entirely summed up, by noble rebelliousness during the Wars of the Roses.[4] Subsequent interpretations have gone on to explain how changes in the sixteenth century drew the crown, the elite and the law much closer together. There was a general decline of elite violence and a greater tendency to serve the state through participation in government rather than by bearing arms or lording it over the provinces. Some historians go so far as to describe what amount to 'constitutional' changes, while others, following a broadly Marxist paradigm, argued for a kind of Tudor revolution of the mind that led an older and warlike 'feudal' elite to adopt the more civic, and civil, values of humanism.[5] In any case, it is generally held that by the early seventeenth century the aristocracy and gentry had adopted the law as the single most important medium for achieving their political and social ambitions, largely because by the time of James I, they had learned effectively how to manipulate it in order to achieve their own objectives.[6]

While aspects of this interpretation remain persuasive, there are nevertheless several reasons for treating it with caution. One principal difficulty is the differential survival of evidence. While there is an abundance of material about the attitudes and actions of the early seventeenth-century gentry, there is virtually nothing for the fifteenth century.[7] Quarter sessions records, which permit a careful analysis of the administration of the law by JPs, are so abundant from the reign of Elizabeth onwards that many series have gone into print, but no such records survive from the reign of Henry VII. All that is established conclusively is that from 1450 there were over forty years of political instability, which included challenges to the thrones of Henry VI, Edward IV and

---

[4] See, for example, J. G. Bellamy, *Bastard Feudalism and the Law* (London, 1989); J. R. Lander, *English Justices of the Peace 1461–1509* (Gloucester, 1989).
[5] M. E. James, *Society, Politics and Culture: Studies in Early Modern England* (Cambridge, 1986).
[6] See, for example, A. Fletcher and J. Stevenson, eds., *Order and Disorder in Early Modern England* (Cambridge, 1985), 'Introduction'.
[7] See below, pp. 294ff and compare with C. Carpenter, *Locality and Polity: a Study of Warwickshire Landed Gentry, 1401–1499* (Cambridge, 1992).

Richard III by greater or lesser numbers of the nobility. But there was at the same time a surprising degree of continuity from one reign to the next in the intermediate levels of the royal bureaucracy and amongst the royal judges at Westminster. Far from reflecting the chronic failure of the rule of law, the early fifteenth century appears to have been a particularly formative period in the history of legal education.[8]

Not surprisingly, historians have come to different conclusions about the evidence that does survive. In the late 1980s, Professors Bellamy and Lander depicted the later Middle Ages as a time when the elite constituted a major threat to social and legal stability. Bellamy wrote of 'gentleman's wars' that arose out of struggles for land. Lander described the gentry as largely negligent and corrupt in their official capacities and argued that their temperamental addiction to violence contributed to the creation of a society in which social anomie reached levels that can only be compared to those of a modern western inner city.[9] Meanwhile Mervyn James sketched a compelling picture of the social attitudes that lay behind this state of affairs. Chivalric values and the importance of honour reinforced ties of lordship made tangible in the practice of retaining, whereby great lords bound lesser men to themselves through written indentures and the payment of a fee.[10]

More recent scholarship has, however, been more cautious. There now seems little reason to accept that the administration of the common law in the late fifteenth century was particularly corrupt, inefficient or dogged by unruliness. In fact levels of litigation were low, but this was most likely caused by difficult late fifteenth-century demographic conditions, and the overall shape and progress of lawsuits differs little from periods before or afterwards.[11] At the same time, although they acknowledge that private interests sometimes interfered with the due administration of justice on the local level, Drs Powell, Carpenter and Harriss also point out that the aristocracy and gentry, as major landholders, depended on the law for the maintenance of their property rights, and were therefore likely to regard an effective legal system as desirable.[12] The widespread use of arbitrations as a means of settling

---

[8] See above, pp. 15–17.

[9] Bellamy, *Bastard Feudalism and the Law*; Lander, *Justices of the Peace*, p. 46.

[10] James, *Society, Politics and Culture*. The subject of retaining is treated most extensively in W. H. Dunham, *Lord Hastings' Indentured Retainers, 1461–1483* (1955).

[11] See above, p. 15.

[12] Christine Carpenter, 'Law, justice and landowners in late medieval England', *Law and History Review*, 1(2) (1983), 205–37; Gerald Harriss, 'Political society and the growth of government in late medieval England', *Past and Present*, 138 (1993), 28–57; E. Powell, 'Settlement of disputes by arbitration in fifteenth-century England', *Law and History Review*, 2(1) (1984), 21–43; J. Gillingham, 'From *Civilitas* to civility: codes of

disputes suggests that 'bastard feudalism' was often a mechanism for the maintenance of order. Dr Harriss argues that by the fifteenth century a legalistic mentality had already replaced a chivalric one.[13] Colin Richmond's biography of Sir John Hopton depicts a country squire who was apparently willing to live in good harmony with his neighbours and who hardly ever indulged in conflict. Dr Moreton thinks that by the later fifteenth century most disputes in fact ended in what is best described as ritualistic stand-offs rather than armed clashes, and Dr Maddern's examination of court records during the first part of the reign of Henry VI has led her to conclude that the criminal justice system worked reasonably well within the parameters it set for itself.[14] While Professor Lander stressed that fifteenth-century gentry JPs were ignorant of the substantive and procedural law, the favoured method for improving local justice was the appointment of more lawyers to the commissions. Although lawyers themselves were often in this period feed retainers of great magnates, they were unlikely to have been uninformed about the law. Lectures on the criminal law, and on the duties of JPs, were given at the fifteenth-century inns. If the example of John Fyneux, serjeant-at-law and judge under Henry VII, who supposedly sat regularly at quarter sessions in Kent, is anything to go by, then even royal judges brought their expertise to the magisterial bench.[15]

These modifications to existing paradigms are even more significant in the light of evidence that nearly all of those offences with which the fifteenth-century gentry is charged – maintenance, tampering with juries and the abuse of power to further private ends – were common enough in the sixteenth and seventeenth centuries for there to be real doubt about the extent of alterations in behaviour.[16] Nevertheless, a persistent strain of legal thought promoted the view that the landed elite was a potentially disruptive element that needed to be brought into line. Judging from the content of petitions to parliament and the preambles to statutes against retaining, rhetoric calling for the restraint of the over-mighty was part of public discourse throughout the later Middle Ages,[17] and it was a natural corollary of perennial language lauding the benefits of the rule of law. Sir John Fortescue warned in *The Governance of*

---

manners in medieval and early modern England', *Transactions of the Royal Historical Society*, 6th series, 12 (2002), 267–90.

[13] Harriss, 'Political society and the growth of governance', pp. 53–7.

[14] C. Richmond, *John Hopton: a Fifteenth Century Suffolk Gentleman* (1981); C. E. Moreton, *The Townshends and Their World: Gentry, Law and Land in Norfolk, c. 1450–1551* (Oxford, 1992); Philippa C. Maddern, *Violence and Social Order: East Anglia 1422–1442* (Oxford, 1992).

[15] Lander, *English Justices of the Peace*, p. 66. ODNB. [16] Below, pp. 285–90.

[17] Carpenter, 'Law, justice and landowners', pp. 229ff.

England that kings should ensure they were richer than anyone else in the realm so that they could easily suppress rebellions like the one that deposed Henry VI.[18] Although Edmund Dudley recognised distinctions between 'the chivalry' and the rest of the population, he maintained that kings had a duty to prevent the oppression of the people by 'great men'.[19] In *Utopia* Sir Thomas More criticised the fact that power and wealth could be used to pervert justice. Although he did not use the word retainers, he disparaged the gentry as an exploitative class and lamented their inclination to 'carry about with them a huge crowd of idle attendants who have never learned a trade for a livelihood'.[20] According to More, one reason for the unproductiveness of the elite was their addiction to service in war rather than in more positive economic and social activities, and Christopher St German made similar points. Although the gentry and nobility were obliged to serve in a military capacity, this did not license them to be ignorant of the laws or expect special treatment. Legal knowledge, he explained, would serve their interests; more importantly, it would be 'a right great gladness to all the people, for certain it is the more part of the people would more gladly hear that their rulers and governors intended to order them with wisdome and justice than with power and great retinues'.[21]

St German may, or may not, have been the first to make an explicit connection between the restraint of the over-mighty and the process of securing the obedience of ordinary people by convincing them that they could expect justice in return for their compliance, but he was certainly not the last. In one of his Star Chamber speeches to JPs, Sir Nicholas Bacon characteristically included an appeal to patriotism in an implicit attack on the deleterious consequences of allowing any kind of attachment to, or respect for, persons to interfere with the administration of the law.[22] In speeches that were evidently addressed to grand jurors in Northamptonshire at the time of the Northern Rebellion in 1569,

---

[18] Sir John Fortescue, *The Governance of England otherwise called the Difference between and Absolute and Limited Monarchy*, ed. C. Plummer (Oxford, 1885), ch. 9.

[19] *The Tree of Commonwealth: a Treatise Written by Edmund Dudley*, ed. D. M. Brodie (Cambridge, 1948), pp. 35–6, 45.

[20] *The Yale Edition of the Complete Works of St Thomas More*, vol. IV *Utopia*, ed. Edward Surtz and J. H. Hexter (New Haven, CT, 1965), pp. 63–5.

[21] Christopher St German, *Doctor and Student*, ed. T. F. T. Plucknett and J. Barton (Selden Society, vol. 91, 1974), pp. 279–81. See also Baker, *Serjeants*, p. 291, for a speech from the time of Henry VIII on the appointment of new serjeants: unable to deal personally with all matters associated with the administration of justice, early kings created dukes, barons, etc. to take over part of the burden from them, 'and after that nobilite begane ons to take litle force of the knowledge of the law they than toke poure men's childrene and made some juges, some serjeants at the law'.

[22] Folger, MS V.a.143, fols. 23–4.

Sir Christopher Yelverton reiterated several times over that the greatest dangers to commonwealths came from the greatest subjects. He warned 'How swiftlie may the rising authoritie of a great Magistrate decline to oppression', and argued that 'We need to obliterate the idea that what is wrong for one person is right for another.' If there were no laws to bridle the great, 'neither could the people live quietly nor the prince rule safelie'.[23]

Although less concerned than Yelverton with the problem of rebellion, William Lambarde's charges to Kentish grand jurors in the 1580s, and his published guides for JPs, stressed how retaining and the influence of great men threatened the appointment of impartial jurors.[24] He also owned and carefully annotated a copy of an anonymous compilation of two centuries' worth of previous legislation concerning liveries and 'reteynours' that was published in 1571.[25] Evidently produced with the blessing, if not the encouragement, of the royal government, and coinciding with the publication of a proclamation warning against the practice, *A Collection* may well deserve to be seen as one of the earliest systematic attacks on 'bastard feudalism', although it does not employ these words. The author noted that retaining was a form of conspiracy that often perverted justice. The statutes showed that some noblemen maintained quarrelsome men, and they illustrated the 'mischiefs' that arose when JPs were also retainers.[26] A statute of Edward III had instructed JPs to do 'equall law and execution of right, to al his subiectes, ryche or poore, w[i]thout hauyng regarde to anye person . . .'.[27] The common law was jealous of justice and hence jealous of any retainers.[28]

Perhaps reflecting changing times, the approach in this tract does not seem to have been repeated, and by the turn of the century, the particular concern with the over-mighty appears to have been folded into general admonitions to live according to the law, which were becoming increasingly common in print.[29] For example, in *De pace regni et regnie*, Ferdinando Pulton gave an eloquent general warning against the evils of forcible entries which was clearly addressed to any of his readers, whatever their station.

---

[23] BL, MS Additional 48109, fols. 37, 37v, 38, 41v.
[24] See above, p. 88. J. P. Cooper, *Land, Men and Beliefs: Studies in Early-Modern History* (1983), pp. 78–96.
[25] *A Collection of the Lawes and Statutes of this Realme concerning Liueries of Companies and Reteynours* (1571) [BL, shelf mark C55.a.28].
[26] Ibid., p. 3r–v.   [27] Ibid., p. 2v. 20 Edward III, c. 6.
[28] Ibid., pp. Aii, 5–6.   [29] See above, pp. 63–5.

Force and violence executed without warrant of law, be contrary to the peace and justice of the realm, as disobedience is to loyaltie, and contempt to government. For whosoever doth make a forcible entry into lands in the possession of an other, doth secretly resolve in his mind, and distrust to himself, that there is no law in the realm to redresse any wrong. He shall assume into his possession by the strength of his arm what the phantasie of his head shall resolve to be his due, whereas the law in convenient time would truely satisfy him.[30]

Nevertheless, Pulton did associate the crime of maintenance (paying for the lawsuit of someone else) with the political and social elite,[31] and the theme was on more than one occasion taken up by no less a figure than Sir Edward Coke. He is, for example, reported to have told a grand jury at Bury St Edmunds that those who used force poisoned their right; he then spoke of oppression either by the purse or when a great man used his public authority for his private purposes.[32] Similarly in 1612, Justice Sir John Dodderidge reminded a grand jury sitting in the King's Bench in London that the articles in the charge compassed the behaviour of all men no matter what their station.[33]

By the early 1620s, Sir John Davies, who was related by marriage to the family of the earl of Huntingdon, drew on an idyllic biblical metaphor in order to illustrate to Yorkshire grand jurors that the particular benefit of the law was that it enabled the weak 'lamb' to lie down in peace with the powerful 'lion'.[34] But at about the same time the attorney and town clerk of Winchester, John Trussell, revealed both his familiarity with the political categories of Aristotle, and the tradition of thought that stressed the importance of law in restraining the over-mighty, in order to produce an account of the origin of the state which explicitly acknowledged the potential for conflict between the rich and powerful and the rest of the population. According to Trussell society had been governed in the beginning by a single individual who ruled with patriarchcal power.

But within short tyme after, when the distinction of propertie by meum and tuum had found out sufficient Combustible stuff to sett Ambition on fyre, and by the reflection therof geve Avarice. . .meanes, a longe, to see how to encrease yts proffytt, as the other to extend yts power, then the weakest went to the wall, And those that were symplie modest were either enforced to serve others, or starve them selves, loosing ether propertie, or libertye, (nay often lyef) to the stronger . . .[35]

---

[30] Pulton, *De pace regis et regni*, p. 34v.   [31] Ibid., pp. 56vff.
[32] Folger, MS V.b.303, fol. 349.   [33] NLW, MS 3648D, item 5.
[34] See above, p. 158.   [35] HRO, MS 107M88/W23.

It would be misleading to exaggerate the degree to which Trussell's apparent class consciousness had become part of wider political discourse by the early seventeenth century, but during the reign of Charles I it seems to have been taken for granted that there had been over the course of English history a gradual growth in the independence of the gentry from the nobility. In deciding for the crown in the case brought to challenge the collection of knighthood fines, Baron Trevor observed that 'It is better now with gentlemen then yt was aunciently [when] most gentlemen did depend upon some Nobleman and now a Gentleman holde*s* himselfe as free as a Nobleman, and the Estates of Gentlemen are greater than they were.'[36] Although he was very unlikely to have been a lawyer, an anonymous author speculating on the relative merits of the learned professions concluded that in past times English laws had given 'great men a tolleracon for killing the poorer sort of people. But now upon better consideracon *and* more mature deliberation such things are iustly repealed.'[37] When Serjeant Francis Thorpe set out to convince a grand jury at York in March 1649 that parliament had done the right thing in executing the king and abolishing the House of Lords, he was not breaking entirely new ground when he cast the argument in terms of the oppression of ordinary people that had always been as characteristic of the nobility as the monarchy.[38]

The landed elite and the law

Of course to identify this criticism of the abuse of power by the elite is not the same thing as being able to demonstrate the success of the law-and-order men in dealing with it. Nor is the effectiveness of governmental initiatives all that easy to weigh up. The retaining of royal justices by great magnates appears to have declined dramatically by the end of the fourteenth century.[39] King Henry VII evidently attempted to execute the laws already in place against the practice of retaining, and he pursued an active policy of keeping the nobles in check, even if some of his methods, such as the use of bonds and recognisances, were thought by contemporaries to reflect his rapacity as much as his pursuit of justice for all of his subjects.[40] Although Henry VIII on more than one occasion

---

[36] ITL, MS Barrington 62, fol. 28.   [37] Petyt MS 583(51), fol. 85v.
[38] *Sergeant Thorpe judge of assize for the northern circuit, his charge, as it was delivered to the grand-jury at York assizes the twentieth of March, 1648* . . . (York, 1649).
[39] Carpenter, 'Law, justice and landowners', p. 215; J. R. Maddicott, *Law and Lordship: Royal Justices as Retainers in Thirteenth and Fourteenth-Century England* (Past and Present Supplement 4, 1978).
[40] J. R. Lander, *Crown and Nobility, 1450–1509* (1976), pp. 267ff.

used parliamentary acts of attainder to do down those members of the nobility, such as the duke of Buckingham, who challenged his power, he also raised up other noble families on whom he depended in times of rebellion, and his vigorous pursuit of war in the 1520s, and again in the 1540s, precluded any attempt to wipe out retaining altogether since the practice remained critical to the raising of military manpower.[41] Nor did the interpenetration of the public office and private interest disappear completely in the sixteenth century. In the 1540s, for instance, John Touchet, the fifth Lord Audley of Heleigh, wrote to Chief Justice Sir Edward Montague to ask his assistance with a cause and explained that he was looking for 'good lordship' from the judge.[42] In the reign of Queen Mary, Sir Robert Broke, chief justice of the Common Pleas, was himself granted a licence to retain.[43]

In the end, retaining, and the particular problems associated with it, eventually declined in the later sixteenth century less as a result of positive crown initiatives than because the more onerous military requirements of the sixteenth century gradually saw the replacement of retinues assembled by the nobility with more centrally organised methods of raising soldiers to fight in wars.[44] Even so, the futile affray led by the earl of Essex in the streets of London in 1601 marks a turning point as the last major challenge to the crown by a single peer of the realm.[45] Although the late date of this rebellion, along with that of the northern earls in 1569, is a reminder of how long the process took, this particular form of threat to the state had evidently subsided sufficiently for the statutes against retaining to have been abrogated without debate by parliament in 1628.[46]

But, if armed intimidation of the state was on the decline, there were other ways to use and abuse landed power, and a fair number of examples survive from the sixteenth and seventeenth centuries. In November 1579, Lord Chief Justice Sir James Dyer became involved in an acrimonious dispute with several Warwickshire JPs, including Sir Fulke Greville, which apparently involved an attempt by a country squire, Sir John Conway, to recover land leased to a widow and her son, who were in trouble about paying the rent. Conway had been very strict in enforcing a stipulation that the rent was to be paid before the sun went down on a certain day. After several bouts of litigation, he sent men to occupy the

---

[41] A. Cameron, 'The giving of livery and retaining in Henry VII's reign', *Renaissance and Modern Studies*, 18 (1974), 17–36.
[42] NCRO, Montagu Papers, original letters and autographs, vol. I, fol. 221.
[43] Dunham, *Lord Hastings*, p. 113.
[44] Penry Williams, *The Tudor Regime* (Oxford, 1979), ch. 4.
[45] James, *Society, Politics and Culture*, ch. 9.   [46] 3 Charles I, c. 5.

house. Alleging his fear of Conway, the local sheriff had failed to remove them, even though he had one hundred men of his own at his disposal.[47]

Dyer, who was sympathetic to the widow, thought the local JPs had 'winked' at Conway's dealings with her. Since she was poor and could not afford counsel, Dyer himself framed indictments against Conway and two others whom he thought guilty of collusion, and he admitted to being 'verrie angrie' with the reluctance of the grand jury at assizes to pass the indictments on for trial, and with both the grand jury and the petty jury for employing delaying tactics. Although the cause and intent of the incident was disputed, a gun was fired off at the start of the assizes, and Dyer's grand jury charge allegedly accused the JPs of ruling the country as they pleased, and of being involved in a number of recent riots and unlawful assemblies.

The dispute came to the attention of the authorities in London because some of the JPs protested to the privy council about Dyer's treatment of them, while Dyer himself was unhappy that after twenty years on the bench, he was being complained of, first by word of mouth to the queen, and then, more formally, to the council. There may therefore have been two sides to the story, and in any case conflicts between judges and squires were probably not all that common.[48] Yet the fact remains that the making of 'entries' in connection with disputes such as that between Conway and the widow were still part and parcel of conflict over property. The nature of the land law, which stressed the importance of occupation (or *seisin*), meant that making an entry in order to lay claim to a house or parcel of property was an unexceptional aspect of any contest. Titles were often encumbered with enfeoffments to use, reversions and other qualifications, which over the course of several generations of occupation presented complex questions of evidence and interpretation that were difficult to disentangle.[49] Under these circumstances taking steps to establish physical possession was an effective, and sometimes necessary, part of the process of making a claim.

Despite the development of the common-law actions of ejectment and trespass on the case during the course of the mid sixteenth century, which offered easier procedures for the peaceful resolution of disputes in court, 'entries' appear to have been widespread in connection with disputes over the enclosure of common lands, and they remained

---

[47] Petyt MS 511(13), fols. 66–7; *Dyer's Reports*, II, pp. 312ff.
[48] In 1602 there was a dispute about precedence on the bench of the Council of the North between justice Christopher Yelverton, who was presiding over *nisi prius* and the lord president of the Council. Baildon, *Cases in Camera Stellata*, p. 417.
[49] See below, pp. 324ff.

commonplace right up till the outbreak of the civil wars.[50] From the point of view of lawyers, entries could involve as little as going into a house and shutting and locking the door, or as much as the use of threatening words and physical violence.[51] The extent of force actually used is difficult to measure precisely because writs of trespass commonly contained the words 'vim et armis' even if no violence had taken place, and many Star Chamber cases allege 'riot', when it was eventually clear to the court that this was also an exaggeration.[52] Even so, entries do appear frequently to have involved precisely the kinds of intimidation that could be mustered by a country squire who had a large band of household servants, or other feed men, at his disposal. Furthermore, squires acting as JPs had statutory powers that enabled them to make restitution of possession pending the outcome of actual trials over title.[53] As was the case in the Warwickshire dispute, there was therefore ample opportunity for the exercise of favouritism towards clients or 'friends', and such practices in the pursuit of disputes over land were sometimes compounded by other illegal activities such as maintenance and interfering with the appointment of juries, or 'labouring' them in favour of one side or another. Although there was considerable scope for litigants to challenge jurors on the grounds of partiality, complaints about undue influence were commonplace. Those defending the conciliar jurisdictions in the north and Wales in the early seventeenth century frequently claimed that local squires who attacked them did so largely because they inhibited gentry influence over jurors.[54] A draft parliamentary bill concerning jurors from 1624 specifically mentioned the ongoing problems associated with labouring juries, including the tendency for 'great men' to prevent witnesses and jurors from showing up for trials. Finally, cases relating to the perversion of juries were frequently brought into Star Chamber.[55]

There is also little doubt that some members of the aristocracy and gentry were willing to take the law into their own hands, or expected special treatment as a result of their social position. In the mid-Elizabethan period Lord Grey of Wilton and a band of his servants assaulted the

---

[50] Roger B. Manning, *Village Revolts: Social Protest and Popular Disturbances in England, 1509–1640* (Oxford, 1988).
[51] Pulton, *De pace regis et regni*, p. 34v.
[52] BL, MS Hargrave 44, fol. 26v; MS Lansdowne 620, fol. 37.
[53] Forcible entries were sometimes the subject of lectures at the inns of court; for example, BL, MS Hargrave 372, fol. 19, a reading by John Wightwick at the Inner Temple in 1632.
[54] See above, p. 127.
[55] Petyt MS 537(17), fol. 248; BL, MS Lansdowne 620, fols. 27, 37v, where it was asserted that embracery of jurors was common in Norfolk.

queen's professor of Greek, John Fortescue, in the streets of London. Brought before Star Chamber, Wilton was imprisoned, but he successfully begged mercy from the queen, apparently because his services to the realm, his mean estate and his need to maintain his 'countenance' as a lord were taken into account.[56] In 1597, the dowager Lady Elizabeth Russell complained to Lord Keeper Egerton about a writ that had been taken out against her and asked whether 'great Ladies persons [be] no more pretious in Law than to be attached by a Base undershrive or Hyghshereve'.[57] Although it is probably an exceptionally severe case, a drawn-out quarrel in the first decade of the seventeenth century between Sir Edward Dimocke and the earl of Lincoln included an exchange of public libels, and ended in 1610 with the imprisonment of the earl for burning Dimocke's house down.[58] At about the same time, the government was also concerned about the difficulty it was having in suppressing duels.[59] Both Sir Edward Coke and Sir James Whitelocke wrote briefs arguing against the practice on the grounds that it represented the completely unacceptable substitution of private revenge for the pursuit of quarrels through the courts,[60] and King James issued a proclamation that led eventually to the re-establishment of a High Court of Chivalry, a jurisdiction before which gentlemen could bring actions of defamation for words 'provocative of a duel'.[61]

Although some account should perhaps be taken of regional peculiarities, the papers of the Wynn family of Gwydir in North Wales provide a particularly detailed insight into the dealings of a gentry family with the law in the first half of the seventeenth century. The patriarch, Sir John Wynn, was accused in 1615 of throwing tenants out on the street at dawn for failing to pay their rents. Subsequently charged with oppression and making forcible entries, he was dismissed from the lieutenancy and the commissions of the peace by the Council in the Marches, but Lord Chancellor Ellesmere recommended leniency on the grounds that Wynn had been willing to submit to the ruling.[62] Later on, in the 1620s, members of the Wynn family were delighted with the appointment of

---

[56] *Dyer's Reports*, II, pp. 296–7.   [57] HEHL, MS Ellesmere 46.
[58] HEHL, MS Ellesmere 2735. Ellesmere also received a complaint against the earl of Stafford for bailing the murderer of a ninety-year-old woman (MS Ellesmere 2717).
[59] HEHL, MS Ellesmere 244 contains an account of the duel between Edward Sackville, 4th earl of Dorset, and Lord Bruce Kinloss in which the latter was killed on August 1613.
[60] BL, MS Additional 25274. See also HEHL, MS Ellesmere 220 for a duel between Edward Morgan and one of Ellesmere's own kinsmen.
[61] *Cases in the High Court of Chivalry 1634–1640*, ed. R. P. Cust and A. J. Hopper (Harleian Society, NS, 18, 2006), p. xii.
[62] Wynn Papers, MSS 713, 719. NLW, MS 339F, fols. 84–5. Ellesmere stressed the importance of the case as an example to others.

John Williams to the lord keepership because they expected him to be a useful ally in their local quarrels, and Williams himself evidently noticed that Chancery was being swamped by Welshmen who assumed that a fellow countryman would be sympathetic to their causes.[63] The Wynns were also pleased to learn that Sir William Jones, recently returned from his commission in Ireland, was sent to the northern circuit, evidently for plotting against Williams,[64] and in general they had a complicated relationship with the local lawyers and members of the judiciary with whom they fraternised regularly during meetings of the assizes and the court of Great Sessions in Wales.[65] In 1625, the future lord keeper, Edward Littleton, sought the patronage of Sir John Wynn in his pursuit of a parliamentary seat. Although Sir James Whitelock, now a justice in Wales, was well regarded by the family, it was noted on one occasion that he had been in conflict with members of the Cheshire gentry, a dispute that sounds similar to Dyer's experience in Warwickshire.[66] A letter of 1625 praises the justices in Wales for being free of partiality in a piece of legal business in which the family was interested, but it also contains a striking observation about the kind of mutual self-interest that continued to bind together the judiciary and the gentry. While the judges were happy to receive 'gifts' that supplemented the quality of their meals, they declared themselves unwilling to continue the 'usual' custom of accepting gold or other money from the JPs.[67]

The gifts in money or in kind referred to in this correspondence were not bribes in which a particular legal outcome was expected in return for a specified payment. They should rather be understood in terms of contemporary social conventions that included the giving of gifts on holidays and other special occasions, and the provision of hospitality for visiting magistrates such as the judges, who were after all undergoing the physical demands and dangers associated with riding assize circuits in order to serve the localities. On the other hand, the Wynns clearly presumed that judges and other prominent lawyers could and should be cultivated, and there were many familial links and cultural mechanisms within elite society that facilitated the process. Yet while this almost effortless interpenetration of public and private interests remained a feature of the relationship between the gentry and the law, its significance must also be balanced by the fact that by the later Tudor period, English law did not bestow all that many favours on the aristocracy and gentry simply as a result of their elevated place in the social order.

---

[63] Wynn Papers, MSS 966, 988, 1096A.   [64] Ibid., MS 1056.
[65] Ibid., MS 1242–3: letters from assizes at Caernarvon, August 1624.
[66] Ibid., MSS 1065, 1113.   [67] Ibid., MS 1365.

Parliamentary peers could, of course, claim special privileges at law, but most of these had more to do with procedure than with substance. Several Elizabethan cases supported the view that peers were entitled to particularly expeditious justice, and there was a maxim that when a peer was a party, the law was otherwise than when the suit was between ordinary persons.[68] Their bodies were not subject to torture (although it was unclear how far they differed in this from other subjects), and it was felony for any servant of the king to kill a lord of parliament. In those cases where a nobleman was arraigned for treason or felony, the right of every Englishman according to Magna Carta to a trial by peers meant that his jury should be composed of men of equal status. However, if a peer was sued or indicted by a common person, he was supposed to be tried by a jury of other common persons. Peers themselves were not subject to ordinary jury service, and their most important practical immunity was probably that they could not be arrested for debt on actions brought in the common-law courts. The theoretical assumption was that a peer would always be in the possession of property that could be distrained as a penalty for failing to answer or appear. But, since procedure through distraint was more costly and time-consuming than arrest, the rule was no doubt a source of considerable frustration for many a tradesman.[69] On the other hand, while peers against whom process was initiated in Star Chamber or Chancery were supposed to receive a letter from the chancellor rather than a formal summons,[70] several important cases debated whether this amounted to a formal legal privilege rather than a mere courtesy.[71] At the same time, while slandering or libelling a peer constituted the statutory offence known as *scandalum magnatum* (1 Richard II, 1 and 2), seventeenth-century discussions tended to equate this with the rights of ordinary persons to seek redress when they thought that their honour or creditworthiness had been damaged, and also warned that peers should not use *scandalum magnatum* as a way of preventing legal actions against them, even if those actions subsequently failed.[72]

---

[68] BL, MS Hargrave 224, fol. 90. A version of the material in this manuscript was printed in the posthumous *Magazine of Honour Or, A Treatise of the severall Degrees of the Nobility of this Kingdome, with their Rights and Priviledges. Also of Knights, Esquires, Gentlemen, and Yeomen, and matters incident to them, according to the Lawes and Customes of England. Collected by Master Bird. But, Perused and enlarged by that Learned, and Judicious Lawyer, Sir Iohn Doderidge Knight, one of his Majesties Iudges of the Kings Bench* (1642). Sir William Bird, a civil lawyer, died in 1624; Dodderidge in 1628.

[69] *Dyer*, 315.   [70] BL, MS Hargrave 224, fol. 86v.

[71] One of the most notable cases, that of the earl of Lincoln in Star Chamber in the 1620s, is reported in BL, MS Lansdowne 620, fols. 38ff.

[72] 12 *CoRep* 96; BL, MS Hargrave 224, fols. 17v, 40ff, 83ff.

Like modern historians, seventeenth-century writers made a point of stressing that noble status (parliamentary peers enjoying the rank of baron or above) was much more circumscribed in England than in other European countries.[73] At its most elementary, therefore, there were only three ranks of people in England according to the common law: the monarch, the nobles and the commons, 'by which generall worde is understood, knights, esquires, gentlemen, yeomen, artificers, and labourers',[74] and amongst these the only legal privilege recognised was the immunity of knights from having to attend meetings of courts leet.[75] Although legal writers regularly acknowledged the commonplace that it was natural for there to be a 'distinction' of persons in a commonwealth, the observation had little substantive significance. By the early seventeenth century (at the latest) contemporaries were aware that peerages and knighthoods had been connected originally with grants of land and feudal tenurial obligations that gave certain landholders both privileges and responsibilities.[76] Thus the well-known 'Treatise concerning the Nobility of England according to the laws of England' noted that in Saxon times earls of counties were not merely personal 'dignities', but 'offices of justice' as well.[77] A parallel work on knighthood pointed out that tenure by knight's service required the service of the tenant in warfare and battle abroad,[78] but this treatise goes on to say that there was nothing more inconstant than the estate men had in lands and livings. Consequently these kinds of tenures had been so 'mixed up' and 'confounded' in the hands of each 'sorte' of people that there was not now any significant note of difference to be gathered from them. It was perfectly possible to envision an individual who claimed the dignity of a knighthood but who was in fact *sans terra*.[79] Peers of the realm, on the other hand, did enjoy an official status in so far as they were sent a writ to attend the House of Lords, but in a view befitting the large numbers of creations in the early Stuart period, Sir Edward Coke

---

[73] Ibid., fol. 1v.   [74] Ibid.

[75] BL, MS Hargrave 325, fol. 8v; *Dyer*, 355a. Another anonymous early seventeenth-century treatise on the 'dignity and degrees of all estates' divided all 'sortes of people' into two, the noble and the ignoble, and appears to include knights and gentry amongst the noble. It also notes that knights should not suffer corporal punishment, since no scandal should be offered to the order, but no references to specific cases are cited (Petyt MS 538 (44), fol. 14).

[76] See below, pp. 334ff.   [77] BL, MS Hargrave 224, fol. 29v.

[78] HALS, MS Gorhambury viii.B.108: 'A treatise of knighthood and matter incident to the degree of knighthood according to the laws of England', no pagination. This manuscript is a more complete version of BL, MS Hargrave 325, but is not the same as Hargrave 224.

[79] Ibid., quoting Lambarde, *Perambulation*, fol. 10 (see above, pp. 84–5).

argued in the *Twelfth Reports* that nobility was derived from the king rather than tenure.[80]

It is true of course that the inclination of contemporaries to distinguish wealthy landholders below the peerage, and educated people such as lawyers, from the mass of the 'baser sort' through the use of status designations such as gentleman and esquire, was reinforced by the Statute of Additions (1415), which required that men be properly 'styled' in legal documents.[81] Furthermore, a decision in the reign of Henry IV was later referred to for the view that knighthood was a 'dignity' whilst 'esquire' and 'gent' were 'but names of worship'.[82] Yet these refinements had little impact on the course of ordinary legal life. Although the failure to style a man accurately according the Statute of Additions was technically a grounds for a non-suit, Elizabethan legal decisions relaxed the level of accuracy required. Coke reported a judgment in which it was held that a man born a yeoman, but styled a gentleman, could be styled as either, a dictum that appears to reflect the reality modern historians have found in the changing use of styles by individuals in the localities.[83] While the creation of the College of Arms in the reign of Henry VIII confirmed that honour was a commodity dispensed by the monarch,[84] this had little to do with the common law. The attempt to revive the High Court of Chivalry in the 1620s and 1630s was based on the premise that members of the gentry would be willing to use the jurisdiction in order to defend slurs on their claims to arms, ancestry or status,[85] but it was successfully attacked as both unlawful and vexatious by the Long Parliament in a campaign that was led by the lawyer, and future royalist, Edward Hyde.[86] As John Selden pithily summarised the situation, in other European countries a gentleman was known by his privileges, but in England in the Court of Chivalry a man was taken to be a gentleman if he could claim to bear arms approved by the Heralds, whilst at Westminster Hall he was a gentleman if he was reputed to be one.[87]

---

[80] 12 *CoRep*, 96: *Countess of Shrewsbury's Case*. However, BL, MS Hargrave 224, fols. 50v–1, does contain some discussion of what happened when a baron by tenure granted away his lands.

[81] G. B. Sitwell, 'The English gentleman', *The Ancestor*, 1 (1902), pp. 58–103.

[82] HALS, MS Gorhambury VIII.B.108.   [83] 6 *CoRep*, 65a and 67a; *Dyer*, 15a.

[84] James, *Society, Politics and Culture*, ch. 8.

[85] Rushworth, *Collections*, II, pp. 1054–6; Cust and Hopper, *Cases in the High Court of Chivalry 1634–1640*; also above, p. 289.

[86] *POSLP*, I, pp. 248–9, 258; II, p. 487. Hyde described the court as an assault on the common law, and John Selden explained that it exercised the 'imperial law', and was consequently outside the common law. The essential questions concerned the jurisdiction of the court to hear pleas of slander regarding claims to gentility. See also G. D. Squibb, *The High Court of Chivalry: a Study of Civil Law in England* (Oxford, 1959).

[87] *Table-Talk*, p. 159.

Magistracy and public discourse

This circumscribed view of elite privilege was also overlain by an elaborate, and long-standing, set of legal ideas centring on the notion that the power of the elite should be harnessed by the crown and the law in the service of good rule in the localities. In this respect the problem of the over-mighty subject had to some degree been resolved, at least at the conceptual level, by the creation in the reign of Edward III of the JPs. Although selected by the crown, and appointed by means of royal commissions under the great seal, JPs were by the early sixteenth century regularly seen by the lawyers as creatures of statute and primarily responsible for the enforcement of statute law. Whatever the shortcomings of the commissions of the peace in practice, the appointment of members of the squirearchy to magisterial offices in the localities conformed to another of the dictums of Sir John Fortescue, who had recommended that the best way to ensure the loyalty of the subjects was to make them officials and servants of the crown.[88] In a similar vein, Sir Francis Bacon in 1617 described the commissions of the peace as a way of knitting together the nobility and gentry of the realm. He thought the fact that the elite added administrative duties to its more traditional involvement in military affairs was one of the significant differences between England and other countries.[89]

Like so many of the legal developments of the Elizabethan period, the closer integration of the nobility and gentry into the commissions of the peace, on which so many historians have commented, appears to have been as much a consequence of political and demographic circumstances as of government policy. In the 1560s, Lord Keeper Bacon, who was generally fairly disparaging about the effectiveness of gentry justices, was apparently thinking of instituting 'reforms' that would have reduced the numbers appointed to the commissions and increased the 'professional' element in their composition, by making a certain number of trained lawyers necessary for a quorum.[90] As it turned out, however, the Elizabethan years saw a steady, and quite substantial, increase in the size of the commissions, and the appointment of a proportionately greater

---

[88] Fortescue, *Governance*, p. 152; Lambarde, *Eirenarcha*, p. 12 refers to Marrow's fifteenth-century reading for the view that dukes, earls and barons were not conservators of the peace, because their titles were mere 'dignities' rather than 'offices'.

[89] *The Works of Francis Bacon*, ed. J. Spedding, R. Ellis and D. Heath (14 vols., 1857–74), VI, pp. 211–12.

[90] See above, pp. 60–1. Lambarde, *Eirenarcha*, p. 38, tactfully declined to comment on whether it was a good or bad idea to have large numbers of JPs.

number of gentry than lawyers.[91] From the point of view of the crown, appointments to the commission became a way to reward loyalty in an age of confessional strife, while the increased affluence of the gentry resulted in a larger pool of squires seeking the local prestige associated with the office.

As was the case from the time of their institution, sixteenth- and seventeenth-century JPs were appointed by the king from lists drawn up by the lord chancellor on the recommendation of local notables. Invariably composed of the wealthiest landowners, and important lawyers, the commissions invested the social elite not only with the responsibility to maintain the peace in their localities, but considerable powers to rule their less well-off neighbours. Indeed, in one of the more remarkable passages in *Eirenarcha*, William Lambarde explained that the emergence of justices appointed by the crown during the reign of Edward III marked the point at which 'the election of the simple Conservators or Wardens of the Peace, was first taken from the people, and translated to the assignment of the king'.[92] On the other hand, as Lambarde also pointed out, apart from a fifteenth-century statutory requirement that the justices should be worth £20 p.a., the principal qualities of those who were appointed to the office were summed up by the words justice, wisdom and fortitude, and of course, 'above all, that he love *and* fear God aright, without whiche he can not be accounted Good at all'.[93] No less important, according to Lambarde, it always took at least one qualified lawyer to constitute a quorum when decisions were being made.[94]

While some of this can, perhaps, be put down to pious rhetoric, the growing gentry presence on the commissions of the peace during the reign of Elizabeth was accompanied by a series of unmistakable developments in the character of landed culture.[95] From the mid sixteenth until the middle of the seventeenth century, increasingly large numbers of the landed elite spent some part of their youth at either the

---

[91] For detailed accounts see J. H. Gleason, *The Justices of the Peace in England, 1558 to 1640: a Later Eirenarcha* (Oxford, 1969); A. Hassel Smith, *County and Court: Government and Politics in Norfolk, 1558–1603* (Oxford, 1974); P. Clark, *English Provincial Society from the Reformation to the Revolution: Religion, Politics and Society in Kent, 1500–1640* (Hassocks, 1977); D. MacCulloch, *Suffolk and the Tudors: Politics and Religion in an English County 1500–1600* (Oxford, 1986).

[92] Lambarde, *Eirenarcha*, pp. 20–1.

[93] 18 Henry VI, c. 11. Lambarde, *Eirenarcha*, pp. 34–5, although he allowed that some account had to be taken of inflation.

[94] Ibid., p. 55. See also pp. 63–5, which lays down the law about limitations on discretion.

[95] This point is developed in James, *Society, Politics and Culture* and *Family, Lineage and Civil Society: a Study of Society, Politics and Mentality in the Durham Region* (Oxford, 1974).

universities, the inns of court, or both.[96] No less important, service in a magisterial capacity was lauded as a critical component of true gentility in influential conduct books such as Sir Thomas Elyot's *Boke named the Governor*, and it was also a good fit with grammar school educations containing a heavy dose of Cicero's *Offices*.[97] A country squire acting as a JP inevitably found himself within the ambit of the quirks and quibbles of the law as well as the rhetoric of juristic humanism that came with them.[98]

Given the much greater survival of evidence from the mid sixteenth century onwards, it is difficult to measure exactly how far there was a qualitative change in gentry values over the course of the later fifteenth and early sixteenth centuries.[99] Nevertheless, the papers of the Palmes family of Yorkshire provide a good illustration of the impact of juristic as well as religious ideas.[100] Although sometimes credited to Guy Palmes, who was born in 1579, and perhaps written out in fair copy by him or at his request, most of the material was probably assembled by his father, Francis Palmes, who owned property in Rutland and Hampshire, but whose family had deep roots in Yorkshire.[101] Having legal interests, but evidently without formal legal training, the elder Palmes may have been a man of affairs as well as a landowner. A member of the Yorkshire commission of the peace, he was returned to parliament for Knaresborough in 1586, when he also sat on the committee considering the fate of Mary Queen of Scots.[102] The thirty-four large folio sheets that he almost

---

[96] L. Stone, 'The Education Revolution in England, 1500–1640', *Past and Present*, 28 (1964), 41–80; W. R. Prest, *The Inns of Court Under Elizabeth and the Early Stuarts* (1972). During the Jacobean period, education and legal training were sometimes mentioned in disputes about whether an individual was qualified for the commissions. HEHL, Hastings MS Box 53 (5), contains a complaint by John Bale that he had been declared unfit because of his 'meaness of birth and education and not having been at university nor inns of court and cant well write or read'. See also, HEHL, MS Ellesmere 6091, for similar allegations against the commissions of the peace appointed for the town of New Windsor (Berkshire).

[97] See above, pp. 27–9.

[98] See above, pp. 65–6. Lambarde, *Eirenarcha*, p. 56, for example, was explicit that while discretion was an inevitable consequence of magistracy, JPs were bound 'fast with chains of laws, customs, ordinances and statutes'.

[99] For two contrasting interpretations see L. Pollock, 'Honor, gender and reconciliation in elite culture, 1570–1700', *Journal of British Studies*, 46 (2007), 3–27 and A. Wood, 'Subordination, solidarity and the limits of popular agency in a Yorkshire valley, c. 1596–1615', *Past and Present*, 193 (2006), 41–72.

[100] YAS, Farnley Hall Papers, DD 146/12/2/19. The manuscript was written by a single late-Elizabethan 'secretary' hand. No pagination.

[101] At least one of the ancestors, another Guy Palmes (d. 1516) was a serjeant-at-law.

[102] For biographical details see, *The House of Commons 1558–1603*, ed. P. W. Hasler (3 vols., 1981). YAS, DD 146/12/2/19 contains a few notes on the case against Mary Queen of Scots.

certainly intended to pass on to Guy, his eldest son, begin with elaborate notes on the times and dates of the birth of himself and his eleven children.[103] There are also accounts of the rent due from tenants as well as records and legal advice concerning the disposition of his various holdings.[104] However, in addition to these records of private affairs, Palmes also collected more general information about legal and public life, much of which was set forth in the form of aphoristic commonplaces and advice.[105]

One of the Palmes took notes on a Star Chamber speech given by Lord Keeper Egerton in 1596, but most of the reflections on government and law are difficult to associate with a single source. A section on 'Impediments to [law]suits', for instance, provides a list of potential hazards: the want of money; the want of a good report of former dealings to give credit to the cause; the want of a circumspect following to produce the best process; the want of good counsel and advice to ground the action; the want of temperance to behave in front of the judge; the want of the good opinion of the judge; and the want of discretion in commencing the suit. Significantly, there is a concluding observation that 'in time of peace, when law governeth, no man can shew himself corragious to withstand violence offerred and not hinder himselfe in prosequition of law.' This sentiment fits nicely with those expressed in a brief essay on 'wisdome and magnanimity', which advocated constancy to oneself and greatness of heart, and there was also a distinctly Stoic quality to the 'Essay on Self-government' which praised patience, wisdom and justice before concluding that 'A wise man wil not troble the publick or comon state or order of people nor will not seike to turne the people unto him, by any new fashion of life.'[106]

As far as government was concerned, the Palmes papers reveal an essentially Aristotelian outlook, which was set out without much reflective comment in the diagrammatic format advocated by the late sixteenth-century philosopher Peter Ramus. Commonwealths consist of magistrates, laws and people. The magistrates govern the people through laws. The law commands things that are to be done and forbids

---

[103] Guy Palmes, the eldest son was born in February 1579/80.

[104] Francis Palmes was involved in a seven-year-long lawsuit to recover lands worth £6 a year. The papers also contain legal advice he was given about how to deal with recalcitrant freeholders who had refused to give evidence to a manorial court at Ashwell.

[105] Another set of Yorkshire papers, those of Francis Stringer of Sharleston, contains similar material, including notes of the payment of servants' wages, and observations from Foxe's *Acts and Monuments*, but is much less concerned with detailed observations on law and magistracy (YAS, MS 311).

[106] YAS, DD 146/12/2/19.

the contrary. In a good commonwealth, 'public commoditie is respected and justice void of partialitie duly ministered',[107] but the government in such a commonwealth could take the form of either democracy, aristocracy, or monarchy.[108] Moreover, Palmes apparently accepted that office-holding was the principal measure of social honour. He noted that a royal judge was a general magistrate throughout the realm and therefore always had 'place' wherever he went. By contrast, a JP only had 'place' in the county where he held office.

Since Francis Palmes was a JP, the papers also contain instructions on the framing of indictments at quarter sessions.[109] In addition, there is a note explaining that Palmes's uncle, 'Mr Thomas Powell' of Shropshire, had written out and sent him 'an ancient form of the charge to be given' at quarter sessions, when he was first appointed to the Yorkshire bench. By the mid Elizabethan period, there were of course already printed guidebooks for the use of justices, but Palmes's notes, which he apparently updated to cover the latest legislation, demonstrate the simultaneous existence of a manuscript tradition that was probably necessary because even after the appearance of the work of William Lambarde, it was difficult to keep up-to-date during the gaps between editions. The most spectacular surviving example is an elaborately written, and lengthy, parchment roll containing all the statutes that were to be read out at the Lancashire sessions around the turn of the sixteenth century, and which was undoubtedly written up by the clerical staff of the commissions for general use.[110] But privately composed commonplace versions which broke down the subject matter under alphabetical heads were still widespread in the seventeenth century. In these each topic was usually accompanied by an entry that outlined the statutory authority and procedures associated with the item of business concerned.[111]

It is unclear from the surviving papers whether Palmes ever actually gave a charge, but at quarter sessions the task was as likely to fall to a country gentleman as it was to a lawyer.[112] An Elizabethan manuscript described as a 'Brief discourse of the ordinary charge given to the juries at quarter sessions' appears to be little more than an eloquent summary of the statutory material by dividing it into matters ecclesiastical and

---

[107] However, some of the advice concerning the use of the law also demonstrates an explicit awareness that magistrates might be corrupt and that bribery and favouritism sometimes enabled 'evil causes' to prosper.

[108] Much of this material is perfectly compatible with, for example, that found in Calvin's *Institutes*. See above, pp. 67–9.

[109] YAS, DD 146/12/2/19.   [110] LRO, MS CPV.

[111] Folger, MS Additional 731 is a particularly good seventeenth-century example. CUL, MS Dd.10.3 is a less comprehensive variation.

[112] See above, p. 22.

matters civil,[113] but by the early seventeenth century the preface was becoming both a minor art form and a matter of honour. In 1632, for example, Justice Richard Hutton was asked by the privy council to investigate a falling-out that had arisen at a meeting of the Leicestershire sessions among Sir Wolstan Dixie, Sir Henry Shirley and Sir Arthur Haselrigge. Dixie, supported by Haselrigge, claimed the right to sit at the head of the table when the justices adjourned for lunch after the opening of the court on the grounds that he had given the charge. Shirley challenged Dixie's right, but Hutton's report to the council recommended that from henceforth it should be made clear that the giver of the charge had precedence, unless a baron or officer of state was also present.[114] Although Hutton expressed some exasperation at the petty nature of the dispute, the importance of the charge itself seems to have been in little doubt, a point summed up by the Yorkshireman Sir John Reresby in a charge he delivered in 1639.[115]

As a Charge is vsuall and fitt for a Session of the Peace, so is a Preface fitt for a Charge. A Charge for your Instruction therein, a preface for your preparation thereto. He that should give a charge should himself be prepared and fitted with the knowledge of the lawes (especially with the statute laws) for the one, and for the other with oratory.[116]

The circulation in manuscript of prefaces by lawyers, as well as printed versions,[117] indicates a demand for off-the-rack material that could be either plundered or used wholesale as a source for the many thousands of such speeches given four times a year, year in and year out. But there was also scope for improvisation, and the process of writing clearly drove some speakers to think seriously about the subjects they were addressing. While humanistic platitudes about the value of indifferent justice, such as those collected by Francis Palmes, undoubtedly figured regularly as part of the standard fare,[118] some writers clearly went further than this, a point illustrated in abundance by the papers of the Warwickshire squire Sir John Newdigate (1571–1610). Since these contain notes on what he read as well as the preambles he composed in

---

[113] NLW, MS Peniarth 377B.   [114] HEHL, Hastings Legal Box 5 (7).

[115] For biographical details see *The Memoirs of Sir John Reresby: the Complete Text and a Selection from His Letters*, ed. Andrew Browning (2nd edn, 1991), pp. xxxviii–xliv.

[116] YAS, MS 329. No pagination.   [117] See above, pp. 87–8, 158.

[118] For example: 'Justice is a quiet agreement of nature found out for the help of many. Justice is not our ordinance, but is set down by God, and is the bond whereby men live together. First fear God and love him that thou maist be loved of him. It is not justice simply not to hurt, but to keep others from hurting' (YAS, DD146/12/2/19).

the first decade of the seventeenth century, it is possible to imagine looking over his shoulder as he scribbled.[119]

Newdigate read Aristotle, Cicero and Sir John Fortescue, but he also took copious notes from compendiums of knowledge on the classical world, politics and religion.[120] He frequently referred to *The Dial of Princes*, a work based on the life of Marcus Aurelius by Antony Guevara, Bishop of Guadix. Although composed originally as a book of advice to princes, the preface of Thomas North's English translation (1568) claims that no other work set out more effectively the omnipotence of God, the frailty of men, the inconstancy of fortune, the vanity of this world, the misery of this life, or the good that mortal men ought to pursue. It was, therefore, a book as fit for the honest, pleasant and 'profitable recreation' of all 'vertous gentlemen' as for the guidance of royal councillors.[121] In addition, Newdigate also read from the same author's translation of *Plutarch's Lives*,[122] and he balanced these somewhat Catholic tastes by drawing wisdom from the Protestant theological and moral compilation, *The Doctrine of the Bible or Rules of Discipline* (1606).

Having read Thomas Wilson's *Arte of Rhetoric*, and compiled notes on 'how to make a fine oratory',[123] Newdigate's approach to charges was probably more eclectic than that which would have been typical of a lawyer. He cast his speeches either in the language of classical precept, Christian religion, English history, or a combination of all three. Yet throughout Newdigate's notes there was a concentration on overlapping or concentric concepts of justice. He stressed that it was impossible to separate individual well-being from a broader concern for the common good. Since everyone aimed for self-preservation, it followed that each person should desire the good of his neighbour.[124] The failure of juries to make presentments, or reach honest verdicts, amounted to the Christian sin of perjury, and the role of the commissions of the peace was most readily explained in terms of familiar agricultural metaphors.

---

[119] V. M. Larminie, *Wealth, Kinship and Culture: the Seventeenth-Century Newdigates of Arbury and their World* (1995).

[120] WCRO, MSS Newdigate B 683–700.

[121] WCRO, MSS Newdigate B 673, 715. *The Dial of Princes, Compiled by the reuerend father in God, Don Antony of Gueuara, Byshop of Guadix, Preacher, and Chronicler to Charles the fifte, late of that name Emperovr. Englished out of the Frenche by T. North* (1568).

[122] WCRO, MS Newdigate B 3475. *The Lives of the Noble Grecians and Romanes, compared together by Plutarke of Chaeronea: translated out of Greeke into French by J. Amyot, Bishiop of Auxerre, and out of French into English* (1579). For another example of the use of Plutarch see HEHL, Hastings School Exercise Box 1 (1), for notes from around 1600, that were probably made by the earl of Huntingdon. In these Lycurgus is described as something of a leveller, but Seneca is quoted for the observation that men should strive for justice and piety.

[123] WCRO, MSS Newdigate B 677, 713.   [124] Ibid.

The law was compared to a hedge or a rake, both of which functioned to prevent the growth of 'weeds' that might devour the good fruit if left unattended.[125] But there was also scope for paternalistic concern and moderation. If there was a chance that malefactors might mend their ways, it was better that they were expostulated with and corrected than judicially punished. 'Winne with lenietcie, not enforce by extremitie. Be an umpire of equitie not a decreer of severitie and bynd by sacred religion [rather] then servile subjection.'[126]

Newdigate apparently did not delve deeply into writings on political thought, but one of his speeches develops a vision of English legal history that reflects contemporary concerns in the first decade of the seventeenth century about the consequences of the Norman Conquest.[127] According to Newdigate, the tyrannical William I replaced the native laws of Edward the Confessor by those of the invaders, which were written in the Norman tongue. However, this 'plague upon the land' had ended with the passage of Magna Carta, and subsequent monarchs had caused the statutes of the realm to be printed in English and proclaimed at every leet and sessions.[128]

Observations such as these do not seem to have had a particular political object for Sir John Newdigate, who in any case marred his local reputation by acting as a harsh landlord. But by the later 1620s, when political controversy erupted over the Forced Loan, country squires were evidently more willing than lawyers to turn similar views on the rule of law into arguments against the exactions of the crown.[129] The Essex squire Sir Harbottle Grimston (I), though not one of the celebrated Five Knights, was imprisoned for refusing to pay, and the petition he addressed to the king pleading for his release made a straightforward appeal to the rule of law in justification of the position he was defending. Taking the law to be that 'rule of justice' which was the 'imp[ar]tiall arbiter' between government and the obedience the subject owed to it, Grimston quoted statutes from the time of Edward I, including Magna Carta, which, he said, showed that the king was not entitled to make levies on the property of the subject without their consent. Though reassured by the royal promise that the Forced Loan would not become a precedent, he was fearful that succeeding ages might see it as a 'strike at the propriety of their goods'.[130]

---

[125] WCRO, MSS Newdigate B 669, 727.   [126] WCRO, MS Newdigate B 721.

[127] See above, pp. 119–22, 156 and Janelle Greenberg, *The Radical Face of the Ancient Constitution: St Edward's Laws in Early Modern Political Thought* (Cambridge, 2001).

[128] WCRO, MS Newdigate B 724.   [129] See above, pp. 167–9.

[130] HALS, MS Gorhambury IX.A.250. This appears to be an autograph copy.

A similar argument was penned and circulated by the West Country gentleman Sir William Coryton.[131] When challenged by the privy council as a result of his actions, Coryton apparently reminded them that the laws on which he was basing his case were agreed on all sides and available for 'every subject' to read in the statute books, which 'every honest Justice of Peace w[hi]ch made care or Conscience what hee did, had . . . ever for his direction'. Acknowledging the great power of the king, and that God commanded obedience for conscience sake, Coryton nevertheless insisted that if there was no law instructing him to pay levies such as the Forced Loan, he was not obliged to do so.[132]

While the position of the loan refusers in 1626 was particularly sensitive because of the political polarisation emerging at the time, it is worth recalling that the public discussion of taxation was apparently much more common than is usually assumed.[133] Furthermore, although surviving examples are even rarer than charges or subsidy speeches, the hustings at the time of parliamentary elections were yet another public forum that gave the gentry the opportunity to think about political and constitutional affairs and share their views with assembled freeholders. In 1624, for instance, the Cheshire squire Sir Richard Grosvenor reminded electors that

A parliament is the most honourable and highest court of the kingdome, haveing an absolute jurisdiction and an unlimited power to dispose of the lives, limms, state, goods, honours and liberties of the subject, ye and of their religion too soe far forth as concerneth the free publique and outward profession thereof. And therefore it behooveth us to bee verie warie whom wee elect.[134]

Grosvenor went on in this speech to explain that although the gentry had selected the candidates, the electors' 'freedome of voyce' was their inheritance, and he was apparently known at the time as a 'patriot' for the position he took up at the end of the 1620s.[135] Yet even those who came to a different conclusion argued the case within a similar rhetorical framework. For instance, although he acknowledged that the Forced Loan was being questioned, Sir Edward Rodney of Stoke Rodney in Somerset gave several speeches encouraging payment. While one of these mentions the fact that the king was accountable only to God, the case was made principally on the grounds that Charles was a diligent king, who had shown that he would never 'Stoppe the course of justice

---

[131] *Coryton's Case* is discussed by R. Cust, *The Forced Loan and English Politics, 1626–1628* (Oxford, 1987), p. 168.

[132] HEHL, MS Huntington 45148, fols. 26–30.   [133] See above, p. 160.

[134] *The Papers of Sir Richard Grosvenor, 1st Bart (1585–1645)*, ed. R. Cust (Record Society of Lancashire and Cheshire, vol. CXXXIV, 1996), p. 1.

[135] Ibid., p. xx.

for all the treasure in the world', and who had proven his piety by agreeing in parliament that, if he married a Catholic, the queen would only be allowed a private chapel. The condition the country found itself in meant that war needed to be financed. While parliament was a very worthy body, when parliament was not in session, a magistrate serving the king had no alternative but to implement royal policies.[136]

Along with his speeches, moreover, Rodney's surviving papers include a single bound manuscript volume, the contents of which cover much of the same ground as the Palmes papers. Born in 1590 and educated at a grammar school in Trowbridge, he spent four years at Magdalen College Oxford before entering the Middle Temple. Having married Frances Southwell a chamber-lady to Queen Anne of Denmark, he then retired to the family seat in Somerset. Although he admitted to having 'only saluted the Law afarre off and misspent his time' at the Temple, Sir Edward wanted posterity to know that his family had not wasted itself in dissipation and maladministration, and his principal exhibits in defence of this proposition were several essays and dialogues on the subjects of law, divine providence, the lord's prayer, and the relationship between Protestantism and popery, that he intended to leave behind him.[137]

Consisting primarily of a series of notes, Rodney's 'Discourse of Lawes' was ambitious but characterised by a profound neo-Stoic distrust of human agency. He thought that God had to be the author of all order within the world because it was evident that men did not even have control over their own bodily functions. He divided laws into those that were divine and those that were human, but the laws of God were difficult to know with any certainty, and his treatment of the law of nations was confounded by the biblical injunction that people should turn the other cheek when an injury was done to them.[138] At this point, Rodney apparently ran out of interest or material, but his meditation on divine providence produced some additional observations on the nature of political authority. Starting with the proposition that all magistracy began with God, he thought that patriarchy (fatherly government) was the first pattern of monarchy and concluded that after time had corrupted the manners of rulers as well as people, laws had been introduced and new forms of government had been devised along the lines of the classical divisions introduced by Aristotle. Of all these monarchy had proven itself the most common and the most effective. Although he

---

[136] BL, MS Additional 34239, fols. 45–51: a speech made at Axbridge in the year 1626 to the Hundreders of Winterstoke, Brent and Bempston, concerning a benevolence demanded by the king.
[137] Ibid., fol. 15.   [138] Ibid., fols. 52–3.

accepted that a judicature based on laws agreed with the subjects and administered by independent courts was the best way to maintain political obedience, Rodney took exception to the idea that the consent of the people was essential to magistracy.[139]

Rodney was eventually sequestered in the 1640s for supporting the royalist cause, but it is unclear whether he wrote his essays before, or after, the Kentish country squire Sir Robert Filmer composed his much more famous work on political theory, *Patriarcha*.[140] Unlike Rodney, Filmer did not back away from drawing out the full implications of the notion that the role of the father within the family, and in particular the authority of the first patriarch Adam, was a pattern for the monarchical authority of modern kings. Although he drew frequently on Aristotle, Filmer, like the French jurist Bodin, rejected the notion that there was a distinction between the nature of the family and the nature of the state. Perhaps most importantly, Filmer was obsessed with the potentially bad consequences of either popular or mixed government. He used historical examples to show how popular states tended towards sedition, a view that seems to have been based on his concern about the fickle and unreliable nature of popular opinion and the fact that the self-interest of individuals tended to lead them to ignore the 'common good'.[141]

Writing in the late 1620s or early 1630s, Filmer blamed a growing division of people into 'patriots', who advocated a popular say in government, and 'royalists', on the 'school divinity' of Jesuits such as Bellarmine and Robert Parsons as well as the writings of John Calvin.[142] But, since one of his objectives was to show that kings alone, rather than kings in parliament, had always had power to make laws, *Patriarcha* also contained a vision of the nature of law that was directly contrary to that which featured in the writings of Sir Edward Coke, and which also appears to have underlain much early seventeenth-century gentry thinking. Arguing that the customs that made up the common law only had authority because they had at some point in the past been acknowledged as law by a king, he also maintained that since the 'public was to be preferred to the private', the force of laws,

must not be so great as natural equity itself – which cannot fully be comprised in any laws, but is to be left to the religious arbitrament of those who know how to manage the affairs of state, and wisely to balance the particular profit with the counterpoise of the public, according to the infinite variety of times, places, and persons.[143]

---

[139] Ibid., fols. 21–5v.
[140] Sir Robert Filmer, *Patriarcha and other Writings*, ed. J. P. Sommerville (Cambridge, 1991).
[141] Ibid., p. 28.   [142] Ibid., p. 3.   [143] Ibid., p. 35.

Far from being invented to bridle or moderate the power of kings, laws were originally created in order to keep the multitude in order. Indeed, while laws were essential to popular states, kingdoms had been successfully governed for many ages without them,[144] and Filmer rather disingenuously drew on the discussion of equity in *Archion*, in order to claim that William Lambarde supported the notion that the king had absolute authority over judicature. Neither the common law or statute law could be taken as any diminution of the 'natural power which kings have over their people by right of fatherhood, but are an argument to strengthen the truth of it'.[145]

Despite the invocation of Lambarde's name, Filmer's profound critique of the position of the common law in relation to equity is unlikely to have appealed much to lawyers. Nor is there conclusive evidence that his references to sedition and popular anarchy were all that convincing to his peers amongst the gentry. Although his treatise is certainly the most sophisticated surviving example of gentry writing on political thought before the civil wars, it was not printed until 1680, during the Tory reaction to the attempt to exclude the future James II from the throne. If, as Filmer argued, England could not in any way be described as a mixed polity, then squires as well as ordinary subjects would have a diminished role in law-making in parliament. If natural equity administered by the king was the supreme law of the land, then royal claims on private property in the name of the common good were no more resistible by the rich than they were by the poor, or the merely moderately well off. Based on their comments about the judges' decision in the Ship Money case, which touched directly on some of these issues, Filmer's fellow Kentishmen seem to have been deeply concerned about the majority verdict because of the extension on royal power that it seemed to imply.[146]

Although they might have agreed with some of Filmer's observations on the diversity of constitutional thought with which early seventeenth-century Englishmen had to contend, even future royalists on the eve of the civil war appear to have taken a more moderate tone, at least in public. In a quarter sessions charge delivered at York in May 1639, Sir John Reresby laid out Aristotle's classification of the different types of government – monarchy, aristocracy and democracy, along with their mixtures – in considerable detail before observing that it is 'an Antient

---

[144] Ibid., pp. 40–1.   [145] Ibid., p. 52. Above, p. 85.

[146] K. Fincham, 'The judges' decision on Ship Money, the reaction in Kent', *Bulletin Institute of the Historical Research*, 57 (1984), 230–7. For details of the case, see above, pp. 201–8.

Schools question and much argued upon' which was the best. He concluded that history seemed to vouch for the durability of monarchy and praised the piety, goodness and care for his people that had been exhibited by Charles I. However, in a second charge that may or may not have been given at a significantly later date, Reresby associated law-making in England with a long history of cooperation between the three estates in parliament in legislating for the common 'profit of civil society'. Cicero said that laws were the soul of the commonwealth, and echoing Fortescue, Reresby went on to say that the laws were the 'very nerves and ligaments' of this kingdom. Any subject with an 'estate' had a need of law as a light to guide them through the darkness of human existence.[147]

The degree to which the landed classes were effectively 'civilised' in the early modern period may be debatable, but they were certainly notable partakers in the rhetoric that made law a central part of the process. If there was a 'baronial' dimension to the opposition to Charles I in 1640–2, the civil wars were emphatically not 'barons' wars' along the same lines as those between the houses of York and Lancaster in the fifteenth century. Aristocratic leaders, such as the earl of Bedford and the earl of Warwick, depended on lawyer allies in the Commons, such as Oliver St John, and their political positions are best understood within the context of the legal, religious and political discourses that had emerged since the middle of the sixteenth century.[148]

[147] YAS, MS 329.
[148] John Adamson, *The Noble Revolt: the Overthrow of Charles I* (2007), pp. 512–13, 518–19.

11 Economic and tenurial relationships

Legal ligaments

For lawyers and country squires a conjuncture of political conditions and intellectual developments evidently made the importance of legal values so obvious and irresistible that they figure in scribblings intended for the edification of children as well as inclusion in public speeches. Furthermore, as Sir John Reresby put it in his charges to the grand jurors at York, the rule of law was a resource that promised to protect the goods, lands and person of every member of the commonwealth, regardless of their station or wealth.[1]

It may be that all this amounts to little more than a demonstration that the early modern English experience is a particularly good illustration of Michel Foucault's contention that *ancien régime* monarchical states were construed as systems of law, which were explained in terms of legal theory, and whose mechanisms of power were articulated through law.[2] By the early seventeenth century, moreover, it was certainly possible to mix the thought of the Florentine Niccolò Machiavelli and the Frenchman Jean Bodin in order to come up with the idea that the due administration of justice was little more than a sop thrown to the volatile 'vulgar sort' in order to prevent those who were rash, heady and devoid of judgment, from becoming discontented with the existing regime.[3]

Nevertheless the purchase of legal rhetoric also reflected the fact that law was much more deeply ingrained into everyday life than has until recently been recognised by most historians. There were social relationships that took place outside the legal matrix, but the list of them is surprisingly short. Quite apart from the ubiquity of courts down to

---

[1] See above, p. 306.
[2] L. Engelstein, 'Combined underdevelopment: discipline and the law in imperial and soviet Russia', *American Historical Review*, 98(2) (1993), 338–53; M. Foucault, *History of Sexuality*, vol. I (1979 edn), p. 87.
[3] HEHL, MS Ellesmere 1174: anonymous early seventeenth-century treatise owned by the earl of Bridgewater.

village level,[4] most men, and many women, from country squires to seamen and urban wage labourers regularly used legal instruments to record many of the most important transactions in their lives: apprenticeship indentures, marriage contracts, last wills, deeds to property, trusts, partnership agreements and, last but hardly least, written penal bonds that could be used to cover anything from a loan of money to a consultation with a physician.[5]

In countries such as France, where the Roman law tradition exerted a greater influence than in England, documents of this kind were formally written out by public notaries, a cadre of licensed lawyers. Furthermore, the registers that notaries kept in order to record the instruments they made were acceptable to courts as evidence that an obligation had been entered into, a technical detail that has made notarial archives a rich historical source for a wide range of social, economic and family relationships.[6] In England, on the other hand, although there were some notable exceptions including the Court of Admiralty and the Lord Mayor's court in London, most jurisdictions refused to accept such registers as evidence. Consequently, with the exception of title deeds and wills, written legal instruments do not survive in great quantities, but this does not mean that they were not widely used. The records of English scriveners, the professionals most closely related to continental notaries, show that they had been engaged in legal writing since the later Middle Ages, and the making of instruments continued to be an important aspect of the work of local lawyers throughout the early modern period.[7]

Like the mortgage agreement on our house, the lease for our flat, and the paperwork associated with banking arrangements early modern legal instruments existed alongside verbal promises as the essential ligaments in the business of living. Enforceable by one sort of court or another, they enabled contemporaries in all walks of life to inscribe relationships, and their efficacy depended on legal certainty and predictability. Indeed, unless we define it as comprising only the property-less or the very young, then it is hard to see how early modern 'popular culture' can be adequately described without including this legal dimension. The

---

[4] See above, pp. 244ff.
[5] C. W. Brooks, 'Les actes juridiques, le cycle de vie, et les relations sociales dans l'Angleterre de la période moderne' in S. Beauvalet, V. Gourdon and F.-J. Ruggiu, eds. *Liens sociaux et actes notariés, 16e–18e siècle* (Paris, 2004), pp. 77–86.
[6] Claire Dolan, *Le famille, le notaire et la Ville (Aix-en-Provence à la fin du XVIe siècle)* (Toulouse, 1998); Renata Ago, 'Enforcing agreements: notaries and courts in early-modern Rome', *Continuity and Change*, 14(2) (1999), 191–206.
[7] C. Brooks, R. H. Helmholz and P. Stein, *Notaries Public in England since the Reformation* (Norwich, 1991), esp. chs. 2, 3, 4.

idealistic sixteenth-century publicist Thomas Phayer was evidently serious when he suggested that legal instruments should be studied by as broad a cross-section of the population as possible, including children.[8] In the wake of the more comprehensive provision of poor relief created by legislation in 1601, even the destitute and the orphaned needed paperwork that would prove they had a 'settlement' entitling them to parish relief. But it was of course those with some material substance who made most use of instruments, and who appeared in court most often in connection with them, a category that included the 'respectable' poor as well as the better-off middling sort and gentry. According to the leading late Elizabethan writer on the subject, William West, the kinds of 'contracts' people entered into were limitless; legal instruments were the means by which individuals separated their property from the 'common fund' of nature, and then traded between themselves in order to support their families.[9] By the mid seventeenth century, the Oxford don and civil lawyer Richard Zouche saw law essentially in terms of human inter-course of this kind, a view that was also central to the more theoretical writings of the most important lawyer of the Restoration period, Sir Mathew Hale.[10] It is suggestive that two of the most important political thinkers of the seventeenth century, John Milton and John Locke, were the sons, respectively, of a London scrivener and a West Country attorney.[11]

Although many practices regarding the most basic of obligations, that between debtor and creditor, were already deeply rooted in the fabric of late medieval society, the acceleration in economic transactions that characterised the later sixteenth and early seventeenth centuries was accompanied by significant legal developments. These tended to priv-ilege economic agency, and they were predicated on a high level of individual self-determination and responsibility. At the same time, it is impossible to discuss the role of law in early modern social and eco-nomic life without looking at other kinds of relationships, including first and foremost those having to do with tenures and the conditions under which land was held and exploited.[12] Here the words that come to mind for the historian are seigneurialism and feudalism, and it is one of the

---

[8] Thomas Phayer, *A Newe Boke of Presidentes* (1543), sig. Aiv–sig. Aiiv.
[9] *Symbolaeographia, Which May be termed The Art, Description, Or Image of Instruments, Covenants, Contracts, etc. OR The Notarie or Scrivener, Collected and Disposed by William West of the Inner Temple, Attorney at the Common Law* (1590), Preface. See also Brooks, Helmholz and Stein, *Notaries Public*, p. 88.
[10] LI, MS Hargrave 13. For Zouche see *ODNB*.
[11] Brooks, Helmholz and Stein, *Notaries Public*, pp. 59, 91; BL, MS Additional 28273.
[12] See below, pp. 322ff.

commonplace assumptions about 'modernisation' that as these declined, contracts between independent legal agents became more important. Yet, the story is complicated because early modern conceptions of landed property flowed out of a set of ideas that were largely distinct from those associated with property in goods or money.

Obligations

Although agriculture was the foundation of early modern economic life, and while much of the work of lawyers concerned interests in land, the records of every law court in the country, from those of the King's Bench and Common Pleas in London, to those of the regional councils or borough courts, indicate that the legal relationship most likely to be entered into by any individual was a transaction involving a sale of goods, or a service rendered, that might ultimately lead to one party being liable to another for a debt. In the central common-law courts, three-quarters of the litigation involved a form of written obligation known as the conditional bond, in which one party agreed with another to repay a sum of money, or take some specified action, and where the penalty for non-performance was normally expressed as an action for debt for double the value of the original obligation. In local courts, including borough tribunals and the pipe-powder jurisdiction, which was exercised in many places whenever there was a market or a fair, actions of debt were by contrast most often brought on verbal agreements, in which one of the parties had promised to pay a certain sum of money, or on informal written agreements, including shop-books and tallies, that might record debts for anything ranging from the purchase of a pair of gloves to the failure to pay a carpenter for a piece of joinery, or a 'score' run up in the alehouse.[13]

Judging from steady increases in the volume of litigation in nearly every kind of court, such transactions became increasingly widespread from the mid sixteenth century onwards, and for every action that found its way into court for one reason or another, there must have been hundreds that went smoothly so that the paperwork was in due course disposed of, burnt or recycled. Furthermore, they affected every sector of the population, including richer and poorer sorts alike. In London, where the City within the walls had long been served by several

---

[13] Brooks, *Lawyers, Litigation*, chs. 2–4; C. Muldrew, *The Economy of Obligation: the Culture of Credit and Social Relations in Early Modern England* (1998), pp. 265, 270; K. Wrightson, *Earthly Necessities: Economic Lives in Early Modern Britain* (New Haven, CT, 2000), p. 175; M. Pelling, *Medical Conflicts in Early Modern London* (Oxford, 2003), ch. 7.

traditional jurisdictions, the Common Council decided in 1518 to establish a small-claims jurisdiction for matters involving less than 40s. where legal procedures were kept to a minimum and where commissioners, rather than juries, would make judgments about who owed and how payments were to be made.[14] In most corporate towns court dockets expanded steadily over the second half of the sixteenth century, and by the 1630s it is evident that the increase in business was accompanied by increased formality and regularity in the record keeping.[15] Market transactions, and the dependence on credit relationships enforced by law, were so important that they constituted a central place in the economic and social culture of the period.[16]

In terms of volume of business, the enforcement of debts and obligations was probably the principal practical manifestation of 'the law' in early modern society. It constituted a large part of the work of local practitioners, principally attorneys, and their involvement in local credit networks is the main reason why some began by the mid seventeenth century to act regularly as brokers between people with money to lend and those who needed to borrow some.[17] Furthermore, although debtor/creditor relations came up only rarely in the reported case law or in law lectures, the subject had some profound social and political consequences, not least because of changing ideas about how someone who claimed to have an obligation owing to them could prove that it existed in the first place.

At the end of the Middle Ages, the default common-law position was that a defendant who was sued in an action of debt based on a verbal promise, or an informal written agreement, could deny the obligation by 'waging their law'. That is, if he or she could find twelve compurgators, or oath-takers, who would swear under oath that there was no obligation, or that it had already been settled, then the plaintiff lost his cause. The evolution of this position reflected a traditional view that the creation of obligations was best done in public, and before witnesses who could, if necessary, vouch for their existence. It also seems apposite to the kind of face-to-face commercial relationships that were doubtless characteristic of a society where the largest provincial towns numbered

---

[14] CLRO, MS Miscellaneous 135.3: typescript historical notes on courts of requests. P. Jones and R. Smith, *A Guide to the Records in the Corporation of London Records Office and Guildhall Library Muniment Room* (1951).

[15] W. A. Champion, 'Recourse to law and the meaning of the great litigation decline, 1650–1750: some clues from the Shrewsbury local courts' in *Communities and Courts*, pp. 179–98. For two other local examples see BLAS, BorBF8; Worcester County Record Office, Worcester, Worcester Court of Pleas, A9 Box 1, 1632–5, 1635–6 and 1645–6.

[16] Muldrew, *Economy of Obligation.*   [17] Brooks, *Pettyfoggers and Vipers*, pp. 196–7.

no more than several thousand people. Nevertheless, it is also clear that formally written, signed, sealed and witnessed legal instruments were already widely used during the fifteenth century, no doubt because many important transactions were entered into without sufficient publicity, or, because the people making the deals were wary of the possibility of perjury if they were not written down.[18] According to William Noy, the Statute of Merchants (13 Edward I), which permitted the enrolment of recognisances of debt before the mayors of towns, had been passed in 1285 at the request of parliament because wager of law provided insufficient security for transactions, a hazard that could lead to the collapse of trade and the impoverishment of the subjects.[19] By the time of Henry VI, legal actions based on formal writings, usually the conditional bond, were already common in the central courts of King's Bench and Common Pleas, and much of the increase in their business over the next two centuries was based on exactly the same legal instrument while the use of wager of law became increasingly less significant.[20]

The chief attractions of the conditional bond were certainty about the terms of the agreement, about what constituted satisfactory performance and about the penalties for defaults. Usually written out by a scrivener or local attorney, bonds were witnessed, signed and sealed by the parties. If the documentation was correct, defendants in actions concerning bonds had little scope for denying the liability, a point reflected in the fact that most of the case law about bonds concerned technical matters, such as whether the conditions, times and places had been set down sufficiently clearly, rather than the nature of the conditions themselves, which were left entirely up to the parties. Indeed, by Elizabethan times it had become common for someone who was entering into a bond to confess a judgment in one of the courts at the same time as they signed it so that the legal record ensured that in the event of a default there would be no question of the defendant contesting the obligation.

On the face of it, the law relating to bonds gave almost unlimited scope to economic agents to make their own agreements. Furthermore, there was an implication that contracts should be enforced strictly according to the letter, and with little regard to mitigating circumstances.[21] But it is at precisely this point that conditional bonds became involved

---

[18] Brooks, *Lawyers, Litigation*, pp. 77–9.
[19] LI, MS Miscellaneous 29, item 3: reading in August 1623.
[20] *Lord Nottingham's Chancery Cases*, ed. D. E. C. Yale (Selden Society, vols. 73 and 79, 1957 and 1961), I, Introduction.
[21] 2 *CoRep*, 9. *Thoroughgood's Case* (1584) addressed the issue of how far an illiterate man might be bound by a written obligation that was read to him incorrectly, either through ignorance or deceit. The ruling was that deceit would in effect void the agreement.

in jurisprudential debates about the relationship between the strict letter of the law and the extent to which this might be relaxed by reference to considerations of natural justice, conscience, or reason, debates central to the way contemporaries understood the relationship between so-called equitable jurisdictions, most notably that of the court of Chancery, and the common-law courts. Christopher St German's classic sixteenth-century treatment of the subject accepted the need for recourse to conscience and equity when the slavish pursuit of the strict letter might lead to injustice. Yet in the wake of the notorious chancellorship of Cardinal Wolsey, St German also made it clear that the discretionary power inherent in equity should be used sparingly, and his prime example of this was a case involving a conditional bond, where the creditor had in fact made the payment, but neglected to cover himself from further legal action by obtaining some form of written receipt to prove it. According to St German, the mitigating circumstance could not be allowed to override the need to interpret bonds strictly. Not enforcing them would lead to uncertainty, and if the power of chancellors was allowed to slip out of control then the common law would in fact be abrogated by the free reign of conscience as exercised by a single individual guided only by his moral values or personal inclinations.[22]

St German went on to point out that the writ of subpoena, the leading process in Chancery, had traditionally been limited by certain conventions,[23] and in practice even the clerical chancellors who succeeded Wolsey were keen to endorse the certainty to be found in the strict enforcement of the bond. During the first two decades of the seventeenth century, however, questions about the relationship between the common-law courts and equity were reignited as part of Sir Edward Coke's quarrel with Lord Chancellor Ellesmere,[24] and the enforcement of obligations inevitably came into the argument. Those who defended the chancellor's position admitted that some litigants resorted to Chancery because it enabled them to gain delays, or breathing space, in paying debts or honouring other obligations, for which they were bound at law.[25] Going even further, Sir John Davies suggested that the confession of judgments in the common-law courts on conditional bonds amounted to little more than the entry of a recognisance and, if this were the case, then the chancellor should be allowed to examine the circumstances which led to the making of such instruments.[26]

---

[22] J. S. Guy, ed., *Christopher St German on Chancery and Statute* (Selden Society, Supplementary Series, vol. 6, 1985), p. 105. Also, see above, pp. 38–9.

[23] Ibid., pp. 106–7, 116ff.   [24] See above, pp. 145ff.   [25] BLAS, MS L28/47, fol. 3.

[26] HEHL, MS Ellesmere 2748. See also BL, MS Hargrave 372, fol. 94: a series of questions about whether recognisances could be taken in any court of record, which

Not surprisingly, those inclined to support equity were aware that there was a certain populist appeal in arguments that strict enforcement of the letter might be relieved by taking account of fraud or the particular circumstances that led to a failure to perform an obligation. The most famous literary representation of this comes, of course, from Shakespeare's play, *The Merchant of Venice*, in which the money-scrivener Shylock ruthlessly enforced a conditional bond where the penalty was a pound of flesh. But bonds were also associated with more mundane stereotypes that often involved the nefarious or the naive (very often heirs with expectations who needed cash) becoming involved in ruinous legal entanglements from which they could not disengage themselves. Furthermore, since it was common for lenders to ask those who entered into conditional bonds to find sureties who would pay the debt if they failed to do so, friends and neighbours, who were simply trying to help out, might also become involved.[27]

If the common law represented the certainty and predictability associated with the merciless enforcement of obligations, equity could be depicted as allowing for a humane relaxation of strict liability on the basis of higher, 'religious' principles, a view that also resonated with contemporary moral prescriptions advising creditors to treat debtors with a degree of kindness and Christian charity. Obligations based on the bond were synonymous with anxiety, but equity, quite literally, offered relief. William Lambarde, himself a sometime Master in Chancery, observed in *Archion* that Englishmen had always had a natural inclination to take their cases before the king and his council, where they could be heard in private and without the encumbrances of strict legal proceedings.[28] Similarly, Sir Anthony Benn must have had a point when he claimed that it was a commonplace with the common people that abstract principles of justice and equity had existed before Magna Carta and the common law.[29] Going even further, Sir Robert Filmer argued in *Patriarcha* that the need for equity was one of the best reasons for thinking that royal authority must ultimately be superior to common law.[30]

notes a decision in 29 Elizabeth that mayors of London and other towns could not take recognisances for debts between parties, except by special prescription.

[27] Brooks, Helmholz and Stein, *Notaries Public*, pp. 99–102; Thomas Powell, *The Art of Thriving . . . Together with the Mysterie and Miserie of Lending and Borrowing . . .* (1635).

[28] William Lambarde, *Archion, or A Commentary Upon the High Courts of Justice in England* (1635), p. 65. Also, above, pp. 85–6.

[29] BL, MS Stowe 177, fol. 196: 'Chancery refuses to be set limits by her younger brother, for equity is older than law.'

[30] Sir Robert Filmer, *Patriarcha and Other Writings*, ed. J. P. Sommerville (Cambridge, 1991), p. 49. Also, above, p. 305.

Although Filmer referred to *Archion,* he failed to mention that Lambarde had also put the other side of the argument, which was that recourse to royal sources of equity in cases determinable at common law would lead to an 'anomy' where everything was in disorder, doubt and uncertainly.[31] In the wake of the dispute between Coke and Ellesmere, moreover, this traditional lawyerly concern about the practical consequences of equity became so intimately tied up with its procedural anomalies, and absolutist implications, that it is difficult to say exactly how far the political influences helped to shape the jurisprudential considerations. Nevertheless, the net result of early seventeenth-century developments was that whatever the wider appeal of taking moral or religious points into consideration, the legal context in which business was done tended towards strictness rather than leniency, although the distinctions remained less than clear cut.

The records of jurisdictions such as Chancery, or the court of Requests,[32] show that litigants regularly maintained that a myriad of special circumstances accounted for the failure to meet their obligations, and there was little juridical dissent from St German's contention that there were cases where the letter of the law, or the exact terms of a conditional bond, had to be overthrown by equitable considerations. Apart from anything else, widows, orphans, or those with diminished mental capacity might need the special care of the courts.[33] But if the sheer volume of cases that were brought into Chancery indicates a plausible expectation of success, and considerable scope for vexatious litigation, the general drift of decision-making appears to have been cautious of leniency. Sir Francis Bacon, who knew from personal experience what it was like to be arrested for debt, was evidently willing to use the authority of Chancery against creditors who had been over-precipitate in bringing legal process in order to collect from those who owed them money.[34] On the other hand, despite his conflicts with Coke, Ellesmere is reported to have held that, except in the case of usurious contracts, he would not intervene to overthrow a bargain merely because it was foolish; indeed a compilation of dicta relating to Chancery practice, which appears to have been made soon after his death, seems to be a pioneering attempt to lay down guidelines for the general application of equitable discretion.[35] Although

---

[31] Lambarde, *Archion,* p. 67.
[32] W. J. Jones, *The Elizabethan Court of Chancery* (Oxford, 1967); T. Stretton, *Women Waging Law in Elizabethan England* (Cambridge, 1998).
[33] John Ritchie, *Reports of Cases Decided by Francis Bacon Baron Verulam, Viscount St Albans, Lord Chancellor of England, in the High Court of Chancery 1617–1621* (1932), p. 57.
[34] Ibid., pp. 62, 122.   [35] CUL, MS Gg.2.31, fols. 437ff.

there is some evidence from the 1620s and 1630s that the common-law judges were increasingly willing to countenance arguments in mitigation of liability for contracts, they do not seem to have deviated very far from rigorous enforcement.[36] At the Oxford assizes in 1624, for example, Justice Jones rejected a plea of duress in upholding the validity of an obligation entered into by a defendant in order to avoid a lawful arrest. In another case, he held that even if it was subsequently annulled, the making of a marriage constituted the satisfactory per-formance of a bond that involved the payment of money to the father of a bride on the condition that she married the promisor's son.[37]

The frequency with which they appear in the records of the court of Common Pleas is proof enough that conditional bonds remained an essential legal ligament, and the growth in the importance of written instruments more generally is also illustrated by two further points. First, yet another attraction of equity courts was that they could be used by one party in a dispute to force the other to disclose relevant docu-ments.[38] Second, forgery and fraud emerged as serious social patholo-gies. One famous Elizabethan case involved the estate of the leading financier Sir Thomas Gresham, and forgery appears to have been an occupational temptation for the more marginal members of the legal profession in London. In response, parliament passed a series of acts aimed at addressing the problem, beginning with the Elizabethan Statute of Frauds (5 Elizabeth I, c. 14), which prescribed the death penalty for anyone found guilty of the offence of forgery for the third time.[39]

Nevertheless, despite the growing importance of writing, the accel-eration in the number and reach of commercial transactions in the six-teenth century was also accompanied by a growth in the number of cases that came before the courts involving informal agreements based either on verbal promises, or on writings (including 'scores' and tallies) that lacked the formality of seals and witnesses. Though such actions had long been entertained in local jurisdictions, including the local courts of London, during the early Tudor period the judges and officials of the central courts, and the court of King's Bench in particular, countenanced the alteration of legal procedures so that suits brought on such 'simple

---

[36] This was in fact the position advocated by the late Elizabethan Edward Hake, *Epieikeia: A Dialogue on Equity in Three Parts*, ed. D. E. C. Yale (Yale Law Library Publications 13, New Haven, CT, 1953).

[37] ECO, MS 168, fol. 8v.   [38] Jones, *Elizabethan Court of Chancery*, pp. 455ff.

[39] Brooks, Helmholz and Stein, *Notaries Public*, pp. 102–3. For other examples of fraud see, HEHL, MS Ellesmere 5962 (which involved a lawyer of Gray's Inn and fraud in connection with a mortgage); Bankes Papers 44/3, 63/43 (forgeries committed by law-writers in Holborn).

contracts' could be heard by juries rather than through the traditional means of waging law and calling on oath helpers.

The critical technical development was the formulation of a legal remedy known as the action on the case in *assumpsit*. The theory in actions on the case, and in *assumpsit* in particular, was that the plaintiff was suing for recompense of the damage he had suffered as a result of the other party having failed to pay his debt or perform the action promised, and the prescribed legal process left it to a jury in the country to assess the value of the monetary damages due.[40] Judging from the evidence of the local court at Shrewsbury, which has been subjected to uniquely detailed study, the prospect of a jury trial appears to have been one of the major attractions of actions of *assumpsit* even in the localities where informal legal agreements, or debts on tallies, were especially important as a way of doing business.[41]

Partly because they often involved relatively small sums of money, actions of *assumpsit* came more slowly into the central common law courts at Westminster, but there was also a significant ongoing judicial break on the process. *Assumpsit* enabled King's Bench to entertain important types of commercial litigation such as charter parties, insurance contracts, partnerships and bills of exchange, but the judges of the court of Common Pleas were much more reluctant to accept them, the argument being that lawsuits that were essentially about debts should be tried according to the traditional common-law writs of debt, detinue and covenant, the first of which involved wager of law. Thus while actions of *assumpsit* were on the one hand becoming a foundation stone in the modern law of contract, a significant section of the judiciary was actively discouraging their use up until the hearing of *Slade's Case*, which finally resolved the conundrum in 1598.[42]

In contemporary terms, there were some weighty reasons for rejecting the innovative forms of action. Arguing against the plaintiff who was attempting to recover his debt in *Slade's Case*, John Dodderidge claimed that the right to wage law in such circumstances was a birthright of freeborn Englishmen. He also pointed out that the records of the courts themselves amounted to a mountain of precedent in favour of the differences between actions on the case (of which *assumpsit* was a variety) and the actions traditionally associated with informal debts. In his report

---

[40] D. J. Ibbetson, 'The development of the Action of Assumpsit 1540–1620' (Cambridge University PhD thesis, 1980), p. 357.

[41] Champion, 'Recourse to law and the meaning of the great litigation decline, 1650–1750', pp. 186–7.

[42] J. H. Baker, *The Legal Profession and the Common Law. Historical Essays* (London, 1986), ch. 21.

of the case, which was heard over the space of years, Sir Edward Coke noted that the judges in making their decision had to balance what he described as clerical precedent against the force of reason and convenience.[43] Expressing surprise that his contemporaries evidently took oaths so lightly, he nevertheless agreed with the majority decision that it was 'good in these days in as many cases as may be done' to prevent defendants from being able to wage their law, 'for otherwise it would be the occasion of much perjury'.[44] His handling of the issue of precedents was no less interesting, particularly in the light of the controversy caused in 1628 by the disputed enrolment in the *Five Knights' Case*.[45] Entries in the records of the courts, he wrote, were merely mechanical and often passed without being challenged. They did not have the same weight as the decisions of judges.[46]

Enforcement

Evolving commercial practices and the demands of litigants were the primary driving forces behind the changes recognised in *Slade's Case*. A similar dynamic also accounts for the other major change in common-law procedure during the sixteenth century, the willingness of the court of King's Bench to allow plaintiffs to cause the arrest and imprisonment of defendants at the early stages of actions involving debts and other kinds of obligations. Traditional common-law procedure followed a pattern in which the series of writs used to summons a defendant to answer the case being brought against him gradually increased in terms of the amount of pressure they brought to bear. If a defendant failed to respond to initial writs requesting him to appear before the court of Common Pleas, for instance, the next step would be writs that enabled the sheriff to distrain his goods, a practice that excluded landed property, domestic cooking utensils and any items that might be considered essential tools of the trade.[47] These procedures enabled defendants to get a clear view of the case being put against them and allowed plenty of time for out-of-court settlements. But they also enabled defendants to delay the progress of the action and hence put off the day on which they would have to satisfy their creditors. Partly to overcome these shortcomings, and no doubt partly to gain a share in the business involved in

---

[43] 4 *CoRep*, 92v, *Slade* v. *Morley*: an action on the case lies for simple contract as well as an action of debt. See also, D. H. Sachs, 'The promise and the contract in early modern England: Slade's Case in perspective' in V. Kahn and L. Hutson, eds., *Rhetoric and Law in Early Modern Europe* (New Haven, 2001), pp. 28–53.
[44] 4 *CoRep*, 95v.   [45] See above, p. 172.   [46] 4 *CoRep*, 95v.
[47] Brooks, *Pettyfoggers and Vipers*, pp. 102, 127–31; BL, MS Hargrave 398, fols. 154ff.

these kinds of action, in the reign of Henry VIII, the judges, clerks and attorneys working in the court of King's Bench began to use a combination of writs known as the Bill of Middlesex and *latitat*, which effectively enabled plaintiffs from the outset of their actions to arrest and hold to bail defendants in cases involving debts, moves that were both cheaper and more draconian than the traditional ones. While this procedure was much more effective from the point of view of plaintiffs, it was sometimes criticised for the pressure it put on defendants and denounced as an infringement of the due process clauses of Magna Carta which were supposed to protect the subject from arbitrary imprisonment before he was clearly aware of the charges that were being brought against him.[48]

The potential to arrest defendants on *mesne process*, as it was known, became the norm in actions of debt by the end of the seventeenth century, but during the Elizabethan years differences in opinion between the judges in King's Bench and Common Pleas about the legality of the procedures, and, it would seem, inertia in the way people were used to doing business,[49] to some degree held back the tide. Even so, an essential feature of litigation on obligations was that the repeated failure of defendants to respond to the summonses of plaintiffs, the inability to find bail, or default on payments once judgment had been given, could lead to detention in a debtors' prison until the creditors were satisfied.[50] Though the ultimate sanctions were enforced only in a tiny minority of cases, by 1600 the law of debt was potentially devastating for individuals and families who ran foul of it. Furthermore, the emergence of the insolvent debtor as a social problem was accompanied by the creation of the 'bankrupt'.

Although common-law procedures allowed for the destraint of moveable property, including stock-in-trade, and rents due to a debtor, landholdings and debts owing to him were exempt. In addition, of course, some debtors endeavoured to conceal their goods and property from creditors so as to avoid paying what they owed, even if they had been imprisoned. Some even went so far as to enter into collusive actions against themselves so that they could transfer assets to one creditor in order to avoid having to pay another, and it was also possible to use imprisonment for one debt as a way of avoiding lawsuits brought by another creditor. Applicable only to those identified as merchants

---

[48] M. Blatcher, 'Touching the writ of latitat: an act of no great moment' in S. T. Bindoff, J. Hurstfield and C. H. Williams, eds., *Elizabethan Government and Society* (1961), pp. 188–211; BL, MS Harleian 6846, fol. 9; N. G. Jones, 'The Bill of Middlesex and the Chancery, 1556–1608', *Legal History*, 22(3) (2001), 1–20.

[49] Brooks, *Pettyfoggers and Vipers*, pp. 63–5.

[50] *Imprisonment of Mens Bodys for Debt, as the practice of England now stands* (1641).

'trading in merchandise', all these potential 'frauds and deceipts', as well as the simpler one of fleeing abroad, were addressed in a series of statutes, beginning in 1543, that labelled debtors who attempted any of them a 'bankrupt', and which made it possible for individual creditors to seek redress by going to the lord chancellor and asking for a commission of bankruptcy.[51] The appointed commissioners could investigate the assets of the debtor and oversee their liquidation in order to pay his debts, and as time went on their powers were increased. According to the statute passed in 1603, frauds and deceits, primarily in the form of fraudulent conveyances, were on the increase, and so commissioners needed the authority to examine anyone who might be involved and to punish perjury.[52] The second Jacobean statute (1624) specified that the wives of debtors might be amongst those interviewed about suspected concealments, and provided that anyone found guilty of fraud in connection with a bankrupt might be put in the pillory and have one of their ears cut off.[53]

The 1624 statute also for the first time specifically named scriveners as one of the occupations liable to bankruptcy, an innovation that was apparently connected with a recent scandal in London that involved money from the City's orphan funds that had been put out to loan by scriveners who had subsequently gone broke.[54] But, although the number of bankrupts appears initially to have been relatively small (around ten a year), they were not an exclusively metropolitan phenomenon,[55] and they increased significantly in the 1630s. In 1638, a least 150 commissions were granted involving people from all around the country in all sorts of trades and occupations.[56] In a case heard at Derby assizes in March 1634, Henry Travis sued one of his creditors for slander, claiming he had been unjustly called a bankrupt and base carrion. It was shown in evidence that Travis either shied away from his creditors by not going to the market or to church, or by disappearing from his house altogether for long periods of time. He was a licensed

---

[51] The first statute, 34 Henry VIII, c. 4, was largely superseded by 13 Elizabeth, c. 7, which became the starting point for subsequent measures.

[52] 1 James I, c. 15.   [53] 21 James I, c. 19.

[54] LI, MS Maynard 57, fol. 3. See also *An Act for the selling of the Lands, Tenements, Leases, Rents, and Annuities of John Moyle of London, Scrivener, for payment of his Debts and relief of his creditors and suerties* (1621); *The Contents of a Bill preferred by the creditors of Thomas Frith, late of London, Scrivener, deceased, for sale of certayne Lands and Leases by him purchased, for the payment of such Moneys, as was owing by him unto them, and are yet unpaid* (1621).

[55] W. J. Jones, 'The foundations of English bankruptcy: statutes and commissions in the early modern period', *Transactions of the American Philosophical Society*, 69 (1979), 3–63.

[56] *A Calendar of the Docquets of Lord Keeper Coventry 1625–1640*, ed. J. Broadway, R. Cust and S. Roberts (List and Index Society, Special Series, 34, 2004), pp. 487ff.

bankrupt who had compounded with seventeen creditors in Manchester, but paid them only a small portion of what he owed them. According to the presiding judge, Sir George Croke, all of this accurately described a bankrupt, and the jury found for the defendant.[57]

While bankrupts were tainted with dishonesty, 'insolvent' debtors who could not pay, and therefore ended up in prison, were regarded a good deal more charitably, though with due regard for the interests of their creditors. The first of what became a long series of royal commissions for relieving insolvent debtors in the King's Bench prison in London was issued in 1585. After reciting the hardships of debtors and their families, it proposed that panels composed of bishops, deans, masters of livery companies and aldermen of the City of London should facilitate the negotiation and settlement of debts, even if this included the sale of some of the goods or lands of the debtor.[58] Commissions along the same lines, but expanded in scope in terms of the jurisdictions covered, were regularly instituted throughout the seventeenth century and beyond, largely because the insolvent continued to be a problem.[59] In local jurisdictions, where the stakes were normally lower, and the debtors poor, courts appear often to have avoided imprisonment by getting debtors to sign up for repayment plans.[60] But since increasingly large numbers of cases from all over the country were going into the central courts, the numbers of people imprisoned in connection with civil actions nevertheless increased as the period progressed. Unique pieces of evidence from Somerset in the later 1620s and 1630s indicate that large numbers of yeoman farmers evidently spent spells in debtors' prison, and it is no less telling that the inhabitants of Ilchester claimed that the economic well-being of the town was largely dependant on the local debtors' prison that was located there.[61] There seems no reason to believe that this example from the West Country was unique, and while the exact number of those imprisoned before 1640 is incalculable, it is likely that their numbers were made up of the middling of one sort or another, rather than the chronically poor.

Prisoners were on occasion unruly or hostile to legal officials, and some of them took undue advantage of the convention that permitted

---

[57] BL, MS Hargrave 44, fol. 9.

[58] HEHL, MSS Ellesmere 6210–14; *The Egerton Papers*, ed. J. Payne Collier (Camden Society, 1st series, vol. 12, 1840), p. 111.

[59] Brooks, *Lawyers, Litigation*, p. 59.

[60] Muldrew, *Economy of Obligation*, pp. 262, 285, estimates that during a four-year sample period in King's Lynn, in the 1660s, 2.7 per cent of adult heads of household spent some time in debtors' prison.

[61] SARS, MSS Phelips DD/Ph/197, 223/50.

debtors to leave prison for periods of time if they were accompanied by a gaoler.[62] Nevertheless, since imprisoned debtors, sometimes accompanied by their families, had to pay for their board and lodgings, there were also complaints about the conditions to which they were subjected as well as criticisms of the principle of imprisonment itself.[63] By the later 1620s it was sometimes argued that both common sense and God's law dictated that it was wrong to imprison debtors since incarceration obviously prevented them from undertaking employment that would enable them to earn the money necessary to pay off their debts. It was also suggested that the practice had a tendency to break up families; that it had no scriptural warrant; and that it was contrary to Christian notions of charity, clemency and compassion. According to one manuscript critique, all punishment was repugnant to charity, and many things required by law were against the nature of right and good, and should therefore be judged by the rule of natural justice and conscience rather than by the strict letter of statute law.[64]

Probably aimed largely at creditors, this is unlikely to have been the sentiment of a common lawyer.[65] Though many lawyers, particularly in the Elizabethan period, made testamentary bequests to poor prisoners, the morality of imprisonment for debt does not seem to have been widely discussed in legal circles.[66] Indeed, the trouble with the language of conscience and natural justice was that it immediately raised the spectre of the jurisdictional issues associated with Chancery and the ecclesiastical courts, the antique problem identified by Christopher St German. Like nearly everyone else, lawyers were both creditors and debtors, on the one hand living in fear of debtors' prison and on the other seeing it as a necessary evil. The need for certainty meant that promises must be strictly enforced.

Tenures

While the dockets of early modern courts were dominated quantitatively by actions about promises and obligations, legal instruments associated

---

[62] HMC, *Report on the Manuscripts of R. R. Hastings of the Manor House, Ashby de la Zouche* (4 vols., 1928–47), II, p. 77.

[63] BL, MS Lansdowne 85, item 53: report of the commissioners appointed to examine the state of the Fleet. A. Jessup, ed., *The Economy of the Fleete* (Camden Society, NS, 25, 1879).

[64] BL, MS Sloane 1926; HRO, MS 44M69L39/72: 'Several Motives and Reasons . . . for freeing mens bodies of imprisonment' in the papers of Henry Sherfield.

[65] In his reading on the Statute of Merchants, William Noy admitted in 1624 that the practice had critics but noted that it was justified by Roman law and the scriptures. LI, MS Misc. 29. Item 3.

[66] Brooks, *Lawyers, Litigation*, p. 87.

with the purchase and transfer of land, and legal questions about the holding of it, were of course of no less importance. Deeds, conveyances and leases are amongst the most ubiquitous documents in the collections of any local archive office, and although they often relate to the holdings of long-established gentry families, those involving people of much more modest means are also common.[67] It has been plausibly argued that the need to be able to read deeds was a good reason for even modest farmers to acquire functional literacy, but as Lord Keeper Coventry intimated in a Star Chamber case in the 1620s, even the illiterate could employ a lawyer to make (and interpret) important documents for them.[68]

By the mid seventeenth century lawyers appear already to have emerged as agents who were regularly involved as middle-men in the property market. Furthermore, the professional interest lawyers had in land was supplemented on a personal level by the fact that some inherited land themselves, and many more invested the profits of their vocation in land. Sir Edward Coke accumulated extensive manorial holdings in Norfolk that laid the foundations for an agricultural dynasty that flourished for centuries after his death.[69] More modestly well-off town-dwellers, on the other hand, such as the Elizabethan judge Francis Wyndham or the Hertfordshire attorney John Skinner, assembled portfolios consisting either of smaller parcels of agricultural land or of urban housing that provided a rental income from tenants.[70] Yet there was surprisingly little general speculation about the nature of land or its qualities. Since issues connected with land and land tenure were normally considered part of the common law, rather than matters determined by statute, they were for the most part only indirectly the subject of lectures at the inns of court. For example, Henry Sherfield mentioned in a reading in 1624 that land had a 'greater dignity' than any other corporal thing, but he did not elaborate very far.[71] It is therefore Coke who left the most memorable observations. In the first part of his *Institutes of the Lawes of England* (1628), an attempt to explain English land law through a commentary on Thomas Littleton's late fifteenth-century treatise on tenures, he noted that land signified any ground, soil, or earth whatsoever, and that this could include, inter alia, meadows, pastures, woods, moors, waters and marshes as well as arable land.[72]

---

[67] For example the 'Ogle roll', which consists of ten parchment membranes of deeds compiled for John Ogle, a freeholder of Whiston (Lancashire), LRO, DD Ww 1.

[68] BL, MS Lansdowne 620, fol. 12v.

[69] R. A. C. Parker, *Coke of Norfolk: a Financial and Agricultural Study, 1701–1842* (Oxford, 1975).

[70] *ODNB*; Brooks, *Pettyfoggers and Vipers*, pp. 256–8.   [71] BL, MS Stowe 424, fol. 53.

[72] *Coke on Littleton* (1628 edn), fol. 4. For Littleton's work see above, pp. 18–19.

In the *Reports*, he said that agriculture and tillage were greatly respected by the common law because they were profitable to the commonwealth and essential in maintaining the social structure as well as the 'policy and good government' of the realm, points he supported by reference to the Roman authors, Cicero, Virgil and Seneca.[73]

No doubt reflecting the active land-market of the late sixteenth and early seventeenth centuries, Coke, like Littleton before him, considered questions about how land could be securely purchased, and Francis Bacon on one occasion noted that certain types of land were little more than merchandisable commodities to be bought and sold on the open market.[74] At the same time, lawyers were interested in how land could be securely distributed to family members through marriage portions or passed on as an inheritance from one generation to the next, issues that constituted the technical background to contemporary gentry pre-occupations with careful management of their patrimonies and the establishment of the kinds of long-settled country 'seats' that figured so prominently in contemporary county histories.[75]

Yet, while it seems legitimate to think to some degree of land as a commodity, the highly idiosyncratic character of English land law, which was memorialised in Coke's writing on Littleton, meant that the social history of land was loaded with a large number of technical complications, many of which seem counterintuitive to a modern observer, and all of which are hard to explain without reference to a centuries-long process of interaction between the interests of holders and the institutional legal learning of the lawyers. Coke, for example, believed that in the state of nature the earth and all its products were equally shared amongst the inhabitants. Hence the individual possession of land was a consequence of human law rather than individual natural right.[76] No less important, early modern land law hardly ever employed the terms now normally associated with it, real property and ownership. In the law reports and lectures at the inns of court, discussions of property, and who had a legitimate claim to property, were developed most often in connection with a form of action known as *trover and conversion*, which plaintiffs could employ to recover goods (not lands) that they claimed had been unjustly taken from them and then sold on to third or fourth parties.[77]

---

[73] 4 *CoRep*, 38v–9. Repeated with some elaboration in *Coke on Littleton*, II. 117.

[74] Ibid., I.1–9; 'The argument in Lowe's Case of tenures in the King's Bench' in *The Works of Francis Bacon*, ed. J. Spedding, R. Ellis and D. Heath (14 vols., 1857–74), VII (2), p. 548.

[75] HEHL, MS Ellesmere 481A: lecture of Ambrose Gilbert on the Statute of Wills, fol. 1.

[76] *Coke on Littleton* (1628 edn), fol. 118v.

[77] For example, stolen spoons sold to a goldsmith. BL, MS Hargrave 44, fol. 29.

It was not a category associated with land. While someone could purchase land, that did not mean they owned it.

The reason why it was nearly impossible to achieve property in land was that, according to the common-law mind, land was held, *seised*, not owned outright. Coke maintained that all landholders were in fact tenants of one kind or another because all the lands and tenements in England were held either immediately, or intermediately, from the king. The law did not recognise *allodium*, outright ownership.[78] Everyone therefore had a lord, and the king was the lord paramount of every parcel of land within the realm. Individuals were said to have an interest in land that was determined by what was known as their 'estate', the period of time during which they (and their heirs) could enjoy the occupation of a piece of land, or make a claim to do so. Hence, for example, an inheritable estate of land held in fee simple was described by contemporaries as a freehold,[79] and came close to a concept of absolute ownership, but it was important that it was not expressed that way. According to Littleton, a tenant in fee simple was one who had lands and tenements to hold to him and his heirs forever, the point being that guaranteed inheritability ensured potentially infinite occupation and use.[80]

The nature of an estate in land was also defined by the form of tenure by which it was held, an historical attribute of a piece of land that could not easily be erased either by purchase or by its opposite, alienation. In his commentary on Littleton, Coke identified ten forms of tenure, each of which stipulated terms and conditions, including 'services' and obligations, either personal or financial, that a tenant owed to his lord.[81] Associated with notions of seigneurialism, 'lords' and (in law French) *seigneurs*, were embedded in the technical language of the land law. According to Littleton, for example, homage was the most honourable service that a free tenant (one who held in fee simple) could do to his lord, and he went on to describe it in terms of unambiguous submission and personal obligation.

[the tenant] shall be ungirt, and his head uncovered, and his lord shall sit and the tenant shall kneel before him on both his knees, and hold his hands together between the hands of the lord, and say thus: I become your man from this day forward of life and limbe, and of earthly worship, and unto you shall be true and faithfull, and beare to you faith for the tenements that I claime to hold of you, saving the faith that I owe unto our sovereign lord the king.[82]

---

[78] *Coke on Littleton*, I.1, and see below, p. 340.

[79] BL, MS Stowe 384, fol. 3.   [80] *Coke on Littleton*, I.1.

[81] Ibid., II.85: escuage, knight service, socage, frankalmoigne, homage ancestral, grand serjeantry, petit serjeantry, burgage, villenage and rents.

[82] Ibid. Fealty is the same as *fidelitas* in Latin, 'when a freeholder doth fealty to his lord, he shall hold his right hand upon a book and say thus. Know ye this, my lord, that I shall

Other forms of tenure, particularly the chivalric, or military tenures, such as knight's fee, were held to involve an obligation to serve the king in his wars, or at least to supply manpower and equipment.[83] Another broad category, socage tenure, was said by Littleton to have originated in the obligation of tenants to bring their ploughs on certain days of the year in order to plough and sow the land of the lord.[84]

The problem for modern students and, indeed, early modern lawyers is that this scheme of *seisin*, estates and tenures did not correspond perfectly to either social or legal reality, a point both Littleton and Coke were well aware of. Littleton observed that the obligation to plough associated with socage tenure had been practised in ancient times but then been transformed by agreement into annual rents.[85] Coke commented that services such as homage and fealty were old but long-since discontinued, and there were hardly any cases in the law reports or readings at the inns of court involving them. Of those services that remained, the most significant were the claims to wardship and *primer seisin* that the king made on those tenants who held (*in capite*) directly from the crown. These had been at the heart of the early sixteenth-century controversy over the legal devices known as uses, which resulted in legislation that aimed to prevent tenants-in-chief from deploying them to defraud the crown of income.[86] As a result, the royal right to tenurial revenues of this kind was institutionalised through the establishment of the court of Wards,[87] but the use itself remained an important legal instrument in the management of intergenerational transfers of land. A form of trust, the key to the use was that a landholder transferred the *seisin* of his lands to a group of feoffees, often lawyers, who were empowered to hold it to the use of a beneficiary (who had made the initial transferral, and, then, whomever he nominated as his heirs). Since the trustees could be replaced when necessary, the trust in effect never died, and all of the conditions arising from the traditional tenures, many of which came into effect at the point of inheritance, were conveniently by-passed.[88]

---

be faithful and true unto you, and faith to you shall bear for the lands which I claim to hold of you.'

[83] Ibid., II. 103.   [84] Ibid., II. 117.   [85] Ibid., II. 119.   [86] See above, pp. 42ff.

[87] H. E. Bell, *An Introduction to the History and Records of the Court of Wards and Liveries* (Cambridge, 1953).

[88] *Spelman's Reports*, II, pp. 192–202; E. W. Ives, 'The genesis of the Statute of Uses', *English Historical Review*, 82 (1967), 673–97; J. M. W. Bean, *The Decline of English Feudalism 1215–1540* (1968); N. G. Jones, 'The influence of revenue considerations upon the remedial practice of Chancery in trust cases 1536–1660' in *Communities and Courts*, pp. 99–114.

The use was attractive because it enabled men to make wills of their land, provide for their children and wives, and pay their debts.[89] It may therefore have fostered a sense of permanent occupation, or ownership, that was missing from traditional common-law doctrine, but it was also a legal instrument as complicated and confusing as a room full of mirrors. The Henrician statutes, and uses, provided the texts for many readings at the legal inns, including those by figures as important as Coke and Sir Francis Bacon, and uses were a regular source of gold for generations of lawyers.[90] Nevertheless, there were always some who expressed disquiet about them. Since the beneficiary of the use, the *cestuy que use*, in effect divested himself of *seisin* in land but continued to enjoy the profits from it, the nature of his estate in the eyes of the common law was problematic. Second, the creation of uses frequently involved legal instruments, such as the 'bargain and sale', which did not require the public notoriety traditionally associated with land transfers. In addition, the provision of a marriage portion for a bride by means of a use excluded her by statute from claiming her right to dower at common law. Consequently from before the passage of the statutes, uses had been associated with secret agreements, which might involve attempts to defraud creditors, or future purchasers of land, and though they were an important instrument of choice, they also contributed to an ongoing anxiety about forgery and perjury associated with titles to land that persisted throughout the first half of the seventeenth century.[91]

Tenurial obligations such as wardship and *primer seisin*, along with those associated with military tenures such as knight's service, were primarily of concern to the aristocracy and greater gentry. But land tenure was of no less importance for smaller landholders stretching from the lesser gentry through the yeomanry and down to husbandmen farmers. While some smaller holdings were composed of largely unencumbered freehold land, the single most important tenure at this level was that known as copyhold, and it gave its name to an entire category of 'tenants', the copyholders.[92] Modern estimates suggest that the exact proportion of copyhold land ranged from about 50 per cent in Lancashire and Northumberland, East Anglia and the Midlands, to between 60 and 80 per cent in the south-west.[93] Consequently, questions about the nature and security of the terms under which copyholders occupied their

---

[89] BL, MS Hargrave 402, fol. 35.   [90] See Baker, *Readers and Readings*, pp. lvii–lviii.
[91] BL, MS Hargrave 402, fols. 34–5.
[92] For example, BL, MS Harleian 1621, fol. 52.
[93] M. Overton, *The Agricultural Revolution in England* (Cambridge, 1996), pp. 33–4.

land have long been critical to the historical understanding of social and economic relations during the period.[94]

The most distinctive feature of copyhold tenure was that it was an integral part of the institution of the manor. It defined the relationship between the lord of the manor and the 'tenants' who owed suit at his court and paid him rent. Copyholders were called copyholders because the proof of their title, whatever its conditions, was a copy of the manorial court roll that recorded the transaction that brought the land in question into their hands.[95] Littleton wrote that copyholders held land of a 'manor within which manor there is a custome, which hath been used time out of mind, that certain tenants within the same have used to have lands and tenements to hold to them and their heirs . . . according to the custom'.[96]

A copyhold estate was therefore defined by the particular customs of particular manors with regard to the inheritability of the parcel of land, services owed to the lord, and the way in which it might be used to provide for widows. Custom also determined the annual rent, as well as the 'entry fine' payable to the lord when one tenant replaced another either as a result of alienation or inheritance. Although they tended to fall into categories such as copyholders by inheritance, or for life, or, indeed, for three lives, there were in theory as many different copyhold tenures as there were manors. Disputes about copyhold tenure frequently involved questions about the nature of a custom and whether it met the test of having been in existence beyond the memory of men. Copyholds and manorial courts were consequently the paradigmatic loci of the role of custom in law. Yet although custom hinged on practices that remained unchanged for long periods of time, the legal understanding of copyhold tenure underwent some significant alterations between 1500 and 1640.

The capacity of the copyholder to call on custom was a distinct advantage, but, according to the lawyers, copyhold tenure was also 'at the will of the lord', and the relationship of the tenant to the lord vested the lord with considerable seigneurial authority. Littleton wrote as if there was little conceptual difference between copyholders and villeins or serfs, unfree, or 'bond', tenants who not only owed services to lords, but who could not leave their land, marry their daughters, or apprentice their

---

[94] For example, E. Kerridge, *Agrararian Problems in the Sixteenth Century and After* (1969); R. Brenner, 'Agrarian class structure and economic development in pre-industrial Europe', *Past and Present*, 70 (1976), 35–75; T. H. Aston and C. H. E. Philpin, eds., *The Brenner Debate* (Cambridge, 1985).

[95] See above, pp. 246, 274.   [96] *Coke on Littleton*, I.73.

sons without the permission of their lord.[97] Furthermore, if copyhold tenure was an unfree tenure, it followed that an individual copyholder was not a freeman of England and therefore could not have an action in the common-law courts to maintain his title or prevent eviction. He was in effect excluded from the due process clauses of Magna Carta and potentially subject to seigneurial oppression, a point reasserted with some authority in the early sixteenth century by Sir Anthony Fitzherbert.[98]

Paradoxically, these legal accounts of copyhold tenure were written when the stagnant demographic conditions of the post-Black Death era meant that copyhold land appears to have been held on very favourable terms. Rents and entry fines were maintained at relatively low levels in order to attract tenants. Many obligations and services had in effect been abrogated.[99] 'Bondmen' of the sort Littleton had in mind had long been thin on the ground when the last of them gained their freedom in the mid sixteenth century, and, while copyholders may not have been permitted to bring questions about their titles to the common-law courts, they could petition Chancery for equitable relief in those circumstances where they claimed to have been unjustly put out of their holdings by landlords.[100] As we have seen, moreover, many other aspects of manorial life were already at this date effectively integrated into the 'national' common-law system.[101] Consequently, when demographic growth from the mid sixteenth century onwards began to put pressure on the value of agricultural land, the position of copyholders was in fact reasonably strong, and they quickly gained a much higher profile in common-law thinking.

Evidently responding to the demands of litigants, who would no doubt have been aided by the growing number of lawyers, the common law judges from the mid-Tudor period onward entertained cases that involved copyhold tenures.[102] Copyholders appeared increasingly often in the court records, and their interests also figured in readings at the inns of court as well as in the reported case law.[103] For example,

---

[97] A. W. B. Simpson, *An Introduction to the History of the Land Law* (Oxford, 1961), p. 151.

[98] C. M. Gray, *Copyhold, Equity and the Common Law* (Cambridge, MA, 1963).

[99] J. Hatcher, 'English serfdom and villeinage', *Past and Present*, 90 (1981), 3–39; R. H. Britnell, 'The feudal reaction after the Black Death in the palatinate of Durham', *Past and Present*, 128 (1990), 28–47.

[100] D. MacCulloch, 'Bondmen under the Tudors' in C. Cross *et al.*, eds., *Law and Government under the Tudors* (Cambridge, 1988), pp. 91–108; Brooks, *Pettyfoggers and Vipers*, pp. 86–7.

[101] Above, p. 248.   [102] *Spelman's Reports*, II, p. 185.

[103] LI, MS Maynard 60, pp. 305–15, notes on the reading of John Ramsey of Gray's Inn on the statute, 2 Ed. 6, c. 8, concerning copyholds; Guildhall, MS 86, fols. 162ff, lecture of Francis Rhodes in 1575 on 18 Edward II, '*de visu franc plegii*'; BL,

a manuscript compilation from the later 1570s contains a number of 'copyholders' cases' covering questions about the conditions under which a copyholder could maintain his holding or be declared to have forfeited it to the lord because of defaults of service. In addition, there were questions about the ability of a tenant to challenge the claims of a lord in a manorial court, the role of the manorial jury in determining the conditions under which land was held, and how customs associated with entry fines or other obligations due when land changed hands should be verified or proven.[104]

Since claims about customs were critical to copyhold tenure, the emphasis from a very early stage was on establishing criteria for deciding whether they existed, to whom they applied, and how they could be proven. A frequently emphasised point was that a custom regarding copyhold tenure could only properly be claimed, collectively, by all of the tenants of an individual manor; prescription by contrast was the process by which an individual could claim a particular right against another person as a result of long usage. In the ideal case, furthermore, a custom was most definitively fixed if it could be shown to have existed from a time before the memory of man, and thanks to the Statute of Westminster, this was defined legally as 1182. Judging from the earliest reported cases, there was never any doubt that written evidence was the best proof of the existence of a custom, providing there was not a problem with forgery. But it was also recognised that written evidence might not be available; in that case, a practice that had existed for however long it took for no one to remember when it had not was judged to constitute a custom.[105] Hence copyholders' cases often involved the collection of evidence from people in the localities about their recollection of customs.

The institutional milieu of the manorial court was perfectly suited to the issues surrounding copyhold tenure, a point frequently alluded to in legal texts by phrases emphasising the mutual dependency of the two. In order to be valid any alienation, inheritance, surrender or admittance involving copyhold land was supposed to be performed in person before the court baron, and recorded by the steward, practices reflected in surviving manorial records. Where there were questions about entry fines or other customs, such as the rights of a copyholder's widow to occupation after his death, or, indeed, whether copyhold could descend to female as well as male heirs, the homage was expected to declare the

MS Hargrave 89, fols. 38ff, Edmund Plowden at New Inn in 1552 on *replevin*; CUL, MS Ff.5.17, fols. 87ff, John Kitchen on the Statute of Leases (32 Henry VIII).
[104] BL, MS Harleian 443, fols. 19ff.   [105] Ibid., fols. 80, 82.

local custom.[106] At Beaminster in Dorset, for instance, the custom was
that if a tenant died and his land was surrendered to another tenant, the
new tenant went to the lord to see if they could agree an entry fine;
if they could not, the matter was left to the homage to decide.[107] At
Wakefield the manorial jury was responsible for determining the inheritance of copyhold land, confirming that the old tenant had died and that
the new one was his rightful heir. Their verdicts were very often submitted on slips of paper signed by people who evidently did not write
very often.[108]

There are several surviving examples, one of them from as late as the
1650s, of manorial stewards recording customs either in verse or song so
that they could be better remembered.[109] But copies of court rolls in
Latin had long been critical to the interests of copyholders, and they
were the sorts of documents that could be kept and referred to lawyers
even if the exact implications were not decipherable by the holder.
Disputes about the keeping of, and access to, records were long-standing.
In the 1520s, for example, tenants of the manor of Holland in Lancashire
brought a bill in Star Chamber claiming it as an immemorial custom that
the records of the manor should be kept in the moot hall so that the
tenants could sustain 'knowledge of their inheritaunce'. The recent
removal of them by the earl of Derby's steward made them fear for their
'estates' and their 'old liberties and customes'.[110]

Although Littleton did not stress the point, mid Tudor and Elizabethan
writing about copyholders assumed that the relationship between tenants and their lords was potentially contentious, but the extent of this
must be kept in perspective. Many cases in the royal courts arose out of
the subleasing of copyhold by tenants, or concerned matters relating to
inheritance and the nature of the interests of widows, rather than the
direct relationship between tenants and manorial lords.[111] Nevertheless,
although the number of landlord/tenant cases may not have been all that
great, it is not surprising that they occurred. Given that the minimum
length of a copyhold tenure was 'one life', and that this often extended to

---

[106] TNA, DL 4/12/16: commission to search the court rolls for precedents confirming any
custom within the manor of Wakefield by which an infant within age or a *feme covert*
may be barred of their claim.

[107] DHC, Acc. 6290.

[108] YAS, MD225/1/329A. Wakefield Court Roll (1603).

[109] Brooks, *Pettyfoggers and Vipers*, p. 200; BL, MS Additional 6681, fol. 126: the liberties
and customs of the lead mines within the wapentake of Wicksworth in Derbyshire,
composed in metre by Edward Manlove, steward of the Barmoot court. Printed in 1653.

[110] TNA, STAC 2/21/125. This and several similar cases were noted in the early seventeenth century by Ellesmere. HEHL, MS Ellesmere 2652.

[111] For example, *Dyer*, 2/192a.

'three lives', or indeed to an indefinite right of inheritance, lords inevitably felt pressure during a period of inflation to increase their rents whenever they could, while tenants were equally reluctant to see them rise over what they had been in the past.

In addition, tenants could also find themselves threatened by forfeitures arising from what was known as 'waste'. Most often, this involved the alleged neglect or destruction of buildings associated with a particular holding, but it also came up in connection with the respective rights of lords and tenants to timber and was associated with disputes about the exploitation of mineral resources such as coal or lead. According to the common-law judges, unless there was a special custom to the contrary, underground minerals belonged to the lord of the manor, and hence could not be touched by the tenant. On the other hand, the tenant could have an action to recover damages if his fields or crops were harmed by the process of extraction.[112]

No less than local custom, case law in the royal courts associated copyhold tenure with a complex web of conditions, and the fact that copyhold land was held 'at the will of the lord' as well as according to the custom had practical as well as symbolic significance.[113] Yet, while their tenure was to this extent uncertain, and sometimes subject to contention, manorial smallholders appear in practice to have been able to maintain their interests reasonably well, or at least well enough that the will of lords did not amount to a licence for absolute oppression.[114] The inheritability, or demisabilty, of holdings depended to some degree on whether copyholds were held for more than a single life (although tenants sometimes had the right to nominate successors even in this case). At the same time, where issues such as the level of entry fines or annual rents were concerned, the manorial institution was a considerable advantage to tenants, who could raise a 'common purse' in order to fight the legal contests that inevitably arose.[115] Nor were copyholders necessarily poor. One of the plaintiffs in a leading Jacobean case involving copyholders was a common-law attorney, for example, and many people owned land

---

[112] BL, MS Harleian 443, fol. 19v. YAS, DD146/11/1/1 (A Palmes family letter, dated 1605, concerning a suit with the inhabitants of Leathley over the cutting of trees); HEHL, Temple of Stowe, Miscellaneous Legal Papers Box 2(7). 5 *CoRep*, 12. ECO, MS 168, fol. 120.

[113] 4 *CoRep*, 21.

[114] R. W. Hoyle, 'Tenure and the land market in early modern England: or a late contribution to the Brenner debate', *Economic History Review*, 43 (2), 1990, 1–20.

[115] Brooks, *Pettyfoggers and Vipers*, pp. 199–203; A. Wood, 'Custom, identity and resistance: English free miners and their law c. 1550–1800' in P. Griffiths, A. Fox and S. Hindle, eds., *The Experience of Authority in Early Modern England* (Basingstoke, 1996), pp. 263, 274, 277.

from more than one manor, or had holdings that combined copyhold and freehold land.

Amongst the judiciary and within the legal profession at large, moreover, copyholder's cases were always discussed in language that reflected a balance between their interests and those of lords, perhaps if for no other reason than that copyholders were an important source of legal work. In a law lecture given at Furnival's Inn in 1574, which subsequently circulated widely in manuscript, and was finally printed in 1635, Charles Calthorpe made a point of saying that he was going to explain how the interests of tenants, as well as lords, were within the compass of the common law.[116] He was, he said, moved to write because of the need to publicise the remedies 'law and custom' made available to tenants. Citing common-law authorities,[117] he discredited Fitzherbert's contention that copyhold tenants were descendants of villeins, stressing instead that royal courts since the time of Henry VII had allowed copyholders to seek redress in London if they had been unjustly disseised by their lords.

The wide circulation of manuscript copies of Calthorpe's reading suggests that it quickly became authoritative. Nor is there much evidence that the ground rules associated with the relationship between copyholders and their lords were a major source of professional debate at any time between the early years of Queen Elizabeth and the outbreak of the civil wars.[118] In his *Fourth Reports*, Coke devoted an entire section to copyholders which outlined their position in connection with a number of critical issues. Although an alienation of copyhold land without the approval of the lord or the manorial court constituted a forfeiture of title, *Brown's Case* affirmed that a copyholder could, according to the custom, claim to possess an estate at law as inheritable as a 'freehold at the common law'. In *Hobart v. Hammond*, which was heard in King's Bench in 1600, the judges declared that in those cases where the entry fines due from copyholders to a landlord were uncertain, then those assessed should be 'fair' and based on an evaluation of the annual value of the land involved. Coke commented on this case that it would be 'inconvenient', that is irrational, if lords were allowed to assess fines at their

---

[116] Baker, *Readers and Readings*, p. 203; *The Relation Betweene the Lord of a Mannor and the Coppy-holder His Tenant. Delivered in the Learned Readings of the late Excellent and Famous Lawyer, Char. Calthrope of the Honorable Society of Lincolnes-Inn . . . Published for the good of the Lords of Mannors, and their Tenants* (1635).

[117] Starting with *Bracton*, going on to fifteenth-century *Year Book* citations and Littleton, and finishing with the recitation of statutes.

[118] Manuscript versions include Folger, MS V.a.151; BL, MS Additional 35957, fols. 84ff; MS Additional 25215, fols. 10–23; MS Harleian 5265; MS Harleian 6690.

pleasure.[119] Drifting even further from the strict letter of the law, he observed in another passage that 'if the Plowman has not a competent profit for his excessive labour and great charge', he would not bother to till the soil for the support of himself and his 'poor family'.[120]

In his commentaries on Littleton, Coke referred readers to these cases, denied any linkage between copyholders and unfree tenants, and, while equivocating a little in order to justify the position of Littleton from which he clearly differed, concluded that a lord could not put out a lawful copyholder at his pleasure without showing some cause of forfeiture. If he did, the copyholder could have an action of trespass against him. Although the copyholder was '*tenens ad voluntatem domini*', the tenure was '*secundum consuetudinem manerii*'.[121]

History, 'feudalism' and seigneurialism

Coke considered Littleton's *Tenures* the most perfect scientific treatise ever written because it was a straightforward didactic work for students that laid down rules of law instead of indulging in either theoretical or historical discussion.[122] Yet, as we have seen, Littleton was aware that 'services' such as homage had been discontinued over time. Coke knew that tenures, and in particular copyhold, had undergone significant alterations since Littleton wrote. Furthermore, the obvious connection between tenures and the fabric of the countryside, as well as the role played by time in the concept of custom, meant that the contemplation of English tenures could lead naturally, if not inevitably, to speculation about their origins and subsequent history. For some lawyers, this line of thought led to a consideration of the entire sweep of English history from before the Conquest in 1066 right down to the seventeenth century.

One of the earliest examples of the historical approach was a well-known reading on the forest laws delivered at Gray's Inn in 1508 by Richard Hesketh.[123] At first sight obscure and highly specialised, the forest laws held an interest for Tudor lawyers because they were seen as arising directly from the royal prerogative and therefore having developed largely outside the ambit of the common law; that is outside the jurisdiction of the courts at Westminster. According to Hesketh, English kings had traditionally created royal forests at will, even if that involved trespassing on the holdings of their subjects. Once established, the

---

[119] 4 *CoRep*, 21–39.   [120] Ibid., 39.   [121] *Coke on Littleton*, 1.77.
[122] Although both Coke and Littleton denied that their works could be taken as infallible guides to the land law.
[123] *ODNB*. Though the work was not printed, at least twelve manuscript copies survive.

bounds of the forests were governed by special laws that included penalties and punishments imposed on those who made encroachments on
timber or wild animals without royal licence. Hesketh argued, moreover,
that these essential qualities of the forest laws could be traced back to the
time of Edward the Confessor and that they had survived the Conquest
to form part of the regime of the early Norman kings. A critical point in
his lectures was that the statute on which he was reading, the Forest
Charter of 1225, had reduced the forest laws to more 'equity and good
reason', by restricting the power of the king to intrude on the inheritance
of the subject.[124]

Hesketh's pioneering interest in the forest laws was pursued in the
Elizabethan period by a fellow Lancastrian, the recorder of London and
legal antiquarian, William Fleetwood.[125] Composed largely to satisfy his
own curiosity rather than for delivery as a law lecture, Fleetwood's work
on the subject deserves notice in the annals of legal history because of his
avowed aim to base the study on the original records of the Honour of
Pickering in Lancashire; in other words, to go back to primary sources.
Furthermore, although his examination was less penetrating and concise
than Hesketh's, it included a treatment of tenures in general, perhaps
reflecting an interest of Fleetwood's evident in an elementary 'tractatus'
that he composed on the first book of Littleton's *Tenures*.[126] Hence,
while one version of Fleetwood's work on the forests contained a highly
nationalistic preface that placed the forest laws within a thoroughly
anti-papal account of the history of English law,[127] another was more
concerned with the history of tenures and the social structures accompanying them. In this Fleetwood associated chapter 3 of Magna Carta,
which dealt with the obligations owed to the king by tenants-in-chief, with
knight's service and military obligation. He connected baronies, which he
held to have been composed of twenty knights' fees, to castles and seigneurial rights over manors, towns and villages.[128] In addition, he was
concerned to delineate pre-Conquest, Saxon, social structure, identifying
the 'bokemen' of that period with freeholders of his own day.[129]

Fleetwood's studies were almost certainly influenced by the recent
publication of William Lambarde's translation of Saxon laws, a work that

[124] LI, MS Maynard 60, fol. 22.
[125] For some of Fleetwood's other writings, see above, pp. 75, 82. Also *ODNB*.
[126] BL, MS Harleian 5225. Consisting of about a dozen folios, this seems likely to be a
synopsis of a larger work (fols. 11v–12).
[127] Guildhall, MS 86, fols. 40, 60.
[128] CUL, MS Dd.9.17, fol. 3. In developing this topic Fleetwood was on a course that
has been followed by many subsequent students of feudalism. See, for instance,
D. Crouch, 'Debate: bastard feudalism revised', *Past and Present*, 131 (1991), 167.
[129] CUL, MS Dd.9.17, fol. 8.

was also referred to by Charles Calthorpe in support of his contention that copyhold tenure had existed before the Conquest.[130] Furthermore, Lambarde himself commented on the relationship between tenure and social structure in his work on his native county of Kent. Since the Kentish men had made a composition with William the Conqueror, their indigenous laws, unlike those of the rest of England, had never been abrogated. Hence they were able to maintain their idiosyncratic tradition of gavelkind tenure, a custom of partible inheritance amongst all the sons of the lands of a father at the time of his death. Manorial structures in the county were therefore virtually non-existent, and, according to Lambarde, Kentish landholders were much less 'bounded to the gentry by copyholds' than those who lived in western England, which explained why many Kentish yeomen, no matter how wealthy, did not care to describe themselves as gentlemen.[131]

Although it would be misleading to exaggerate professional interest in the history of tenures, many of the points raised by Fleetwood and Lambarde, as well as an interpretation of the recent case law on copy-holders, appear to have been brought together in an anonymous early seventeenth-century manuscript 'Treatise on Manours' that was eventually published in Coke's name after his death, although it is far from clear that he actually wrote it.[132] After establishing the point that the equivalents of freehold and copyhold tenure existed in Saxon times, this author accepted that the Normans had introduced the modern form of the manor when the Conqueror rewarded those who had served with him by making grants of land.[133] In any event, under either the Saxons or the Normans, the ancestors of copyhold tenants would have been subject to the will of lords, who could, 'sometimes without any colour of reason, sometimes by discontentment or mere malice, make evident to

---

[130] W. Lambarde, *Archaenomia, sive de priscis anglorum legibus libri* (1568).

[131] William Lambarde, *A Perambulation of Kent. Containing the Description, Hystorie and Customes of that Shyre* (1576), pp. 5, 11.

[132] CUL, MS Gg.3.26, fols. 159ff. *The Complete Copy-Holder Wherein is contained a Learned Discourse of the Antiquity and Nature of Manors and Copy-Holds . . . by Sir Edward Coke* (1641). The preface, signed 'W. C.', says that the work had been 'perused, and reverenced by men learned in the Laws'. The text contains, with a few minor alterations, the material in the manuscript version, as well as some additions. There is little in the style of the work to support the authorship of Coke. It is clearly written, and contains hardly any references either to case law or other works by Coke. Instead there are a number of references to writers such as Thomas Smith and William Fulbecke. Subsequent editions often included the reading of Calthorpe: *The Compleat Copy-Holder Wherein is contained a Learned Discourse of the Antiquity and Nature of Mannors and Copy-holds . . . by Sir Edward Coke . . . Whereunto is newly added The Relation between the Lord of a Mannor and the Copy-holder his Tenant by that Worthy Lawyer Charles Calthrop* (1650).

[133] CUL, MS Gg.3.26, fols. 162–3.

the world the height of their power and authority', and expel out of house and home their poor copyholders, leaving them helpless and remedyless by any course of law.[134] Nevertheless, the critical point was that over time a great 'alteration' in the point of service had occurred, so that 'nowadays' it was nearly impossible to distinguish between freehold and copyhold lands. As long as the copyholder performed the duties required of him, he knew himself 'safe and not w[i]thin any danger, for if the Lordes anger growe to expulsion, the Lawe hath provided him severall weapons of remedy, . . . and thus in many respects tyme hath dealt verye favourably w[i]th Coppyholders'.[135]

The history of this implied development is not charted in any detail, but the outcome was that, although copyholders retained the taint of base tenure, this was of little practical consequence. There had over time been a process of social change that caused a redistribution of land, and property rights, out of the hands of the very few, and into those of the fairly numerous. Under the Normans, and for some time thereafter, manors were thought fit only for nobles and other men of high calling. At the end of the sixteenth century by comparison, many manors were held by individuals who could claim nothing like such status. In the modern day, because of the changes caused by generations of transferrals, a knight or a lord might very well find himself holding copyhold land, and a peasant freehold land.[136]

Noe wonder then that nobles turn copyholders and many peasants and pedanes turn freeholders. No marvaile, I say, that men of all sorts and conditions are promiscouslie both freeholders and copyholder since there is such small respect had unto the qualitie of the land in the definition of services.[137]

This tract appears in effect to depict the decline of seigneurialism, a process of tenurial and social change that on the one hand weakened the power of the nobility by undermining private jurisdictions, and on the other, incorporated a mass of smaller landholders into something like a unified state where the common law was the ultimate arbiter over all disputes about land. Furthermore, this perspective was articulated at

---

[134] Ibid., fol. 161. The source of these observations were, interestingly, the medieval legal writers *Bracton* and *Fleta*.

[135] Ibid.

[136] Ibid., fol. 163. This writer also captured perfectly some of the ambiguities in the status the manor, an institution that was partly seigneurial, partly royal and partly communal. Thus he noted that fines and amerciaments administered through the manor were seen by some authorities as a pecuniary punishment for offences committed against the lord of the manor, but, according to others, they were penalties imposed by the steward 'for the breache of any law (made either for the profit of the whole kingdom, or for the benefitt of 'their little Common wealth w[i]thin themselves)'.

[137] Ibid., fol. 160v.

just about the same time as what has come to be known as the 'feudal' interpretation of history was beginning to be known and discussed in English legal and historical circles.[138]

An interpretation of tenurial relationships transmitted through the Roman law schools of continental Europe, 'feudalism', and 'feudist history', as contemporaries described it, depicted social and political systems in which kings had granted land to subordinate lords in return for military services, and those lords in turn made grants to lesser tenants, once again stipulating services, and, sometimes, granting certain reciprocal privileges such as security of tenure and the capacity to make intergenerational transferrals. Points along these lines had been made by William Fleetwood, but the most likely direct source of a genuinely 'feudal' interpretation of English tenures was probably the distinguished Scottish jurist Sir Thomas Craig, who composed a Latin work on the history of Scottish law, *Jus feudale*, which also showed that the legal systems of England and Scotland had a common ancestor in the 'feudal law', which Craig considered a European-wide phenomenon.[139] Given his subject, and the fact that Craig subsequently served on the commission appointed by the king to negotiate the union of laws, it is very unlikely that his approach was not known to English lawyers and historians. In any case, the terms 'feudal' or 'feudist' began to make an appearance in England during the first decade of the seventeenth century. The leading English authority on the subject, the Norfolk squire and antiquary Sir Henry Spelman, advocated the study of English tenures from the feudal perspective in a paper he delivered to the Society of Antiquaries sometime before it was dissolved in 1607.[140] A reference to 'feudist' history also appeared in a widely circulated reading on benefices delivered at the Middle Temple in 1619 by James Whitelocke.[141]

---

[138] The seminal work on this subject is J. G. A. Pocock, *The Ancient Constitution and the Feudal Law: a Study of English Historical Thought in the Seventeenth Century. A Reissue with a Retrospect* (Cambridge, 1987; first published in 1957). See also Susan Reynolds, *Fiefs and Vassals: the Medieval Evidence Reinterpreted* (Oxford, 1994). For a fuller treatment of some of the points discussed below see, Christopher Brooks, 'Contemporary views of "feudal" social and political relationships in sixteenth and early seventeenth century England' in Natalie Fryde, Pierre Monnet and O. G. Oexle, eds., *Die Gegenwart des Feudalismus . . . The Presence of Feudalism* (Göttingen, 2002), pp. 109–36.

[139] *ODNB*. There is a translation by James Avon Clyde, *The Jus Feudale by Sir Thomas Craig of Ricarton* (Edinburgh, 1934). Craig also published two tracts in support of the Union.

[140] *Reliquiae Spelmannianae. The Posthumous Works of Sir Henry Spelman Kt. Relating to the Laws and Antiquities of England. Published from the Original Manuscripts* (Oxford, 1698, though printed in London), pp. 98–9.

[141] BL, MS Hargrave 198, fol. 48v. See also Paul Christianson, *Discourse on History, Law and Governance in the Public Career of John Selden 1610–1635* (Toronto, 1996), esp. p. 55.

Although the articulation of the feudal interpretation of medieval and early modern history represents a landmark (for better or worse) in both 'popular' and professional perceptions of western European history, its ideological significance in the early seventeenth century was not straightforward.[142] The association of Craig's feudal legal history with the pro-union position is unlikely to have made it all that popular, especially since he argued that Scottish kings had never done homage to English kings, and was categorical that feudalism had been introduced by William I at the time of the Conquest.[143] Yet, according to some English thinkers, the feudal interpretation could be argued without attaching particular significance to the Conquest, and, indeed without necessarily seeing it as the starting point for centuries of oppressive seigneurialism.[144] Spelman, for example, believed that 'feudal' tenures introduced at the Conquest had positive advantages over those recognised by the Saxons. Most notably, they gave lesser tenants the right to pass on land to their heirs, and this demisability, or inheritability, was an essential prerequisite for a genuine concept of landownership.[145]

Although he differed from Spelman on the significance of the Conquest, a similar point was made in a treatise composed by an otherwise obscure barrister, Robert Hill, at about the time of the parliamentary debates over the Great Contract in 1610. Evidently writing at the request of the master of the court of Wards, the earl of Salisbury, Hill explored Roman history, and, more briefly, the history of other European nations to come to the conclusion that tenures *in capite* had their origins in land granted by kings for military defence.[146] Taking the lead of continental writers, he held that the English, Germans, French, Italians and Spanish, all took their customs and ordinances of fees 'at the second hand' from the ancient Gauls.[147] Hill had a distinctive view of feudalism in the context of European as well as English, and Scottish, history, but he also argued that the system was already effectively in place under the Saxons. Although the Normans had been oppressive, and created wardship, they had not installed new institutions.[148]

---

[142] See, for example, P. Anderson, *Lineages of the Absolutist State* (London, 1979 edn), pp. 18, 402–3. For a notable assault on the usefulness of 'feudalism' in medieval history see Reynolds, *Fiefs and Vassals*, esp. pp. 3, 7, 22.

[143] Craig, *Jus feudale*, I.7.2. Also, see above, pp. 131–3.

[144] See above, pp. 121–3.   [145] *Reliquiae Spelmannianae*, pp. 5–6.

[146] BL, MS Harleian 4750: Hill claimed to have written at the suggestion, or through the offices of, Thomas Hesketh, who was appointed attorney of the court of Wards in 1597. Bell, *An Introduction to . . . the Court of Wards and Liveries*. Cecil is mentioned by name in the preface.

[147] BL, MS Harleian 4750, fols. 38vff, 52v–53.   [148] Ibid., fols. 18v–21v.

Since Hill was writing in order to provide a convincing case for the king's prerogative rights, and was also an advocate of union, it is interesting that he concluded with a powerful and striking political assessment of his findings. If feudal tenures were ancient, then they could not be associated with aspersions of bondage or slavery that might follow if they were linked to the Conquest. Indeed, Hill went so far as to say that accepting the Norman origins of tenures would make it necessary to accept that the 'pillars' of the English state were based on 'three degrees of slavery': peers of the realm would be 'honourable slaves'; gentry would be 'worshipful slaves'; and the commons would be whatsoever it 'pleased any man to stile them'.[149]

This same line of thought may have been in the mind of Sir Edward Coke when he was commentating on Littleton. Although he never offered a detailed account of the earliest history of tenures, he did at one point refer to *Bracton* and Lambarde, to explain their origins.[150] It 'appeared', he said, that the earliest kings of England at first had all the lands of the country in their own hands, but then, after reserving to themselves the greatest manors, they had enfeoffed the barons with the rest for the defence of the realm.[151] Indeed, Coke's use of the term *allodium* in connection with his explanation of why land was *seised* but not owned appears to correspond closely with a description of feudal tenure that Spelman offered in the later 1630s. According to Spelman, the feud was defined as

a right which the Vassal hath in Land or some immoveable thing of his Lord's, to use the same and take the profits thereof hereditarily: rendring to his Lord such feodal duties and sevices as belong to military tenure: the meer propriety of the soil always remaining unto the Lord . . . For in feodal speech the tenant or vassal hath nothing in the propriety of the soil itself which remains the Lords. Seignory is the term given to this interest of the lord. Seignory and feud joined together, seem to make that absolute and complete estate of inheritances, which the feudists call allodium.[152]

The existence of some form of early feudal polity could therefore explain the single most important characteristic of English land law, which was that all land was held from the king, but this was not always the primary concern of contemporaries when they discussed feudal history. Some, including Robert Hill and Francis Bacon, were attracted by the idea that military tenures ensured that some landholders might

[149] Ibid., fol. 26.
[150] Spelman as well as later writers criticised Coke for not exploring the history of tenures more thoroughly.
[151] *Coke on Littleton*, I.73.   [152] *Reliquiae Spelmannianae*, p. 3. See above, p. 325.

also be subject-soldiers who were either equipped to defend the realm, or at least obliged to pay for it, a point that was exploited at length by Oliver St John at the Ship Money trial.[153] Although he was not a practising lawyer, Spelman's antiquarian expertise was utilised by the crown mainly in Ireland. In 1617, he made the first of three visits to the lordship as a result of his appointment to a royal commission to settle titles of land in connection with the plantation policy.[154] One of the most complete expressions of his interpretation of England's feudal history appears in a brief he wrote at the end of the 1630s in connection with a legal dispute about whether royal regrants of land titles were justified in naming the tenures, a point hinging on whether or not knight's service could be said to have been introduced before, as opposed to after the Conquest.[155]

At the same time, as we have seen, most English legal thought on the subject assumed that even if England had once been a feudal polity (either before or as a result of the Conquest), there had subsequently been significant changes. Manorial courts were royal, not private seigneurial jurisdictions.[156] Copyholders had come within the ambit of the common law. Even Spelman acknowledged that time had introduced changes that had in effect drawn 'the propriety of the soil from the Lord unto the Tenant'.[157] The intellectual rise of 'feudalism' in the very early seventeenth-century apparently coincided with a perceived decline in seigneurialism, and the two points were never altogether reconciled. That there was a potential problem is suggested by Henry Sherfield's struggle in a lecture given in 1624 to separate the feudal foundations of the English monarchy from the different kind of state that had subsequently emerged. Going out of his way to make a distinction between tenures as a way of holding land, and tenures as a source of jurisdiction or military service, his key point was that the power to rule, sovereignty, did not rest on the control of land, but in the services of men.[158]

Agrarian tensions and political discourse

The essentially unresolved quality of early seventeenth-century thinking about the nature and significance of tenurial relationships was reflected both in agrarian disputes and in the wider political rhetoric of the early seventeenth century up to the time of the civil wars.

---

[153] See above, p. 204.   [154] See above, pp. 128ff.
[155] 'The original, growth, propagation and condition of feuds and tenures by knight-service, in England', printed in *Reliquiae Spelmannianae*, pp. 1ff.
[156] See above, pp. 247–8.   [157] *Reliquiae Spelmannianae*, p. 2.
[158] BL, MS Stowe 424, fol. 53r-v.

While it was hardly endemic, agrarian unrest was not unknown in the period and much of it revolved around manorial institutions and copyhold tenure. At the end of the 1590s, for example, when economic conditions, including shortages of food, were particularly acute, general social tensions were accompanied by serious unrest in the Midland counties, which was capped by a small-scale and ultimately abortive rising in Oxfordshire in 1596. Although the principal participants were mainly village artisans rather than agriculturists, they were explicitly hostile to local men who had recently bought manors, and they called for greater access to common land and an end to enclosures that were undertaken to convert arable land to pasture.[159]

While some disputes about access to commons were between lords and copyhold tenants, many, including those in Oxfordshire, in fact arose out of another characteristic of the land law, which was that a common was usually attached to a manor, and the right to commons was normally, though not always, defined as a right of a tenant rather than an inhabitant, or resident, of a village or township. Hence disputes about commons, like those in Oxfordshire, were most often the result of a growth in the non-landholding population of a locality, and the regulation of access to commons was as much a matter of interest to the ordinary tenant farmers as it was to lords.[160] It seems likely that in many areas, perhaps in smaller townships in particular, common land was recognised as a resource that might be made available to the poor,[161] but the connection between common land and tenure was strongly reasserted by the decision in *Gateward's Case* (1603), which was explicit that rights to common, including access to estovers (firewood), could only be claimed as a consequence of some proprietary, tenurial, interest in the land.[162] This meant that a copyhold tenant would certainly have a claim, but a landless cottager would not, even though there is some evidence that juries, not to mention those denied access, did not always agree with the ruling.[163]

---

[159] J. Walter, 'The "rising of the people"? The Oxfordshire rising of 1596', *Past and Present*, 107 (1985), 90–143.

[160] See above, p. 271. V. Skipp, *Crisis and Development: an Ecological Case Study of the Forest of Arden 1570–1674* (Cambridge, 1978).

[161] Sara Birtles, 'Common law, poor relief and enclosure: the use of manorial resources in fulfilling parish obligations 1601–1834', *Past and Present*, 165 (1999), 74–106.

[162] 6 *CoRep*, 59. Though the decision dates from 1607; the case was brought in 1601 from Horsington, Lincolnshire.

[163] For example, BL, MS Hargrave 44, fol. 57v: jury gives common rights twice against the direction of the judges. For some popular reactions to enclosures, see J. Walter, 'Public transcripts, popular agency and the politics of subsistence in early modern England' in M. J. Braddick and J. Walter, eds., *Negotiating Power in Early Modern Society* (Cambridge, 2001), pp.123–48.

Similarly, although the enclosure of common land by the gentry for the erection of parks was sometimes a grievance of smaller landholders, most enclosure, including that associated with the conversion of arable to pasture, took the form of what is known as 'enclosure by agreement' and as often involved smaller yeoman farmers, who might well be copyholders, as it did members of the gentry.[164] Nevertheless, since the time of Wolsey and Sir Thomas More, enclosure that led to rural depopulation and a decline in arable land had been identified as a greed-driven social evil warranting the attention of government.[165] Hence, although Coke, as attorney general, advocated a strikingly hard line against the ringleaders of the Oxfordshire rising by insisting that they be indicted for treason, it has been plausibly suggested that the experience of the revolt may have led to his own expressions of concern about rural depopulation, and in 1597 parliament passed two statutes that laid down complex provisions for preventing it, essentially by prohibiting arable land with a house attached to it from being converted to pasture.[166]

The lawyers and other MPs who drew up this legislation were evidently unconcerned about claims the holders of such lands might have made about their rights as proprietors to do with them as they pleased. The question is not mentioned in the acts, nor does it seem to have been raised subsequently in the courts, but it did evidently occur to those who fell within the compass of the legislation.[167] Writing enthusiastically in support of the Caroline commissions to enforce the statutes in the late 1630s, the Somerset attorney Robert Powell acknowledged that many landholders would ask 'is it not lawful for me to do what I list with my owne, to pull or let down my own houses, or alter the property of my own soil?' His answer was not altogether to deny the existence of such a property, but to remind readers that there were two kinds of justice. One of these, the rule of commutative justice, 'observes an arithmeticall proportion in all exchanges, contracts, covenants and commerce, betweene man and man, strictly looking upon the equality of the thing bought, sold, bartered, or exchanged, without respect of the person, party in the bargaine', and was the rule normally exercised in 'all entercourses of buying, selling and dealings whatsoever . . .' But, although an encloser

---

[164] Joan Thirsk, *Tudor Enclosures* (1959); *CroCar*, 845, *Case of the Forest of Dean*. 8 Car I.
[165] See above, pp. 27, 199.
[166] Walter, 'A "rising of the people"? ', 137–8. 39 Elizabeth, c. 1 & 2. See also CUL, Ll. 3.2, fol. 10. *Gave* v. *Pickering*. Easter 6 James: it is lawful to put in only one man's cattle for trial of the title to avoid multiplicity of suits. In common cause it is lawful to make a common purse.
[167] E. F. Gay, 'The Midland revolt and the inquisition of depopulation of 1607', *Transactions the Royal Historical Society*, 18 (1904), 195–244.

might well claim to be acting on the basis of legal relationships of this kind, his actions also had to take into account notions of distributive justice, which looked more to the common good. These could, moreover, be illustrated by pointing to similar measures in previous periods and supported as social values by referring to the traditional role of manorial courts in preventing 'common nuisances'.[168]

Powell put his finger directly on the tensions in early Stuart society (and law) between a growing tendency towards commercial, even capitalist, ideas about proprietorship and what historians have subsequently come to describe as the idea of a 'moral economy', where social problems, such as enclosure, or the hoarding of food supplies in times of dearth, were seen as causes of unacceptable hardship and dislocation that had to be addressed by government, even if that meant interfering with individual property rights.[169] Addressing himself to Attorney General Bankes, and explaining in some detail why the private interests of individuals who caused depopulation had a deleterious impact on the public condition of the state, Powell retailed several recent Star Chamber prosecutions of enclosers and fully endorsed the crown's policy of creating commissions to investigate them.

Yet, in its attempts to exploit its own crown lands, the early Stuart monarchy was not exactly a model of benevolent lordship. Jacobean attempts to raise income from rents were accompanied by a number of incidents in which crown surveyors met with the hostility of copyhold tenants.[170] At Wakefield, for instance, there was a classic clash between the king, who claimed as lord of the manor that entry fines were arbitrary, and the tenants who, it was alleged, had combined and confederated together to maintain that they were fixed, and who demanded that the rent be set according to standard calculations based on the annual value of the land. Although an agreement was eventually reached after the king offered a 'benevolent' compromise, the dispute was clearly acrimonious and the tenants demanded, and got, a private act of parliament in order to seal the deal.[171]

After 1625, of course, many aspects of Caroline 'fiscal-feudalism' reflected symptoms of seigneurial exploitation. In the late 1620s,

---

[168] *Depopulation Arraigned, Convicted and Condemned . . . A Treatise Necessary in these Times By R. P. of Wells, one of the Societie of New Inne* (1636), pp. 42–3.

[169] J. Walter and K. Wrightson, 'Dearth and the social order in early modern England', *Past and Present*, 71 (1976), 22–42.

[170] R. H. Hoyle, ed., *The Estates of the English Crown 1558–1640* (Cambridge, 1992). See also Bankes Papers, MS 5/9.

[171] *Wakefield Manor Book, 1709*, ed. John Charlesworth (Yorkshire Archaeological Society, Record Series, vol. 101, 1939), pp. 19–24.

commissions were issued to recover 'concealed' royal lands that had been encroached upon by subjects, some of whom were members of the gentry. Several cases were also brought to reassert traditional, but neglected, royal claims to land that bordered on tidal rivers in London and other towns.[172] Most significantly, the means used to exploit the forest laws for profit, including the holding of eyres, or courts, and the appointment of jurors to identify encroachments could have come straight out of any manorial steward's handbook.[173] Yet there is no clear evidence that any of this was seen as a 'feudal' initiative in the strict sense of the word.[174] Instead, the attempt by the crown to investigate its landed resources with the aim of exploiting them more effectively is best regarded as little more than a logical reaction to changing social and economic conditions. In this respect, the king's position was much the same as that of other landlords, and so the inevitable question is how far there was a general trend to more ruthless exploitation of land in the early seventeenth century, and where the law stood with respect to it.

It is certainly true that by 1640 many more lords of manors were employing professional lawyers as manorial stewards than had been the case in 1550, and the main reason for this must have been a desire for the more effective exploitation of their holdings.[175] As far as anecdotal evidence goes, it is worth noting that Sir Lawrence Tanfield, a Jacobean baron of the Exchequer, was a notably oppressive landlord in Oxfordshire,[176] and the duke of Buckingham was involved in a Chancery case about the level of entry fines at his manor of Hartington in Derbyshire.[177] Lord Chancellor Ellesmere and his son, the earl of Bridgewater, had run-ins with their tenants in Shropshire and Buckinghamshire over entry fines in disputes that seem to mirror exactly the one at Wakefield.[178] The JP Sir John Newdigate was severely criticised by his neighbours for setting up enclosures in Warwickshire,[179] and in Cambridgeshire, the antiquarian Sir Robert Cotton used his expertise to

---

[172] BL, MS Hargrave 30, fols. 30 (*Case of Stepney*), 266 (*Corriton's Case*). Bankes Papers, 20/7: abstract of the orders made by the commissioners for defective titles at their last sitting, 17 June 1636.

[173] Bankes Papers, 16/7: memorandum concerning a commission to enquire into encroachments on forests. Counties of York, Nottingham and Derby.

[174] See above, pp. 194–5. [175] Brooks, *Pettyfoggers and Vipers*, pp. 197–202.

[176] Prest, *Barristers*, pp. 170–1, provides additional examples.

[177] HEHL, Hastings Box 1(18). Buckingham allegedly claimed arbitrary fines; the tenants refused to accept those set by the steward.

[178] HEHL, MSS Ellesmere 233 and 6488: Bridgewater to Noy concerning a dispute with tenants at Great Gaddesden in 1631. He had had difficulties with these tenants since the death of his father.

[179] Walter, 'Public transcripts, popular agency and the politics of subsistence', pp.129–30, 135–7. For Newdigate's public speeches, see above, pp. 300ff.

search his family's court rolls in order to see if the estate could be exploited more effectively.[180]

Judging from an unsystematic evaluation of the evidence from the central courts, including Star Chamber and Chancery, while there were a fair number of similar cases, many of which may have involved a good deal of hostility, they probably did not involve a very significant proportion of the huge amount of land that was held with tenurial encumbrances.[181] Furthermore, although it seems clear that there was more judicial emphasis on the need to provide effective proofs of customs, there does not seem to have been a significant change in judicial opinion from that reported by Coke. The Caroline bench ruled that customs relevant to the existence of inheritable copyhold estates would be strictly interpreted regardless of whether they favoured copyhold by inheritance or not.[182] In a case in which a lord of the manor had attempted to raise entry fines to two and a half times the annual value in 1630, they followed earlier precedent in declaring this unreasonable, and suggesting that one and a half years' improved rent was 'high enough'.[183]

As had always been the case, the fate of manorial tenants depended most on whether their customary holdings amounted to inheritable estates or whether they were for no more than one life, and/or whether rents could be set at the will of the lord, but even in these circumstances there seems to have been some possibility of relief. Ellesmere is reported to have said that he would hear in Chancery the cases of individual tenants who thought they had been subjected to arbitrary entry fines, though not a petition from a whole 'rout' of copyholders in a similar position, whose only recourse would be to an Act of parliament.[184] He also allowed a composition between a group of copyholders and their lord which changed their custom by mutual consent from one which assumed the youngest son would inherit to one that permitted the eldest to inherit while at the same time offering more favourable interests to widows. This judgment was arguably problematic, and possibly contrary to common law, since it involved the disseisin of future generations of younger sons, but Ellesmere said he would enforce the agreement because otherwise 'all the copyholders of that manor or any other manor of England, which have altered their customes in like case, by consent, shall be perverted and altered and nothing will be certain'.[185]

---

[180] R. B. Manning, 'Antiquarianism and seigneurial reaction: Sir Robert and Sir Thomas Cotton and their tenants', *Bulletin of the Institute of Historical Research*, 63 (1990), 277–89.

[181] The relevant Chancery classes are TNA, C 3 and C 33. For example, see C3/330/1, 3.

[182] BL, MS Hargrave 30, fol. 225v.   [183] *CroCar*, 772.   [184] CUL, Gg.2.31, fol. 473v.

[185] Ibid., fol. 476.

Although imperfect, the surviving evidence indicates that the legal advice offered to Jacobean and Caroline lords tended to follow the same general guidelines about the position of copyholders with regard to entry fines and forfeitures as had been laid down in Elizabethan writings on the subject.[186] The publication of Calthorpe's reading in 1635, and the appearance of similar works thereafter, suggests that the relationship between manorial lords and customary tenants continued to be one of potential conflict, but also one where the lawyers claimed to take an interest in both sides of the argument. While some of the court cases that have come to light reveal attempts at petty tyranny by the lords of manors, they also demonstrate unequivocally that even the powerful found that groups of copyholders could make formidable opponents.[187] Holding land at the 'will of the lord' must always have seemed precarious to the smallholder, and it could also involve irksome obligations. But, on the other hand, the 'customs of the manor' provided a significant legal space for negotiation, and the institution of the manorial court made for strength in numbers. Armed with common purse, copyholders used lawyers, and lords often accused them of either making false claims or endeavouring to forge evidence. The relationship between lords and tenants at its worst seems, therefore, to be well summed up by a letter sent by a local official, Thomas Challoner, to the chancellor of the duchy of Lancaster in 1633. Reporting on the difficulties he was having in negotiations with copyholders about entry fines on the royal manor of Duffield (Derbyshire), Challoner noted that he had just been to a meeting where he expected to explain to the assembled tenants the new demands that were being put to them. But only two showed up, and one of them, John Stanley, was 'audaciously refratorious' about the matter. Stanley said that he and his fellow tenants would see themselves arrested and arrested again before they would pay any more than the 'ancient fines'.[188]

Given the economic and demographic conditions of the later sixteenth and early seventeenth centuries, there is little doubt that there was an intense, potentially contentious, 'politics' associated with customary land tenures. Furthermore, the rhetoric of landlord/copyholder relationships

---

[186] HEHL, Temple of Stowe Miscellaneous Legal Papers, Box 2(7). Advice to Sir Thomas Temple, dated 1625. If a copyholder commit waste, be behind for rent, or deny the same at his term, the lord may enter and seize his copyhold.

[187] Roger B. Manning, *Village Revolts: Social Protest and Popular Disturbances in England, 1509–1640* (Oxford, 1988), pp. 45, 50, 106, 132, 136–7, 152–3, 316.

[188] TNA, DL 41/37/1. Clearly frustrated, Challoner noted that if some measure was not speedily taken against Stanley, who was worth about £40 p.a. in copyhold land, he might 'easely infect' many others.

also acquired a wider political resonance, which meant that it was not confined either to the court room or to conversations around the parish pump. Metaphors that referred to seigneurialism, some of which raised the spectre of 'feudalism' itself, were particularly prominent in the later parliaments of the 1620s, and they continued to be used when the Long Parliament met in 1640. If the king could make financial demands on his subjects, or question their titles without their consent, then he was ruling them not as a lawful king but as a seigneurial one who claimed an interest in the lands and goods of his subjects similar to that of a manorial lord over his tenants at will.[189]

Speaking in the House of Commons in 1628, Sir Dudley Digges maintained that a king who was not tied to laws was a king of slaves. Sir Edward Coke pointed out that while a lord might tax his villeins 'high and low . . . this is against the franchise of the land for freemen' of England'.[190] The judge Sir Robert Berkeley used the same trope in his argument for the king in the Ship Money case in 1637. Although the King 'hath a monarchical power, and hath *jura summae majestatis*, and hath an absolute trust settled in his crown and person for the government of his subjects, yet his government is to be *secundum legis regni* . . . By those laws the subjects are not tenants at the King's will. . . .'[191] The barrister MP Edward Bagshawe merely echoed these points when he told the House of Commons in November 1640 that peace and justice were the prerequisites of prosperity. Since the people of England were '*liberi homines*' and not '*villani*', they needed to be protected from illegal arrests and imprisonments.[192]

Oddly, lawyers such as Bagshawe and Coke apparently found no difficulty in discussing freemen of England in a general political context when they must have been aware that much of the land in the country was held according to tenures that explicitly recognised 'the will of the lord'.[193] Equally, while the language of the land law was used in parliament and in the celebrated cases for polemical purposes, the fact of the matter was that the issues at stake normally applied not to land, but to property in goods, a point that was correctly recognised by Lord Saye and Sele at the end of the 1630s, when he brought an action of *trover and conversion* to recover property that had been taken from him as a result of

---

[189] See above, pp. 190–1.
[190] *PP 1628*, II, pp. 64, 66, 358; III, p. 494. In another debate Coke asked who would engage in a profession of any kind if he was but a 'tenant at will of his liberty'. *PP 1628*, III, p. 358.
[191] J. P. Kenyon, *The Stuart Constitution, 1603–1688: Documents and Commentary* (Cambridge, 1966), p. 111.
[192] Rushworth, *Collections*, pt 3(1), p. 26.   [193] Above, p. 334.

his failure to pay Ship Money in the hopes that it would lead to another court case on the matter that might overthrow the decision in *Rex* v. *Hampden*.[194] Nevertheless, in contrasting 'freemen' with words such as villeinage, slavery and bondage, the implications of tenurial discourse would seem to be that while England may at some point in the past have been a country where all titles, from those of tenants-in-chief down to those of the smallest holders, were in some way or another arbitrary or insecure, by the early seventeenth century, the situation had changed. In this respect, the views of the lawyer-politicians were compatible with legal and historical analyses such as those reflected in the treatises on copyholders discussed earlier, but, as we have seen in chapter 8, they also reflected the opinion of writers such as Bodin who maintained that one of the standard tests of the legitimacy of a monarchy was the degree to which it could be distinguished from a seigneurial or 'feudal' one.[195]

One way through the intellectual confusion may have been provided by the perception that many copyhold tenants, even if they held at the will of the lord, nevertheless enjoyed an estate protected by law that could be treated much as a freehold in an increasingly commercialised land market, and which also enfranchised them to vote in parliamentary elections as the legal equivalents of forty shilling freeholders.[196] This same outlook, along with the relative success of customary tenants in maintaining their economic position during the early seventeenth century, also explains why tenurial issues on their own do not go very far in accounting either for civil war allegiance or the fate of demands for more revolutionary change in the wake of the abolition of the monarchy in 1649. It has been argued that traditional manorialised regions were more inclined to support the royalists than parliament, but the case is hardly conclusive.[197] Indeed, some contemporary observers instead reiterated the point that the overall course of tenurial history in the recent past had been to undermine an older, and probably largely imagined, paternalistic relationship between manorial lords and their tenants. One Leveller writer, for instance, argued that remnants of seigneurial power were already obsolete: 'nowadays', manors were often held by men who were

[194] *CroCar*, 1053.
[195] Above, p. 191. *The Six Bookes of a Commonweale: a Facsimile Reprint of the English Translation of 1606 Corrected and Supplemented in the Light of a New Comparison with the French and Latin Texts*, ed. Kenneth D. McRae (Cambridge, MA, 1962), p. 176.
[196] D. Hirst, *The Representative of the People: Voters and Voting Under the Early Stuarts* (Cambridge, 1975). Below, p. 424.
[197] D. Underdown, *Revel, Riot, and Rebellion: Popular Politics and Culture in England 1603–1660* (Oxford, 1985).

not gents, let alone aristocrats. No man any longer valued his landlord more than another just because he paid rent to him.[198] In a similar vein, John Selden is reported to have observed that the creation of more economic rents had broken down whatever loyalty tenants may once have rendered to their lords. If they might have been willing in the past to fight for them, 'nowadays . . . if but a constable bid them, they shall [be the first] to lay the landlord by the heels'.[199]

Property in land as well as goods was a principal bone of contention at the famous debates of the general council of the New Model Army that were held at Putney in 1647, but the critical issue was the nature of property in general rather than the details of tenures. Oliver Cromwell echoed the law of obligations in maintaining that it was important for the Army to honour its undertakings to serve parliament. Depending heavily on the traditional common-law notion that property was a creation of human law rather than a natural right, Commissary General Henry Ireton, a sometime solicitor from Nottinghamshire, applied the term 'leveller' to the Agitators who advocated the extension of the parliamentary franchise to all adult males, his point being that a parliament representing the landless would be inclined to legislate away, or confiscate, the property of the better-off. Far from embracing the abolition of property, however, some of the Levellers responded by suggesting that the problem he raised could be solved by the recognition of a right to property that was beyond the reach of statute.[200] Similarly, while some Leveller printed works advocated a complete root and branch reform of the system of tenures, including the abolition of the manorial court and all of the law that went with it, by no means all of them did. Gerrard Winstanley and the 'True Levellers' went so far as to maintain that there was a 'common freedom' in the earth and all of its fruits that belonged to the poor by the right of the Law of Creation and scriptural equity. But Winstanley was a hard-up refugee from London, and the attempt he and his fellow Diggers made to occupy and plant a common in Surrey in 1649 was vigorously opposed by local copyholders.[201] In his *Appeal to all Englishmen*, Winstanley declared that the abolition of the monarchy meant that lords of manors could no longer compel their

---

[198] *The Lawyers Bane or, The Lawes Reformation, and New Modell: Wherein the Errours and Corruptions both of the Lawyers and of the Law it selfe are Manifested and Declared by John Nicholson* (1647).

[199] *Table-Talk*, p. 178.

[200] *Puritanism and Liberty: Being the Army Debates (1647–9) from the Clarke Manuscripts with Supplementary Documents*, ed. A. S. P. Woodhouse (London, 1950), pp. 26, 55, 59, 61. Thomas Rainborough tried to prove a right to property according to the law of God (p. 59).

[201] *ODNB.*

copyholders to come to their courts, act as jurors, do homage, or pay entry fines and other rents.[202] But, however irksome the services and obligations that accompanied them may have been, the tenures associated with what he described as the 'old law of the manor' were precisely the context within which many smallholders could make some claim to a 'propriety' in the lands they occupied. In this respect, it is not surprising that such superficially appealing proposals evidently enjoyed relatively little support.

---

[202] Gerrard Winstanley, *An Appeale to all Englishmen, to Judge between Bondage and Freedome, sent from those that began to digge upon George Hill in Surrey, but now are carrying on that publick work upon the little Heath in the Parish of Cobham* . . . (1650).

12 The household and its members

Public and private interests

In the 1620s, the Puritan lawyer Henry Sherfield evidently felt completely comfortable in describing his relationship to God in contractual language that referred to the terms of a conditional bond between them.[1] By the time of the outbreak of the civil wars, the occupation of land was increasingly seen largely as a commercial relationship between landlord and tenant. Thus in terms of both obligations and tenures, early modern men (and women, too) apparently exercised considerable individual agency, and this was matched by an increasing acknowledgment in public rhetoric and political thought that individuals might expect to have 'private' interests that were distinct from those of the 'state' or the community at large.

In fact, the distinction between public and private interests was implicit in some of the standard views expressed from time to time about the origins of political society itself, namely that it was the heads of households (patriarchs) who had eschewed a warlike state of nature to live under a rule of law that would protect their property and their families.[2] Thus the early seventeenth-century judge Sir John Dodderidge on at least one occasion explained to grand jurors that commonwealths were essentially aggregations of 'private families'. Apparently following Aristotle, he then went on to divide the law into that part which dealt with the polity in general, and that which dealt with 'oeconomick', or household, matters concerning the 'private carriage of each man in his particular domain'. Amongst these were questions about the relationships between husbands and wives, fathers and children, and masters and servants.[3]

Yet, if early modern lawyers were aware of a 'private sphere', it was not a subject that figured significantly in readings at the legal inns or, very often, in systematic treatises. At the end of the sixteenth century,

[1] HRO, MS 44M69/L36/12/1.   [2] See above, pp. 28, 85–6.
[3] NLW, MS 3648D; BL, MS Harleian 583, fols. 3v–4 (1619). Both charges were to grand juries sitting in the King's Bench for London.

the ecclesiastical lawyer Henry Swinburne composed a treatise on the law of marriage as it was administered by the English church courts. Unpublished until the 1680s, it nevertheless became an authoritative work on a major subject.[4] By contrast, the only common-law text along similar lines was *The Lawes Resolutions of Womens Rights* (1632). A compilation of material relating primarily to the economic provision for wives that was apparently gathered together by the little-known barrister Thomas Edgar, it is unusual for a work of its type insofar as it does not appear to have come out of a distinct manuscript tradition; nor is there much evidence that it was considered particularly important at the time.[5]

Nevertheless, in running to just over 400 pages, and in organising its material broadly around the life-cycle of women as they moved from being daughters to wives and then widows, *The Lawes Resolutions* demonstrates that lawyers had to consider various aspects of family formation. Similarly, though much of it seems lacking in any clearly formulated structural principles, the litigious sixteenth and seventeenth centuries produced a large corpus of common-law thought on issues that can be broadly organised around households and the domestic 'oeconomy'. This material often brings us as close as the sources allow to a consideration of concepts such as 'privacy' and 'patriarchy', which frequently figure in historical discussions of the period, but which were rarely treated by contemporaries from the same perspective as we might expect them to be treated today. Apart from anything else, there were no clearly articulated 'human rights', such as a right to privacy, that formed the basis of the arguments being made. Instead, insofar as they used general principles at all, early modern lawyers began with a few basic assumptions about the nature of 'being human'. Here, 'natural love' and affection, as expressed, for example in the care of a father for his children, figures more prominently than might be expected, but the focus was often on elemental material needs such as shelter, the provision of food, and the protection of life and limb. There may have been an implicit understanding that it would have been unreasonable that any householder should enjoy less security and protection from civil society than had been expected by those patriarchs who had originally entered into it,[6] but juridical expressions were normally a good deal more oblique than this. Take, for instance, Coke's claim in his *Institutes* that

[4] Henry Swinburne, *A Treatise of Spousals or Matrimonial Contracts* . . . . (1686).
[5] T[homas] E[dgar], *The Lawes Resolutions of Womens Rights: or the Lawes Provision for Women* (1632). For the attribution to Edgar see W. R. Prest, 'Law and women's rights in early modern England', *The Seventeenth Century*, 6(2) (1991), 169–87.
[6] See, for example, *The History of Great Yarmouth by Henry Manship, Town Clerk*, ed. C. J. Palmer (Yarmouth, 1654), p. 23.

land with a house attached to it had precedence over land without a house. The reason was that houses were for the preservation of man, and 'every thing as it serveth more immediately or meerly for the food and use of man hath the precedent dignitie before any other'.[7]

'Everyman's house is his castle'

It is frequently asserted by early modern historians that contemporaries living in a largely face-to-face society had only a limited sense of an inviolate private sphere, and there was much in both theory and practice to support this view.[8] For example, cases brought into the ecclesiastical courts involving allegations of fornication or adultery were often based on testimony from servants and other individuals who stated that they had made discoveries while peeping through doors or overhearing something through thin partition walls.[9] In what appears to have been an entirely similar vein, James Whitelocke once mentioned in a charge that grand juries should take it upon themselves to see that each citizen practised good manners and that each family was well ordered.[10]

Yet if the early modern household was in these respects open for inspection by the commonwealth, there were other dimensions in which the membrane that set it off from the rest of the body politic was a good deal less porous. Apprenticeship indentures routinely specified that young men who entered into service should not reveal the secrets of their masters. One of the standard reminders in charges to manorial courts was that leet juries should present 'evesdroppers', anyone who lurked under the windows of their neighbours in order to spy on them or overhear their conversations, and it was evidently taken for granted in a late Elizabethan case that a Londoner should expect to enjoy a degree of privacy in his back garden.[11] Even more tellingly, one of the least controversial legal commonplaces of the period was the maxim 'everyman's house is his castle'. Traceable at least as far back as the reign of Henry VII, Coke made a significant reference to it in his *Fifth Reports*, at which

[7] *Coke on Littleton* (1628), fol. 4.
[8] See, for example, K. Thomas, *Religion and the Decline of Magic* (1971), p. 629; I. Archer, *The Pursuit of Stability: Social Relations in Elizabethan London* (Cambridge, 1991), p. 77.
[9] G. Quaife, *Wanton Wenches and Wayward Wives: Peasants and Illicit Sex in Early Seventeenth Century England* (1979); M. Ingram, *Church Courts, Sex and Marriage in England 1570–1640* (Cambridge, 1987).
[10] Whitelocke Papers, vol. xxi, fol. 109.
[11] Guildhall, MS 9384, fol. 44v: if you make windows into my garden, 'this is a wrong done unto us for by this means I cannot talk with my friends in my garden without your servants seeing what I do'.

point it appears to have achieved a common currency in seventeenth-century legal discourse.[12]

'Castle' in this formulation may have resonated with a (perhaps romanticised) notion of a fortified space, one that might even have enjoyed certain legal privileges,[13] but it is notable that seigneurial or status implications were distinctly insignificant. In a speech of 1619 Justice Dodderidge hit the most regularly recurring themes when he noted that 'our houses' were places of residence, repose and refuge.[14] By the time he was speaking, furthermore, the words had been explored in connection with cases that arose, not about castles, but about housing in growing towns such as Norwich, York[15] and London, and from the development of industrial processes such as the burning of lime or the manufacture of starch that put the stiffness in Tudor and Stuart collars.[16]

Brought by plaintiffs who feared windows and light would be blocked by new construction, or by those who found that neighbouring premises had become the source of noxious smells or noise, such cases were normally argued by the lawyers in terms of questions about what was 'necessary' for human life.[17] No one seems to have dissented from the view that the purpose of a house was to defend against wind and weather and to delight or give comfort to the inhabitants. On the other hand, although a pleasant prospect might be a 'great commondation' in a house, it could not be judged necessary, and therefore could not be protected by law. More controversially, while light and air were recognised as important for health, there was some question about how 'necessary' they were. Roger Manwood, a baron of the Exchequer, who had apparently grown accustomed to living next to a blacksmith's yard in London, maintained that an action at law could only lie where there was some measurable damage to the plaintiff, and this could not be proved in connection with light and air, which were not necessary things 'of profit' but merely for pleasure. To support his position, moreover, he quoted the custom of London which permitted buildings to be erected adjacent

[12] *Spelman's Reports*, II, p. 316. 5 *CoRep*, 91v referred to a *Year Book* case from 21 Henry 7.
[13] In his reading on Magna Carta, Francis Ashley, following Coke's report of *Semayne's Case*, stressed the point that a man was entitled to guard his house as if it were a castle. BL, MS Harleian 4841, fol. 47v.
[14] BL, MS Harleian 583, fol. 5.   [15] BL, MS Lansdowne 1075, fol. 23.
[16] For an excellent discussion of the 'public policy' implications see T. G. Barnes, 'The prerogative and environmental control of London building in the early seventeenth century: the lost opportunity', *California Law Review*, 58 (1970), 1332–62.
[17] The leading London case was an action for damages brought by Reginal Hewes, an attorney of the King's Bench, in 1610 against a neighbour who erected a new house on the sight of an old one which blocked windows in Hewes's house. The best report is BL, MS Lansdowne 1075, fols. 22ff. But fuller details of some of the arguments are given in Guildhall, MS 9384, fols. 29vff.

to one another so that light was blocked on the sides, but not in the front and rear, and he also argued that urban development in a 'great and populous city' would be impossible if unlimited rights to light and air were respected.[18] A similar line of thought was advanced in a Jacobean case between two neighbours in Harleston, Norfolk, when one of them erected a 'hog pen' in an orchard next door to the house of the other. In response to the plaintiff's claim for damages, counsel for the defendant argued that 'one ought not to have such a delicate nose that he cannot bear the smell of hogs'. Nevertheless, the judges ruled that the hog pen was a nuisance, and the reasoning in this case, which was reported by Coke, was also applied to lime-kilns and instances where damage was done by dye running into a pond.[19]

The prevalent common-law view appears to have been that whoever took something from a man that was essential to his health in his castle or house did him a wrong equivalent to denying his freehold. Thus the turning-away of water in order to drive a water mill, or the breaking of a water supply pipe were actionable wrongs, and legal remedies could also be sought against anyone with a 'horrible illness' who refused to depart from a house, against those who dumped 'filth' in or near a house, or anyone who built a house so high that it was liable to fall down on another one.[20] Although light and air, like land, had originally been in common, they were commodities that could be made 'private' by the act of building a house, and, once established, they could not be taken away. Hence the settled rule on the blocking of light to windows was that an action would lie against anyone who built a new house that cut off the light that had customarily been enjoyed by a pre-existing one (also known as prescription of light).

While these cases recognise qualities of a house that were necessary for health, residence and repose, the idea of the house as refuge was equally significant. Burglary was considered a particularly heinous criminal offence because the burglar broke the safety of the house and threatened the inhabitants within. As a complicated Caroline case demonstrated, determining whether the offence of burglary had been committed depended not on the ownership or title to the house, but on the presence or absence of family members when it was committed.[21] The same approach to the sanctity of the home also explains the unambiguous judicial view that it was legitimate for a householder to use force, up to and including manslaughter, against an intruder.

---

[18] Guildhall, MS 9384, fols. 41v–5.   [19] 9 *CoRep*, 57v.
[20] Guildhall, MS 9384, fol. 30.   [21] ECO, MS 168, fol. 66. See also 11 *CoRep*, 36v.

Yet, if the house was not to be violated by other individuals, the question of how far officials of one kind or another might be permitted to enter was more debatable.[22] In *Semayne's Case*, which arose from Blackfriars in London in 1605, and in the report of which Coke constantly repeated 'everyman's house is his castle', the question was whether a sheriff could break the door of a house in order to deliver a writ that arose out of a personal legal action.[23] During the course of arguments, it was apparently held as uncontroversial that a sheriff in the process of making an arrest, or otherwise executing process in the king's name, could make a forcible entry, having first made known to the inhabitants the purpose of his visit, because he was acting for the good of the commonwealth. However, a variety of opinions were expressed about the exact point in question, which was whether a sheriff was entitled to take such action in the course of serving writs associated with ordinary legal business between two parties. On the one side it was asserted that since a sheriff was *custos comitatas*, it could not be presumed by any subject that his presence could cause any harm. Furthermore, if sheriffs could not use such measures in serving process, defendants could constantly evade it, a point that had some validity given the notorious inclination of debtors to avoid their creditors by staying inside their houses, even if this meant missing divine service on a Sunday, or absence from the marketplace.[24]

Despite all this, however, Coke's report of *Semayne's Case* began with a reassertion of the point that although the life of man was 'much favoured at law', killing in defence of the household was not murder, and he went on to expand at some length on the decision of the court that it was not lawful for an official serving ordinary legal process to enter a house without permission. Though sheriffs were men of great authority and trust, writs were frequently delivered by bailiffs, and other persons of little value. It would be 'inconvenient' if men should 'as well in the Night as in the Day ... have their houses broke, by colour whereof great damage and mischief might ensue, on any feigned suit ... and so men would not be in safety or quiet in their own houses'.[25] Following the same line of thought, Justice Jones ruled in the 1620s that a sheriff's officer could not break down a door, or enter a house at night, in order to serve civil process, and that if he happened to be killed while doing so, the 'tenant' would not be in danger of an indictment for murder, because his house was his castle.[26]

---

[22] 9 *CoRep*, 65v. *Mackalley's Case*.   [23] 5 *CoRep*, 91v.

[24] Archer, *The Pursuit of Stability*, pp. 78–80.   [25] 5 *CoRep*, 92v.

[26] ECO, MS 168, fol. 120v. See also *CroCar*, 532, accidentally killing a man who was thought by the householder to be breaking into his house was neither murder or manslaughter.

Even more interestingly, a Star Chamber case of the late 1620s generated differences of opinion amongst the judges on the question of whether a constable could force his way into a house in order to apprehend someone who was merely suspected of felony. It was universally agreed that it was an offence for a constable to enter by force without first asking to be let in. However, Lord Keeper Coventry was doubtful whether a constable could at common law break into a house unless he could justify the grounds of his suspicion. Aware of the practical difficulties this fine point might cause, Coventry declared that the court would not punish a constable in such circumstances, even though the action was not, strictly speaking, legal, but two other judges, Hyde and Richardson, were less inclined to recognise the technicality he raised. They maintained that a complaint made to a constable was sufficient warrant for him by virtue of his office to pursue those suspected of felony. If constables had to verify the truth of every complaint before they sought out felons, some might escape altogether because of the delay.[27]

Thinking along these same lines probably also explains why the supposed sanctity of the household laid down in *Semayne's Case* evidently did not extend to the poor, or at least to those who were in receipt of poor relief. A set of instructions for overseers of the poor in the localities, which was issued in 1623, explicitly ordered such officials to enter the houses of poor labourers to search for stolen goods, and to examine what kinds of fuel they had been gathering for the upcoming winter months.[28] But since paupers who took relief came within the jurisdiction of officers working in the name of the commonwealth, the orders differ less than at first sight might seem to be the case from the general principles implied in *Semayne's Case*, which were that whilst a person in his house could expect to enjoy privacy, respite and refuge against any other individual subject, he could not claim them unequivocally when the king's peace, or some other matter associated with the common good, came into the question.

Patriarchy and gender

In the most general terms, there was much in the legal maxim 'everyman's house is his castle' that appears to correspond closely to commonplace assumptions about the household, and in particular the householder,

---

[27] BL, MS Lansdowne 620, fol. 69r-v. 21 James I, c. 19, specifically granted commissioners of bankrupts powers to break into houses and warehouses to search for goods.
[28] Bodleian, MS Tanner 73, fol. 390: A true copy of the charge to overseers in every town, 19 December 1623.

that were prevalent in other spheres of contemporary life. Becoming a householder was taken to represent the transition from youth to adulthood. Householders in towns served on juries and were often qualified to vote for town governors or in parliamentary elections. Householders paid poor rates and were usually the individuals identified as liable for other forms of taxation. Clerical authorities stressed the role of the householder in cultivating the religious values of his family, and the maintenance of a well-ordered household was one standard against which true manliness was measured as well as a test of the health of the most basic unit in civil society.[29] As we have seen in the case of Sir Robert Filmer, moreover, it was possible to join all this with the Fifth Commandment in order to project a social and political order that was based not just on the household, but on the primacy within it of the male patriarch.[30] Yet in reality the limits on patriarchy were much the same as those on privacy within the household; insofar as the affairs of the household came into the public domain, patriarchy in any meaningful sense of the word was effectively undermined.

The most unambiguous reflection of patriarchalism in common-law thought was the doctrine of 'petty treason',[31] which drew an explicit analogy between taking the life of the king, and the killing of husbands, fathers, or heads of households (either male or female) by wives, children or apprentices. Yet, although those convicted of petty treason were executed by being burnt at the stake rather than being hung, the subject was treated surprisingly infrequently as a particular branch of law. Lawyers, no less than the rest of the population, were fascinated by the bizarre and melodramatic circumstances associated with domestic homicide: murders of husbands by wives and their lovers; cases of poisonous porridge with lesbian overtones; attorneys murdered by their clerks.[32] Compared with the interest in such subjects reflected in the popular imagination, however, there was relatively little comment about their legal distinctiveness.[33] Explaining petty treason to a grand jury in 1638, Harbottle Grimston noted that the offence applied to people who killed those they were supposed to obey 'that have a civil soveraignety over

---

[29] See A. Shepard, 'From anxious patriarchs to refined gentlemen? Manhood in Britain circa 1500–1760', *Journal of British Studies*, 44 (2005), 281–95.

[30] Sir Robert Filmer, *Patriarcha and other Writings*, ed. J. P. Sommerville (Cambridge, 1991), p. 35. See above, p. 304.

[31] '*Petite*' treason in law French.

[32] *Dyer's Reports*, II, pp. 404, 406, 408. 'The poysoning of Sir Euseby Andrew. My opinion at the assises in Northampton demaunded in court . . . by John Cotta', printed in *Tracts (Rare and Curious Reprints, MS, etc.) Relating to Northamptonshire* (1881).

[33] BL, MS Hargrave 44, fol. 40, is a note of a case of petty treason tried at Monmouth in 1631, but with no comment on the technical legal issues.

them', but he then went on to explain that the only difference between petty treason and murder was that murder could be said to be committed by a stranger, whereas petty treason was confined to those within the narrow bounds of 'previty'.[34]

The other point sometimes made about petty treason was that it dated from the Middle Ages, and that it originated as an offence associated with monks or nuns who took it upon themselves to kill their religious superiors.[35] While this analogy may well have seemed strained in post-Reformation England, it is probably best understood as a way of seeing the patriarch as the head of a petty polity, an idea that sometimes received a practical manifestation in the penchant for the heads of aristocratic and gentry families to lay down sets of regulations for the better government of their households. For example, according to the preamble of the instructions composed by the earl of Bridgewater for his Shropshire household in the 1630s, the 'Common course' of man's life demonstrated that not only in the mightiest monarchies, but even in the meanest towns and the 'smallest Companies' of men, 'Godly governments' had been embraced by virtuous and well-disposed people in order to make laws to restrain bad dispositions. So for the better government of the family it was wise to establish rules to encourage the well inclined and punish the 'wickedly disposed'.[36]

Confined largely to the social elite, household regulations of this kind were in any case not enforceable in public courts. Furthermore, while the common law allowed that heads of households were entitled to use corporal punishment as a means of chastising and correcting members of their biological and social family, including wives, children and living-in servants, the acceptable parameters of this appear to have been surprisingly limited both in practice and according to the law.[37] In *Eirenarcha*, his guidebook for JPs, the gentle William Lambarde noted that a parent was 'suffered (with moderation)' to chastise a child, and, 'if not outragiously', to chastise his wife. A page later he reminded husbands and masters that they should always behave 'honestly' and treat their wives as though they were their own flesh.[38]

[34] R. Campbell, 'Sentence of death by burning for women', *Journal of Legal History*, 5(1) (1984), 44–59; HMC, *Report on the Manuscripts of the Earl of Verulam, preserved at Gorhambury* (1906), p. 191.

[35] See John Cowell, *The Interpreter or Booke Containing the Signification of Words* (1607), under petty treason.

[36] HEHL, MS Ellesmere 1180.

[37] For differing theological positions see K. Davies, 'Continuity and change in literary advice in marriage' in R. B. Outhwaite, ed., *Marriage and Society: Studies in the Social History of Marriage* (1981), pp. 58–80.

[38] Lambarde, *Eirenarcha*, p. 136.

Yet, if contemporaries clearly had some idea of the existence of a boundary between what was acceptable and unacceptable domestic chastisement, neither law reports nor other kinds of sources make it clear exactly how the lines were supposed to be drawn. Cases involving apprentices frequently mention beatings so violent that they caused open wounds on the back into which salt was rubbed, but this formula appears so often that it is difficult to be sure whether what was being alleged was merely for the court record, and hence whether it gives anything approaching a reliable picture of the issues at stake.[39] There is not all that much more to go on in connection with the chastisement of wives.[40] It is clear that town authorities, and even guilds,[41] took it upon themselves in the sixteenth century to interfere in family relations, and the notorious case of Mervyn Audley, the earl of Castlehaven, who was tried in 1631 for orchestrating the rape of his wife by his servants, demonstrated that there were limits to patriarchal power, particularly in connection with wives. After sentencing, Castlehaven warned his fellow peers that he had been unjustly convicted for exercising a husband's right to manage his household as he saw fit, but this line of argument appears to have had little purchase during his trial in London, which was also notable for judicial decisions that permitted a wife to give evidence against her husband.[42]

By the Elizabethan period, and especially in rural areas, it seems likely that the most typical recourse for either party involved in domestic violence was to take the case before a local magistrate. Since at least the late fifteenth century, the law relating to JPs included the provision that wives, or husbands, could sue out a recognisance that obliged one party to 'keep the peace' against the other, and by the mid seventeenth century this was certainly a common practice around London.[43] Requiring an

---

[39] C. W. Brooks, 'Apprenticeship, social mobility and the middling sort, 1550–1800' in J. Barry and C. Brooks, eds., *The Middling Sort of People: Culture, Society and Politics in England, 1550–1800* (Basingstoke, 1994), pp. 74–5.

[40] The mid-Tudor proposals for the reform of ecclesiastical law (which were never implemented) criticised the ill treatment of wives, but maintained that husbands had the power to coerce them, 'in whatever ways are necessary', if they were rebellious, obstinate, petulant, scolds or of ill behaviour, so long as the husband did not exceed the limits of 'toleration and fairness'. Bray, *Reformatio*, p. 271.

[41] A. Crawford, *A History of the Vintners' Company* (London, 1977), p. 87, S. Thrupp, *A Short History of the Worshipful Company of Bakers of London* (London, 1933), p. 88.

[42] *ST*, III, cols. 402–18. See also C. B. Herrup, *A House in Gross Disorder: Sex, Law, and the 2nd Earl of Castlehaven* (New York, 1999).

[43] CUL, MS Hh. 3.6, fols. 74–116: Marrow's reading *De pace terre et ecclesie et conservacione eiusdem*. The point is repeated by Lambarde in *Eirenarcha*. See also Jennine Hurl-Eamon, 'Domestic violence prosecuted: women binding over their husbands for assault at Westminster Quarter Sessions, 1685–1720', *Journal of Family History*, 26(4), (2001), 435–54.

appearance before the magistrates, and the necessity of finding sureties that would guarantee that the terms of the recognisance were observed, such bonds were relatively private, but they also alerted family and neighbours to the existence of a problem. The framework could also be used to deal with some very difficult cases. For example, early seventeenth-century correspondence of the Temple family in Northamptonshire provides rare insights into one family's reaction to abusive behaviour by a husband. When it emerged in 1625 that one of Sir William Temple's daughters was beaten so badly by her husband, Sir William Andrew, that her face was black-and-blue and her body so badly bruised that she nearly fainted, her father and brothers sought both to make her safe and to prosecute the husband.[44] The social position, and magisterial connections, of the Temples were certainly an advantage, but it seems unlikely that recourse to such help was limited to the rich.[45] Suing the peace against a husband was a relatively cheap process to take out, and in a world where there was hardly any chance of a divorce which permitted remarriage, such a course of action, which did not place a husband's earning-power in jeopardy, had advantages. It is true that husbands accused of cruelty by their wives in the ecclesiastical courts sometimes referred to their right to chastise their wives, but they also often indicated that the violence in question was the result of a moment of hot blood or a loss of rational control, including drunkenness. Equally, if they could be proved to the satisfaction of the ecclesiastical court authorities, accusations of cruelty were an effective plea for wives who were attempting to gain separations from their husbands, and remain in receipt of alimony.[46]

Nevertheless, while patriarchalism within the family clearly had limits, gender, and in particular the status of married women, was one of the most profoundly important distinctions between kinds of 'persons' within English law.[47] It was a commonplace in formal early modern thought that women were subject to various legal disabilities as a consequence of, or in perpetual atonement for, Eve's disobedience in the

---

[44] HEHL, MS Temple of Stowe Legal Box 2(a). Andrew also bragged that he would starve his wife. Their servants were reportedly concerned. Eventually, articles were taken out in High Commission against Andrew.

[45] See, for example, *The Casebook of Sir Francis Ashley, 1614–35*, ed. J. H. Bettey (Dorset Record Society, vol. 7, 1981), p. 49 (a husbandman farmer bound over for beating his wife 'often times'), p. 84 (parents complain that their daughter's husband beat her and then poisoned her with raisins).

[46] Joanne Bailey, *Unquiet Lives: Marriage and Marriage Breakdown in England 1660–1800* (Cambridge, 2003), pp. 26, 114, 132, 200.

[47] The question led the author of *The Lawes Resolutions*, p. 5, to speculate on hermaphrodites; not on whether they existed, 'but what persons they bee'.

Garden of Eden, the act which directly precipitated the Fall of man, and which therefore made the rule of law a necessary evil.[48] The reign of Elizabeth, which was of course the subject of controversy, may have made it unfashionable to deprecate individual female capacity, but early seventeenth-century figures seem to have had little doubt about female legal inferiority.[49] In the House of Commons in 1621, both Thomas Crew and Sir Edward Coke argued against allowing a woman to give evidence before the House, with Coke rather curiously referring to a dictate of St Bernard that women should not be allowed to speak 'in the congregation'.[50] Modern historians have shown that juries of women were sometimes appointed to determine whether condemned felons were pregnant and therefore qualified to have their executions postponed, or to obtain the names of fathers from the bearers of illegitimate children.[51] Yet the author of the *Lawes Resolutions of Women's Rights* was anything but controversial in stating that women had no place in public office or in fora such as parliament or courts leet, where laws were made and promulgated.[52]

Furthermore, although Sir Francis Ashley said in his reading at the Middle Temple in 1616 that women as well as men were entitled to the rights guaranteed by Magna Carta,[53] the *Lawes Resolutions* categorically described the legal position of women in terms of their relationship with men: women were either daughters under the rule of their fathers who were waiting to be married; wives whose property was subsumed into that of their husbands according to the doctrine known as coverture; or widows, who enjoyed certain benefits as a result of their marriages.[54] This litany appears to outline a female life-cycle characterised by legal subordination, and it goes some way towards explaining why the content of the *Lawes Resolutions of Women's Rights* does not seem to modern

---

[48] Ibid., p. 6.
[49] See for some of the theoretical arguments, A. N. McLaren, *Political Culture in the Reign of Elizabeth I. Queen and Commonwealth 1558–1585* (Cambridge, 1999).
[50] *Journals of the House of Commons, 1547–1714* (17 vols., London, 1742), II, p. 519. 13 February 1621.
[51] R. A. Houlbrooke, 'Women's social life and common action in England from the fifteenth century to the eve of the Civil War', *Continuity and Change*, I (1986), 171–89; L. Gowing, 'Ordering the body: illegitimacy and female authority in seventeenth-century England' in M. Braddick and J. Walter, eds., *Negotiating Power in Early Modern Society: Order, Hierarchy and Subordination in Britain and Ireland* (Cambridge, 2001), pp. 43–62.
[52] *The Lawes Resolutions*, p. 2.
[53] BL, MS Harleian 4841, fol. 8, *'liber homo'* comprehends both sexes.
[54] *The Lawes Resolutions*, 'Epistle' and p. 6: 'All [women] are understood either married or to bee married and their desires are subject to their husband, I know no remedy though some women can shift it well enough. The common Law here shaketh hand with Divinitie.'

readers to live up to the expectations of its title. Yet the author himself was aware that there was something odd about the fact that these limitations on the rights of women should serve as a preface to a work of some 400 pages dealing with the law as it related to them. Indeed, the point about women's rights was not that they did not have any, but that they were in fact highly elaborated and, to a limited extent, frequently contested. Although men such as Sir Anthony Benn fulminated against the propriety of women appearing in court, as much as a third of litigation in most types of jurisdiction involved females, either directly or indirectly, as at least one of the parties.[55] The interests of women also appeared surprisingly often in both the reported case law and in exercises at the inns of court, and while one early seventeenth-century wag concluded that the 'law of England was a husband's law', it is also possible to see how the Elizabethan judge Sir James Dyer could comment on the need for the judiciary to protect the 'lawful liberty of women at common law,' especially since they had no voice in the making of statute law in parliament.[56]

The key determinant of the legal position of women with regard to property, the doctrine of coverture, stipulated that the legal personality of a married woman was subsumed into that of her husband. As a default position, coverture meant that a married woman could not hold property in her own name, enter into a business transaction or contract, or make a will. Yet, while it might be expected that such a radical submersion of married women's rights would have prevented questions regarding their property from entering the courts, the reality appears to have been exactly the opposite. One reason for this was the obvious one that not all women (spinsters and widows) were married, but there were also exceptions to coverture, and it was not the only dimension of the economic relationship between men and women within marriage.[57] The most straighforward exception was the recognised custom of London, according to which married women could choose to exercise trades, and enter into legal transactions in their own right.[58] At the same time, while coverture extinguished the separate property rights of married women, early modern wives were in reality the ones that went to the market and

---

[55] Brooks, *Lawyers, Litigation*, pp. 71–2, 75, 86, 111, 129. See, generally, T. Stretton, *Women Waging Law in Elizabethan England* (Cambridge, 1998).

[56] *Dyer's Reports*, I, p. lx.

[57] See A. L. Erickson, *Women and Property in Early Modern England* (1993); M. McIntosh, *Working Women in English Society, 1300–1620* (Cambridge, 2005).

[58] LI, MS Maynard 60: notes on the Sheriff's courts of London. M. McIntosh, 'The benefits and drawbacks of *feme sole* status in England 1300–1630', *Journal of British Studies*, 44 (2005), 410–38.

did the shopping. Hence there were problems in determining where contractual liability lay for many of the transactions they entered into.[59]

On the one hand, it was recognised that husbands had a responsibility to provide their wives with 'necessaries', namely food, shelter and clothing.[60] On the other, wives were understood to have been acting as the 'agents' of their husbands when they entered into transactions connected with the running of their households, which in effect meant that husbands were deemed responsible for any debts that accrued.[61] Failure to provide necessaries was an argument that figured in cruelty pleas in the ecclesiastical courts, and questions about the use or abuse of agency may have come up frequently in local courts. But by the early seventeenth century, the cases reported from the central common-law courts most often involved disputes over whether particularly expensive items of clothing or jewellery were necessary, lawsuits that must have been to some degree a warning to tradesmen that they might not get paid for supplying what could be described as an extravagant item (a gown made of velvet rather than wool, for example) to a wife without the explicit consent of her husband.[62] Nevertheless, the overall position was summed up in 1628 by Justice Jones when he noted at Hertford assizes that while a married woman (*feme covert*) could not generally make a contract without the consent of her husband, she could do so in case of 'necessitie', or, as was the issue in the case at hand, where she needed to sustain herself in sickness (*'in maladie'*).[63]

Another peculiarity of coverture was of course that it only applied to married women. When a wife became a widow she was suddenly endowed with the capacity to hold property. Furthermore, according to common-law tradition and in local custom, widows were entitled to dower, which enabled them to enjoy during their lifetimes one-third of the goods and property accumulated during marriage. Widows' right to dower had considerable ideological significance. It was protected by chapter 2 of Magna Carta, and readings on the statute were sometimes used in order to explain the law surrounding it to students.[64] In practice,

---

[59] *Readings and Moots*, p. 293. See also C. Muldrew, ' "A mutual assent of her mind"? Women, debt litigation and contract in early modern England', *History Workshop Journal*, 55(1) (2003), 47–71.

[60] *Readings and Moots*, p. 289. A grant of '*victus*' includes food, drink, clothing, a bed and a house to lie in. '*Necessaria*' includes all the above plus washing, fuel to burn and the like.

[61] This branch of law later came to be known as the law of agency.

[62] 2 *Dyer*, 234b. *Sir Nicholas Poines's Case*. ECO, MS 168, fol. 185, *Philips and Stanley*. Dodderidge ruled that the husband was responsible for giving warning to the tradesmen if he was unwilling to pay. See also *Moor KB*, 354, *Vicountess Bindon's Case*.

[63] ECO, MS 168, fol. 178v.

[64] For example, CUL, MS Hh.2.6, fols. 2–27; BL, MS Hargrave 87, fols. 195–218.

however, during the course of our period, both dower and coverture were circumvented to a significant degree by methods of managing family financial affairs that involved marriage settlements and the creation of uses, or trusts, that were administered by lawyers for the benefit of wives and other family members. One of the first clauses in the preamble to the Statute of Uses of 1536 proclaimed that a prime evil of the practice was that use undermined the common-law right of dower,[65] but there seems little reason to doubt that lawyers found a way to create uses because heads of families wanted greater control over what would happen after their deaths in terms of provision for widows, and for male as well as female children.[66]

The overall result of the passage of the Statute of Uses, and its companion Statute of Wills (1541), was that a woman had to decide at the time of her marriage whether she would accept provision made for her widowhood through a marriage settlement involving a trust (a 'jointure'), or whether she would claim her common-law right to dower.[67] No less significantly, the legitimisation of uses also made it possible for wives to enjoy property in their own right, and thereby added greatly to the complications associated with coverture. Land settled on daughters by fathers at the time of their marriage could be put in a trust to the use of the wife alone, often with the provision that it should go to the children on her death.[68] Although the Statutes of Uses and Wills established that the beneficiary was effectively the legal owner of a trust, the courts accepted forms of uses that evaded the rules of coverture. Hence there were reported cases at the turn of the sixteenth century in which it was held that the signature of both the wife and the husband was necessary before property in her name could be alienated,[69] and during his tenure as lord chancellor, Bacon ruled that the equitable separate property of a *feme covert*, including leaseholds and money, was not liable for the debts of her husband, a decision that in effect meant that a husband could end

---

[65] 27 Henry VIII, c. 10. Above, pp. 42ff.

[66] Points made explicitly by Henry Sherfield in his reading on uses in 1624. BL, MS Stowe 424, fol. 40v.

[67] Ibid., fol. 48v. Sherfield maintained that the choice had to be made at the start of the marriage, otherwise husbands might seek to defraud their wives of dower by coercing them into accepting jointures. See also, Lincoln's Inn Library, MS Miscellaneous 29. The lecture of Edmund Escote in Lincoln's Inn, on a branch of statute 27 Henry 8, c. 10, which concerned the provision of jointures in recompense for dower at common law (1618).

[68] Erickson, *Women and Property in Early Modern England*.

[69] 2 *CoRep*, 57, *Beckwith's Case*: '[If] the Husband may declare the Use of his Wife's Land, great inconvenience would follow, and Wives might be disinherited and deceived by their Husbands, which would be inconvenient.'

up in debtors' prison even if his wife was of sufficient means to have met his obligations.[70]

The private conveyances to trustees who held land for the use of third parties, which was the essence of the paperwork associated with marriage settlements, sometimes led to them being associated with fraud.[71] Moreover, such arrangements could be the source of domestic discord when husbands wanted property that wives were unwilling to surrender, a point reflected in the observation of one seventeenth-century law lecturer that the best way to secure a wife's separate property was to ensure that control of it was as remote from her as possible.[72] On the other hand, when a wife became a widow she was very likely to become involved in her husband's estate as an executor of his will. In addition, a feature of litigation about women's separate property was that it was often brought by remarried widows who were making a claim, along with their second husbands, for lands, goods, or money that had been alienated when they had been married to the first.[73]

By the early seventeenth century, the interesting cases at common law involved women who were moving either out of or into coverture, and those where, for one reason or another, the limits of coverture were tested. In the 1620s, there was a discussion in Star Chamber about how far a husband might be responsible for an obligation entered into by his wife when she was a *feme sole*, which appears to have concluded that he would be liable for any debts she brought with her, but not for any arising from a legal action against her that had concluded before the marriage.[74] Coke reported a judgment in which it was held fraudulent for a widow to put property in trust for herself prior to a remarriage without telling her new husband of her wealth, but in another case it was ruled that a widow could enter into a marriage contract with her future husband which would be binding on them once they were married. In the 1630s, this principle was cautiously extended in a ruling that a widow could enter into a contract with a man she was about to marry to keep separate property that belonged to her and her children by a first marriage.[75] In yet another case, it was decided that a lease made by a *feme sole* continued to be valid after her marriage, although any act in

---

[70] John Ritchie, *Reports of Cases Decided by Francis Bacon Baron Verulam, Viscount St Albans, Lord Chancellor of England, in the High Court of Chancery 1617–1621* (1932), p. 128.

[71] For example HEHL, MS Ellesmere 6077: fraud against a married woman by a trustee and counsel.

[72] HEHL, MS Huntingdon 106, fol. 49.   [73] Stretton, *Women Waging Law*, chs. 5–6.

[74] BL, MS Lansdowne 620, fol. 18.

[75] *CroCar*, 779, *Crowle* v. *Dawson*: if a man covenant that the woman he is about to marry shall quietly enjoy all her goods, and after the marriage he takes the goods and detains them, it is a breach of the covenant.

connection with the income she received would have to be made in conjunction with her new husband. Lawyers even expressed a rather amused interest in what should happen when a *feme sole* or widow entered into litigation with a man and then subsequently married him while it was still in progress, and it was literally a moot point whether a man could be described as legally imprisoned if he was in a gaol where his wife served as gaoler.[76]

It is true that women's separate property secured through uses and trusts was often controlled ultimately by fathers, husbands and trustees. While the wife literally had the use of it during her lifetime, it was not directly in her hands to dispose of as she liked, and after her widowhood and death, it would descend to others, most often children, without her having much say in the matter. Yet it is worth recalling that much of the property of males was tied up in similar legal constructions,[77] and for contemporaries questions about female property were as often associated with ways of providing for wives and daughters as with preventing them from having anything. An Elizabethan version of the laws and customs of London, for example, was critical of husbands who attempted to disinherit their wives, even if they were thought to have been undutiful; the point was supported by the assertion that the customs of the City had been founded on the notion that marriage was based on love and affection between man and wife.[78]

By the early seventeenth century, the legal position of a married woman could not in any case be discussed simply in terms of coverture, because there were inevitably questions about other kinds of civil liability, and, most importantly, where women stood with respect to the criminal law.[79] This is not to say that there was any inclination to overthrow the distinctions associated with coverture. In 1633, for instance, the indictment of a married woman, Elizabeth Cullington, for the offence of barratry, or stirring up lawsuits, was overturned by the King's Bench on the grounds that a *feme covert* could not be a barrator; she had to be indicted as a scold instead.[80] But there were other circumstances in which the application of the simple rule seemed more doubtful. In 1593, for instance, there was a question about whether a wife should be named with her husband in an action of negligence

---

[76] BL, MS Hargrave 44, fol. 1; MS Harleian 924, fols. 59–60.

[77] See above, pp. 326–7.

[78] *A Breefe Discourse Declaring and Approving the Necessarie and Invioable Maintenance of the Laudable Customs of London* (1584), pp. 26ff.

[79] The bankruptcy statute of 1624 (21 James I, c. 19), alleged that wives frequently colluded with husbands in concealing property from debtors.

[80] BL, MS Hargrave 24, fol. 112v.

brought against a medical man the husband had engaged to cure a problem she was having with her leg, the conclusion being that it was legitimate for her to be named because she was a significant party in the transaction.[81] There was a discussion on the Oxford assize circuit in the 1620s about whether to accept a plea of negligence that named both a husband and his wife as liable for causing a fire that burned down a neighbouring house. Counsel for the couple argued that the case should have been brought against the husband alone because the wife was responsible merely as his servant. But the judges ruled that the fact that the wife had no separate property was not relevant in a case of negligence.[82] Similarly, in a case where a husband was indicted for keeping an illegal alehouse, it was queried whether his wife could be indicted if she continued to run it. The argument against the indictment was that only a husband could be said to keep a house, but Justice Jones and Attorney General Noy argued that the relevant statute had made it an offence to sell ale and for this the wife as well as the husband could be indicted.[83]

Although women enjoyed certain special privileges, most notably the right of pregnant women convicted of felonies to have their executions postponed until they had given birth,[84] the general drift of the criminal law was that they were to be treated little differently from men and not to enjoy special consideration because of their sex.[85] There was back-handed recognition of this in a statute passed in 1624 that extended benefit of clergy to women in all those circumstances where it had previously been available only to men.[86] Nor is there much evidence to suggest that men, or lawyers acting in the name of men, saw the bodies of wives and daughters as the possessions of husbands and fathers. Although it was always difficult to prove, and although accusations had the best chance of succeeding if they fell into certain patterns, it is clear that rape was considered a crime against the person of the female concerned rather than an offence against the property of a father or husband.[87]

---

[81] BL, MS Hargrave 34, fol. 217, *Blachford and Wife* v. *Buckingham*. In the late 1620s, Coventry noted that one reason for naming a wife along with the husband in a case of battery was so that the wife could recover damages in case her husband died. BL, MS Lansdowne 620, fol. 58v.

[82] ECO, MS 168, fol. 81.   [83] BL, MS Hargrave 24, fol. 112v.

[84] In a case of 1625, the assize judges struggled when a convicted female felon appeared to have been pregnant for over a year. ECO, MS 168, fol. 62.

[85] *The Lawes Resolutions of Womens Rights*, p. 2; Garthine Walker, *Crime, Gender and Social Order in Early Modern England* (Cambridge, 2003), p. 37.

[86] 21 James I, c. 6.

[87] R. F. King, 'Rape in England 1600–1800: trials, narratives and the question of consent' (Durham University MA thesis, 1998).

The case of Ann Davies, reported by Coke and frequently referred to thereafter, was a precedent for the idea that a woman could sue for slander if someone had questioned her moral probity in such a way as to cost her the prospect of a marriage.[88] The large numbers of cases brought by women, often married women, against other women in the ecclesiastical courts show both that women valued their sexual reputations and were evidently assiduous in making sure that others lived up to the same standards.[89] Women also sued at common law for damages in other cases where their business, credit, or professional competence was slandered.

Even the most draconian statute of the period regarding women, the 'Infanticide Act' of 1624, may, paradoxically, have been as much a reflection of female agency as the product of patriarchal gender bias. Directed against the crime of 'child murder', the statute specified that when an unmarried woman had concealed her pregnancy and the childbirth, and the baby was subsequently found dead, the mother would be assumed to have killed it unless she should could find some means to prove her innocence.[90] The measure was harsh because most infanticidal mothers appear to have been unmarried girls in service who were no doubt suffering mental duress because of their predicament.[91] Remaining on the statute books until the early nineteenth century, it was also justly notorious because it denied the right of the accused to be considered innocent until proven guilty by a jury of her peers.[92]

Although there is little evidence about the introduction or passage of the bill in parliament, some insight into its origins may be provided by an account recorded by one of the members of the 1624 parliament, Sir Francis Ashley, in the notebook he kept of cases that came before him as a magistrate in Dorchester. In 1623, just a year before the statute became law, Elizabeth Lowes, a servant in the household of the town gaoler suddenly gave birth to a child in the scullery. Two of her fellow servants soon thereafter found the dead baby boy propped up in a small pan. Elizabeth, who was distraught, claimed that the child had 'dropped suddenly' and died because of head injuries. Ashley took depositions from Elizabeth's fellow servants, the wife of the gaoler and a midwife,

---

[88] 4 *CoRep*, 17–20.

[89] L. Gowing, *Domestic Dangers: Women, Words and Sex in Early Modern London* (Oxford, 1996).

[90] 21 James I, c. 27: 'An Act to prevent the destroying and murthering of Bastard Children'.

[91] K. Wrightson, 'Infanticide in earlier seventeenth-century England', *Local Population Studies*, 15 (1975), 10–22.

[92] ECO, MS 168, fol. 105, noted the execution of several women on the statute soon after it was passed, and raised further points about it, most notably whether there might be physical evidence of a miscarriage, and the severe nature of the rule about concealment.

who had been called in to give expert testimony, which included a familiar forensic test: if the baby's hands were clenched, then it had not been born dead but had taken breaths and subsequently been killed. Ashley did not record the outcome of the case, but given his predicament in having to weigh up evidence as difficult as this, it is perhaps possible to see why he would have been in favour of legislation that made it easier for male magistrates to reach decisions in difficult circumstances that were likely to be dominated by females.[93]

As Tim Stretton has suggested, it is probably a mistake to attempt to weigh up too finely the disadvantages and advantages of early modern women-at-law or to speculate too confidently about whether their position was improving or getting worse.[94] The parameters of marriage and domestic economies were so different from what they are today that value-laden comparisons of the component parts seem pointless. The relative accessibility of courts, and the widespread propertied interests of women, led them to be involved in litigation surprisingly frequently in comparison with subsequent periods.[95] Paradoxically, the doctrine of coverture and its complications may have made women more, rather than less, aware of their legal circumstances. The chance survival of a few signed copies show that early modern women sometimes owned law books.[96] Predictably, these were exclusively genteel women, but the evidence from the courts suggests that everyday life may well have brought many others into contact with the law in one way or another. Judging from a proclamation which explicitly attempted to keep them away, London women flocked in large numbers to be present at the case of the earl of Castlehaven.[97] More mundanely, the medical and demographic realities of the early modern period meant that many married women found themselves having to look after the economic affairs of their families when, as frequently happened, they were appointed executors of the wills of their husbands.[98] By the early eighteenth century, the tradition of composing legal guidebooks for and about women, which began with *The Lawes Resolutions*, resulted in further works. Bearing titles such as *Baron and Feme*,[99] they generally had less to do with the

---

[93] *The Casebook of Sir Francis Ashley, 1614–35*, ed. J. H. Bettey, pp. 18–20.

[94] Stretton, *Women Waging Law*, pp. 229–40.   [95] Brooks, *Lawyers, Litigation*, p. 111.

[96] For example, Elizabeth Brereton owned a copy of Pulton, *De pace regis et regni* . . . ., Bodleian Library, Oxford, shelf mark 35 e. 26.

[97] *ST*, III, cols. 402ff.

[98] ECO, MS 168, fol. 124v, *Stanton* and *Darling*: a question of how far lunacy of the husband might serve to put the government of children into the hands of the wife.

[99] *Baron and Feme: A Treatise of the Common Law Concerning Husband and Wives* (1700); *The Laws Respecting Women, As they Regard their Natural Rights, or their Connections and Conduct. . .Also the Obligations of Parent and Child* (1777).

emotional relations between husbands and wives than with property-holding and the legal obligations associated with parenting that married women might find themselves having to know about.

While lawyers sometimes mulled over the nature of patriarchy in their private musings, individual biographies suggest that the reality of gender relations was rarely reducible to legal technicalities, or, indeed, theological prescriptions. Sir Edward Coke appears to have been driven to distraction, even to the point of kidnapping, as a result of his stormy relationship with his second wife, the formidable widow of Sir Christopher Hatton.[100] On the other hand, it was said that Sir George Croke, one of the two judges who held out against the legality of Ship Money, was influenced to do so as a result of the promptings of his wife. Since they were frequently away from home, lawyers must have been more aware than most of the importance of having a reliable spouse to handle affairs in their absence.[101] The point was famously illustrated by the heroic defence of Corfe Castle during the civil wars by the wife of Sir John Bankes, one of the most steadfast supporters of Charles I, but it is even more telling that Lady Bankes had always kept the family accounts, which include notes of the fees Sir John was due as chief justice of the Common Pleas.[102] Even a misogynistic scribble by the highly conservative Sir Anthony Benn, which speculated on the dangers of allowing women to learn to read, was premised on the observation that the problem lay precisely in the fact that women would be able to make just as much out of the opportunity as men.[103] Both his will and the paternalistic advice he wrote for his daughter, Amabella, reveal an unexpected idealisation of the marriage he himself had enjoyed and a cloyingly sentimental view of family life.[104]

Servants and children

The relationship between husbands and wives was the central co-ordinate in the ideal household, but not all households contained it, and since many households, from those of middling artisans to peers of the realm, included living-in servants as well as biological family members, the

---

[100] C. W. Brooks, 'The common lawyers in England, c. 1558–1642' in W. R. Prest, ed., *Lawyers in Early Modern Europe and America* (1981), p. 60.
[101] Prest, *Barristers*, pp. 115–26.
[102] George Bankes, *The Story of Corfe Castle, and of Many who have lived there . . .* (1853). DHC, D/BKL 8c, 64.
[103] BLAS, L28/46, fol. 102.
[104] Barbara Carroll, ed., *Advice to Amabella: Sir Anthony Benn to his Daughter* (Melbourne, Australia, 1990). TNA, PROB 11/132, sig. 97.

household was conceived more broadly than it normally is today. In technical legal terms the point came up in the 1630s in the form of a question about whether a servant could be indicted for committing burglary against a household in which he lived,[105] and servants, as well as wives, were liable to be tried for petty treason if they killed their master.[106] More generally, Sir Anthony Benn mused that the ideal housekeeper provided bounty and good cheer amongst his own and amongst those 'whom by the law of nature and reason he was bound to provide'. The man who kept his eye on his household and made certain that its members did not eat their bread in idleness was profitable to himself and to the commonwealth.[107]

Of course, the quality of household management doubtless ranged from something approaching Benn's ideal to the notoriously disordered households of Lord Chancellor Bacon and the earl of Castlehaven.[108] But the fact remains that while the law gave householders power over those living under their roofs, it also demanded responsible behaviour in return, a point made forcefully by Coke in a charge at Bury St Edmunds where he is said to have warned against misgovernment within households, and pointed out that masters could be made to answer for the misdemeanours of their servants. The first example that came to his mind was that of unmarried girls in service, like Elizabeth Lowes, who became pregnant, and who were in theory not supposed to be dismissed before the end of their term of employment. But he also made the more general point that it was wrong for masters to dismiss servants without lawful notice. According to Coke, the bad treatment of servants was objectionable because it drove young people to the alehouse and might eventually cause them to fall into roguery.[109] From the more narrowly legal perspective, however, he may also have been thinking about the body of statute law, dating back to the time of Richard II (Statute of Labourers), and updated as recently as 1604, which empowered JPs to set wages annually for servants and enforced the established practice that the term of employment, especially for those in agricultural service, should be set at one year.[110]

---

[105] BL, MS Hargrave 44, fols. 40ff.   [106] See above, pp. 359–60.
[107] BLAS, L28/46, fol. 124v.
[108] Then, as today, a telling statistic is that between 1550 and 1650 most homicides occurred within the household. J. A. Sharpe, 'Domestic homicide in early modern England' *Historical Journal* 24(1) (1981), 29–84; Walker, *Crime, Gender and Social Order*, ch. 4.
[109] Folger, MS V.b.303, fol. 349.
[110] See, generally, A. Kussmaul, *Servants in husbandry in early modern England* (Cambridge, 1981).

The law relating to masters and servants, both inside and outside the domestic sphere, and in both urban and rural agricultural settings, had a long history.[111] Mid-sixteenth-century compilations of precedents record cases dating back to the fifteenth century in which masters brought legal actions against people who had lured their servants away, presumably for higher wages or to gain some other economic advantage (such as a trade secret).[112] A Henrician statute made it a felony for a servant to embezzle the goods of his master;[113] another passed in the reign of Edward VI forbade workers from entering into any combination or conspiracy in order to gain increases in wages.[114] In general, however, there are few, if any, lengthy expositions of the master/servant relationship either in readings at the inns of court or in the law reports, presumably because this aspect of law was left largely to JPs who were supposed to operate according to statutory authority that gave them considerable power, particularly in the setting of wages. For example, a long chronological run of wage assessments from early seventeenth-century Somerset was written out on large parchment sheets, which were probably posted in marketplaces, or during meetings of sessions. Following the statutory instructions, the preamble to each assessment states that it had been made after taking the advice of 'grave' persons within the county, and that it applied to artificers, labourers, servants in husbandry and apprentices. Most importantly, the assessments set maximum limits on the wages servants in named categories were allowed to take for one-year periods of service. Qualified artificers were to have no more than 40s.; male servants in husbandry over twenty no more than 33s. 4d.; females over eighteen no more than 24s. Males under twenty, and females under eighteen, were not to get any wages at all, although they were supposed to be supplied with sufficient meat, drink and other necessaries, which probably included clothing and, possibly, medical care.[115]

At face value, this statutory legislation, and the wage assessments that went with it, were a potentially powerful means of controlling the conditions of employment in the interest of employers,[116] but the master/servant relationship was also characterised by other legal and paternalistic

[111]   During the eighteenth and nineteenth centuries, master and servant law became the basis of what today is described as employment law.

[112]   Brian William Napier, 'The contract of service: the concept and its application' (Cambridge University PhD thesis, 1975), p. 34.

[113]   1 *Dyer*, 5a-b. Action on the statute 21 H 8, c. 7 touching servants embezzling their master's goods.

[114]   Napier, 'The contract of service', p. 33; 2 & 3 Edward VI, c. 15.

[115]   SARS, Q/AW. Wage assessments 1604–41.

[116]   Napier, 'The contract of service', p. 34.

qualifications that most people probably considered appropriate for a dependent relationship. Masters could be held responsible for an injury caused to a third party as a result of an action undertaken on his orders by his servant.[117] In one early seventeenth-century case it was ruled that a master could dismiss, and then sue out an action on the case against a servant in husbandry for failing to keep sheep according to a contract, but the judges also noted that even if he was dismissed early, a servant could sue in debt for the wages that were due to him for the entire year.[118] The final clauses of the Jacobean statute on masters and servants, 2 James I, c. 6, specifically singled out the cloth industry as one in which the setting of wages was directly connected with an assumption that employers would be obliged to pay them, and the act also prohibited clothiers who were JPs from setting the wage rates for weavers, tuckers, spinsters, or other artisans who made cloth. In the 1630s when Chief Justice Bramston was in Essex attempting to quell disquiet that had resulted there from a severe depression in the cloth trade, he was clear that master clothiers who were themselves in difficult circumstances should be obliged to continue to pay artisans they had contracted with. As if echoing the thoughts of Coke some years earlier, one of the workers to whom Bramston spoke at the time summed up his predicament by pointing out that if he did not receive his wages, he would be forced either to go to London to beg, or to join in with actions by workers to stop the export of grain from the county.[119]

As Douglas Hay has pointed out in connection with the eighteenth century, it is one thing to show that judges were sensitive to the position of servants, but quite another to be confident about how far, given their ages and economic condition, they were able to enforce their rights before local magistrates.[120] Indeed, in this respect living-in servants in particular may have been in a weaker position than the other principal class of household members, apprentices. Most typically (but not exclusively) involving male teenagers who were literally moving away

[117] See YAS, DD 146/12/ 2/19, notes concerning the responsibility of masters for their servants in making entries and disseisins.

[118] ECO, MS 168, fol. 165v.

[119] Essex Record Office, Chelmsford, D/Deb 7/1–22. See *CSPD 1633–34*, p. 164, for a report from Sir William Jones and Sir Thomas Trevor about similar problems in Gloucestershire in 1633. See, also, J. Walter, 'Grain riots and popular attitudes to the law: Maldon and the crisis of 1629' in J. Brewer and J. Styles, eds., *An Ungovernable People: the English and Their Law in the Seventeenth and Eighteenth Centuries* (1980), pp. 47–85.

[120] D. Hay, 'Master and servant in England: using the law in the eighteenth and nineteenth centuries' in W. Steinmetz, ed., *Private Law and Social Inequality in the Industrial Age: Comparing Legal Cultures in Britain, France, Germany and the United States* (Oxford, 2000), pp. 227–64.

from their biological family into another household in order to learn a trade or occupation, apprenticeship was based on a three-cornered agreement between the youth, his parent, who provided an up-front sum of money known as the 'premium', and the master, who took the premium in return for providing room, board and training for the young person.

Apprenticeship was given a legislative basis in 1563 by the Statute of Artificers, which used the traditional customs of London as a model to be applied nationally.[121] The key legal point was that service for a period of seven years became a prerequisite for entry into named trades, and hence essential for the gaining of the freedom of a town, which was necessary in order for an individual to carry on a trade when he became an adult. Because of the importance of being able to prove the period of service, apprenticeship was normally accompanied by a written document (the indenture) that detailed the relationship between the master and the apprentice, even though the apprenticeship premium was supplied by the parent. Indentures were so common that by the mid-seventeenth century they were available as printed forms, and the terms of the agreement were largely formulaic. The apprentice undertook to obey his master, to keep his household secrets, and not to haunt ale-houses or engage in fornication. The master on the other hand obliged himself to feed and accommodate the apprentice, to teach him his trade, and to see that he eventually became a freeman of the relevant company, guild, or town. Amongst the issues that might have been negotiable, and hence specially mentioned in indentures, were clothing, and who would be responsible in case the apprentice fell into ill health.[122]

Parenting and the maintenance of apprentices were such closely related activities that the approach of individual householders to the one was likely to have influenced his or her approach to the other. In both cases, the doctrine of reasonable chastisement permitted the head of household to enforce his discipline. Clerics and the writers of advice books also regularly reminded young people that the biblical Fifth Commandment required them to submit to the discipline of their masters as well as that of their fathers and mothers. On the other hand, there is a wealth of evidence that parents were extremely careful to find a placement for their sons in which they would be well treated and properly brought up. They are known to have used legal means to intervene in situations where they thought their children were being abused in one way or

---

[121] 5 Elizabeth, c. 4. For the opinion of William Fleetwood and Peter Osborne on the origins and early implementation of the statute see BL, MS Lansdowne 38, fol. 36.

[122] For an overview see, Brooks, 'Apprenticeship, social mobility and the middling sort'.

another.[123] Furthermore, it is by no means clear that the judiciary necessarily favoured the most draconian interpretations of any kind of domestic authority. In his private meditations, for example, the Caroline judge Sir Robert Heath, expressed his personal abhorrence of corporal punishment, concluding that it was more fit for dogs than his own sons.[124] Exactly how such an outlook might have affected decisions on the bench is uncertain, but allegations of serious sexual or physical abuse of young people within households were evidently taken seriously when they were uncovered and brought to the attention of the authorities.[125]

Nevertheless, given all of the ingredients in the practice of apprenticeship – youth, the authority of surrogate parents, and the relatively low life expectations on all sides – there was a great deal of scope for breakdown in the relationship. On the whole, the view of the judges at Westminster was that legally recognised apprenticeship should be enforced mainly in towns rather than in rural communities, and that in any case quarter sessions and other local jurisdictions were the proper places for dealing with questions that arose from it. Judging from the records of the Lord Mayor's court in London, for example, such cases often involved a wide range of circumstances, stretching from bad treatment by the master to dangerous conditions in the workplace or failure to teach the craft.[126] Equally, apprentices were sometimes disobedient, stayed out late at night, stole money, or ran away, and for this reason urban magistrates exercised powers that enabled them to administer short-term punishments on those accused by their masters of particularly bad behaviour.[127] Indeed, one of the few cases reported from the common-law courts, *Gilbert* v. *Fletcher*, illustrates many of the complications and ambiguities in the relationship. The question was whether a master could sue for breach of covenant if an apprentice

---

[123] K. Thomas, *Rule and Misrule in the Schools of Early Modern England* (Reading, 1976). Folger, Bacon-Townshend Collection, L.d.748: information from Agnes Howsgo of Wells (Norfolk) to JPs about the maltreatment and death of her son, who was apprenticed to a tanner, October 1606. Greater London Record Office, Calendar of Sessions Rolls, vol. 1611, pp. 110; vol. 1612, pp. 91, 110, 186, 216. WJ/SP/1646/1 (sessions papers): 'The humble petition of Hanna Lovering, widow, on behalf of her poor daughter Elizabeth'.

[124] BL, MS Egerton 2982, fol. 25v. BLAS, L28/46, fol. 115.

[125] M. Ingram, 'Child sexual abuse in early modern England' in Braddick and Walter, eds., *Negotiating Power*, pp. 63–84.

[126] For example, CLRO, 'Mayor's court original bills', p. xix; MC 2G/1; 'Mayor's court precedent book, 1603–05', fols. 5–6; Large Suits box 1.ll, items 1–4, 6–7; Small Suits box 2.49.

[127] Betty Masters, *The Chamberlain of the City of London 1237–1987* (London, 1988), pp. 13, 96; Greater London Record Office, Typescript sessions calendar, 1638–44, pp. 28, 128, 105, 123.

bound himself for seven years and then left the service without permission. The view of two of the judges was that the action was not good because the Statute of Artificers had been designed to compel service, not to provide damages to the master. Nevertheless, the reporter of the case seems to have had some sympathy with the contrary view, which was that the statute said that the apprentice was to be bound as though he were of full age, presumably with the intent that he should be considered liable for the loss of service that resulted if he absconded.[128] Yet, whatever appeal this analysis may have had in terms of the law of obligations, it must have been evident that it was untenable in connection with a relationship in which up to a third of the boys involved departed before the completion of their terms. Consequently, in occupations where significant sums of money were at stake, it was common for fathers to enter into bonds in which they agreed to make up for any losses that arose to masters from apprentices who stole or absconded.[129]

As in clerical thought, so, too, in legal thought there was a presumption that parents had a responsibility for nurturing their children and preparing them for adult life. Just as husbands were supposed to care for the needs of their wives, they were also liable for providing necessities for their children. Thus in a case from the Caroline period in which the master of St Edmund Hall, Oxford, sued a father for college bills run up by his son, it was remarked that while a father would not be obliged to pay his son's alehouse tab, he might be liable in this case because he had paid for other expenses associated with being a student, including college fees.[130] In effect, the apprenticeship indenture recognised these responsibilities by recording the transferral of them from the biological parent to the master, and this feature of the practice helps to explain why apprenticeship was sometimes associated with attempts to solve more general social problems such as underemployment, poverty, or the predicament of orphaned children, and why they met with very mixed results.

The so-called 'Slavery Act' of 1548 was an attempt to cure unemployment and vagrancy by empowering JPs to bind vagrants and 'runagate' servants into a two-year period of service, complete with permission for masters to use shackles and other harsh treatments as a means of punishment, but the scheme soon collapsed, at least in part because it was difficult to find masters anxious to take on difficult

---

[128] BL, MS Hargrave 24, fol. 28v.
[129] GL, MS 15,860/1. See also P. Seaver, 'The puritan work ethic revisited', *Journal of British Studies*, 19(2) (1980), 40–1.
[130] ECO, MS 168, fol. 5v.

servants.[131] A statute of 1610, on the other hand, noted that a large
number of charitable gifts had been made in rural as well as urban areas
in order to provide apprenticeships for poor children, and laid down
regulations to facilitate the process, primarily by prescribing that masters
who took such apprentices should give back the premium once the
period of service had ended.[132] In 1631, the Caroline *Book of Orders*
instructed JPs to fund the binding into service of children from poor
families as a way of alleviating poverty and helping to ensure that they
were properly prepared for adult life.[133] Once again, however, forcing
masters to take such children, even if the parish provided money for an
apprenticeship premium, was a source of friction. Furthermore, although
apprenticeship arrangements appear to have been widely used from the
early seventeenth century onwards as a way for parishes to put children
who had lost their parents into the care of new families,[134] it is clear that
not all poor families were content to see their children removed from
them when the parents were still alive. One of the questions about the
Book of Orders put by JPs to the royal judges for clarification was what to
do about 'poor parents' who either refused to put their children into
service or attempted to lure them away from it once they had been
apprenticed. The answer was that they were to be sent to the house of
correction.[135]

While it appears that the poor, or at least those in receipt of relief, had
no inalienable right to determine the future of their children, for the
better-off, the problem of parental control was, of course, more likely
to arise in connection with marriage. Since money or land was often
involved even in the marriages of people with modest means,[136] lawyers
probably inclined to the view that parents should exercise as much
control as possible, but this was complicated by the fact that the English

---

[131] 1 Edward VI, c. 3. The act also provided that the children of beggars could be bound
apprentices. It was repealed by 3 & 4 Edward VI, c. 16. C. S. L. Davies, 'Slavery and
Protector Somerset: the Vagrancy Act of 1547,' *Economic History Review*, 2nd series,
19(1) (1966), 533–49.

[132] 7 James I, c. 3. HEHL, MS Ellesmere 2521: observations on the statute concerning
rogues and vagabonds, noted that vagrant parents should provide for children if they
could, but if the parents were overburdened with children then they should be put out
as apprentices.

[133] *Bulstrode's Reports*, pp. 1176–83.

[134] SARS, Bridgwater Borough Records, B/B/bw: apprenticeship indentures for orphans,
1583–1609. The numbers were particularly high in the 1590s. Girls, who were usually
apprenticed into 'domestic science' or housewifery, are included as well as boys. One
child was four years old.

[135] HALS, MS Gorhambury xii.A.15.

[136] D. O'Hara, *Courtship and Constraint: Rethinking the Making of Marriage in Tudor
England* (Manchester, 2000).

ecclesiastical courts' interpretation of canon law allowed that a valid marriage could be undertaken by people as young as twelve and fourteen without the consent of their parents or anyone else, and that it was not necessary for the act to be consecrated in a church service.[137] In the late 1530s Lord Chancellor Audley is said to have been concerned about the marriage of minors (according to the common law, where the age of majority was twenty-one) without the consent of their parents,[138] and the proposals produced in the later years of Henry VIII's reign for the reform of church law, the *Reformatio legum ecclesiasticarum*, contained a provision that marriage of children should not be undertaken without parental consent.[139] Although it is unclear whether he had these proposals in mind, a collection of manuscript essays by the recorder of London William Fleetwood contains a rumination on the 'greate question . . . whether . . . children maie marrie or contracte them selfes w[i]thout the consent of the parent*es*'. Referring briefly to the *Institutes* of Justinian, but evidently finding little in common or statute law to support his position, Fleetwood relied largely on scripture for his conclusion that the commandment that children should honour their parents was not limited merely to 'putting of[f] the capp and making Curtesie' but in obeying them in all 'thing*es* lawfull and honest', including the making of marriage.[140]

In fact, since the average age of marriage for both men and women was in the late twenties,[141] the marriage of young people in their teens was primarily a concern of the aristocracy and greater gentry, who generally married younger than the rest of the population. Some of the associated anxieties had been addressed in both common and statute law by the creation of the offence of abduction and by allowing guardians to sue out actions of trespass against those who 'carried off' underage girls with the intention of marrying them. A statute passed in the 1550s laid it down that a girl under the age of sixteen would in effect be disinherited if she married without the permission of her father or guardian, and it imposed a penalty of two-years' imprisonment on the man involved.[142]

In much the same spirit, canons passed by Convocation in 1584 and 1603 specified that parental consent was required for the making of

---

[137] Swinburne, *Treatise of Spousals*, pp. 45ff.

[138] G. R. Elton, *Reform and Renewal: Thomas Cromwell and the Commonweal* (Cambridge, 1973), p. 153.

[139] Bray, *Tudor Church Reform*, pp. cxxv, 249.   [140] Folger, MS V.b.9, fols. 73–9v.

[141] E. A. Wrigley and R. S. Schofield, *The Population History of England 1541–1871: a Reconstruction* (Cambridge, 1981).

[142] 4 & 5 Philip and Mary, c. 8: 'An act for the punishment of such as shall take away maidens that be inheritors'.

marriages of those who were under the ages of twenty-one for men, and eighteen for women respectively, and there was a concurrent attempt by the church to enforce banns, licenses and church weddings as the only reliable way to prove that a legal marriage had taken place.[143] Yet the ecclesiastical courts were understandably reluctant to undo consummated unions once they had in effect taken place, and this meant that in individual cases, parents could find themselves less than content with the outcome. A tragicomic instance of this emerged from a Caroline Star Chamber case in which a lawyer called Moody was found guilty of libelling the church courts after one of them had declared, despite his wishes, that the marriage of his daughter was legitimate. In a letter written to his sister-in-law, Moody apparently accused the ecclesiastical court officials of living by 'rapine', and making their 'lowman and cruel' jurisdiction a market in which they took money for the 'wrongfull selling of poor innocent virgins'.[144]

Moody claimed in his defence that the marriage had been unlawfully 'contrived' [plotted or arranged] by this same sister-in-law, and illicit 'practising' in the making of marriages was, indeed, an offence that could be heard in Star Chamber. In the early 1580s, a Lancashire squire, William Farrington, sued out bills against a Westmoreland widow, Elizabeth Benson, allegedly because she was playing two suitors at once for the hand of her daughter, who was being courted both by Farrington's son and by a lawyer, Sergeant Rhodes. Accompanied by various melodramas that would not be out of place in a City comedy, including a serious loss of face by Farrington, senior, when he was served with legal process during a meeting of the assizes at Lancaster Castle, the case also involved financial interests, since Elizabeth Benson and her daughter, who was also a widow, were apparently attempting to conceal some of the latter's property from her previous marriage.[145]

Since financial considerations of some kind, ranging from dowries given with daughters to land settled on the new couple by the father of the groom, were so ubiquitous in early modern marriages, cases like that of Farrington, including the associated emotional turmoil, must not have been all that uncommon. In fact, most of the reported common-law cases concerning marriage arose from circumstances in which fathers or mothers had entered into penal bonds for the payment of money or goods to a prospective groom, on condition that a marriage was made,

---

[143] *Lawes Resolutions*, p. 53, noted that the approval of parents was desirable 'in regard of honestie', but not of necessity, according the canons of the Church.
[144] BL, MS Lansdowne 620, fol. 37.   [145] LRO, MS DDF 1049.

but where there was a subsequent default, either in the making of the marriage, or in the payment of the sum promised.[146]

If more serious allegations of deceit were involved, then Star Chamber might be resorted to. For example, a reported Caroline case, *Woodrowe v. Crispe*, was concerned with the 'contrived' marriage of Thomas Woodrowe, the son and heir of a London mercer, who was reputedly worth £15,000, but who had been declared a lunatic by the court of Wards at the instigation of his mother. According to the bill, Mrs Woodrowe had hired Alice Crispe, a Berkshire widow, to help effect a cure of her son, but Crispe managed instead to convince Thomas to marry her daughter Dorothy in their local parish church. In the event, the ecclesiastical court officials refused to recognise the marriage, and the Star Chamber imposed fines of £500 on the Crispes to show the magnitude of their crimes, even though it was accepted that they were much too poor to pay them.[147] Summing up his own opinion in the case, Chief Baron Walter covered a number of the relevant legal points concerning the necessity of parental consent in marriage, noting in particular that most of the statutory provisions related to young women under the age of sixteen. But he went on to declare that 'contriving' marriages, whether they involved males or females, and regardless of their age, was an 'evil in itself at common law; and punishable in this court', because children were the 'special goods' of their parents.[148]

Privacy, patriarchy and community

Late twentieth- and twenty-first-century historians have placed considerable weight on privacy and patriarchy in understanding crucial transformations in early modern society. In one of his most persuasive articles, Christopher Hill argued that a consequence of the Reformation was a growing emphasis on the heads of households as intermediaries between their extended families and religious truth, and as secular heads of the most basic unit of early modern society. By the mid seventeenth century, according to Hill, the result was the emergence of a much more private sense of the family and the simultaneous degeneration of a broader sense of community.[149] Joining this insight with work that highlighted a corresponding emergence of what might be described as clerical Fifth-Commandment patriarchy, Lawrence Stone drew a powerful picture of the early seventeenth-century emergence of a 'closed domesticated

---

[146] 1 *Dyer*, 13a; BL, MS Hargrave 372, fol. 71; ECO, MS 168, fol. 36.
[147] BL, MS Lansdowne 620, fol. 19.   [148] Ibid., fol 21v.
[149] C. Hill, *Society and Puritanism in Pre-Revolutionary England* (1964), pp. 443–86.

nuclear family'. Largely isolated from kin and community, the early modern household was dominated by the patriarch whose authority was conceptualised in much the same way as that of the early Stuart kings, and who ruled his wife and married off his daughters as a petty absolute monarch.[150]

A major methodological problem with formulations such as these is, of course, that it is difficult to measure how far religious ideas, most often expressed in sermons, corresponded to life as lived in real families. Much the same may be said of legal practices and ideas. Lawsuits and reported case law almost always arise from the exceptional circumstance rather than the typical one, and it is no easier to prove the take up of legal ideas by the population at large than it is religious ones. On the other hand, the nature of the English legal system meant that legal discourse was influenced as much by the cases that came before it as by the internal logic of law, and the lawyers who had to think about the affairs of households and families almost all lived in them themselves.

In so far as it can be taken as a reliable guide, legal thought reflects some of the categories that Hill and Stone were talking about, while suggesting some important ways in which contemporaries might have modified them. The qualified conception of private domestic space encapsulated in the phrase 'everyman's house is his castle', and the 'rights' that were associated with it, emerge particularly strikingly in the early seventeenth century, but the phrase itself, and some of the legal learning that went with it, existed as far back as the late fifteenth century.[151] No less important, in 1640, as in 1500, it was still conceptually impossible to imagine a private sphere that would be absolutely impervious to the claims the law might make on it in the name of common morality, the common good, or the community.

Although the clerical emphasis on the Fifth Commandment, and Filmer's attempt to prove a connection between the power of fathers and the power of monarchs reflect the pervasiveness of the patriarchal ideal within early Stuart culture, it had only a limited impact at law.[152] At least one reason for this was that most of the principal relationships within households, including those between husbands and wives, and those between masters, servants and apprentices, were often discussed in terms of the word 'contract', and most of them were testable in courts. Judges were evidently as likely to weigh up the question of whether

---

[150] L. Stone, *The Family, Sex and Marriage in England 1500–1800* (1977).
[151] See above, pp. 354–5.
[152] The classic statement of the contrary view is Gordon J. Schochet, *Patriarchalism in Political Thought: the Authoritarian Family and Political Speculation and Attitudes Especially in Seventeenth-Century England* (Oxford, 1975).

'love and natural affection' were a sufficient consideration for making a contract as they were to reinforce fatherly authority. In the speeches that the recorder of King's Lynn, Francis Parlett, made on the appointment of mayors there in the 1630s, a deliberate projection of a patriarchal political vision was based on analogies with the family and, in particular, that between husbands and wives. Time after time, the conclusion he drew was that love and mutual affection were the essential ingredients in determining the relationship between the body of the people and their governors.[153]

Yet, while these thoughts were in tune with the kinds of political rhetoric being expressed at the same time in Caroline court masques,[154] most English lawyers would probably have agreed with Aristotle and Richard Hooker that there was a difference between life within families and the nature of political authority, and a natural corollary of this was that there should be scope for civil intervention in the private lives of families, even if this was at the expense of fathers.[155] In the early stages of the civil war, the polemicist Henry Parker was able to score an effective point about the limits of political patriarchalism simply by recounting the most common form of legal intervention in domestic violence. While the king might be described as the head of the commonwealth in the same way that fathers were the heads of households, everyone knew that in cases where there was abuse by a father or a master, even servants were obliged to bring the disorder to the attention of the magistrates.[156]

[153] NRO, King's Lynn Borough Records, MF/RO 396/13, fols. 6v, 10.
[154] K. Sharpe, *Criticism and Compliment: the Politics of Literature in the England of Charles I* (Cambridge, 1987).
[155] *Of the Laws of Ecclesiastical Polity by Richard Hooker, Books 1–4*, ed. R. Bayne (London, 1907), p. 191.
[156] [H. Parker] *Jus populi. Or A discourse Wherein clear satisfaction is given, as well concerning the Rights of Subiects, as the Right of Princes* . . . (1644), pp. 31–4.

13   The person, the community and the state

Earning a living

If it was thought perfectly natural that law and the 'public interest' should intervene in the private lives of families, it follows as self-evident that it should also have been involved in those aspects of 'political economy' that took place beyond the household, in the streets, the alehouse, the guildhall or the marketplace. This was of course most uncontroversial in connection with obvious infractions of the criminal law, where mutual protection mandated collective vigilance. As the complier of statutes Ferdinando Pulton put it, while private suits might be considered private matters, criminal cases were the 'concern of all men', and since all men benefited from the common peace, all were required from time to time to participate in the maintenance of it.[1] Yet, as many historians have pointed out, the use of legal sanctions to govern personal behaviour in the early modern period often seems to have been more comprehensive than this, and, according to some accounts, it was also the source of hegemonic power that the social elite could use to exercise political and social control. Consequently, the aim of this chapter is to investigate the relationship between the individual person and society at large, primarily by examining the nature and extent of constraints on what could be said in public and what could be done in public spaces outside the household.

As we shall see, some of the issues at stake involved parliamentary legislation, decisions at common law and the activities of JPs. By the 1610s some of the relevant questions were addressed in language that celebrated the liberties and freedoms of the English in potentially emotive rhetoric. Yet the fact of the matter is that many cases arose not in connection with the relationship between the individual subject and the state, but as a result of his or her relationship with their local communities, and the way these were articulated through lesser political bodies,

---

[1] Pulton, *De pace regis et regni*, p. 23.

including franchise jurisdictions and, especially, incorporated towns. Although historians have recently concentrated their attention on the regulation of what might be described as social and moral behaviour, early modern questions about the liberty of the subject were arguably more often concerned with economic activity. Even for people of very modest means, the capacity of a court leet, a guild, or an urban corporation to restrict their opportunities to trade and earn a living was inevitably of profound importance.

As a starting point, it is worth recalling that the relationship between lesser political bodies and the common law adjudicated by the judges at Westminster was incompletely resolved.[2] A long-standing tradition of judicial interrogation of local customs and practices was reflected in the use by the crown of *quo warranto* proceedings to challenge town charters, and statutory legislation passed during the reign of Henry VII mandated that all new guild ordinances should be approved by royal justices or crown law officers before they were implemented.[3] On the other hand, by 1600 lawyers had for years been employed in London and major provincial towns to record and systematise local bylaws and procedures, and on the whole there was an inclination on the part of the judiciary to accept these if they could be shown to be based either on valid customs or charters granted by the crown.[4] London itself was the most important single site of legal exceptionalism within the realm, and its privileges, which were endorsed by Magna Carta and by frequent parliamentary confirmation, were normally upheld at common law.

Thus although it is an exaggeration, indeed a misconception, to say that the early modern judiciary, and Sir Edward Coke, in particular, were advocates of 'economic liberalism', if that is taken to mean a complete hostility to privileges or restrictions that affected business and trade, legal thinking had for a long time been informed by a distinction between regulations that could be shown to be beneficial to trade and those that were prejudicial either to individuals or to the public at large.[5] The preamble to the early Tudor statute 19 Henry VII, c. 7, which aimed to regulate the making of bylaws by guilds, fraternities and other corporate bodies, and which was itself an updating of earlier legislation, mentioned the harm caused by the use of such powers to fix the price of

---

[2] See above, pp. 241–3.
[3] 19 Henry VII, c. 7; *John Spelman's Reading on Quo Warranto, delivered in Gray's Inn (Lent, 1519)*, ed. J. H. Baker (Selden Society, vol. 113, 1997).
[4] See, for examples, Brooks, *Pettyfoggers and Vipers*, pp. 209–17, and also, HMC, *Report on the Records of the City of Exeter* (1916), pp. vii, xii, 51.
[5] For an earlier debate on this subject see, B. Malament, 'The "economic liberalism" of Sir Edward Coke', *Yale Law Review*, 76 (1967), 1321–58.

goods, while asserting that local acts or ordinances should not be against the 'common profit of the people'. Similar issues were raised in the mid-Tudor period in connection with the royal grant by Queen Mary of a monopoly to import malmsey wine into the town of Southampton, which was declared by the judges to be illegal because it was damaging to the broader public interest.[6]

In the light of this tradition of interpretation, the Elizabethan practice of granting courtiers monopolistic powers through letters patent that enabled them to control named trades, such as the making of starch or the importation of German wines, was generally seen as a legal abuse, and at least in the minds of some, such royal grants were associated with a dislike of monopolies of any kind, including those connected with the privileges of corporate towns or guilds.[7] The decision in *Darcy* v. *Allen* (1602), which declared illegal a royal patent of monopoly over the importation and sale of playing cards, was based in part on the point that the grant damaged the interests of domestic manufacturers.[8] An anonymous tract, probably written at about the time when James I granted monopolistic control over the exportation of cloth to a newly formed company of Merchant Adventurers, criticised the damage this did to free competition in foreign trade and alleged that grants of corporate powers to particular towns tended to prohibit the free concourse of merchants and traders. It maintained that the existence of 'private societies and companies', including guilds, probably did more harm than good to the commonwealth.[9]

Never going so far as this, judicial arguments and decisions in the age of Coke generally maintained corporate powers, but they also regularly reiterated the importance of trade and commerce to the good of the commonwealth while at the same time accepting the need for the 'good governance' of occupations, and the utility of some special privileges or customs. In *George Hanger's Case*, for example, which concerned the exemption of citizens of London from paying import duties on wine, counsel for the defendant argued that London was the equivalent to a 'university' for the training of merchants. The exemption, which had been granted by a charter from King Edward I, aimed for the 'advancement and good of merchandising and trading which are as it were the blood which giveth norishment into the whole body of the kingdom'. It should therefore be given a favourable and benign construction, because it was

---

[6] *Dyer's Reports*, I, p. 50.
[7] See, for example, Bodleian, MS North a.2, fols. 67ff: petition of the Grocers of London, concerning the monopoly in starch, with the answer of the Company of Starchmakers (1608).
[8] 11 *CoRep*, 85.   [9] BL, MS Lansdowne 811, fol. 101v.

a positive encouragement to trade.[10] Similarly, in the 1560s, it was held that despite the provisions of the Statute of Artificers, which prescribed a seven-year apprenticeship as a prerequisite for entering into named trades, citizens of London could legitimately claim a customary privilege to leave the trade in which they were trained in order to take up another one, a judgment which, of course, explains why an association with a named City livery company is not necessarily a good guide to the actual occupation of one of its members. While the general argument hinged on customs of London guaranteed by Magna Carta, it was also claimed that the privilege was necessary because of the particular hazards associated with doing business there, including the danger of losses on the high seas due to piracy and misadventure, as well as the higher risk of ill-health and physical disability.[11]

While these cases stressed the benefits of customary privileges to citizens, those restrictive of outsiders were sometimes more rigorously questioned. The *Case of the City of London* (1610), for example, was brought on a writ of *habeas corpus* by James Wagoner, a non-citizen, who had been imprisoned as a result of a prosecution in the Mayor's court for breaching customs of London that prohibited the sale of goods, apart from foodstuffs, within the City walls by anyone who lived outside them who was not a freeman. Clearly reflecting the expansion of the suburbs that accompanied the overall demographic growth of London, the decision in the case went ultimately in favour of the City, but while its ancient privileges were taken note of, the judgment in fact established tests for the validity of such a custom, including a consideration not only of its efficacy for the City, but its utility for the realm as a whole. The first test was in this case passed relatively easily; since citizens of London had to pay taxes (scot and lot) within the City, and hold office, they were entitled to the sole privilege of buying and selling there. The discussion of the second test, on the other hand, was more long-winded and involved (perhaps strained) considerations of public policy. Restrictions on outside traders prevented the excessive confluence of people in the metropolis that might otherwise lead to the depopulation and impoverishment of the rest of the country. Equally, by controlling the flow of people into the capital, the restriction helped to prevent the outbreak of plague and pestilence, and the degeneration of the city into a state of ungovernability as a result of over-population, a matter of importance to the country as a whole. When London was governed well, all parts of the 'kingdom are kept in better order'. If the City became so populous that it was not subject to searches for faulty wares, 'fraud and decit would

---

[10] BL, MS Lansdowne 1075, fols. 6–11.   [11] Ibid., fols. 9v–11.

increase' to the prejudice of the king and the entire realm as well as the City itself.[12]

By contrast, the other major case reported by Coke with regard to corporate control of trade, the *Case of the Merchant Tailors of Ipswich* (1615), reflects a more sceptical judicial view of the utility of regulation. The Merchant Tailors brought the case in order to collect a fine of £3 13s. 4d. they imposed on William Sheninge, a tailor who had qualified through apprenticeship, for failing to present himself to the wardens of the society before exercising his trade in the town. Although the circumstances were unusual in that Sheninge claimed to have acted as a domestic servant to another inhabitant of the town, rather than by setting up a shop on his own, Coke nevertheless used the report to enunciate what subsequently became a famous dictum, namely that at common law no man could be prohibited from working at any lawful trade.

Coke developed the point through a discussion of the passage, and subsequent repeal, of statutes in the reign of Edward III which demonstrated that restrictions on an individual practising more than one art or mystery had been found discommodious to the commonwealth.[13] This led him to the conclusion that restrictions on the right to earn a living could only be introduced by parliament. Thus restraints beyond those laid down in that Statute of Artificers, including those instituted by the Merchant Tailors, were against the law. Hence, while Coke reiterated the familiar point that guild ordinances for the good order and government of trades were lawful, those that restrained anyone from practising a lawful mystery were not. Such measures were contrary to the liberty and freedom of the subject, and in the past they had been used as 'a means of extortion in drawing money . . . or of oppression of young tradesmen, by the old and rich of the same trade, not permitting them to work in their trade freely'.[14]

Despite the damning rhetoric of these last few lines, however, judicial opinion was not implacably hostile to guilds and corporations. While some decisions may have put limits on their powers, they did not aim to undermine them altogether. The provisions of the Statute of Artificers, which made a period of apprenticeship in a named trade a prerequisite for gaining the freedom of the town, and hence the right to do business there, were comfortably integrated into the long-established guild tradition that already existed in towns.[15] The number of people who became involved in guilds increased, and a significant number of new

---

[12] 8 *CoRep*, 127b.
[13] 37 Edward III, c. 6, which was repealed by the subsequent parliament.
[14] 11 *CoRep*, 54a.   [15] 1 *Saunders*, 311–12.

guilds were introduced in London and most other major towns in the early seventeenth century.[16] In the 1630s, furthermore, the crown explicitly drew on the claim that corporate organisation provided an element of government essential to the success of any trade in order to justify a large number of new incorporations in London, even though these were by this date manifestly tied to the king's needs for money.[17]

It is clear that disputes of the kind Coke reported, as well as conflicts between groups of guildsmen, were fairly common. For example, a controversy at Chester in the 1620s, which arose when the Company of Ironmongers tried to prevent a tradesmen from opening a shop, evidently threw the town into several days of political turmoil that included threats of violence, demonstrations in the streets, confrontations at the town hall and recourse to legal counsel.[18] Furthermore, those who felt that their economic interests were inhibited by company privilege sometimes argued that monopolistic restrictions were an impeachment of broader liberties of Englishmen. In 1629, for instance, brokers in the City of London complained about monopolies of the Goldsmiths Company in connection with pawning that put 'limits on the rights men have in their property to dispose of it as they will'.[19]

Yet, given the potential for friction, the number of central-court cases involving challenges to corporate privileges was probably not very great, at least judging from what survives in the manuscript and printed law reports. The Cokean distinction between restriction from trade and governance or regulation was probably more easily compromised over than argued out in court. Although urban corporate bodies were no doubt irksome to those excluded from them, they were useful forms of association for the many tradesmen, artisans and merchants who worked within their framework. In Jacobean London, for instance, the so-called 'working' goldsmiths frequently referred to the written constitution of their company in their attempts to make the governing body take more account of their interests. In the late 1620s, they united with their leaders in consulting leading lawyers, including Coke and Selden, to find the best way to prevent the erection of a new Royal Exchange in London.[20] At the same time, on the level of interpersonal relations, one of the avowed purposes of urban guilds was to promote a sense of fraternity that would make the kind of conflict epitomised by lawsuits unnecessary.

---

[16] Christopher Brooks, 'Apprenticeship, social mobility and the middling sort, 1550–1800' in J. Barry and C. Brooks, eds., *The Middling Sort of People: Culture, Society and Politics in England, 1550–1800* (1994), pp. 52–83.
[17] See above, pp. 197–8.   [18] BL, Harleian MS 2054, fols. 89ff.
[19] Goldsmiths Company, Goldsmiths Hall, London, Court Minute Book R, pt 1, fol. 160.
[20] Goldsmiths Company, MS D.I.1; Court Minute Book, Q, pt 1, fols. 57, 80.

Charity and love amongst the brotherhood were supposed to translate into honest behaviour that precluded disharmony, and judges were not inclined to question these values.

Damaging words

The emphasis in urban corporate thought on non-contentious behaviour corresponded with similar values found in 'community' or 'neighbourhood' institutions such as manorial courts, and there is no reason to doubt that contemporaries took such notions seriously.[21] Yet, at the same time there was a concurrent preoccupation with slanderous speeches, written libels and treasonous words. Notable growth areas in the law, they would seem to suggest high levels of conflict rather than neighbourly consensus. Slanderous words arose from relationships in the street, or in the alehouse, as well as those in the guildhall or the House of Commons. Thus while the story of dangerous words needs to take account of attempts by the crown and its agents to suppress political dissent,[22] it is no less significant that contemporaries evidently relished attacking each other with verbal barrages that mixed deeply held views with vile personal invective.[23] Men and women of middling status sued each other for slander on a scale that we might associate primarily with politicians, pop stars and other media 'celebrities'.[24]

In an account of the court of Star Chamber written at the very beginning of the 1620s, William Hudson claimed that libels (or written slanders) had been particularly targeted by the court when Sir Edward Coke was attorney general,[25] and the large number of notorious cases brought before it in the later 1620s and 1630s would appear to be proof enough of the government's concern about them in those years as well.[26] Speaking and writing about political matters seem almost certain to have increased across our period as a whole, not least because of the wider availability of paper, yet, as some contemporary authors pointed out, questions about what one person could say in public about another also had a long history.

---

[21] See above, pp. 250–1, 258–9.   [22] See above, pp. 94–7, 108–9.

[23] M. Ingram, 'Law, litigants and the construction of honour: slander suits in early modern England' in P. Coss, ed, *The Moral World of the Law* (Cambridge, 2000), pp. 134–60.

[24] For some comparative figures see Brooks, *Lawyers, Litigation*, ch. 4; L. Gowing, *Domestic Dangers: Women, Words and Sex in Early Modern London* (Oxford, 1996).

[25] [William Hudson], 'A Treatise of the Court of Star Chamber' in Francis Hargrave, ed., *Collectanea Juridica. Consisting of Tracts Relative to the Law and Constitution of England* (2 vols, n.d.), I, p. 100.

[26] Above, pp. 177–85.

Hudson himself retailed a fascinating case from the time of Henry VII when, he said, the books of all the tradesmen in the City of London had been examined at the Guildhall in order to match the handwriting in them with that of a libeller. For Hudson, this was proof that libels had been 'severely punished' throughout the ages, a view endorsed by Lord Chancellor Ellesmere who once observed that before the Conquest, in the times of Kings Edgar and Ethelbert, slanderers had been punished by losing their tongues.[27] Yet, although the punishment of political libels was no doubt a perennial concern of governments, the history of libel and slander was not quite as straightforward as these accounts suggested. A late sixteenth-century treatment of the subject by an anonymous legal antiquarian claimed that there was in fact no traditional 'common-law' remedy for words spoken by one ordinary person against another.[28] There was insufficient evidence to demonstrate that damages had been recovered before 1066 for words such as thief, extortioner, briber or the like. Intriguingly, this writer also argued that before the reign of Edward I, it had been 'free to every man to descant on the government of the realm'. The Edwardian treason laws had been passed because many people in the localities were 'inventing and publishing news', whereby discord grew between the king and his subjects. Subsequently, these statutes were reinforced in the reign of Richard II by legislation relating to the offence of *scandalum magnatum*, which made it a crime to speak ill of the nobility and certain royal officials, and which, according to this author, had the broader purpose of preventing distrust between the commonalty and the nobility.[29] Yet, despite these developments, the common-law courts had remained reluctant to hear accusations of slander between ordinary subjects, whose only recourse was to bring actions in either the ecclesiastical courts or in franchise jurisdictions.[30]

Whatever the accuracy of these remarks about the history of political slanders, the attempt to chart a parallel history for words against governments and interpersonal slanders between ordinary subjects is a telling reflection of the relationship between them at the turn of the sixteenth century. Furthermore, the overall picture of the gradual historical development of a common-law action for slander fits well with one of the most significant features of early modern legal history.[31] Throughout

---

[27] Hudson, 'Star Chamber', p. 100. Baildon, *Cases in Camera Stellata*, p. 45. BL, MS Stowe 422, fols. 118ff.

[28] BL, MS Harleian 4317, fols. 11ff.   [29] 2 Richard II, c. 5.

[30] BL, MS Harleian 4317, fols. 11ff.

[31] *Wiltshire: the Topographical Collections of John Aubrey*, ed. John Edward Jackson (Devizes, 1862), p. 13, reports a conversation amongst lawyers in which it was said that before the Reformation, 'one could hardly in a year find an Action of the case for Slander'.

the Middle Ages, those who thought their personal reputations had been impugned in public had to seek redress through manorial or ecclesiastical courts, but during the course of the early sixteenth century such cases were increasingly being brought successfully before the major courts at Westminster.[32] By the early seventeenth century this became a tidal wave in which money damages were sought for slanderous words.

Along with the apparent keenness of litigants to sue for slander, the development of the common-law action was facilitated by the willingness of early Tudor judges to hear lawsuits brought as 'actions on the case', which alleged that the slanderous words constituted a wrong done to one of the king's subjects that could only be remedied by the payment of damages. It has also been plausibly argued that the recourse of litigants to the common-law courts was an early manifestation of dissatisfaction with the ecclesiastical jurisdiction,[33] perhaps because the church courts could only offer a successful plaintiff the pleasure of seeing his adversary suffer the humiliation of a public penance whereas at common law there was a prospect of a jury trial and significant compensation. Given the relative ease with which people found themselves able to take out legal actions, it is consequently difficult to say exactly how far the remarkable growth in the common-law action was a reflection of a growing sensitivity to the damaging power of words, or merely a form of legal opportunism, which at the same time exposes fractious interpersonal relationships and high levels of general social anomie.[34]

Far from decreasing as a result of the development of the common-law remedy, the numbers of defamation cases in the ecclesiastical courts actually increased, and they appear to have been particularly popular amongst married women who felt the need to protect their reputations.[35] In fact, although some business of this kind was channelled into the common-law courts through the medium of prohibitions, this only reinforced the importance of maintaining a flawless sexual reputation.[36] Meanwhile the commonplace books of late Elizabethan and early Stuart common lawyers were filled with long lists of phrases divided into those that would support an action and those that would not. Sir Mathew Hale's autograph 'Black Book of the New Law', which he began compiling in

---

[32] R. H. Helmholz, *Select Cases on Defamation to 1600* (Selden Society, vol. 101, 1985), pp. xlivff.

[33] *Spelman's Reports*, ii, p. 238.

[34] Lawrence Stone, *The Crisis of the Aristocracy, 1558–1641* (Oxford, 1965), pp. 240–42, and 'Interpersonal violence in English Society, 1300–1980', *Past and Present*, 101 (1983), 22–33; J. A. Sharpe, 'Debate: the history of violence in England. Some observations', *Past and Present*, 108 (1985), 206–15; Lawrence Stone, 'A rejoinder', *Past and Present*, 108 (1985), 216–24.

[35] Gowing, *Domestic Dangers*.   [36] Above, pp. 109ff.

the 1620s, contained nearly 400 entries under the heading of action-on-the-case for words, more than for any other single category.[37] One the one hand, actions for slander demonstrate the inclination of contemporaries to hurl the vilest invectives at each other, but, on the other, they were evidently part of a culture in which public reputation was held to have a quantifiable value, and where it would have been very difficult for any prudent person to ignore the possibility of being called to account for what they said about someone else.[38]

According to William Hudson, the Star Chamber's jurisdiction over libel and slander was based on the idea that offensive words might lead to a breach of the peace,[39] a point memorably illustrated in the 1630s by a case in which it was remarked that disparaging remarks about a nobleman's bald head were actionable because they might provoke overheated men of honour to indulge in duels.[40] Yet while contemporaries clearly thought that the provision of legal remedies for libel and slander were important as a means of preventing the escalation of interpersonal violence,[41] many of the cases reflected more practical and pecuniary considerations. At common law, the underlying theory was that a slander was a personal injury equivalent to a physical assault or a trespass on land, a quantifiable damage to the reputation and livelihood of the plaintiff who brought the case and specified the damages to which he thought himself entitled. As they had evolved by the early seventeenth century, there were two broad categories of actionable words: those that impugned the professional competence, or creditworthiness, of people such as doctors, lawyers, craftsmen or merchants, and those that could be taken to imply that the defamed individual had committed a misdemeanour or criminal offence:[42] thief, forger, perjurer, witch,[43] whore and so on, and which if true might warrant legal proceedings.[44] Hence there was something of the counting house about many actions of slander, as well as a prudential concern about the consequences of allowing a malicious rumour to remain unchecked, particularly in those circumstances

---

[37] LI, MS Hale 191.

[38] 9 *CoRep*, 59v. It was possible for an individual to read, and even laugh at a libel without being prosecuted, so long as he did not publish, or spread it about.

[39] Husdon, 'Star Chamber', p. 102.

[40] BL, MS Lansdowne 620, fol. 55.

[41] 5 *CoRep*, 125, *De libellis famosis*. Coke wrote that 'although the Libel be made against one, yet it inciteth all those of the same family, kindred, or society to revenge, and so may be the cause of shedding of blood, and of great inconvenience'.

[42] *CroCar*, 1015.

[43] *Les reports de Sir William Jones . . . un des justices del banck le roy. . .* (1675), p. 198.

[44] *CroCar*, 285. *Kercheval* v. *Smith and others*: action on the case against defendants, who were churchwardens, because they presented the plaintiff, '*falso et malitiose*', on a 'pretended fame' of sexual incontinency.

where the words might form the basis of legal action. The cases reflect a world where a reputation for professional competence, or the ability to pay one's debts, was thought to have a direct bearing on individual livelihoods, and where traditional values such as honest dealing and civil conversation were accompanied by a willingness to denounce those who appeared not to live up to them.[45]

The exact quantitative dimensions of common-law actions of slander are difficult to establish, but by the early seventeenth century they had evidently reached such proportions that there were judicial efforts to stem the tide.[46] A statute of 1624 laid it down that no more costs than damages could be awarded by the courts in cases of slander where the damages amounted to less than the small sum of 40s.,[47] and the judges endeavoured to tighten the criteria for bringing a plausible case. In the 1630s it was ruled that only words implying a felonious wrong, as opposed to those alleging a mere trespass or civil injury, should carry an action;[48] in the same spirit the judges maintained that calling someone a witch was actionable only if the words might be presented in a criminal prosecution.[49] Most significantly of all, perhaps, by the end of our period it was also possible to argue that intoxication in effect rendered slanderous words less harmful than they would have been had the speaker been in complete control of his faculties.[50] Nevertheless, it is clear that a prudent, and sober, person needed to be circumspect about what he said in the alehouse about his business associates or neighbours, not to mention about how he expressed his religious opinions, or his views on the virtues and vices of particular Scottish kings of England. Although satirical, even scatological, libels were powerful and popular, they were undeniably dangerous for those who uttered them, or indeed those who read or laughed at them.[51]

The widespread use of actions of libel and slander may have made it safer for someone who thought they had a grievance against another person to resort to litigation, or to a criminal prosecution, than to make a

---

[45] HL, MS Ellesmere 2727, includes a case brought in Star Chamber by Smallbrooke, a mercer of Birmingham, who had been libelled for his 'manner of living and selling of wares, usury, and cosenage'.

[46] For the problems regarding numbers see Brooks, *Lawyers, Litigation*, chs. 3–4.

[47] 21 James I, c. 16, § 6: An Act for limitation of Actions, and for avoiding of Suits in Law.

[48] BL, MS Hargrave 24, fol. 29v.

[49] *The Reports of that Reverend and Learned Judge, Sir Richard Hutton Knight* . . . (1656), p. 133.

[50] R. H. Helmholz, 'Civil trials and the limits of responsible speech' in R. H. Helmholz and T. A. Green, *Juries, Libel, and Justice: the Role of English Juries in Seventeenth- and Eighteenth-Century Trials for Libel and Slander* (Los Angeles, CA, 1984), pp. 3–36.

[51] BL, MS Lansdowne 620, fol. 35, A. Fox, 'Ballads, libels and popular ridicule in Jacobean England', *Past and Present*, 145 (1994), 47–83.

potentially slanderous public declaration of the facts as they saw them. Unless they could be shown to have malicious intent, actions of slander were unlikely to be successful if the accusatory words were the basis of legal proceedings. At the same time, the character of legal proceedings in Chancery and Star Chamber actually invited statements by the plaintiff about the bad character or immoral behaviour of the defendant. However, there were limits beyond which it was unsafe to venture. Both courts punished plaintiffs who submitted bills that were deemed to be either malicious or unseemly, or where the evidence was insufficient to support the original allegation.[52]

Not surprisingly, legal proceedings themselves often resulted in frustrations that led to untoward words.[53] Every early modern judge, from the lowest to the highest, had the power to bind over or fine individuals whose words or deeds in court could be described as contemptuous.[54] While it was apparently not slanderous to criticise a jury verdict, so long as there was no imputation of illegal action by individuals, litigants who complained too vigorously or persistently about the behaviour or decisions of judges could find themselves accused of libel or slander. In the early Elizabethan period, Sir James Dyer collected a long list of precedents about the punishments that could be meted out to those who slandered judges.[55] Both Ellesmere and Coke considered taking action against individuals who defamed their judicial reputations,[56] and in the 1630s Attorney General Bankes brought Star Chamber proceedings against a couple involved in a custody and inheritance case who had allegedly slandered Lord Keeper Coventry. Putting the case in court,

---

[52] BL, MS Lansdowne 620, fol. 66, to put in a scandalous bill against the defendant and not prosecute it is the same as publishing a libel, for which the defendant may punish the plaintiff (1628). See also S. Hindle, 'The shaming of Margaret Knowsley: gossip, gender and the experience of authority in early modern England', *Continuity and Change*, 9(3) (1994), 391–419.

[53] DHC, DC/DOB/8/1. Mayor's Court Offenders Book, fol. 196, 30 December 1633. John Gardiner deposed against for saying he cared not a straw for the gentlemen of the county and especially the JPs, particularly Sir Francis Ashley and Sir Walter Earl. He said he had been done badly by in connection with a parcel of land.

[54] HL, MSS Ellesmere 2740, 2652: examples of public corporal punishment for slandering great men, including judges. BL, MS Hargrave 34, fols. 273ff. Cases of words uttered against JPs: 'he hath receyved money of a thief that was apprehended and brought before him and for stealing of certain sheep, to let him escape and to keep him from Gaol'.

[55] *Dyer's Reports*, II, pp. 337, 378.

[56] *CroCar*, 753, *Jeffe's Case* (1630): a libel on a person who had been a judge, charging him with perjury during the time he was in office, is an indictable offence. Bankes Papers, 28/16. Copy of a judgment in Star Chamber (1604) in a case Coke brought as attorney general against Forth for slandering Ellesmere.

Bankes praised Coventry's record in general terms, and argued that in slandering the king's principal law officer, the defendants had in effect slandered the king himself.[57] Given these precedents, it is perhaps easier to understand why Bankes also argued effectively against Thomas Harrison for slandering Sir Richard Hutton in connection with the case of Ship Money, despite the fact that Harrison was arguing a position that supported the authority of the king.[58]

For the historian interested in either high politics or the 'politics of the parish', actions of libel and slander are both illuminating and paradoxical. They are illuminating because the court cases often reveal the strength of the opinions held as well as the vehemence with which they might be expressed. On the other hand, rashly expressed opinions could have dangerous consequences for the speaker, and this seems to reflect a deeply engrained set of social values as much as the reaction of government in particularly paranoid periods of monarchical insecurity. Clergymen warned against the evils of a loose tongue,[59] decorous speech was demanded in manorial courts, in the meetings of guilds and in the proceedings of borough councils.[60] When speakers of the House of Commons asked kings at the beginning of each new session for freedom of speech in parliament, they were requesting an immunity that would have been recognised in the guildhall as well as in the king's council. Contemporaries might reasonably claim that legal actions provided an outlet for legitimate grievances, but there was no such thing as a genuinely open public forum, and it is not clear that very many contemporaries, no matter what their social station, would have argued that there should be.[61]

Nevertheless, there was some awareness that limits on speech could be oppressive insofar as they might make it very difficult to express any significant opinion whatsoever. In the notes he made of Star Chamber proceedings against Bonham Norton, a bookseller who accused Coventry of taking bribes, the earl of Bridgewater was at pains to remind himself that it had to be legitimate for people to bring forward justifiable complaints against royal ministers.[62] At the same time, potentially defamatory words were an everyday feature of the fractious world of

---

[57] Bankes Papers, 44/2: *Case of James and Alice Maxwell*.

[58] See above, pp. 216–17.

[59] J. W. Spargo, *Juridical Folklore in England Illustrated by the Cucking-Stool* (Durham, NC, 1944), pp. 114–15, 121.

[60] See above, pp. 258–9.

[61] D. Shuger, *Censorship and Cultural Sensibility: the Regulation of Language in Tudor-Stuart England* (Philadelphia, 2006).

[62] HEHL, MS Ellesmere 7950. Star Chamber 1630.

town politics, and cases arising from them pushed judges towards considering the boundaries of acceptable speech.[63]

The most important reported example from the early seventeenth century was probably that of James Bagge, Sr, who brought a writ of *mandamus* in the King's Bench in 1616 after he had been dismissed from his place as a burgess of the town of Plymouth[64] because of contemptuous words he spoke against the mayors and chief governors of the town over a period of eight years. He allegedly invited one mayor to 'kiss his arse'. He said of another that he had carried 'himself foolishly in his place', and encouraged the other inhabitants of the town to join together to throw him out and select a 'wiser man in his place'. In addition, Bagge was accused of openly criticising a customary local impost on the sale of wine and of disparaging the town's new Jacobean charter.[65]

In a complicated and surprisingly controversial decision, Coke and his fellow justices of the King's Bench appear to have followed an absolutely conventional line in ruling that the mayor of Plymouth could certainly fine Bagge, or take sureties for his good behaviour, given that some of his ruder words were held to be '*contra bonos mores*'. However, they did not accept that rude or critical words were a sufficient grounds for disenfranchisement at the will of the mayor alone. This could only be justified if there was a specific warrant for it that was legitimated either by prescription or the words of the town charter. In any case such an action would still have to conform to chapter 29 of Magna Carta; that is it would have to involve due process and a trial by peers, neither of which had been the case in Plymouth.[66]

The judges were clearly aware that the case raised the question of how dissent might legitimately be expressed within a corporation. Coke's report suggested that if critical words alone were the measure, then nearly every citizen or burgess in the country might find himself disenfranchised at one time or another, and he noted that new charters, new courts and new fees frequently caused trouble in towns because they

---

[63] *CroEliz*, 33: King's Bench orders the restoration of a man to the freedom of the City of London after he had been disenfranchised for taking a case to Westminster which he had been ordered not to do by the lord mayor. *Cases collect et report per Sir Francis Moore, chivaler, serjeant del ley* (1663), p. 412: a bylaw that a mayor can imprison for opprobrious words is not legal. 3 *Bulstrode* 189: does drunkenness make a person unfit for government? Baildon, *Star Chamber*, p. 372.

[64] See P. D. Halliday, *Dismembering the Body Politic: Partisan Politics in England's Towns 1650–1730* (Cambridge, 1998), for the use of *mandamus* in the later seventeenth century.

[65] 11 *CoRep*, 96–7.

[66] A manuscript report of the case by Timothy Turner notes that Coke's own argument in the case depended heavily on Magna Carta. BL, MS Additional 35957, fol. 7v. Also, see below, pp. 420–1.

were seen as overthrowing the existing public weal.[67] Sir John Dodderidge apparently agreed that it had to be possible for a member of a
corporation to criticise the mayor in connection with the performance
of his office, otherwise the mayor could do what he liked without any
control. To accept this, Dodderidge said, was essentially to allow a
mayor the same privileges as had been claimed by the pope, who by his
neglect of duty had allowed thousands to go to Hell, while suppressing
all objections to his policies and theology.[68]

Dodderidge's popish analogy presumably carried considerable weight,
but it also had potentially wide implications, which may explain why his
words were not reported in published versions of the case. Equally, while
Bagge's case, like the more celebrated words of Sir John Eliot in parliament in 1628, demonstrates the contested nature of the limits of speech
in the pre-civil war period, it was hardly a resounding victory for the
right to speak openly and without reserve. Coke's report of the case was
one of those Lord Chancellor Ellesmere construed as demonstrating that
the Lord Chief Justice was seeking popularity.[69] In his own printed
account of it, Coke sarcastically advised the reader to note that during
the course of the hearing, much was said to exhort citizens and burgesses
to yield obedience and reverence to the chief magistrates in their cities
and boroughs. They derived their authority from the king, and '*obedentia
est legis essentia*'. Hence it was shown how those who committed 'any
contempt against them' might be punished.[70]

Personal behaviour

If sober adult males and females had to be careful about what they said,
it was no less important that they should be circumspect in their actions,
and, as was the case with words, the reasons owed as much to traditional
community values as to legislation or judicial decisions. In fact, at common law there were few restrictions on personal behaviour beyond
long-established misdemeanours and felonies such as assault, petty
theft, grand theft, burglary and murder. In an Elizabethan case, for
instance, the judges explained that the haunting of taverns or the playing
of games were not offences (*mala in se*) according to common law, but
had to be prohibited by statute.[71] In the famous case of monopolies,
Darcy v. *Allen*, one of the moves used in the successful argument against

---

[67] Ibid., fol. 7.   [68] Ibid.
[69] L. A. Knafla, *Law and Politics in Jacobean England: the Tracts of Lord Chancellor Ellesmere*
(Cambridge, 1977), pp. 297ff.
[70] 11 *CoRep*, 100.   [71] 3 *Dyer*, 255.

the power of the crown to grant a monopoly over the manufacture of playing cards was that playing at cards and other forms of gambling were not offences at common law, and therefore could not be regulated by patents from the crown, even if these were allegedly made with a patriarchal care for the good of the subjects.[72] Yet, having said this much, there was no general jurisprudential precept that limited either legislative or customary restrictions on what a person could or could not do. As we have seen already at a number of points, borough courts and manorial courts had traditionally supervised personal behaviour.[73] Frequently employing fines or shame punishments such as sitting in the pillory, and sometimes whipping, they dealt with a range of offences stretching from the selling of unhealthy food to assaults, drunkenness, wife-beating, fornication and unruly apprentices.[74] Similarly, the ecclesiastical courts had long enforced the penalty of public penance for 'crimes' such as fornication, drunkenness and disorder in the parish church.

In fact, the 'local' punishment of relatively minor offences was an important aspect of the contemporary approach to general problems of crime and disorder. By the second half of the seventeenth century, the failure of earlier correction to instil reform frequently figured in popular biographies of convicted felons.[75] But the link had been made at least a century earlier in the speeches Lord Keeper Nicholas Bacon delivered to MPs and JPs as they were about to depart from London for the provinces in the 1560s and 1570s.[76] He reminded lords of manors that they should maintain their leet jurisdictions. He was keen that JPs should regularly attend quarter sessions in order to enforce the wholesome laws available for keeping the peace, and, famously, he concluded that it was better that thousands should be whipped than that one person should go to the gallows, the point being that the early correction of misbehaviour was the best method for preventing more serious offences.[77]

It was in much the same spirit that other Elizabethan law-and-order men such as William Lambarde and William Fleetwood emphasised to grand jurors that they should be diligent in reporting offenders,[78] and Lord Keeper Bacon's son, Sir Francis, once went so far as to tell jurors at London's court of the Verge that it was better to live in a society where

---

[72] 11 *CoRep*, 85.   [73] See above, pp. 269–72.

[74] For an enlightening treatment of the subject see M. Ingram, 'Shame and pain: themes and variations in Tudor punishments' in S. Devereaux and Paul Griffiths, eds., *Penal Practice and Culture 1500–1900: Punishing the English* (Basingstoke, 2004), pp. 36–62.

[75] P. Rosenberg, 'Sanctifying the robe: punitive violence and the English press 1650–1700' in ibid., pp. 157–82.

[76] See above, pp. 59–60, for the context.

[77] Folger, MS V.a.143, fols. 15 (1559), 22, 63 (1565), 66.   [78] See above, p. 58.

nothing was lawful than in one where everything was. His point was that presenting juries should bring forward accusations because, 'of two evils it were better mens doeings were looked into over strictlie and severlie than that there should bee a notorious impunitie of malefactors'.[79] Given the social and economic conditions of the late sixteenth and early seventeenth centuries, it is hardly surprising that those with some stake in their communities appear to have been willing to comply with such advice. Statistical studies of crime and punishment have shown that increasingly large numbers of individuals suspected of petty misdemeanours, as well as more serious felonious crimes, were presented at courts at all levels as the period progressed.[80] Furthermore, the rhetoric and action of magistrates was sometimes driven on by a 'Godly' belief that there was a need for a reformation of manners employing every available means, either civil or ecclesiastical, to suppress sin of all kinds. William Lambarde once went so far as to draw up a version of what he described as articles inquirable before JPs drawn out of the Ten Commandments.[81] In the 1620s, Henry Sherfield was pressed by one of his parliamentary constituents at Salisbury to encourage measures against the idleness of local shopkeepers and artisans, who were, so it was alleged, more addicted to the alehouse than to the care of their families.[82] In one of his own speeches as recorder of Southampton, Sherfield noted that the local minister had recently reminded the inhabitants that only 'a true and real reformation of the city', which attacked Sabbath breaking, profane swearing and idleness, could adequately express their thanks to God for delivering them from a recent outbreak of plague. Eschewing what he described as the easy course of concentrating on the 'weaker sort', who could not effectively complain, Sherfield stressed that the programme of moral reform had to be strictly enforced, even if it made 'many enemies' for magistrates and presenting jurors amongst their friends and neighbours, and even though it might lead them to be described as 'cruel magistrates'.[83]

Indeed, there were so many mechanisms, particularly at the local level, for the regulation of behaviour, that it is hard to dissent entirely from Alison Wall's assertion that in the early modern period, community and neighbourliness often meant little more than that 'little brother' was watching.[84] Yet, since so many of the cases were brought by individuals

---

[79] CUL, MS Gg.3.26, fols. 135ff.

[80] J. Sharpe, *Crime in Early Modern England 1550–1750* (1984); S. Hindle, *The State and Social Change in Early Modern England* (Basingstoke, 2000), pp. 118–19.

[81] BL, MS Egerton 3676.   [82] HRO, MS 44M69/L30/78. The letter is anonymous.

[83] HRO, MS 44M69/L38/54/2, no date.

[84] Alison Wall, *Power and Protest in England 1525–1640* (2000), p. 115.

within the context of traditional institutions, it seems inappropriate to identify this with a consistent programme of social control managed by the authorities in London without the willing concurrence of people in the localities. Furthermore, if legalistic viewpoints were often perfectly consistent with the acceptance of local regulation in the interest of broader social, or indeed, religious aims, the common law was also the means by which it was contested.

In his guidebook for JPs, Michael Dalton pointed to a subtle, but significant shift in attitudes towards the meaning of the king's peace between the early sixteenth and early seventeenth centuries. While Sir Anthony Fitzherbert had described peace as the 'amity', confidence and quiet that is between men, Dalton said that it was more commonly taken in his own day to be an 'abstencie from actual or injurious force, and so is rather a restraining of hands than a uniting of minds',[85] and this was a point acknowledged even by lawyers with puritan sympathies such as Henry Sherfield or Francis Parlett of King's Lynn.[86] In one of his charges to jurors, Sir John Dodderidge stressed that law enforcement was necessary to the common good but also insisted that punishments should be proportionate to crimes and that convictions could only result from proper indictments and arraignments.[87] Apparently referring to the due process clauses of Magna Carta, Sir Francis Bacon moderated the more severe views he shared with the Verge court with the observation that the English were lucky in that they could not be deprived of life, lands or goods, by flying 'rumours' and 'slandering fames', or by the reports of 'secret' or 'privy' inquisitions.[88]

From about the mid 1570s, moreover, there were a growing number of civil actions that challenged local regulatory authority, civil as well as ecclesiastical. The Elizabethan judiciary was increasingly willing to grant writs of *habeas corpus* to individuals who claimed they had been unjustly imprisoned or unjustly punished by either JPs or urban magistrates, and the numbers of such cases increased during the course of the early seventeenth century.[89] In 1588, for example, there was a famous case involving two gentlewomen of 'good behaviour' who had been arrested

---

[85] M. Dalton, *The Countrey Justice, Conteyning the Practise of the JPs out of their Sessions . . . .* (1619 edn).

[86] NRO, King's Lynn Borough Records, MF/RO 396/13, fol. 5v: 'God's law punisheth the sin of pride in the heart, but our law punisheth not that sin until it comes into act . . .'

[87] NLW, MS 3648D.

[88] CUL, MS Gg.3.26, fol. 136.

[89] J. H. Baker, 'Personal Liberty under the Common Law of Engalnd, 1200–1600' in R. W. Davis, ed., *The Origins of Modern Freedom in the West* (Stanford, 1995), pp. 178–202. See *Dyer's Reports*, I, p. lxxii, for examples. Professor Paul Halliday will soon publish an authoritative account of *habeas corpus* in the early modern period.

by constables while they were walking in the streets of London after dark. Although they were neither indicted nor given an opportunity to defend themselves, two sheriffs of London, Skinner and Catcher, ordered that they should be stripped naked from the waist upwards and publicly whipped as common harlots. During the hearing of the case in Star Chamber that was brought against the sheriffs on behalf of the women by the attorney general, counsel for Skinner and Catcher argued that they had ordered the punishments in accordance with the customs and Charter of the City of London. However, the court found the sheriffs guilty of acting contrary to due process of law, sentenced them to a spell in prison, and obliged them to make a public apology to the women as well as payment in compensation for the wrong.[90] When passing judgment, Lord Treasurer Burghley was reported to have quoted chapter 29 of Magna Carta before remarking that the 'freedom' it enshrined in protecting the subjects from unlawful imprisonment without due process of law was something that 'noe Countrye butt ours (noe nott Fraunce) can chalenge by the laws of their Realme'.[91]

A well-known decision such as this one, which was reinforced by a number of other Star Chamber judgments against over-zealous JPs, may well have made local officials and magistrates cautious about whom they arrested or punished for offences such as nightwalking or other forms of vice.[92] Indeed, a statute passed in the first parliament of James I, which enabled officials such as constables to claim triple damages if they were found not to be guilty of abuse in connection with the performance of their duty, suggests there was already an awareness that regular recourse by individuals to civil actions for false or unlawful imprisonment, or assault and battery, was making life potentially difficult for those charged with law enforcement.[93] Nevertheless, while Burghley was clear that Skinner and Catcher had acted unlawfully because they had punished the women without allowing them a proper hearing, he acknowledged that whipping was a customary means of punishing moral offences in London, and even in the seventeenth century it appears to have been necessary for the judges to remind local officials that an 'honest' person, for example a wife visiting the chambers of her husband at one of the legal inns, might have a legitimate reason for being out after dark.[94]

---

[90] A fairly full account of the case is given in BL, MS Additional 48064, fols. 207–8. See also *Acts of Privy Council, 1588*, pp. 246–306.

[91] BL, MS Harleian 358, fol. 201v. This report is included in a volume of collections relating to the ecclesiastical jurisdiction. For the significance of this, see below, pp. 405–6.

[92] See below, pp. 417–19.

[93] 7 James I, c. 5; continued and expanded in 21 James I, c. 12.

[94] ECO, MS 168, fol. 117v.

The point that customary practices could be used to justify the regulation of personal behaviour was reiterated in the case of Philip Haines, a citizen of Exeter, who brought an action in Star Chamber in the 1620s against the town's mayor, Ignatius Jordan. Haines claimed that Jordan had acted illegally in having him imprisoned, whipped and subjected to moral indoctrination by a local clergyman for having allegedly committed fornication and adultery. Counsel for Haines, including William Hudson, raised *Skinner and Catcher's Case* as a precedent for their client, and they also put forward a clever technical argument that attempted to show that the mayor and the city of Exeter were acting in derogation of the authority of the local ecclesiastical courts because they had in effect established a 'consistory' with jurisdiction over matters such as adultery, which were normally within the purview of the church courts. In addition it was alleged that Jordan, a figure notorious for his pursuit of godly reformation, had acted excessively. But, while the judges accepted that the argument about consistory courts might have been compelling in some circumstances, they ruled against Haines because Exeter was able to demonstrate the customary nature of the powers that had been exercised. Furthermore, two royal judges, Chief Justice Hyde and Chief Baron Walter, made a point of commending Jordan as a regular church-attender and a diligent magistrate.[95]

The outcome in this case would appear to reflect the degree to which the royal legal authorities were content to delegate regulatory powers either to towns or, in the 1630s, to various types of company or guild organisation.[96] But it is equally clear that some individuals were willing to challenge it. The Star Chamber case *Remington* v. *Remington*, which arose in the early 1620s in Nottinghamshire, involved a protracted conflict between churchwardens and a group of parishioners whom they accused of holding a 'parliament' at an alehouse during divine service. The parishioners responded to the churchwardens' presentment to the ecclesiastical courts by bringing accusations of barratry against them at quarter sessions, and a lengthy legal quarrel escalated from there.[97] In 1631, a man called Weston, a resident of the Puritan stronghold of Banbury, brought a civil action for assault and false imprisonment against three constables who took out a warrant against him for drinking late one night in an alehouse and threatened to put him in the stocks for

---

[95] BL, MS Lansdowne 620, fol 92. See also K. Thomas, 'The puritans and adultery: the act of 1650 reconsidered' in Donald Pennington and Keith Thomas, eds., *Puritans and Revolutionaries: Essays in Seventeenth-Century History Presented to Christopher Hill* (Oxford, 1978), pp. 257–81.

[96] See above, pp. 197–200.   [97] BL, MS Lansdowne 620, fol. 4.

refusing to pay the relatively small fine of 3s. 4d.[98] In an even more intriguing case from 1629, a plaintiff called Lea sued the mayor of Walsall for unlawfully imprisoning him for refusing either to pay a fine (3s. 4d.) or enter into a recognisance when he was caught bowling at an alley within a mile of town. When the case came before the assize judges, the critical issue was whether an Henrician statute outlawing certain games was still in force. The presiding judge, Sir William Jones, was certain that it was, and Lea dropped his case, but Jones nevertheless launched an unusually vehement attack against the mayor. Apparently thinking that he had been badly influenced by a notorious local clergyman, Jones advised him to be more temperate and not to be led by factious ministers. The judge said he knew of no other corporation that was so 'forward' with this particular penal law.[99]

Such cases demonstrate the means through which the enforcement of various kinds of social and behavioural regulation could be challenged, especially when some abuse of power, or neglect of due process, could be alleged against local officials. Furthermore, it seems quite likely that judicial sensitivity about local enforcement also owed something to the arguments of Elizabethan 'Puritan' lawyers such as James Morice, and his colleague Robert Beale, whose attacks on the ecclesiastical oath *ex officio* led them to a more general questioning of the kinds of regulatory jurisdictions that were epitomised by the church courts.[100] Perhaps surprisingly given his impeccable credentials as an advanced Protestant, Moricen came as close to being what might be described as a 'libertarian' lawyer as the early modern period was likely to produce. Although his campaign against the church courts and the oath *ex officio* became well known thanks to the plight of deprived minsters brought before High Commission, he also had a broader vision. He and Beale were pioneers in collecting evidence of individual cases from the Essex area in order to demonstrate how the use of the oath by officials of the consistory court of London had led ordinary lay people of modest means to suffer trouble, expense and even periods of imprisonment, in connection with minor disciplinary matters.[101] One of the cases involved a tanner from Royston, who had asked his servant to put out some skins to dry on a

---

[98] BL, MS Hargrave 44, fol. 27v.
[99] Ibid., fol. 6v. The clergyman was Mr Lapthorne who had caused trouble elsewhere (in Tamworth and Gloucester).
[100] See above, pp. 97ff. for the broader religious and political context.
[101] BL, MS Additional 48064, fols. 76–87, contains papers relating to complaints against ecclesiastical jurisdiction in Essex, and more generally in the diocese of London in 1584–5. Similar material appears in Morice's 'A iust and necessarie defence of a briefe treatise made ageinst generall oathes . . . .' (LPL, MS 234).

Sunday, and who subsequently wound up spending days in gaol because his service as a constable made it difficult for him to attend the church court in order to answer for not having properly kept the Sabbath.[102] Another, rather surprisingly, concerned an elderly man who was reputed to have had sex with one of his servants.[103]

In the extensive manuscript treatise that he wrote on the oath *ex officio*, Morice claimed that the church court officials normally only applied it to people of modest means, primarily because the 'greater sort' would not stand for the 'servitude and thraldome' that it represented in breaching the principles of due process at common law that were enshrined in chapter 29 of Magna Carta.[104] Furthermore, Morice was concerned that the 'contagion of this injustice and wrong will in time spirall and enlarge yt selfe to the subversion of our pollicie and commonwealth', civil as well as ecclesiastical. The trouble with the oath was that it tended toward the 'inquisitorial discovery of faults', and was therefore an 'enemie to societies in houses and commonweales, so that no man shall dare communicate anie thing to him or to her that he is nearest to' for fear of being exposed by a friend or relative who was subjected to interrogation. According to Morice, moreover, there was a distinct danger that inquisitorial methods were infecting the procedures of JPs, an allegation he illustrated by describing how his own son had been obliged to answer questions put to him by a magistrate in London after he had returned home from a trip to the Continent.[105]

The critical point about this line of attack on the ecclesiastical courts was that the principles of due process at law laid out in chapter 29 of Magna Carta (legal indictments and jury trials) were put forward as a native, English standard against which the inquisitorial procedures of the church courts were measured and found wanting. The men and women who feature in Morice's illustrative cases are regularly quoted as having said on being tendered the oath that it was their understanding that, according to the law of England, they were not required to make an answer to any 'criminal' cause unless there had been either a private suit, a formal accusation or an indictment.[106] Morice and Beale themselves pointed out that, according to the laws of the realm, a 'nightwalker' brought before a magistrate could refuse to answer questions put to them, and they quoted *Skinner and Catcher's Case* in support of the view that neither the pope nor king can take 'from the Common people their right of inheritance, which they have in the Common Lawe'.[107]

---

[102] LPL, MS 234, fol. 14v.   [103] BL, MS Additional 48064, fol. 76v.
[104] LPL, MS 234, fol. 45.   [105] LPL, MS 445, fol. 442; MS 234, fol. 20v.
[106] Ibid., fols. 14–19, 42.   [107] BL, MS Additional 48039, fol. 80v.

Furthermore, while Morice's concern 'for the due administration of law and justice'[108] focused more on procedural than substantive rights in face of various kinds of moral and behavioural regulation, he, and others, were also hostile to the existing practices of the ecclesiastical courts at least in part because they seemed to entrap people in endless expense and controversy about relatively trivial matters while much more serious ones, such as the bearing of bastard children, were largely ignored.

As we have already seen, the effective use by litigants of writs of prohibition constituted an ongoing challenge to the ecclesiastical courts that existed alongside the use of writs of *habeas corpus* to challenge the jurisdiction of secular local authorities. From the point of view of the common lawyers the issues were conceptually similar because of the importance of due process in both, and because the defence of the ecclesiastical courts and of secular authorities was essentially that they were justified by custom and usage, not that they conformed to general principles of common law.[109] Consequently, for lawyers like Morice, the 'correction of manners' was to be sought, 'not by new imagined devices, but according to positive laws' enacted by parliament that were subject to common-law standards of due process.[110]

Regulatory legislation

The nature and extent of community control over the behaviour of individuals must be seen largely in terms of the sometimes contested authority of local secular and ecclesiastical jurisdictions, but, as Morice's words suggest, there was also a statutory dimension through which parliament and the state could lay down laws that aimed for a broader 'reformation of manners'. In fact, there was nothing new in this. According to the common lawyers, the jurisdiction exercised by justices through the commissions of the peace was entirely based on statute. Similarly, legislation about matters such as the playing of unlawful games or the regulation of apparel stretched back as far as the fifteenth century, and some of it specified that enforcement should be carried out through the jurisdiction of the court leet, where offenders might be found guilty by presentment alone, and therefore denied the full access to due process prescribed by Magna Carta.[111] Equally, although generations of modern historians have quoted a passage in *Eirenarcha* where William Lambarde mentioned the heavy weight of the stacks of statutes JPs were responsible for enforcing, he was writing just as the privy council was launching a project to weed out

---

[108] LPL, MS 234, fol. 52.   [109] See above, pp. 106, 402–4.
[110] LPL, MS 234, fol. 188v.   [111] Above, pp. 268–72.

and consolidate the accumulation of penal laws built up over previous centuries.[112] His observations do not, therefore, necessarily reflect on the passage of regulatory measures in his own time, and the picture that emerges from a more careful examination of the subsequent legislative history of the period is more ambiguous than is usually acknowledged.

The regulatory issues that were of most interest to Elizabethan and early Stuart parliaments appear to have fallen into several broad categories: those having to do with the church courts and their operation; those connected with the keeping of Sunday and other religious observances; measures involving alehouses and drunkenness; extravagant apparel; swearing; and, finally, illegitimate children. Yet, even these often attracted little more than intermittent parliamentary attention, particularly in periods when other issues, such as the union of the crowns, Roman Catholic terrorism, or disagreement over taxation were more pressing. For example, of 267 proclamations issued during the reign of James I, only thirty were directly concerned with social or moral regulation, and even in the legislatively active parliament that sat between 1604 and 1610, regulatory bills made up no more than 15 per cent of the total introduced, and 10 per cent of the total number passed.[113]

Furthermore, those measures that received a hearing often had a rough passage or failed to become law. A problem connected with bills for the better keeping of the Sabbath, for example, was that they threatened to interfere with the customary privileges of places that had traditionally held fairs or market days on Sunday.[114] Another difficulty was that their most ardent supporters insisted on an absolute ban that extended to the service of legal process. This controversial issue was still giving rise to civil litigation in the 1620s and 1630s, but some of the considerations at stake lay behind a joke that the Essex barrister Edward Glascock made at the expense of a bill proposed in 1584 that would have rendered legal contracts made on a Sunday null and void. When he asked whether this should be taken to include marriage contracts, he apparently won howls of laughter from the other members.[115]

[112] William Dunkel, *William Lambarde, Elizabethan Jurist 1536–1601* (New Brunswick, NJ, 1965), p. 118. Lambarde was amongst the group of lawyers appointed to undertake the task. See above, p. 64.

[113] I owe these points to material assembled by Ms Yvonne Hardman in a Durham University undergraduate dissertation (1999).

[114] CUL, Dd.5.14, fols. 93v–9v. A moot discussion at one of the inns of chancery in 1614 about the legality of holding fairs, markets and courts of pipe powder (market courts) on Sunday apparently accepted that the honour of God was to be more respected than the safety of the subjects and their commerce.

[115] David Dean, *Law-Making and Society in Late Elizabethan England: the Parliament of England, 1584–1601* (Cambridge, 1996), p. 120.

For all of these reasons, though bills for the better-keeping of the Sabbath had been frequently introduced, none of them was passed until 1625, and that statute (1 Charles I, c. 1) was concerned mainly with quarrels, bloodsheds and other great inconveniences caused by people venturing outside their home parishes on a Sunday in pursuit of various sports and pastimes. Given its focus, it would appear that the measure was aimed primarily at events such as a very bloody football match in the Midlands with which the lord lieutenant of Leicestershire, the earl of Huntingdon, had recently had to deal.[116] While it also included the imposition of fines of 3s. 4d. on those who used illegal or outlawed pastimes within their own parishes, these were unspecified and presumably included only those which had not been declared legitimate by James I in the *Book of Sports* he issued only a few years earlier.[117]

As is well known, the subject of Sunday sports was divisive in a very religious society, but a charge given by the country squire Sir Robert Phelips in Somerset in the later 1620s provides an insight into how contemporaries viewed the alternatives. Reminding the quarter sessions grand jury of the recent legislation for preserving the Sabbath, he praised the *Book of Sports*, and criticised the 'judicial strictness' around which an unnamed group of 'ill-humoured' men [i.e. Puritans] were trying to draw a party by bringing prosecutions.[118] Equally, although a follow-up statute passed in 1628 (3 Charles I, c. 1) banned butchers and those involved in any part of the carrying trade (carriers, drovers of cattle, etc.) from working on a Sunday, no other form of business activity was specifically outlawed, which presumably meant that the task of restricting them was left either to the ecclesiastical courts, or to local secular jurisdictions, some of which had long enforced such measures through the passage of bylaws.

By comparison with measures regarding Sunday, proposals to regulate apparel, and in particular to create a kind of social coding by associating permissible levels of vestimentary finery with prescribed social status, were even less successful in the period after 1550, despite the fact that such legislation had been common in the Middle Ages.[119] Although one line of thought stressed the need to inculcate more thrifty housekeeping

---

[116] HMC, *Report on the Manuscripts of R. R. Hastings, of the Manor House, Ashby de la Zouche* (4 vols., 1928–47), IV, p. 206. Letter dated 23 June 1624.
[117] *The Kings Maiesties Declaration to His Subiects, concerning Lawfull Sports to be Used* (1618).
[118] SARS, MS DD/PH221/15.
[119] Folger, MS V.a.143, fol. 64. In 1565, Lord Keeper Bacon had quite a lot to say about the need to enforce such measures, because it was important to be able to distinguish between the different degrees of men.

by outlawing the purchase of clothing on credit,[120] the measures were doubtless doomed by the prospect of the very rich being denied the right to dress in as much gold and silver thread as they liked, and by the hostility of the wives of rich merchants and lawyers, groups well represented in parliament, who were not keen to have legislative limits put on their access to the latest fashions.[121]

Swearing, on the other hand, was an easier target, but while the matter had been discussed frequently in parliaments going back to the reign of Elizabeth, no legislation was passed against profane swearing until 1624, when a measure was introduced alongside a bill for maintaining the Sabbath.[122] One obvious difficulty was that enforcement was bound to involve endless citations of people who were obliged to pay relatively small fines, and the circumstances of the passage of the Act in 1624, during difficult political times, may suggest that it was successful largely because it was the sort of measure around which it was possible to generate uncontroversial moral consensus.[123] This is not to say, however, that it was regarded lightly. Lord Keeper Coventry on several occasions mentioned the value of the Act, and the need to enforce it, when he addressed the judges as they were about to go on circuit.[124] At least one man, Thomas Peynell of Castle Hedingham in Essex, was investigated by Attorney General Bankes for swearing and allegedly saying that he 'cared not a fart' for a recent royal proclamation concerning the measure.[125] But, since the fine for breaches of the statute amounted to only 12d., it is not surprising, perhaps, that there appear to be no reported cases in which the meaning of the words proscribed were explored.[126]

Of all the regulatory issues considered in Tudor and Stuart parliaments those concerning alehouses and the perceived problems of drunkenness were undoubtedly highest on the agenda, and there were in contemporary terms good reasons for thinking this appropriate. By the early seventeenth century, policy-makers often maintained that the sale of food and drink at retail outside London had been limited historically to

---

[120] See BL, MS Sloane 326, for a discussion of the 1575 bill of apparel.

[121] Joan R. Kent, 'Attitudes of members of the House of Commons to the regulation of "personal conduct" in late Elizabethan and early Stuart England', *Bulletin of the Institute of Historical Research*, 46 (1973), 41–71.

[122] 21 James I, c. 20: An Act to prevent and reform prophane Swearing and Cursing.

[123] C. Russell, *Parliaments and English Politics* (Oxford, 1976), p. 157.

[124] For example, Rushworth, *Collections*, II, p. 299. By 1635, an office had been set up by letters patent in order to collect the fines.

[125] Bankes Papers, MS 63/64.

[126] But for another example of enforcement see DRO, DC/DOB/8/1. Mayor's Court Offenders Book, fol. 196, 30 December 1633. 'Thomas Sustrode did on friday night last between xi and xii of the clock being in Richard Boyes house, an alehouse, sweare 6 times by the name of God, for an oath, and twice by the eternal god. Ordered to pay 8s.'

fair-days and inns, places that accommodated travellers away from home on legitimate business.[127] Over time, however, the retailing of ale became common all over the country, and it was recognised that the first steps to control alehouses had been taken in the reign of Henry VII through legislation that empowered JPs to grant licences, and which, not for the last time, associated alehouses with vagrancy.[128] This law was, probably inadvertently, abrogated by new vagrancy legislation passed in the reign of Edward VI,[129] but the gap was quickly filled by a fresh measure that required alehouse-keepers to be approved (licensed) by at least two JPs in public sessions and to enter into recognisances for their good behaviour. According to one seventeenth-century source, who thought that the first Edwardian Act was intended to outlaw alehouses completely, the licensing approach had been adopted because it was appreciated at the time that the complete abolition of alehouses would be hard on travellers and on the 'poorer sort', who were the main frequenters of such establishments.[130] Licensing gave JPs the power to suppress or permit alehouses at their discretion, and legislation from the time of Henry VIII standardised, or 'assized', the price and measures of beer and ale. Even so, at the end of the reign of Elizabeth, there were no regulations about the number of alehouses or the crucial matter of opening hours.

Although relatively little survives from parliamentary debates about their origins, statutes passed at the beginning of James I's reign appear to have been made with these outstanding issues in mind. The preamble to the first of them briefly recited the history outlined above, and stipulated that the general opening times of alehouses should be restricted to an hour around 'dinner' time, when various kinds of manual workers might expect to take their midday breaks for food and drink. There was also an intention to restrict access to 'travellers' and those who were, literally, joining them for a drink since the statute also provided that alehouse-keepers should be fined if they served anyone who resided within a two-mile radius of the premises at any time other than midday.[131]

The two-mile limit was mocked by Edward Glascock as a 'mere Cobwebb to Catch pore Flyes in' when it was discussed in the House of Commons in 1585, and there is not much evidence of systematic

---

[127] *Hutton's Reports*, 100. Inns, places which provided accommodation, were distinguished from alehouses, and were considered outside the remit of legislation regulating ale-houses.

[128] 11 Henry VII, c. 2.   [129] 3 & 4 Edward VI, c. 16.

[130] Bankes Papers, 66/12: papers relating to Sir William Bellenden's propositions for the reform of alehouses, p. 2.

[131] 1 James I, c. 9: An Act to restraine the inordinate haunting and tipling in Innes, Alehouses, and other Victualling houses.

enforcement of the Jacobean measure.[132] In any case, contemporaries remained convinced that the number of alehouses was increasing. Sir William Bellenden, who claimed in the 1630s to have made an analysis of recognisances taken out in connection with the granting of licences, calculated a ten-fold rise between 1560 and 1603, followed by a further five-fold increase thereafter, and he did not count unlicensed 'tippling houses'.[133] Consequently, in the 1630s, there were discussions in government circles about the number of alehouses and the need for reform, but by then the line between earnest concerns about the moral and social damage done by alehouses and the need of the king for additional sources of revenue had become distinctly blurred.

Bellenden himself proposed that JPs should continue to license but that the process should in the future be supervised by the crown with the king taking a fee (of not more than 20s. a year) for each licence granted. Though simple enough in conception, the problem with the scheme, as Bellenden acknowledged, was that the Edwardian statute apparently put licensing into the hands of JPs, and without a new parliamentary statute, it was not clear on exactly what basis the crown could intervene.[134] But in addressing this question Bellenden found language typical of that associated with the numerous projects of the Caroline period. Alehouse-keeping was not a recognised trade under the Statute of Artificers. Even according to the Edwardian statute, moreover, alehouses were a kind of 'newtrall thing left under caution to arbitrary discretion', and there was no reason why they should not be suppressed altogether by the crown '*pro bono publico*'. The king's will had to be a 'guide and limitation to the discretion of the subject' in a matter where there was no public law or private interest to the contrary. In any case, private interests were not to have any weight where the question trenched a point of state, 'of which the king is and ought to be under god, the supremest judge director and reformer'.[135]

Although the crown's lawyers did not fully endorse this last line of thought, the scheme appears to have been approved by Bankes, and it was strongly supported by Sir Robert Heath, who had evidently been asked to look into it by the privy council.[136] A practical point in its

---

[132] Dean, *Law-Making and Society*, p. 177–8.   [133] Bankes Papers 66/12, p. 4.

[134] As Bellenden also acknowledged, his scheme ran the risk of association with Sir Giles Momposson's notorious patent to license inns, which had been vigorously attacked as a monopoly by parliament in 1621, at least partly because it encroached on the powers of justices. Bankes Papers, 66/12, p. 18.

[135] Bankes Papers, 66/12, pp. 6–7.

[136] Ibid., at p. 18, there is an endorsement, probably in the hand of Bankes, which acknowledges the legal sticking point, but which nevertheless concludes that 'For great conveniences of this reformation, it seemeth that these orders are not contradictory to

favour was that the introduction of a fee for a licence would create a financial interest in enforcement that had hitherto been lacking. In addition, information could be gathered from 'churchwardens, ministers, and overseers' about existing premises and the number of alehouses they thought appropriate for their localities. According to Heath, the king could use this to take measures for the 'suppressing of drunkenness and saving the expense of corn' that was used to make beer by regulating licences. 'Reformation' could thereby be linked to the addition of a 'considerable yearly' sum to the king's revenue, which, according to one estimate, would amount to £9,000–10,000 per annum.[137]

Perhaps because of the legal questions, but more likely because of the administrative difficulties associated with implementation, Bellenden's proposal remained on the drawing board. Instead, the 'state' turned for control of the drinks trade to the other trusty device of the Personal Rule, the use of the royal prerogative to grant corporate powers, much like those traditionally exercised by guilds, to individuals who would, it was supposed, simultaneously regulate themselves and exclude outsiders from operating.[138] One of the many schemes either proposed or implemented was, for example, a grant of corporate powers to brewers in Essex who agreed in return to pay a composition to the king. The idea was that the 'company' so created would limit a growth in numbers because it would be in the interest of existing members to do so, and, in addition, the brewers agreed as part of the deal to supply ale only to licensed alesellers.[139]

While measures such as this had the virtue of involving those associated with the trade in its regulation, they were also pursued largely for the financial gain of the crown, and, no doubt, for that of those who participated as well. By contrast, statutes passed against the effects of consuming too much alcohol, rather than to control the sale of it, reflect less ambiguous social and moral concerns. Often associating it with newly discovered evils such as tobacco-smoking, contemporaries commonly blamed drunkenness for most of the social problems that beset them, from affrays and murders to the neglect of trades and the financial ruin of families as the result of the debt and bad management it

---

[137] law or reason.' Bankes Papers, 64/9 is a letter signed by Heath, and addressed to My Lord, dated 4 December 1634.
Bankes Papers, MS 66/12, p. 18.
[138] See above, pp. 197–8. Bankes Papers, 5/12: note by Bankes about brewing by innkeepers and alehouse-keepers (1637–8); also, 5/14; 12/3; 12/20. See also P. Slack, *From Reformation to Improvement: Public Welfare in Early Modern England* (Oxford, 1999), ch. 3.
[139] Bankes Papers, 12/27, 14 February 1637/38: warrant to the privy council to draw up a charter of incorporation for the brewers of the county of Essex.

caused.[140] Although alehouses and drunkenness were seen primarily as evils affecting the poor and the young, Puritan anxieties about the evils of drunkenness also reflected urban 'family' values that stressed thrift, honesty and hard work, and which were traditionally enforced in local jurisdictions. At the same time, judges were sometimes dismayed by the connection they saw between drunkenness and deaths resulting from quarrels between men who regularly carried knives and sometimes used them.[141] Sir James Dyer, for example, noted a case from the 1560s in which a man was hung for murder after an alebench discussion of taxation apparently led to a fatal exchange of blows.[142]

Early modern magistrates would certainly have found it unacceptable for large numbers of inebriated people to congregate in London or provincial towns after dark, but there is little evidence of the extent to which they either failed or succeeded in preventing it, and the lack of comment may even suggest that it was not identified as a problem. Preambles and charges to grand juries do not mention drunkenness all that often, and when they do, it appears that the problem was seen as one that affected society primarily as a result of its impact on individuals.[143] These considerations, along with the perceived difficulty of enforcement, may explain why the Jacobean statute against drunkenness does not seem particularly draconian, especially for people of at least modest means. Though lingering too long in an alehouse was specifically mentioned, the nature of the offence was otherwise left largely undefined, and the penalty for committing it was the payment of a fine of 3s. 4d. While the fine was not excessive, it would certainly have been harder on the young or the less well-off, an eventuality anticipated by a stipulation that those who were unable to pay could be sentenced instead to a spell of public humiliation in the pillory, the means by which unruly behaviour had long been punished in towns and manorial courts.[144]

---

[140] See for example, HRO, 44M69L30/78: a letter written in the 1620s from a constituent to Henry Sherfield complaining about idleness amongst the tradesmen and shop-keepers of the town. The alehouse was a principal cause of the neglect of wives and children.

[141] *The Casebook of Sir Francis Ashley, 1614–35*, ed. J. H. Bettey (Dorset Record Society, vol. 7, 1981), p. 91: an account of a 'duel' between a parson's servant and another man after they had been drinking beer.

[142] *Dyer's Reports*, II, p. 424.

[143] A charge by Bulstrode Whitelocke at Abingdon in 1632 mentioned the necessity of enforcing laws against the viciousness and ill-manners of the inhabitants of the town, including those relating to the alehouse and unlawful games. The Jacobean statutes had, he said, been aimed at those 'drones' who used their time unprofitably 'to themselves and the commonwealth' (Whitelocke Papers, vol. 31, fol. 231).

[144] 1 James I, c. 9. The measure was renewed and amended by 21 James I, c. 7.

A feature of statutes against drunkenness and swearing, as well as those for keeping the Sabbath, was that they contained 'saving clauses' which pointed out that although the measures enacted were positive laws to be enforced by secular authority, they did not preclude or prohibit citations being made in the ecclesiastical courts for any offences that had formerly been heard in them. Nevertheless, they did little to reinforce, and something to undermine, the spiritual courts. Statutory offences were by definition temporal as well as spiritual, and hence prohibitions from the common-law courts were available to those prosecuted for them in the ecclesiastical courts.[145] In any case by the 1630s, excommunication, the ultimate sanction of the church courts, had been rendered largely ineffective by the fact that no official or individual litigant had a financial interest in enforcing it.[146] By contrast with this, of course, the statutory offences not only involved the payment of a fine, but each of them also specified that this should go into local poor relief funds, thereby directly recycling the wages of sin into charity, and in theory at least reducing the burden of the poor rate.

The statutory measures can therefore be seen as moving responsibility for the matters concerned from traditional local authorities, and the ecclesiastical courts, to the JPs, but however diligent they were JPs were likely to be more distant, at least in rural areas, than neighbours who sat on the presentment juries at a manorial court. In this respect it may well be the case that community invigilation of certain kinds of behaviour was actually on the decline rather than increasing during the course of the early seventeenth century. No less important, by this date, it is clear that local attorneys and barristers were available, particularly in cases of misdemeanours, both to speak for those accused, and bring legal actions on their behalf in those cases where some form of official misconduct could be alleged.[147]

Nevertheless, some of the newer legislation did have procedural implications that also have to be taken into consideration in assessing the character of enforcement. The first Jacobean statute on drunkenness (4 James I, c. 9), for example, provided that offenders should be brought

---

[145] *CroCar*, 870, *Starre* v. *Buckhold*. To call a man a drunkard is a temporal offence.

[146] At least this is the claim made in 1627, and again in the mid 1630s, by Henry Cogane and Thomas Knyvett, who petitioned the king for a commission that would empower them to collect fines due to the king on the writ *excommunicato capiendo*. Their point was that since no one had an interest in collecting the fines they were not enforced. The scheme was approved in 1634 by Bankes and Littleton (Bankes Papers, MS 17/25).

[147] Brooks, *Pettyfoggers and Vipers*, pp. 189–91. The Kenyon of Peel papers in the Lancashire Record Office, Preston, provide a number of examples of correspondence between an early seventeenth-century clerk of the peace and local lawyers acting on behalf of clients.

forward either through the traditional means of presentment, or by indictment before a JP. However, when the act was 'continued' in 1624, it was specified that a JP acting singly could administer an oath to one witness, and on this basis a fine could be levied.[148] All of the other measures discussed above subsequently followed this pattern of permitting a summary conviction on the basis of one or two sworn witnesses rather than prescribing a full hearing and jury trial. In the 1580s there had been some controversy in the House of Commons when a Shropshire lawyer raised the due process chapters of Magna Carta during the course of a debate on a bill that proposed to employ similar procedures in order to impose fines for failing to attend church.[149] But while these kinds of objections may have contributed to the delay in the passage of some regulatory measures, the pattern that they eventually came to follow clearly controverted the very high standards James Morice wanted enforced in English courts. The relatively small value of the fines involved as well as the similarity between the kind of regulation being imposed by statute and that which had long been allowed on presentment, or summarily, in local courts, no doubt made it seem unnecessary to demand full hearings and jury trials. At the same time, civil litigation was always available to those who thought they had been unjustly arrested or over-harshly punished, points the Acts themselves recognised by specifying that officials named in such actions could plead the statutes in justification, and claim 'good' damages if plaintiffs were unsuccessful in making a convincing case against them.

The idle and disorderly

Despite these safeguards, therefore, the statutes regulating personal behaviour can justifiably be seen as part of a movement towards the granting of more extensive summary powers to both urban and rural JPs, and in this respect they had much in common with measures for dealing with problems of poverty that had been evolving gradually since the time of the early Tudors. As is well known, over the course of the sixteenth century, parliament drew on the example of measures first developed in towns in order to pass legislation, which finally reached a settled form in the Poor Law of 1601, and which depended on a distinction between those who were unable to work to support their families, either because of incapacity (old age, physical infirmity) or a lack of available employment, and those who were able to work, but who refused to do so. Thus the 1601 Act provided for parish rates to supply relief to the impotent

---

[148] 21 James I, c. 7.   [149] Dean, *Law-Making and Society*, p. 124.

and unemployed poor, but at the same time parallel legislation permitted the punishment of 'idle persons' who allegedly refused to work, and there were also statutory measures that dealt with the early modern equivalent of the homeless, 'rogues and vagabonds', who were commonly thought to be responsible for serious crime as well as general disorderliness.[150]

As was the case with the provision for the deserving poor, the punishment of the idle and disorderly had long been characteristic of English towns, the best single example being the practice in London whereby masters appealed to the lord chamberlain to administer summary punishment to unruly apprentices.[151] Significantly, however, these powers were put on an important new footing in the 1550s as a result of a royal charter, which created what came to be known as the first 'house of correction' at Bridewell hospital. No doubt partly because of the high degree of geographical mobility amongst young people at the time, the idea appears thereafter to have spread rapidly to other places. A statute of 1576 permitted localities to raise a rate in order to fund a 'bridewell'. By 1600, at least thirteen towns outside London had one, and legislation passed in 1601 made it mandatory for every locality to have a house of correction. By 1640, the institutions had become common across the entire country.[152]

A key component of what has been described as the house of correction project was the idea that bridewells should combine punishment with the provision of work, or, ideally, some form of basic job training. In practice, however, a lack of organisation and a shortage of funding led to a concentration on short-term imprisonment and corporal punishment, which usually involved a whipping consisting of a specified number of lashes. Probably because the first bridewells were founded either on the basis of a royal charter, as was the case in London, or as offshoots of existing urban jurisdictions, the exact procedures involved in a committal were initially ambiguous, but since they tended towards the summary, they were fairly quickly perceived by some as subject to challenge in courts such as Star Chamber.[153] Bridewell charters empowered governors to search for, inquire of and seek out idle ruffians, tavern haunters, vagabonds, and all persons of evil name and fame, and then to lock them up and punish them at their discretion. But a brief written in the later

---

[150] 43 Elizabeth, c. 2. P. Slack, *Poverty and Policy in Tudor and Stuart England* (1988).
[151] See above, p. 377.
[152] Joanna Innes, 'Prisons for the poor: English bridewells, 1555–1800' in F. Snyder and D. Hay, eds., *Labour, Law and Crime: an Historical Perspective* (1987), pp. 42–122.
[153] For an account of reactions amongst Londoners see P. Griffiths, 'Contesting London Bridewell, 1576–1580', *Journal of British Studies*, 42 (2003), 283–315.

sixteenth century either by the recorder of London, William Fleetwood, or by Sir Francis Bacon, pointed out that since the king could not grant away by commission or charter the rights guaranteed to the subject by custom or common law, such summary powers were in fact directly contrary to Magna Carta.[154] If this were true, then incarceration in a bridewell, like the punishments administered in *Skinner and Catcher's Case*, was challengeable in the courts and potentially illegal.[155]

As this work goes on to point out, however, the problem could be overcome relatively easily by passing parliamentary legislation that granted discretionary powers to magistrates, and by the early seventeenth century this course was usually followed as the best means of 'legalising' the bridewell jurisdiction so that committals could in effect be carried out summarily by a single JP. Subsequent justifications of bridewell procedures were usually based on a statute of 1610 that explicitly empowered JPs to summarily punish rogues, vagabonds, the idle and nightwalkers by ordering periods (usually a matter of days) of incarceration in a house of correction. In addition, the scope of the jurisdiction was further extended to include unmarried mothers whose children were likely to become a burden on the parish.[156]

In parliamentary debates, speakers from time to time questioned the wisdom of putting so much discretionary power in the hands of JPs, and the nature of discretion also received a good deal of judicial attention as well. In his *Fifth Reports*, for example, Coke referred to Aristotle for the view that the best laws were those that left the fewest things to the discretion of judges, and he noted that the use of discretion needed to be bounded by the rule of law and reason so that it did not become merely the expression of the will of the magistrate or his 'private Affections'.[157] He also maintained that the royal judges and Star Chamber should oversee the actions of JPs in this connection, and there were a number of early seventeenth-century cases brought against magistrates who had

---

[154] Given the date of composition and the fact that he was recorder of London, Fleetwood seems the most likely author. It is not clear on exactly what basis the tract was assigned to Bacon by the editors of his collected works. Guildhall, MS 9384, fols. 1ff: 'A brief treatise or discourse of the vallidity, strength, and extent of the charter of Bridewell, and how far Repugnant both in Matter, sence and meaninge to the great Charter of England. Worthily Composed by Mr Serieant Fleetwood Sometymes Serieant at Law' is the fullest version. That attributed to Bacon is CUL, MS Ee.2.30.

[155] See above, p. 403.

[156] 7 James I, c. 4: An acte for the due execution of divers Lawes and Statutes heretofore made against rogues Vagabonds, and Sturdie Beggers, and other lewde and idle persons. CUL, MS Dd.5.49, fols. 72–4v, is a particularly good example of bridewell procedure at this time.

[157] 5 *CoRep*, 100 (*Rooke's Case*). See also the earlier views of Lambarde in *Eirenarcha*, pp. 428ff.

allegedly abused their powers by ordering over-harsh whippings, especially in the cases of young women.[158] Indeed, having pointed out that a 1601 statute against pilferers was the first that empowered JPs to order a whipping,[159] Chief Justice Sir Thomas Richardson spoke at length in the Star Chamber in the mid 1620s about the need to make certain that punishments of this kind were justified by law and that officials who abused their powers were disciplined severely and made an example to the public. The case to which he was speaking involved an alehouse-keeper, Grice, who was sent to the house of correction and given twenty lashes by a Yorkshire JP for the saucy words and behaviour he had addressed to him as a result of a summons to appear. The court concluded that the punishment was excessive, fined the JP 200 marks, and ordered that he pay Grice £40 in damages. Apparently summing up the opinion of others present, including Coventry and Bishop Neile, Richardson concluded that although the plaintiff was a poor man, 'he is a freeman [and] whipping is for a slave, and he thereby is destroyed, yet neither by lawful judgment, nor by judgement of his peers'.[160]

Thus although those committed to the houses of correction were not completely without legal recourse, petty thieves, rogues, vagabonds, the bearers of illegitimate children,[161] the idle and those who were out after dark without a reason acceptable to the authorities were effectively denied the benefits of due process as laid down in the Great Charter. To some extent this should no doubt be put down to perceived administrative necessity. It also reflected the traditional jurisdictional world out of which the houses of correction had emerged, and that world, too, could sometimes be arbitrary. In his Star Chamber speech, for example, Richardson mentioned a case from Suffolk where a scold had been put in the ducking stool by neighbours who had not bothered to make a presentment at the court leet. No less important, since most of the individuals caught up in the net were likely to have been young, and very often homeless, contemporaries would no doubt have maintained that they fell outside the normal definitions of freemen, or, indeed, free-women. In this respect the houses of correction were certainly the most paternalistic of all Tudor and Stuart legal institutions, and in the minds of many this was probably one of their principal virtues. Coke famously, and probably optimistically, wrote that everyone committed to a house of correction came out better than they had gone in, while all of those

---

[158] Baildon, *Cases in Camera Stellata*, p. 98; L. A. Knafla, *Kent at Law, 1602*, vol. 1, *The County Jurisdiction: Assizes and Sessions of the Peace* (1994), p. 193.

[159] 43 Elizabeth I, c. 7.   [160] BL, MS Lansdowne 620, fol. 39.

[161] *CroCar*, 476. The judges thought it unjustifiable, however, that a JP should commit a bastard-bearer to a house of correction 'for life'.

committed to the common gaol invariably came out worse.[162] As has often been noted, the development of the houses of correction created the scope for reformatory punishments that were an alternative to formal indictments. They were the period's most distinctive contribution to criminal law.

The liberties of the English

It is difficult to draw up a balance sheet about the posture of the individual person with respect to his or her community and the secular and religious arms of the state. According to at least one contemporary observer, the general impact of the opinions expressed in Coke's *Reports* was to undermine the authority of lesser secular authorities as well as that of the ecclesiastical jurisdictions.[163] Yet Caroline government, in particular, was perfectly content both to support such local institutions and to create new ones in the forms of 'companies' empowered to regulate trades. At the same time JPs were increasingly charged by statute with summary powers that permitted them to correct moral misdemeanours such as drunkenness or vagrancy.

On the other hand, lawyers like James Morice were concerned about the potential spread of 'arbitrary' or discretionary justice from the ecclesiastical to secular jurisdictions, and challenged both with rhetoric recalling the 'liberties of Englishmen' while at the same time clarifying the legal remedies that could be used to contest them. By the second decade of the seventeenth century, moreover, these technical concerns with 'due process' had become linked to more general political issues such as the proposed union of England and Scotland, as well as Coke's quarrel with Ellesmere about the jurisdiction of Chancery. As we have seen in chapter 6, Francis Ashley's reading on chapter 29 of Magna Carta at the Middle Temple in 1616 cast the subject partly in terms of the struggle to block the 'exorbitant' power of the churchmen, and partly as a reflection of the centuries-old struggle of the English people to maintain native 'freedoms and liberties'.[164] Yet Ashley's detailed treatment was both more and less profound than his prefatory rhetoric suggests. Although he was clear the crown could not lawfully grant public powers of enforcement by letters patent, as had been done recently in connection with patents of monopoly, he also stated without qualification that kings had the power to imprison subjects suspected of serious crimes against the state without pressing charges against them, the same

---

[162] Sir Edward Coke, *The Second Part of the Institutes of the Lawes of England* (1642), p. 734.
[163] BL, MS Stowe 153, fol. 39.   [164] See above, pp. 156–7.

position he maintained, though with some qualification, when he was asked by the House of Lords in 1628 to comment on the position of the Five Knights.[165]

Far from concentrating on matters of state, however, Ashley's lectures were devoted primarily to an examination of the powers of lesser political bodies, such as guilds and townships, as well as those of JPs. Citing cases from the mid-Elizabethan period up till the time he wrote, many of which had been published recently by Coke, his reading seems, more than most, to have been addressing current legal issues. In the course of attempting to make sense of them, moreover, much of Ashley's discussion centred on whether the authority of corporate bodies or magistrates could, or could not, be justified according to the extent to which legitimate 'special' customs deviated from 'general customs' expressed in Magna Carta or common law.

Organised around a series of questions fashioned from the words of chapter 29, the subheadings, or divisions, of the reading asked who was a freeman of England; what were arrest and imprisonment according to the statute; what were the liberties of the English and what constituted a disseisin of those liberties; what was the difference between free customs and special customs; what were trial judgment, condemnation and punishment; and, finally, what was the law of the land (*lex terrae*) according to the statute.[166] Ashley argued that the statute offered remedies against every exaction, vexation, extortion or oppression that grieved the free subject and threatened the illegal imprisonment of his body or disseised his property.[167] He showed that it was contrary to the statute for the lord of a manor to raise excessive entry fines from either copyholders by inheritance or those who held for lives.[168] Referring to well-known cases reported by Coke, he explained that it was only as a result of a special custom that the City of London could imprison executors who failed to turn over funds to the Orphans court, or merchants who neglected to have their broadcloth weighed at Blackhall.[169] Furthermore, if they were not justified by customs, royal grants to corporations or towns, or to monopolistic patentees, could not include new powers to imprison. Most importantly, Ashley reiterated the basic principle of due process at common law, which was that fines or imprisonments could only occur as a result of a legal hearing, where there were indictments, proofs and evidence, and a trial before a jury of peers. Hence a JP was not entitled to

---

[165] See above, pp. 174–5.
[166] BL, MS Harleian 4841, fols. 8ff. Frustratingly, since the surviving manuscripts of the reading do not contain complete notes under each heading, some of the answers are less full than others.
[167] Ibid., fol. 3.   [168] Ibid., fol. 50.   [169] Ibid., fols. 9, 47v.

set excessively high sureties for individuals bound over to keep the peace
unless they were justified by statute. Nor could a magistrate fine or
commit to prison without a proper trial, even if the offender had confessed to a crime.[170] The remedies against unjustified imprisonments
were actions on the case, which could be brought against gaolers for false
imprisonment, or writs of *habeas corpus* sued out of King's Bench, which
required those holding a prisoner to bring him before the court and
explain the grounds on which he was being held.[171]

Not surprisingly in the light of recently passed legislation discussed
earlier in this chapter, Ashley had nothing directly to say about the
summary jurisdiction of JPs, houses of correction,[172] or debtors imprisoned in connection with legal actions that were taken out against them
by other subjects. Nevertheless, Ashley made a strong case for the rights
of subjects at large, particularly in the face of the oppressive exercise of
power by lesser polities within communities or by agents of the crown
such as JPs. Although he accepted the standard argument that special
customs might permit controls over individuals that were contrary to
the principles of due process, he like Coke was aware that that these
might be tested against standards of reasonableness and economic
utility. Local privileges ought not to prohibit anyone from exercising
their common-law right to earn a living. It was wrong that trade should
be impeded by excessive tolls levied for passing through towns or
crossing bridges.

There is no evidence that Ashley's reading was controversial at the
time, or, indeed, that it circulated widely in manuscript. Nevertheless,
the case law remained familiar thanks to Coke's *Reports*. It also indis-
putably outlined remedies lawyers could make available to those inclined
to challenge local authorities through the courts, and it seems equally
clear that a significant number of people took advantage of them. Magna
Carta, Ashley claimed, had delivered the subjects from a great thraldom
and tyrannical oppression; it gave them property in their goods, title to
their lands, liberty of their persons and safety of their lives. These were
after all the qualities that distinguished freemen from bondmen and
subjects from slaves.[173]

---

[170] Ibid., fol. 10v.   [171] Ibid., fol. 3.
[172] *Casebook of Sir Francis Ashley, 1614–35*, pp. 10, 28–9, 31, shows that Ashley often dealt
with such matters as a magistrate, but the lecture does not refer to this experience,
though it does address the powers of justices sitting out of sessions.
[173] BL, MS Harleian 4841, fol. 3.

14   Conclusion

The powerful rhetorical connection Francis Ashley drew in his reading on Magna Carta between the law of England and the liberties and franchises of its freemen reflects one of the most striking features of the culture of the rule of law in the early modern period: the existence of a language of liberty. Furthermore, the subject matter of Ashley's lecture, which was concerned primarily with lesser polities and the ecclesiastical courts, as well as his later involvement in the *Case of the Five Knights* in the 1620s, suggests that he was expressing a version of early modern 'rights speak' associated as much with ordinary subjects going about their daily business as with the predicament of country squires imprisoned at the will of the crown.

On the other hand, while there was often an explicit recognition in early modern legal rhetoric of a principle of self-preservation that lay at the heart of all legal and political relationships, and a growing awareness of a distinction between the private interests of individuals and the public interests of the state, the liberties Ashley and other jurists praised were not based to any very significant extent on systematic theories of natural right. The Ciceronian values expressed so often in late sixteenth and early seventeenth-century charges at assizes and other local courts either explicitly or implicitly identified the rule of law with the protection of the subject, his family, his lands and his goods. But rights to landed property were seen ultimately as a consequence of human laws rather than inherent natural right. The Aristotelian teleology of the state implied that since the polity had been created for the good of the subjects and civil society as a whole, it was logically impossible that any of its acts should be detrimental to an individual member of it. In this respect statutes aimed at regulating the alehouse or prohibiting swearing were part of the same jurisprudential mindset that led legal writers such as the Somerset attorney Robert Powell to argue that the right of the subject to use his land as he saw fit had to be weighed against the 'common good' and the deleterious social consequences of depopulating enclosures.[1]

---

[1] See above, pp. 343–4.

In his speech at the Ship Money trial the solicitor general, Edward Littleton, made an unexceptional point when he noted that the private interests of the subject and those of the commonwealth were ultimately indistinguishable.[2] As Ashley stressed in his lecture, the liberty he had in mind was liberty under the law, not 'lawless liberty', whereby men may live like 'libertines'.[3]

Furthermore, while the liberties of Englishmen as enshrined by the Great Charter might be described as part of the law of the land, lawyers also gave considerable weight to claims for customary local privileges and franchises that might to a degree curtail them. A telling illustration of this apparent paradox can be found in a collection of cases involving disputed parliamentary elections that were put together by lawyers who sat on the committees of the House of Commons that heard them in the 1620s. While these make it clear that the default position according to 'common right' was that every male householder should have a say in elections in towns, most of the cases involved questions from boroughs about the extent to which royal charters, or prescriptive rights, justified limitations on the franchise to more select groups of voters.[4]

Significant aspects of the legal history of the early modern period must therefore be written in terms of the relationship between a national common law, administered by the judges at Westminster and involving the legal profession trained at the inns of court, and a plurality of other jurisdictions with which it interacted. Sir Edward Coke himself once described the laws of England as consisting of over a dozen different varieties, only one of which was the common law determined by the judges at Westminster.[5] Yet even in the 1560s, John Kitchen apparently found it so easy to incorporate manorial jurisdictions into a system of national law that their place as customary courts had in a sense to be reinvented in the seventeenth century.[6] It is very difficult to find any evidence at any point during this period of the existence of a distinctively 'folk justice' that existed outside one kind of local jurisdiction or another, and which was therefore completely out of touch with the common law. Furthermore, although there were of course instances of social discontent and riot in the late sixteenth and early seventeenth centuries, these were in fact relatively infrequent. Often including demands by participants that justice should be done, this was usually identified according to what was already taken to be the law of the land, and most historians

---

[2] See above, p. 204.   [3] BL, MS Harleian 4841, fol. 1v.

[4] John Glanville, *Reports of Certain Cases, Determined and Adjudged by the Commons in Parliament in the Twenty-first and Twenty-second Years of the Reign of King James the First* (1775), esp. pp. 107, 142.

[5] See above, pp. 11–15 and *Coke on Littleton* (1628 edn), fol. 11v.   [6] See above, p. 248.

who have studied such episodes have been struck more by their law-abiding character than any demands for root and branch change to the existing legal or political regime.[7]

The king's judges at Westminster were naturally inclined towards jurisdictional imperialism, and the waves of litigation that came into the central courts during the years from 1550 to 1640 can justly be seen as contributing both to the growth of the state and to the reach of London law ever more deeply into social and economic life.[8] Yet the process was associated with an enduring tendency to privilege customary practices, and many lesser jurisdictions continued to flourish until well after the Restoration. Far from seeing legal centralisation as a way of increasing its authority, the government of Charles I and the judges who sat for the king appear to have been quite happy to support local institutions and to create more lesser polities as a way of dealing with social problems and improving the finances of the crown. In all of these respects, it is perfectly understandable in juridical terms that people in the provinces petitioned for a redress of grievances during the first two years of the Long Parliament and then either closed their city gates to both sides, or banded together into formal neutrality pacts, once civil war began.[9]

Given this respect for custom, English common law has often been described as intellectually insular, and insofar as there was relatively little direct reference to either Roman civil or canon law in connection with arguments made in court, there is considerable truth in this view. Yet one of the most distinctive features of the sixteenth and seventeenth centuries was the way in which the political history of the British Isles made it inevitable that English lawyers give some thought to the inter-section of different legal cultures. In the case of Wales, law was seen as a vehicle for integrating different peoples on either side of an ancient border. In the case of Ireland, it was a tool for facilitating social engineering and a 'civilising process'. In the case of the proposed union between England and Scotland, there was a perceived danger associated

---

[7] See, for example, J. Morrill and J. Walter, 'Order and disorder in the English Revolution' in A. Fletcher and J. Stevenson, eds., *Order and Disorder in Early Modern England* (Cambridge, 1985), pp. 137–65; J. Walter, 'Grain riots and popular attitudes towards the law' in J. Brewer and J. Styles, eds., *An Ungovernable People: the English and their Law in the Seventeenth and Eighteenth Centuries* (1980), pp. 47–84; J. Walter, *Understanding Popular Violence in the English Revolution: the Colchester Plunderers* (Cambridge, 1999).

[8] For expressions of this view see M. Braddick, *State Formation in Early Modern England, c.1550–1700* (Cambridge, 2000) and S. Hindle, *The State and Social Change in Early Modern England, 1550–1640* (Basingstoke, 2000).

[9] J. S. Morrill, *The Revolt of the Provinces: Conservatives and Radicals in the English Civil War, 1630–1650* (1976).

with the rewriting of the law of England itself at the very beginning of the reign of a foreign king with potentially dangerous political ideas.[10]

The impact of these conjunctures, as manifested in the prefaces to Coke's English reports, and those of Sir John Davies for Ireland, was a natural inclination both to praise English law, and to validate it by depicting it as having evolved hand-in-glove over the centuries with English society and the English people despite potentially disruptive events such as the Norman Conquest or the union of the crowns of England and Scotland in 1603.[11] In ordinary case law, however, although custom was respected, it was always balanced against tests of reasonableness. There are plenty of examples where Coke expressed this view in his decisions, and Davies's entire project was based on the need to completely obliterate Brehon law and customs.[12] Nevertheless, in law lectures such as that of Francis Ashley, and in countless public speeches before meetings of quarter sessions, assizes or manorial courts, rhetorical appeals to nationality and ethnicity lent emotional appeal to accounts of the liberties of Englishmen that were protected by common law. Although it is ultimately impossible to judge the impact of this oratorical onslaught, it was undertaken with a self-consciously educative purpose, and at the very least constant repetition must have made the language familiar even in the most remote village.

Essentially populist accounts of English history helped to institutionalise and create vernacular versions of some of the general ideas about the role of law in society that Elizabethans seemed to have soaked up so readily from classical sources such as Cicero and Aristotle.[13] But it is no less evident that well before 1600, formulations of the history of English law were also beginning to be shaped in parallel with accounts of the long-term history of the English church. From at least the time of John Hales in the mid sixteenth century, it was possible to construe a history of both that was structurally identical.[14] A time of primitive purity had been cut short or interrupted by a foreign incursion, either in the form of the conquest of William the Bastard, or papal hegemony over the native church, and the subsequent history of each was then depicted as one of recovery of suppressed, but not lost, religious and legal liberties. Indeed, it is hard to resist the conclusion that this template of historical struggle made it easier rather than harder for contemporaries to imagine the kind of conflict that emerged in the 1640s between a stubborn king, who stood on his prerogative, and his people

---

[10] See above, pp. 124–35.   [11] See above, pp. 130, 132.   [12] See above, p. 129.
[13] See above, pp. 89–92.   [14] See above, pp. 83–5.

as represented in parliament, who identified his rule with popery and a betrayal of native liberties.[15]

Yet, despite this, and the obvious impact that evangelical Protestantism had on lawyers and laymen alike, it is no less significant that some of the most dynamic jurisdictional interactions of the entire period were those between the common-law and the ecclesiastical courts. These were accompanied by professional and ideological conflicts between the lawyers and the clergy that were endemic for most of the period, but which became particularly acute during the 1620s and into the 1630s and 1640s. The ecclesiastical jurisdiction was sanctioned by the 1559 settlement which created the Church of England by statute, and a civilian like Richard Cosin could plausibly argue in the 1590s that its juridical institutions, no less than manorial courts, had long been a customary part of the English polity.[16] But the use of the judicial machinery of the church to discipline deprived clergymen spurred the attack on the church courts that was pioneered by James Morice, and which ultimately focused on the authority of the jurisdiction as much as its procedures. According to Morice, the struggle over the oath *ex officio* had the effect of putting the words of chapter 29 on the lips of many an ordinary subject. Ironically, it was the questionable status of the spiritual jurisdiction in the eyes of the common lawyers that to a degree at least undermined the concurrent tendency of English society in this period to use legal means to more thoroughly invigilate personal behaviour.[17] At the same time, Morice's introduction of an act to confirm Magna Carta in 1593 was a direct predecessor of the campaign for the Petition of Right in 1628.[18]

From a jurisprudential point of view, the jurisdictional issues raised by the composite nature of the English monarchy, and by the disputes over the place of the church in the English polity, appear to have led the principal legal figure of the early seventeenth century, Sir Edward Coke, to espouse a theory about the nature of law that owed more to the past than to the future. While men younger than Coke, most notably John Selden and the Cromwellian and Restoration judge Sir Mathew Hale, developed positivist theories that located the authority for law in the command of a sovereign power (be that either the king, or the king in parliament), Coke, like Fortescue before him, maintained that English

---

[15] See, for example, Nathanial Bacon, *The Continuation of an Historicall Discourse, of the Governmennt of England, Untill the End of the Reigne of Queene Elizabeth. With a Preface, being a Vindication of the Anceint Way of Parliaments in England* (1650).
[16] See above, p. 106. [17] See above, pp. 405–7. [18] See above, pp. 108, 176.

legal institutions were rooted in the historical past.[19] But, like most sixteenth-century lawyers, Coke was probably more interested in the place of law in society than in interrogating the authority on which it was based. The rule of law brought civilisation to a potentially brutish state of nature. It provided the ligaments of civil society. It promised the security of possessions, households and families, while at the same time taking due regard for the common good; these were, after all, the reasons why men subjected themselves to authority in the first place. It was only in a limited sense redistributive, but it provided a playing-field on which the poor and the middling could co-exist with the rich.[20]

Contemporaries were well aware that equality before the law could be subverted by wealth. Nor was the early modern legal system by any means completely free of bureaucratic corruption and peculation. Yet these problems must ultimately be weighed against the fact that the law was evidently more extensively resorted to between 1560 and 1640 than at any other period in English history. While there were some calls for law reform during the 1640s and 1650s, those that were not hopelessly utopian usually amounted to little more than a tinkering with details. Although the influence of lawyers in inhibiting radical reform was no doubt significant, the survival of most aspects of the secular legal regime during a period which saw the nearly complete deconstruction of the English church is probably a fair measure of its intrinsic place in social and political life.[21]

Although it was rarely worked out in a systematic way, most early modern legal rhetoric presumed that the ultimate source of law was the community. The fact that statutes were the only subjects of lectures at the legal inns is proof enough that parliament's function as the maker of positive law rendered it an indispensable institution. Yet the monarch and the royal prerogative were also essential cornerstones in the legal edifice. Royal mercy in the form of pardons was an increasingly important element in the administration of the criminal law as the period progressed,[22] and the crown's provision of equity in courts such as Chancery mitigated the rigour of the common law. Since the monarch was

---

[19] See for a exceptionally clear exposition of this point, M. Lobban, *A History of the Philosophy of Law in the Common Law World 1600–1900* (Dordrecht, 2007).

[20] See above, pp. 25–6, 58–9, 85–6, 158, 353.

[21] For an attempt to put the 1640s and 1650s in a broader context, see C. W. Brooks, 'Litigation, participation and agency in seventeenth- and eighteenth-century England' in D. Lemmings, ed., *The British and their Laws in the Eighteenth Century* (Woodbridge, 2005), pp. 155–81.

[22] C. Herrup, 'Negotiating grace' in T. Cogswell, R. Cust and P. Lake, eds., *Politics, Religion and Popularity in Early Stuart Britain* (Cambridge, 2002), pp. 125–32; K. J. Kesselring, *Mercy and Authority in the Tudor State* (Cambridge, 2003)

thought at least in theory to have had a seat in the principal common-law court, the eponymous King's Bench, there was even much to be said for the view that the common law was the king's law, and that the king was the principal fountain of justice in the realm. This argument was from time to time used by lawyers in their debates with the churchmen, and there was no inevitable reason for law and the prerogative to conflict. But, as Sir John Fortescue made clear in *De laudibus*, while the king was the titular head of the legal system, he did not need to bother himself with the details of adjudication, because in England this was left to his judges.[23] Similarly, legal education at the inns of court and inns of chancery in the fifteenth and sixteenth centuries fostered the idea that the law was a body of common erudition shared and developed in the course of an ongoing dialogue between lawyers, judges, students and litigants. Associated with a large number of technical, sometimes arcane, rules and moves, but incompletely systematised into a set of general principles, legal lore could only be mastered by years of immersion in the arguments of previous as well as present generations of lawyers and judges. This process constituted the 'artificial reason' that was the intellectual core of the common law, and which made the judges the ultimate keepers of its content.

If Queen Elizabeth was frequently praised for respecting this concept of law in the way her progenitors had supposedly done, James VI and I was almost certainly more inclined to favour the idea that it was the king rather the judges who made the law, a point illustrated by his frequent confrontations with Coke, and underlined by the appointment of Bishop Williams as lord keeper in 1621.[24] While Coke promoted the idea that the judges, and the law that they determined, could adjudicate the relationship between the king and his people, he was forced after his dismissal from office in 1616 to do so from a seat in the Commons rather than from the judicial bench. Although King Charles consistently aimed to secure judicial approval for his actions, by the later 1620s this was accompanied by the even more blatant application of pressure on the judiciary. Although the narrow, and narrowly constructed, judicial decision in 1637 in favour of his right to levy Ship Money was probably a less sinister betrayal of the liberties of Englishmen than it was portrayed as in the Long Parliament, it is nevertheless easy to appreciate why it was seen that way at the time.[25] Once confrontation between king and parliament began to escalate, moreover, the relatively underdeveloped state of English public law made it difficult for the artificial reason of the common law to give a clear resolution to the conflict. Legal discourse

---

[23] See above, pp. 23–7.   [24] See above, pp. 150–2.   [25] See above, pp. 229–32.

certainly contributed to the rag-bag of ideas we call English political thought, but while lawyers made arguments about particular cases, they did not for the most part engage in systematic treatise writing, and by the 1640s, if not the 1620s, the kinds of arguments that were being made about the nature of authority in the English polity could no longer be comfortably resolved in a court of law.

On a more mundane but no less important level, however, judge-made law and artificial reason perfectly captured the way in which much of the law discussed in chapters 9–13 was made, or 'discovered'. Based on a myriad of technical rules and maxims that related to particular issues rather than the systematic development of judgments from general principles, common-law judging is much easier to describe as a process than to explain as a coherent set of ideas about social, political or economic issues. Although legal reasoning was found in the corpus of learning stored in the *Year Books* or reports of previous decisions, these were guidelines rather than binding sources of authority, and judicial decision-making was also influenced from time to time by commonplaces about the social good, or the nature of human existence more generally.

The early modern legal regime operated as an open forum offering the prospect of remedies to those who thought they had a grievance. The victims of crime, famously, had to rely largely on self-help and the assistance of unpaid amateur constables in order to bring the perpetrator to justice. In much the same way, those who thought themselves slandered or owed an unpaid debt consulted a lawyer and took out a writ. Cases that reached a public hearing were either settled out of court or before a jury, and any interesting legal reasoning that arose from them was likely to be written down and subsequently discussed or reformulated by lawyers dealing with similar or slightly different cases. Indeed, the well-known tendency of lawyers to narrow down the scope of a question as far as possible further limited the general applicability of any particular ruling.

These characteristics of English law were not badly suited to a period of significant social and economic change. It adapted to new conditions and new problems within the parameters of relatively fixed procedures and traditional ways of looking at questions regarding fundamental matters such as obligations and tenures. Yet it was no doubt this sense of change in relation to new circumstances and new cases that accounts for the anxiety expressed by lawyers and laymen alike at the begining of the seventeenth century about the alleged uncertainty of the common law. Indeed, innovative judicial decision-making in response to new kinds of problems sometimes pointed to a more liberal interpretation of the relationship between the strict letter of the law and its relaxation according to conscience or other general principles associated with English notions of judicial equity. Nevertheless, the tendency to head in this direction was rendered problematic (at least on the theoretical plane) by quarrels such as that between Coke and Ellesmere, and, probably, by the outbreak of the civil war in the 1640s. Equitable jurisdictions such as the court of Chancery, or those associated with the provincial councils in the north and Wales, were called into question before the wars because of their association with the royal prerogative, and the threat they posed to the known common law of the land. Conversely, as civil war approached, arguments based on general principles of natural justice, or about the relative place of king and people in the constitution, looked more like abstract arguments in equity than cases that could be settled according to traditional reasoning or the known common law.

It is likely that the principal impact of the two mid-century decades of civil war and political turmoil was to drive the lawyers in the direction of a greater reliance on legal formalism and a stress on known and established rules. Prior to the civil wars, by contrast, English law was in a state of ongoing contestation within a long-established and reasonably widely accepted set of conventions. Constituting social relationships and providing much of the language that described them, it might even be described as a 'public transcript' that prescribed behaviour over a range of human interactions. The institutions and processes of English law made it subject to an ongoing process of negotiation participated in by a broad cross-section of the population.[26] Advertised by contemporaries as a source of security, it is certainly true that the security protected was primarily that of those who could claim in one way or another to have some stake in civil society. But, then again, even the poorest person could legitimately expect to be protected from assault, pilfering or other violations of him or herself by neighbours or the broader community. It is often asserted that early modern society was characterised by patriarchal or hierarchical values, but the lack of a systematic expression of such ideas in connection with the legal life of the realm is worth reiterating and perhaps significant enough to raise questions about the assumptions that are so often made about them. Equally, while the extensive use of law courts that was such a characteristic feature of this

---

[26] The idea of the 'public transcript' is developed in the works of James C. Scott, including, *Domination and the Arts of Resistance: Hidden Transcripts* (New Haven, CT, 1990). The subject is discussed in M. Braddick and J. Walter, eds., *Negotiating Power in Early Modern Society: Order, Hierarchy, and Subordination in Britain and Ireland* (Cambridge, 2000), but the editors' introduction gives only cursory consideration to the place of law in this connection.

period is not in itself definitive proof that the rule of law was accepted as a cultural value by the poorest as well as the richest members of society, the law did provide a space for words such as 'freedom' and 'liberty'. Like his contemporary Anthony Benn, Francis Ashley noted in his reading on Magna Carta, that '*nullus liber homo*', the Latin words with which chapter 29 began, immediately came to the mind of 'every vulgar understanding' whenever they felt threatened by exactions, oppressive violence or any other 'grievance in the commonwealth'.[27]

---

[27] BL, MS Harleian 4841, fol. 4.

Manuscript bibliography

ALL SOULS COLLEGE, OXFORD

MS 180   Speeches of Sir John Croke as recorder of London

BEDFORDSHIRE AND LUTON ARCHIVES SERVICE, BEDFORD

L28/46	Essays of Sir Anthony Benn, Knt, Recorder of London
L28/47	'A Problem Whence it comes to passe that the Courte of Chancery of late especially now in the time of the present Chancellor is so frequented above other the Common law Courtes at Westminster'
L28/49	'God before all and all after the King' by Sir Anthony Benn
BorBF8	Bedford Borough Court of Pleas minute books, 14 Henry VII–1651
BF11/4a–4b	Bedford Borough view of franckpledge and sessions of the peace 1586–1604

BODLEIAN LIBRARY, OXFORD

Bankes MSS	Papers of Sir John Bankes as attorney general
North a.2	Early seventeenth-century political collections
North c.4	North family correspondence
Rawlinson C.85	Elizabethan law readings and tracts
Tanner 73	Collection of letters and papers, 1621–4
Tanner 84	Copies of political and historical tracts
Tanner 288	Legal and political papers, including autographs by Sir Henry Spelman

BRITISH LIBRARY, DEPARTMENT OF MANUSCRIPTS, ST PANCRAS, LONDON

MS ADDITIONAL

149	Transcripts of state papers by Ralph Starkey (d. 1628)
756	Entry book of reports of the commissioners for Ireland, 1622
6681	Woolley collection relating to Derbyshire lead mines

433

10114   Memoranda book of John Harrington
11405   Miscellaneous papers of Sir Julius Caesar
12515   Miscellaneous collection
16169   Elizabethan law readings
18016   Speeches of Sir Heneage Finch, recorder of London, 1620–7
23151   Court book of the manor of Nettleton (Wilts.)
25215   Cases relating to copyholds
25220   Reports of cases belonging to Oliver St John
25249   Privileges and customs of London compiled by William Fleetwood
25274   Treatises on duels by Coke and others
25278   Commentary on St Paul's Epistle to the Ephesians by Oliver St John
25285   Theological commonplace book of Oliver St John
27380   The reading of Sir Thomas Tempest at Lincoln's Inn, 16 Charles I
28201   Classified catalogue of manuscripts connected with English
        history and literature by John Bruce
28273   Memorandum book of John Locke, attorney and solicitor, father
        of the philosopher, 1623–55
32092   'Le methode de Monsieur Dodderige en son practize del ley dengleterre'
34239   Rodney of Stoke Rodney papers
34324   Collection of political papers belonging to Sir Julius Caesar
35957   Law reports and law readings collected by Timothy Turner
36079   Law readings by Sir Anthony Fitzherbert, 1521
36080   Law readings and select cases, Elizabethan
36081   Legal papers including James Morice's reading on the prerogative
40010   Fountains Abbey rentals and court papers
41613   Miscellaneous Jacobean tracts
46500   Letters and papers of Roger Hill
48016   (Yelverton) Notes on sermons, probably by Sir Henry Yelverton
48023   (Yelverton) Miscellaneous papers of Robert Beale and
        Thomas Norton
48039   (Yelverton) Papers of Robert Beale
48047   (Yelverton) Political treatises, including a charge to jurors
48064   (Yelverton) Papers of Robert Beale
48104   (Yelverton) Treatise approving the monarchical government
        of this kingdom from the Saxons' time
48109   (Yelverton) Speeches and letters of Sir Christopher Yelverton

MS COTTON

Cleopatra F.I   Tracts on prohibitions
Cleopatra F.II   Collections regarding ecclesiastical affairs
Faustina C.II   A discourse touching the reformation of the laws
                 of England (fols. 5ff)

MS EGERTON

2651   Barrington family papers
2711   Charges and notes of John Harrington

2978   (Heath and Verney) Political papers
2982   (Heath and Verney) Essays of Sir Robert Heath and his sons
3376   Miscellaneous tracts, including James Morice on the royal prerogative
3676   'A Charge for ye Peace by order of ye Decalogue' by William
        Lambarde

MS HARGRAVE

15   Reports and readings, Elizabeth-James I
24   Reports of cases, 1625–33
27   Reports and papers, mostly by Sir Nicholas Hyde
30   Reports of Arthur Turner; James I, Charles I
34   Law papers, including reports on *Bate's Case*
35–6   Select arguments in parliament and other courts by Sir Henry
        Calthorpe
44   Circuit cases before the judges of assize and *nisi prius*, 4–11
        Charles I
46   Reports of Sir Richard Hutton
87   Readings on statutes
89   Tudor law readings
91   Readings on statutes, James I–Charles I
132   Parliamentary and political papers
198   James Whitelocke's reading on benefices, 1619
206   Edward Bagshawe's reading at the Middle Temple,
        24 February 1639/40
224   'A treatise concerning the Nobilitie of England according to
        the Lawes of England'
325   'Of knights and matters incident to the degree of knighthood
        according to the laws of England'
372   Law readings at the Inner Temple, Charles I
398   Elizabethan law commonplace book that probably belonged to
        Henry Yelverton
402   Collections of law readings
407   Commonplace book of Sir John Dodderidge
419   Collections concerning the laws and customs of London, possibly by
        William Fleetwood

MS HARLEIAN

37   Stuart parliamentary and political papers
72   Law readings and tracts
141   Elizabethan treatises on Wales by George Owen
160   Seventeenth-century miscellany of tracts and papers
249   Elizabethan tracts and papers
358   Tracts and papers relating to ecclesiastical affairs
361   Legal tracts and papers
367   Miscellaneous Elizabethan papers
443   Elizabethan legal tracts and law reports

555   Sir Anthony Brown's succession treatise
583   Miscellany including charges by Jacobean judges
849   Edmund Plowden's succession treatise
924   Humfrey Rant's law notes
1222   Miscellaneous early seventeenth-century tracts and papers
1603   Seventeenth-century law notes and precedent books
1621   Treatise on Littleton's tenures by someone other than Coke
2054   Tracts and papers relating to the town of Chester
4317   Treatise of the origins of the laws of England
4750   Robert Hill's treatise on tenures
4841   Francis Ashley's lecture on the liberty of the subject
4850   Legal papers relating to the Forest of Dean
4943   Privy council letters and papers, c.1570–80
4990   Sixteenth-century law tracts and papers
5153–4   Commonplace books of William Fleetwood
5220   Sir John Dodderidge's treatise on the royal prerogative
5225   Sixteenth-century readings and tracts
5265   Calthorpe on copyholders
6234   Law tracts including Fleetwood's '*Itinerarum ad Windsor*'
6846   Papers relating to parliamentary and public affairs

MS LANSDOWNE

38, 68, 82, 85   Papers and correspondence of William Cecil, Lord Burghley
119   Treatises on Elizabethan political and religious affairs
155   Miscellaneous collection including the 'devices' of Thomas
           Norton (fols. 105ff)
157, 174   Papers of Sir Julius Caesar
620   Lightfoot's Star Chamber reports, 1625–8
621   Elizabethan collections relating to the court of Chancery
798   Miscellaneous collection
811   Miscellaneous seventeenth-century treatises
1075   Cases concerning the customs of the city of London by Henry
           Calthorpe
1134   Collection of readings. Edward VI-Elizabeth
1138   Readings on *statuta antiqua*
1172   Elizabethan and Jacobean law reports

MS SLOANE

326   Speeches in parliament 1570–87
1608   John Hales' treatise on the succession to the crown
1818   Miscellaneous tracts and papers
1926   Miscellaneous tracts and papers
2716   Legal tracts and papers
3479   Jacobean law tracts and papers
4359   Michael Dalton's Breviary of the State of the Roman (or Western)
           Church and Empire

MS STOWE

153   Miscellaneous papers 1540–1629
177   State papers and correspondence of Sir Thomas Edmonds
382   Seventeenth-century analysis of St German's doctor and student
384   Law treatise in 23 chapters on real property
415   Elizabethan collections relating to Chancery
420   Notes on prohibitions in ecclesiastical courts
422   Legal treatises and speeches
423   Legal collections
424   Legal and political miscellanies, including law readings

CAMBRIDGE UNIVERSITY LIBRARY, CAMBRIDGE

MS Additional 3295	William Fleetwood's treatise on JPs
MS Additional 9212	'Certaine errors upon the Statute made the xxvth yeare of King Edward the third of children borne beiond ye sea conceiued by Seriant Browne and confuted by Seriant Fair fax in maner of a Dialogue'
Dd.3.85	Miscellaneous seventeenth-century manuscripts
Dd.5.14	Readings, moots, anecdotes (1611–14)
Dd.5.49	Precedent book of a justice of the peace
Dd.9.17	Historical discourse by William Fleetwood
Dd.14.3	Seventeen-century justice's notebook
Dd.15.3	Law commonplace
Ee.2.30	Seventeenth-century tracts
Ee.6.3	Readers' cases from the Middle Temple
Ff.5.17	Sixteenth-century readings on statutes
Gg.2.31	Early seventeenth-century Chancery miscellanea
Gg.2.5	Seventeenth-century reports
Gg.3.26	Seventeenth-century reports and tracts
Gg.6.18	Sixteenth-century readings on statutes
Hh.2.1	Sixteenth-century readings and reports
Hh.2.6	Fifteenth-century readings on statutes
Hh.3.6	Sixteenth-century law readings
Ll.3.2	Jacobean Star Chamber reports
Mm.1.51	Collection of transcripts including James Morice's remembrance of 'certain matters' concerning the clergy and their jurisdiction.
Mm.6.62	Sir Edward Littleton's collections on parliament
Mm.6.63	Sir Edward Littleton's speeches

CORPORATION OF LONDON RECORD OFFICE, THE GUILDHALL, LONDON

Papers of the Lord Mayor's Court of London

DORSET HISTORY CENTRE, DORCHESTER

DBKL   Bankes of Kingston Lacey. Papers [uncatalogued] of
              Sir John Bankes and his family
DC/DOB/8/1   Mayor's Court Offenders Book

MANORIAL COURT RECORDS

Badbury Hundred
Beaminster
Broadwindsor
Kingston Lacy
Litton Cheney
Netherbury Yondover
Portesham
Stafford West

ESSEX RECORD OFFICE, CHELMSFORD

Papers of Sir John Bramston (D/DEb)

EXETER COLLEGE LIBRARY, OXFORD

Manuscripts of Sir William [and Charles] Jones

FOLGER SHAKESPEARE LIBRARY, WASHINGTON, DC

Additional 731 Commonplace book of a justice of the peace

BACON–TOWNSHEND COLLECTION

V.a.143   Speeches of Sir Nicholas Bacon
V.a.151   'A treatise concerneinge the tenure of Coppyholders . . .'
           dedicated by Philip Chapman to Sir Thomas Lucy
V.a.197   Speeches of Sir Nicholas Bacon
V.a.278   Register of Star Chamber cases, 1–16 Charles I
V.b.9   Treatises on English law by William Fleetwood dedicated to the
           Mayor and Aldermen of London
V.b.303   'The Somme [or some point*es*] of my L. Cookes charge at
           Burye the 26 of July 1609' (fols. 348ff)
X.d.337   Five Caroline Star Chamber cases

GOLDSMITHS COMPANY, GOLDSMITHS HALL, LONDON

Court minutes and miscellaneous papers

GUILDHALL LIBRARY, LONDON

MS 86   Autograph notes and legal treatises by William Fleetwood
MS 9384   Seventeenth-century compilation relating to London

HAMPSHIRE RECORD OFFICE, WINCHESTER

MSS 44M69   Jervoise manuscripts. Papers of Henry Sherfield
MS 107M88/W23   John Trussell's 'The Origins of Cities' transcribed by
                   T. Atkinson

HENRY E. HUNTINGTON LIBRARY, SAN MARINO, CALIFORNIA

Ellesmere manuscripts   Papers of Thomas Egerton, Lord Ellesmere
                               and his son, John, earl of Bridgewater
Hastings manuscripts
Huntington MS 106   Seventeenth-century law lectures
Temple of Stowe manuscripts

HERTFORDSHIRE ARCHIVES AND LOCAL STUDIES, HERTFORD

Gorhambury MS   Papers of Sir Harbottle Grimston

INNER TEMPLE LIBRARY, LONDON

Barrington manuscripts
Petyt manuscripts

INSTITUTE OF HISTORICAL RESEARCH, LONDON

Whitelocke Papers: Microfilms of papers of Sir James and Bulstrode
                      Whitelocke at Longleat House, Wiltshire

LAMBETH PALACE LIBRARY, LONDON

MS 234   'A Iust and Necessarie Defence of a Briefe Treatise made
                 ageinst generall oathes exacted by Ordinaries and Iudges
                 Ecclesiasticall to answer to all such articles as pleaseth them
                 to propounde, and against their forced oathes, Ex Officio
                 Mero. And Consequently A iustification of the lawes,
                 liberties and Iustice of England impugned by Richard
                 Cosyn, doctor of the ciuill lawe in his Appologie for sondrie
                 proceedings by Iurisdiction Ecclesiasticall, By James
                 Morice'
MSS 3391, 3470   (Fairhurst papers) Miscellaneous collections of letters and
                 papers

LANCASHIRE RECORD OFFICE, PRESTON

CPV	'Articles to be given in Charge at Sessions of the Peace'
DD Ar 21–2	Archibald of Rusland papers
DD F/1049	Account of Star Chamber dispute between William Farrington of Wodden and Elizabeth Benson, widow
DD Pt/46/1	Judge Walmesley's commonplace book
DD Ke	Kenyon of Peel papers
DD Ww 1	The Ogle Roll

LEEDS CITY ARCHIVES

DB 205/Box 6	Hatfield Chase Court Rolls

LINCOLN'S INN LIBRARY, LONDON

Hale 12	Law notes and collections by John Selden
Hale 191	Sir Matthew Hale's Black Book of the Law
Hargrave 13	Treatise on the law of nature attributed to Sir Matthew Hale
Maynard 57	John Barkesdale's reading on the statute of bankrupts (21 James I, c. 19)
Maynard 60	Collection of law readings and notes
Maynard 72	Cases relating to parliamentary elections, 1620s
Maynard 75	Reports (1630–4) and parts of a treatise on Chancery
Maynard 83	Collection of materials regarding the proposed Anglo-Scottish union
Miscellaneous 29	Jacobean readings and reports
Miscellaneous 586	Notes on practice and procedure in the courts, early seventeenth century
Miscellaneous 599	Autograph copy of Lambarde's *Archion*

THE NATIONAL ARCHIVES, KEW, LONDON

C 3	Chancery bills and answers
C 33	Chancery orders and decrees
DL 1	Duchy of Lancaster equity pleadings
DL 4	Duchy of Lancaster depositions and examinations
DL 5	Duchy of Lancaster entry books of decrees and orders
DL 41	Duchy of Lancaster miscellanea
E 215	Papers of the early Stuart commissions on fees
KB 165	King's Bench plea side *scire facias* rolls
SP 46	State papers supplementary
STAC 2	Star Chamber proceedings, Henry VIII

NATIONAL LIBRARY OF WALES, ABERYSTWYTH

MS 3648D	Miscellany of seventeenth-century legal treatises

MS 339F   Letter book containing deeds and documents relating to the Council in the Marches of Wales
MS Peniarth 377B   Seventeenth-century miscellanea
Wynn of Gwydir Papers

NEW COLLEGE LIBRARY, OXFORD

MS 9502   Diary of Robert Woodeford, attorney of Northampton

NORFOLK RECORD OFFICE, NORWICH

King's Lynn Borough Records, MF/RO 396/13 (microfilm), Book of Francis Parlett

MANORIAL RECORDS

Blickling (NRS 10924, 11261, 11265, 11275, 21034)
Felbrigg (WKC 2/118)
Gimmingham (NRS 16738; MSS 5827, 5876, 6000, 16739–40, 22556)
Paston (MS 3370, 3372)
Worstead (DCN 60/38)

NORTHAMPTONSHIRE RECORD OFFICE, NORTHAMPTON

Finch-Hatton Manuscripts
Montague of Broughton Papers
   Original letters and autographs, vol. 1, 1537–1643
   Letters to the Montague family from various personages, 1612–50

NORTHUMBERLAND RECORDS OFFICE, WOODHORN, NORTHUMBERLAND

Allendale MS   Hexham court records

SHAKESPEARE'S BIRTHPLACE TRUST, STRATFORD-ON-AVON

Archer Collection Box 83

SHROPSHIRE ARCHIVES, SHREWSBURY

Bridgewater Collection
Shavington Collection

SOMERSET ARCHIVE AND RECORD SERVICE, TAUNTON

B/B/bw   Bridgwater borough records
D/B/ch   Chard court records

DD/PH   Phelips papers
DD/SP   Records from the Exchequer Chamber at Taunton Castle
Q/AW   Quarter sessions wage assessments 1604–41

STAFFORDSHIRE RECORD OFFICE, STAFFORD

MS P/399   Letters and papers of John Bridgeman, bishop of Chester

UNIVERSITY COLLEGE LONDON

MS Ogden 29   Notebook of Timothy Turner

WARWICKSHIRE COUNTY RECORD OFFICE, WARWICK

CR 136/B   Newdigate papers
CR 136/L6/29   Lucy manorial papers

WILTSHIRE AND SWINDON RECORD OFFICE, CHIPPENHAM

MANORIAL RECORDS

Broad Town (192/2)
Broughton Gifford (34/21)
Selkley Hundred (192/12)
Trowbridge Manor Court (192/19)

YORKSHIRE ARCHAEOLOGICAL SOCIETY, LEEDS

DD 146   Farnley Hall papers
MD 225   Court rolls of the manor of Wakefield
MS 311   Papers of Francis Stringer of Sharleston
MS 329   Poems and essays by Sir John Reresby, 1638–45

Index